Resilience and Growth in the Small States of the Pacific

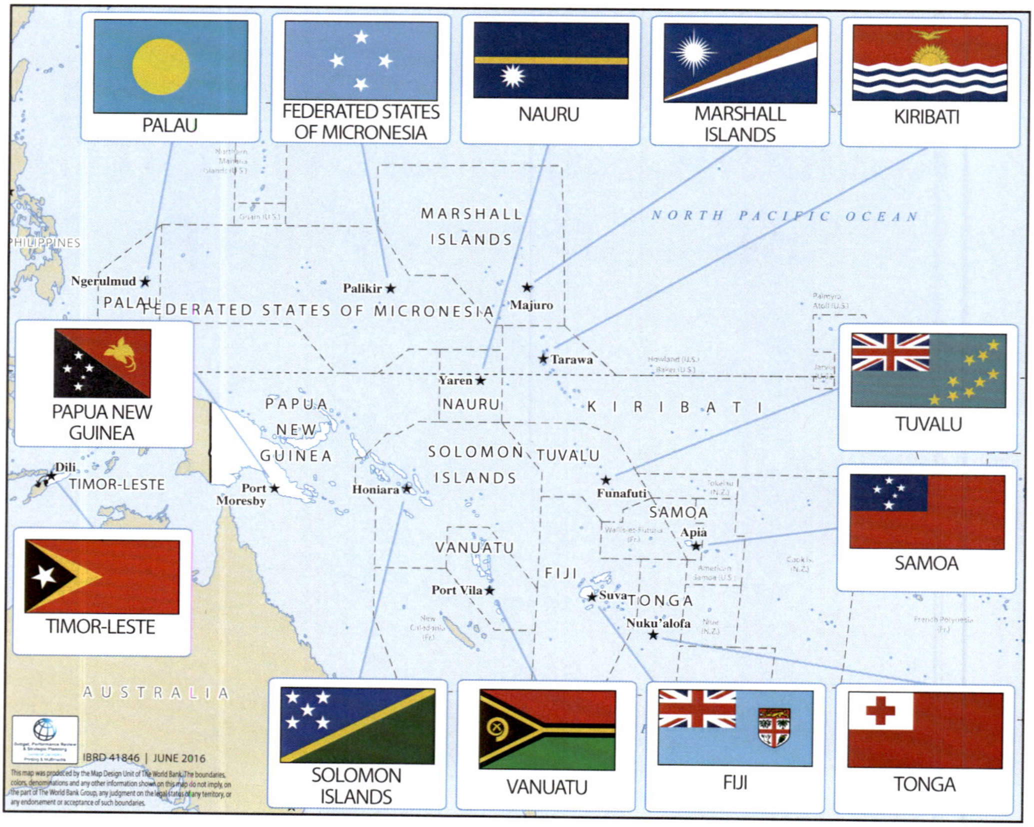

PALAU
FEDERATED STATES OF MICRONESIA
NAURU
MARSHALL ISLANDS
KIRIBATI
PAPUA NEW GUINEA
TUVALU
SAMOA
TIMOR-LESTE
SOLOMON ISLANDS
VANUATU
FIJI
TONGA
NORTH PACIFIC OCEAN
PHILIPPINES
Ngerulmud
Palikir
Majuro
Tarawa
Yaren
Port Moresby
Honiara
Dili
Funafuti
Apia
Port Vila
Suva
Nuku'alofa
AUSTRALIA
IBRD 41846 | JUNE 2016
This map was produced by the Map Design Unit of The World Bank. The boundaries, colors, denominations and any other information shown on this map do not imply, on the part of The World Bank Group, any judgment on the legal status of any territory, or any endorsement or acceptance of such boundaries.

Resilience and Growth in the Small States of the Pacific

EDITORS
Hoe Ee Khor, Roger P. Kronenberg, and Patrizia Tumbarello

INTERNATIONAL MONETARY FUND

Cover design: IMF Multimedia Services Division

Cataloging-in-Publication Data
Joint Bank-Fund Library

Names: Khor, Hoe Ee. | Kronenberg, Roger P. | Tumbarello, Patrizia. | International Monetary Fund.
Title: Resilience and growth in the small states of the Pacific / editors: Hoe Ee Khor, Roger P. Kronenberg, and Patrizia Tumbarello.
Other titles:
Description: Washington, DC: International Monetary Fund, 2016. | Includes bibliographical references and index.
Identifiers: ISBN 978-1-51350-752-1 (paper)

Subjects: LCSH: Islands of the Pacific—Economic conditions. | Economic development—Islands of the Pacific.

Classification: LCC HC681.R475 2016

Please send orders to:
International Monetary Fund, Publication Services
P. O. Box 92780, Washington, DC 20090, U. S. A.
Tel.: (202) 623-7430 Fax: (202) 623-7201
E-mail: publications@imf.org
Internet: www.elibrary.imf.org
www.imfbookstore.org

Contents

Foreword

Policymakers in the small Pacific states face unique challenges in increasing their growth potential. These countries tend to be highly remote and dispersed, exposed to severe shocks, vulnerable to natural disasters and the effects of climate change, face infrastructure gaps, and have very narrow production and exports bases. These problems are particularly acute for microstates—countries with populations under 200,000. Capacity constraints are a key challenge for all small Pacific states.

Recognizing these challenges, continuous engagement with Pacific islands has long been a priority for the IMF. In 1993 it established the Pacific Financial Technical Assistance Center—the first of the IMF's regional technical assistance centers—to help foster capacity building with the support of development partners. The IMF's work in the region has intensified in recent years, particularly amid its growing engagement in small states. This can clearly be seen in the production of major analytical studies on small-state issues, high-level conferences focusing on the most pertinent policy questions small states face, and the more visible participation of IMF management in high-profile events involving small states. The IMF recently issued a guidance note—tailored to the particular conditions of small states—to better inform IMF staff working in these countries.

Resilience and Growth in the Small States of the Pacific gathers recent analytical work on the challenges Pacific island countries face and the policy responses they could consider to overcome them. Many of the chapters in this book are based on papers that were presented and discussed during two high-level regional conferences on the Pacific islands, jointly organized by the IMF and the governments of Samoa in 2012 and Vanuatu in 2013. They have thus benefited from the views and insights of the conference participants, which included policymakers, leading scholars specializing in small states and Pacific island issues, and representatives from the donor community and private sector. The policy advice in this book contributes significantly to the literature on the best policy options for decision makers in Pacific island countries and for small states generally.

This book raises awareness about the challenges faced by Pacific island countries, and offers policy options that should help authorities overcome their development needs and leverage their full potential in achieving inclusive and sustainable growth.

Min Zhu
Deputy Managing Director
International Monetary Fund

Preface

Economic growth in the small island states of the Pacific has been disappointing for more than a decade.[1] During the 10 years leading up to the 2008–09 global financial crisis, real GDP growth for the group averaged just 2 percent a year, considerably lower than in the countries of the Eastern Caribbean Currency Union (4 percent), other small states (4½ percent), and low-income countries of Asia (7 percent). Average real income per capita in the Pacific island countries has increased by less than 10 percent since 1990, compared with 40 percent in the Eastern Caribbean, 25 percent in the group of all small states, and about 150 percent in emerging Asia. Growth in the Pacific island countries in the 2000s was the lowest in four decades. As of 2014, average gross national income per capita in these countries was just one-third that of the Caribbean countries. Among Pacific island countries recovery from the global financial crisis has also generally lagged that in Asian low-income and emerging market economies.

This book examines the factors that have contributed to the low rates of economic growth in the region and seeks to identify policies that could help enhance resilience and raise growth performance in a way that is both inclusive and sustainable. Most chapters are based on papers presented at three high-level regional conferences that were organized by the International Monetary Fund (IMF) and hosted by the governments of Fiji, Samoa, and Vanuatu between 2012 and 2015.[2]

The picture that emerges is that the Pacific island countries' below-par growth performance can only partly be explained by the region's unique physical characteristics, including their very small populations and internal markets, extreme geographic isolation, vulnerability to natural disasters and climate change, narrow production bases, and the depletion or unsustainable exploitation of natural resources. In addition to these physical characteristics, economic growth in the region has also been constrained by policy-related factors, such as weak macroeconomic policy frameworks and implementation capacity, lack of financial depth, laws and customs that limit the flexibility of product and factor markets, particularly the real estate market, and, in some cases, high levels of public debt, dependence on foreign aid, and history of political instability.

Chapters in this book are grouped into four sections, examining growth and resilience, spillovers and vulnerabilities, macroeconomic policy, and structural impediments to growth. The main message is that there is scope for the Pacific island countries to strengthen the policy environment and improve growth performance. However, to do so, governments in the region need to put in place policies that foster macroeconomic stability and debt sustainability, build institutions through reforms, strengthen confidence in the policy framework, promote the development of financial markets, and improve the business environment to attract foreign direct investment. Another challenge the authors identify is finding the right balance between the need to build fiscal buffers to enhance resilience and the need to fund development spending. Finally, the reader may be interested in the appendices, which provide economic profiles of each of the 12 countries covered in this book.

[1] The group of Pacific island nations examined in this book consists of Fiji, Kiribati, Marshall Islands, Micronesia, Palau, Papua New Guinea, Samoa, the Solomon Islands, Tonga, Tuvalu, and Vanuatu, all of which are members of the IMF. Timor-Leste is also included, because it shares similar prospects and challenges with these Pacific island countries.

[2] Participants in the conferences included finance ministers, central bank governors, and other policymakers from the region, as well as officials from international financial institutions and regional agencies (the Asian Development Bank, the IMF, the Pacific Forum Secretariat), representatives of major bilateral donors (Australia, China, the European Union, Japan, Korea, New Zealand), leading academics, and private sector representatives. For more information on the conferences, see http://www.imf.org/external/np/seminars/eng/2012/PIC; http://www.imf.org/external/np/seminars/eng/2013/PIC; and https://www.imf.org/external/np/seminars/eng/2015/fiji.

SETTING THE STAGE: THE QUEST FOR RESILIENCE AND GROWTH IN THE PACIFIC ISLANDS

In the first part of the book, contributors explore the factors that have adversely affected growth in the region, as well as economic vulnerabilities and how to build resilience to them. Chapter 2, by Ezequiel Cabezon, Patrizia Tumbarello, and Yiqun Wu, identifies characteristics that have been shown to impede growth in Pacific island countries, including small populations, geographical isolation, narrow export and production bases, the lack of economies of scale, limited access to both domestic and international capital markets, exposure to shocks (including natural disasters and climate change), a heavy reliance on foreign aid, high fixed costs of establishing public services, a limited range of economic policy instruments, and a high cost of doing business. The chapter points to the importance of building policy buffers to enhance resilience and of improving the composition of public spending, especially in education, to lift potential growth.

Small states are inherently more vulnerable economically than other groups of countries. Nevertheless, small states can succeed if they adopt policies conducive to good economic, social, and political governance. In Chapter 3, Lino Briguglio highlights the importance of setting policy directions and priorities that focus on strengthening the resilience of small states, presenting a framework for understanding the benefits of good political, economic, social, and environmental governance in countries with high vulnerability to external economic shocks.

In Chapter 4, Yongzheng Yang, Hong Chen, Shiu Raj Singh, and Baljeet Singh zero in on slow growth rates and tepid recovery in Pacific island countries following the global financial crisis, comparing them with other groups of countries with similar characteristics. The chapter sheds some light on slowing growth in the 2000s, and attempts to tease out the roles played by natural conditions and policy-related factors.

The Pacific island countries are among the most susceptible to natural disasters in the world. The combination of location and small size heightens their vulnerability to earthquakes and weather-related extremes such as cyclones, tsunamis, hurricanes, and floods. Furthermore, climate change poses risks to the very survival of some Pacific atoll islands. Natural disasters have a negative impact on both short-term and longer-term potential growth, as well as on public finances. In Chapter 5, Ezequiel Cabezon, Leni Hunter, Patrizia Tumbarello, Kazuaki Washimi, and Yiqun Wu present the first cross-country IMF study assessing fiscal indicators and the consequences of natural disaster damage and losses for growth in Pacific island countries as a group. The chapter offers policymakers a policy framework for boosting resilience to natural disasters. It also clarifies the role the IMF can play in helping Pacific island countries face the challenges posed by natural disasters in the design and formulation of their macroeconomic policy.

MANAGING EXTERNAL SPILLOVERS, SHOCKS, AND VULNERABILITIES

The four chapters in this section of the book elaborate on the vulnerability of Pacific island countries to external shocks, particularly commodity price shocks, and spillovers from within the region and globally. In Chapter 6, Fazurin Jamaludin, Niamh Sheridan, Patrizia Tumbarello, Yiqun Wu, and Tlek Zeinullayev show that the Pacific island countries have become more closely integrated with the economies of Australia, New Zealand, and emerging Asia over the past two decades, with a corresponding increase in inward spillovers from the region. China has become a major market for commodity exports, making spillovers from China increasingly important.

Chapter 7, by Patrick Colmer and Richard Wood, highlights the importance of natural resource endowments, economic integration, debt levels, and macroeconomic imbalances in explaining differences in growth performance. Although the onset of the global financial crisis in 2008 did not have a substantial direct impact, given their generally low levels of financial development, the Pacific island countries did experience a significant adverse impact from the ensuing global recession, operating mainly through exports and remittances. The negative impact was greatest for the smallest, most fragile countries, particularly those with foreign trust funds.

In Chapter 8, Xuefei Bai, Patrizia Tumbarello, and Yiqun Wu study inflation in Pacific island countries since the early 2000s. Spillovers of international commodity (especially food) prices and exchange rates have been rapid and significant. However, owing to more prudent macroeconomic policies and more diversified import sources, these countries also appear to have become more resilient to external inflationary shocks.

Chris Becker, in Chapter 9, provides further evidence that the small populations and extreme geographic isolation of the Pacific island countries—both from major global markets and from each other—have had significantly adverse consequences for growth performance, and ranks Tuvalu, Kiribati, Marshall Islands, Micronesia, and Palau as the five most vulnerable countries in the world. The lack of arable land is a significant constraint in many of the countries.

TAILORING MACROECONOMIC POLICIES TO THE SMALL STATES OF THE PACIFIC

Five chapters are devoted to analyzing the importance of policy instruments to support growth. In Chapter 10, Ezequiel Cabezon, Patrizia Tumbarello, and Yiqun Wu explore how policies can best support economic growth given the extent of the natural impediments and limited policy options available to the national authorities. The unique characteristics of Pacific island countries make fiscal management more challenging than in most other countries, including other small states. Nevertheless, strengthening fiscal frameworks is the key to long-term growth. Given the large development needs that these countries face, a key challenge for policymakers is the trade-off between building fiscal buffers to foster resilience to shocks and funding additional investment spending. The chapter examines the opportunity cost of building such buffers.

Owing to small size and a lack of scale, the government sector plays a significant role in the economies of small states, particularly the remote and dispersed Pacific island countries. Sergei Dodzin and Xuefei Bai, in Chapter 11, present a practical framework that links fiscal aggregates, GDP, public and private sector employment, and other factors to analyze fiscal multipliers and the impact of fiscal policies on growth, with applications to Kiribati and Palau.

During the global financial crisis, central banks in some Pacific island countries eased monetary policy to stimulate growth. However, the monetary policy transmission mechanism was weak, according to the findings detailed in Chapter 12 by Yongzheng Yang, Matt Davies, Shengzu Wang, Jonathan Dunn, and Yiqun Wu. The chapter highlights the importance of developing domestic financial markets, and stresses the need to coordinate macroeconomic policies and to use all macroeconomic tools available in designing countercyclical policies, including exchange rate flexibility.

Vulnerability to commodity price shocks poses challenges to monetary policy in Pacific island countries. The high degree of exchange rate pass-through to headline inflation and weak monetary transmission mechanisms suggest exchange rate changes are more effective than monetary policy in managing inflation. To assess the trade-off between the use of the exchange rate and monetary policy in macroeconomic stabilization, Shanaka Peiris and Ding Ding use a model-based approach to examine the optimal policy in response to the historical distribution of exogenous shocks in a Pacific island country. The empirical evidence and model simulations they describe in Chapter 13 favor employing exchange rate policy given the close relationship between exchange rate changes and headline inflation and low interest rate sensitivity of aggregate demand.

In Chapter 14, Jan Gottschalk revisits the issues of excess liquidity and interest rate pass-through in the Pacific and argues that the effectiveness of monetary transmission in the Pacific is inhibited by the absence of a number of channels that are available to central banks in advanced economies. Monetary transmission is therefore dependent on interest rate pass-through, which has been ineffective in the Pacific. Although very little can be done to improve the functioning of the interest rate channel in the short term, policy options are available over the longer term to improve the functioning of the banking sector, in terms of both enhanced competition and market infrastructure.

REMOVING STRUCTURAL IMPEDIMENTS TO GROWTH

The final section of the book looks at the structural impediments to growth, including public financial management, trade, and banking sector characteristics, taking a look back at the roles played by these obstacles to growth, and then forward to strategies that, if implemented, could help lift Pacific island countries to greater prosperity. Chapter 15, by Tobias Haque, Richard Bontjer, Mary Betley, and Ron Hackett, argues that the economic vulnerability of the Pacific island countries is exacerbated by weaknesses in their public financial management systems. In view of the severe shortage of expertise and implementation capacity in many countries in the region, reform should be carefully prioritized to address the most serious and binding constraints affecting each individual country, instead of attempting to implement all facets of "international best practice" standards in a comprehensive single stage. Efforts should focus initially on improving functions that are likely to have the greatest impact on the countries' development priorities and objectives, such as building the revenue base, achieving a better alignment between government spending programs and social and economic objectives, and ensuring greater resilience to economic volatility and natural disasters.

International trade is vital for economic prosperity in Pacific island countries, but their trade performance has been generally weak over the past decade, with the exception of resource-rich countries. In Chapter 16, Hong Chen, Lanieta Rauqeuqe, Shiu Raj Singh, Yiqun Wu, and Yongzheng Yang note that the Pacific island countries have much scope to diversify trade into Asian markets. The authors argue that the emergence of Asia as a dynamic global economic region presents the Pacific island countries with an unprecedented opportunity to develop trade, particularly in tourism. Moreover, if stronger synergies can be established between tourism, agriculture, and fisheries, countries stand a better chance to improve broad-based growth.

In Chapter 17, Nooman Rebei investigates the determinants and implications of high spreads between bank deposit and lending interest rates. Such high spreads may be an indication of low competition in the banking industry, which can hinder access to credit by the private sector and impede growth, as well as reduce the effectiveness of the credit channel for the transmission of monetary policy, both of which are identified in earlier chapters as impediments to growth. Rebei uses an innovative set of macroeconomic and bank-specific data for the Solomon Islands to develop his theory. He concludes that some scope exists for increasing competition in the Solomon Islands' banking sector, but financial deepening also requires the development of nonbank institutions.

In Chapter 18, Matt Davies, John Vaught, and Ezequiel Cabezon provide comparative information on interest rate levels, key profitability indicators, and capital adequacy across the Pacific island countries and vis-à-vis other selected regions, to better contextualize regulatory actions and reforms that are needed to increase the depth, breadth, and efficiency of the financial sector in the Pacific. Although the focus of efforts must necessarily be at the national level, coordinated regional action also has a role to play, particularly given similarities in the underlying regulatory systems.

Acknowledgments

This book is the product of a strong partnership among Pacific island policymakers, development partners, academics, experts, and IMF staff. Most of the papers contained in this volume have been presented at the IMF high-level regional conferences in Samoa, Vanuatu, and Fiji, in 2012, 2013, and 2015 and greatly benefited from the discussion with the Pacific small states' authorities and other stakeholders.

This book would not have been possible without the support and encouragement of IMF Deputy Managing Director Min Zhu and of Changyong Rhee, Director of the Asia and Pacific Department. Special thanks go to our colleagues for their help in ensuring the successful completion of this book. We would like to thank in particular Sergei Dodzin for leading the production of the country annexes in strong collaboration with country teams. We are very grateful to Dongyeol Lee, Kazuaki Washimi, and Yiqun Wu who made the production of this book possible and to Ezequiel Cabezon and Tlek Zeinullayev for updating all the charts and tables. Gabriel Alvim, Justin Flinner, and Kathie Jamasali provided excellent administrative assistance. Fazurin Jamaludin coordinated all stages of production.

We are in debt to Joanne Creary from the IMF's Communications Department who edited the manuscript and together with Patricia Loo provided exceptional collaboration in coordinating the publication of this book.

Contributors

Xuefei Bai, a national of China, is a section chief in the International Department of the People's Bank of China, and works on regional financial cooperation issues. He also served for one year in the Asia and Pacific Department of the IMF as a special appointee economist, working on Kiribati and Tuvalu.

Chris Becker, a national of Australia and Germany, works at the Reserve Bank of Australia (RBA) as the head of domestic liquidity management, and also consults to the IMF providing advice and technical assistance on monetary and foreign exchange market policies and operations. He has held a variety of managerial positions at the RBA in departments covering economic analysis, domestic and international financial markets, as well as financial stability. He worked at the IMF Board from 2010 to 2012, where he represented members including Australia, Korea, New Zealand, and several Pacific island countries.

Mary Betley, a British national, works as a consultant providing advice and technical assistance in the areas of public financial management, public expenditure management, and budgetary policy and planning. She has experience assisting governments with budget and public financial management reforms in numerous countries in east Asia and the Pacific, central and south Asia, Africa, and eastern Europe. She has also participated in a number of IMF Fiscal Affairs Department missions.

Richard Bontjer, a national of Australia, is Director of Public Financial Management Advice in the Pacific Division of the Australian Department of Foreign Affairs and Trade (DFAT). Prior to joining DFAT, Mr. Bontjer served as an advisor for the Fiscal Affairs Department of the IMF, focusing on countries affected by conflict, and as a fiscal specialist consultant to the World Bank and the Panel of Experts for the Organisation for Economic Co-operation and Development Partnership for Democratic Governance (PDG). He also has held a variety of positions in the Australian Department of Finance.

Lino Briguglio, a national of Malta, is the Director of the Islands and Small States Institute of the University of Malta and a Professor of Economics at the same university. He is known internationally for his seminal work on the "Vulnerability Index," which measures the extent to which countries are exposed to external economic shocks. He has also pioneered work on the measurement of economic resilience. He has acted as consultant to various international organizations on studies and reports relating to small states.

Ezequiel Cabezon, a national of Argentina, is an economist in the IMF's European Department, and the desk economist for Albania. Before this, he was in the Asia and Pacific Department of the IMF, where he worked on the Pacific island countries, and he has also worked at the Inter-American Development Bank, focusing on the South American region.

Hong Chen, a national of China, is a senior researcher at the China Institute of Economic Transformation and Opening, Lingnan (University) College, Sun Yat-Sen University, China. She has been a consultant for the United Nations Economic and Social Commission for Asia and the Pacific and the United Nations Population Fund, working on projects related to trade and development.

Patrick Colmer, a national of Australia, works as a consultant providing advice and technical assistance in the subject areas of foreign investment, indirect tax, government relations, and development. His clients include governments in the Asia-Pacific region. He was previously the general manager of the International Finance and Development Division of the Australian Treasury. He has 25 years' experience as a senior policy advisor with various Australian government agencies.

Matt Davies, a division chief in the IMF's Fiscal Affairs Department. He has worked extensively in Asia and the Pacific, including as coordinator of the IMF's Pacific Financial Technical Assistance Centre based in Fiji. Prior to joining the IMF he worked in the United Kingdom and Papua New Guinea governments.

Ding Ding, a Chinese national, is a senior economist in the IMF's Asia and Pacific Department. He is currently the desk economist on Korea and mission chief for Kiribati. He has worked on a number of advanced and emerging market economies, including Australia, New Zealand, and Sri Lanka, and has published on a variety of topics such as macro-financial linkages, monetary policy transmission, and macroeconomic modeling and forecasting. He holds a PhD in Economics from Cornell University.

Sergei Dodzin, a senior economist in the Asia and Pacific Department (APD). He led missions to Kiribati and worked on various IMF country teams, including Malaysia, Singapore, Myanmar, Fiji, and, prior to joining APD, Serbia during the global financial crisis. As a member of the APD Small States Unit he was extensively involved in the analytical and policy work on small states. He also worked on an external assignment at the U.K. Financial Services Authority in 2007–08, where he participated in supervisory assessment of complex financial institutions and research and supervisory projects. His research interests include international economics, finance, and macro-financial linkages. Mr. Dodzin holds a PhD in Economics from Harvard University.

Jonathan Dunn is currently the IMF's resident representative to Vietnam and Lao P.D.R. He has been a deputy division chief at the IMF and the IMF mission chief for Fiji, Maldives, and Tajikistan. During 2009–11 he coordinated work on the Pacific islands in the IMF's Asia and Pacific Department. He has also been the IMF's resident representative in Azerbaijan, Bangladesh, Georgia, and Nigeria.

Jan Gottschalk, a national of Germany, is a senior economist in the IMF's Fiscal Affairs Department. He was previously the macroeconomic advisor at the IMF's Thailand Technical Assistance Office and prior to that the macroeconomic advisor at the IMF Pacific Financial Technical Assistance Centre (PFTAC) during 2010 to 2013. At PFTAC he helped build capacity for macroeconomic analysis and forecasting at ministries of finance and central banks in the Pacific. Before joining the IMF in 2001, he worked on business cycle research and forecasting in Germany.

Ron Hackett is Public Financial Management Advisor in the IMF Pacific Financial Technical Assistance Centre. Prior to joining the IMF in 2011, he served for 15 years as a project manager and hands-on advisor for several fiscal reform projects in developing countries funded by the U.S. Agency for International Development. His international development work was preceded by 20 years of budget management experience related to financing education, public employee pensions, and human services in the Minnesota State Budget Office.

Tobias Haque, a New Zealand national, is an economist at the World Bank, working on public financial management, economic policy, and debt management issues. Based in Washington, he previously spent three years based in the IMF Pacific Financial Technical Assistance Centre office in Suva, Fiji, and earlier lived in Honiara while working as the World Bank country economist for the Solomon Islands. He has published several research papers and policy reports promoting context-appropriate approaches to public financial management and economic management in Pacific island countries.

Leni Hunter, a New Zealand national, joined the Asia and Pacific Department of the IMF in 2013, working primarily on Pacific island countries and Timor-Leste. During 2011–13 she served on the IMF's Executive Board as the senior advisor from New Zealand. Prior to joining the IMF she spent 11 years at the Reserve Bank of New Zealand in various roles. She holds a Master of Commerce Degree in Economics from the University of Auckland.

Fazurin Jamaludin, a Malaysian national, is an economist in the Small States Unit of the IMF's Asia and Pacific Department. His country work experience at the IMF includes the Central African Republic, Maldives, the Solomon Islands, and Timor-Leste. Prior to joining the IMF, he worked on capital market development and regulatory issues in emerging markets and developing economies.

Hoe Ee Khor is the Chief Economist of the ASEAN+3 Macroeconomic Research Office (AMRO) and former deputy director of the IMF's Asia and Pacific Department. He started his career as an economist at the IMF in 1981 and has worked on a wide range of economies from the Caribbean and Pacific islands to southeast Asia, Korea, and Mexico. He was the IMF resident representative in China during 1991–93, and has written papers and reports on a wide range of topics and countries, focusing primarily on macroeconomic, monetary, and financial issues. He worked at the Monetary Authority of Singapore during 1996–2009 and was assistant managing director (Economics) responsible for monetary policy, financial stability, and international relations. He was also chief economist at the Abu Dhabi Council for Economic Development during 2009–12.

Roger P. Kronenberg is a macroeconomic and financial policy consultant. He retired from a 29-year career with the IMF in 2010. As an advisor in the IMF's Asia and Pacific Department, Mr. Kronenberg coordinated work on the Pacific island countries, and headed IMF mission teams for a diverse group of countries, including Australia, Brunei Darussalam, Fiji, Malaysia, Mongolia, New Zealand, Papua New Guinea, and Samoa.

Shanaka J. Peiris is the IMF's resident representative to the Philippines and covers ASEAN macro-financial surveillance for the Asia and Pacific Department. Prior to this he was a senior economist in the Asia and Pacific and Monetary and Capital Markets Departments of the IMF covering ASEAN countries and south Asia. He was also a mission chief to Pacific island countries and led a subworking group on asset price risks for the G-20 Mutual Assessment Program. He has published papers in academic journals on a wide range of topics, including inclusive growth, monetary policy and inflation, bond markets, banking and finance, and macroeconomic models for emerging markets, and has coauthored a book on poststabilization economics in sub-Saharan Africa.

Lanieta Rauqeuqe, a national of Fiji, is currently a senior economist at the Reserve Bank of Fiji, and previously worked as a local economist at the IMF's Resident Representative Office for the Pacific Islands, based in Suva, Fiji.

Nooman Rebei is a senior economist in the IMF's Middle East and Central Asia Department. He has a PhD in Economics from the University of Quebec at Montreal, specializing in macroeconomics and monetary and fiscal policies. Before joining the IMF, he was a principal economist in the central banks of Canada and Spain. He also worked at the African Development Bank as a research economist.

Niamh Sheridan, a national of Ireland, is a senior economist in the IMF's Asia and Pacific Department, the mission chief for Samoa, and desk economist for Malaysia. Before this, she worked on Fiji, Australia, and Singapore. She has also worked in the IMF's Institute for Capacity Development, training government officials on a broad range of macroeconomic topics.

Baljeet Singh, a national of Fiji, is a lecturer at the University of the South Pacific, Fiji. Before this, he was an economic planning officer at the Ministry of National Planning, Fiji. His research focuses on development issues in the Oceania region.

Shiu Raj Singh, a national of Fiji, is a Senior Public Finance Management Officer in the Asian Development Bank's Pacific Department, and the country economist and country officer for Samoa. Before this, he worked in the IMF's Asia and Pacific Department as a desk economist for Samoa and Tuvalu. He has also worked as an economist for the Government of Fiji.

Patrizia Tumbarello is the unit chief of the Small States Unit of the Asia and Pacific Department of the IMF. She oversees the work on the small states of the Pacific, and she is currently also the mission chief for the Solomon Islands. She has also worked on Australia, Vietnam, Albania, Moldova, Algeria, and Morocco. Prior to working in the Asia and Pacific Department, she spent time in the IMF's Strategy, Policy, and Review and Middle East and Central Asia Departments, focusing on emerging markets and economies in transition. Her research interests and publications have focused on enhancing macroeconomic resilience to natural disasters and climate change, fiscal frameworks, trade, and corporate and bank vulnerabilities.

Jon Vaught was formerly the Financial Sector Supervision Advisor at the IMF Pacific Financial Technical Assistance Centre (PFTAC). Prior to joining PFTAC, he provided technical assistance to a number of countries under the IMF technical assistance program, including Swaziland, where he was resident advisor for three years.

Shengzu Wang is currently the China Economist at Barclays Capital Asia, based in Hong Kong SAR. He was previously an economist in the European Department of the IMF covering the euro area and Greece. Since joining the IMF in 2009, he has also worked on economic surveillance and lending programs on a variety of advanced and emerging market economies in Asia-Pacific and Africa. Dr. Wang received his PhD in Economics from McGill University. He also served as an assistant professor at Fudan University, China.

Kazuaki Washimi, a national of Japan, is an economist in the IMF's Asia and Pacific Department, and the desk economist for Papua New Guinea, Samoa, and Timor-Leste. Prior to joining the IMF, he worked as an economist in the Research and Statistics Department of the Bank of Japan.

Richard Wood was formerly a policy advisor at the Australian Treasury, and represented Australia at the Organisation for Economic Co-operation and Development and the Paris Club.

Yiqun Wu, a Chinese national, is an economist in the IMF Asia and Pacific Department (APD), and the desk economist for the Solomon Islands. His country experience at the IMF includes Kiribati, Palau, and Papua New Guinea. He has also worked in APD's Regional Studies Division and coauthored several analytical chapters in the *Regional Economic Outlook: Asia and Pacific*.

Yongzheng Yang is currently a deputy division chief in the Asia and Pacific Department of the IMF and the IMF's mission chief for Myanmar. Prior to this, he was the IMF's resident representative in Pacific island countries from 2010 to 2014 and served as the mission chief for Papua New Guinea and Samoa. Mr. Yang has also worked on countries in Africa and Central Asia, as well as on IMF policies toward low-income countries. Before joining the IMF in 2001, he was a senior lecturer at The Australian National University, where he taught for 10 years. His most recent research focuses on economic growth, exchange rate policy, and monetary policy transmission mechanisms in Pacific island countries and the role of emerging donors in the economic development of low-income countries.

Tlek Zeinullayev, a national of Kazakhstan, is a research analyst in the Small States Unit of the IMF's Asia and Pacific Department. Prior to joining the IMF, he worked as a consultant at the World Bank in the Europe and Central Asia Chief Economist Office. He holds an MPhil in Economics from Oxford University.

PART I

Setting the Stage: The Quest for Resilience and Growth in the Pacific Islands

CHAPTER 1

Economic Growth in the Pacific Island Countries—Challenges, Constraints, and Policy Responses

ROGER P. KRONENBERG AND HOE EE KHOR

Economic growth among the Pacific island countries (PICs) has lagged most peer groups for more than a decade. This chapter provides an overview of the policy issues and challenges faced by these countries, and discusses the factors that have contributed to the low rates of economic growth in the region. It seeks to identify policies that could help raise growth performance in a way that is both inclusive and sustainable. The countries examined are Fiji, Kiribati, the Marshall Islands, Micronesia, Palau, Papua New Guinea, Samoa, the Solomon Islands, Timor-Leste, Tonga, Tuvalu, and Vanuatu. All are IMF members.

The picture that emerges is that the below-par growth performance of PICs can be partly explained by the region's unique characteristics. But policies also matter.

THE ECONOMIC SETTING

PICs seem stuck on a low-growth path (see Chapter 6). During the 10 years preceding the global financial crisis, real GDP growth in these countries averaged just 2 percent a year, considerably lower than in the countries of the Eastern Caribbean Currency Union (4 percent), other small states (4½ percent), and Asia's low-income countries (7 percent) (Figure 1.1). Real average income per capita in PICs has increased by less than 10 percent since 1990, compared with 40 percent in the Eastern Caribbean, 25 percent in the group of all small states, and about 150 percent in Asia's emerging market economies. PIC growth in the 2000s was the lowest in four decades. As of 2013 average gross national income per capita in PICs was just one-third that of the Caribbean countries. The PICs' recovery from the global financial crisis has also generally lagged Asia's low-income countries and emerging market economies. Meanwhile, differences in growth performance among PICs have widened over the past decade, with the natural-resource-rich countries (Papua New Guinea, the Solomon Islands, Timor-Leste) generally outperforming the others, particularly since 2008 (Figure 1.2).

The below-par growth performance can be partly explained by the region's unusual geographic, demographic, climatic, and other characteristics. These include:

- Small populations and small internal markets that result in diseconomies of scale and high fixed costs of production.
- Extreme geographic dispersion and isolation, implying low connectivity.
- Vulnerability to natural disasters and climate change, including cyclones, droughts, and rising sea levels.
- Narrow production and exports bases due to smallness and therefore lack of economies of scale.
- Depletion or unsustainable exploitation of natural resources, including forestry products, minerals, energy resources, and marine resources.

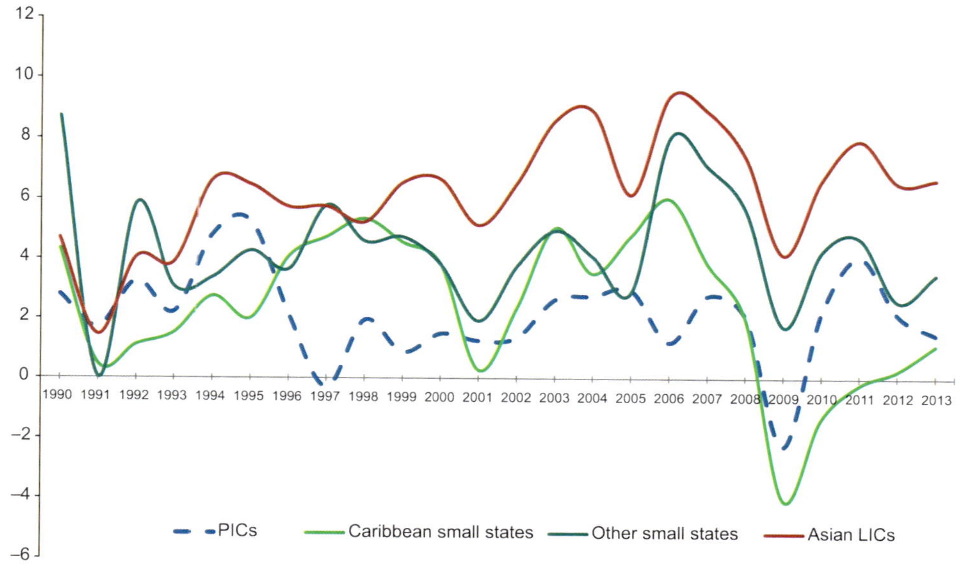

Figure 1.1 Growth Performance: Pacific Island Countries and Selected Comparators (*Percent*)

Source: IMF, World Economic Outlook database.
Note: LICs = low-income countries; PICs = Pacific island countries.

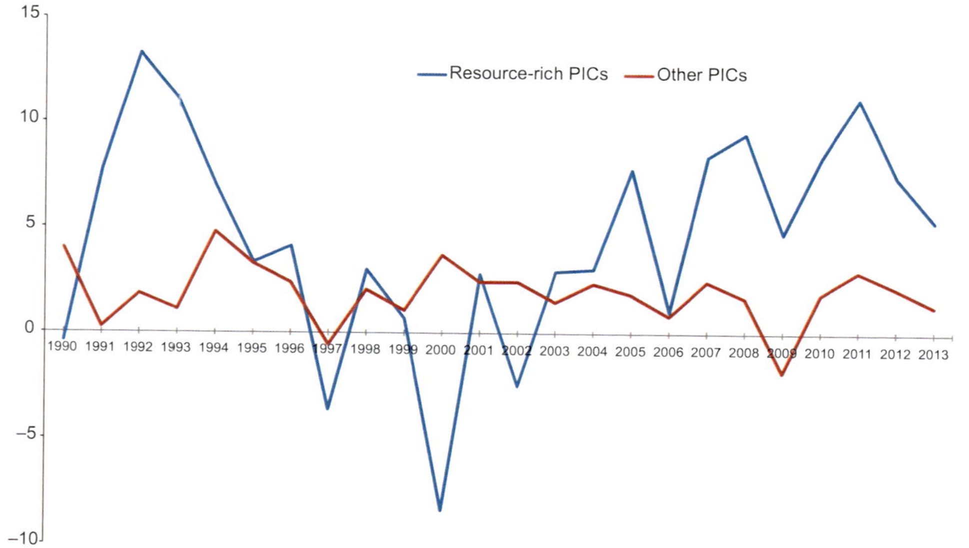

Figure 1.2 Growth Performance among Pacific Island Countries (*Percent*)

Source: IMF, World Economic Outlook database.
Note: LICs = low-income countries; PICs = Pacific island countries.

In addition to the effects of these physical characteristics, growth in some PICs has been further constrained by policy-related factors, such as:

- Weak macroeconomic policy frameworks, which led at times to unsustainable exploitation of natural resources.
- Capacity constraints, including weak policy implementation capacity.
- Limited financial depth.
- Laws and customs that limit the flexibility of product and factor markets (for example, land tenure).
- High levels of public debt (Samoa, Tonga, Tuvalu).
- High dependence on foreign aid; for example, microstates reliant on Compacts of Free Association with the United States (Marshall Islands, Micronesia, Palau); and remittances (Samoa, Tonga, Tuvalu).
- Political economy factors such as periods of political instability or lack of security (including, at various times, Fiji, Papua New Guinea, the Solomon Islands, Timor-Leste, and Tonga), which hamper investment and the development of sound institutions.

While there is broad agreement about the factors that have contributed to slow growth in PICs, it is less obvious how policymakers can overcome these constraints. Small domestic markets, remote locations, and poor natural resource endowments do not lend themselves to quick or easy solutions. Even so, policies do affect economic outcomes in broadly predictable ways, and even the smallest countries can achieve higher economic performance with the right policy mix, good governance, and a skilled labor force.

There is scope for PICs to strengthen the policy environment and improve growth performance. However, to do so, their governments need to put in place policies that foster macroeconomic stability and debt sustainability, build institutions through reforms, strengthen confidence in the policy framework, promote the development of financial markets, improve the business environment, and address rigidities in product and factor markets to attract foreign direct investment. Another challenge is to find the right balance between the need to build fiscal buffers to enhance resilience and the need to fund development spending.

The foundation of a growth-enhancing policy strategy must start with a credible macro-fiscal framework that sets clear, achievable targets for a sustainable medium-term debt position. Here, one of the biggest challenges is striking the right balance between policy rules that can help anchor confidence and policy flexibility to enable the authorities to respond to unanticipated macro-critical shocks, including natural disasters, which can be severe in PICs. For countries with significant natural resource endowments, such as Papua New Guinea, the Solomon Islands, and Timor-Leste, the fiscal framework and minerals taxation regime should facilitate the transformation of nonrenewable underground and undersea wealth into income-generating wealth through investments in domestic infrastructure, human capital, and a diversified, low-risk portfolio of foreign financial assets.

The challenges of doing so should not be underestimated, particularly in countries where technical capacity and the ability of the economy to absorb higher levels of development spending may be very limited. Development programs therefore need to be scaled up in line with capacity improvement to ensure effective use of resources. Governments and central banks also need to hold adequate international reserves for precautionary purposes. Although it is an important form of protection, self-insurance in itself is not enough and needs to be complemented by international safety nets and pooling of risks through regional arrangements (see Chapter 5). Other key policy elements include:

- Monetary and exchange rate arrangements that facilitate the maintenance of low inflation, ensure competitiveness, and promote adjustment to large terms-of-trade swings or supply shocks in a manner consistent with a country's institutional and administrative capacity.

- Developing sound financial institutions capable of mobilizing savings and channeling them to productive investments.
- Policies to address structural rigidities in land tenure systems. These rigidities reduce the efficiency of land use by placing constraints on the ability to transfer ownership of land, using land for loan collateral, and putting land to nontraditional uses.
- Regional arrangements to mitigate the diseconomies of scale, enhance competition, protect and promote regional interests, and allow greater specialization in areas of comparative advantage.
- Closer trade and investment linkages with fast-growing partners, including Australia, New Zealand, and east Asia's rapidly growing economies.

CHALLENGES AND CONSTRAINTS TO GROWTH

Small Populations and Remote Locations

With the exception of Papua New Guinea (population: 7.2 million), the PICs and Timor-Leste are small states.[1] Of these, seven (Kiribati, Marshall Islands, Micronesia, Palau, Samoa, Tonga, Tuvalu) can be classified as microstates, with populations under 200,000.

Small populations limit market size and can affect growth and income levels through their impact on competition, the diversity of labor market skills, diversification of production, and the ability to achieve economies of scale in producing public services ranging from health care to financial supervision and tax administration. Most PICs also have very small land areas, although the maritime areas within their exclusive economic zones (EEZs) can be very large (Figure 1.3).

PICs are also among the most remote countries in the world. Distances to even their closest neighbors—Australia, New Zealand, and countries in east Asia—are measured in hundreds, if not thousands, of kilometers. While advances in telecommunications technology have reduced some of the costs of remoteness, PICs have, on the whole, been slow in introducing and adding capacity in new technologies. Indeed, it could even be argued that technological advances have left PICs even more commercially isolated from the major centers of global economic activity than before, since there is now less need for modern aircraft and ships to call at PICs for refueling or resupply.

Trade among PICs is also constrained by geography. In the same way that they are far from large markets, the distances separating PICs from each other are also considerable, and there are few complementarities in their production structures to encourage trade among them. Even domestic commerce can be constrained by remoteness. Micronesia, for example, comprises 65 inhabited islands in four separately governed states. Kiribati's 21 inhabited islands have a total area of just 811 square kilometers in an EEZ covering some 3.4 million square kilometers of ocean, and two of the country's three island chains have no air services. Even in Papua New Guinea, the most populous PIC and the one with the largest land area, transportation between different parts of the country can be extremely difficult because of the rugged terrain and limited road infrastructure.

Vulnerability to Natural Disasters and Climate Change

Climate, geography, geology, and weak infrastructure leave PICs exposed and vulnerable to natural disasters. Natural disasters have included major cyclones (Fiji, Samoa, Tonga, Vanuatu), tsunamis (Samoa, the Solomon Islands), severe drought (Marshall Islands, Tuvalu), flooding (the Solomon Islands), and volcanic eruption (Papua New Guinea). And then there is the looming existential threat to some low-lying coral island countries (Kiribati, Marshall Islands, Tuvalu) posed by rising sea levels from climate change. Faced with this bleak prospect, the government of Kiribati has

[1] Small developing countries/small states have populations of under 1.5 million. See IMF (2014).

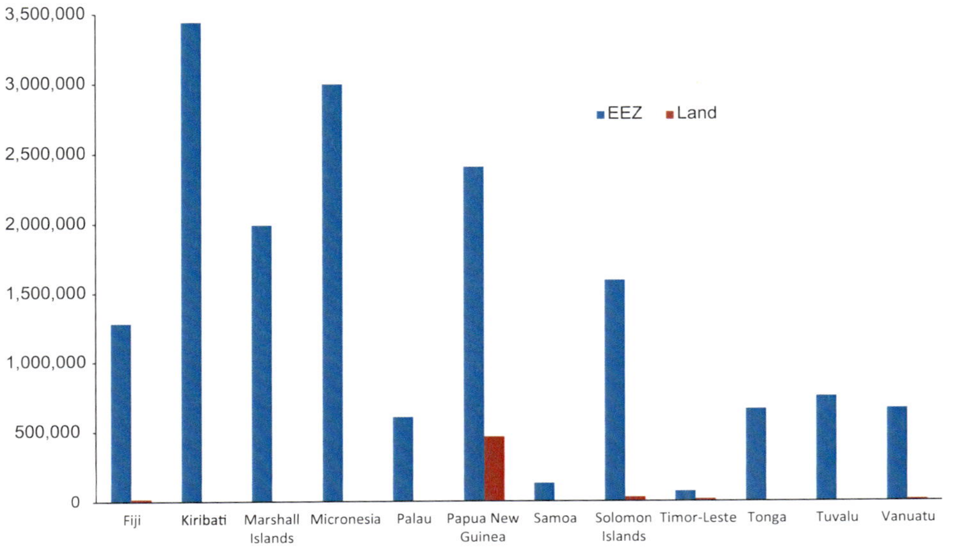

Figure 1.3 Pacific Island Countries: Exclusive Economic Zones and Land Mass (*Square kilometers*)

Source: Sea Around Us database.
Note: EEZ = exclusive economic zone.

bought land in Fiji and asked Australia and New Zealand to open their borders to immigrants from Kiribati in anticipation of a possible evacuation of the islands.

Natural Resources and Tourism

The natural resource endowments of PICs span a huge range. In Timor-Leste, for example, oil and natural gas account for about 80 percent of GDP and 90 percent of government revenue, making the economy highly dependent on energy prices and the exploration of new fields. The country needs to successfully diversify its currently narrow economic base. Natural resources, including gas, oil, copper, and gold, also play a very important role in Papua New Guinea's economy. A large-scale liquefied natural gas development was successfully completed in 2014 and production is expected to continue for about 20 years. Gold was once an important export for Fiji and the Solomon Islands, with the latter also having untapped reserves of nickel and bauxite. In contrast, some other PICs, including some of the smallest, have no commercially exploitable mineral wealth, relatively little arable land, and precarious supplies of fresh water.

The sustainable management of natural resource wealth can present huge policy challenges for low-income countries. Unlike most other forms of economic activity, the extraction of energy and mineral resources can occur only once. For sustainable and inclusive growth to take place after the exhaustion of mineral wealth, these countries must set aside a portion of mining sector income for investment in income-generating assets for the future. Good examples include Kiribati, which has built up a significant sovereign wealth fund from its phosphate deposits, and Timor-Leste, which has also built up a sizable sovereign wealth fund from its energy exports since 2005.

Several PICs have important forestry and agricultural sectors, but the resource base in some of them has been depleted by unsustainable rates of harvesting. Forestry remains an important export sector for the Solomon Islands, for example, though the country faces unsustainable rates of logging that will lead to rapid depletion of logging stocks. Sugar production in Fiji has been declining for

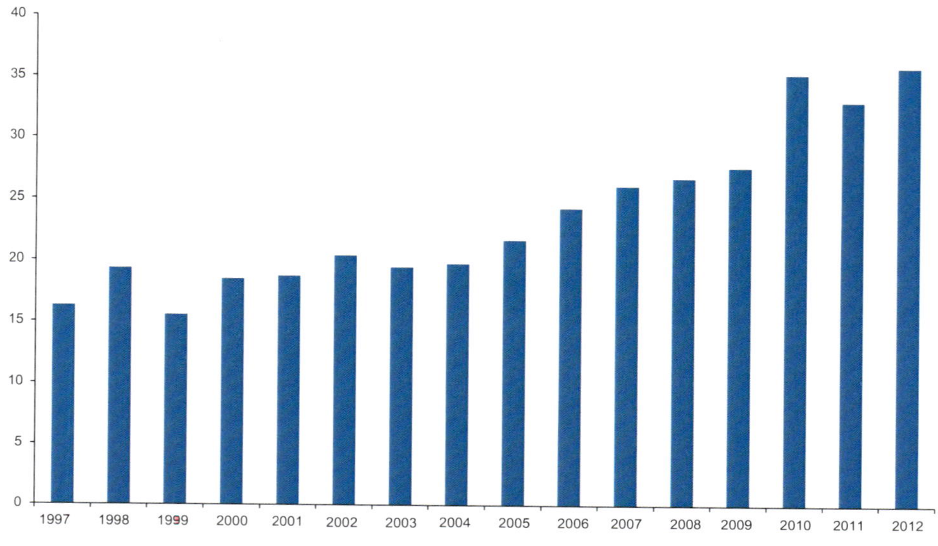

Figure 1.4 Parties to the Nauru Agreement: Share of Global Tuna Catch *(Percent)*

Sources: Western and Central Pacific Fisheries Commission (WCPFC), *Tuna Fishery Yearbook* (2012); and WCPFC estimates as of July 2014.
Note: The parties to the Nauru Agreement Concerning Cooperation in the Management of Fisheries of Common Interest are Kiribati, Marshall Islands, Micronesia, Nauru, Palau, Papua New Guinea, the Solomon Islands, and Tuvalu.

many years because of the phasing out of trade preferences in Europe, low crop yields, the inefficiency of its manufacturing plant, and the emigration of growers. Recent restructuring efforts have partially reversed this trend. Samoa, Tonga, and Vanuatu are producers of agricultural commodities, including root crops, copra, and coconut oil. The small atoll islands of Micronesia have very little in the way of onshore natural resources, including arable land.

The Pacific islands occupy some of the world's richest fishing waters, but managing these resources has been a major challenge. The EEZs claimed by the eight parties to the Nauru Agreement Concerning Cooperation in the Management of Fisheries of Common Interest cover some 14.3 million square kilometers—roughly 1½ times the size of China or the United States—and account for 25–30 percent of the world's tuna supply (Figure 1.4).[2] Foreign vessels operating under licensing arrangements account for more than 80 percent of the total catch in the EEZs of PICs, and monitoring their activities across such large swathes of ocean presents major logistical challenges for these countries.

The natural beauty and rich cultural heritage of the Pacific islands are enormous assets for the tourism industry. In the tourism-based economies (Fiji, Palau, Samoa, Vanuatu), tourism receipts on average account for about 30 percent of GDP—in Palau the share is 58 percent—compared to 19 percent in the Caribbean small states (Figure 1.5). In the other Pacific countries, tourism is still in relatively early stages of development, but the potential is large for niche activities such as diving and ecotourism.

Despite having these critical components, developing a sustainable tourism industry poses significant challenges for policymakers in the region. In infrastructure this requires sufficient guest accommodations, airports able to handle long-haul aircraft, and airlines interested in providing a

[2]The parties to the agreement are Kiribati, Marshall Islands, Micronesia, Nauru, Palau, Papua New Guinea, the Solomon Islands, and Tuvalu.

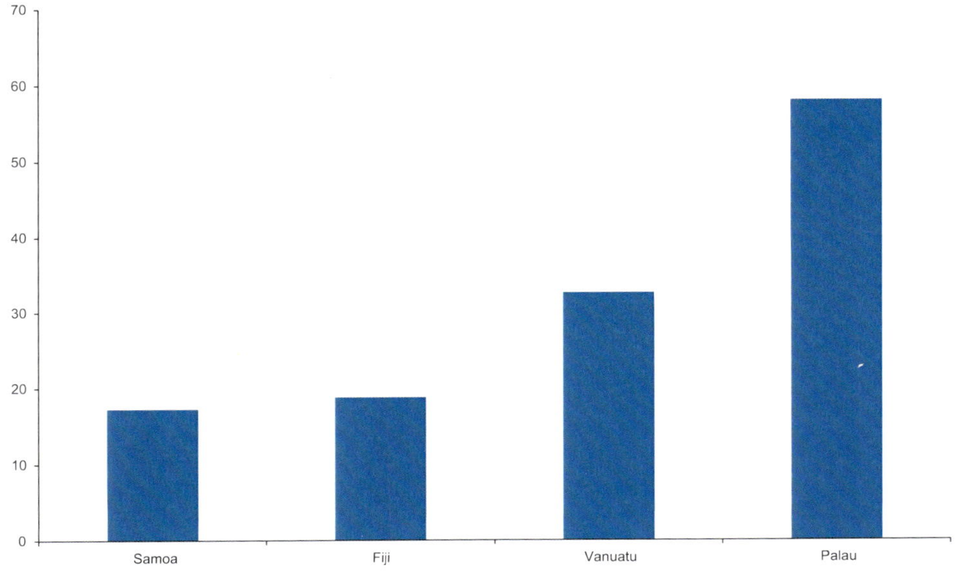

Figure 1.5 Tourism-Intensive Pacific Island Countries: Tourism Receipts (*Percent of GDP*)

Source: IMF staff estimates.

service. The large, up-front costs of building this infrastructure can create considerable sequencing problems for small, remote countries, as there is a natural desire on the part of investors to want other infrastructure components in place before committing their resources. While it is clearly in the interest of policymakers to try to coordinate policies and investment decisions, the difficulty of the task is substantial—and the history of tourism development in the Pacific has numerous examples of very costly failures. Fragile environmental conditions and free-ridership issues add to the challenges and complexity of developing tourism in the region.

Political and Social Stability

Political and social stability are important catalysts for investment, sustainable economic growth, and inclusive development. Yang and others (Chapter 4) find that political stability has had an overall positive impact on the growth performance of the PIC region compared with other small states, but individual country experiences have differed sharply. Broadly speaking, the smaller Polynesian and Micronesian countries have experienced greater political stability than the larger Melanesian countries, which also happen to be the ones with greater endowments of natural resource wealth.

Recent political developments in the region have been quite encouraging. Timor-Leste, which experienced severe civil strife in recent decades, has successfully held democratic elections and is making significant progress in rebuilding national institutions and strengthening governance. With domestic security restored, the government was able to complete the withdrawal of the United Nations-sponsored multinational police force in 2012. Similarly, the regional police force requested by the Solomon Islands to help restore order following a period of social unrest has started to gradually wind down as the situation is normalized. Fiji, which had been ruled by a military junta since 2006, adopted a new constitution in 2013 and held a general election in September 2014. The successful transition to a democratic government has generated tremendous interest among foreign investors and is likely to lead to higher foreign investment.

POLICY RESPONSES TO STRENGTHEN GROWTH POTENTIAL

PICs have been significantly disadvantaged by their small populations, remote locations, weak administrative capacities, and limited arsenal of policy instruments. But what can the authorities do to secure a more prosperous and stable future? The chapters in this book suggest there is scope for policies to reduce the vulnerabilities of PICs and strengthen growth potential. Success will depend, to a large extent, on the ability of the authorities to put in place medium-term macro-fiscal frameworks, sound monetary and exchange rate policies, and structural reforms to improve the business environment, investment climate, and flexibility of markets. And to do this while finding new ways to turn the region's unique resources and environment to its own greater advantage.

Macro-Fiscal Frameworks and Sovereign Wealth Funds

Fiscal policy serves multiple purposes in PICs. It must be designed to meet countries' highest priorities for infrastructure, human capital formation, and the provision of public services, which is made more costly and difficult by their small size, remote location, and limited scope for a high level of labor force specialization. Fiscal policy must also be sustainable, which is particularly important and difficult in countries that are heavily dependent on exhaustible natural resources. The tax system should be as neutral and nondistortionary as possible, while also being administratively enforceable and not imposing excessive compliance costs. And the fiscal regime must establish the right balance between fiscal anchors, which generate confidence and predictability in the economic environment for domestic residents and foreign investors, and providing the authorities with adequate discretion to respond flexibly to unanticipated shocks or new opportunities.

Given the vulnerability to large shocks and revenue volatility, fiscal policy in the PICs should be grounded in a credible medium-term macro-fiscal framework (see Chapter 10). Fiscal frameworks for resource-rich PICs like Timor-Leste and Papua New Guinea recognize the importance of investing a significant share of their natural resource revenue in productive assets that can continue to generate a stream of income indefinitely after mineral or energy resources have been depleted. However, only five of the PICs have adopted a multiyear budget framework to help smooth the expenditure path over the medium term.

The appropriate policy response to a negative shock depends in part on the individual country's fiscal space (see Chapter 6). While Papua New Guinea, the Solomon Islands, and Vanuatu still have fiscal space, the scope for countercyclical policies is more limited in those countries with high public debt (Marshall Islands, Samoa, Tonga, Tuvalu).

A critical issue for policymakers in resource-rich, low-income countries is how resource revenues should be used to promote sustainable growth. Traditionally, the emphasis was on setting aside a significant proportion of extractive resource revenues for the international reserves of the central bank. The revenues were typically invested in highly rated liquid financial assets, such as the government securities of reserve currency countries, which could generate steady, safe, and predictable streams of income, while providing a precautionary buffer to negative shocks.

In recent years, with yields on such instruments becoming very low and often negative in real terms, greater attention has turned to sovereign wealth funds and the need to maintain a broader, more balanced portfolio of international assets, including equities and other alternative assets, with the objective of improving investment returns while containing overall risk. The sovereign wealth funds of Kiribati and Timor-Leste, for example, are mandated to invest in diversified portfolios of bonds and equities. To assist the Timorese authorities in achieving these objectives, the government has retained the services of major international investment advisors to manage the portfolio of its fund, subject to the government's prudent and transparent investment guidelines.

Thinking has also evolved somewhat on domestic investments. In particular, increased attention has been given to the need for low-income, resource-rich countries to invest in domestic infrastructure and human capital to facilitate the diversification of their economies away from minerals or energy extraction. This is so that growth can become more broadly based and sustainable, as natural resource extraction peaks and eventually declines (IMF 2012). At the same time, it is important to recognize that PICs have quite limited absorptive capacity and that pushing too hard to scale up domestic investment can be inflationary and even wasteful, and have adverse consequences for competitiveness.

The economic policy frameworks of Marshall Islands, Micronesia, and Palau are structured around their Compacts of Free Association with the United States. These provide for the disbursement of sector grants by the United States and the establishment of trust funds that have been funded mostly by the United States. The purpose of the trust funds is to contribute to economic advancement and to achieve budgetary self-reliance ahead of the projected expiration in 2023–24 of U.S. grants to these countries. The trust funds are invested in a mix of assets (bonds and equities) and are subject to the oversight of joint committees with U.S. participation. For Marshall Islands and Micronesia, no disbursements from the funds are allowed until 2023. For Palau, the government was allowed to withdraw up to US$5 million annually until 2013, and it can gradually increase maximum annual withdrawals up to US$13 million in 2023 under the proposed new agreement. These three countries have adopted the U.S. dollar as their national currencies, reflecting the importance of the compacts in their policy frameworks as well as their small size. Tuvalu also participates in a large trust fund, which is jointly owned by the Tuvaluan government and several key development partners. The fund can be drawn down only when its value exceeds a benchmark that is indexed to Australia's consumer price index, and the maximum that can be drawn is the portfolio value in excess of the benchmark.

Monetary and Exchange Rate Arrangements

Monetary policy can help maintain macroeconomic stability and smooth business cycles. However, its effectiveness depends, in part, on the strength of the pass-through of interest rates set by the central bank to bank deposit and lending rates. Gottschalk (Chapter 14) finds that this pass-through is weak in most PICs, which have large amounts of excess liquidity. In addition, the up-front fixed costs of establishing effective monetary policy institutions, instruments, and capacity can be extremely large for very small countries. Therefore, it is not surprising that the smallest PICs have adopted other reserve currencies, either the U.S. dollar or the Australian dollar, as their legal tender.[3] Timor-Leste, which is a larger country, also uses the U.S. dollar, partly reflecting the importance of oil and natural gas exports (which are denominated in U.S. dollars) to its economy and its relatively underdeveloped financial markets. However, unlike the other smaller countries using the currencies of larger nations, Timor-Leste has established a central bank, both to supervise local financial institutions and to build research and other central banking capabilities.

Exchange rate flexibility can enhance the effectiveness of monetary policy and facilitate adjustment to economic shocks, particularly in countries subject to large terms-of-trade shifts and other external shocks. However, floating exchange rate regimes require foreign exchange markets that are sufficiently deep and liquid to prevent excessive volatility. Reflecting the small size of their foreign exchange markets, most of the PICs that have their own currencies maintain exchange rates pegged to a basket of foreign currencies (Fiji, Samoa, the Solomon Islands, Tonga, Vanuatu). Papua New Guinea, the country with the largest economy and banking sector in the region and a resource-based economy, is the only PIC with a flexible exchange rate regime.

Regional Initiatives

The exceptionally small size of PICs means that regional initiatives have the potential of generating economies of scale that could not possibly be achieved by individual countries. Regional initiatives

[3] Kiribati and Tuvalu use the Australian dollar, given Australia's importance as a trading partner.

also have an important role to play in cases where the actions of one country have externalities—positive or negative—for their neighbors, and in cases where multiple countries may be prone to the same shocks, such as cyclones.

There are success stories of regional cooperation in the Pacific. In education, the University of the South Pacific is a shining example of how regional cooperation can mitigate diseconomies of scale. Fisheries is another area where collective efforts have met with considerable success. Historically, the domestic fishing industry in PICs has suffered from a low number of jobs, poor earnings from employment, and a low impact on poverty alleviation and food security. PICs' domestic fishing fleets are estimated to account for only about 20 percent of the catch in the waters of their EEZs. The 17-nation Pacific Islands Forum Fisheries Agency (FFA) was established as an advisory body to assist member countries to manage their fishery resources in a sustainable way. Under the Harmonized Minimum Terms and Conditions for Access to FFA Member EEZs by Foreign Fishing Vessels, which has been agreed by all FFA members, foreign fishing vessels operating in the region must identify themselves to the FFA Vessel Monitoring System using an automatic location communicator. In addition, the eight countries that are parties to the Nauru agreement, which are also FFA members, have implemented a Vessel Day Scheme, which apportions the total allocation of fishing days among its members and allows for the purchase and trade of fishing days among the parties. The scheme's purpose is to constrain catches of tuna species to sustainable levels and increase the rate of return from access fees paid by the Distant-Water Fishing Nations.

To mitigate the disadvantages from small country size and remoteness, much more needs to be done to increase regional cooperation. Air and sea transportation is an area where greater cooperation is urgently needed to reduce the fragmentation of regional networks, which continues to hamper trade and tourism development. On the trade policy front, liberalization under the Pacific Island Countries Trade Agreement was established to deepen regional trade integration and prepare PICs to form a regional free trade agreement—the Pacific Agreement on Closer Economic Relations Plus—with Australia and New Zealand. But progress has been slow and so far has brought only limited and uneven benefits to PICs, though this is not surprising given the similarities of resource endowments among these countries. A key challenge for PICs is to formulate a broad strategy that would enable them to secure greater access for their labor and agricultural products in Australia and New Zealand. At the same time, PICs should increase efforts to tap into Asia's rapidly growing markets, particularly the tourism market. This calls for greater openness to trade and foreign direct investment across the board, and nondiscriminatory liberalization over time to maximize the benefits of economic integration with both traditional and emerging trade partners.

Other Policy Issues

Making efficient use of their very limited land resources has posed problems for many PICs. Land tenure in most of these countries is typically based on some form of communal land ownership, which can reduce the incentives for making land improvements and other forms of investment, as well as inhibit the development of mortgage-type financial instruments. Land rights issues have been particularly important in some of the resource-rich PICs, where disputes have arisen over the division of natural resource revenues among various parties, including central and local government and groups with competing land ownership claims. In Fiji, for instance, differences between smallholders in the sugar industry, who are mostly descendants of immigrants, and landowners, who are from the indigenous population, have resulted in poor agricultural practices and lack of investment in farms leading to low yields. The recent establishment of the Land Bank is a welcome step toward creating a predictable and stable supply of land with lease for long-term investment.[4]

[4] Through a land bank, indigenous landowners can allow the government to use their property for development purposes and on-lease it at market rates.

The small size of PIC markets has hindered the development of financial and capital markets in the region. With a perceived shortage of bankable projects, many banks (mostly foreign) hold an unusually high share of their deposits in the form of government and central bank securities and excess reserves. They also rely heavily for their income on fee-based services such as foreign exchange transactions, rather than intermediating between domestic savers and potential users of funds. Bank penetration in these countries is also quite low, reflecting the high cost of setting up branches in remote areas. However, with advancements in computer and telecommunications technology, banks in Fiji, Papua New Guinea, and the Solomon Islands are developing mobile-phone-based banking and microfinance, which can facilitate the expansion of banking services to the broader population.

CONCLUSIONS

Small size, remote location, high vulnerability to natural disasters, and poor natural resource endowments do not lend themselves to quick or easy fixes. Nevertheless, policies still play a critical role in reducing vulnerability to shocks and mitigating some of the disadvantages of small size and remote location.

Being able to address these constraints effectively will, to a large extent, depend on the authorities' success in implementing a medium-term macro-fiscal framework appropriate to the particular characteristics of each individual country, and adopting sound monetary and exchange rate policies to maintain low inflation and promote adjustments to external shocks. Addressing these constraints will also depend critically on their success in implementing structural reforms and investments aimed at strengthening institutions and the governance framework, upgrading human capital, building physical infrastructure, and improving the flexibility of labor, capital, and goods markets.

Finally, PICs should cooperate through regional initiatives to strengthen their capacity to harness the region's natural resources, including the vast marine resources of the Pacific Ocean, for the economic and social development of their populations. And income from these natural resources needs to be invested in income-generating assets for future generations.

REFERENCES

International Monetary Fund (IMF). 2012. "Macroeconomic Policy Frameworks for Resource-Rich Developing Countries." Background Paper 1, Supplement 1, Washington.

———. 2014. "Staff Guidance Note on the Fund's Engagement with Small Developing States." IMF Policy Paper, Washington.

CHAPTER 2

Raising Potential Growth and Enhancing Resilience to Shocks

EZEQUIEL CABEZON, PATRIZIA TUMBARELLO, AND YIQUN WU

The small states of the Asia and Pacific region face unique challenges in raising their growth potential and living standards. Small populations, geographical isolation and dispersion, narrow export and production bases, lack of economies of scale, limited access to international capital markets, exposure to shocks (including climate change), and heavy reliance on aid leave them particularly vulnerable. In providing public services, they face higher fixed government costs than other states because their governments must provide these services regardless of small population size. In small states, limited access to credit by the private sector is an impediment to inclusive growth, and capacity constraints are another key challenge. These challenges seem to be particularly acute in microstates (countries with populations of less than 200,000). But as well as these challenges, Asia and Pacific small states face higher volatility than other small states in GDP growth per capita, changes in the terms of trade, aid, current account balances, and revenue.

This chapter's econometric analysis confirms that the Pacific island countries (PICs), many of which are small states and microstates, have underperformed relative to their peers over the last 20 years. After controlling for standard variables that explain GDP growth per capita, PICs suffer a disadvantage in this measure of about 2 percentage points, compared with an average small state.

They also have more limited policy tools. Five out of 13 developing small states in Asia and the Pacific covered in this chapter do not have a central bank, and the scope for diversifying their economies is narrow.[1] Given their large development needs, fiscal policies have been procyclical at times. Within the Asia and Pacific small states, the microstates are subject to more vulnerability and macroeconomic volatility than the rest.

Despite the limited availability of policy tools, policies *do* matter and they can help build resilience and raise potential growth. Indeed, because of sound policies and strong links with resilient economies in the region, and despite all the challenges, PICs did slightly better than some comparators during the recent business cycle. Some Asia and Pacific small states have also made progress in building policy buffers. Nevertheless, growth rates have remained quite low. Given their high vulnerability to external shocks, these countries should continue to rebuild buffers and improve the composition of public spending for education, health, and infrastructure to better foster inclusive growth (see also Chapter 10).

The Asia and Pacific small states have enormous untapped marine resources, which require more effort to properly exploit and manage them. These states should continue to pursue regional solutions, mainly in fisheries, information technology, and aviation safety. Further integration with the broader Asia and Pacific region should help raise growth potential.

This chapter is based on IMF Working Paper 13/123 (Tumbarello, Cabezon, and Wu 2013). The authors thank Peter Allum, Luis Breuer, Ian Davidoff, Sergei Dodzin, Romain Duval, Tubagus Feridhanusetyawan, Craig Fookes, Leni Hunter, Sonali Jain-Chandra, Fazurin Jamaludin, Nghi Luu, Vance Martin, Koshy Mathai, Brad McDonald, Shanaka Peiris, Alexander Pitt, Jack Ree, Neil Saker, Werner Schule, Niamh Sheridan, Shiu Singh, Olaf Unteroberdoerster, Yongzheng Yang, Akihiko Yoshida, and the participants of the Small Islands Club at the IMF for their comments; and Hoe Ee Khor for his guidance throughout the project. Shari Boyce provided excellent editorial assistance.

[1]The 13 comprise Bhutan, Fiji, Kiribati, Maldives, the Marshall Islands, Micronesia, Palau, Samoa, the Solomon Islands, Timor-Leste, Tonga, Tuvalu, and Vanuatu. With the exception of Bhutan, Maldives, and Timor-Leste, they are all PICs. The microstates are Kiribati, the Marshall Islands, Micronesia, Palau, Samoa, Tonga, and Tuvalu.

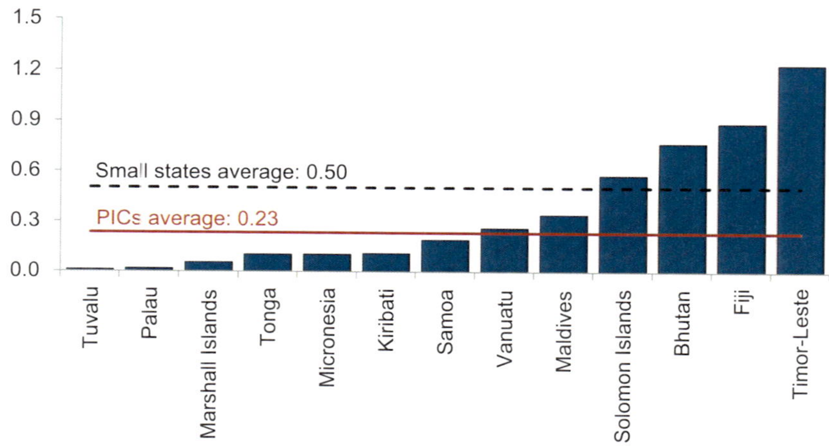

Figure 2.1 Asia and Pacific Small States: Population, 2014 (*Millions*)

Sources: IMF, World Economic Outlook database; and World Bank, World Development Indicators database.
Note: PICs = Pacific island countries.

TABLE 2.1

Geographical Dispersion: Average Sea Distance between Two Inhabitants of the Same Country

Country	Distance (Kilometers)
Micronesia	706
Kiribati	691
Marshall Islands	280
Solomon Islands	267
Vanuatu	210
Tuvalu	177
Tonga	105
Fiji	71
Samoa	19
Palau	14
The Bahamas	96
Trinidad and Tobago	9
St. Kitts and Nevis	9
Antigua and Barbuda	2

Source: IMF staff calculations, based on country censuses.
Note: This is equivalent to computing the average distance between islands of the same country weighted by population.

CHARACTERISTICS OF SMALL STATES IN THE ASIA AND PACIFIC REGION

As noted, the region's small states face unique challenges in raising growth potential and living standards, which distinguishes them from the broader group of small states in other regions. Yet even among them, heterogeneity is high, with the microstates subject to more vulnerability and macroeconomic volatility than the other Asia and Pacific small states.[2]

[2] See Chapter 9 for a discussion of the importance of geographic isolation as a source of vulnerability and on the higher fixed costs of government in PICs.

Many small states in the Asia and Pacific region are remote, widely dispersed, and sparsely populated (Figure 2.1). Their remoteness from major markets and trading partners—unlike small islands in other regions—raises transport costs and keeps these economies relatively isolated. Their wide dispersion, shown in Table 2.1, precludes the exploitation of geographical agglomeration effects. Most PICs consist of hundreds of islands scattered across the Pacific Ocean in a space occupying 15 percent of the earth's surface—and these are by far the most remote countries in the world, according to different indicators. These include the United Nations' liner shipping connectivity index, which measures countries' connectedness to global shipping networks based on the status of their maritime transport sectors and geographical distance (Figures 2.2 and 2.3). Two PICs are the IMF's smallest members by population—Tuvalu and Palau—and the average population in PICs is half that of small states outside the Pacific.

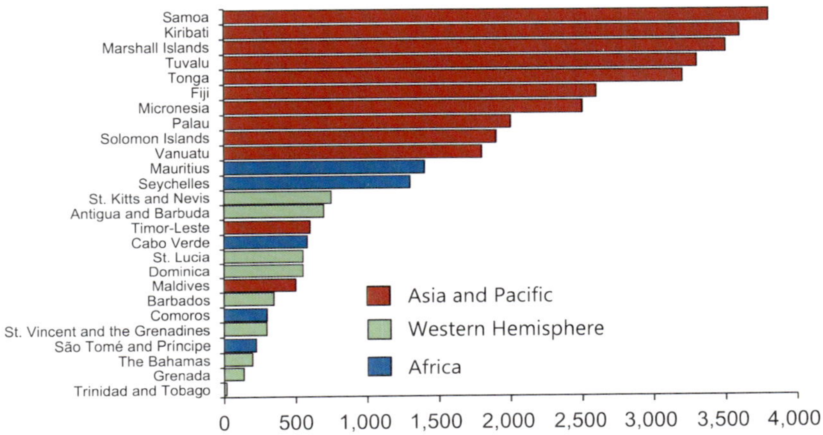

Figure 2.2 Small States: Distance to the Closest Continent (*Kilometers*)

Sources: South Pacific Applied Geoscience Commission; United Nations Environment Programme; and IMF staff calculations.

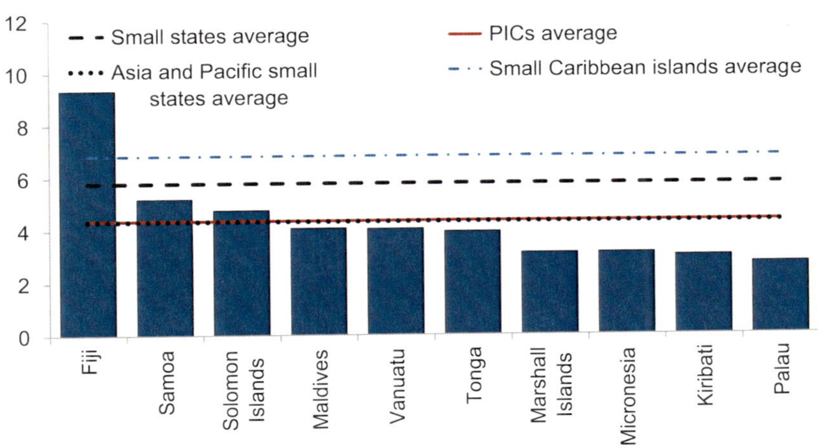

Figure 2.3 Asia and Pacific Small States: Liner Shipping Connectivity Index, 2004–13[1]

Source: WorldBank, World Development Indicators database.

Note: PICs = Pacific island countries.

[1] A smaller number indicates lower connectivity/high transportation costs. Countries with maximum connectivity = 100.
Non-small states mean = 25.3.

In providing public services, the Asia and Pacific small states face higher fixed (per capita) government costs relative to other small states (Figures 2.4 and 2.5). This is because government must provide public services regardless of the population size. In the island states, remoteness and wide dispersion compound this effect, creating an inverse relationship between the size of the country and the size of government. Large dispersion and small populations increase input costs and worsen the diseconomies of scale in creating public institutions and providing public goods and services, such as education, justice, social services, and infrastructure. Current government spending as a share of GDP is generally higher in the microstates than in all other groups (Becker 2012).

These countries are quite heterogeneous but they all have narrow export and production bases. Some rely primarily on tourism (Fiji, Maldives, Palau, Samoa, Vanuatu), and some on fishing and fishing license fees (Kiribati, Marshall Islands, Micronesia, Tuvalu—Table 2.2). Some are commodity or energy-resource based (Bhutan, the Solomon Islands, Timor-Leste). While scope for export diversification remains limited, with the exception of Fiji and Samoa, niche or ecotourism is gradually developing in Kiribati, Marshall Islands, and Micronesia. Recent experiences in setting up joint ventures for marine processing are also effective as ways to move up the value-added chain.

PICs appear to be less open than comparators (Figure 2.6), which reflects their remoteness, underdeveloped infrastructure—which is hurting tourism—and low competitiveness. Poor connectivity and high transportation costs have prevented greater trade integration with the rest of the region. Trade openness, however, has increased in these countries over time and integration has benefited the Asia and Pacific small states. Yet this also poses challenges because shocks are transmitted more rapidly in a more interconnected world.

Financial depth is generally below that of small states in other regions and access to credit is more limited (Figure 2.7). Land tenure systems favoring communal land also constrain credit growth and private sector development, leading to less inclusive growth. Land in most PICs is owned by the government and large families rather than by individuals. Family tenure makes property rights unclear and limits the use of land as collateral; and if banks are unable to secure their lending effectively with land as collateral, lending becomes costly. This leaves the spread between lending and borrowing rates very high in PICs (see Chapter 17).

Yet commercial banks in PICs, which are mainly foreign banks, are well capitalized and highly profitable, despite relatively low lending growth in recent years. This reflects high levels of noninterest income (higher than some comparators), largely from foreign exchange activities and fees and charges (Table 2.3—see Chapter 18).

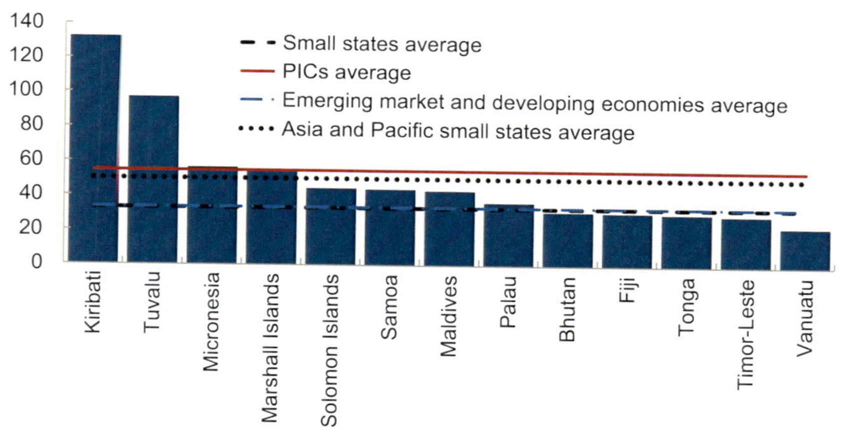

Figure 2.4 Asia and Pacific Small States: Government Expenditure, 2014 *(Percent of GDP)*

Sources: IMF, World Economic Outlook database; and IMF staff calculations.
Note: PICs = Pacific islands countries.

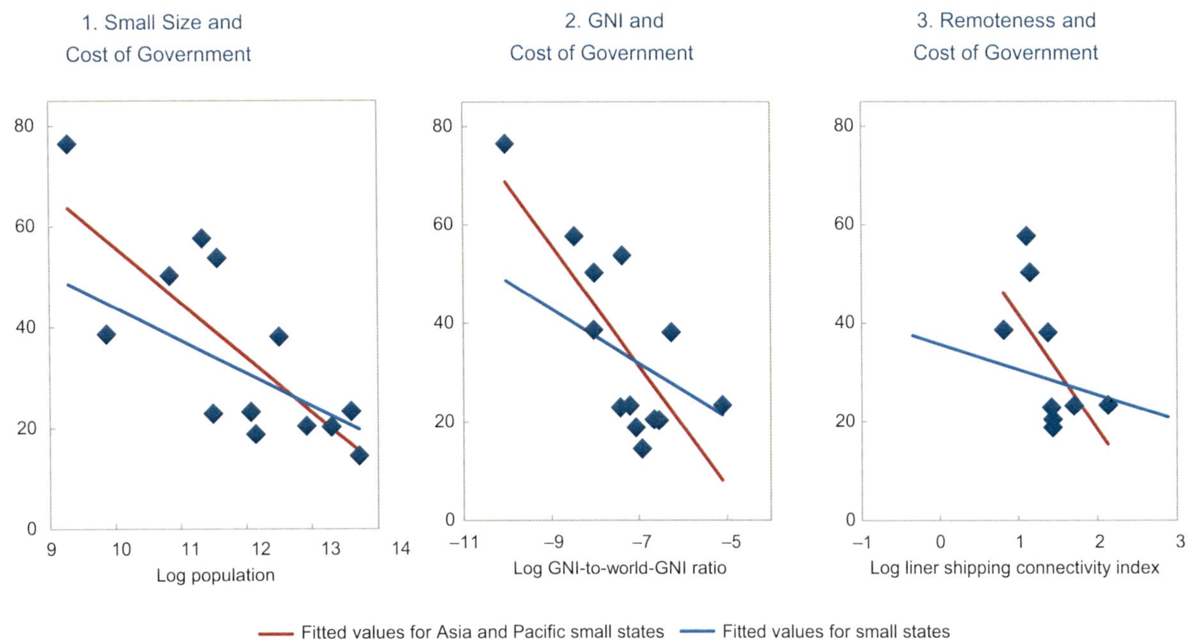

Figure 2.5 Asia and Pacific Small States: Cost of Government, 1990–2010 (*Percent of GDP*)

Sources: World Bank, World Development Indicators; and IMF staff estimates.
Note: GNI = gross national income.

TABLE 2.2

Asia and Pacific Small States: Main Exports of Goods and Services

Country	First Good or Service	Second Good or Service
Bhutan	Hydroelectricity	Minerals
Maldives	Tourism	Fish
Timor-Leste	Oil	Coffee
Pacific Island Countries		
Fiji	Tourism	Sugar
Kiribati	Fish	Copra
Marshall Islands	Fish	Copra
Micronesia	Fish	Copra
Palau	Tourism	Fish
Samoa	Tourism	Copra
Solomon Islands	Logs	Fish
Tonga	Agriculture (squash)	Tourism
Vanuatu	Tourism	Copra
Tuvalu	Fish	Copra

Sources: Country authorities; and IMF staff reports.

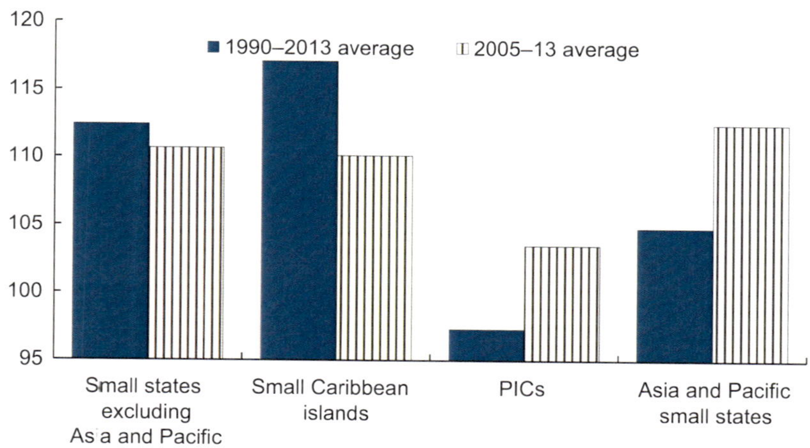

Figure 2.6 Small States: Trade Openness (*Percent of GDP*)

Sources: Penn World Tables; World Bank, World Development Indicators; and IMF staff calculations.
Note: Trade openness measured as exports plus imports of goods and services. PICs = Pacific island countries.

The private sector's limited access to credit impedes inclusive growth (Figure 2.8). Indeed, a simple regression suggests a negative relationship between inequality (proxied by the Gini coefficient) and the share of private credit as a percent of GDP.

Greater use of mobile phone networks for basic financial services is one recent method used in Fiji, Samoa, the Solomon Islands, and Tonga to support private sector growth that fosters financial inclusion. This also helps lower the cost of sending remittances to the Pacific from Australian banks, which, likewise, fosters financial sector intermediation.

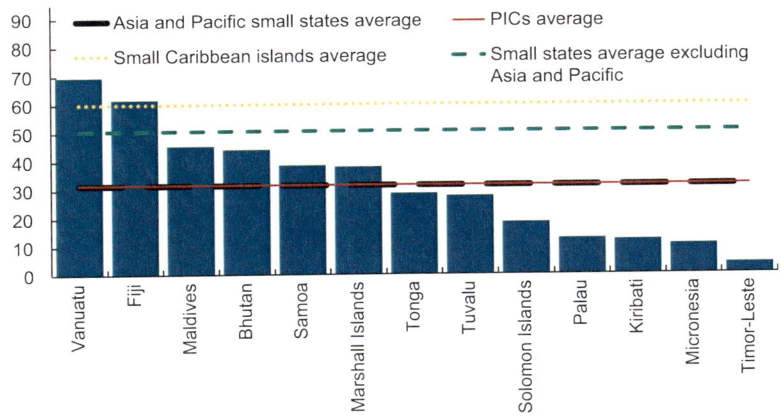

Figure 2.7 Asia and Pacific Small States: Domestic Credit to the Private Sector, 2013
(Percent of GDP)

Sources: World Bank, World Development Indicators; and IMF staff calculations.
Note: PICs = Pacific island countries.

TABLE 2.3

Small Pacific Island Countries: Interest and Noninterest Income of Commercial Banks, 2013

	Net Interest Income (Percent of total assets)	Noninterest Income (Percent of total assets)
Fiji	3.4	2.7
Marshall Islands	5.9	1.4
Samoa	5.5	3.6
Solomon Islands	4.4	4.1
Tonga	4.5	4.3
Vanuatu	4.1	3.0
Memorandum:		
Pacific island countries (average)	4.6	3.2
Small Caribbean states (average)	3.0	2.9
Small African states (average)	2.4	1.2

Sources: Davies, Vaught, and Cabezon (2014); and central bank data.

International market access is also very limited. Because of capacity and structural impediments, including legal and administrative frameworks, these countries have still not been able to tap international capital markets and attract capital inflows. With the exception of Fiji and Maldives, their market access to private capital flows is almost nonexistent.

Indicators on the business environment are weaker in the Asia and Pacific small states than in some comparators. According to the World Bank's *Doing Business 2015* report, procedures for starting and closing a business are more expensive in the small PICs than in the other Asia and Pacific small states as well as in the Caribbean island countries. Weak private sector development impedes sustainable growth (Figure 2.9).

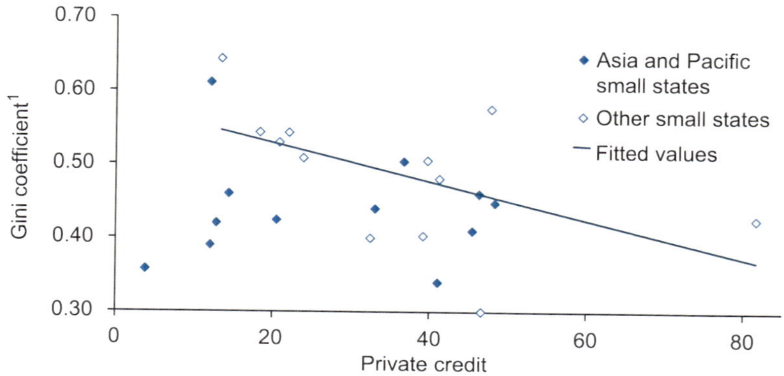

Figure 2.8 Asia and Pacific Small States: Financial Development and Income Inequality, 1990–2013 (*Percent of GDP*)

Sources: ADB (2012); World Bank, World Development Indicators; and IMF staff calculations.
[1] One indicates maximum inequality.

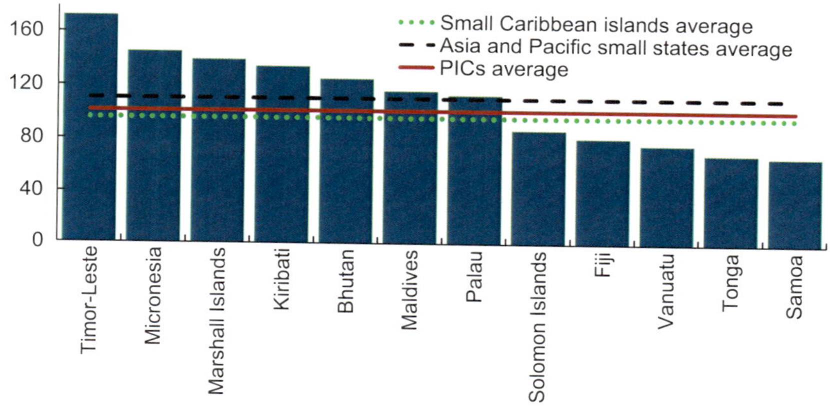

Figure 2.9 Asia and Pacific Small States: Ease of Doing Business Index

Sources: World Bank (2015), *Doing Business Report*; and IMF staff estimates.
Note: A lower number indicates a more business-friendly climate. PICs = Pacific island countries.

Policy tools are also limited. Five out of the 13 countries examined in this chapter have, as noted, no central bank (Kiribati, Marshall Islands, Micronesia, Palau, Tuvalu). The Australian dollar is legal tender in Kiribati and Tuvalu, and the U.S. dollar in Marshall Islands, Micronesia, and Palau. The use of dollarization or either fixed or managed exchange rate regimes for the Asia and Pacific region's other small states reflects the fixed costs of operating an independent monetary policy as well as weak monetary transmission mechanisms. The latter are largely the result of structural characteristics of undeveloped financial markets, such as shallow money markets, the absence at times of institutions such as credit bureaus that facilitate bank lending, and small markets (see Chapter 12).

Capacity constraints are larger in PICs relative to comparators, another major challenge impeding economic potential. For example, school enrollment is lower than in other small states (Figure 2.10). A recent analysis suggests that in the small PICs capacity constraints in the public service are associated with small size and that this explains the underperformance on public financial management reforms (Haque, Knight, and Jayasuriya 2012). That said, Fiji, the Solomon Islands, and Vanuatu have recently taken meaningful steps to strengthen public financial management and promote budget transparency and accountability.

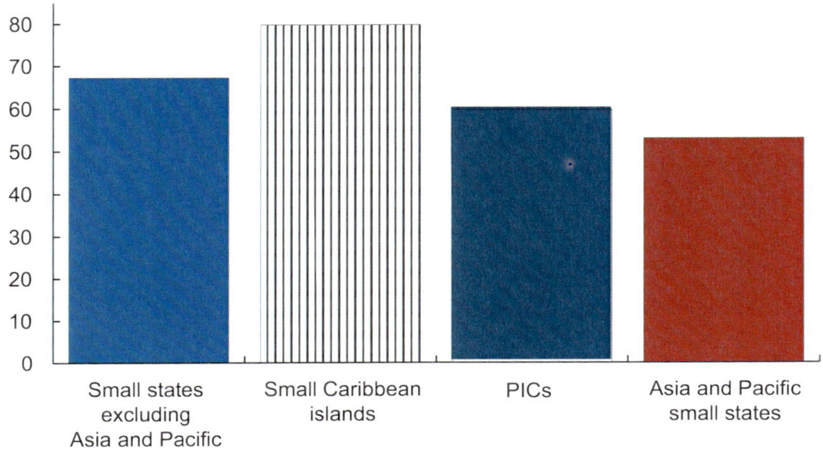

Figure 2.10 Asia and Pacific Small States: Secondary School Enrollment (*Percent of population 12–17 years old, 1990–2012 average*)

Sources: World Bank, World Development Indicators; and IMF staff calculations.
Note: PICs = Pacific island countries.

MANAGING SHOCKS, VULNERABILITY, AND VOLATILITY

Shocks

Small states in Asia and the Pacific are heavily exposed to shocks. Some shocks are related to external economic developments, some to weather and environmental events, and some are homegrown, such as political shocks. The main channels of spillover from the global economy are terms of trade, remittances, tourist flows, and financial channels. In particular:

- *All PICs remain especially vulnerable to global commodity price shocks*—This is especially so for food and fuel, given their large share in total imports (about 50 percent). The change in commodity prices and their greater volatility in recent years has meant that terms-of-trade shocks have translated into large output shocks.[3] Higher import prices in 2008 had also raised production costs and reduced real household income. The opposite effect has been in place since the fall in commodity prices that started in 2011.
- *External demand and financial shocks are also important*—The main channels of contagion are changes in remittances (in Samoa, Tonga, Tuvalu and, to a lesser extent, Fiji) and tourism receipts (Fiji, Maldives, Palau, Samoa, Vanuatu—Figure 2.11). A fall in stock prices in advanced economies would also affect PICs with large trust funds whose assets are invested offshore (Kiribati, Marshall Islands, Micronesia, Palau, Tuvalu), as happened during the global financial crisis (Figure 2.12).

Aid flows proved resilient during the 2009 turmoil as Australia, the main donor in the Pacific region, weathered the global financial crisis relatively well. However, high dependence on foreign aid is a source of fiscal vulnerability. Much weaker than expected economic activity in Australia and to a lesser extent New Zealand would hit PICs particularly hard, as both countries are the main trading partners for most of the Pacific islands. Even in the case where donors do not decide to cut grants further, in the Solomon Islands grants are expected to gradually decline (in terms of GDP) over the medium term.[4] Aid from the United States has a big impact on Marshall Islands, Micronesia, and

[3] See Chapter 6 for an assessment of the impact on PICs of external shocks from global and regional economies.

[4] The Regional Assistance Mission to Solomon Islands, which commenced in 2003 following the period of civil conflict known as the "ethnic tensions" (1998–2003), started to scale down its operations in 2013.

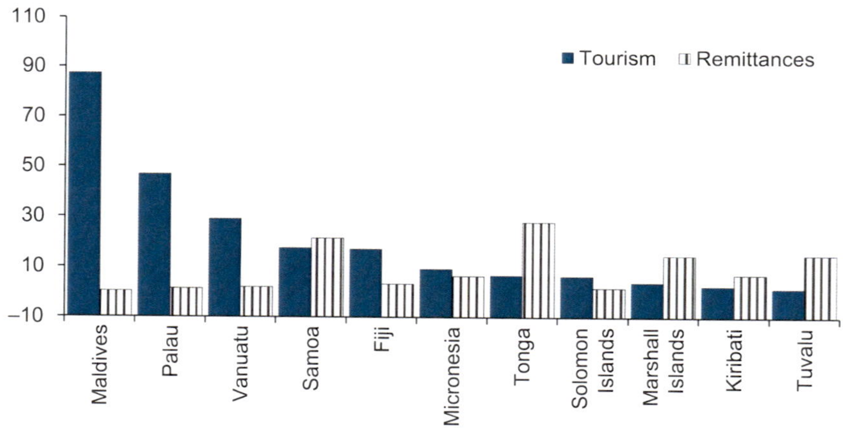

Figure 2.11 Asia and Pacific Small States: Tourism and Remittances (*Percent of GDP, 2005–14 average*)

Sources: Country authorities; and IMF staff calculations.

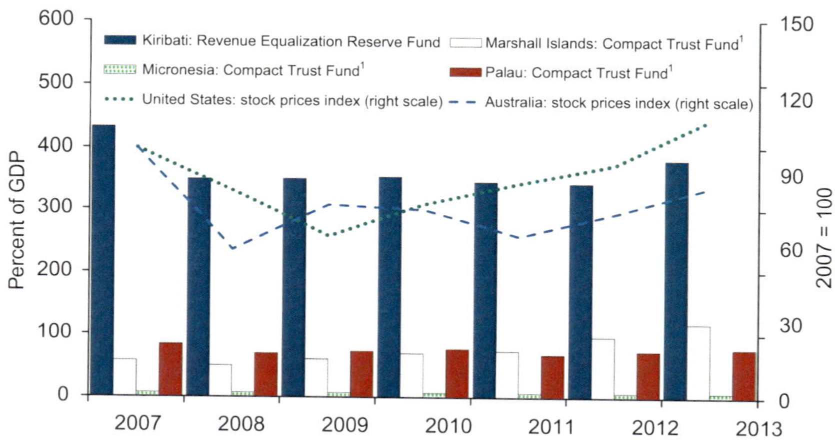

Figure 2.12 Asia and Pacific Microstates: Sovereign Investment Fund Balances

Sources: Country authorities; and IMF staff calculations.
[1] Fiscal year.

Palau through the bilateral Compact of Free Association agreements (Figure 2.13). This aid represents over 65 percent of total aid in Palau and 90 percent of total aid in Marshall Islands and Micronesia. These PICs finance a large portion of their budget and balance of payment needs with compact grants, scheduled to expire in 2023/24.

PICs are also severely affected by natural disasters and climate change (Figure 2.14). Of the 20 countries in the world with the highest average annual disaster losses measured by GDP, eight are PICs (Cook Islands, Fiji, Marshall Islands, Micronesia, Niue, the Solomon Islands, Tonga, Vanuatu). Several small island countries in the Asia and Pacific region are low-lying coral islands, with their populations and infrastructure concentrated along coastlines (Kiribati, Maldives, Marshall Islands, Tuvalu). This makes them highly vulnerable to the effects of sea-level rises and coastal erosion associated with climate change. While worldwide databases are available to account for the costs of natural disasters, the costs of climate change (including fiscal costs), which are likely substantial in the Asia and Pacific small states, have for the most part not been estimated.

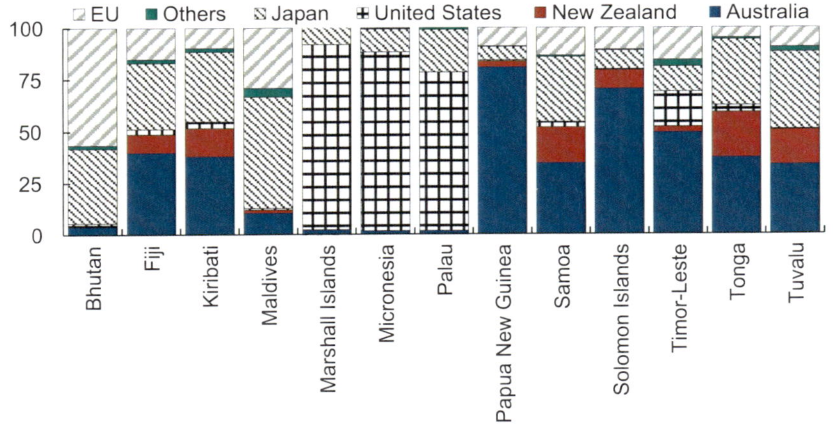

Figure 2.13 Asia and Pacific Small States: Official Development Assistance by Donors (*Percent of total aid, 1990–2012*)

Source: World Bank, World Development Indicators.
Note: EU = European Union.

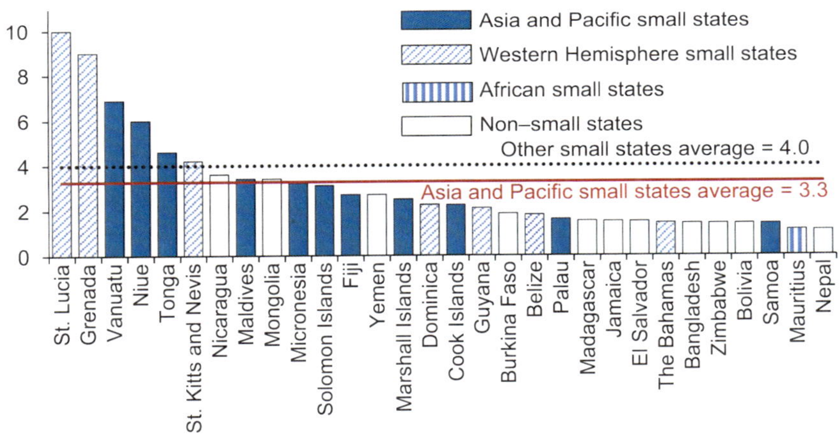

Figure 2.14 Average Impact of Natural Disasters (*Percent of GDP*)

Source: World Bank and United Nations (2012), *Natural Hazards, UnNatural Disasters: The Economics of Effective Prevention.*
Note: Excludes the cost of climate change.

The frequency of shocks is also higher in the small PICs than in other comparators (Figure 2.15). Our event analysis shows that political, terms-of-trade, and natural disaster shocks are more frequent relative to other low-income small states.

Vulnerability

Reliance on aid and remittances to finance structural trade deficits remains a key vulnerability (Figures 2.16 and 2.17). Small domestic markets, coupled in most cases with poor resource endowments, result in large trade deficits. The Asia and Pacific small states rely heavily on imports given the shortage of arable land. Most PICs are net importers of energy and food, and they also import capital goods because of their dependence on imported technologies and other consumer goods.

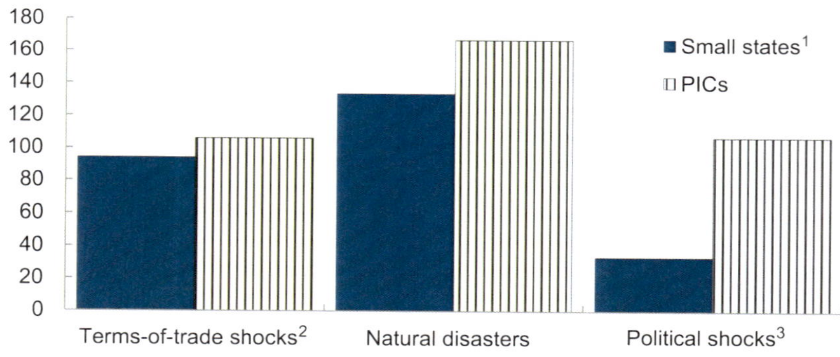

Figure 2.15 Small States: Frequencies of Shocks (*Low-income countries = 100*)

Sources: United Nations, Natural Disaster database; Polity IV Project; and IMF staff calculations.
Note: Based on events during 1970–2007. PICs = Pacific island countries.
[1]Low-income countries only.
[2]Change in the terms of trade larger than 10 percent.
[3]Defined as a deterioration by three points or more in the political stability index (Polity index) from Marshall and Jaggers (2009), complemented with country information.

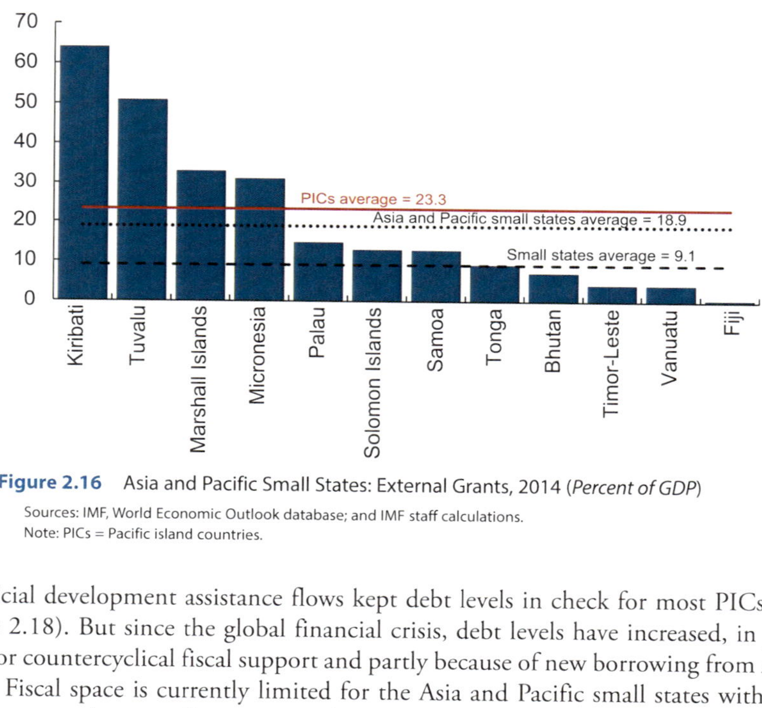

Figure 2.16 Asia and Pacific Small States: External Grants, 2014 (*Percent of GDP*)

Sources: IMF, World Economic Outlook database; and IMF staff calculations.
Note: PICs = Pacific island countries.

Large official development assistance flows kept debt levels in check for most PICs until recent years (Figure 2.18). But since the global financial crisis, debt levels have increased, in part because of the need for countercyclical fiscal support and partly because of new borrowing from Asia's emerging markets. Fiscal space is currently limited for the Asia and Pacific small states with high public debt, which narrows the scope for countercyclical policies should a cyclical slowdown materialize. As of November 2015, according to the debt sustainability analysis for low-income countries, which applies to 10 small states in the Pacific, based on the latest IMF Article IV staff reports, only one was at low risk of debt distress (Timor-Leste). Four were at high risk of debt distress (Kiribati, Marshall Islands, Micronesia, Tuvalu) and five at moderate risk (Bhutan, Samoa, the Solomon Islands, Tonga, Vanuatu).

The literature presents different indices of vulnerability to shocks. The Becker index (see Chapter 9) provides a vulnerability ranking based on different dimensions of vulnerability (such as small population, volume of arable land, and distance). The analysis also shows that using gross national income (GNI) per capita to determine the income status of small states can be misleading

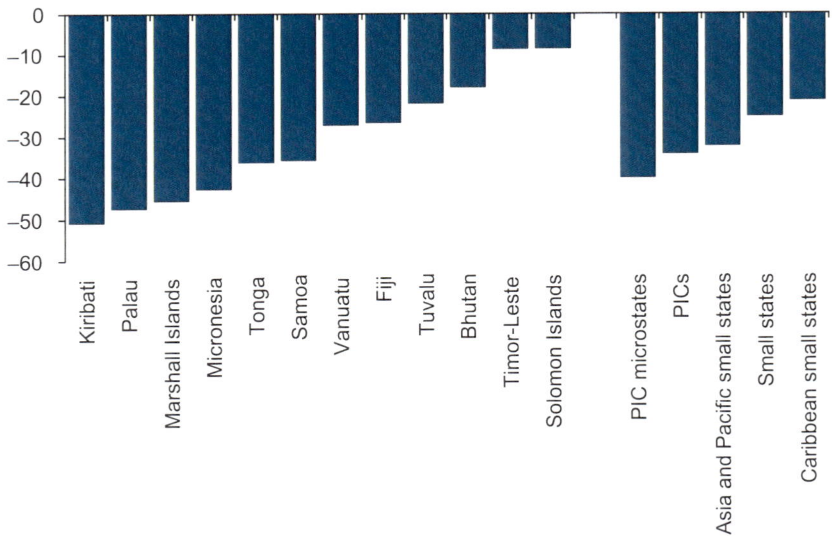

Figure 2.17 Asia and Pacific Small States: Current Account Balance Excluding Grants (*Percent of GDP, 2005–14 average*)

Sources: IMF, World Economic Outlook database; and IMF staff calculations.
Note: PICs = Pacific island countries.

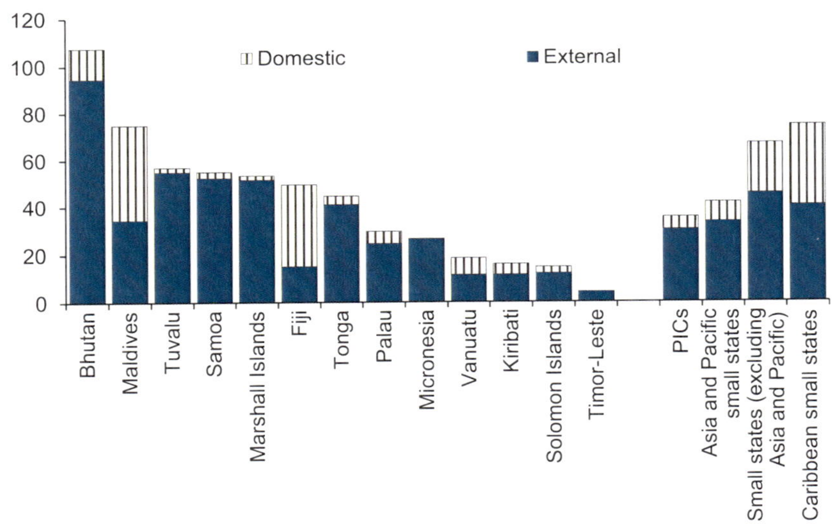

Figure 2.18 Asia and Pacific Small States: Public Debt, 2014 (*Percent of GDP*)

Sources: IMF, World Economic Outlook database; and IMF staff calculations.
Note: PICs = Pacific island countries.

when the population is very small and dispersed. This is because a much higher proportion of income in microstates covers government fixed costs, such as establishing institutions and providing public services, especially in countries composed of scattered islands. Per capita indicators therefore tend to overstate the economic conditions of microstates. Because of high fixed costs and distance from the rest of the world, the effective purchasing power of these states is actually quite low, despite a not-so-low GNI per capita. Similar vulnerability indices have been developed by Briguglio (Chapter 3) and the Commonwealth Secretariat (Easter, Atkins, and Mazzi 2000).

Volatility

The small states of the Asia and Pacific region face greater volatility than other small states in GDP growth per capita, changes in the terms of trade, aid, current account balance, and revenue, as the following shows:

- *GDP per capita*—During 1990–2010, the volatility of GDP per capita (Figure 2.19) was higher in Asia and Pacific small states—especially the microstates, which are all PICs—than in other small states. Tuvalu experienced the highest variability among the PICs, while Timor-Leste and Maldives faced higher GDP volatility than other small Asian states. Consistent with the literature on the negative impact of output volatility on growth, higher output volatility was associated with lower economic growth during 1990–2010 in Asia and Pacific small states and a lower quality of governance, after controlling for other variables (Figures 2.20 and 2.21).
- *Terms of trade, aid, and current account balance volatility*—The terms of trade in the Asia and Pacific small states during 1990–2014 were more volatile than in other small states. Aid flows were also more volatile, especially to the microstates. Over the last 20 years, this volatility reflected a drop in assistance from traditional European donors and the emergence of Australia as the largest aid provider in the Pacific. In the microstates, the greater aid volatility may also reflect the fact that aid flows generally finance specific one-off projects. The volatility of terms of trade and aid has resulted in greater current account volatility (Figure 2.22).
- *Revenue volatility*—Revenue volatility is higher in the Asia and Pacific small states, especially the microstates, than in other small states (Figures 2.23 and 2.24, and see Box 2.1). The main source of volatility in the region's microstates is nontax revenues, particularly fishing license

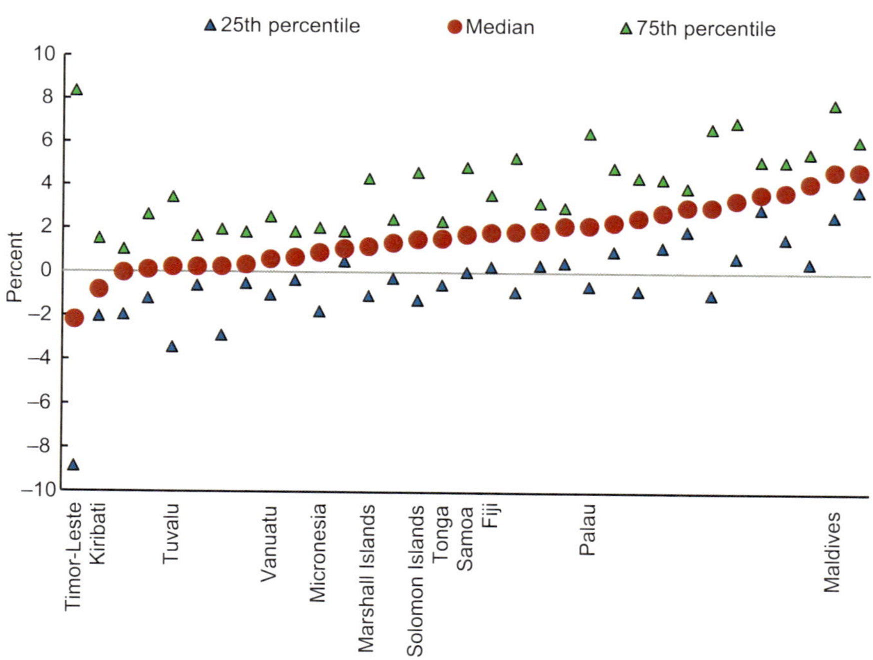

Figure 2.19 Asia and Pacific Small States: Volatility of Real GDP Growth per Capita, 1990–2014

Sources: World Bank, World Development Indicators; and IMF staff calculations.

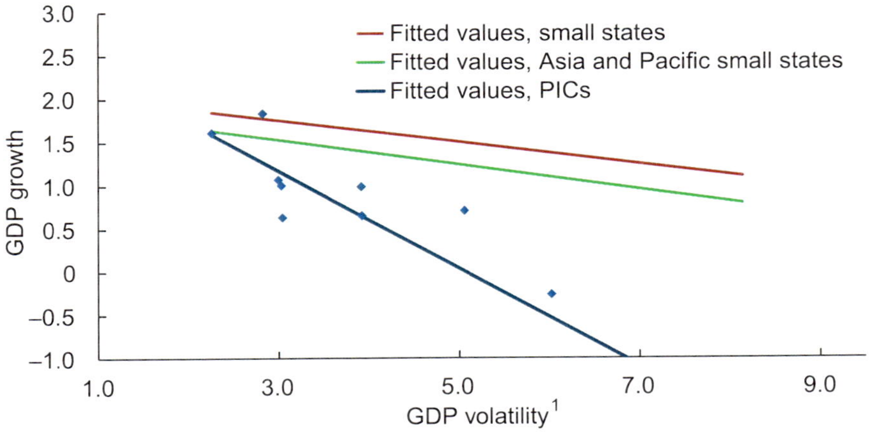

Figure 2.20 Asia and Pacific Small States: Real GDP per Capita Volatility and Growth, 1990–2013

Sources: World Bank, World Development Indicators; IMF, World Economic Outlook database; and IMF staff calculations.
[1]Volatility measured as the five-year backward-looking standard deviation of real GDP per capita growth.
Note: PICs = Pacific island countries.

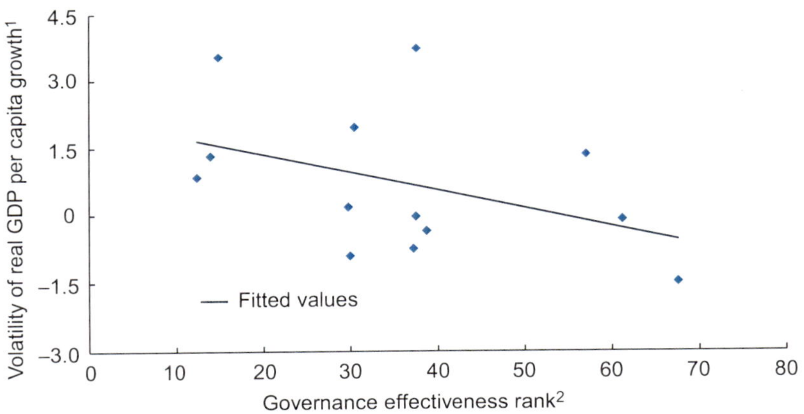

Figure 2.21 Asia and Pacific Small States: Volatility of Real GDP per Capita Growth and Governance, 1990–2013

Sources: World Bank, Worldwide Governance Indicators; and IMF staff calculations.
[1]Controlling for inflation and terms-of-trade volatility.
[2]Small values represent a low level of government effectiveness.

fees, which represent about 40 percent of their revenues. Managing revenue volatility is a major challenge for the Asia and Pacific small states as such volatility can foster fiscal policy procyclicality (that is, expansionary fiscal policy during upturns and contractionary policy during downturns). Indeed, fiscal policy appears to have been procyclical in many Asia and Pacific small states in recent years. Only five out of 13 countries have adopted a multiyear budget framework to help smooth the expenditure path over the medium term. And only one, Timor-Leste, has a fiscal rule and a stabilization fund to manage the volatility of fiscal revenue and ensure intergenerational equity in the distribution of earnings from its natural resources.

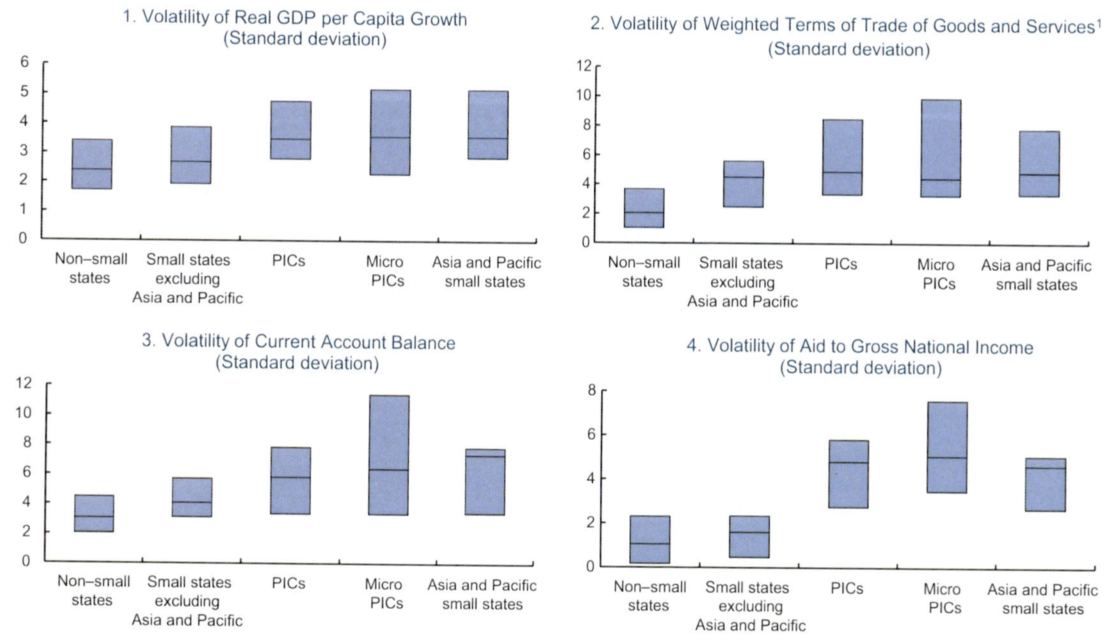

Figure 2.22 Asia and Pacific Small States: Volatility of GDP Growth, Terms of Trade, Current Account Balance, and Aid, 1990–2014

Sources: IMF, World Economic Outlook database; World Bank, World Development Indicators; and IMF staff calculations.

Note: — represents the median. The boxes represent 50 percent of the observations, between the 25th and 75th percentiles. PICs = Pacific island countries.

[1]Weighted terms of trade indicates the changes in the prices of exports and imports weighted, respectively, by the share of exports and imports in GDP.

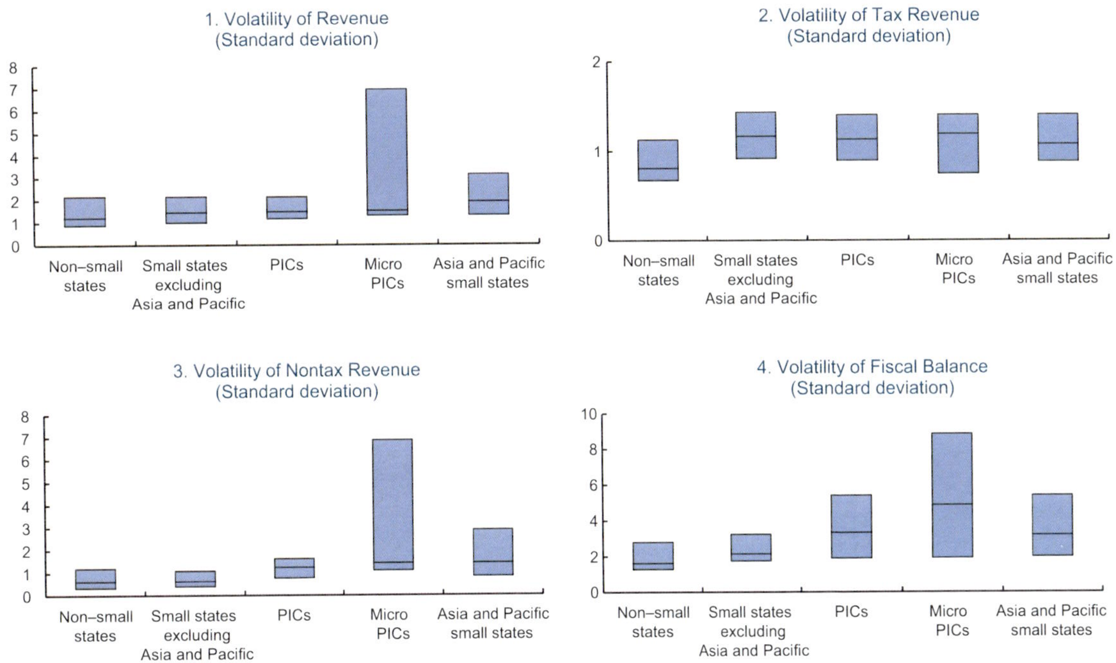

Figure 2.23 Asia and Pacific Small States: Fiscal Volatility, 1990–2014

Sources: IMF, World Economic Outlook database; World Bank, World Development Indicators; and IMF staff calculations.

Note: — = median. The boxes represent 50 percent of the observations between the 25th and 75th percentiles. PICs = Pacific island countries.

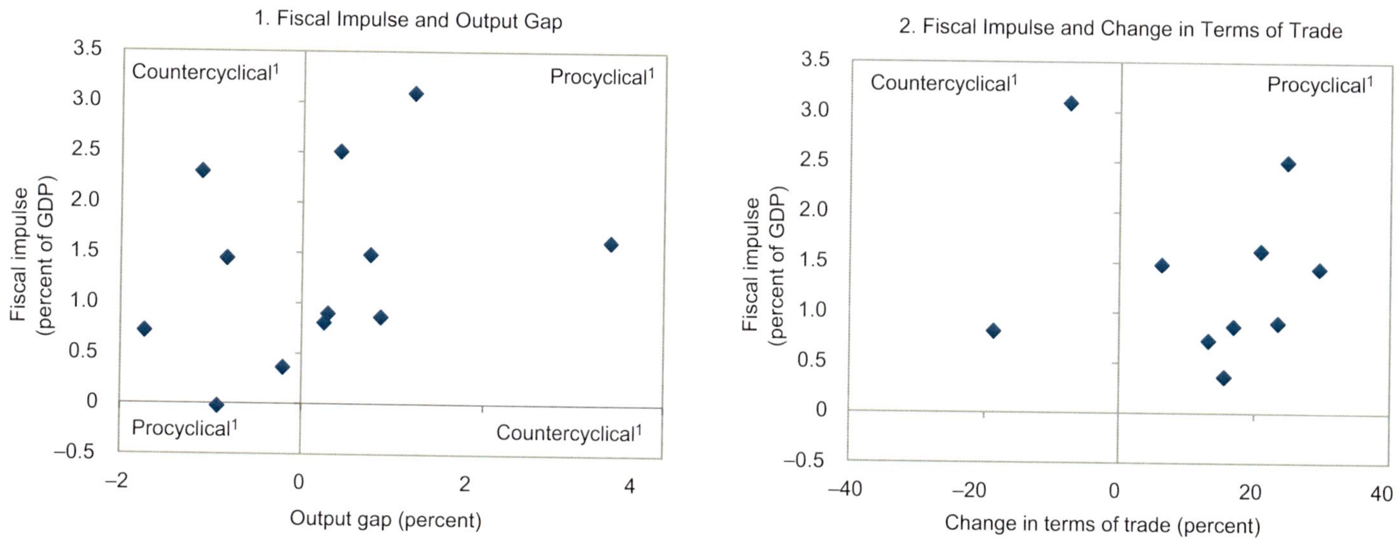

Figure 2.24 Asia and Pacific Small States: Procyclical Bias in Fiscal Policy, 2005–10

Source: IMF staff calculations based on World Economic Outlook database.

Box 2.1. Special Challenges Facing Pacific Island Microstates

Pacific island microstates face several special challenges, including:

- *More volatility*—Microstates face more volatility in their GDP growth, revenue, aid, terms of trade, and current accounts relative to the rest of the Asia and Pacific small states and other small states outside the region.
- *Climate change*—Rising sea levels are a big threat for Kiribati, Marshall Islands, and Tuvalu, and individual countries cannot internalize the costs of climate change. And because development spending is sometimes redirected to building seawalls and other climate-change mitigation, it may crowd out other project-financing aid unless the aid envelope expands substantially.
- *High aid dependency*—Pacific island microstates depend heavily on aid to finance their large external and internal imbalances and their development needs. The expiration of grants under the Compact of Free Association agreements with the United States in 2023/24 will create both fiscal and external difficulties for Marshall Islands, Micronesia, and Palau if they fail to implement reforms to achieve self-sufficiency.
- *Fragility*—Kiribati, Marshall Islands, Micronesia, and Tuvalu are classified as fragile states.[1]

[1] IMF (2015). The other Asia and Pacific small states in fragile situations are the Solomon Islands and Timor-Leste.

UNDERSTANDING GROWTH AND PERFORMANCE

As a result of these factors, real GDP per capita of PICs is among the lowest of the small states (Figure 2.25). Since 1990, real GDP per capita in purchasing-power-parity terms in PICs has increased less than 25 percent, compared with 45 percent in the Eastern Caribbean Currency Union and more than 30 percent in small states (IMF 2013a, 2013b). PICs have not been able to benefit from growth in Asia's emerging market economies, where GDP has increased by about 120 percent since 1990.

Data on income per capita show a similar pattern (Figure 2.26). During 1990–2010 income per capita in purchasing-power-parity terms in PICs grew by 77 percent, compared with 130 percent in the Eastern Caribbean Currency Union and less than 85 percent in small states. Income per capita in Asia's emerging market economies grew by over 250 percent during the same period.

As of 2013, the average GNI per capita for PICs was one-third the average income of Caribbean countries. While GNI per capita in Tuvalu and to a lesser extent Marshall Islands and Micronesia appears relatively high, it overstates public spending capacity in these countries. In Tuvalu, for example, GNI exceeds GDP by 60 percent because of sizable government investment income from its sovereign trust fund, which has its assets invested abroad.[5]

In Tuvalu, however, much of the government investment income cannot be spent because the multilateral agreement governing the country's trust fund stipulates that its real value, indexed to Australian inflation, be maintained. This places limits on the use of earnings for budget support. The inflation component of earnings is some two-thirds of total earnings, or about 10 percent of GNI; this is the amount needed every year to maintain the value of the fund constant in real terms. Marshall Islands and Micronesia are bound by a similar bilateral agreement with the United States governing the management of their trust funds until 2023/24.

PICs seem to be stuck on a low-growth path. Growth in these countries has been weak over the last two decades, and even more so relative to other small states (Figure 2.27). Because of their demographics, the underperformance of PICs, in per capita terms, is also more striking.

While PICs have done slightly better than comparators during the recent business cycle, growth rates remain quite low, especially among the net commodity importers. Strong linkages with resilient

[5] Tuvalu's trust fund was established in 1987 by several development partners. The trust funds of the Marshall Islands and Micronesia were established by the amended Compact of Free Association agreement between the United States and these countries, which came into force in 2004.

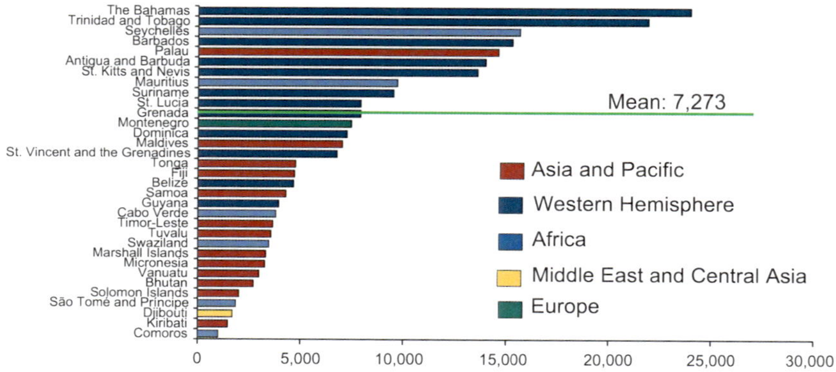

Figure 2.25 Asia and Pacific Small States: GDP per Capita, 2014 (*U.S. dollars*)

Sources: IMF, World Economic Outlook database; and World Bank, World Development Indicators.

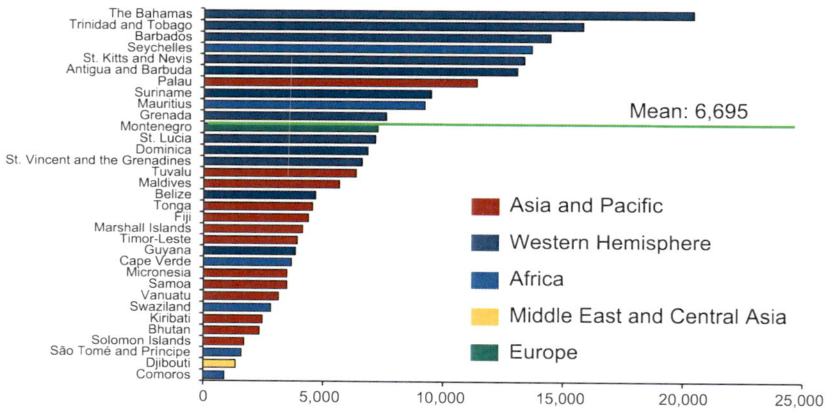

Figure 2.26 Asia and Pacific Small States: GNI per Capita, 2013 (*U.S. dollars*)

Source: World Bank, World Development Indicators.

Note: For The Bahamas and Barbados, data are as of 2012. For Djibouti, data are as of 2009.

economies in the region (Australia and, to a lesser extent, Asia's emerging markets) helped cushion the downturn in all PICs during the global financial crisis.

Since then, some Asia and Pacific small states have made progress in rebuilding policy buffers, but they need to do more (see Chapter 6). Their reserve position, on balance, has improved relative to 2004–07, but more than half of the PICs emerged from the crisis with somewhat less comfortable fiscal buffers from higher debt and larger fiscal deficits than before the crisis.

ECONOMETRIC ANALYSIS: GROWTH DETERMINANTS IN ASIA AND PACIFIC SMALL STATES

Our econometric analysis confirms that PICs have underperformed relative to their peers (Table 2.4). After controlling for some standard variables that explain GDP growth per capita, PICs suffer a disadvantage in GDP growth per capita of about 2 percentage points, compared with an average small state.

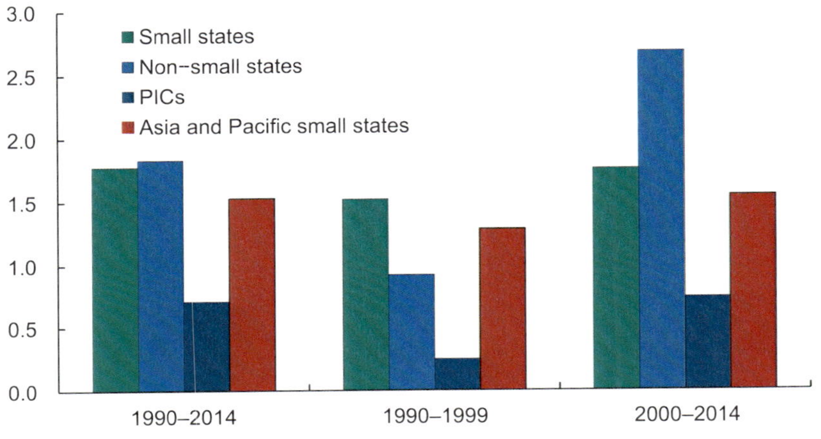

Figure 2.27 Asia and Pacific Small States: Real GDP per Capita Growth (*Percent, 1990–2014 average*)

Sources: IMF, World Economic Outlook database; and World Bank, World Development Indicators.
Note: PICs = Pacific island countries.

All variables have the expected sign. Trade openness and a well-educated population have a positive impact on real GDP growth per capita, while public debt, GDP volatility, and government consumption do not. High government consumption crowds out productive investment. Our analysis shows that, while small states have grown 1¼ percentage points less than big states (model 1 in Table 2.4) after controlling for other variables, PICs have grown by 3 percentage points less than non–small states (model 2)—reflected in the sum of the coefficients of the PIC and small states dummies.

TABLE 2.4

Determinants of Real GDP per Capita Growth

	Model 1	Model 2	Model 3	Model 4	Model 5	Model 6
Small states	–0.0126***	–0.0098**	–0.0105**	–0.0084*	–0.0070	–0.0066
PICs	. . .	–0.0197**	. . .	. . .	–0.0161	. . .
Asia and Pacific small states	. . .	. . .	–0.0111	. . .	. . .	–0.010
Oil exporters	–0.0150**	–0.0149***	–0.0150***	–0.0167***	–0.0163***	–0.016***
OECD	–0.0094**	–0.0094**	–0.0095**	–0.0085*	–0.0087*	–0.0087**
Openness	0.0084***	0.0079***	0.0081***	0.0085***	0.0081***	0.0082***
Initial GDP per capita	–0.0017***	–0.0018***	–0.0018***	–0.0017***	–0.0018***	–0.0017***
GDP volatility	–0.4184***	–0.4160***	–0.4178***	–0.4206***	–0.4183***	–0.4200***
Education	0.0064	0.0042	0.0054	0.0086	0.0064	0.0077
Debt-to-GDP ratio	–0.0089***	–0.0092***	–0.0091***	–0.0088***	–0.0092***	–0.0090***
Government-consumption-to-GDP ratio	–0.0913***	–0.0811***	–0.0876***	–0.0939***	–0.0852***	–0.0905***
Distance	. . .	. . .	. . .	–0.0011*	–0.0009	–0.0011*
Constant	0.0565***	0.0583***	0.0574***	0.0575***	0.0587***	0.0581***
Observations	1,741	1,741	1,741	1,741	1,741	1,741

Source: Authors' calculations.
Note: Panel regressions, 1990–2010. All regressions include a full set of regional dummies. The dependent variable is the real GDP growth per capita. The estimation period starts in 1990 because of a lack of data for many PICs soon after independence. OECD = Organisation for Economic Co-operation and Development; PICs = Pacific island countries.
*$p < 0.1$, **$p < 0.05$, ***$p < 0.01$.

Our econometric results show that the geographic disadvantage of PICs undermines their growth performance. Once distance is included in the regression, the dummies for the PICs and other small states become insignificant (model 5). This suggests that distance is a key variable in explaining the difference in growth performance in small states—especially the PICs—even after controlling for other factors. Remoteness is proxied by distance to the closest continent and the coefficient has the expected negative sign. This result is in line with other studies (see Chapter 4). The Asia and Pacific small states as a whole have also underperformed relative to the average small states, but this difference is not statistically significant (models 3 and 6). Finally, higher fixed government costs, capacity constraints, less openness, and higher GDP volatility relative to other small states help explain the difference in growth performance.

Further econometric analysis shows that Asia and Pacific small states are indeed different from other small states. To quantify the importance of different growth determinants of PICs relative to comparators, we regressed each explanatory variable used in Table 2.4 on the same set of regional dummy variables as well as on the dummies for small states and PICs. Compared with an average small state, PICs have lower initial income, less openness, lower education, and lower debt (as expressed by the negative sign of the coefficients of the PIC dummy in Table 2.5), but they have greater GDP volatility and higher government consumption, as expressed by the positive sign of the coefficients of the PIC dummy in the same table.

Combining the results of Tables 2.4 and 2.5, we can disentangle the relative impact of each determinant in explaining growth in the PICs relative to other small states. For example looking at model 4 in Table 2.4, PICs' lower initial income has a positive effect on growth. Based on the convergence hypothesis we found in the regression, the lower initial income has allowed PICs to grow about ½ percentage point (= –2.3* – 0.0017) faster than an average small state. However, this positive factor, together with the lower debt level of the PICs relative to other small states, which has increased their growth by about 0.1 percentage point (= –0.113* – 0.0088), has been negatively offset by other factors that have been detrimental to their growth performance. These include lower education, greater distance, higher government consumption relative to GDP, less openness, and high GDP volatility. For example, higher government consumption relative to GDP has a large negative growth effect for the PICs (0.167* – 0.0939 = –1.6 percentage points). Table 2.6 shows the same exercise for all Asia and Pacific small states.

TABLE 2.5

Pacific Island Countries: Growth Advantages and Disadvantages

Dependent Variable/ Independent Variables[1]	Initial Real GDP per Capita	GDP Volatility	Openness	Education	Debt-to-GDP Ratio	Government-Consumption-to-GDP Ratio	Distance
Pacific island countries	–2.303	0.001	–0.279	–0.130	–0.113	0.167	3.102
Small states	–0.086	–0.002	0.356	0.180	0.009	0.048	3.182

Source: Authors' calculations.
Note: OECD = Organisation for Economic Co-operation and Development.
[1] All regressions include, in addition to Pacific island countries and small states, a full set of regional dummies, dummies for the OECD, and dummies for oil exporters.

TABLE 2.6

Asia and Pacific Small States: Growth Advantages and Disadvantages

Dependent Variable/ Independent Variables[1]	Initial Real GDP per Capita	GDP Volatility	Openness	Education	Debt-to-GDP Ratio	Government-Consumption-to-GDP Ratio	Distance
Asia and Pacific small states	–1.82	0.002	–0.403	–0.14	–0.223	0.156	2.098
Small states	–0.094	–0.002	0.422	0.193	0.052	0.037	3.144

Source: Authors' calculations.
Note: OECD = Organisation for Economic Co-operation and Development.
[1] All regressions include, in addition to Asia and Pacific small states and small states, a full set of regional dummies, dummies for the OECD, and dummies for oil exporters.

POLICY IMPLICATIONS: HOW TO RAISE GROWTH POTENTIAL AND ENHANCE RESILIENCE

Decisive policy measures by the governments of small states in the Asia and Pacific region can go a long way toward addressing the challenges they face. Given their high vulnerability to external shocks and still low potential growth, these countries should continue to rebuild policy buffers in a way that reinforces efforts to implement growth-enhancing reforms. This could be done by:

- *Strengthening domestic revenue mobilization to support the rebuilding of policy buffers.* Revenue compliance is extremely challenging to enforce, especially in widely scattered islands. Further progress in strengthening revenue collection, including by streamlining and simplifying existing tax and customs regimes with technical assistance provided by development partners, would help create fiscal space to meet critical development spending needs.
- *Improving the composition of public spending in education, health, and infrastructure.* This will be essential for fostering inclusive growth. Public investment in infrastructure could help "crowd in" private investment, thereby promoting more broad-based growth, including by attracting foreign direct investment and stimulating more tourism. Increasing investment in education would also raise potential growth.
- *Sound structural policies to enhance long-term resilience to shocks and boost growth potential.* Implementing growth-oriented structural reforms that enhance the business environment can boost investor confidence and private sector growth. The Asia and Pacific small states have enormous untapped marine resources and further efforts are needed to properly leverage and manage them.
- *Strengthening institutions and improving governance.* This should be a key part of the reform agenda of governments and the capacity-building programs of development partners. Bolstering public institutions, particularly through public finance management reforms, would also improve expenditure efficiency. Strengthening public finance by introducing a multiyear budget framework would help bring about realistic fiscal plans and guard against procyclical policies. A multiyear fiscal framework built around simple fiscal anchors could also contribute to a better balance between rebuilding buffers and allocating sufficient budget resources for priority needs. From a political economy standpoint, this would also help build consensus on the appropriate sequencing of development projects and contain spending pressures in the near term. It would also help to better calibrate the pace of spending by taking capacity constraints into account (see Chapter 10).

Scope exists for increasing competition in the banking sector, but financial deepening also requires the development of nonbank institutions. These include finance companies, foreign exchange dealers, and microcredit institutions that have the potential to be competitive, apart from the main commercial banks. Financial-inclusion initiatives, such as lowering the cost of remittances and mobile phone banking, can also help foster private sector development.

Regional solutions to common problems should continue to be pursued. This approach can help individual countries mitigate the challenges associated with small size and high dispersion, for example, by increasing economies of scale through cooperation. Regional approaches can encourage the alignment of regulations and laws across the Pacific, lower transaction costs, and reduce the need for country-specific knowledge on regulatory approaches. They can also promote regional integration and the exchange of knowledge, best practices, and experience. Regional solutions to natural disaster risk insurance should be pursued, and a start has already been made in five PICs.[6]

---

[6] In January 2013 Japan, the World Bank, and the Secretariat of the Pacific Community teamed up with Marshall Islands, Samoa, the Solomon Islands, Tonga, and Vanuatu to launch the Pacific Catastrophe Risk Insurance Pilot (see Chapter 5).

Key sectors of common interest include fisheries, information and communication technology, and aviation safety. Progress has been made in the fishery sector through the Nauru Agreement Concerning Cooperation in the Management of Fisheries of Common Interest to increase the bargaining power of license-issuing countries and enhance regional actions to stop illegal fishing. Further collective efforts are required to remove barriers to labor and investment. The seasonal employment scheme opened to PICs and Timor-Leste, first introduced by New Zealand in 2006 and followed by Australia, is a successful case of enhanced integration with neighboring countries that has generated income opportunities and increased the skills of Pacific island workers in countries with labor shortages.

Further integration with the Asia and Pacific region through trade and investment should help raise growth potential. While the Pacific islands are geographically scattered and remote, their closest markets are among the most dynamic in the world. And the resilience of Australia and Asia's emerging market economies in recent years has played an important role in helping the recovery of PICs.

REFERENCES

Asian Development Bank (ADB). 2012. *Key Indicators for Asia and the Pacific*. Manila: ADB.

Easter, Christopher D., Jonathan P. Atkins, and Sonia Mazzi. 2000. "A Commonwealth Vulnerability Index for Developing Countries: The Position of Small States." Economic Paper 40, Commonwealth Secretariat, London.

Haque, Tobias, David Knight, and Dinuk Jayasuriya. 2012. "Capacity Constraints and Public Financial Management in Small Pacific Island Countries." Policy Research Working Paper 6297, World Bank, Washington.

International Monetary Fund (IMF). 2013a. "Macroeconomic Issues in Small States and Implications for Fund Engagement." Board Paper, International Monetary Fund, Washington. www.imf.org/external/np/pp/eng/2013/022013.pdf.

———. 2013b. "Caribbean Small States: Challenges of High Debt and Low Growth." Board Paper, International Monetary Fund, Washington. www.imf.org/external/np/pp/eng/2013/022013b.pdf.

———. 2015. "IMF Engagement with Countries in Post-Conflict and Fragile Situations—Stocktaking." Board Paper, International Monetary Fund, Washington. http://www.imf.org/external/np/pp/eng/2015/050715.pdf.

Tumbarello, Patrizia, Ezequiel Cabezon, and Yiqun Wu. 2013. "Are the Asia and Pacific Small States Different from Other Small States?" IMF Working Paper 13/123, International Monetary Fund, Washington.

World Bank Group, 2014. *Doing Business 2015*. Washington: World Bank.

CHAPTER 3

Building Resilience in the Pacific Island Countries

LINO BRIGUGLIO

Many studies on small island states focus on their economic vulnerability and conclude that, as a group, these countries are highly exposed to the harmful effects of external shocks.[1] This chapter shows this reality applies to the Pacific island countries (PICs).

Despite such exposure, GDP per capita in many small island states is relatively high compared to other developing economies. Briguglio (2004) termed this reality "the Singapore paradox," referring to the possibility that a very vulnerable small country could actually be very successful economically. This chapter argues that the juxtaposition of economic vulnerability and economic resilience can explain this apparent contradiction.

ECONOMIC VULNERABILITY

The word "vulnerability" originates from its Latin root *vulnerare*, meaning "to wound." This etymology associates the word with exposure to damage or harm and with precariousness. When applied to the macroeconomy, the term is generally used to refer to a country's susceptibility to harm by external forces as a result of exposure to such forces. Several vulnerability indices have been constructed (Briguglio 1995, 1997, 2014; Atkins, Easter, and Mazzi 2000; Crowards 2000; Briguglio and Galea 2003; UNDESA 2011).[2] The indices proposed in this chapter define vulnerability by the inherent features that expose countries to external shocks, including high trade openness exacerbated by high export concentration and dependence on strategic imports.

Most economic vulnerability indices conclude that small states, particularly island ones, tend to be more inherently economically vulnerable than other groups of countries, regardless of differences in the components of the indices and the approaches utilized. The literature shows a high degree of consensus in this regard. Seven out of the eight vulnerability indices reviewed in Cordina (2008) had statistically significant positive correlation coefficients between country size and vulnerability scores. This implies that, in general, the indices tend to agree that small countries are more economically vulnerable than larger ones.

ECONOMIC RESILIENCE

The word "resilience" comes from *resilire*, Latin for "rise again." Briguglio and others (2006) define economic resilience as an economy's ability to withstand or rebound from the negative effects of

[1] Other characteristics of small states pose economic disadvantages but do not lead directly to economic exposure to external economic forces. These include a limited ability to exploit economies of scale—mainly because of overhead-cost indivisibilities associated with small-scale operations—as well as limitations in the effectiveness of domestic competition policy, owing to the ease with which a few firms can monopolize or dominate a small market. For many small states that are also islands, insularity, remoteness, dispersion (in archipelagoes), proneness to natural disasters, and vulnerability to climate change are associated with additional economic disadvantages.

[2] Gonzales (2000) points out that, for various vulnerability classifications: "While small developing states on average emerge as being comparatively vulnerable, rankings of individual countries can differ substantially between alternative indices."

external shocks, and the authors associate such ability with policy measures. Guided by this definition, they constructed a resilience index consisting of four components, namely macroeconomic stability, market efficiency, social development, and good political governance.[3] These variables are, to a large extent, influenced by policy and are associated with an economy's ability to absorb or counteract the harmful effects of external shocks. In general, the authors found that the 86 countries covered by the index exhibited a wide range of resilience scores, with high-income countries generally ranking higher in this regard than middle- and low-income countries. Briguglio (2014) confirms this tendency.

JUXTAPOSING VULNERABILITY AND RESILIENCE

According to Briguglio and others (2006), the juxtaposition of vulnerability and resilience would indicate an economy's overall risk of harm by external shocks, as Figure 3.1 explains. It shows that such risk increases with economic vulnerability and decreases with economic resilience. A major implication of the vulnerability and resilience framework is that small states can succeed economically, despite their economic vulnerability, if they adopt policies conducive to good economic, social, and political governance.

Briguglio and others (2006), applying this framework and using the vulnerability and resilience indices they constructed, classified 86 countries into four categories, as Figure 3.2 shows. The results indicated that (1) countries with high resilience and low vulnerability scores are mostly large developed countries with relatively good economic, political, and social governance; (2) countries with low resilience and vulnerability scores are mostly large developing economies with relatively weak governance; (3) countries with high vulnerability and resilience scores are mostly small states with relatively good governance; and (4) countries with relatively high vulnerability and relatively low resilience scores include many small states with relatively weak governance. Briguglio (2014), covering 183 countries, confirmed these general tendencies.

Because vulnerability refers to inherent characteristics that make countries prone to external shocks, vulnerability scores for a particular country should not differ much over time. It is therefore not expected that countries will move vertically along the quadrants of Figure 3.2, but they can move horizontally from the left to the right quadrant if they adopt measures that build resilience.

Defining vulnerability by inherent features and resilience by policy-induced changes has a number of advantages. First, the vulnerability index would refer to permanent (or quasi-permanent) features over which a country can exercise no practical control, and which, therefore, cannot be attributed to inadequate policies. In other words, countries scoring high on the index cannot be accused of self-inflicted vulnerability through misguided policy. Second, the resilience index would refer to what a country can do to mitigate or exacerbate its inherent vulnerability. Third, the combination of the two indices would indicate the overall risk of harm by external shocks owing to inherent vulnerability features counterbalanced to different extents by policy measures.

VULNERABILITY AND RESILIENCE OF PICS

Briguglio (2014) constructed and computed vulnerability and resilience indices for 183 countries, including nine PICs,[4] based on the methodology developed in Briguglio and others (2006). The

[3] Briguglio and others (2006) also identified environmental management as a possible component of their resilience index, but did not include it because of the lack of relevant data. An environmental management index was included as a resilience index component in Briguglio (2014).

[4] The nine are Fiji, Kiribati, Marshall Islands, Micronesia, Papua New Guinea, Samoa, the Solomon Islands, Tonga, and Vanuatu. Data were insufficient to construct an economic vulnerability index for the Cook Islands, Nauru, Niue, Palau, and Tuvalu.

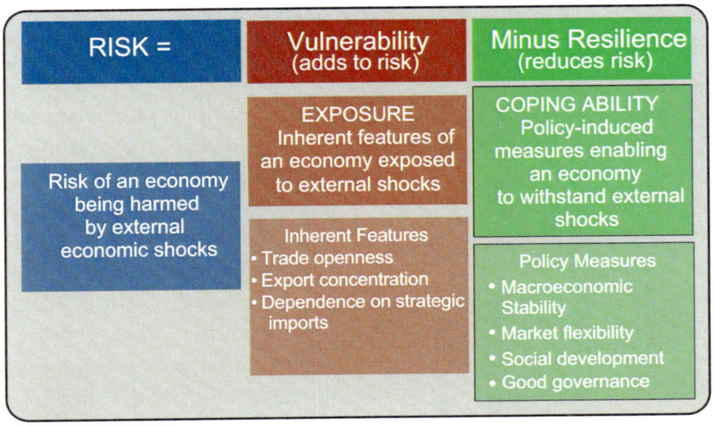

Figure 3.1 Risk of Harm by External Economic Shocks

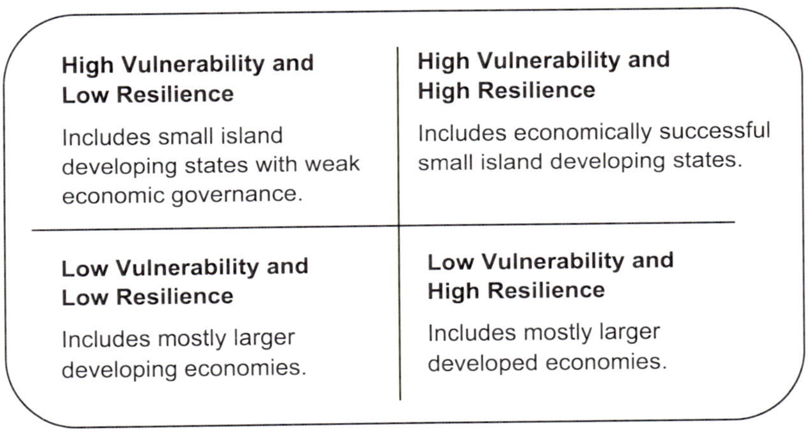

Figure 3.2 Vulnerability-Resilience Nexus

nine PICs were all found to be highly economically vulnerable (with vulnerability index scores in the top 25 percent among 183 countries). Samoa topped the list, with Vanuatu taking second place.

In general, PICs tended to have very open economies not much different from the average for the rest of the small island developing economies.[5] Their dependence on strategic imports was in general also on the high side, but slightly lower than the average for the rest of the small island developing economies. But PICs' exports were in general markedly more concentrated than those of other small island developing economies.

In addition, four PICs (Fiji, Samoa, Tonga, Vanuatu) are highly prone to natural disasters. Their average vulnerability score was higher than the average for the rest of the small island developing economies, although individual country scores revealed many exceptions. On the whole, PICs' vulnerability scores were much higher than the average score for non-small-island developing economies, whether high, middle, or low income, indicating that economic vulnerability is highly related to small size and insularity.

[5]The comparator small island developing states were members of the Alliance of Small Island States: Antigua and Barbuda, The Bahamas, Barbados, Belize, Cabo Verde, Comoros, Dominica, Dominican Republic, Grenada, Guinea-Bissau, Guyana, Haiti, Jamaica, Maldives, Mauritius, São Tomé and Príncipe, Seychelles, Singapore, St. Kitts and Nevis, St. Lucia, St. Vincent and the Grenadines, Suriname, and Trinidad and Tobago. Timor-Leste was not included because of insufficient data.

To measure resilience, Briguglio (2014) produced an economic resilience index, again using the methodology developed in Briguglio and others (2006), which indicated that the PICs' resilience rankings were not on the high side, mainly because of their relatively low scores on political governance, social development, and environmental management. The macroeconomic stability scores were, on average, higher than the average for the rest of the small island developing economies, due to PICs' lower debt ratios, among other things. Their average overall economic resilience index scores were about the same as those for the rest of the small island developing economies.

A correlation analysis between economic resilience index scores and country size indicated that these two variables are not related. But a statistically significant positive correlation exists between countries' income per capita and resilience scores, suggesting that, as expected, countries with the best economic performance tend to be those with the highest resilience scores. It should be noted that these tendencies conceal considerable differences between individual countries in each grouping.

Briguglio (2014) classified the nine PICs according to the categories shown in Figure 3.2, and found that Fiji, Samoa, Tonga, and Vanuatu—countries that are highly economically vulnerable, with moderately well-governed economies—marginally fit in the northeast quadrant (that is, on the left side of that quadrant). In contrast, Kiribati, Marshall Islands, Micronesia, Papua New Guinea, and the Solomon Islands, which are also highly economically vulnerable, but with weaker resilience scores, fit marginally in the northwest quadrant (that is, on the right side of that quadrant).

IMPLICATIONS FOR PICS

The vulnerability and resilience framework just described has a number of implications for PICs and for small island developing states in general. The framework may be useful to support decision making in PICs, especially for setting policy direction and prioritizing resilience-building actions. In particular, the analysis can help to disseminate information on and draw attention to issues relating to resilience building, encourage quantitative estimation of resilience building, and promote the idea of integrated action in this regard. In general, the framework can foster a better understanding of the benefits of good political, economic, social, and environmental governance in a country's efforts to better withstand and recover from external economic shocks.[6]

A major policy implication for PICs associated with this framework is that, in view of their high economic vulnerability, resilience building is very important for these states, and it therefore pays for them to embed resilience-building measures into their plans.

The framework has additional implications for attracting investment to small states. That is, everything else remaining equal, an economically well-governed country with political and social stability is more likely to attract both domestic and foreign investment than a badly governed and socially unstable country. Small states tend to be disadvantaged in attracting investment because of their small domestic markets and general difficulty in diversifying their economies. But good economic governance could partly make up for these inherent deficiencies.

---

[6]The vulnerability and resilience framework proposed in Briguglio and others (2006) led to considerable interest among international organizations working in the interests of small states. This framework also formed the basis of work with the Commonwealth Secretariat to examine and develop a resilience framework, which led to vulnerability/resilience profiles in Seychelles, St. Lucia, and Vanuatu, as explained in Briguglio and others (2010). The vulnerability and resilience framework was also referred to in the report of the UN Secretary-General (http://www.un.org/ga/search/view_doc.asp?symbol=A/65/115&lang=E) on the occasion of the Five-Year Review of the Mauritius Strategy for the Further Implementation of the Program of Action for the Sustainable Development of Small Island Developing States. The United Nations Economic and Social Commission for Asia and the Pacific (ESCAP, ADB, and UNDP 2010) sought to assess the impact of the global financial crisis by developing a vulnerability index. Their report (Appendix 3) also cited the approach introduced in Briguglio and others (2006). The United Nations Department of Economic and Social Affairs, in preparation for the Third International Conference on Small Island Developing States in Samoa in 2014, has also embarked on developing a vulnerability-resilience framework, building on the approach pioneered by Briguglio and others (2006); see http://www.sids2014.org/content/documents/260attrdlu7.pdf.

Regional collaboration is also relevant to PICs. Largely because of the indivisibility of certain overhead costs, some regulatory frameworks required for good economic governance may be prohibitively expensive for a single small state on its own, but affordable regionally. For this reason PICs could benefit through further regional cooperation by jointly undertaking policy measures conducive to resilience building. Such cooperation could, for example, cover competition law and policy, telecommunications regulations, air and shipping services, and pooling of expertise for various purposes, including for international negotiations.

The high vulnerability scores of PICs also suggest that economic vulnerability is not often given due importance in development assistance, especially when these states are classified as middle-income countries, even though their vulnerability poses serious disadvantages. It would, therefore, be beneficial to vulnerable small island developing economies if donor countries and organizations devise development support schemes that *effectively* factor in a vulnerability criterion.[7] This would be especially relevant when support is intended to strengthen the economic resilience of PICs.

CONCLUSION

The main message of this chapter is that even though small states tend to be economically vulnerable, that should not be construed as an argument for complacency among them. Rather, several resilience-building policy options can enable small states to minimize or withstand negative external economic shocks. This suggests in turn that small states should assign major importance to resilience-building policies and embed them in national plans and strategies.

The donor community, in its quest to support the economic development of small states, should likewise heed this message. Official development assistance and other forms of aid should include resilience building as an important motive for support to economically vulnerable states.

REFERENCES

Atkins, J., C. Easter, and S. Mazzi. 2000. *A Commonwealth Vulnerability Index for Developing Countries: The Position of Small States.* Commonwealth Secretariat Economic Report 40. London: Commonwealth Secretariat.

Briguglio, Lino. 1995. "Small Island States and their Economic Vulnerabilities." *World Development* 23 (9): 1615–32.

———. 1997. "Alternative Economic Vulnerability Indices for Developing Countries." Report prepared for the United Nations Department of Economic and Social Affairs.

———. 2004. "Economic Vulnerability and Resilience: Concepts and Measurements." In *Vulnerability and Resilience of Small States*, edited by L. Briguglio and E. J. Kisanga. Commonwealth Secretariat and the University of Malta, London.

———. 2014. "A Vulnerability and Resilience Framework for Small States." In *Building the Resilience of Small States: A Revised Framework*, edited by D. Lewis-Bynoe. London: Commonwealth Secretariat.

Briguglio, Lino, Gordan Cordina, Nadia Farrugia, and Stephanie Vella. 2006. "Conceptualising and Measuring Economic Resilience." In *Building the Economic Resilience of Small States*, edited by L. Briguglio, G. Cordina, and E. J. Kisanga. Malta: Islands and Small States Institute of the University of Malta in collaboration with the Commonwealth Secretariat.

Briguglio, Lino, Gordan Cordina, Stephanie Vella, and Constance Vigilance. 2010. *Profiling Vulnerability and Resilience: A Manual for Small States.* Commonwealth Secretariat and Islands and Small States Institute of the University of Malta, London.

Briguglio, Lino, and W. Galea. 2003. "Updating and Augmenting the Economic Vulnerability Index." Occasional Reports on Islands and Small States 2004 2003/4, Islands and Small States Institute of the University of Malta, Valetta.

---

[7]The word "effectively" should be emphasized in this context. This is because even in the case of graduation from least-developed country status, where a vulnerability index is used as a criterion, its effect may be negligible due to the fact that economic vulnerability is just one of three graduation criteria, and graduation requires that a country fulfill at least two of the three criteria. In addition, if the national income per capita of a least-developed economy rises to a level at least double the graduation threshold, the country will be deemed eligible for graduation regardless of its performance under the other criteria. See UNCTAD (2013). On this issue, see also the statement by the Government of Maldives (2009).

Cordina, Gordan. 2008. "The Macroeconomic and Growth Dynamics of Small States." In *Small States: Economic Review and Basic Statistics*. London: Commonwealth Secretariat.

Crowards, Tom. 2000. *An Index of Economic Vulnerability for Developing Countries*. Barbados: Caribbean Development Bank.

Economic and Social Commission for Asia and the Pacific (ESCAP), Asian Development Bank (ADB), and United Nations Development Programme (UNDP). 2010. "Achieving the Millennium Development Goals in an Era of Global Uncertainty." Asia-Pacific Regional Report 2009/10.

Gonzales, Anthony. 2000. "Policy Implications of Smallness as a Factor in the Lomé, FTAA and WTO Negotiations." Final Report 7/9/00.

Government of Maldives. 2009. "Impacts of Graduation from Least Developed Countries." Background paper prepared by the Ministry of Foreign Affairs for the Maldives Partnership Forum in Maldives, March 23–24. http://www.maldivespartnershipforum.gov.mv /pdf/Impacts%20of%20LDC%20Graduation.pdf.

United Nations Conference on Trade and Development (UNCTAD). 2013. *The Least Developed Countries Report*. New York: United Nations. Geneva: UNCTAD. http://unctad.org/en/PublicationsLibrary/ldc2013_en.pdf.

United Nations Department of Economic and Social Affairs (UNDESA). 2011. "LDC Criteria." http://www.un.org /en/development/desa/policy/cdp/ldc/ldc_criteria.shtml#evi.

CHAPTER 4

The Pacific Speed of Growth: How Fast Can It Be and What Determines It?

YONGZHENG YANG, HONG CHEN, SHIU RAJ SINGH, AND BALJEET SINGH

Economic recovery in most Pacific island countries (PICs) following the global financial crisis was mixed.[1] Although the region's two resource-rich countries, Papua New Guinea and the Solomon Islands, rebounded strongly on the back of high commodity prices after the crisis, most other PICs are still struggling with slow growth, with annual GDP growth averaging about 2 percent in 2011–14. Slow income growth has made it more challenging to reduce poverty and youth unemployment, both major socioeconomic issues in the region that need to be urgently addressed.[2]

With such a tepid recovery, a key challenge is how to raise the growth rate in PICs over the medium term. The slow economic recovery in many of these countries partly reflects their low growth rates when the global financial crisis began—and weak recovery is often associated with weak growth. But what is more worrying is the secular decline of economic growth in the non-commodity-exporting Pacific islands during 2001–14, again, with some exceptions. This is in sharp contrast with developing economies in other parts of the world, most of which managed to raise quite strong growth over this period. Of particular interest is the comparison with low-income countries, which grew three times as fast as PICs during the 2000s after growing at a similar rate during the 1990s.

Does this mean that PIC economies are performing below their potential? A large body of literature examines the economic growth performance of PICs compared with other country groups and relative to their own growth potential. Economic geography suggests that small states such as PICs are disadvantaged in economic growth: their small size makes it harder to exploit economies of scale, and remoteness and insularity increase the cost of transportation for international trade and technology dissemination. The empirical results are inconclusive, however, and complicated by how to take into account the unique characteristics of small states in terms of country size and geographical location.

Against this background, we address the following questions in this chapter: To what extent has economic growth in PICs been slower than in other small states and other similar country groups over the past decades? Have natural conditions, such as small size and geographical location, and external shocks, such as fuel prices and changing trade preferences, played a role in determining the long-term growth of PICs? Why did growth in these countries slow during 2001–10? And how might economic and other policies have affected their growth performance?

This chapter is based on IMF Working Paper 13/104 (Yang and others 2013) prepared for the Joint IMF–Government of Samoa Conference on Pacific Island Countries, held March 23, 2012, in Apia, Samoa. The authors thank Hoe Ee Khor, Tobias Haque, Matt Davies, Patrizia Tumbarello, Alexander Pitt, Jim Walsh, Nghi Luu, Craig Fookes, Ian Davidoff, Biman Chand Prasad, and Tiru Jayaraman for helpful comments. Tobias Haque kindly shared the initial World Bank database that is used in the econometric analysis, and Jan Gottschalk provided helpful input in the formative stage of the research.

[1] The focus of this study is the 11 PICs that are IMF members: Fiji, Kiribati, Marshall Islands, Micronesia, Palau, Papua New Guinea, Samoa, the Solomon Islands, Tonga, Tuvalu, and Vanuatu. Timor-Leste is not included in this study.

[2] See the forum communiqué of the Forty-Second Pacific Islands Forum, Auckland, September 7–8, 2011, and Noble, Pereira, and Saune (2011).

We use a unique data set for small states to examine the growth performance of PICs and its determinants in comparison with other countries that have similar characteristics. Previous attempts to analyze growth in PICs tend to lump them together with other small states or examine them in isolation. We also take a long-term perspective in analyzing their growth and pay particular attention to the declining performance during 2001–10. In doing so, we examine the broad international environment as well as internal factors, including through case studies, that may have contributed to the slowing growth.

These questions are put into context by providing an overview of the economic performance of PICs over past decades in a regional and global context, and the growth constraints in small states are briefly reviewed. This is followed by an overview of the methodology and data used in the econometric analysis, and an attempt to identify and quantify growth determinants in small states, and PICs in particular, with the aim of distinguishing the role of natural conditions from policy-related factors. This chapter tries to shed some light on why growth in PICs slowed in 2001–10, and closes with a discussion on the implications of the empirical findings for economic policies.

GROWTH PERFORMANCE: STYLIZED FACTS

Our focus on growth performance does not imply that this should be the sole criterion for assessing economic success. As many note, PICs have made considerable progress in many aspects of development, including the Millennium Development Goals. Nevertheless, as recognized in the development literature, inclusive growth is fundamental to poverty reduction and broad human development, and its continued improvement is crucial for sustaining development in the Pacific.

Overall, economic growth in PICs has lagged behind peer groups (Figure 4.1), especially if we exclude Papua New Guinea and the Solomon Islands. In the 1970s PIC economies grew at a respectable rate of just below 4 percent a year, albeit still not as fast as low-income countries (LICs) and other small states on average.[3] The 1980s was a slow-growth decade for PICs, but the performance of LICs and small states was also weaker. The 1990s saw PIC growth rebound and nearly catch up with LICs, but this was followed by a sharp divergence during the 2000s. Although the acceleration of LICs contributed most to this divergence, it is also evident that PICs had the weakest growth in four decades, at just one-third the rate of LICs.[4] Although growth rates during 2011–14 have been in aggregate higher for the PICs than in the previous decade, the average marks wide differences within the group.

There has been considerable variation in economic growth across PICs (Figure 4.2). The two resource-rich economies in the region, Papua New Guinea and the Solomon Islands, riding world commodity booms and investment in the commodity sector, had a dramatic change in fortune during 2001–14, outperforming their non-resource-rich peers after a long period of weak growth during 1970–90. In fact, Papua New Guinea grew well above the regional average even in the 1990s. Fortunes have also changed in the opposite direction. Fiji, for instance, after outperforming most of its neighbors for most of the 1990s, registered one of the region's slowest growth rates in the past decade, until recently. As we discuss later, this was largely a result of domestic developments.

---

[3]The definition of LICs is based on the current IMF classification. It should be noted that, as pointed out by Winters and Lim (2010), the growth performance of LICs tends to be understated, as some countries that were once LICs moved out of the group because of their faster economic growth. The classification of small states is based on Commonwealth Secretariat and World Bank (2000), with a population below 1.5 million except for Papua New Guinea. Of these countries, Annex 4.1 lists those with data available for econometric analysis. The Eastern Caribbean Currency Union members are Anguilla, Antigua and Barbuda, Dominica, Grenada, St. Kitts and Nevis, St. Lucia, and St. Vincent and the Grenadines.

[4]Despite the food and fuel price shocks and the global financial crisis, average growth during 2007–10 was similar to that during 2001–06.

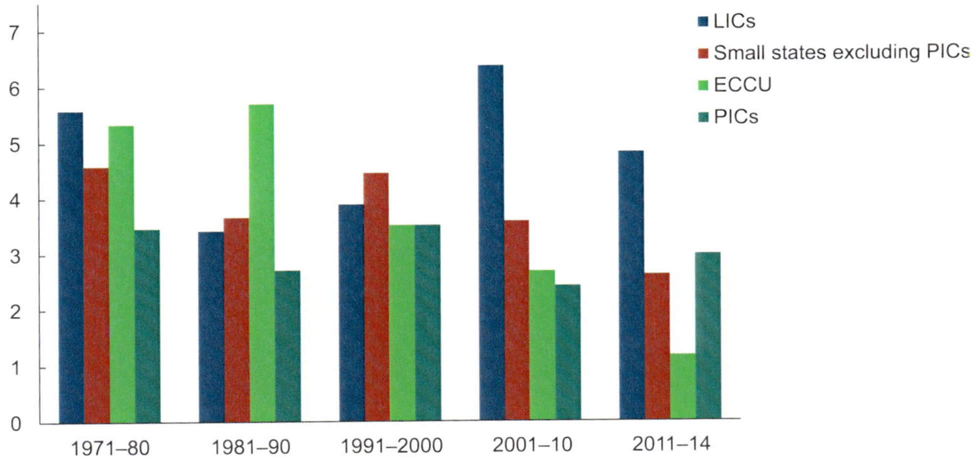

Figure 4.1 Annual Average Real GDP Growth (*Percent*)

Sources: IMF, International Financial Statistics database; and IMF staff estimates.
Note: ECCU = Eastern Caribbean Currency Union; LICs = low-income countries; PICs = Pacific island countries.

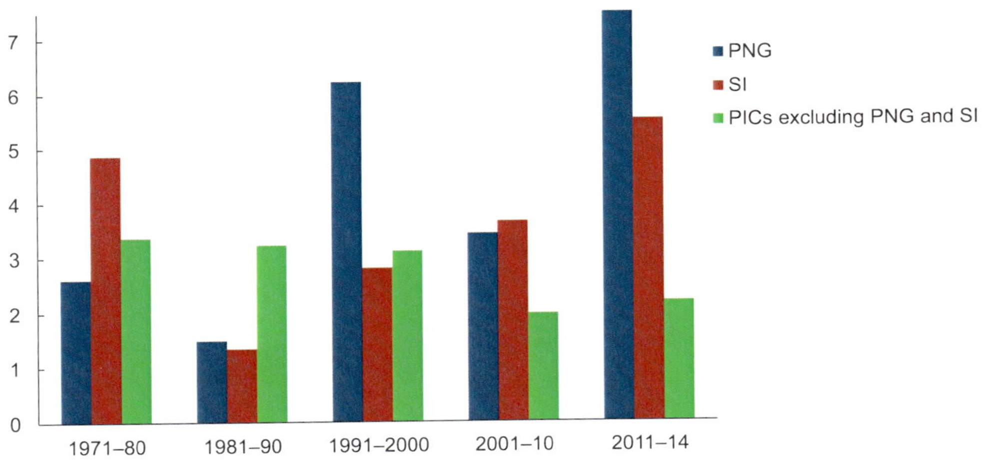

Figure 4.2 Annual Average Real GDP Growth (*Percent*)

Sources: IMF, International Financial Statistics database; and IMF staff estimates.
Note: PICs = Pacific island countries; PNG = Papua New Guinea; SI = Solomon Islands.

PICs' growth has been volatile but, on average, at similar levels of volatility as other groups of developing economies (Figure 4.3). It is worth noting that growth volatility was high in the 1970s and 1980s, at least in those countries with available data. In the 1990s volatility remained high for all the regional groups except the Eastern Caribbean Currency Union. In the 2000s volatility declined noticeably in all groups except the Eastern Caribbean Currency Union, which experienced its most volatile period in four decades when growth slowed. Growth volatility was lower in PICs in the 2000s, along with the slowest growth rate of the regional groups. Volatility declined in all groups in 2011–14.

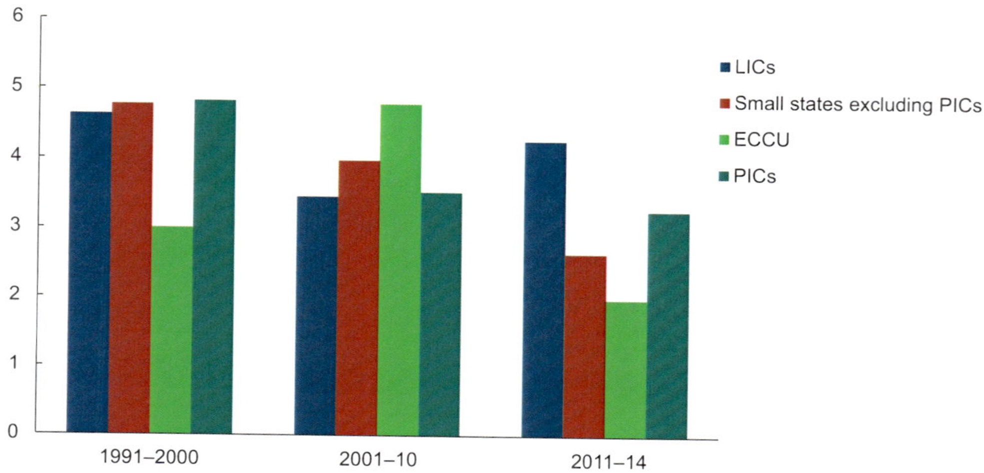

Figure 4.3 Standard Deviation of GDP Growth

Sources: IMF, International Financial Statistics database; and IMF staff estimates.
Note: ECCU = Eastern Caribbean Currency Union; LICs = low-income countries; PICs = Pacific island countries.

GROWTH CONSTRAINTS IN SMALL STATES

So why have PICs tended to grow less rapidly than peer groups and why did growth slow during 2001–14? In this section, we focus on the first question and leave the discussion of the second to later.

Research on the determinants of growth and volatility in PICs has been closely related to "special problems of small states" (Streeten 1993).[5] These are inevitably linked to country size and geographic location and the issues they entail, particularly in PICs. Small populations give rise not only to diseconomies of scale if the domestic market is relied upon as the main source of demand, but also difficulties with industrial clustering, which is used in modern manufacturing (for example, electronics and toys) and service industries (for example, financial and information technology) to reduce production costs.[6] The location of many small states, and PICs in particular, makes them remote and insular from major international markets, raising the cost of transportation and communication. Coupled with the effect of country borders (including trade restrictions),[7] this means that countries with small populations are less able to exploit economies of scale and hence suffer from lower productivity (if not lower growth of productivity).[8] Small states also face high unit costs in providing public goods because of the indivisibility of such goods (World Bank 2010; Commonwealth Secretariat and World Bank 2000; and see Chapter 2 in this volume).

Thus, theory suggests that PICs are particularly disadvantaged by their small populations and location in terms of production costs and economic integration. Figure 4.4 shows that not only are many PICs small, but they also tend to be more remote than most other small countries.

[5]There is no consensus on the definition of small states—not only have several variables (for example, population, GDP, and geographic area) been used as a criterion, but also various thresholds for the same variable. The threshold for population, the most commonly used variable, has ranged widely from about 1 million to 15 million (see Armstrong and Read 2003). The IMF defines small developing states as those with a population of 1.5 million or less, excluding advanced economies (as defined by the IMF *World Economic Outlook*) and fuel-exporting countries.

[6]The literature also discusses the potential advantages of small size. These include flexibility in adapting to changes in the external environment, a more homogeneous population, size-induced greater openness, and a lower chance of implementing costly import substitution. See Streeten (1993), Easterly and Kraay (2000), and Armstrong and Read (1998, 2003).

[7]See McCallum (1995), Wei (1996), and Anderson and van Wincoop (2004) for the effect of international borders on trade. McCallum found that Canadian provinces trade up to 22 times more with each other than with states within the United States.

[8]Milner and Westaway (1993) explore the medium-term growth effects of country size through possible capital shallowing, restricted structural change, barriers to catching up, and limited domestic technology diffusion. The authors find some evidence of capital shallowing and greater barriers in technological diffusion.

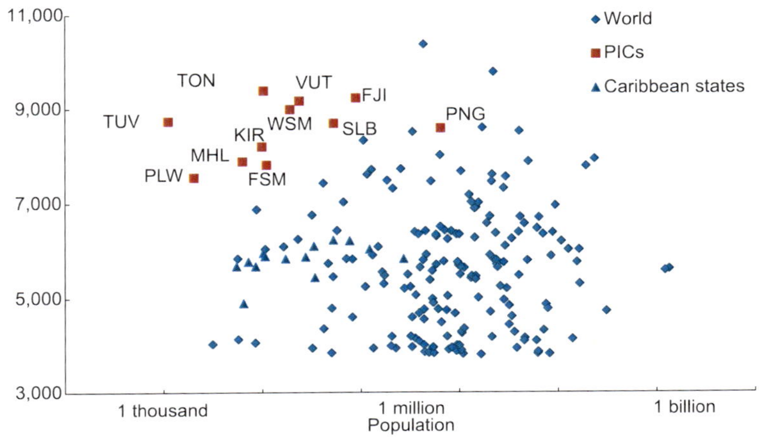

Figure 4.4 GDP-Weighted Distance (*Kilometers*)

Source: Gibson and Nero (2007).

Note: PICs = Pacific island countries. Country labels in the figure use International Organization for Standardization abbreviations.

Smallness may not be a disadvantage if a country is surrounded by large, advanced economies (for example, Luxembourg) that offer large markets without significant trade barriers. But in PICs, their small size and location reinforce their disadvantages, and remoteness increases their transportation costs, raising the costs of exporting and importing, which in turn raise the cost of domestic production and exports.[9] At the same time, smallness tends to add to transportation costs, either because of weak competition (for example, fewer airlines and shipping companies), higher infrastructure costs (for example, fewer resources for building efficient ports), or small transportation volumes (for example, containers not fully utilized). Distances between the islands of the same country also add to production costs. So, while small can be beautiful, remoteness is not, as far as economic efficiency is concerned.

In contrast to the theory, empirical evidence on the effects of smallness and remoteness on income and economic growth is inconclusive. In an extensive survey, Armstrong and Read (2003) conclude that there is no evidence that small states grow more slowly, despite earlier expectations. Evidence is also weak on the negative impact of "islandness" on growth. This is, however, somewhat surprising given that the literature has demonstrated that landlocked countries—which face similar challenges to island countries in isolation-induced transportation and communication costs—tend to grow more slowly than coastal countries (Gallup, Sachs, and Mellinger 1998; Hausmann 2001). If these conclusions are correct, there must be some intrinsic characteristics of small states that enable them to offset their geography-related disadvantages.

Greater trade openness has been found to be one such offsetting factor. Small states tend to have higher trade-to-GDP ratios than larger countries. Easterly and Kraay (2000) find that the benefits of this greater trade openness offset the adverse impact of greater output volatility in small states.[10]

[9] Redding and Venables (2004) find that the geography of access to markets and sources of supply is an important determinant of income levels across countries. Their results indicate that halving a country's distance from all of its trade partners increases its income per capita by about 25 percent. Similarly, using data on costs of doing business, Winters and Martins (2004) show that for both clothing and electronics assembly, microeconomies have cost inflation factors of 36 percent, and that for tourism the factor is 58 percent. The last is driven substantially by high costs for personal travel (and the high share of such travel in overall packages).

[10] Srinivasan (1986) argues that smallness is neither a necessary nor sufficient condition for slow growth and development. Milner and Westaway (1993) find there is no obvious link between medium-term growth performance and a range of attributes of country size.

In the sample that they used, small states have a ratio of trade to GDP that is 54 percentage points higher than the average economy and the effect of this greater openness is 2½ times larger than the negative effect of greater output volatility. The authors conclude that, even if output volatility is one of the consequences of openness, the greater openness of small states is, on balance, a positive factor for their growth. Of course, greater volatility is not the only (or even the most important) disadvantage that small states face.

Because of greater trade openness, the growth performance of small states is more closely linked to that of their major trading partners. Countries in more dynamic and prosperous regions are likely to grow faster than those in stagnating regions, and vice versa. Empirical research finds supporting evidence for this hypothesis (Armstrong and Read 2000). In a similar vein, Gibson and Nero (2007) find that growth in small states is heavily influenced by the growth of neighboring countries located within 35 degrees of latitude or longitude (a distance of approximately 3,900 kilometers, or 2,423 miles, at the equator).[11] Their results show that each percentage point increase in the average growth rate of this neighboring area raises the GDP growth rate of small states in the region by 0.54 percentage point. Looking at this type of growth linkage from a different angle, Bertram (2003) finds that the GDP per capita of small island economies and its growth through time are explained to a large extent by the closeness of the political linkages tying each island to a corresponding advanced economy and the level of GDP per capita in that advanced economy. Estimates show that for every U.S. dollar increase in the GDP per capita in the advanced economy, there is a US$0.30 to US$0.56 increase in the GDP per capita of island states.

MODEL, DATA, AND METHODOLOGIES

Model Specification

The review on growth constraints in small states suggests that it is not clear how important geography-related disadvantages are in determining the growth performance of small island states relative to common constraints facing all countries. In what follows, we take a more comprehensive approach to the analysis of growth determinants, using a cross-section data set covering 1992–2008 for 45 small states (see Annex 4.1, Table 4.1.1 for the list of countries). Our aim here is to test within this relatively homogeneous group of small island states what differentiates the growth performance of PICs from their peers. Once growth determinants are identified, we evaluate their relative magnitude of impact. This allows us to assess potential benefits from policy actions to influence these determinants. Our approach is to start with parsimonious specifications and move on to more comprehensive and sophisticated specifications.

The model employed in the current study is the growth-initial level model, which is also called the beta-convergence model. The development of the beta-convergence literature has reached a high level of sophistication, owing to the efforts of Mankiw, Romer, and Weil (1992), Barro and Sala-i-Martin (2004), and Islam (2003a, 2003b). The basic form of the growth-initial level equation can be expressed as follows:

$$\begin{aligned} gy_i = &-(1-e^{-\lambda\tau})\ln(y_{i,0})+(1-e^{-\lambda\tau})\cdot\frac{\alpha}{1-\alpha}\cdot[\ln(s_i)-\ln(n_i+g+\delta)] \\ &+(1-e^{-\lambda\tau})\cdot\ln A_{i,0}+g\cdot(t-e^{-\lambda\tau})+\gamma\cdot X+\varepsilon_i \end{aligned} \tag{4.1}$$

where gy is the average growth of GDP per capita over the period under study; the subscript denotes province i; $-(1-e^{-\lambda\tau})$ captures the convergence effect, with $-(1-e^{-\lambda\tau})<0$ providing

[11] Gibson and Nero (2007) also find that long-term growth in small states is also hurt by output volatility and language diversity.

evidence that economies converge to their respective steady-state levels of income, that is, beta-convergence; while $-(1 - e^{-\lambda\tau}) > 0$ indicates beta-divergence. The rate of convergence, λ, can be restored from the estimated coefficient, y_0 is real GDP per capita in the initial year, s is the share of gross fixed capital formation in GDP, n is the growth rate of the total population, g denotes technological progress, δ is the physical capital depreciation rate, and X is a variable matrix representing variables other than those related to beta-convergence in determining economic growth. In this study we set $g + \delta = 5$ percent.[12] Furthermore, by making the restriction that the coefficients of $\ln(s)$ and $\ln(n + g + \delta)$ have identical magnitudes but different signs as in equation 4.1, one is able to obtain the output share of physical capital, α. However, if this restriction is not supported by empirical analysis, as in the current study, the growth-convergence model should have the following expression:

$$gy_i = \beta_0 + \beta_1 \ln(y_i,0) + \beta_2 \ln(s_i) + \beta_3 \ln(n_i + g + \delta) + \gamma \cdot X_i + \varepsilon_i \tag{4.2}$$

where $\beta_1 = -(1 - e^{-\lambda\tau})$.

Data Description

Our data are from the databases of the IMF, United Nations, and World Bank. All money values are in constant 2005 prices in U.S. dollars. In general, 45 small countries are covered in the study, but owing to limitations on data availability for certain series, some regressions cover 39 or 40 countries. Statistics of the relevant series are summarized in Annex Table 4.1.2. The following are used as relevant growth determinants with average real growth of GDP per capita over 1992–2008 (denoted by gy) as the dependent variable:

- GDP per capita in 1992, denoted by $\ln(y_0)$, captures the convergence effect.
- Investment-to-GDP (percent), denoted by ln(investment rate). Values of this variable are averaged over 1992–2008.
- Population growth together with the physical capital depreciation rate and cost of technological progress (percent), denoted by $\ln(n + g + \delta)$. Values of this variable are averaged over 1992–2008.
- The ratio of foreign aid to gross national income (GNI; percent), denoted by Aid/GNI. Because of data limitations, the most recent data (2007) were used. The validity of this proxy is supported by a strong linear correlation between the aid-to-GNI ratio in 2007 and the average aid-to-GNI ratio over different available years during 1992–2007.
- The political stability series is obtained from the World Bank's Worldwide Governance Indicators database (Kaufmann, Kraay, and Mastruzzi 2011). The data are averaged over available years during 1996–2008. We also tried other governance indicators from the same source, but only the political stability indicator was found robust.
- Exports-to-GDP ratio (percent), denoted by Exports/GDP, measures export openness. We also tried imports-to-GDP and trade-to-GDP ratios, but found them less robust. Values of this variable are averaged over 1992–2008.
- Growth volatility is measured by the standard deviation of GDP growth rates over the period under study. The volatility-growth nexus has been widely discussed in the literature. Some studies, such as Kormendi and Meguire (1985) and Grier and Tullock (1989), found that volatility is positively associated with growth, while others, such as Ramey and Ramey (1995), Aizenman and Marion (1999), and Easterly and Kraay (2000), showed a negative relationship. However, as noted in the literature and our observations in the analysis, the impact of volatility

[12] Most studies in the literature assume a same value of $g + \delta$ for all countries, and the most frequently used value is 0.05. See, for example, Mankiw, Romer, and Weil (1992), Islam (1995), Yao and Zhang (2001), and Chen (2012).

on growth is often linked to some other factors that directly affect growth. For instance, volatility may arise from political instability and trade openness.

- Remoteness, measured by GDP-weighted distance to the capital cities of major overseas markets, is denoted by ln(distance). We tried several measures of remoteness, such as distance to the top three trading partners; distance to the top three trading partners weighted by GDP; weighted distance to the top three export markets, import sources, and trading partners; average distance to other countries; and distance between producers and consumers within a country. We found only the GDP-weighted distance to the capitals of major overseas markets helped effectively explain growth in the current study.
- A set of dummy variables to represent continents/regions and the country of Equatorial Guinea, with the latter capturing its exceptional growth with the exploration of oil resources. This set of dummy variables is found to be important in controlling for country heterogeneity and mitigating the heteroscedasticity problem. Apart from this set of dummies, we also tried dummy variables to represent oil producers, oil exporters, commodity exporters, and advanced economies, but none was found significant across various regressions in the current study.

We also considered a number of other factors but found they are statistically insignificant. For example, we tested the importance of smallness as measured by population size. The insignificance of population size in our study of small states, together with the significance of the same indicator in the literature (see, for example, Easterly and Kraay 2000), suggests the impact of smallness on growth may not be linear. This is not surprising given the relatively homogeneous sample used. Other insignificant factors identified include education, inflation, government expenditure, imports, size of agriculture and manufacturing, urban population ratio, arable land ratio, terms of trade, disaster indicators, trade-weighted external demand, and external demand measured by the top three export destinations' GDP growth. Of course, the performance of these variables could be limited by data quality.

Estimation Methodologies

The analysis in this chapter is based on cross-sectional data on up to 45 countries. Such a relatively small sample can yield unstable results if large heterogeneity exists among observations. However, it is not the case in this study, as our regression results across various specifications are quite consistent, a benefit of the homogeneity of the sample. This benefit is also evident in the consistently high adjusted *R*-squared values across regressions and the consistency between cross-sectional analysis and panel-data analysis that we carried out, with heterogeneity of countries controlled for by country fixed effects.[13]

Another issue worth noting is the causality between dependent and explanatory variables. For instance, the causality between investment and growth is believed to be bidirectional. See, for example, Feeny (2005). Endogeneity of aid also receives considerable attention in the aid-growth literature (Mosley 1980; Ali and Isse 2005). Similarly, bidirectional causation between volatility and growth is also widely discussed in the literature (Easterly and Kraay 2000; Malik and Temple 2009). Given this, addressing the endogeneity problem is important in our analysis, as least squares estimates in the presence of endogeneity are biased and inconsistent. Instrumental variables estimators should be applied instead. The Sargan test and Hausman test are employed in our study to detect overidentification of external instruments and endogeneity, respectively. Based on test statistics, we found investment and aid do not pose an endogeneity problem to estimation, while growth volatil-

[13] In our panel data exercise, the whole sample period 1992–2008 is divided into four: 1992–96, 1996–2000, 2000–04, and 2004.

ity does.[14,15,16] Therefore, the two-stage least squares estimator is employed to estimate those regressions in which growth volatility is included as a regressor; otherwise the least squares estimator is applied.

The estimation of the specified model follows a simple-to-general strategy; namely, we first test for the neoclassical growth theory by assessing effects of $\ln(y_0)$, $\ln(s)$, and $\ln(n + g + \delta)$ jointly, and then add and test for additional control factors one at a time.[17] This approach helps us identify relevant determinants while avoiding biased estimates caused by omitted relevant variables and minimizing the loss in the efficiency of estimates caused by including irrelevant variables.

DETERMINANTS OF GROWTH IN SMALL STATES

Regression results suggest that geography has a large influence over economic growth in PICs (Table 4.1).[18] After controlling for a number of variables found to be statistically significant as determinants of growth, PICs are shown to suffer a distance-related disadvantage in GDP per capita growth of about 1½ percentage points compared with an average non-Pacific small state.[19] To put this in perspective, PICs' annual average GDP per capita growth over 1992–2008 was a little over 0.7 percent. Without the geographical disadvantage, PICs could have grown more than three times as fast in this period.

As important as it is, geography is not the only factor that has contributed to the slower growth of PIC economies compared to other small states. Growth in small states is influenced by a number of other variables—initial income levels, investment, population growth, aid, export openness, growth volatility, and political stability, all of which were found to be statistically significant. When combined, these variables lower GDP per capita growth in PICs by about another percentage point, compared with an average small state, with some variables making positive contributions and others negative. To start with, PICs' initial income works to their advantage as they were, on average, poorer than other small states in the early 1990s, the period our initial income calculations is based

[14] To test investment endogeneity, manufacturing and mining output relative to GDP and agricultural output relative to GDP were used as external instruments for the investment-to-GDP ratio. The Sargan test statistic is 0.811 with a p-value of 0.617, therefore the null hypothesis that external instruments are valid is not rejected. However, the Hausman test statistic of 1.618 with p-value of 0.203 provides strong evidence that the null hypothesis of exogeneity is not rejected.

[15] For the aid-to-GDP endogeneity test, we considered external instruments such as the education index, deaths caused by natural disasters, government expenditure to GDP, and primary industry output to GDP. Only government expenditure to GDP and primary industry output to GDP are found to be valid external instruments based on the Wald parameter test (F-statistic = 13.45). Overidentification of parameters is confirmed by a Sargan chi-squared statistic of 0.453 with p-value of 0.5011. However the Durbin-Wu-Hausman test (with a chi-squared statistic of 0.46481 and p-value of 0.495) provides no evidence that the aid-to-GNI ratio in the analysis is endogenous. Nonetheless, the two-stage least squares estimator was applied to address any potential endogeneity, but the results obtained are similar to those using the ordinary least squares estimator.

[16] To test for endogeneity of growth volatility, we used political stability and the exports-to-GDP ratio as external instruments. The Sargan test statistic of 0.111 with p-value of 0.739 strongly indicates that external instruments are valid, and the Hausman test statistic of 9.316 with p-value of 0.002 provides strong evidence that volatility is endogenous.

[17] We also tried a specification with human capital as a growth determinant. We used various proxies for human capital, such as the United Nations' education and human development indices and the secondary school enrollment rate, but none were found statistically important in explaining growth experience in small states. Data limitation in terms of time coverage may have affected the results.

[18] Discussions hereafter are based on regressions 2 and 3 in Table 4.1.

[19] Small states in Africa also suffer a geography-related disadvantage, but PICs are subject to by far the greatest disadvantage among small states. We run two models: one using trade-weighted distance and the other regional dummies to capture the impact of geography on growth. Not surprisingly, we found the two variables are correlated, and including one in the regression would render the other insignificant. Moreover, the estimated impact of the two sets of variables on PIC growth is similar, confirming that distance is the main obstacle to growth. Distance is measured as GDP-weighted physical distance to the capital cities of major markets.

TABLE 4.1

Regressions on GDP per Capita Growth of Small Island Countries

Estimation Method	(1) OLS		(2) OLS		(3) OLS		(4) 2SLS	
Variable[1]	Coefficient	[t-statistic]	Coefficient	[t-statistic]	Coefficient	[t-statistic]	Coefficient	[t-statistic]
Pacific	−3.13	[−3.33]	−1.90	[−2.11]			−1.77	[−2.01]
Constant	7.00	[1.56]	15.68	[3.47]	35.09	[2.90]	15.41	[3.34]
ln(y_0)	−0.13	[−0.58]	−1.30	[−3.80]	−1.36	[−4.77]	−0.87	[−3.36]
ln(investment rate)	1.23	[2.11]	1.05	[1.78]	1.08	[2.20]	1.72	[3.20]
ln($n+g+\delta$)	−3.21	[−2.04]	−4.06	[−2.61]	−3.94	[−3.32]	−4.62	[−2.84]
Aid/GNI			−0.05	[−2.09]	−0.06	[−2.44]	−0.07	[−2.83]
Political stability			1.25	[2.50]	1.41	[3.19]		
Exports/GDP			0.03	[2.07]	0.04	[2.79]		
Growth volatility							−0.36	[−2.69]
ln(distance)					−2.31	[−1.91]		
Sample size	45		40		39		40	
Adjusted/centered R^2	0.8161		0.8786		0.9068		0.8818	
Variance inflation factor (mean VIF)	2.33		2.33		1.99		–	
Breusch-Pagan (p-value)	0.3634		0.4534		0.7104		–	
Sargan statistic	–		–		–		0.7387	

Source: Authors' calculations.

Note: GNI = gross national income; OLS = ordinary least squares estimator; 2SLS = two-stage least squares estimator. Regressions 1 to 3 employ the ordinary least squares estimator, and regression 4 employs the two-stage least squares estimator.

[1] y_0, representing initial per capita income in 1992, measures convergence effect; saving rate is gross fixed capital formation out of GDP; $n + g + \delta$ is population growth, g is technological progress rate, and δ is capital depreciation rate. $g + \delta = 0.05$ is adopted in this study. Political stability is one of the governance indicators provided by the World Bank. Growth volatility is measured by the standard deviation of GDP per capita growth rate. Distance is weighted distance to major overseas markets. Dummy variables are included to represent Equatorial Guinea, Pacific island countries, and continents such as Africa, North America, and Europe, which help to control for the heteroscedasticity problem. Growth volatility is found to be endogenous in the current study, and political stability and exports/GDP are used as instrument variables for growth volatility whose validity as efficient instruments is confirmed by the Sargan statistic. Further details on the endogeneity test are in footnote 15. As noted in the regressions, impacts of political stability and the exports-to-GDP ratio not only work on growth directly, but also indirectly by affecting growth volatility. Variance inflation factor (mean VIF) is used to detect the colinearity of the regressors with the constant. A mean VIF of less than 10 can be taken as no evidence of a colinearity problem. The Breusch-Pagan test is employed to test for heteroscedasticity. A p-value greater than a preferred significance level can be taken as no evidence of heteroscedasticity. All regressors are significant at least at the 10 percent level, with most of them significant at either the 1 percent or 5 percent level.

on. According to the convergence effect found in the regressions, this lower initial income has allowed PICs to grow about ½ percentage point faster than an average non-Pacific small state.

Lower investment (as a percent of GDP) partly explains the slower growth in PICs. Over 1992–2008, investment in PICs averaged 22½ percent of GDP, about 6 percentage points lower than the average of all small states. Had PICs been able to achieve the average investment rate of non-Pacific small states, their real GDP growth per capita would have been about ¼ percentage point higher. Given the data limitations, we were not able to disaggregate the investment data into public and private components or by economic sector.[20] A detailed analysis is needed to identify at the country level what type of investment would be most productive, but the results here suggest that PICs do have to catch up when benchmarked against other small states. Moreover, there are considerable variations in the investment rate among PICs, which are often as large as between PICs and other small states.

Greater export orientation makes a strong positive contribution to growth in small states. On average, each increase of 10 percentage points in the exports-to-GDP ratio raises GDP growth per capita by about 0.3 percentage point. Since the exports-to-GDP ratio in PICs is 24 percentage points lower than the average of non-Pacific small states, this implies that PICs could have grown by 0.6 percentage point faster had they exported as much as other small states (in percent of GDP). We find that greater imports as a percent of GDP have no statistically significant impact on growth. This suggests that, unlike evidence found for some other countries, imports have not been associated with technological transfers that benefit growth in small states. This, in turn, may reflect the fact that imports in small states more often consist of consumer goods, rather than intermediate

[20] We did include secondary education in the regression in an attempt to capture the effect of human capital on growth. However, the results are statistically insignificant.

inputs or capital goods that embody newer technologies and help improve local productivity. Moreover, imports in smaller PICs are more likely to be linked to aid-funded projects that tend to have weaker linkages with the local economy. Similarly, we also find no evidence that openness measured by the ratio of trade turnover (exports plus imports) to GDP has any positive impact on growth.

Some of the benefits from greater export openness are offset by increased output volatility arising from larger exports (as a percent of GDP). Estimates show that each change of 10 percentage points in export openness is associated with a 0.2 percentage point change in the standard deviation of GDP growth.[21] Given this, less than one-fourth of the growth benefits from greater export openness are nullified by the associated increase in output volatility, leaving PICs worse off by about 0.5 percentage point from their lower openness compared with other small states.

Aid is found to be associated with slower GDP growth. In almost all the regressions we tested, the relationship between aid and growth is negative. For each increase of 10 percentage points in aid as a percent of GDP, growth is lower by 0.6 percentage point. Our preliminary tests show that there is no reverse causality. In other words, slower growth does not lead to more aid; it is more aid that leads to slower growth. It is not clear how aid might slow growth in small states, though the most commonly cited mechanism is Dutch disease—a phenomenon of weak export competitiveness resulting from real exchange rate appreciation caused by capital inflows, such as aid. That said, it must be noted that the negative relationship found between aid and growth should not be interpreted as aid lowering economic welfare. In fact, much aid is often aimed at reducing poverty rather than increasing economic growth.[22] Unfortunately, we are unable to disaggregate aid into different categories in this analysis, so the estimated impact here applies to total aid rather than to the part of aid that is likely to enhance growth, such as aid used for improving infrastructure and increasing investment in other productive sectors. Furthermore, if aid helps improve living standards in terms of education and health, it could help raise growth in the long term that may not have been captured in this analysis.

Political stability is an important source of faster growth. Measured by the World Bank Political Stability and Absence of Violence/Terrorism indicator, PICs score more favorably on political stability than other small states. This gives PICs, on average, an advantage of 0.3 percentage point in growth over other small states. It should be noted, however, that political stability varies substantially among PICs themselves. Other things being equal, the highest-scoring country in the region has a growth advantage of more than 1 percentage point over the lowest-scoring country.

To sum up the results, PICs have relatively low export openness and investment, but do better than other small states in maintaining political stability. On balance, these policy-related factors, together with geography-related disadvantages, have led to growth rates that are much lower than in other small states. Figure 4.5 shows a rough decomposition of the impact of the various determinants on PICs' growth, benchmarked against the average growth rate of non-Pacific small states. The first bar depicts the GDP per capita growth rate of non-Pacific small states during 1992–2008. Each of the bars to the right shows, cumulatively, the impact of a growth determinant, with red segments showing the negative impact, blue segments the remaining growth rate after the negative impact, and green segments representing the positive impact. The third bar shows the results when using distance to capture the effect of geography instead of regional dummies, shown in the second bar. The blue bar at the far right shows the actual growth rate in PICs during 1992–2008. The chart reflects that lower export openness, aid, and investment, along with the geographical disadvantage of PICs, are the main contributors to their lower growth compared with other small states.

---

[21] This result is illustrative only. Our estimates are significant only at the 83 percent confidence level, and the sample size is small (28 observations). However, the result is consistent with that reported in Easterly and Kraay (2000).

[22] The relationship between aid and growth is a hotly debated subject in the Pacific, as it is globally. See Bowman and Chand (2008), Rao, Sharma, and Singh (2008), Pavlov and Sugden (2006), and Hughes (2003).

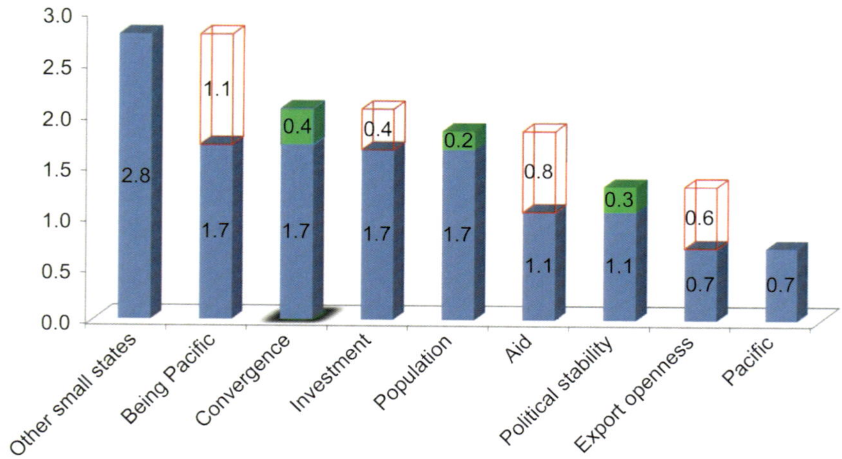

Figure 4.5 Factors Affecting Pacific Islands' Growth (*Percent*)

Source: Authors' calculations.
Note: See text for explanation of graph.

The results presented in Figure 4.5 should, however, be interpreted with caution. Data quality is always an issue in such exercises, and this is especially true for data on small states. While the results are generally consistent across model specifications, they are subject to data limitations and should be further tested for robustness as data and other information improve. And perhaps even more important, the interpretation of the results should be guided by economic conditions pertaining to the countries in question. For instance, while we found that greater export openness is good for growth, it may not be equally feasible for all PICs to increase exports of goods or nonfactor services, particularly for microstates that have few resources to produce such exports. Similarly, while low investment is generally a constraint on growth in PICs, countries need to identify what impediments investors might be facing and what projects could bring the highest social returns.[23] Moreover, any scaling up of investment should take into account debt sustainability if it is financed by borrowing. Capacity constraints at any particular time may also affect the effectiveness of investment.

WHY HAS GROWTH SLOWED IN PICs?

The analysis just discussed provides a broad explanation for the relatively slow growth in PICs over the long term, but it sheds little light on why growth slowed in many PICs during 2001–10. In this section, we use the framework established in the previous section to explore possible explanations of the growth slowdown in 2001–08. Statistical tests suggest there were no significant structural breaks in growth for the entire sample of small states. Given this, the same set of regression coefficients from the previous section can be used to predict growth rates based on the level of the determinants in the two subperiods.

It appears that a decline in the exports-to-GDP ratio is a major contributor to the recent growth slowdown. Investment increased slightly, which should have helped raise growth, as should lower output volatility. The positive effects of these developments should add up to over one-half percentage point. On the other hand, the average export openness ratio fell by as much as 4½ percentage

[23]A growth diagnosis approach could be employed in such an analysis. See Duncan and Nakagawa (2006) for a growth diagnosis for six PICs.

points in the 2000s from its 1990s level. There are undoubtedly other factors, including country-specific ones, that have not been included in the model but that contributed to the slower growth in the 2000s. Even so, the decline in export openness, though far from fully explaining the growth slowdown, does point to a weakness in an area that is key to mitigating an obstacle to growth in small states—integration with the global economy.

While the decline in trade openness over 15 years may partly reflect external shocks, it may also indicate weakening competitiveness in some cases. In several PICs, growth began to decelerate well before the increases in world food and fuel prices in 2007–08. At least seven out of the 11 PICs that are the focus of this study had slower growth in 2001–06 than in 1991–2000. For the 11 as a group, average growth in 2001–06 was a little over half the rate of the 1990s and was similar to the average growth of 2007–10, a period full of adverse shocks. In some cases, external shocks seem to have had a lasting impact on productive capacity and weakened growth fundamentals, as in the experience of Samoa following the devastating 2009 earthquake and tsunami and the global financial crisis (Box 4.1). Countries in such circumstances may need to reassess their competitiveness position and adapt their strategies to regain growth momentum.

Real exchange rate appreciation may have played an important part in weakening competitiveness in a number of PICs. In contrast to the 1990s, when only the Solomon Islands experienced an appreciation of its real effective exchange rate, 2001–15 saw the rate appreciate, on average through the entire period, in all six countries with their own currencies, with only Tonga depreciating since 2012 (Figure 4.6).[24] With the exception of Papua New Guinea, which has a de jure floating exchange rate regime, the other five countries' currencies are pegged to a basket of currencies that include the Australian and U.S. dollars, among other key trading partner currencies.[25]

While domestic prices have been rising more rapidly than those in trading partners, there have been limited movements in nominal effective exchange rates in the 2000s, leading to considerable real appreciation in some cases, as in Fiji, Tonga, and Vanuatu, even before the increases in global food and fuel prices. For Papua New Guinea and to a lesser extent the Solomon Islands, the appreciation after 2008 was driven by commodity booms, which boosted export earnings and foreign direct investment inflows. In the five PICs that do not have their own currencies, those that use the Australian dollar (Kiribati, Tuvalu) experienced real appreciation until 2012 (Figure 4.7), whereas those using the U.S. dollar (Marshall Islands, Micronesia, Palau) have seen real appreciation only since 2012 as a result of strengthening of the U.S. dollar.

It should be noted that exchange rate appreciation did not in general lead to declines in foreign reserves. In fact, in most cases, reserves as measured by import coverage have risen since the global financial crisis. In some cases, this partly reflects weak import demand resulting from slow economic activity, but also generous donor support.

The evolution of the current account is indicative of the change in external competitiveness over time. While the 2007–08 food and fuel price increases and global financial crisis certainly contributed to this development in PICs in recent years, the deterioration started before these shocks (Figure 4.8). The trade account has also deteriorated (Figure 4.9). It is worth noting, however, that the North Pacific states (Marshall Islands, Micronesia, Palau) saw an improvement in the trade balance in the 2000s. On the other hand, countries that had real effective exchange rate appreciation experienced larger increases in their trade deficits than other countries. Again in the case of Papua New Guinea, it should be noted that the deterioration of the current account also reflects the investment boom associated with its liquid natural gas project. The deterioration of Samoa's current account was largely due to increases in imports for post-tsunami and more recently post-cyclone

[24] The six are Fiji, Papua New Guinea, Samoa, the Solomon Islands, Tonga, and Vanuatu.

[25] From April 2014, the kina (the currency of Papua New Guinea) has reduced its volatility and followed a trend within a 2 percent band against the U.S. dollar. Accordingly, the de facto exchange rate arrangement was reclassified from floating to a crawl-like arrangement, effective April 11, 2014.

Box 4.1. Samoa: Managing Shocks and Regaining Its Growth Momentum

The Samoan economy was growing strongly until the mid-2000s when it lost momentum. Well-coordinated reforms in the mid-1990s and sound macroeconomic policies delivered an annual average GDP growth rate of 5 percent during this period. Investment in the lead-up to the 2007 Pacific Games provided another boost before a series of shocks hit the country—the food and fuel price hikes, the global financial crisis, and two devastating natural disasters (a tsunami in 2009 and a cyclone in 2012). Economic growth has since slowed significantly despite a large boost to government expenditure in 2009/10–2012/13, with an average overall fiscal deficit of about 4 percent of GDP. Real GDP growth between 2006/07 and 2012/13 averaged only 0.2 percent, the slowest since the mid-1960s (Figure 4.1.1).

The government's large infrastructure rebuilding and reconstruction effort following the tsunami and the cyclone was well supported by development partners through grants and concessional loans. However, Samoa's public debt continued to rise, reaching 55 percent of GDP at the end of 2013/14. Meanwhile, tourism and remittances, two pillars of the economy, have recovered only slowly, and production at the Yazaki automotive component plant, one of Toyota Australia's biggest component suppliers, has been declining since the global financial crisis. Agricultural production has also been declining for a number of years, though it has seen a recent modest recovery.

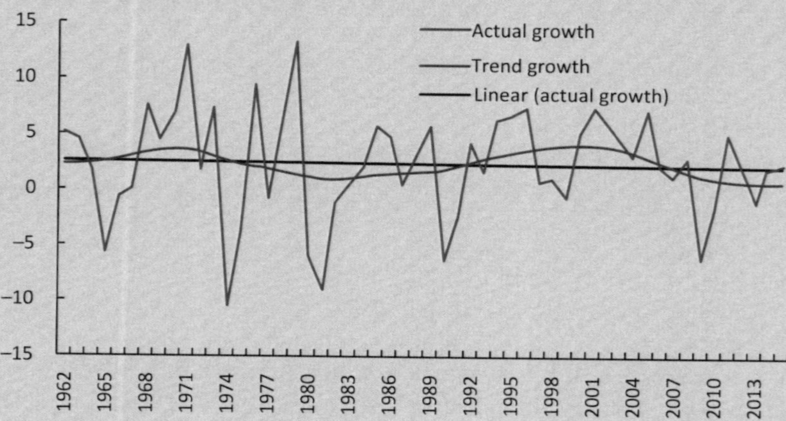

Figure 4.1.1 Samoa: Actual and Trend Real GDP Growth (*Percent*)

Sources: IMF, World Economic Outlook database; and IMF staff calculations.

Samoa now faces a difficult path to wind down its fiscal deficits because the private sector has not picked up the slack. The government is committed to reducing public debt to a more sustainable level to maintain hard-won macroeconomic stability. While the fiscal consolidation is essential for long-term sustainability, it is also important to safeguard economic growth and social spending. Given weak global demand, a great effort will be needed to strengthen competitiveness and revitalize private-sector-led growth.

Samoa's experience highlights the vulnerability of a small island economy's competitiveness to exogenous shocks, including natural disasters. Competitiveness can be undermined quickly by such shocks, and it will take coordinated efforts to regain it. A reassessment of the economy's underlying strength and growth potential is needed to help establish a macroeconomic framework to regain competitiveness and to maintain macroeconomic stability over the medium term. Structural reform needs to progress further to provide a more favorable environment for the private sector to take a lead role in economic development. Samoa has a strong track record of reform, however, and the government's continued commitment to keeping this record bodes well for future progress.

reconstruction, although the strong tala may also have helped boost imports. It is also useful to note that the increase in the trade deficit in Fiji, Palau, Samoa, and Vanuatu occurred despite the recent rapid growth of tourism exports.

Given the real exchange rate appreciation and deteriorating export performance in many PICs, it is tempting to link weakening competitiveness to the aid-induced Dutch disease effect referred to

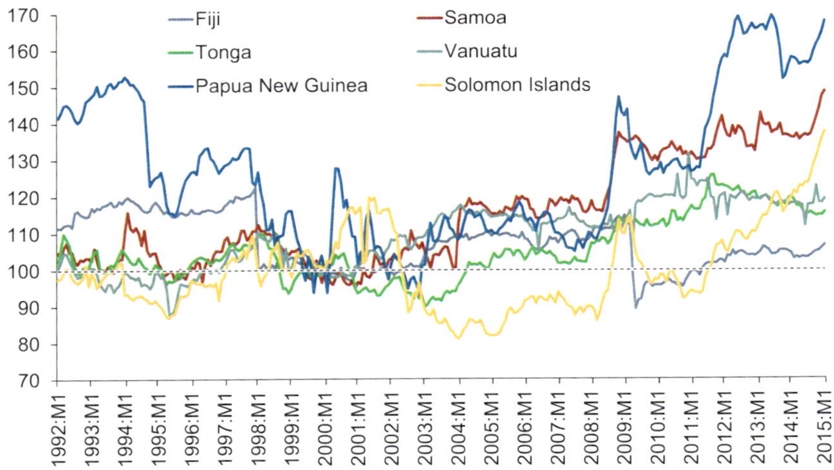

Figure 4.6 Real Effective Exchange Rates of PICs with Central Banks (*Index, January 2000 = 100*)

Sources: IMF, International Finance Statistics database; and IMF staff estimates.
Note: PICs = Pacific island countries.

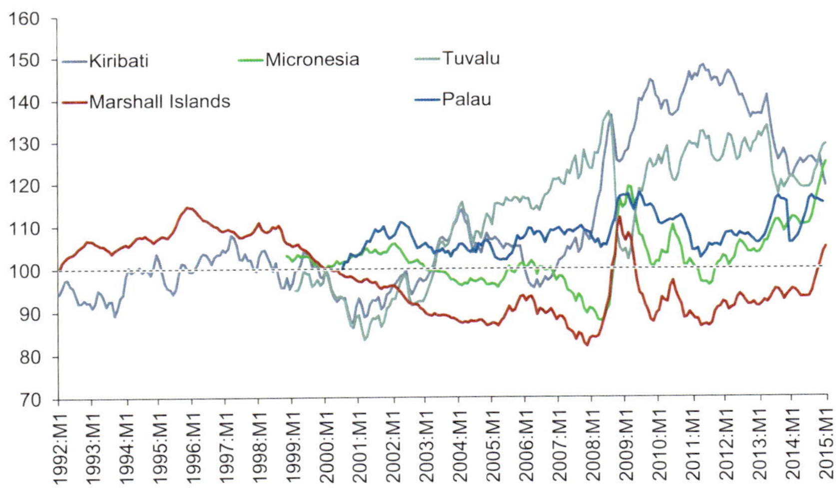

Figure 4.7 Real Effective Exchange Rate of PICs without Central Banks (*Index, January 2000 = 100*)

Sources: IMF, International Finance Statistics database; and IMF staff estimates.
Note: PICs = Pacific island countries.

earlier in the econometric analysis. However, the competitiveness of PICs may have also been affected by the changing external trade environment. As part of the African, Caribbean, and Pacific Group of States, PICs have benefited from nonreciprocal trade preferences under successive Lomé Conventions (first signed in 1975) and subsequently the Cotonou Agreement (signed in 2000). Fiji's sugar exports, at higher than world prices, are one example of such benefits. But trade preferences under the Cotonou Agreement have been eroded or are being phased out, reducing the export competitiveness of PICs. Nonreciprocal trade preferences offered by Australia and New Zealand under the South Pacific Regional Trade and Economic Co-operation Agreement, which took effect

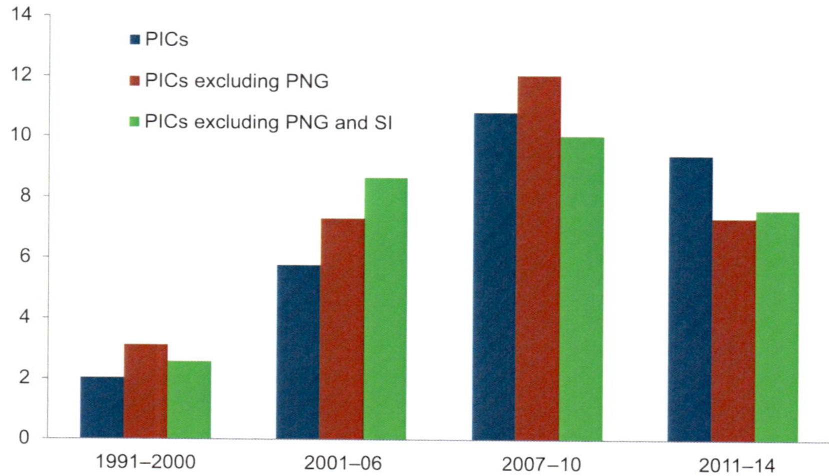

Figure 4.8 Current Account Deficit (*Percent of GDP*)

Sources: IMF, World Economic Outlook database; and IMF staff estimates.
Note: PICs = Pacific island countries; PNG = Papua New Guinea; SI = Solomon Islands.

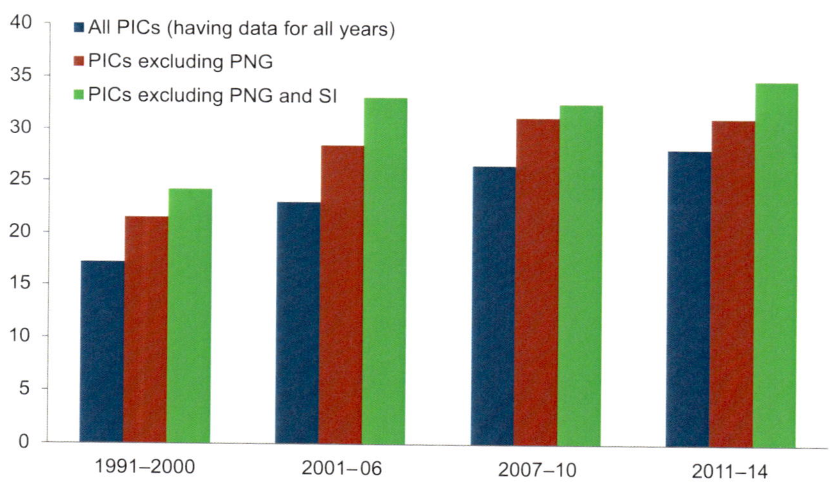

Figure 4.9 Goods and Services Deficit (*Percent of GDP*)

Sources: IMF, World Economic Outlook database; and IMF staff estimates.
Note: PICs = Pacific island countries; PNG = Papua New Guinea; SI = Solomon Islands.

in 1981, are also being eroded as the two countries liberalize their trade. Under the agreement, for example, Fiji was able to export large volumes of garments to Australia and New Zealand, but as preference margins shrank so have Fiji's exports, especially when restrictions under the Agreement on Textiles, Clothing, and Footwear were phased out in 2005.[26] Negotiations on a Pacific Agreement on Closer Economic Relations Plus (PACER-Plus) to achieve the long-term goal of a single regional

[26]The textiles, clothing, and footwear industry accounted for 26 percent of Fiji's total domestic exports in 1997, contributing 3.5 percent of GDP and providing employment for about 18,000 people (16 percent of those in total paid employment). In 2010, the industry reportedly employed only 4,000 people.

market among Pacific Islands Forum members have moved slowly.[27] In recent years, PICs have not joined any regional trade arrangements in Asia and the Pacific. Among them, only Papua New Guinea is a member of the Asia-Pacific Economic Cooperation (APEC), and none are members of any other major regional grouping or regional trade arrangements in Asia.

The trade patterns of PICs in recent years may have reflected these developments in the trade policy environment. As is the case with all other groups of developing economies, PICs' traditional markets—the European Union and North America—have become less dominant.[28] Developments in the Australian and New Zealand markets have affected resource-rich and non-resource-rich PICs differently. Both markets have become more important for Papua New Guinea and the Solomon Islands, while their importance to other PICs has fallen. In the nontraditional markets, the two PIC groups have also gone in different directions. While Papua New Guinea and the Solomon Islands have shifted to China from other Asian countries,[29] the other PICs[30] moved in the opposite direction, reflecting the growing importance of southeast Asia's markets. Non-resource-rich PICs are the only group of countries that have seen less of their exports going to fast-growing China due mainly to their lack of mineral resources and supply constraints on other commodities. Taking Asia as a whole, however, these PICs have diversified their exports to the region.

To fully understand the export performance of PICs, one also needs to take into account service exports, especially tourism. Of the 11 PICs covered in this chapter, five (Fiji, Palau, Samoa, Tonga, Vanuatu) have significant tourism exports, with earnings from the sector accounting for between 10 percent (Tonga) and 70 percent (Palau) of GDP and serving as an important source of economic growth in all five countries.[31] Growth as measured by tourist arrivals has varied considerably in this group (Figure 4.10). As with merchandise exports, North America, Europe, Australia, and New Zealand are the traditional tourism markets and still dominate in all countries in the group except Palau, which has diversified into Asian markets in recent years. As Box 4.2 illustrates, both economic policy and geography played an important role in the recent recovery of tourism in the five countries.

Developments in the cost of international transport may have worked to the disadvantage of PICs in recent years. It is commonly assumed that advances in transport technology should reduce disadvantages facing more remote countries. The introduction of jet engines in the late 1950s and containerized shipping in the late 1950s substantially increased the efficiency of air and ocean transportation. But according to Hummels (2007), technological advances in ocean shipping have been largely trumped by fuel price increases, leaving ocean transport costs (as a percent of the values of shipped goods) in the early 2000s much as they were in the 1950s.[32] Moreover, rapid increases in transport costs during 2001–10, especially for air transport, led to a sharp decline in the proportion of airlifted goods in trade after a long period of steady increases (Figures 4.11 and 4.12). For PICs, the increase in air transport costs has added substantially to the transport cost of perishable products. These trends were somewhat mitigated by the substantial fall in global fuel prices starting in mid-2014.

Other key developments in international transport have also had mixed impacts on trading costs in PICs. It is worth noting that containerized shipping was introduced in PICs much later (mostly in the late 1970s and 1980s) than in other parts of the world because of the substantial investment involved, including in port facilities. Furthermore, competition in the air and ocean transport industries in PICs

[27] Negotiations on PACER-Plus were started under PACER in 2007.

[28] Data are available only for Fiji, Papua New Guinea, Samoa, the Solomon Islands, Tonga, and Vanuatu.

[29] IMF (2011) discusses the growing economic ties between low-income countries and the BRICS (Brazil, Russia, India, China, and South Africa).

[30] Other PICs exclude Papua New Guinea and the Solomon Islands from the group of PICs used in this study.

[31] Using a panel regression, Thacker and Acevedo (2011) find a significant positive association between tourism and growth. A 10 percent increase in tourist arrivals per capita raises economic growth by about 0.2 percent.

[32] Note that the weight-based measures tend to overstate the decline in transport costs because the composition of shipped goods tends to shift toward lighter, higher-value goods over time.

Box 4.2. Why the Recovery in Tourism Varies So Much across PICs

Recent experience with the recovery of tourism in PICs shows the importance of linking to Asian markets and the role of economic policy in determining tourism growth. Figure 4.2.1 shows the tourism market by visitor arrivals in Fiji, Palau, Samoa, and Vanuatu.

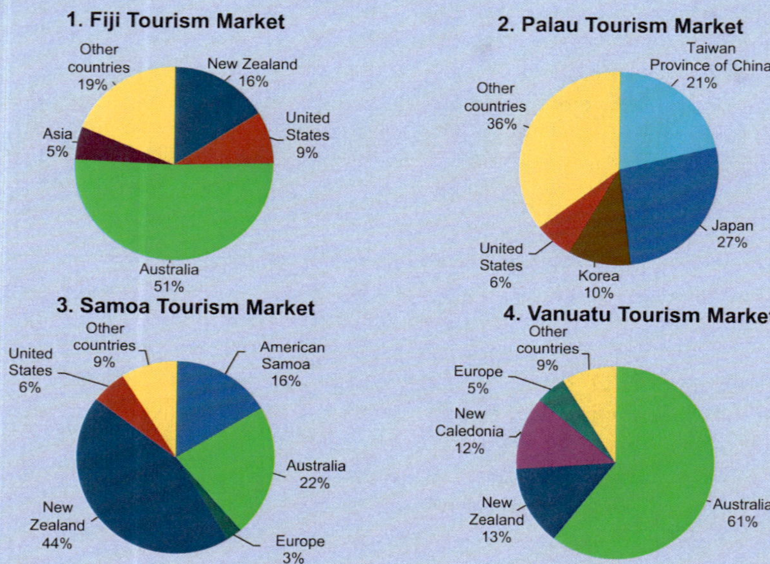

Figure 4.2.1 Tourism Market by Visitor Arrivals

Sources: Samoa Bureau of Statistics; Palau Visitor Authority; Samoa Bureau of Statistics; and Vanuatu National Statistics Office.

Being much closer to Asia than other PICs, Palau has benefited immensely from the region, with Taiwan Province of China and Japan accounting for some two-thirds of the country's total tourist arrivals in recent years. Tourist arrivals from these and other Asian countries have increased rapidly, helped by more charter flights. However, in 2013, Palau's tourism industry was hit by the cessation of direct flights from Asia's emerging market economies, the stronger U.S. dollar, and high tourism-related fees. The industry rebounded in 2014 on strong tourist arrivals from China.

In contrast, Fiji, Samoa, Tonga, and Vanuatu rely on Australia and New Zealand for tourism, which together account for two-thirds to three-fourths of total arrivals to these countries. Fiji's tourism has grown strongly while that of Samoa, Tonga, and Vanuatu has been slow or stagnating, despite all of these countries benefiting from the sustained growth of Australia and New Zealand. Successful elections in Fiji in September 2014 and its return to democratic government created a favorable environment to attract tourism. The devastating Cyclone Pam in March 2015 is expected to severely impact Vanuatu's tourism sector in the near term.

As with merchandise trade, exchange rate policies seem to have played an important part in explaining the varying performances of the tourism industries of these countries. The Fijian dollar was devalued by 20 percent against the U.S. dollar in April 2009, and the increased competitiveness from the devaluation temporarily helped boost Fiji's tourist arrivals, by 17 percent in 2010 and 7 percent in 2011. Palau uses the U.S. dollar as its legal tender, and the currency's strength since the second half of 2014 relative to Asian currencies has affected Palau's competitiveness. In contrast, Fiji, Samoa, Tonga, and Vanuatu peg their currencies to a basket of currencies that includes the Australian dollar. The weak Australian and New Zealand dollars since mid-2014 could undermine tourist flows to the Pacific islands from these countries.

There may be substitution among PICs as tourist destinations. This means that if every PIC devalues its currency, the region as a whole may not attract more tourists. However, given the region's relatively small market share in total Australian and New Zealand tourists, the substitution effect could be easily overstated. In any case, the effect should be limited among Asian tourists.

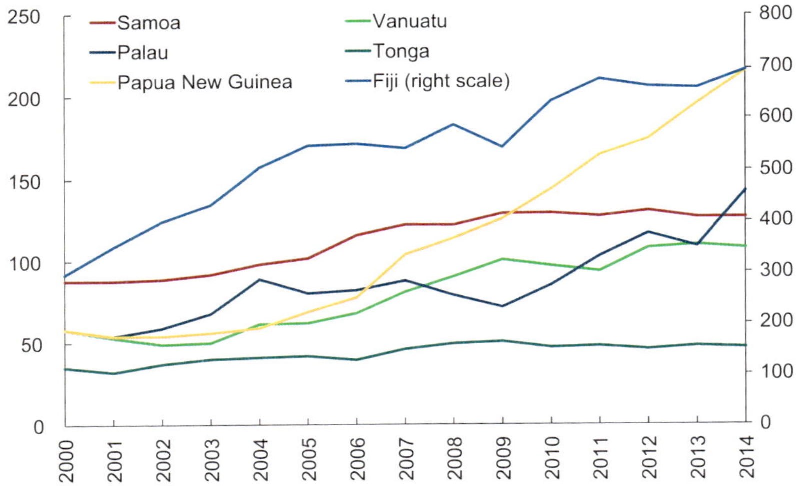

Figure 4.10 Annual Visitor Arrivals (*Thousands*)

Sources: Country authorities; and national tourism statistics.

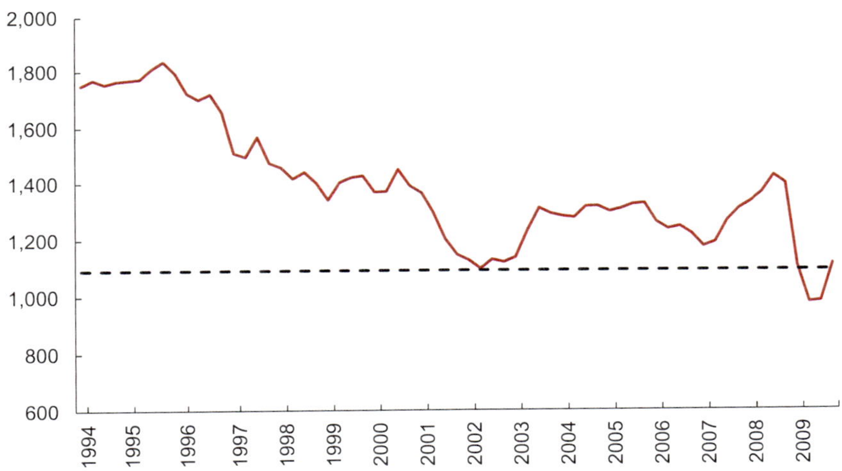

Figure 4.11 International Containerized Freight (*Simple average cost in U.S. dollars, TEU deflated by U.S. GDP deflator*)

Source: Containerisation International.
Note: TEU = twenty-foot-equivalent unit.

is limited because of small market size and state monopolies. As a result, the benefits of technological advances may not have been passed on to consumers as much as in other parts of the world.[33]

One of the major benefits from technological advances over the past decades has been faster speed and greater reliability in shipping. This, in principle, would have helped island countries lower transport costs relative to their competitors. However, remote small states such as PICs do not appear to have been able to take much advantage of large, more efficient vessels because of their small trade volumes and the need for ships to stop more frequently to serve small and often widely dispersed destinations. Paradoxically, the

[33] Kleinert and Spies (2011) find that trade partners with 10 percent more exports enjoy 0.8 percent lower transportation costs. Favaro, Halewood, and Rossotto (2008) show how the lack of competition in the telecommunications industry in Samoa raised costs to consumers.

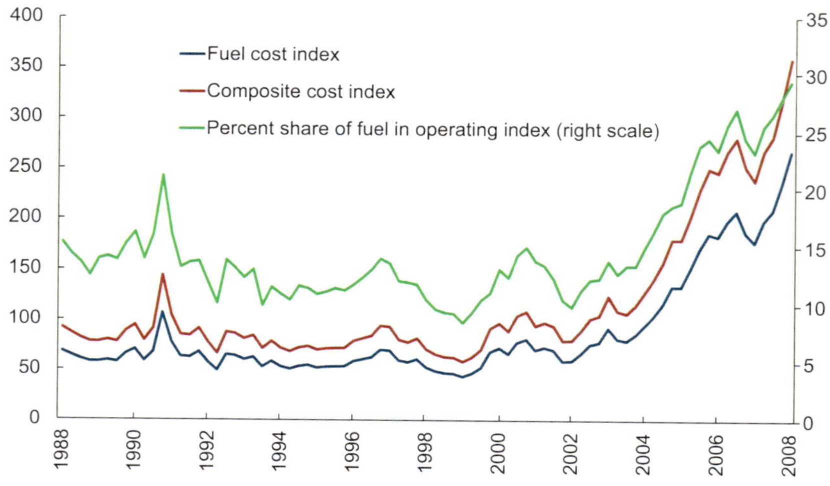

Figure 4.12 Trends in Airline Costs (*Index, left scale; percent, right scale*)

Source: Hummels (2009).

technological advances appear to have given a greater advantage to exporters of manufactured goods, as large vessels and greater speed and reliability allow finer segmentation of value chains. Associated with this, the cost advantage enjoyed by high-end goods is growing over time as the spread between high-priced and low-priced goods in each product category widens (Hummels 2007, 2009). Thus, without high-value-added exports, PICs could be increasingly disadvantaged by transportation costs.

POLICY IMPLICATIONS

One of the key findings of this econometric analysis is that PICs do seem to face lower speed limits in economic growth because of their remoteness. Moreover, growth volatility in PICs has often been higher than in larger economies. It is important for policymakers to recognize the existence of such limits because unrealistic expectations for growth could lead to overly ambitious targets. Moreover, growth volatility also entails prudent planning and maintaining larger policy buffers in good times.

Admittedly, there are significant challenges in raising growth, including finding a more effective way to allow aid to contribute to long-term domestic productive capacity as well as reducing poverty and fostering inclusive growth. When a country is small and relatively poor, it is likely to receive more aid (relative to GDP) than a large country, and so there is no need to have a more depreciated real exchange rate to keep a balanced trade or current account. This allows small countries to enjoy a higher living standard than they would otherwise, through better public services and cheaper imports. However, it also means that the export sector has to be very efficient to be able to compete on the world market even when it enjoys a comparative advantage. While it seems difficult to fully overcome the effects of aid-supported strong exchange rates, PICs should nevertheless take measures to alleviate them by directing more aid to productivity improvements and accelerating structural reforms.

This analysis highlights the importance and difficulty of macroeconomic policies in creating a competitive environment in small states. As shown, neither a fixed nor flexible exchange rate regime guarantees such an outcome. Most PICs maintain a pegged exchange rate regime, which provides a useful nominal anchor. Historically, however, PICs tend to have higher inflation than their trading partners (as many developing economies do), and periodically the fixed exchange rates become unsustainable and large-step devaluations become necessary to correct external imbalances. On the other hand, a flexible exchange rate (or using a foreign currency) can also lead to rapid appreciation when there are large foreign exchange inflows, such as aid and resource rents. Such appreciation may be necessary for maintaining macroeconomic stability (that is, controlling inflation), but it may not be consistent with the objective of maintaining competitiveness. In principle, such inflows can be sterilized through reserve accumulation, but countries often do not fully sterilize inflows because of the costs involved in mopping up local currency liquidity and the resulting higher domestic interest rates. This tends to cause higher inflation and real exchange rate appreciation. Furthermore, foreign exchange markets are shallow in PICs, and a floating exchange rate regime may result in heavy exchange rate volatility, which would be harmful for trade.

This calls for better coordination of macroeconomic policies to maintain competitiveness and stability. When a country maintains a fixed exchange rate regime, monetary policy must be subordinate to the exchange rate policy and ensure that inflation is not consistently higher than levels in trading partner countries. Similarly, fiscal policy must be prudent to avoid pressure on domestic prices and debt sustainability.[34] Large windfall inflows could be saved—for example, through a sovereign wealth fund—for intergenerational distribution and consumption smoothing. Since the global financial crisis, macroeconomic policies in PICs have been geared toward supporting growth through accommodative monetary and fiscal policies. These are appropriate given the circumstances. However, as noted earlier, higher inflation resulting from rising world food and fuel prices has led to significant real exchange rate appreciation in a number of countries since 2008. At the same time, increased aid inflows in response to the global financial crisis have allowed many PICs to maintain or accumulate foreign reserves. However, as economic recovery strengthens with import demand increasing and aid inflows reverting to normal levels, these countries may face challenges to return their real exchange rates to more sustainable and competitive levels.

Structural reforms are critical to mitigating the effects of strong exchange rates through higher productivity. When a country has a fixed exchange rate and faces persistently higher inflation than its trading partners, raising productivity at a pace faster than its trading partners is essentially the only way to avoid periodic devaluations.[35] Empirical research indicates that productivity growth in PICs has generally been slow and low investment is a key constraint on higher growth, as demonstrated in the case of Fiji.[36] This is consistent with our findings that PICs need to raise the level of investment to grow faster, a self-evident conclusion, but nevertheless a particularly pertinent one given the low investment rates of PICs compared with peer countries. Our findings that political stability is important for growth in PICs are similarly conventional, but they should nevertheless reinforce the resolve of these countries' governments for better governance.

Improving competitiveness will be difficult without aggressively reducing the costs of distance and insularity, a principal source of the growth disadvantage in PICs. As in the manufacturing sector, the transportation and communication industries also exhibit economies of scale, and this again puts small and remote countries at a disadvantage. The challenge is not only to scale up investment in transportation, communication infrastructure, and connectivity, but also to continue with reforms and appropriate regulation to ensure rigorous competition in these industries. Greater regional cooperation could also help mitigate the effect of diseconomies of scale, as shown by the establishment of the Pacific Forum Line[37] and the Pacific Islands Telecommunications Association.[38]

---

[34] Chapter 12 discusses macroeconomic policy coordination in the context of strengthening monetary policy transmission.

[35] One thinks of the Chinese experience in recent years—the yuan has faced pressure for appreciation despite China having higher inflation than its trading partners.

[36] Chen and Singh (2011) estimate that total factor productivity growth in Fiji during 1983–2007 was only 0.5 percent a year, less than half the rates in Asia and other Pacific countries.

[37] Pacific Forum Line was a multi-government-run shipping line. It was born of PICs' concern over the deterioration of traditional island tramp services due to containerization. Samoa recently acquired all outstanding PIC shares in Pacific Forum Line.

[38] The Pacific Islands Telecommunications Association is a nonprofit organization formed to represent the interests of small island nations in the Pacific region in the field of telecommunications.

The ultimate way to overcome smallness and distance is further integration with the global economy, and trade policy can play an important role in this process. PICs need to adapt to a rapidly changing landscape in world trade and finance. As trade preferences under colonial ties are phased out or are being eroded, PICs should seek deeper integration with metropolitan countries, particularly in trade in labor services. Much progress has been made in the temporary migrant workers programs with New Zealand and Australia, but the potential remains large relative to the size of labor forces in PICs. In some, particularly the smaller ones that have fewer natural resources or are constrained in developing such resources, increased trade in labor services provides a critical source of income generation, which in turn boosts domestic activities. Given the limited job opportunities at home, there is little risk of brain drain. PACER-Plus provides a useful framework for further integration with Australia and New Zealand and, to this end, greater efforts could be made to accelerate the negotiations.

Further integration with the global economy should also include strengthening trade and financial ties with Asia. Our analysis suggests that PICs without mineral resources still have untapped opportunity to leverage the fast-growing Asian markets. This is not surprising given that exporting nonmineral products to Asian markets needs reliable supply and marketing. Some emerging market economies in Asia offer duty-free and quota-free entry of goods from the PICs' least-developed economies.[39] However, constraints on domestic supply have meant that these opportunities have not been fully utilized. For the other PICs, it is important to engage with Asian countries to ensure that goods from the Pacific are not discriminated against as Asian countries expand their free trade agreements. Given the supply constraints in PICs, it may seem irrelevant to secure market access to Asia at this stage, but doing so may encourage foreign investment and increase the awareness of goods that PICs can offer. Entrepreneurs in Asia could help bring capital as well as fill in skills and marketing gaps in PICs. As such, a proactive policy toward Asia is important.

CONCLUSIONS

In many respects, the findings presented in this chapter are unsurprising, yet they have received little empirical support. PICs do face special challenges in economic growth because of their disadvantages arising from geography. It is also unsurprising that there is plenty of room to raise growth by increasing investment and promoting trade openness as well as ensuring political stability. By reaching the levels of other small island states in these areas, PICs could substantially speed up their economic growth. The key question is how to increase investment and openness. The good news from this study is that lower investment and exports in the Pacific do not seem to be entirely the result of geography. This implies that economic and other policies can make a difference in speeding up growth in the region, including by enhancing connectivity through better composition of public spending. The large variations in the performance across countries provide some evidence that policies do matter. Thus, the main challenge is to identify and implement policies that would be most effective in increasing openness and productive investment based on individual country circumstances.

It is important to recognize the differences in natural endowments and economic circumstances across PICs. Microstates may well face quite different challenges from their relatively large neighbors, principally Melanesian countries. These may necessitate different priorities and approaches to promoting investment and trade. To this end, detailed case studies would be highly desirable for formulating policy recommendations. The fact that growth in most PICs during 2001–14 has lagged behind other small states suggests some fundamental changes may have been taking place—either in policy settings or the external environment—making country size and location more determinant factors than previously thought.

---

[39] United Nations–defined least-developed countries in the Pacific include Kiribati, Samoa, the Solomon Islands, Tuvalu, and Vanuatu.

It is tempting to suggest that a competitive exchange rate is essential to inducing higher investment and greater trade openness. While external shocks to trade and commodity prices seem to have contributed to the weakening competitiveness in some PICs, evidence also points to the role played by macroeconomic policies. In the face of substantial size- and geography-induced cost disadvantages and large aid inflows, PICs need to manage their macroeconomic policies to ensure that their exchange rates allow domestic producers to compete in the world market in areas in which they have a comparative advantage. This may prove critical for pursuing private-sector-led growth.

Maintaining competitiveness also entails structural reforms to improve efficiency in production, transportation, and communication. Many reforms have been carried out over the years, and the payoffs have been significant in some areas, as shown by marked declines in the cost of telecommunication following the industry's deregulation. However, as the quest for faster and more inclusive growth continues, PIC governments will need to keep searching for such high-payoff reforms. The ever changing global environment should only strengthen the resolve of PIC governments to accelerate such reforms.

ANNEX 4.1. COUNTRY LIST AND DATA DESCRIPTION

ANNEX TABLE 4.1.1

Country List

Africa (14)	Americas (12)	Europe (4)	Pacific (9)	Asia (6)
Botswana	Antigua and Barbuda	Estonia	Fiji	Bahrain
Cabo Verde	The Bahamas	Malta	Kiribati	Bhutan
Comoros	Barbados	Montenegro	Micronesia	Brunei Darussalam
Djibouti	Belize	San Marino	Palau	Maldives
Equatorial Guinea	Bermuda		Papua New Guinea	Qatar
Gabon	Dominica		Samoa	Timor-Leste
The Gambia	Grenada		Solomon Islands	
Guinea-Bissau	Guyana		Tonga	
Lesotho	St. Kitts and Nevis		Vanuatu	
Mauritius	St. Lucia			
Namibia	St. Vincent and the Grenadines			
São Tomé and Príncipe	Suriname			
Seychelles				
Swaziland				

Source: Authors' compilation.

ANNEX TABLE 4.1.2

Average Values of Relevant Series, 1992–2008

	Small Economies	Non-Pacific Small Economies	Pacific Island Countries
Convergence effect ($\ln Y_0$)	7.98	8.15	7.40
Investment [ln(investment/GDP)]	3.26	3.33	3.04
Population growth [$\ln(n + g + d)$]	1.88	1.88	1.87
Aid (aid/gross national income, percent)	7.96	5.69	20.01
Political stability	0.49	0.53	0.57
Exports (percent of GDP)	52.11	56.97	35.08
Volatility (growth rate standard deviation, percent)	4.61	4.36	5.48
GDP growth per capita (percent)	2.38	2.87	0.64
GDP-weighted distance to major overseas markets (ln)	9.01	8.93	9.25

Source: Authors' calculations.

REFERENCES

Aizenman, Joshua, and Nancy Marion. 1999. "Volatility and Investment: Interpreting Evidence from Developing Countries." *Economica* 66 (262): 157–79.

Ali, Abdiweli M., and Hodan S. Isse. 2005. "An Empirical Analysis of the Effect of Aid on Growth." *International Advances in Economic Research* 11 (1): 1–11.

Anderson, James, and Eric van Wincoop. 2004. "Trade Costs." *Journal of Economic Literature* 42 (3): 691–751.

Armstrong, Harvey W., and Robert Read. 1998. "Trade and Growth in Small States: The Impact of Global Trade Liberalization." *The World Economy* 21 (4): 563–85.

———. 2000, "Comparing the Economic Performance of Dependent Territories and Sovereign Microstates." *Economic Development and Cultural Change* 48 (2): 285–306.

———. 2003. "The Determinants of Economic Growth in Small States." *The Round Table* 92 (368): 99–124.

Barro, Robert J., and Xavier I. Sala-i-Martin. 2004. *Economic Growth.* Second edition. Cambridge, Massachusetts: MIT Press.

Bertram, Geoffrey. 2004. "On the Convergence of Small Island Economies with Their Metropolitan Patrons." *World Development* 32 (2): 343–64.

Bowman, Chakriya, and Satish Chand. 2008. "Size Matters: The Impact of Aid on Institutions." *Pacific Economic Bulletin* 23 (2): 145–65.

Chen, Hong. 2012. *Convergence, Total Factor Productivity and Industrial Growth: Growth Empirics in Post-Reform China.* Saarbrücken: Lambert Academic Publishing.

Chen, Hong, and Baljeet Singh. 2011. "Total Factor Productivity in Fiji over 1983–2007." In *Fiji Economy Update,* Suva, Fiji.

Commonwealth Secretariat, and World Bank. 2000. "Small States: Meeting Challenges in the Global Economy." From the final communiqué of the Sixty-First Meeting of the Development Committee, Washington, April 17.

Duncan, Ron, and Haruo Nakagawa. 2006. "Obstacles to Economic Growth in Six Pacific Island Countries." Working Paper, World Bank, Washington.

Easterly, William, and Aart Kraay. 2000. "Small States, Small Problems? Income, Growth and Volatility in Small States." *World Development* 28 (11): 2013–27.

Favaro, Edgardo, Naomi Halewood, and Carlo M. Rossotto. 2008. "From Monopoly to Competition: Reform of Samoa's Telecommunications Sector." In *Small States, Smart Solutions: Improving Connectivity and Increasing the Effectiveness of Public Services,* edited by Edgardo Favaro. Washington: World Bank.

Feeny, Simon. 2005. "The Impact of Foreign Aid on Economic Growth in Papua New Guinea." *Journal of Development Studies* 41 (6): 1092–1117.

Gallup, John L., Jeffrey D. Sachs, and Andrew D. Mellinger. 1998. "Geography and Economic Development." Working Paper 6849, National Bureau of Economic Research, Cambridge, Massachusetts.

Gibson, John, and Karen L. Nero. 2007. "Are Pacific Island Economies Growth Failures? Geo-Political Assessments and Perspectives." Report for the Pasifika Project, Institute of Policy Studies, Victoria University of Wellington.

Grier, Kevin B., and Gordon Tullock. 1989. "An Empirical Analysis of Cross-National Economic Growth, 1951–80." *Journal of Monetary Economics* 24 (2): 259–76.

Hausmann, Ricardo. 2001. "Prisoners of Geography." *Foreign Policy* 122 (1): 44–53.

Hughes, Helen. 2003. "Aid Has Failed the Pacific." Issue Analysis No. 33, Centre for Independent Studies, St Leonards, Australia.

Hummels, David. 2007. "Transportation Costs and International Trade in the Second Era of Globalization." *Journal of Economic Perspectives* 21 (3): 131–54.

———. 2009. "Globalization and Freight Transport Costs in Maritime Shipping and Aviation." Working Paper 3, International Transport Forum, Paris.

International Monetary Fund (IMF). 2011. "New Growth Drivers for Low-Income Countries: The Role of BRICs." Washington.

Islam, Nazrul. 1995. "Growth Empirics: A Panel Data Approach." *Quarterly Journal of Economics* 110 (4): 1127–70.

———. 2003a. "What Have We Learnt From the Convergence Debate?" *Journal of Economic Surveys* 17 (3): 309–62.

———. 2003b. "Productivity Dynamics in a Large Sample of Countries: A Panel Study." *Review of Income and Wealth* 49 (2): 247–72.

Kaufmann, Daniel, Aart Kraay, and Massimo Mastruzzi. 2011. "Worldwide Governance Indicators 2011 Update," Washington, World Bank.

Kleinert, Jörn, and Julia Spies. 2011. "Endogenous Transport Costs in International Trade." Discussion Papers 74, Institut für Angewandte Wirtschaftsforschung, Tübingen.

Kormendi, Roger, and Philip Meguire. 1985. "Macroeconomic Determinants of Growth: Cross-Country Evidence." *Journal of Monetary Economics* 16 (2): 141–63.

Malik, Adeel, and Jonathan R. W. Temple. 2009. "The Geography of Output Volatility." *Journal of Development Economics* 90 (2): 163–78.

Mankiw, N. Gregory, David Romer, and David N. Weil. 1992. "A Contribution to the Empirics of Economic Growth." *Quarterly Journal of Economics* 107 (2): 407–37.
McCallum, John. 1995. "National Borders Matter: Canada-U.S. Regional Trade Patterns." *American Economic Review* 85 (3): 615–23.
Milner, Chris, and Tony Westaway. 1993. "Country Size and the Medium-Term Growth Process: Some Cross-Country Evidence." *World Development* 21 (2): 203–11.
Mosley, Paul. 1980. "Aid, Savings, and Growth Revisited." *Oxford Bulletin of Economics and Statistics* 42 (2): 79–95.
Noble, Cameron, Natalie Pereira, and Nanise Saune. 2011. *Urban Youth in the Pacific: Increasing Resilience and Reducing Risk for Involvement in Crime and Violence*. Suva, Fiji: UNDP Pacific Centre.
Pavlov, Vlad, and Craig Sugden. 2006. "Aid and Growth in the Pacific Islands." *Asian-Pacific Economic Literature* 20 (2): 38–55.
Ramey, Garey, and Valerie A. Ramey. 1995. "Cross-Country Evidence on the Link between Volatility and Growth." *American Economic Review* 85 (5): 1138–51.
Rao, B. Bhaskara, Kanhaiya L. Sharma, and Rup Singh. 2008. "Estimating Aid-Growth Equations: The Case of Pacific Island Countries." *Pacific Economic Bulletin* 23 (2): 82–96.
Redding, Stephen, and Anthony J. Venables. 2004. "Economic Geography and International Inequality." *Journal of International Economics* 62 (1): 53–82.
Srinivasan, Thirukodikaval N. 1986. "The Costs and Benefits of Being a Small Remote Island Landlocked or Ministate Economy." *World Bank, Research Observer* 1 (2): 205–18.
Streeten, Paul. 1993. "The Special Problems of Small Countries." *World Development* 21 (2): 197–202.
Thacker, Nita, and Sebastian Acevedo. 2011. "A Cross-Country Perspective on Growth in the Caribbean: The Role of Tourism and Debt." Paper presented at the University of the West Indies, Central Bank of Barbados, and IMF conference "Options for the Caribbean after the Global Financial Crisis," Bridgetown, Barbados, January 27–28.
Wei, Shang-Jin. 1996. "Intra-National Versus International Trade: How Stubborn are Nations in Global Integration?" Working Paper 5531, National Bureau of Economic Research, Cambridge, Massachusetts.
Winters, L. Alan, and Wonhyuk Lim. 2010. "Economic Growth in Low Income Countries: How the G20 Can Help to Raise and Sustain It." Economics Department Working Paper Series 8–2010, University of Sussex, Brighton.
Winters, L. Alan, and Pedro M. G. Martins. 2004. "When Comparative Advantage Is Not Enough: Business Costs in Small Remote Economies." *World Trade Review* 3 (3): 347–83.
World Bank. 2010. "Solomon Islands Growth Prospects: Constraints and Policy Priorities." Discussion Note, World Bank, Washington.
Yang, Yongzheng, Hong Chen, Shiu Raj Singh, and Baljeet Singh. 2013. "The Pacific Speed of Growth: How Fast Can It Be and What Determines It?" IMF Working Paper 13/104, International Monetary Fund, Washington.
Yao, Shujie, and Zongyi Zhang. 2001. "On Regional Inequality and Diverging Clubs: A Case Study of Contemporary China." *Journal of Comparative Economics* 29 (3): 466–84.

CHAPTER 5

Strengthening Macro-Fiscal Resilience to Natural Disasters and Climate Change in the Small States of the Pacific

EZEQUIEL CABEZON, LENI HUNTER, PATRIZIA TUMBARELLO, KAZUAKI WASHIMI, AND YIQUN WU

The Pacific island countries (PICs) are among the most susceptible to natural disasters in the world. The combination of location and small size heightens their vulnerability to earthquakes and weather-related extremes such as cyclones, tsunamis, hurricanes, and floods. And climate change poses risks to the very survival of some Pacific islands.

This is the first IMF study to quantify the impact of natural disasters on Pacific island economies using a cross-country approach. Previous IMF analyses have been conducted on a country-by-country basis. After a disaster occurs, the IMF typically assesses the impact of the event on the macroeconomic framework and debt sustainability (using a debt sustainability analysis) jointly with the World Bank Group and in collaboration with the Asian Development Bank (ADB).

Assessing the prospective fiscal costs and growth impact of natural disasters is vital to evaluate the long-term economic prospects of PICs. Mainstreaming estimates within the macro framework before an event occurs can help enhance countries' disaster risk management and thus their ability to cope with such events. It can also help tailor better IMF policy advice. Integrating such prospective costs into the debt sustainability analysis could determine ex ante the magnitude of the need for fiscal and financial buffers and other sources of financing. It can also determine the fiscal space available for building infrastructure to address natural disasters and climate change. The chapter also presents a multipillar strategy that involves national, regional, and multilateral responses, including the engagement of the IMF. This integrated framework can provide a more strategic and less ad hoc framework for strengthening the resilience of PICs to natural disasters and climate change both before and after events.

STYLIZED FACTS FOR THE PACIFIC ISLANDS

PICs, on average, have been more heavily affected by natural disasters relative to other small states, and the evidence for this holds across a large range of metrics:

- *Occurrence*—During the last four decades, PICs have suffered more natural disasters than small states in other regions. PICs have experienced about 2,400 tropical cyclones in the last 60 years (World Bank 2013), and their occurrence has increased over time in line with global trends (Figures 5.1 and 5.2).

We are grateful to the Pacific island country authorities for their thoughtful comments and suggestions. We also wish to thank Sebastian Acevedo, Pedro Conceicao, Gail Hurley, Vladimir Klyuev, Nicole Laframboise, Wojciech Maliszewski, Catherine McAuliffe, Christine Richmond, Mariusz Sumlinski, and Sofia Bettencourt for their useful comments and Hoe Ee Khor for his guidance throughout the project. We thank Rosanne Heller and Antoinette Kanyabutembo for excellent editorial and administrative assistance, and Tlek Zeinullayev for outstanding research assistance.

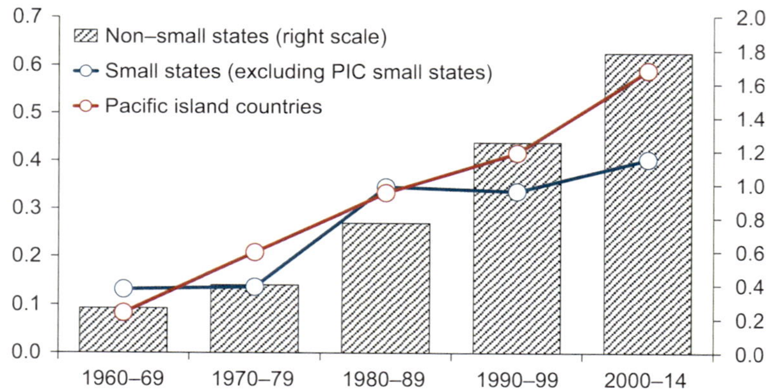

Figure 5.1 Average Number of Natural Disasters Each Year

Sources: Emergency Events Database (EM-DAT); and IMF staff estimates.
Note: PIC = Pacific island country.

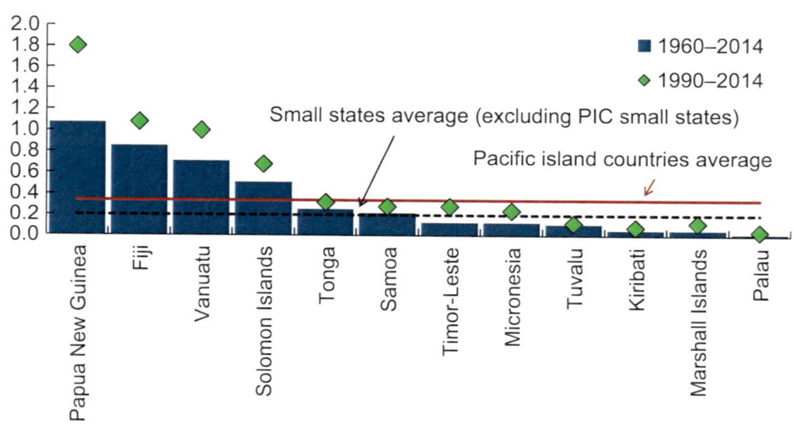

Figure 5.2 Pacific Island Countries: Average Number of Natural Disasters Each Year

Sources: Centre for Research on the Epidemiology of Disasters, International Disaster Database; and IMF staff estimates.
Note: PIC = Pacific island country. Averages refer to 1960–2014.

- *Probability of a natural disaster*—Based on historical frequency, the probability of a natural disaster averages more than 20 percent a year across the small Pacific states and Papua New Guinea. Given that PICs are geographically dispersed, natural disasters do not hit all countries at once, although they may hit more than one country, as Cyclone Pam did in March 2015, inflicting heavy damage on Vanuatu and Tuvalu. The joint probability of the occurrence of natural disasters in more than one PIC is generally below 5 percent, with a maximum of 12 percent for Fiji and Papua New Guinea (Figures 5.3 and 5.4).
- *World Risk Index*—According to the World Risk Index, a composite measure of a country's exposure to natural hazards and of its ability to cope with them, the Pacific islands have the highest risk of suffering a disaster. Among the 171 countries covered by the index, six Pacific islands rank among the 16 countries with the highest risk of experiencing a natural disaster, topped by Vanuatu (Figures 5.5 and 5.6).
- *Damage and losses*—Annual damage and losses, a better measure of the vulnerability of countries to natural disasters, averaged 2.3 percent of GDP in the PICs during 1980–2014, higher than in peers and non–small states. For example, even though disasters are more frequent in

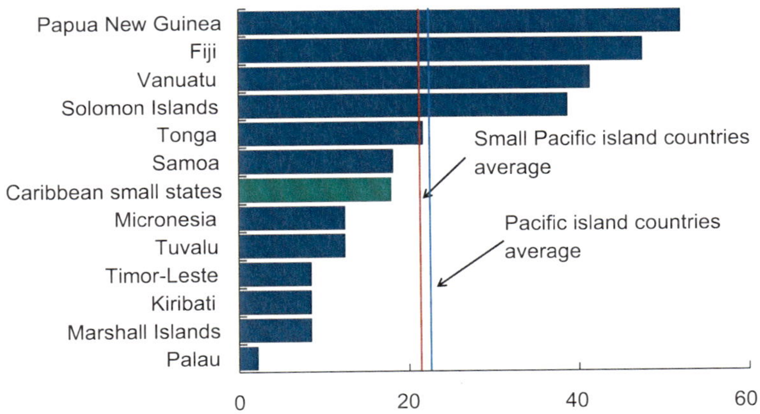

Figure 5.3 Probability of Occurrence of Natural Disasters during 1970–2014 (*Percent*)

Sources: Centre for Research on the Epidemiology of Disasters, International Disaster Database; and IMF staff estimates.

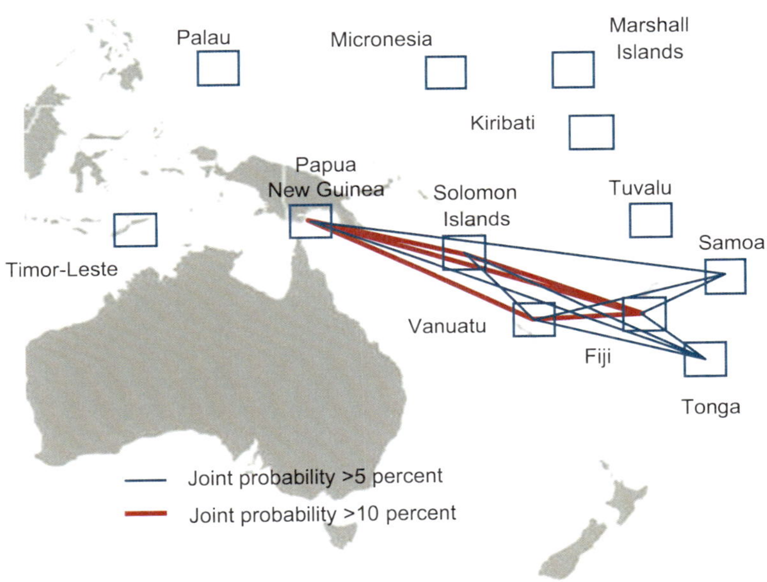

Figure 5.4 Pacific Island Countries: Joint Probability of Occurrence of a Natural Disaster during 1970–2014

Source: IMF staff estimates based on data from the Centre for Research on the Epidemiology of Disasters, International Disaster Database.
Note: Probabilities below 5 percent are not shown.

Papua New Guinea and Fiji, damage and losses seem to be far higher in Samoa and Vanuatu. This suggests that the intensity of natural disasters and resilience to these events vary across countries. Cross-country studies (Raddatz 2009; Cavallo and Noy 2010) show that the economic effects of natural disasters depend on a range of variables, including income level, stage of development, country size, disaster type, and disaster severity. Moreover, natural disasters generally hit less-developed economies harder than developed economies. Developed economies are more highly exposed to wealth losses, whereas large and diversified economies can better absorb shocks (Auffret 2003). Damage and losses are in fact lower in Papua New Guinea, which is not a small state, than in other PICs, even though disaster occurrence is the highest

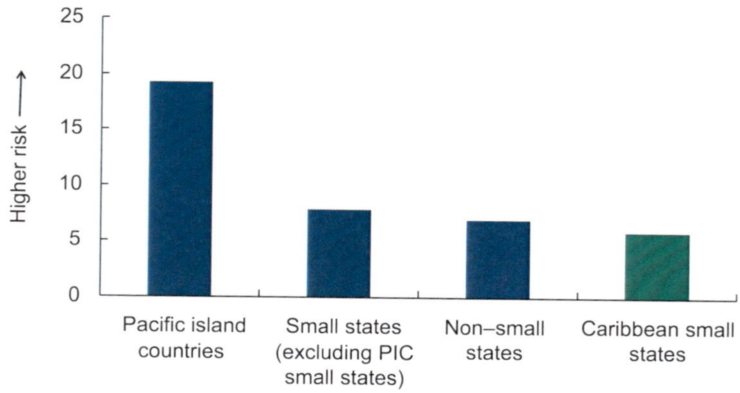

Figure 5.5 Natural Disaster Risks: World Risk Index, 2014 (*Percentage points*)

Sources: Alliance Development Works, *World Risk Report 2014;* and IMF staff calculations.
Note: High value indicates high risk. Maximum risk country = 36 percentage points.

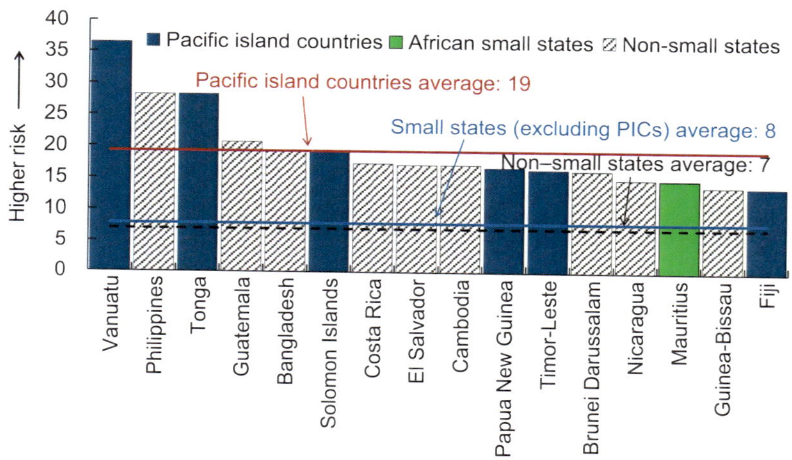

Figure 5.6 Natural Disaster Risks: World Risk Index, 2014, Top 16 (*Percentage points*)

Source: Alliance Development Works, *World Risk Report 2014.*
Note: PICs = Pacific island countries. Index combines exposure to natural hazards, coping, and adaptive capacities. Samoa is not included in the database.

in the region. And damages and losses are also lower in Fiji, a middle-income country. Lack of diversification also heightens vulnerability to natural disasters and other shocks (Figures 5.7 and 5.8).

Cyclone Winston, which hit Fiji in 2016, Cyclone Pam, which devastated Vanuatu and Tuvalu, and Typhoon Maysak, which hit Micronesia, both in 2015, are reminders of the Pacific islands' vulnerability to weather-related disasters. Other events include flash floods in the Solomon Islands (April 2014), Cyclone Lusi in Vanuatu (March 2014), Cyclone Ian in Tonga and Fiji (January 2014), Typhoon Haiyan in Palau (November 2013), Cyclone Evan in Fiji and Samoa (December 2012), and a tsunami in Samoa (September 2009). Damage and losses from these events in percent of GDP averaged (median) 10 percent of GDP (Table 5.1).

Climate change poses risks to the survival of some Pacific islands. Low-lying atolls such as Kiribati, Marshall Islands, and Tuvalu are the most vulnerable to rising sea levels. But climate change also threatens agricultural income in higher islands such as Papua New Guinea and the Solomon Islands, especially by increasing water salinity in rural areas. Sea levels are already rising, and recent studies (ADB 2013; IPCC 2013) suggest they will rise further, between 1.0 and 1.7 meters in some

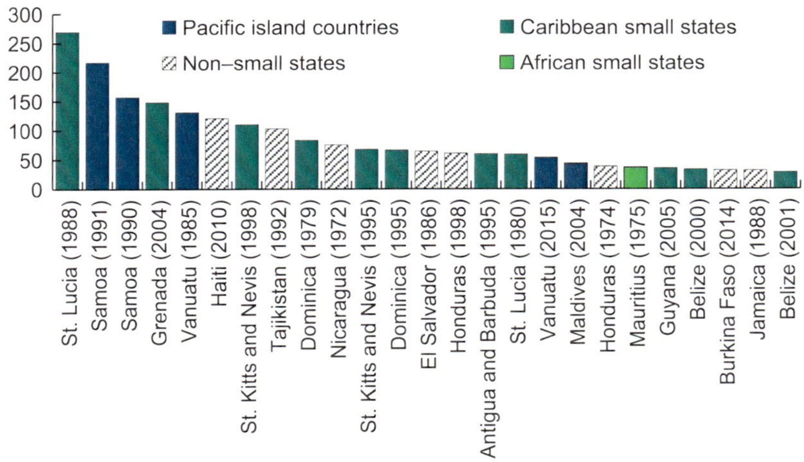

Figure 5.7 Damage and Losses of Extreme Disaster Events, Top 25 during 1970–2015 (*Percent of GDP*)

Sources: Emergency Events Database (EM-DAT); and IMF staff estimates.

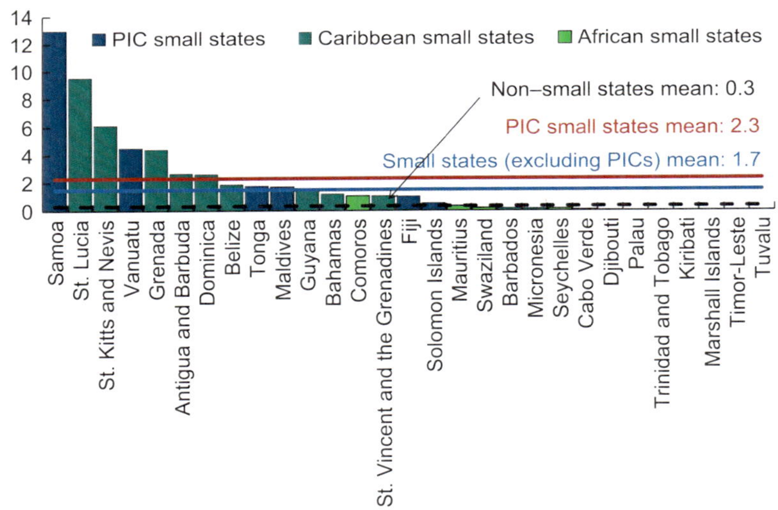

Figure 5.8 Average Annual Damage and Losses during 1980–2014 (*Percent of GDP*)

Sources: Emergency Events Database (EM-DAT); and IMF staff estimates.

cases. For example, a rise of 50 centimeters would lead to a loss of 80 percent of the land in the Majuro Atoll of the Marshall Islands, and the habitability of other islands would be threatened well before lands are lost.

The interaction of climate change and natural disasters affects the Pacific islands to varying degrees. Rising temperatures are widely predicted to increase the frequency of, and risks associated with, natural disasters. Higher-elevation islands would also be hit hard, given their concentrations of population, socioeconomic activity, and infrastructure in coastal zones.[1]

[1] Indeed, IOC/UNESCO and others (2011) find that more than half the population of the Pacific islands lives within 1½ kilometers of the coast.

TABLE 5.1

Most Recent Natural Disasters: Damages and Losses

	Millions of U.S. Dollars	Percent of GDP
Fiji	940 (2016)	20.0
	108.8 (2012)	2.6
Micronesia	8.5 (2015)	3.0
Palau	1.2 (2013)	0.5
Samoa	210 (2012)	30.0
	152.1 (2009)	25.0
Solomon Islands	100 (2014)	9.0
Tonga	45.4 (2014)	10.0
Tuvalu	11.9 (2015)	33.6
Vanuatu	20 (2014)	2.5
	467 (2015)	61.0
PICs mean	187.7	20.1
PICs median	104.4	20.0

Sources: Country authorities; Emergency Events Database (EM-DAT); and IMF staff estimates.
Note: PICs = Pacific island countries.

MACROECONOMIC IMPACT OF NATURAL DISASTERS

Framing the Issue

Natural disasters and climate change pose macro-critical challenges to PICs, with varying degrees of severity (Figures 5.9 and 5.10). As well as their devastating human cost, natural disasters and climate change destroy or damage infrastructure and other capital, creating considerable macroeconomic volatility. Natural disasters contribute to the higher revenue volatility experienced by PICs, relative both to other small states and to non–small states. Disasters can damage growth prospects and contribute to the low potential growth rates of PICs, and they typically worsen fiscal positions. In Chapter 10 of this volume the authors show that a natural disaster that affects 1 percent of the population in the Pacific islands causes a drop in real revenue of 0.4 percentage point, double that in other small states where the revenue drop is 0.2 percentage point. Natural disasters often expand public debt by triggering more borrowing, owing to lower revenues or increased spending, thereby intensifying balance of payments pressures.

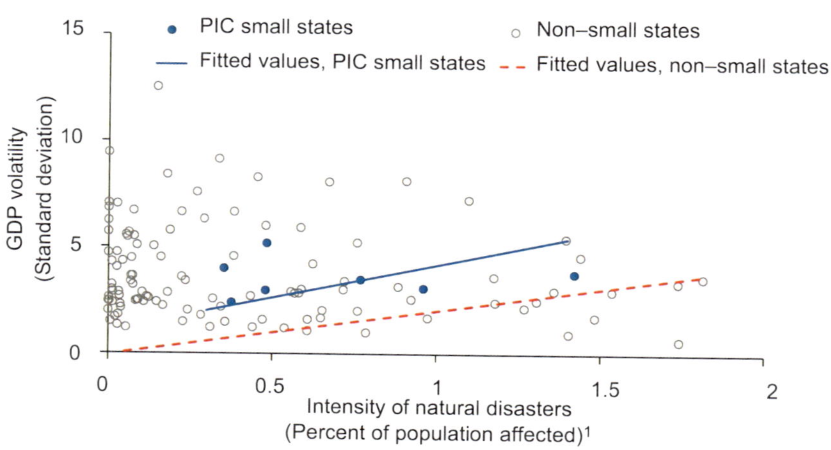

Figure 5.9 GDP Volatility and Intensity of Natural Disasters, 1990–2013

Sources: Emergency Events Database (EM-DAT); and IMF staff estimates.
[1] Intensity = [(number of deaths + 0.33*number of people affected)/population]*100.

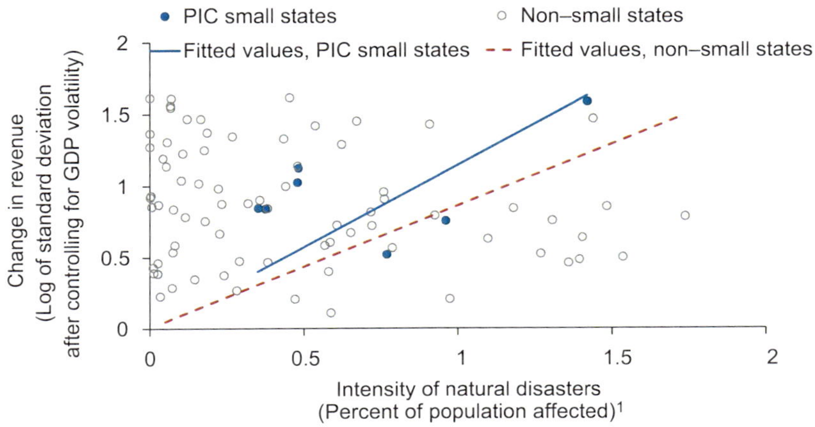

Figure 5.10 Revenue Volatility and Intensity of Natural Disasters, 1990–2013

Sources: Emergency Events Database (EM-DAT); and IMF staff estimates.
[1] Intensity = [(number of deaths + 0.33*number of people affected)/population]*100.

Recent Empirical Analyses

The literature reveals that the economic impact depends on the type of disaster and its magnitude, despite the stimulus of rehabilitation activity. Fomby, Ikeda, and Loayza (2013) find negative effects on growth from droughts and storms and no statistically significant effect on aggregate GDP growth from earthquakes. Raddatz (2009) finds small countries are hurt more by windstorms, but helped by moderate floods; the latter result seems to derive from higher electricity-generating capacity given more plentiful water supply. Acevedo (2014) finds negative effects from both storms and floods in Caribbean countries. Loayza and others (2009) find that although small disasters may have a positive effect in the short term (owing to reconstruction boosting growth, for example), the short-term effect of large disasters on growth is always negative.

Some international organizations have estimated the cost of natural disasters and climate change in terms of reduced economic growth. According to the World Bank (2014), natural disasters in the PICs cause damage, every year on average, of nearly 2 percent of GDP (about US$248 million). For climate change, the ADB estimates economic costs for the Pacific islands of 2.2 to 3.5 percent of GDP annually, which could rise as high as 12.7 percent by the end of the century (ADB 2013). The ADB also estimates that preparing for the effects of climate change may cost between 1½ and 2½ percent of GDP a year.[2]

ESTIMATING THE MACRO-FISCAL IMPACT OF NATURAL DISASTERS

As noted at the start of this chapter, this is the first cross-country IMF study assessing the impact of natural disasters on growth in the Pacific islands as a group. We use the Emergency Events Database (EM-DAT) maintained by the Centre for Research on the Epidemiology of Disasters, and the following three methodologies: (1) a panel vector autoregression model to estimate the short-term impact on growth and on the fiscal balance and its components (revenue and expenditure), (2) a

[2]The ADB study's policy recommendations include mainstreaming climate change actions in development planning, adopting a forward-looking adaptation strategy, using a risk-based approach to adaptation and disaster-risk management to help prioritize climate change actions and increase the cost efficiency of adaptation measures, climate proofing of infrastructure, and improving knowledge and capacity to deal with climate uncertainties.

panel autoregressive distributed lag model to estimate the long-term effect on GDP growth, and (3) an event analysis to study growth and fiscal performance during and after natural disasters.

Vector Autoregression Model

We use annual panel data for five countries (Fiji, Samoa, the Solomon Islands, Tonga, Vanuatu) for 1970–2013 to measure the impact of natural disasters on fiscal aggregates and growth. The panel is unbalanced because a long time series for these countries is unavailable owing to data weaknesses and because many of them became independent in the late 1970s.

The model specification includes the following variables: real GDP growth, total government spending as a percent of GDP, tax revenue as a percent of GDP, the overall fiscal balance as a percent of GDP, and a measure of natural disaster intensity. Following Fomby, Ikeda, and Loayza (2013), the disaster intensity is proxied by the share of the fatalities and of the overall affected population and defined as:

$$Intensity_{i,t} = 100 * \left(\frac{fatalities + 0.3 * total\ affected}{population} \right).$$

The identification strategy assumes that natural-disaster damage affects real GDP growth and fiscal variables in the current period, while natural disasters are exogenous.[3] This assumption is implemented with a Choleski decomposition. The vector autoregression is described by the equations below, with the lag structure set to one in order to minimize the number of parameters estimated:

$$Y_{i,t} = A_{i,0} + A_{i,1} Y_{i,t-1} + B_{i,0} X_{i,t} + B_{i,1} X_{i,t-1} + u_{i,t},$$

where

$$y_{i,t} = \begin{bmatrix} \Delta Overall\ fiscal\ balance_{i,t} \\ \Delta Tax\ revenue_{i,t} \\ \Delta Total\ government\ expenditure_{i,t} \\ Real\ GDP\ growth_{i,t} \end{bmatrix},$$

$$X_{i,t} = [Natural\ disaster\ intensity_{i,t}],$$

with i = {Fiji, Samoa, the Solomon Islands, Tonga, Vanuatu}.

The estimation results show that natural disasters reduce short-term growth. The effects of a natural disaster with an intensity affecting 1 percent of the population are shown in the impulse responses plotted in Figure 5.11. The shock causes growth to contract by about 0.5 percentage point in the year of the disaster. A natural disaster that causes damage and losses equal to 1 percent of GDP causes an average drop in GDP of 0.7 percentage point in the year of the disaster. This is equal to an annual drop on average of 2.1 percent for all the Pacific islands, based on historical data on damage and losses (Figure 5.12).

Natural disasters also worsen the fiscal positions of PICs. For damage and losses equal to 1 percent of GDP, the fiscal balance deteriorates by 0.5 percent of GDP in the year after the disaster. Spending rises by 0.7 percentage point of GDP in the year of the disaster, while tax revenue falls by 0.2 percentage point of GDP before rising by the same amount in the following year. The fiscal deterioration is not as large as the drop in tax revenue and increase in expenditure suggest, which can be explained by the role that grants play in those PICs experiencing natural disasters. Tax revenue seems to rebound faster than GDP.[4]

---

[3]The fiscal variables are first-differenced to guarantee stationarity. See the annexes for further details.

[4]A natural disaster reduces tax revenue for two reasons: first because of lower GDP and second because of possible disruption in the payment infrastructure system (or the infrastructure used to collect taxes). In the year of the disaster there could be a disruption of the services through which taxes are collected (for example, banks or tax office). The year after the disaster this issue dissipates and tax revenue starts to grow at a higher rate than GDP. Furthermore, firms and households allocate funds to emergency expenditure and delay tax payments, which are resumed the year after the disaster.

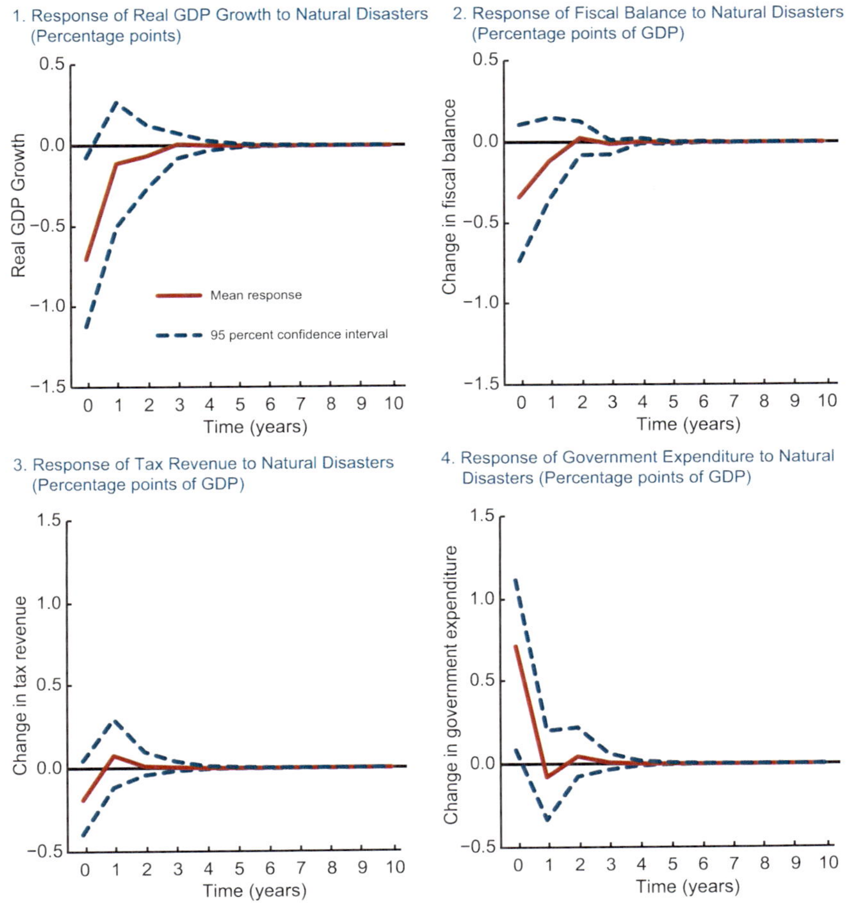

Figure 5.11 Response of Growth and Fiscal Aggregates to a Natural Disaster with Intensity Equivalent to 1 Percent of the Population Affected

Sources: Emergency Events Database (EM-DAT); and IMF staff estimates.

These results are robust to an alternative definition of disaster intensity (Figure 5.13). This includes damage and losses in percent of GDP as the disaster variable instead of disaster intensity.[5] The results are broadly similar; the main difference is that GDP growth returns to the predisaster trend faster than in the first specification and that spending consistently picks up in the year after the disaster, with possible delays in reconstruction activity. It also takes longer for the fiscal balance to return to the preshock trend.

The results are also robust to global shocks and different lag specifications. Estimations that include two and three lags present analogous impulse responses, in terms of the sign of the responses. Including real world GDP growth and changes in oil prices as measures of global shocks affects the estimations minimally.

[5]The EM-DAT Glossary notes: "The economic impact of a disaster usually consists of direct consequences (e.g., damage to infrastructure, crops, and housing) and indirect consequences (e.g., loss of revenues, unemployment, and market destabilization) for the local economy. The estimated damages and losses are in thousands of U.S. dollars."

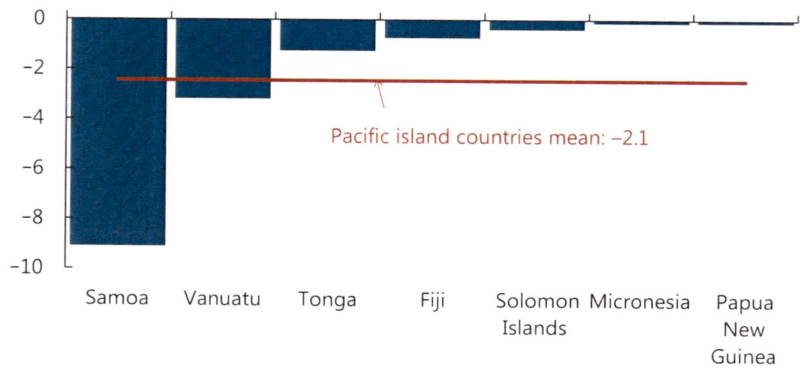

Figure 5.12 Pacific Island Countries: Short-Term Impact of Natural Disasters on GDP Growth (*Percentage points*)

Sources: Emergency Events Database (EM-DAT); and IMF staff estimates.
Note: According to the vector autoregression model, for every incident of damage and losses equivalent to 1 percent of GDP, GDP growth drops by 0.7 percentage point.

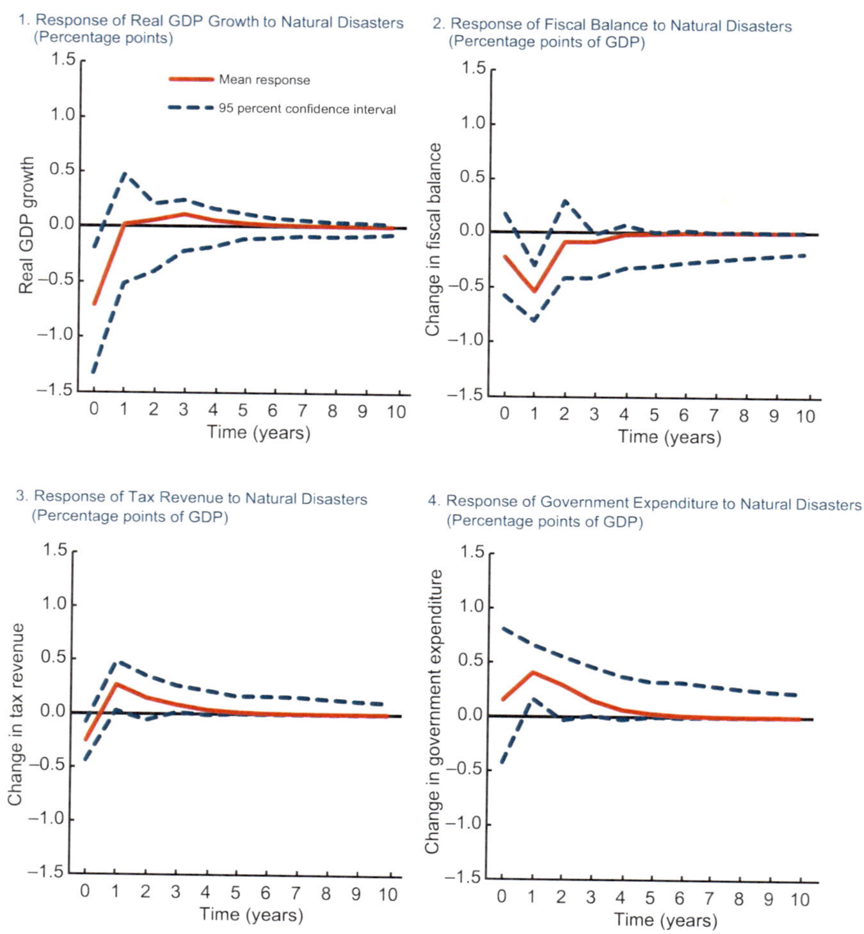

Figure 5.13 Response of Growth and Fiscal Aggregates to 1 Percent of GDP Damage Shock

Sources: Emergency Events Database (EM-DAT); and IMF staff estimates.

Autoregressive Distributed Lag Model

We estimate the impact of natural disasters on long-term growth using a panel autoregressive distributed lag model with fixed effects. We use annual panel data for five countries (Fiji, Papua New Guinea, Samoa, Tonga, Vanuatu) for 1970–2014. The dependent variable is real GDP (in log). The explanatory variables are population, capital stocks (both in log), and damage and losses (in percent of GDP). The capital stock series is constructed applying the perpetual inventory method.

The econometric result shows that for damage and losses equal to 1 percent of GDP, growth in PICs falls on average by 0.3 percentage point over 10 years (Figure 5.14 and Annex 5.1). This means that during 1980–2014 trend growth was 0.7 percentage point lower than it would have been without natural disasters. The actual average growth for the PICs during the same period averaged 2.6 percent; without natural disasters, the average would have been 3.3 percent (Figures 5.15 and 5.16).

The long-term impact of natural disasters on GDP growth is substantial. Assume that before a disaster, GDP grows at 3 percent. The 10-year growth on a cumulative basis would then be 34 percent. After a disaster, with damage and losses equal to 60 percent of GDP, growth falls by 18 percentage points (that is, 60 multiplied by 0.3), resulting in a 10-year growth loss of 16 percent on a cumulative basis (Table 5.2).

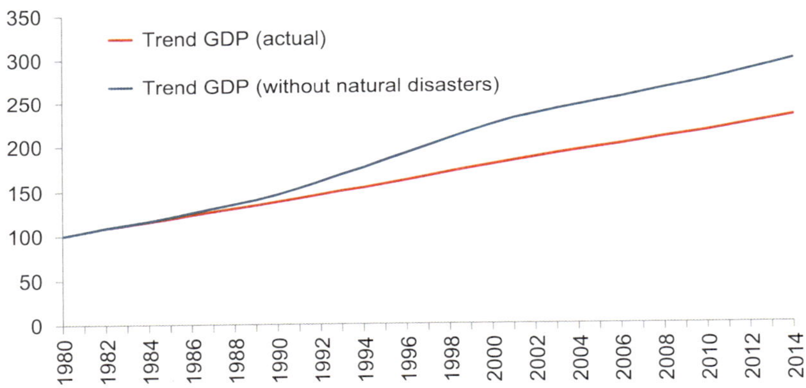

Figure 5.14 Pacific Island Countries: Long-Term Impact of Natural Disasters on Trend GDP (*1980 = 100*)

Sources: Emergency Events Database (EM-DAT); and IMF staff estimates.
Note: Trend GDP is calculated as a 10-year moving average of real GDP.

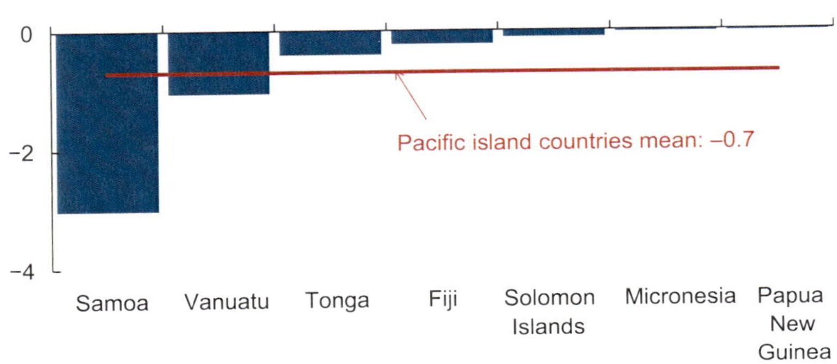

Figure 5.15 Pacific Island Countries: Long-Term Impact of Natural Disasters on Trend Growth (*Percentage points*)

Sources: Emergency Events Database (EM-DAT); and IMF staff estimates.
Note: According to the panel autoregressive distributed lag model, for every incident of damage and losses equivalent to 1 percent of GDP, GDP growth drops by 0.3 percent over 10 years. Given historical data on damages and losses, the average GDP growth drop during 1980–2014 was 0.7 percentage point.

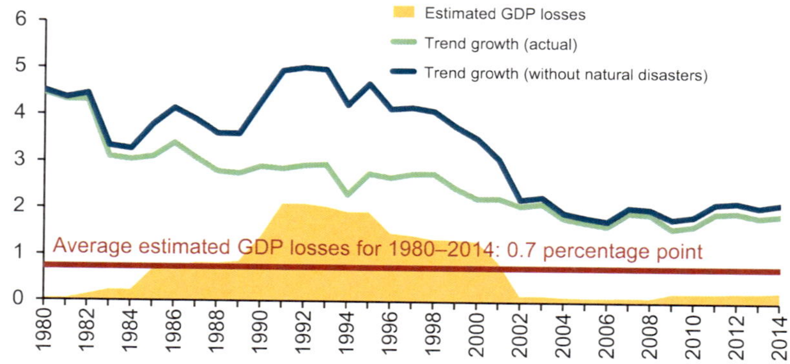

Figure 5.16 Pacific Island Countries: Long-Term Impact of Natural Disasters on Trend Growth[1] *(Percent)*

Sources: Emergency Events Database (EM-DAT); and IMF staff estimates.
[1] Trend growth is calculated as a 10-year moving average of real GDP growth.

TABLE 5.2

Illustration of Long-Term Impact of Natural Disasters on GDP Growth

	Before Natural Disaster	After Natural Disaster	Difference
Annual GDP growth (in percent)	3.0	1.3	1.7
Cumulative GDP growth over 10 years (in percent)[1]	34.0	16.0	18.0

Source: Authors' calculations.
Note: Assumes damage and losses of 60 percent of GDP. The number 18 is equivalent to 0.3*60. See Annex Table 5.1.1 for the coefficient on damage and losses. Since real GDP is in log while damage and losses are expressed in percent of GDP, the coefficient 0.003 is multiplied by 100.
[1] Calculated as $(1 + \text{annual growth rate})^{10}$.

Event Analysis

Using an event analysis, we study growth performance during and after natural disasters. We define a natural disaster episode as one that results in damage and losses of at least 10 percent of GDP. In contrast to the other two econometric models, event analysis focuses on the relationship between growth performance and natural disaster shocks before, during, and after an episode. While event analysis does not attempt to determine the direction of causality, it represents a useful complement to econometric models because it allows us to uncover the nonlinear dynamics of economic relationships that are likely to be missed by standard econometric specifications.

A main finding is that a loss in output relative to the predisaster GDP growth trend persists after two years, with the fiscal balance remaining as negative as in the year of the disaster. While not a conclusive determinant of the growth effects of natural disasters, these events were probably dominant factors affecting the economies at the time. On average growth was zero in the year of the disaster. While growth rebounds fairly quickly (on average two years after the disaster), it is below the growth rate prior to the disaster. The still-large fiscal balance deterioration is consistent with the results of the vector autoregression and may reflect infrastructure rehabilitation and rebuilding (Figures 5.17 and 5.18).

INCREASING MACRO-FISCAL RESILIENCE BY ENHANCING DISASTER RISK MANAGEMENT: A MULTIPILLAR FRAMEWORK

Policies that support strong fundamentals can foster resilience. Some PICs have rebuilt or made progress in rebuilding fiscal buffers since the global financial crisis. But more than half still have less-comfortable buffers (higher debt, lower fiscal balances and reserves) than before the crisis. Enhancing resilience to natural disasters and climate change demands a multipillar strategy at the national, regional, and multilateral levels, and it also requires enhancing countries' risk-management capacity (Figure 5.19). The key pillars of disaster risk management before the event include (Laframboise and Loko 2012):

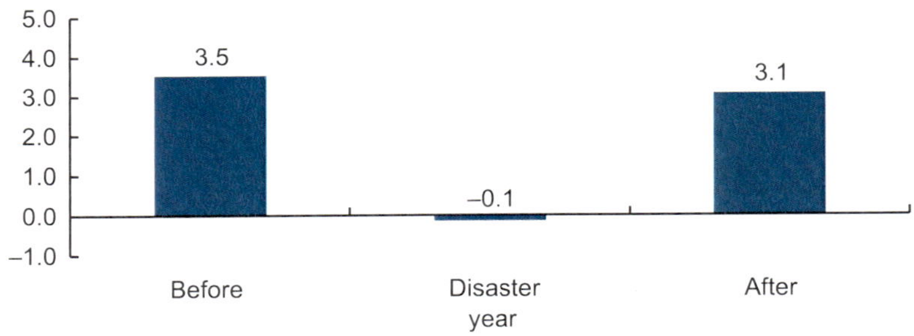

Figure 5.17 Event Analysis: Real GDP Growth before and after Natural Disasters (*Percent*)

Sources: Centre for Research on the Epidemiology of Disasters, International Disaster Database; and IMF staff estimates.
Note: Based on *natural* disasters with damage and losses larger than 10 percent of GDP during 1970–2013. Average of two years before and average of two years after. The median damage of these natural disasters was 26 percent of GDP.

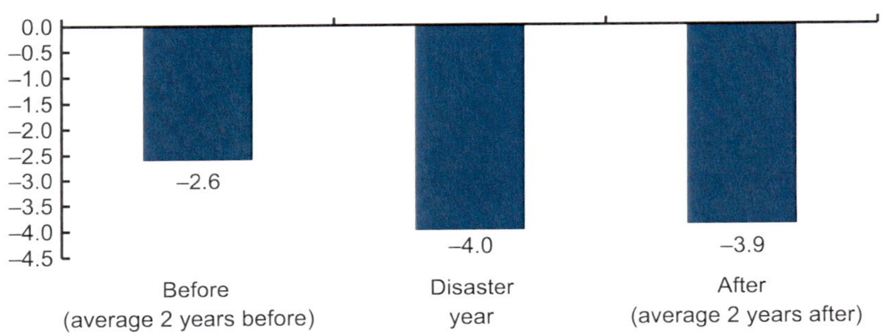

Figure 5.18 Event Analysis: Fiscal balance before and after Natural Disasters (*Percent*)

Sources: Center for Research on Epidemiology for Disasters, International Disaster Database; and IMF staff estimates.
Note: Based on *natural* disasters with damage and losses larger than 10 percent of GDP during 1970–2013. Average of two years before and average of two years after. The median damage of these natural disasters was 26 percent of GDP.

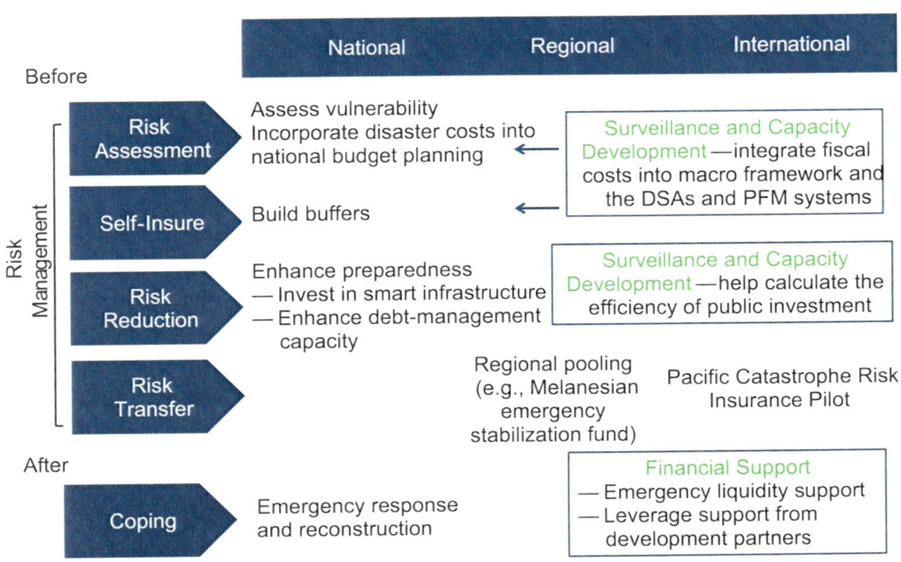

Figure 5.19 Multipillar Framework: Strengthening Resilience before and after Disasters

Note: DSAs = debt sustainability analyses; PFM = public financial management. Green shows the role of the IMF.

- Identifying and undertaking risk assessment. At the national level, building resilience before an event entails identifying risks and explicitly integrating these risks into the fiscal frameworks and budget planning.
- Providing self-insurance by building policy buffers to enhance resilience to shocks (lower debt, higher fiscal balances and reserves).
- Reducing risks by enhancing preparedness, including by investing in "smart" infrastructure that can better cope with climate change and natural hazards and by enhancing debt-management capacity.
- Transferring risk through private or sovereign insurance and through multilateral risk sharing (that is, international safety net):
  - Insurance is provided through the Pacific Catastrophe Risk Insurance Pilot for the Pacific islands, a joint initiative between the Secretariat of the Pacific Community, the World Bank Group, and the ADB, with financial support from the government of Japan and the Global Facility for Disaster Reduction and Recovery. This very innovative scheme, covering Marshall Islands, Samoa, the Solomon Islands, Tonga, and Vanuatu, was launched in January 2013 and concluded its first phase in October 2014. The pilot began its second phase in November 2014 and is expected to be concluded in October 2015. The scheme offers immediate funding in the wake of severe natural disasters (World Bank 2013) to currently participating countries: the Cook Islands, Marshall Islands, Samoa, Tonga, and Vanuatu. The government of Japan provided an additional US$1 million to fund premium subsidies for four of the participating countries (the Cook Islands is self-funding). The pilot uses "parametric triggers" such as cyclone intensity or earthquake magnitude to determine payouts. In January 2014 Tonga became the first country to benefit from a payout under the pilot of US$1.3 million, and Vanuatu received US$1.9 million after Cyclone Pam.[6] Damages and losses were US$45.4 million in Tonga and US$467 million in Vanuatu.
  - Membership in multilateral organizations could be seen as a risk-pooling mechanism.
  - Some PICs are currently discussing the establishment of a subregional reserve pooling arrangement. Member countries of the Melanesian Spearhead Group (Fiji, Papua New Guinea, the Solomon Islands, Vanuatu) are holding discussions on setting up an emergency stabilization fund to assist members in balance of payments crisis situations, particularly when members encounter imminent risks of erosion of foreign exchange and the consequent inability to finance imports and external debt.

Coping with natural disasters coupled with ensuring a resilient recovery is the main pillar of disaster risk management after an event. The main actions at the national level include emergency response and reconstruction efforts. A sound reconstruction program should consist of measures to reduce risks, such as resettlement away from coastlines, where feasible, and infrastructure investment. Reconstruction can provide an opportunity to accelerate broader growth-enhancing structural reforms.

Donor financing will remain important in enhancing resilience to cope with natural disasters and climate change as the PICs are too small and the costs too high to be fully internalized by building buffers. Moreover, building buffers also has an opportunity cost. Participation in insurance mechanisms is very promising, but so far the disbursement has been limited. However, increased global resources are being made available for climate change finance under the United Nations Framework Convention on Climate Change, with a new target of raising US$100 billion a year by 2020 to cover rising climate change costs. But access to global funding for the PICs is challenging because of capacity constraints, so bilateral funding remains critical. Moreover, the complexity of numerous financing

[6] The Solomon Islands chose not to continue its participation in the insurance pilot because it did not qualify for a payout after the flood in April 2014. Disbursements are linked to specific physical parameters (for example, the wind speed triggering a cyclone) that were not triggered during the flood.

instruments can add to the overall donor coordination challenge (Annex 5.2). Donor funding is a necessary part of resilience for small Pacific island states. Donor coordination should also be strengthened among multilateral institutions, donors, national authorities, and civil society, especially given the limited administrative capacity of these countries.

THE ROLE OF THE IMF

The IMF is increasingly incorporating macro-critical challenges posed by natural disasters and climate change into its work. The IMF has been looking at how to help countries respond through policy advice (surveillance), financial support, and technical assistance and training to build capacity (IMF 2012). The IMF recently published a staff guidance note on small states that recognizes the importance of natural disaster management and climate change (IMF 2014a). Among other policy messages, the note emphasizes the need to enhance resilience to shocks and climate change. It incorporates several of the lessons cited in this chapter, including the potential for recovery programs to pursue growth-enhancing reforms. The guidance note recognizes the complex nature of climate-change-financing arrangements and the problems posed by lack of capacity in accessing climate change resources. As such, in their consideration of fiscal space in the surveillance context, the IMF staff is advised to be sensitive to the long-term implications of climate change for the public investment needs of small states and to be ready to consider how these might be financed.

Surveillance

The 2013 IMF Board paper on small states (IMF 2013a) indicates that fostering resilience before the event requires:

- Integrating natural disaster risks into macro frameworks to determine the magnitude of the buffers (or self-insurance) needed and of the required outside insurance.[7]
- Ensuring sufficient flexibility to help redeploy spending rapidly.
- Ensuring sufficient policy space (external reserves and low debt) to help mitigate potential balance of payments shortfalls.

After the event, an efficient response—that is, in the area of resilience—requires greater transparency to ensure the effective use of disaster assistance, strengthening coordination among development partners and authorities, and pursuing growth-enhancing structural reforms.

The costs of natural disasters and climate change are also included in the debt sustainability analysis and scenario analysis in the Article IV consultations. Kiribati's recent Article IV reports (IMF 2011, 2014b) describe climate change vulnerabilities that have slowed Kiribati's achievement of poverty reduction goals owing to the need to divert resources from development spending to building seawalls. Debt sustainability analyses on Kiribati have highlighted the fiscal risks arising from uncertain climate change costs and the importance of external assistance for concessional finance (IMF 2011). The 2014 Article IV Consultation Staff Report for Tonga (IMF 2014c) assessed the impact of Cyclone Ian, which hit the country in January 2014 provoking damages and losses of about 10 percent of GDP. The 2015 Article IV Consultation Staff Report for Samoa analyzed the impact of natural disasters on debt (IMF 2015b).

Financial Support

The IMF offers financing to meet a broad range of urgent balance of payments needs, including those arising from natural disasters. Although sometimes limited in magnitude, IMF financial support

[7]The costs and policy frameworks will differ from country to country; therefore policy advice needs to be carefully tailored.

catalyzes external finance from other sources. IMF financing to support countries hit by natural disaster includes:

- The *Rapid Credit Facility* (RCF), which provides rapid financial support in a single, up-front payout for low-income countries facing urgent financing needs. Financial assistance under the RCF is provided as an outright disbursement to Poverty Reduction and Growth Trust (PRGT)-eligible members that face an urgent balance of payments need, and where a full-fledged economic program is either not necessary or not feasible. Financing under the RCF carries a zero interest rate through 2016 and has a grace period of 5½ years and a final maturity of 10 years. The *Rapid Financing Instrument* (RFI) is similar to the RCF and designed for situations where a full-fledged economic program is either not necessary or not feasible. Financial assistance provided under the RFI is subject to the same financing terms as the Flexible Credit Line, the Precautionary and Liquidity Line, and Stand-By Arrangements, and should be repaid within 3¼ to 5 years. Both lending facilities are designed for members that do not require a full-fledged economic reform program (for example, because of the transitory and limited nature of the shock) or where such a program is not feasible because the need is urgent or policy implementation capacity is limited.
    - ***Samoa*** was hit by Tropical Cyclone Evan in December 2012, leading to loss of life and damage estimated at 30 percent of GDP. A request for a one-off disbursement of US$8.6 million under the RCF facility was approved by the IMF Board in May 2013 (IMF 2013b). In 2009, Samoa was hit by a tsunami whose damage and losses were estimated at 25 percent of GDP, and IMF financial assistance (equivalent to US$9.3 million) was also provided (IMF 2010).
    - ***Vanuatu***, in June 2015, received financial support from the IMF following the devastating cyclone of March 2015. The IMF Board approved a disbursement of about US$11.9 million under the RCF and disbursement of about US$11.9 million under the RFI (IMF 2015a). As in the case of Samoa, this financial assistance was intended to help Vanuatu cope with its immediate balance of payments needs and to catalyze critical donor support for the recovery.
- *Augmentation of an existing program*—When a country with an IMF-supported program is hit by a natural disaster, augmented financing under the existing program could be the usual channel for providing additional financial support.
- *IMF Catastrophe Containment and Relief (CCR) Trust*—This replaced the Post-Catastrophe Debt Relief Trust in February 2015. It allows the IMF to join international debt relief efforts when poor countries are hit by catastrophic natural disasters or public health disasters. The IMF can provide debt relief to free up resources to meet exceptional balance of payments needs created by the disaster, rather than having to assign those resources to debt service. The Catastrophe Containment and Relief Trust is available to 38 low-income countries eligible for concessional borrowing through the Poverty Reduction and Growth Trust that also have either income per capita below US$1,215 or, for small states, a population below 1.5 million and income per capita below US$2,430. Among the PICs, only the Solomon Islands meets these criteria. A country qualifies under the trust if it is hit by a disaster that directly affects at least one-third of the population and destroys more than a quarter of productive capacity. This is estimated by such early indications as destroyed structures and the impact on key economic sectors and public institutions, or by damage exceeding 100 percent of GDP.

Capacity Development

IMF policy advice on coping with natural disasters is also supported by technical assistance and training. For example, technical assistance on public financial management, which improves budget planning and enhances transparency of public funds, helps improve the foundation on which PICs seek natural disaster and climate change assistance. A sound public financial management system is essential to enhancing risk management related to these events by incorporating disaster risk into fiscal planning. The IMF also supports public financial management reform needed for climate change access through Public Expenditure and Financial Accountability assessments.[8]

Public financial management reform and more transparent aid management policies enhance the effectiveness and quality of public expenditure, and so offers benefits that extend beyond climate change and natural disaster management. A Nauru case study by the Pacific Islands Forum Secretariat (2013a) offers several lessons on this, including the benefits of integrating climate change into national plans, policies, and budgets, and of tracking spending through budget systems. The study also cites the difficulties in quantifying the extent of external financing available for climate change and distinguishing this financing from existing development assistance. These challenges are likely to divert capacity from other aspects of core policy management.

The IMF also provides technical assistance to all members interested in adopting environmental tax reforms. Fiscal policies should take center stage in trying to get energy prices to reflect the harmful environmental side effects associated with energy use, notably climate change (de Mooij, Keen, and Parry 2012).[9]

The Pacific Financial Technical Assistance Centre, in coordination with the World Bank's Disaster Risk Financing and Insurance Program, held a regional workshop in March 2015 hosted by the Pacific Islands Forum Secretariat on incorporating natural disaster risks into the fiscal planning process. The workshop addressed such issues as special budgetary procedures for providing rapid access to emergency funding, the macroeconomic and fiscal impact of natural disasters, incorporating disaster risk into the fiscal planning process, and disaster risk financing.

CONCLUSIONS

Pacific island countries face severe challenges from natural disasters and climate change. These events have an impact on both potential growth and public finances.

A more strategic approach is needed to help countries deal with the increasing frequency and magnitude of these events. Explicit recognition of the costs of natural disasters and climate change in baseline macro frameworks and debt sustainability analyses is important, particularly given the risks that these events will become increasingly severe over time. While building policy buffers is especially relevant in the small states of the Pacific to enhance resilience before these events occur, these countries will need to continue to be supported by access to external assistance and insurance schemes. In addition to providing financing support, the IMF can also help by continuing to provide technical assistance and training to enhance countries' risk-management capacities, thereby continuing to also foster resilience before disasters occur.

---

[8]The Public Expenditure and Financial Accountability framework is one of the tools that helps assess the health of public financial management systems. The Pacific Islands Forum Secretariat (2013b) developed a Pacific Climate Change Financing Assessment Framework, which assesses a country's ability to access and manage climate change resources, and its reports provide a baseline for the framework.

[9]See also a speech by IMF Managing Director Christine Lagarde at the Center for Global Development in July 2014, which can be found at https://www.imf.org/external/np/speeches/2014/073114.htm.

ANNEX 5.1. AUTOREGRESSIVE DISTRIBUTED LAG MODEL

The autoregressive distributed lag (ARDL) methodology is valid regardless of whether the regressors are exogenous or endogenous, and irrespective of whether the underlying variables are integrated of order 1 or zero, as shown in Annex Table 5.1.1.

ANNEX TABLE 5.1.1

Fixed Effects Estimates of the Long-Term Effects Based on the ARDL Model

Dependent Variable: Real GDP (log)	
Capital stock (log)	0.344***
Population (log)	0.628***
Damage and losses (percent of GDP)	−0.003**
F-statistics for cointegration	4.851***
Observations	225
Number of countries	5

Source: Authors' compilation.

Note: The lag length was selected using Schwarz's Bayesian criterion. Estimation period: 1970–2014.

*** $p<0.01$, ** $p<0.05$, * $p<0.1$.

ANNEX 5.2. SOURCES OF INTERNATIONAL FINANCING TO COPE WITH NATURAL DISASTERS AND CLIMATE CHANGE

ANNEX TABLE 5.2.1

Selected Programs and Funds

Institution	Programs/Funds	Purpose	Period	Amounts	Comments
Asian Development Bank (ADB)	Pacific Climate Change Program (PCCP)	Climate change	2011–14	US$240 million	The ADB is delivering an integrated program to its Pacific Developing Member Countries (DMCs) to address both mitigation and adaptation to climate change, focusing on climate and disaster proofing of the investment portfolio and scaling up renewable energy. In the Pacific, the ADB has facilitated access to international climate financing primarily as cofinancing of investments. The ADB has set up dedicated climate facilities funded by its own resources and bilateral partners. Out of the ADB's own funds, approximately US$172 million funded adaptation and mitigation costs of projects during 2011–14. In addition, the ADB mobilized about US$68 million from global funds from the Least Developed Country Fund (LDCF) and the Climate Investment Fund's Pilot Program for Climate Resilience (PPCR).
ADB	Asia Pacific Disaster Response Fund (APDRF)	Natural disasters		US$3 million per event	Incremental grant resources for developing member countries impacted by a major natural disaster, with quick-disbursing grants to assist ADB DMCs to restore life-saving services and augment aid provided by other donors. Since 2011, ADB has approved eight APDRF projects in the Pacific.
ADB	Disaster Response Facility (DRF)	Natural disasters	Since 2011	US$26 million	The DRF supports emergency assistance, restoration, and rehabilitation and reconstruction needs. The assistance is provided in the form of grants or loans depending on a country's status. In the case of a disaster, countries eligible for financing by the Asian Development Fund can get up to 100 percent of their annual performance-based allocation (PBA) or US$3 million per disaster, whichever is higher; a blend country can receive up to 3 percent of its annual PBA. Since 2011, the ADB has helped Pacific countries access US$26 million from the DRF through three projects (in Samoa, the Solomon Islands, and Tonga).
European Union	African, Caribbean and Pacific (ACP)-EU Building Safety and Resilience in the Pacific	Disaster risk reduction and climate change adaptation	2013–18	€20 million	Strengthen the capacity of PICs to address existing and emerging challenges with regard to the risks posed by natural hazards and related disasters, while maximizing synergies between disaster risk reduction (DRR) strategies and climate change adaptation (CCA).

(continued)

ANNEX TABLE 5.2.1 (*Continued*)

Selected Programs and Funds

Institution	Programs/Funds	Purpose	Period	Amounts	Comments
European Union	ACP-EU Natural Disaster Risk Reduction Programme (NDRR)	Disaster risk reduction and climate change adaptation	2011–20	Total: €80 million Indicative Pacific: €13.7 million	Address prevention, mitigation, and preparedness in response to natural hazards in ACP member states, focusing on mainstreaming disaster risk reduction, risk identification and assessment, early warning systems and communication on DRR, and risk transfer and integration of DRR into recovery.
European Union	Intra-ACP Global Climate Change Alliance (GCCA)	Climate change adaptation and mitigation	2012–16	€37 million Indicative Pacific: €8.0 million	Integrated strategies, mainstreaming climate change in national development planning and budgeting, institutional and capacity strengthening, and fostering dialogue and exchange of experiences to address climate change in developing ecomomies.
European Union/ UNESCAP/ILO/UNDP	Enhancing the Capacity of Pacific Island Countries to Address the Impacts of Climate Change on Migration	Climate change and migration	Ends in 2016	€2.1 million	Capacity building on climate-change-induced migration financed through the European Initiative for Democracy and Human Rights (EIDHR).
European Union	Global Index Insurance Facility (GIIF)	Disaster risk reduction	2008–16	€24.5 million (all ACP countries)	Reduce the vulnerability of the ACP population to external shocks/ natural disasters through expansion of the use of index insurance as a risk management tool in ACP countries. GIIF seeks to introduce a new and more efficient approach (indexed or parametric insurance) for mitigating weather/catastrophic risks in developing economies.
European Union	Global Climate Change Alliance (GCCA) South Pacific	Mainstreaming adaptation	2011–15	€10 million	Secretariat of the Pacific Community, Secretariat of the Pacific Regional Environment Programme: Overall development and poverty reduction, coastal zone management, health, infrastructure, and water and sanitation.
European Union	Global Climate Change Alliance (GCCA) Papua New Guinea	UN-REDD – Forest	2013–17	€8.6 million	Contributes to the implementation of the national REDD readiness plan.
European Union	Global Climate Change Alliance (GCCA) Samoa	Mainstreaming adaptation/disaster risk reduction	2012–15	€3.0 million	Contributes to the implementation of the national Water for Life Sector Plan – Water and sanitation.
European Union	Global Climate Change Alliance (GCCA) The Solomon Islands	Mainstreaming adaptation	2011–14	€2.8 million	Overall development and poverty reduction. Contributes to the implementation of the Solomon Islands National Adaptation Programme of Action (NAPA) priorities and the National Disaster Risk Management Plan.
European Union	Global Climate Change Alliance (GCCA) Timor-Leste	Mainstreaming adaptation	2013–18	€4.0 million	Overall development and poverty reduction, forests, agriculture, and natural resource management.

European Union	Global Climate Change Alliance (GCCA) Vanuatu	Mainstreaming adaptation/disaster risk reduction	2010–14	€3.2 million	Overall development and poverty reduction, agriculture, natural resource management, and water and sanitation. Contributes to the implementation of the measures identified in the NAPA.
European Union	Pro-Resilience Action	Building resilience in response to food crises	2014–20	Indicative €65 million a year (worldwide)	Supporting the poor and food insecure to react to crises by addressing the effects of the crises and strengthening their resilience. The action is worldwide, and Pacific small island developing states can access support if they are stricken by a food crisis. The program does not respond specifically to natural disasters. However, the program can be activated if a natural disaster has impacts in terms of food and nutrition security.
European Union	Adapting to Climate Change and Sustainable Energy (ACSE)	Climate change	2014–19	€35.5 million	ACSE will help 15 Pacific island countries (PICs) adapt to adverse effects of climate change and enhance their energy security at national, provincial, and local/community levels. The objectives are: (1) create and/or strengthen national technical expertise on climate change adaptation and sustainable energy, (2) improve cost-effective and efficient energy systems to reduce fossil fuel dependency, and (3) improve communities' adaptive capacity to cope with climate change challenges. Another aim of the ACSE program is to enhance sustainable livelihoods through the support of government institutional efforts and empowering communities to increase their self-reliance and their ability to cope with the effects of climate change through appropriate practices in agriculture and coastal fishery, by disseminating improved plant varieties that are resistant to saltwater, by securing their daily water supply, and by improving their access to energy, among other initiatives.
United Nations	Adaptation Fund (AF)		Established 2001		The Adaptation Fund was established to finance concrete adaptation projects and programs in developing-country parties to the Kyoto Protocol that are particularly vulnerable to the adverse effects of climate change. The Adaptation Fund is financed from the share of proceeds of the clean development mechanism (CDM) project activities and other sources of funding. The share of proceeds amounts to 2 percent of certified emission reductions (CERs) issued for a CDM project activity. The Adaptation Fund is supervised and managed by the Adaptation Fund Board (AFB). The AFB is composed of 16 members and 16 alternates and meets at least twice a year.

(continued)

ANNEX TABLE 5.2.1 (*Continued*)

Selected Programs and Funds

Institution	Programs/Funds	Purpose	Period	Amounts	Comments
World Bank/United Nations	Global Facility for Disaster Reduction and Recovery (GFDRR)	Reduce vulnerability to natural disasters and climate change	Established 2006	For projects US$100,000 to US$1 million	GFDRR is a partnership of 35 countries and six international organizations committed to helping developing economies reduce their vulnerability to natural hazards and adapt to climate change. The partnership's mission is to mainstream disaster risk reduction and climate change adaptation in country development strategies by supporting a country-led and country-managed implementation of the Hyogo Framework for Action (HFA).
World Bank Group, International Development Association (IDA)	Immediate Response Mechanism (IRM)	Natural disasters	Established December 2011	5 percent of undisbursed IDA project balances, or SDR 5 million.	The IRM allows IDA countries to rapidly access up to 5 percent of their undisbursed IDA investment project balances following a crisis (natural disasters and economic shocks). Small states and countries with small undisbursed project balances will be able to access up to US$5 million. The IRM complements longer-term emergency response tools available to IDA countries, such as the Crisis Response Window.
World Bank Group, IDA	Pacific Catastrophe Risk Assessment and Financing Initiative (PCRAFI)	Natural disasters	November 2012 to November 2014	US$45 million in aggregate coverage	Participating countries select per-peril coverage and option of coverage attaching at loss levels of a severity of recurrence of 1 in 10, 15, or 20 years (or less frequent). Five PICs participated in the initial 2012–13 pilot, which had an aggregate limit of US$45 million and an annual expected loss of US$1 million. The scheme covers Marshall Islands, Samoa, the Solomon Islands, Tonga, Vanuatu, and the Cook Islands.
World Bank Group (Trustee)	Climate Investment Funds (CIF)	Climate change	Established 2008		The CIF provides funding to 48 developing and middle-income countries. Funding is from contributor countries, with co-funding sought from the private sector. The CIF fosters partnerships through a programmatic approach, whereby CIF countries, with support from the multilateral development banks, lead investment planning and implementation. The CIF has four funding windows: (1) the $5.5 billion Clean Technology Fund (CTF); (2) the $639 million Forest Investment Program (FIP); (3) the $1.3 billion Pilot Program for Climate Resilience (PPCR); and (4) the $551 million Scaling Up Renewable Energy in Low Income Countries Program (SREP).

World Bank Group	IDA	Climate and disaster resilience	2011–15	US$150 million	The IDA-17 Replenishment requires Country Partnership Frameworks to incorporate climate and disaster risk considerations, and for all IDA operations to be screened for short- and long-term climate change and disaster risks, integrating resilience measures as appropriate. This includes both concessional credits and IDA grants that are used to support climate and disaster resilience.
World Bank Group	International Bank for Reconstruction and Development (IBRD)	Climate and disaster resilience	2011–15	US$15 million	The IBRD aims to reduce poverty in middle-income countries and creditworthy poorer countries by promoting sustainable development through loans, guarantees, risk-management products, and analytical and advisory services.
Australian Department of Foreign Affairs and Trade (DFAT)	DFAT	Climate change	Total funding for 2010/11 and 2012/13 was A$599 million		Support to developing countries to adapt to climate change, reduce their carbon emissions, and pursue cleaner development. Focus is on least developed countries and small island developing states. Efforts will build on work to reduce emissions from deforestation, pilot low emission development pathways, and engage in key international development and environment forums.
Japan	Japan's Assistance Package for PICs at the 7th Pacific Islands Leaders Meeting (PALM7)	Climate change	2015–17	US$450 million	Japan will provide assistance to PICs that are battling rising sea levels and natural calamities as a result of global warming. Focus is on disaster risk reduction, climate change, environment, people-to-people exchanges, sustainable development, maritime issues and fisheries, and trade, investment, and tourism.

Source: Authors' compilation.
Note: ILO = International Labour Organization; UNDP = United Nations Development Programme; UNESCAP = United Nations Economic and Social Commission for Asia and the Pacific; UN-REDD = United Nations Programme on Reducing Emissions from Deforestation and Forest Degradation, a collaborative initiative of the Food and Agriculture Organization, UNDP, and the UN Environment Programme.

REFERENCES

Acevedo, S. 2014. "Debt, Growth and Natural Disasters." IMF Working Paper 14/125, International Monetary Fund, Washington.

Asian Development Bank (ADB). 2013. *The Economics of Climate Change in the Pacific*. Manila: ADB.

Auffret, P. 2003. "High Consumption Volatility: The Impact of Natural Disasters?" Policy Research Working Paper 2962, World Bank, Washington.

Cavallo, E., and I. Noy. 2010. "The Economics of Natural Disasters." Working Paper Series IDB-WP-124, Inter-American Development Bank, Washington.

De Mooij, R. A., M. Keen, and I. W. H. Parry (eds.). 2012. *Fiscal Policy to Mitigate Climate Change: A Guide for Policymakers*. Washington: International Monetary Fund.

EM-DAT Glossary, Centre for Research on the Epidemiology of Disasters. http://www.emdat.be/glossary/9.

Fomby, T., Y. Ikeda, and N. V. Loayza. 2013. "The Growth Aftermath of Natural Disasters." *Journal of Applied Econometrics* 28 (3): 412–34.

International Monetary Fund (IMF). 2010. "Samoa: Request for Disbursement Under the Rapid-Access Component of the Exogenous Shocks Facility—Staff Report." IMF Country Report 10/46, Washington.

———. 2011. "Kiribati: 2011 Article IV Consultation—Staff Report, Informational Annexes, Debt Sustainability Analysis… ." IMF Country Report 11/113, Washington.

———. 2012. "Enhancing Resilience to Shocks and Fostering Inclusive Growth in the Pacific Islands." Speech by Min Zhu, Deputy Managing Director, International Monetary Fund in Apia, Samoa, March 23.

———. 2013a. "Macroeconomic Issues in Small States and Implications for Fund Engagement." IMF Board Paper, Washington.

———. 2013b. "Samoa: Request for Disbursement under the Rapid Credit Facility—Staff Report." IMF Country Report 13/162, Washington.

———. 2014a. "Staff Guidance Note on the Fund's Engagement with Small Developing States." Washington.

———. 2014b. "Kiribati: 2014 Article IV Consultation—Staff Report; Press Release; and Statement by the Executive Director for Kiribati." Washington.

———. 2014c. "Tonga: 2014 Article IV Consultation—Staff Report." IMF Country Report 14/240, International Monetary Fund, Washington.

———. 2015a. "Vanuatu: 2015 Article IV Consultation and Request for Disbursement under the Rapid Credit Facility and Purchase under the Rapid Financing Instrument—Press release; Staff Report and Statement by the Executive Director for Vanuatu." Washington.

———. 2015b. "Samoa: Article IV Consultation—Press Release; Staff Report; and Statement by the Executive Director for Samoa." IMF Country Report 15/191, International Monetary Fund, Washington.

Intergovernmental Oceanographic Commission (IOC)/United Nations Educational, Scientific and Cultural Organization (UNESCO), International Maritime Organization, Food and Agriculture Organization of the United Nations, and United Nations Development Programme. 2011. *A Blueprint for Ocean and Coastal Sustainability*. Paris: IOC/UNESCO.

Intergovernmental Panel on Climate Change (IPCC). 2013. *Fifth Assessment Report*. Geneva: IPCC.

Laframboise, N., and B. Loko. 2012. "Natural Disasters: Mitigating Impact, Managing Risks." IMF Working Paper 12/245, International Monetary Fund, Washington.

Loayza, N., E. Olaberría, J. Rigolini, and L. Christiaensen. 2009. "Natural Disasters and Growth: Going Beyond the Averages." Policy Research Working Paper 4980, World Bank, Washington.

Pacific Islands Forum Secretariat. 2013a. Nauru Case Study Final Report.

———. 2013b. Pacific Climate Change Finance Assessment Framework—Final Report.

Raddatz, C. 2009. "The Wrath of God: Macroeconomic Costs of Natural Disasters" Policy Research Working Paper 5039, World Bank, Washington.

United Nations University Institute for Environment and Human Security (UNU-EHS) and Alliance Development Works. 2014. *2014 World Risk Report*. Bonn: UNU-EHS; Berlin: Alliance Development Works.

World Bank. 2013. *Pacific Catastrophe Risk Assessment and Financing Initiative, Risk Assessment–Summary Report*. Washington: World Bank.

———. 2014. "Helping Small Island States Cope with the Aftermath of Natural Disasters." Treasury Case Study, World Bank, Washington.

PART II

Managing External Spillovers, Shocks, and Vulnerabilities

CHAPTER 6

Global and Regional Spillovers to Pacific Island Countries

FAZURIN JAMALUDIN, NIAMH SHERIDAN, PATRIZIA TUMBARELLO, YIQUN WU, AND TLEK ZEINULLAYEV

The Pacific island countries (PICs) have been integrating economically with Australia, New Zealand, and Asia's emerging market economies over the last two decades, creating big economic opportunities for them.[1] This integration has greatly benefited PICs, but it has also posed challenges because shocks are transmitted more rapidly in a more interconnected world. Indeed, PICs have become more exposed to regional business cycles. Yet strong linkages with resilient economies—notably Australia and Asia's emerging markets—helped cushion the downturn in the aftermath of the global financial crisis.

The PICs' strong linkages with Australia and New Zealand are well established. Australia is by far the largest provider of aid and foreign direct investment (FDI) to these countries, and Australia and New Zealand account on average for one-third of trade with PICs. Remittances from Australia and New Zealand account for about 60 percent of total remittances to Fiji and Samoa, while 60–70 percent of total tourist arrivals in Fiji, Samoa, and Vanuatu come from these two countries. Australian banks, meanwhile, dominate the banking sector in PICs. PICs have also been establishing more substantial links with Asia's emerging market economies, including China, especially over the last 10 years.

Today, spillovers from regional economies are more important for PICs than advanced economies outside the region. Australia is the main source of direct and indirect spillovers, both over the short and long term, except for the compact agreement countries (Marshall Islands, Micronesia, Palau), for which the United States is the most important partner, consistent with the large volume of U.S. aid. Over the last decade, shocks from Asia's emerging market economies have had a greater impact on the business cycles of PICs, while the role of more traditional partners, such as Japan, has declined. In the short term, the elasticity of PICs' output with respect to the GDP of regional partners has at times been higher than one, pointing to the critical role for policies to stabilize business cycles.

While strong linkages with Asia and the Pacific would help in the event of a global downturn, PICs remain particularly vulnerable to global commodity price shocks. The 50 percent decline in crude oil prices between mid-2014 and October 2015 broadly supported their macroeconomic prospects, with the exception of fuel commodity exporters such as Papua New Guinea and Timor-Leste, despite lingering global economic uncertainties. But a jump in oil prices of, say, 50 percent above the baseline would have a substantial negative impact on growth given PICs' relatively heavy

This chapter is based on IMF Working Paper 12/154 (Sheridan, Tumbarello, and Wu 2012). We thank Peter Montiel, Richard Wood, and the other participants in the 2012 Pacific Islands conference in Samoa for their valuable comments. We also thank Ben Hunt and Keiko Honjo from the IMF Research Department for providing the data underlying the global shock scenarios, and Sri Joedianna Pg Hj Mohammed for collecting the information on the financial sector used in the section Assessing Spillovers to the Financial Sector. We greatly benefited from comments by Roberto Cardarelli, Matt Davies, Huidan Lin, Shanaka Peiris, Haiming Tan, John Vaught, and Aki Yoshida. We are very thankful to Professor Vance Martin for all his suggestions on the econometric analysis. We are in debt to Branan Karae and Ambassador Mack Kaminaga for liaising with the authorities in the Pacific island countries and providing the data underlying this analysis. Safieh Hekmat provided excellent editorial assistance.

[1]The PICs covered in this chapter are the IMF Pacific island members Fiji, Kiribati, Marshall Islands, Micronesia, Palau, Papua New Guinea, Samoa, the Solomon Islands, Timor-Leste, Tonga, Tuvalu, and Vanuatu.

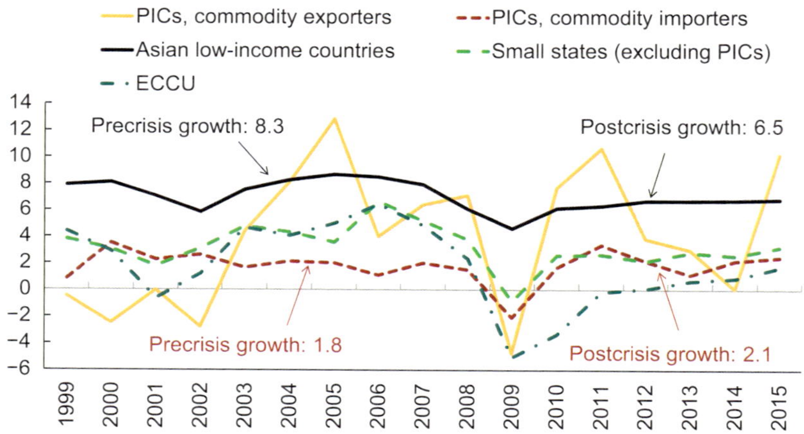

Figure 6.1 Real GDP Growth (*Percent*)

Sources: Country authorities; and IMF staff calculations and projections.
Note: ECCU = Eastern Caribbean Currency Union, and includes Antigua and Barbuda, Dominica, Grenada, St. Kitts and Nevis, St. Lucia, and St. Vincent and the Grenadines. PICs = Pacific island countries.

reliance on oil imports—and in some cases the impact would be larger than from a negative global demand shock.[2]

The increasing regional links of these countries could help mitigate the downside risks generated by business cycles in nonregional advanced economies. Even so, sound policies can enhance resilience, and the Pacific island countries should continue to rebuild policy buffers, undermined during the global financial crisis, and implement growth-oriented structural reforms to ensure sustained and inclusive growth.

THE SETTING: PICS BEFORE AND AFTER THE GLOBAL FINANCIAL CRISIS

Growth in PICs has been weak over the last decade. The global financial crisis compounded the problem by reducing growth further, especially among the commodity importers. While many PIC economies have recovered, headwinds remain amid the global economic uncertainty. In the event of a negative global demand shock, adverse spillovers would occur mainly through regional partners. But the linkages with Australia, New Zealand, and Asia's emerging market economies would help offset the downturn, owing to the strong fundamentals of these countries.

Most PICs seem to be stuck on a low-growth path. Figures 6.1 and 6.2 show that in the 10 years preceding the global financial crisis, PIC growth averaged just 2 percent a year—much lower than comparator countries, namely Asia's low-income countries (6 percent), the Eastern Caribbean Currency Union countries (4 percent), and other small states (4½ percent). Relative growth performance has been uneven, favoring commodity exporters, which have benefited from global price trends for the better part of the last decade.

PICs recovered from the global financial crisis at different paces (Figure 6.3). This suggests differing levels of resilience—and vulnerability—to shocks in the future. Excluding the net commodity exporters (Papua New Guinea, the Solomon Islands, Timor-Leste), average real GDP fell to

[2] Global scenarios involving a negative global demand shock and a sharp increase in oil prices are described, for instance, in the IMF's April 2012 *World Economic Outlook*. The January 2015 *World Economic Outlook Update* highlights global economic uncertainties as well as a significant drop in oil prices.

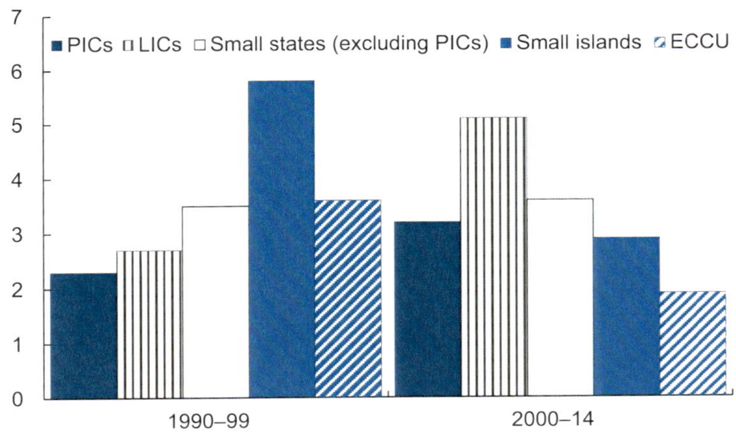

Figure 6.2 Real GDP Growth (*Percent*)

Sources: IMF, World Economic Outlook database; and IMF staff calculations.
Note: ECCU = Eastern Caribbean Currency Union; LICs = low-income countries; PICs = Pacific island countries.

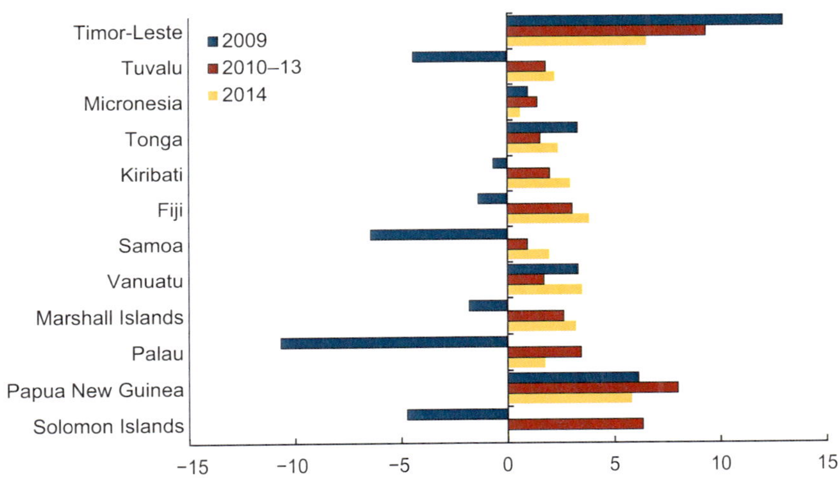

Figure 6.3 Real GDP Growth Following the Global Financial Crisis (*Percent*)

Sources: Country authorities; and IMF staff calculations.

-2.0 percent in 2009. Despite a rebound—growth averaged 1.6 percent and 3.3 percent in 2010 and 2011, respectively—average growth in non-resource-rich countries remained about 2 percent in the five years after the crisis. By contrast, real GDP growth averaged above 6 percent during 2010–14 in Papua New Guinea and the Solomon Islands on the back of the development of the liquefied natural gas sector in the former and strong mining and logging in the latter. Nonetheless, being a commodity exporter does not guarantee sustained growth. The depletion of finite natural resources and lower production—due to lower commodity prices and high costs—can weigh on growth and prove challenging for countries like the Solomon Islands, a wood and gold exporter.

The vulnerability of PICs to natural disasters can also affect growth (see Chapter 5). The 2009 flood in Fiji and, in the same year, the earthquake and tsunami in Samoa, as well as cyclones and floods in Fiji, Samoa, the Solomon Islands, and Vanuatu in 2013–15 are just some of the major natural disasters in the last five years that have had a harmful economic impact.

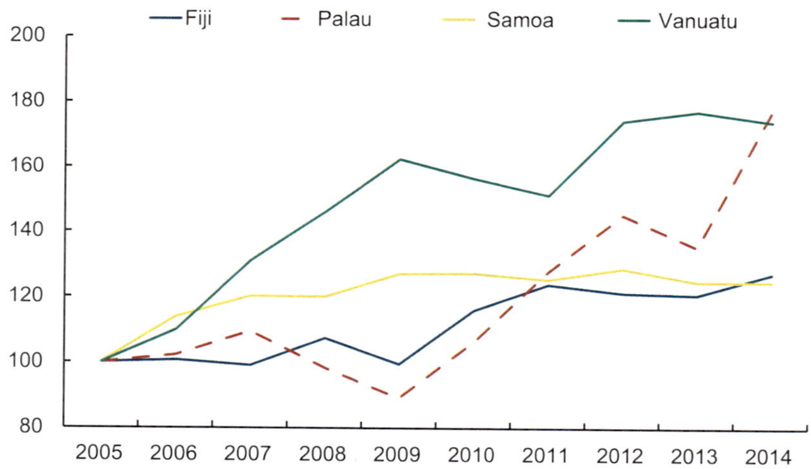

Figure 6.4 Tourist Arrivals (*2005 = 100*)

Source: IMF staff calculations.

Although growth in PICs regained precrisis rates, their growth performance is still low relative to other low-income countries. This reflects the relatively small export bases of PICs, which preclude a large increase in external demand associated with global recovery. Helped in part by Australia's economic resilience during the crisis, PICs recovered more strongly than some comparator regions, such as in the Eastern Caribbean Currency Union, which is tied more closely to the U.S. business cycle. Strong Australian and New Zealand dollars supported the PIC tourist sector for most of 2010–14 (Figure 6.4), although the depreciation of both currencies is expected to affect tourism flows in the medium term.[3]

A closer look suggests that PIC net commodity importers generally recovered more slowly than in previous recessions. Over the past four decades, PIC importers experienced economic contractions in 1975, 1980, 1987, 1997, and 2009. Only 1975 and 2009 coincided with global recessions. The 2009 contraction was comparable to previous PIC downturns, yet the recovery was weaker (Figure 6.5). For net commodity exporters, however, the contraction was milder than in previous episodes and the recovery much faster (Figure 6.6).

What explains the slow recovery of PIC commodity importers relative to past episodes? Using a vector autoregression analysis following Berg and others (2010), we find that terms-of-trade shocks, to which PICs are most exposed, result in a far greater output loss than shocks to external demand and imply a faster recovery too. Because the 2009 recession was driven by external-demand shocks, this may explain the milder drop in growth rate relative to the precrisis level during 2009 and slower recovery relative to previous episodes. In contrast, external-demand shocks have a larger impact on output in Asia's low-income countries, which may help explain the greater impact of the global recession on those economies.

Terms-of-trade shocks have a larger impact than external-demand shocks on PICs for several reasons. Given their narrow export and production bases and geographical remoteness, most PICs have structural trade deficits (IMF 2015a). With the exception of Papua New Guinea, the Solomon Islands, and Timor-Leste, PICs are commodity importers and therefore vulnerable to swings in commodity prices. However, heavy reliance on the imports of commodities, particularly fuel, is characteristic of commodity exporters and importers alike in many of these countries, especially when

[3] Both the Australian and the New Zealand dollars depreciated by about 25 percent against the U.S. dollar between September 2014 and September 2015.

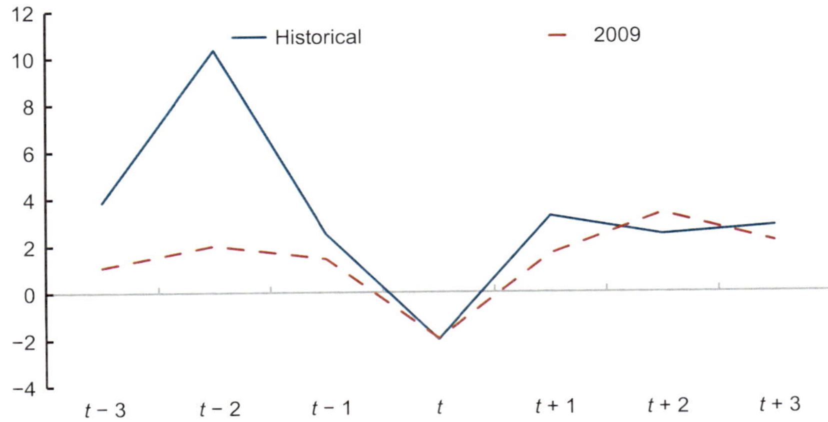

Figure 6.5 Commodity Importers among Pacific Island Countries: Real GDP Growth around Downturns (*Percent*)

Source: IMF staff calculations.
Note: Historical is average of four downturns.

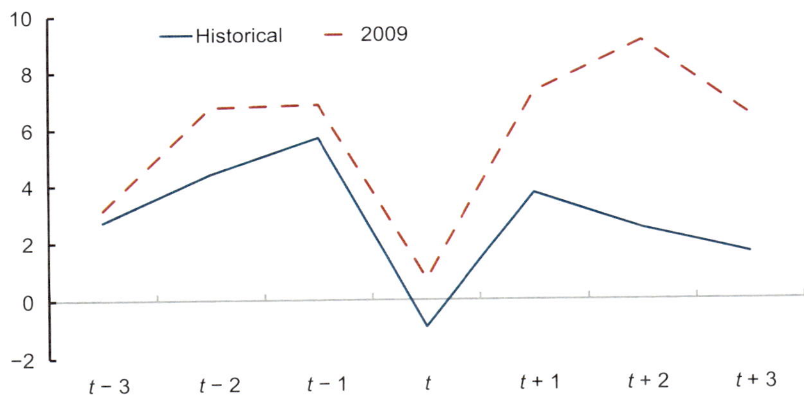

Figure 6.6 Commodity Exporters among Pacific Island Countries: Real GDP Growth around Downturns (*Percent*)

Source: IMF staff calculations.
Note: Historical is average of four downturns.

compared to peers. Given greater commodity price volatility in recent years, terms-of-trade shocks have translated into larger output shocks. Changes in import prices have also affected the cost of production and real household income.

CHANNELS OF SPILLOVER

If the global economy were to slow or contract again, the channels of contagion would also vary across PICs. The main channels are:

- *Tourism, remittances, and FDI*—Fiji, Palau, Samoa, and Vanuatu would be hurt by a fall in tourism, which accounts for between 20 percent and 50 percent of their GDP (Figure 6.7), with spillovers affecting the broader economy through reduced tourism-related FDI.

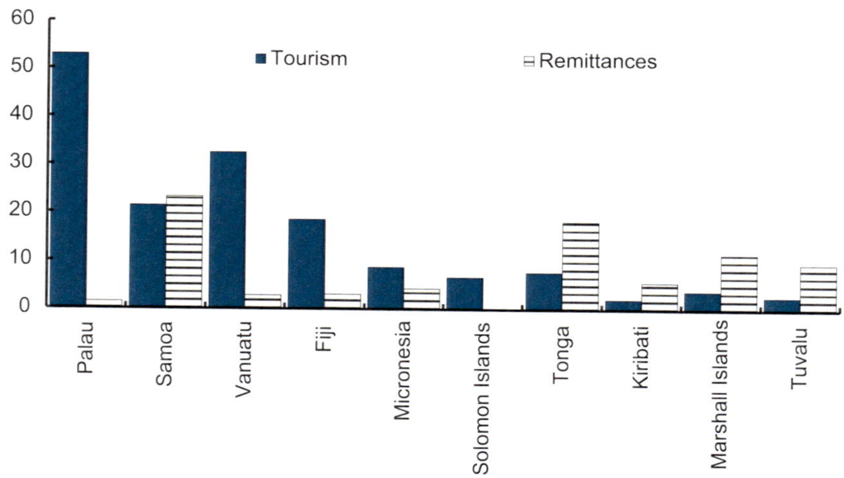

Figure 6.7 Tourism and Remittances (*Percent of GDP, 2014*)

Sources: Country authorities; and IMF staff estimates.
Note: Data are the latest available.

Remittances would be one of the main channels of contagion in Samoa, Tonga, and Tuvalu, and to a lesser extent in Fiji, Kiribati, Marshall Islands, and Micronesia. Tourist arrivals and remittances declined during the global financial crisis (Figure 6.8).

- *Terms of trade*—Movements in relative prices that result in a drop in fuel commodity prices would hurt the trade position in Papua New Guinea and Timor-Leste. Among the commodity importers, the decline in food and fuel prices could provide some relief to household budgets because (1) rising real income will increase consumption, (2) production costs will fall due to lower costs of energy, (3) the external position will improve substantially, and (4) inflation will ease.
- *Financial channels*—A fall in stock prices in advanced economies would also affect PICs with large trust funds—Kiribati, Marshall Islands, Micronesia, Palau, and Tuvalu—whose assets are invested offshore. A large decline in the value of these trust funds, as happened during the global financial crisis, could worsen fiscal sustainability over the medium and long term.
- *Foreign aid*—High dependence on foreign aid flows, averaging over 20 percent of GDP in PICs in 2014, is a source of fiscal vulnerability (Figure 6.9). In the past decade, approximately 40 percent of these countries' total fiscal receipts consisted of foreign grants. Even under the baseline scenario, the scheduled expiration in 2023/24 of U.S. aid under the compact grant scheme is set to present a fiscal cliff, as these grants make up a significant share of budgets in Marshall Islands, Micronesia, and Palau. In the Solomon Islands, donor assistance will gradually decline (in terms of GDP) over the medium term with the phased withdrawal, starting in 2013, of the Regional Assistance Mission to the Solomon Islands.[4]
- *Exchange rates*—Only six of the 12 PICs discussed in this chapter have their own national currencies (Fiji, Papua New Guinea, Samoa, the Solomon Islands, Tonga, Vanuatu). Marshall Islands, Micronesia, Palau, and Timor-Leste use the U.S. dollar; Kiribati and Tuvalu use the Australian dollar. Apart from Papua New Guinea, all the countries with their own currency and

[4]Technical assistance from the Regional Assistance Mission to the Solomon Islands started in 2003, after the civil war, as a partnership between the government of the Solomon Islands and 15 Pacific countries. The assistance focuses on security, justice, law, and economic growth.

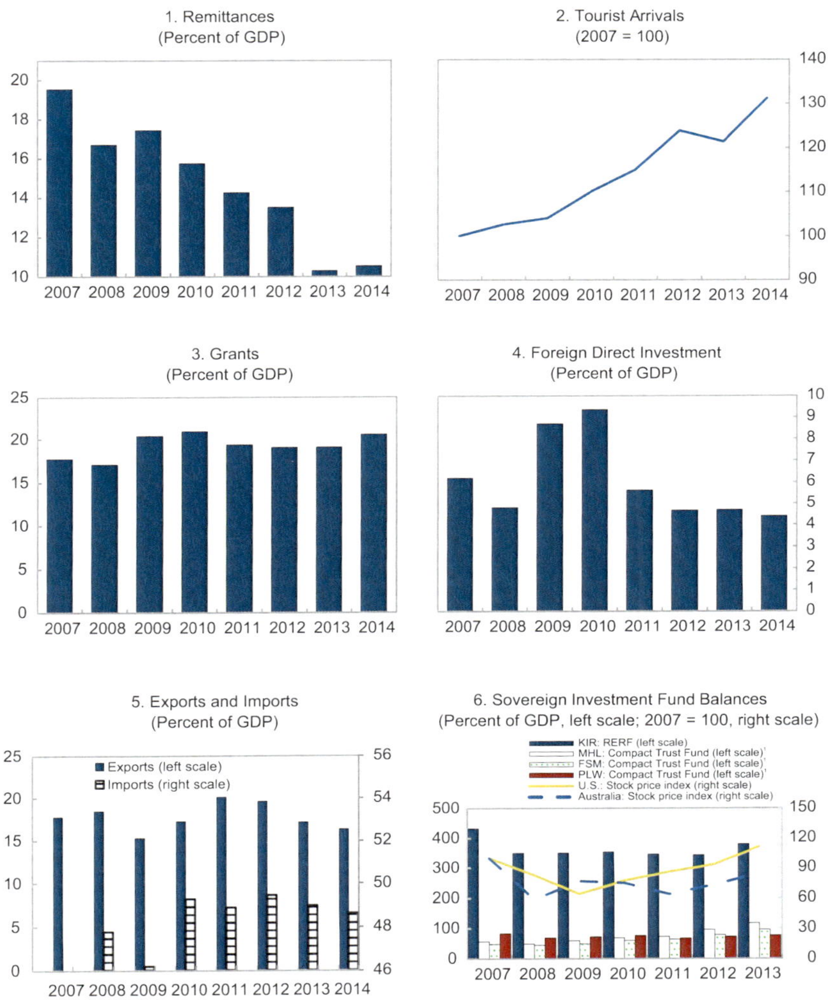

Figure 6.8 Pacific Island Countries, Channels of Spillover: Stylized Facts

Sources: Country authorities; and IMF staff calculations.

Note: FSM = Federated States of Micronesia; KIR = Kiribati; MHL = Marshall Islands; PLW = Palau; RERF = Revenue Equalization Reserve Fund; U.S. = United States.

[1]Fiscal year.

exchange rate implement some form of currency peg. As a result, PIC economies are vulnerable to U.S. dollar and regional currency movements. The depreciation of the Australian and New Zealand dollars against the U.S. dollar and PIC currencies that started in 2014, for instance, could be expected to reduce the size of remittances, aid flows, tourist arrivals, and return on investments.

ASSESSING GROWTH SPILLOVERS

To understand how external shocks from the global economy can affect PICs, one must understand growth spillovers from the region. Stylized facts suggest that direct exposure to Europe is limited. The impact of a global slowdown on PICs would occur through spillovers from regional economies and, to a lesser extent, from the United States.

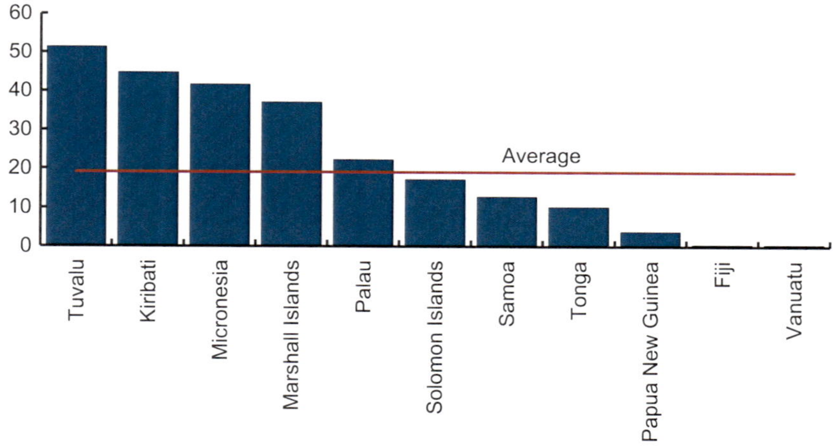

Figure 6.9 Grants to Pacific Island Countries (*Percent of GDP, 2014*)

Sources: Country authorities; and IMF staff estimates.

Linkages with Australia and New Zealand, as noted, are strong and well established, stemming from the strong exposure of PICs to these economies through trade, tourism, remittances, FDI, aid, and financial channels. Trade with Australia and New Zealand accounts, on average, for one-third of PICs' trade, while remittances from Australia and New Zealand account for about 60 percent of total remittances in Fiji and Samoa (Figure 6.10). Tourist arrivals from Australia and New Zealand represent 60–70 percent of total arrivals in Fiji, Samoa, and Vanuatu (Figure 6.11). Australian banks dominate the PICs' financial sectors, which is discussed later, and Australia is by far the largest provider of aid. Among Organisation for Economic Co-operation and Development countries, Australia is also the largest foreign investor (Figures 6.12 and 6.13) in PICs.

The United States has a large impact on some PICs, especially the compact agreement countries. U.S. aid represents over 65 percent of total aid to Palau and 90 percent to Marshall Islands and Micronesia. Remittances from the United States account for 50 percent of total remittances in Tonga (IMF 2012a).

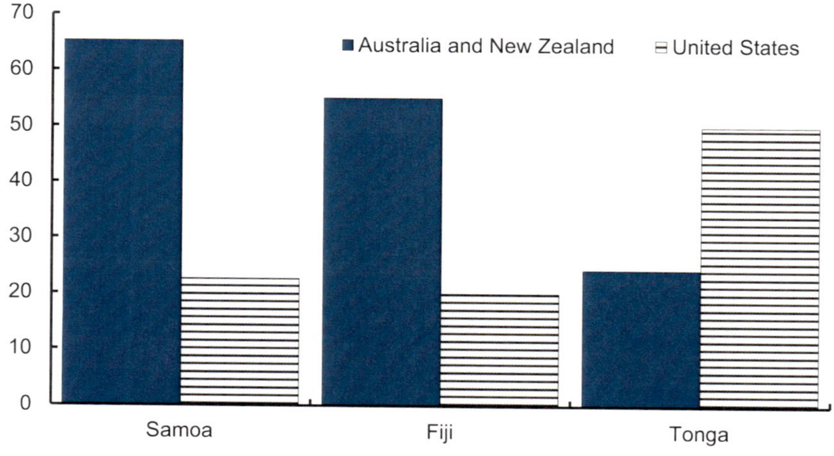

Figure 6.10 Remittances by Country of Origin (*Percent of total remittances*)

Sources: Country authorities; and IMF staff calculations.

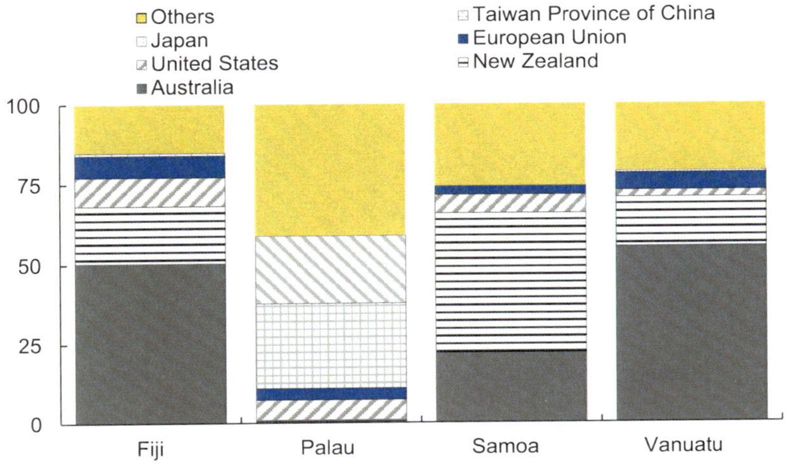

Figure 6.11 Tourists by Country of Residence (*Percent of total arrivals, 2014*)

Sources: Country authorities; and IMF staff calculations.

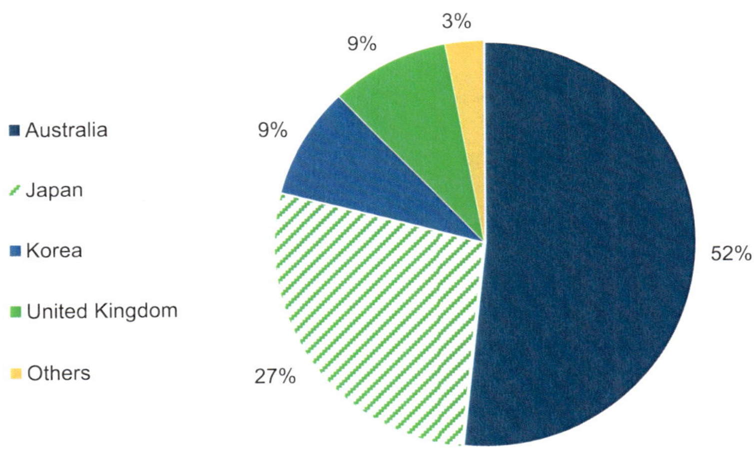

Figure 6.12 Foreign Direct Investment by OECD Countries (*Percent of total foreign direct investment, 2005–12 average*)

Source: Statistics from the Organisation for Economic Co-operation and Development (OECD).

Note: Excludes Belgium, Denmark, Greece, Italy, Netherlands, and Norway.

Linkages between PICs and Asia's emerging market economies have grown over the last decade. Direction of trade data point to a large increase in China's share of PICs' trade, with trade with China increasing sevenfold on average since the early 2000s (Figure 6.14). China is now the Solomon Islands' top trading partner, and external financing from China is substantial for Tonga (Figure 6.15). FDI patterns have become more diverse, with the share of inward FDI from China and other east Asian trading partners, notably Korea, growing at the expense of traditional investors such as Japan (Figure 6.16).

Quantitative Analysis

Can growth from fast-growing neighboring economies spill over to PICs as tailwinds to an economic recovery process or buffers during a downward scenario? A simple correlation analysis

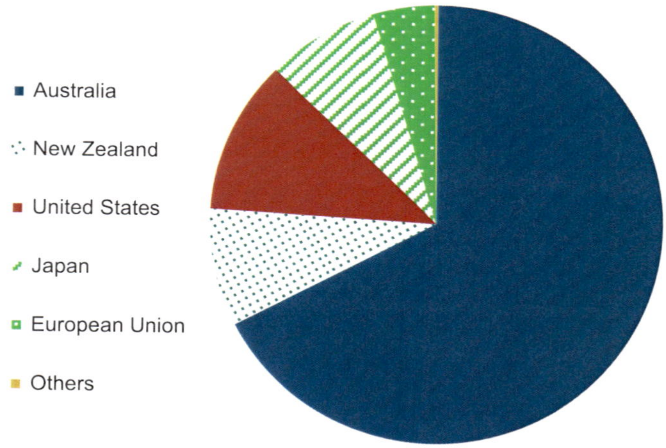

Figure 6.13 Official Development Aid by Donors (*Percent of aid, 2012*)

Source: World Bank, *World Development Indicators*.

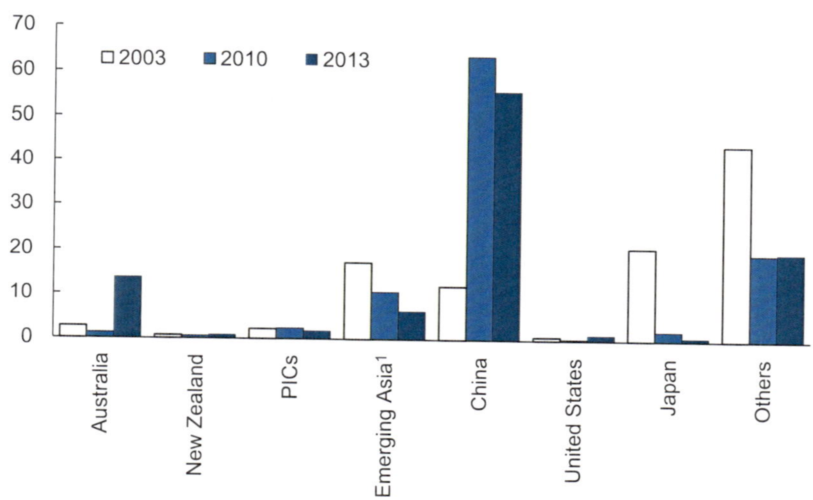

Figure 6.14 Solomon Islands: Exports by Destination (*Percent of total*)

Sources: Country authorities; and IMF staff calculations.
Note: PICs = Pacific island countries.
[1]Excludes China.

between the real GDP growth rates of Australia, New Zealand, and Asia's emerging markets suggests an increasing comovement between the business cycles of PICs and their neighboring economies over the last two decades, with the correlation increasing over the last 10 years (Figure 6.17).

Econometric Analysis: Baseline Scenario

The econometric analysis further investigates the relevance of potential growth spillovers from the global and regional economies. We use a vector error correction model for each PIC to gauge the impact of global and regional growth spillovers on individual PICs. We use annual data from the late

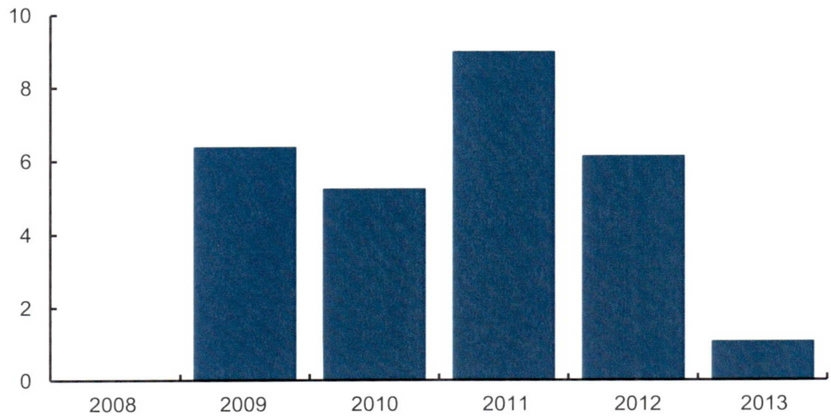

Figure 6.15 Tonga: Loan Disbursements from China (*Percent of GDP*)

Source: Country authorities.

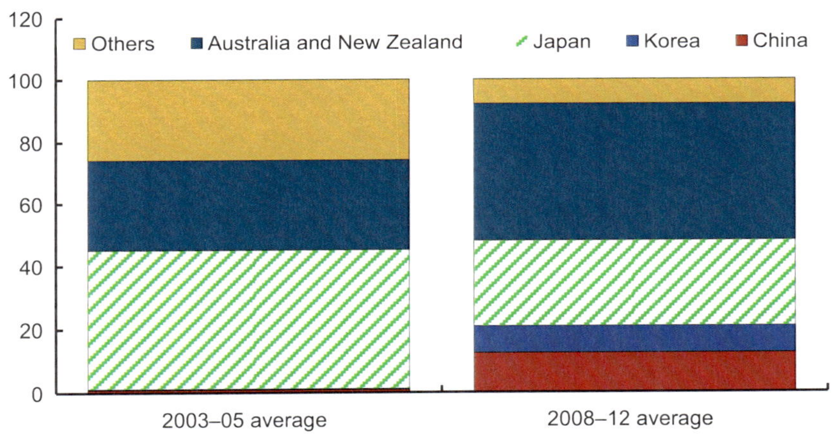

Figure 6.16 Foreign Direct Investment (FDI) by Country of Origin (*Percent of total FDI*)

Sources: Data from the Organisation for Economic Co-operation and Development; and United Nations Centre for Trade and Development.

Note: Includes Australia, China, Korea, Japan, France, Germany, Italy, Luxembourg, Netherlands, New Zealand, Sweden, United Kingdom, and United States.

1970s through 2011.[5] The analysis examines both short- and long-term dynamics using historical data. We use a cointegration technique to identify the long-term relationship between GDP in PICs and the GDP of their main trading partners, using variables expressed in levels.[6] We use that long-term relationship to build a structural model that captures both long- and short-term dynamics, which is then employed for scenario analysis. Focusing on individual PICs—rather than treating them as a homogeneous group—sheds light on spillovers specific to each country.

[5] A shorter sample period may apply, depending on country data availability.

[6] Cointegration models are preferable to single equation models, with variables expressed in percentage changes, because the former can capture both long- and short-term relationships among variables, not just the short-term ones.

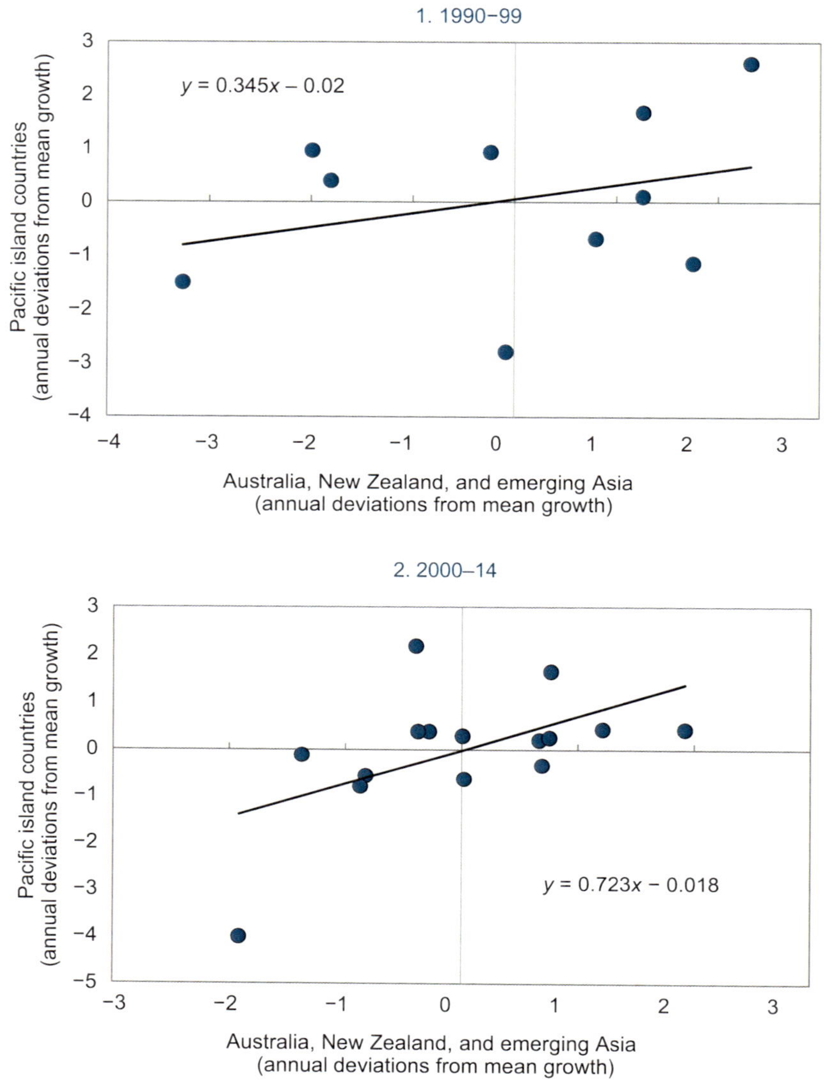

Figure 6.17 Pacific Island Countries: Correlation of Real GDP Growth with Australia, New Zealand, and Emerging Asia (*1990–99 and 2000–14*)

Sources: Country authorities; and IMF staff calculations.

Our main findings are summarized as follows (with technical details in Annex 6.1):

- Using a subsample analysis, PICs appear to be more integrated with Australia's, New Zealand's, and Asia's emerging market economies than they were 20 years ago, suggesting an increase in growth spillovers from the region.
- Australia is by far the main source of direct and indirect spillovers, both in the short and long term, with the exception of the compact agreement countries. Australia sometimes has an indirect impact on PICs through New Zealand. Direct spillovers from New Zealand are also highly relevant for several PICs.
- Over the last decade, shocks from Asia's emerging market economies had a greater impact than in the past on PICs' business cycles (that is, the short term). This suggests that the role of Asia's

emerging markets in explaining output in PICs has increased, while that of more traditional partners, such as Japan, has declined.

- In the short term, the elasticity of output with respect to regional partners is at times higher than one, suggesting greater scope for policies to stabilize the business cycle.
- In the short term, the main channel of spillovers is commodity prices, consistent with the analysis presented earlier. The adverse-oil-shock scenario discussed in the following section shows a larger and more negative impact on growth than the global-demand-shock scenario, confirming that PICs are very vulnerable to commodity price shocks. Conversely, this also suggests that the potentially protracted decline in commodity prices—including oil prices—starting in mid-2014 will provide some support for their economic prospects, despite lingering global economic uncertainties (Box 6.1).

Econometric Analysis: Downside Scenarios

We simulate the impact on PICs' growth of two external downside scenarios consistent with two global scenarios developed using the IMF's Global Economy Model.[7] Using the econometric models already discussed, we estimate the spillovers to individual PICs from global and regional economies.

The first downside global scenario assumes a negative global demand shock due to financial turmoil in the euro area. This scenario implies that global growth falls short of baseline projections by about 1½ percentage points in the years $t + 1$ and $t + 2$, with the euro area growth rate declining by 2.5 percentage points in $t + 1$ and a further decline of 1.1 percentage points in $t + 2$. The direct spillovers from stress in the euro area to PICs are estimated to be limited. The slowdown in global growth would spill over to PICs within the same year through their regional partners and the United States.[8] For the commodity importers, the decline in GDP growth is estimated, on average, at a little over ½ percentage point each year, compared with the baseline. For the PIC commodity exporters, the impact on growth would be much larger, declining by almost 1 percentage point in each year of the shock. The milder impact on commodity importers depends on the fact that oil prices would decline under this scenario because of lower global growth (Figures 6.18 to 6.21).

The impact on PICs' growth from an adverse-oil-shock scenario—the second scenario—would be substantial. This assumes a negative oil-price shock triggered by geopolitical uncertainty in the Middle East that would raise the real oil price by 50 percent, relative to the baseline, for at least two years. Global output growth would thus be lower than the baseline by about ½ percentage point in $t + 1$ and a little more than 1 percentage point in $t + 2$. Simulations using the vector error correction model suggest that negative spillovers spurred by higher oil prices will reduce all PIC growth rates in both years, except for the commodity exporters Papua New Guinea and Timor-Leste, whose terms of trade would improve.[9] The decline would average about 1½ percentage points of GDP for fuel commodity importers—where the baseline trend growth is already low, at about 2 percent. On average, this impact on PIC growth would be larger than in the previous scenario (where the financial turmoil in the euro area intensifies). In part, the greater sensitivity of PICs to global oil and commodity prices reflects the large weight of fuel and food in the consumer price index basket, the comparatively high dependence on fuel imports, and the relatively larger share of imported items in consumption and investment, owing to their smaller domestic manufacturing base. It also reflects the fact that PICs would have to cope with higher oil prices amid slower growth among their trading partners.

[7] See IMF (2012b) for a description of these scenarios.

[8] The U.S. growth rate is assumed to fall by 0.75 percentage point at $t + 1$ and by 0.6 percentage point at $t + 2$. In Asia's emerging market economies, growth is assumed to decline by 0.8 percentage point at $t + 1$ and by 0.4 percentage point at $t + 2$. For other countries (a grouping of countries in the Global Economy Model that includes Australia and New Zealand, among others) growth is estimated to decline by 1½ percentage points at $t + 1$ and by ½ percentage point at $t + 2$, relative to the baseline.

[9] The sensitivity of PICs' growth rates to global commodity price shocks is similar to that described in Chapter 13.

Box 6.1. Impact of Lower Oil Prices on Pacific Island Country Oil Importers

Commodity prices fell by almost one-fifth in the first nine months of 2015, mainly driven by sharply lower fuel prices. Between June 2014 and September 2015, crude oil prices fell by 57 percent on account of strong supply and concerns about future demand (Figure 6.1.1). In the October 2015 *World Economic Outlook* (IMF 2015c), average oil prices were projected to fall by 46 percent in 2015, and to decline further in 2016.

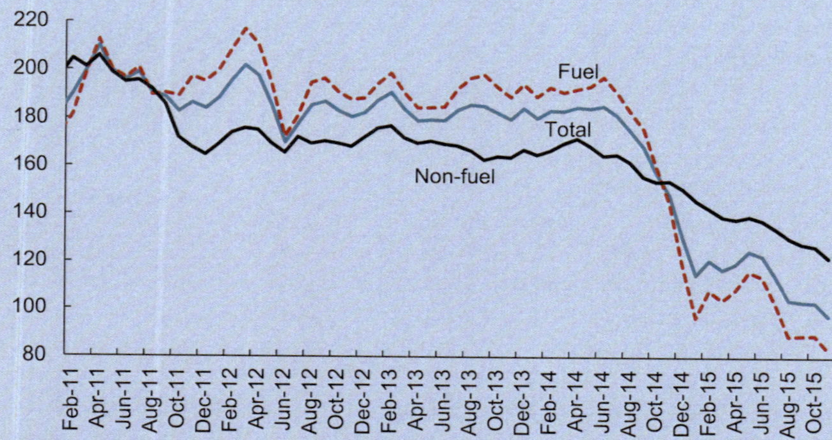

Figure 6.1.1 IMF Commodity Price Indices *(2005 = 100)*

Sources: IMF World Economic Outlook database.

Based on our findings, a 40 percent drop in commodity and oil prices implies a boost to economic growth in Pacific island countries (PICs) by an average of 2 percentage points, all other things being equal.[1] This positive effect on growth appears to be broadly confirmed by growth forecast revisions for PICs following the downward revision in oil price forecasts in October 2015. While PIC average growth outlook in 2015 was weighed down by a number of negative shocks—including the devastation wrought by Cyclone Pam—the overall growth trajectory appears to receive a boost from lower oil prices (Figure 6.1.2).

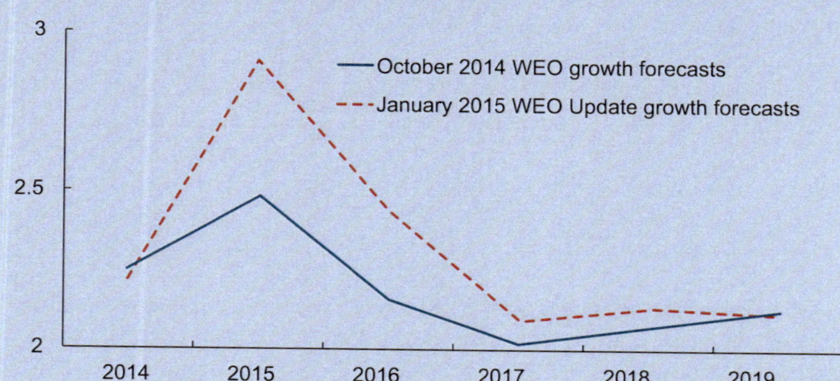

Figure 6.1.2 PIC Oil Importers: Growth Projections under Different Oil Price Assumptions *(Percent)*

Sources: IMF, World Economic Outlook (WEO) database, October 2014 and January 2015; and IMF staff calculations.
Note: Oil price forecasts in the October 2014 WEO were US$98/barrel for 2015 and $93 a barrel for 2016; forecasts in the January 2015 WEO Update were $51 a barrel for 2015 and $59 a barrel for 2016. PIC = Pacific island country.

[1] Based on results for Fiji, Kiribati, Marshall Islands, Micronesia, Palau, and the Solomon Islands, for which a statistically significant relationship between oil and commodity prices is found.

Box 6.1. (*Continued*)

More broadly, estimates for PICs from IMF country teams, amid expectations of lower oil prices, also point to lower input costs supporting growth, lowering inflation, strengthening current account balance, and marginally improving the fiscal position of oil importers in 2015 and 2016 (Figure 6.1.3).

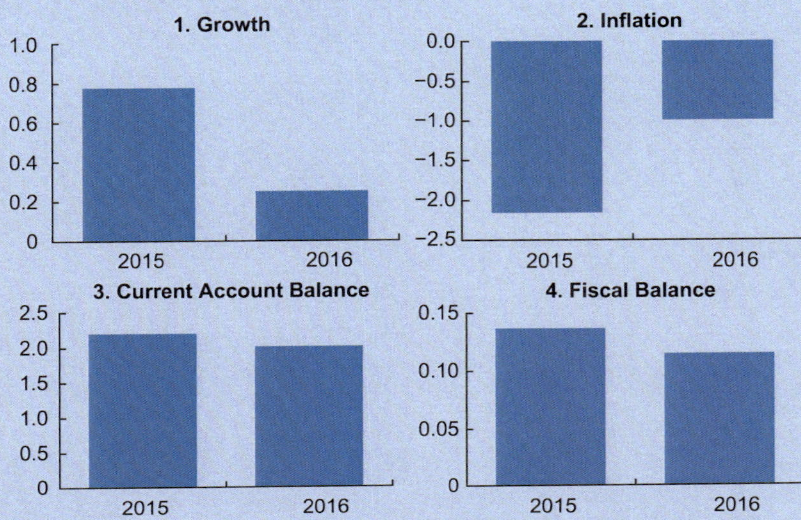

Figure 6.1.3 Impact of Lower Commodity Prices on PIC Oil Importers: Average Differential from Baseline Projections (*Percentage points*)

Source: IMF staff calculations.
Note: PICs = Pacific island countries. Based on simple averages. In both scenarios, countries with an independent monetary policy are assumed to be taking monetary policy action. The differential is calculated as the difference from the latest baseline projections as of December 2014.

ASSESSING SPILLOVERS TO THE FINANCIAL SECTOR

The financial sector in PICs is also closely integrated with regional economies. It consists mainly of foreign-owned banks—primarily Australian—and large provident or trust funds. Banks from other countries include a Papua New Guinea domestic bank (Bank South Pacific), which has operations in Fiji, Samoa, the Solomon Islands, and Tonga, and France's BRED Bank, which is present in Fiji and Vanuatu (see Annex Table 6.2.1 for a list of commercial banks in the PICs). Over the last few years, a number of domestically incorporated banks have entered the financial sector in PICs and in at least a number of cases, these have also been funded through the injection of foreign capital. Foreign banks in PICs have been profitable and proved resilient to the global financial crisis. Reflecting their asset allocation mix and large exposure to global financial markets, the provident and trust funds did not cope as well with the global financial crisis.

The size of the banking sector varies across PICs. Not surprisingly, total bank assets (in U.S. dollar terms) are greatest in the largest economies, although not as a percent of GDP. Relative to GDP, the size of the banking system is broadly in line with Asia's low-income countries. Reflecting the small size of PIC economies, the banking sector consists generally of a small number of commercial banks or even just one bank, as in Kiribati and Tuvalu (Figures 6.22 and 6.23).

The banks are well capitalized, with high total capital and Tier 1 capital adequacy ratios. This provides a buffer against financial shocks (Figures 6.24 and 6.25). Reflecting the vulnerability of PICs to shocks, the authorities have in many cases opted for a capital requirement ratio in excess of the Basel II minimum requirements. Furthermore, several banks exceed the required minimum ratio, which varies widely across the islands.

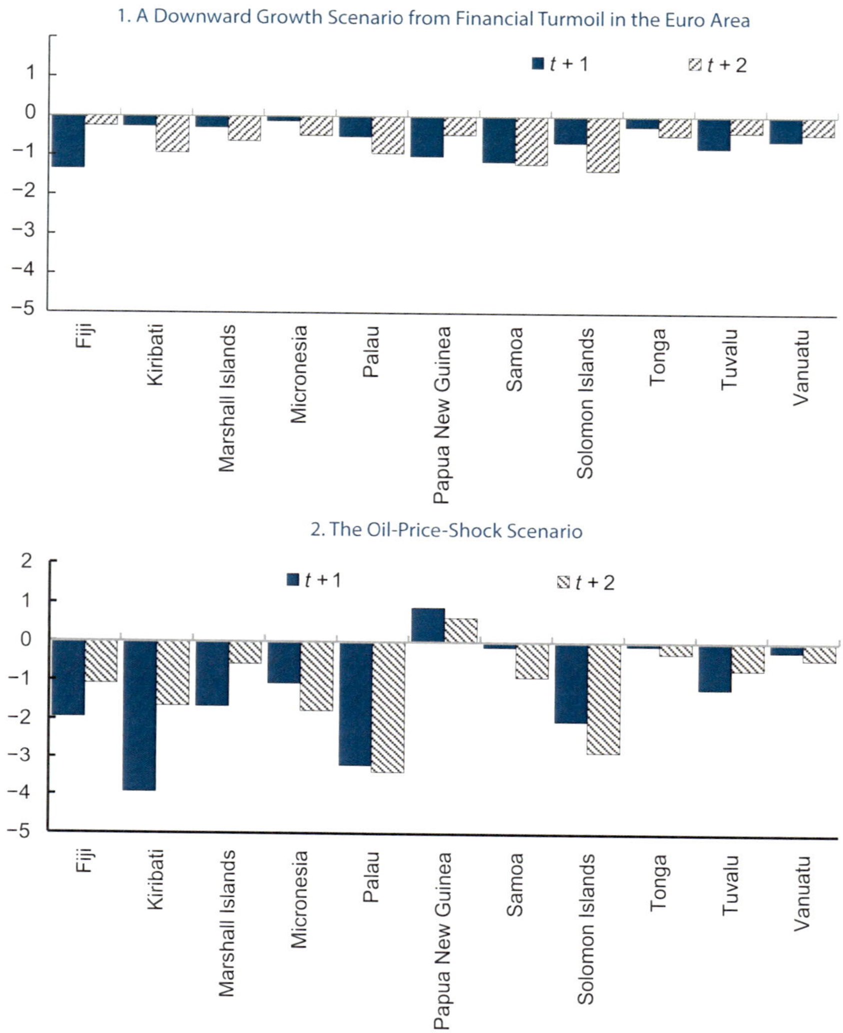

Figure 6.18 Pacific Island Countries: Change in Growth under Different Scenarios (*Percent*)

Source: IMF staff calculations.

Because banks rely largely on domestic deposits for funding, the funding structure provides an additional buffer against turmoil in international financial markets. The lower loan-to-deposit ratios in Papua New Guinea and the Solomon Islands reflect the large excess liquidity these countries have faced since the global financial crisis. Given the large bank capitalization, high loan-to-deposit ratios do not necessarily imply reliance on wholesale funding. These ratios have been generally stable in recent years, with the exception of Tonga and the Solomon Islands, where banks have improved their funding profiles since 2008 by increasing their reliance on deposits (Figures 6.26 and 6.27).

The quality of loans in PICs appears to be relatively good, with some variation reflecting country-specific circumstances, including collateral laws.[10] The ratio of loan-loss provisioning to total

[10] In most PICs, land is owned by the government and by families (communal land) rather than individuals. This often makes property rights unclear and constrains the use of land as collateral.

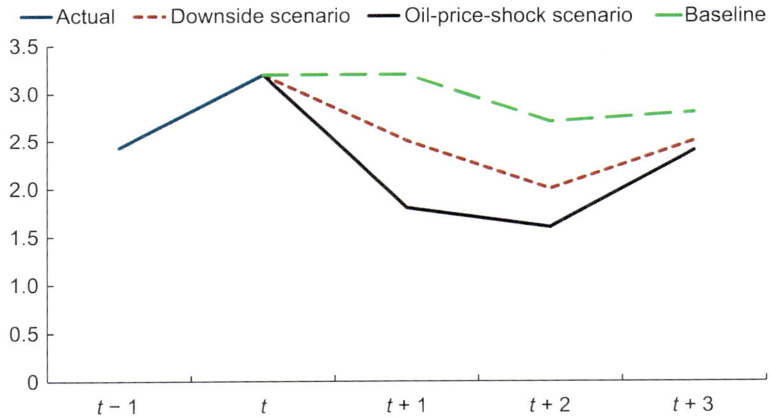

Figure 6.19 Pacific Island Countries: Real GDP Growth under Different Scenarios (*Percent*)

Source: IMF staff estimates.

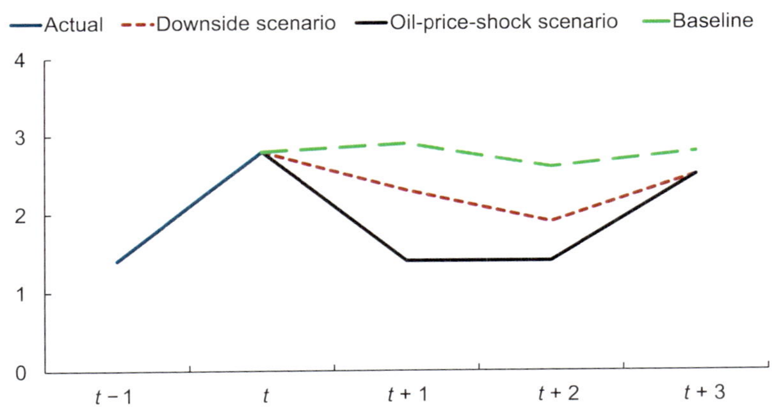

Figure 6.20 Pacific Island Countries: Real GDP Growth for Commodity Importers (*Percent*)

Source: IMF staff estimates.

loans—a proxy for loan quality—suggests an improvement across almost all PICs after the global financial crisis (Figure 6.28).

Provident and Trust Funds

A more direct effect of a global economic slowdown will occur through the impact on PICs' provident and trust funds. These are large, relative both to GDP (Table 6.1) and to the size of the domestic banking systems. In some cases, the objective of the funds is to provide retirement benefits, while in others it is to finance budget deficits. The experience during the global financial crisis highlights the vulnerability of these funds, as demonstrated by the negative returns on investment exceeding 20 percent for the compact trust funds of Micronesia and Marshall Islands (Table 6.2).

The domestic versus foreign investment split of asset portfolios differs considerably across PICs. The difference naturally means that the implications for the vulnerability of the funds to external shocks vary.

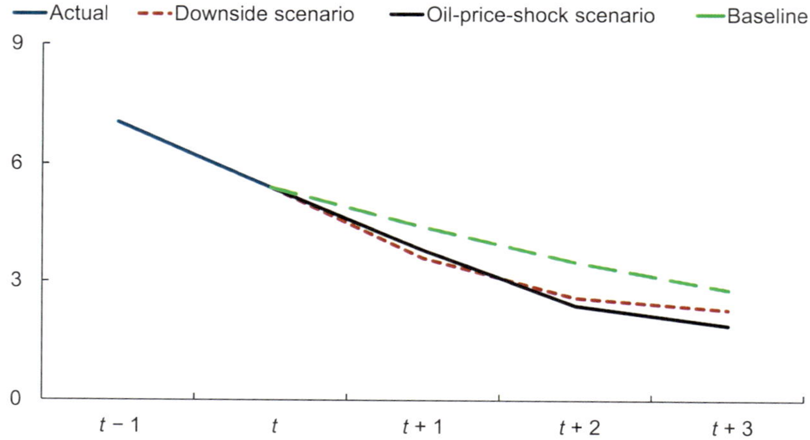

Figure 6.21 Pacific Island Countries: Real GDP Growth for Commodity Exporters (*Percent*)

Source: IMF staff estimates.

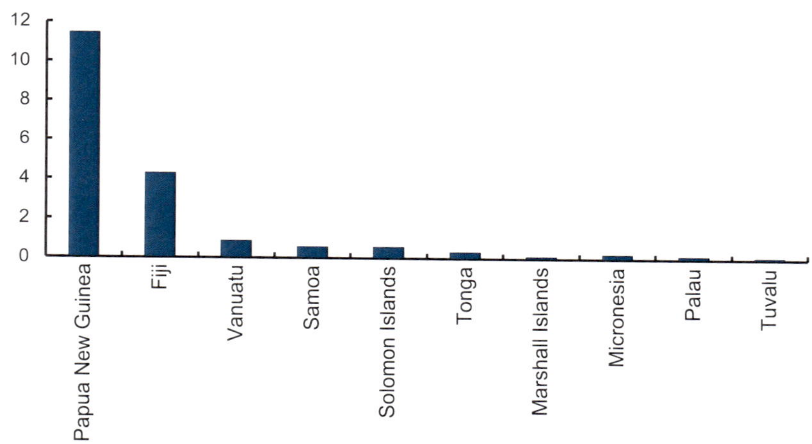

Figure 6.22 Banking Sector Total Assets (*Billions of U.S. dollars, 2014*)

Sources: Country authorities; and IMF staff estimates.

Note: The National Bank of Tuvalu performs some monetary functions, including the holding of government accounts and foreign assets.

Spillovers from a Downside Scenario

Although banks in PICs seem somewhat sheltered from shocks through their ownership and funding structures, the financial systems of PICs remain vulnerable to any worsening in the global economy.

Financial stress could occur through a fall in stock prices, which could affect PICs with large provident and trust funds whose assets are invested offshore (Kiribati, Marshall Islands, Micronesia, Palau, Tuvalu). Lower GDP growth attributable to a fall in remittances and tourism receipts would weaken the quality of loans and reduce banks' profitability, which in turn would affect banks' liquidity. Noninterest income, arising largely out of foreign exchange activities, plays a key role in deter-

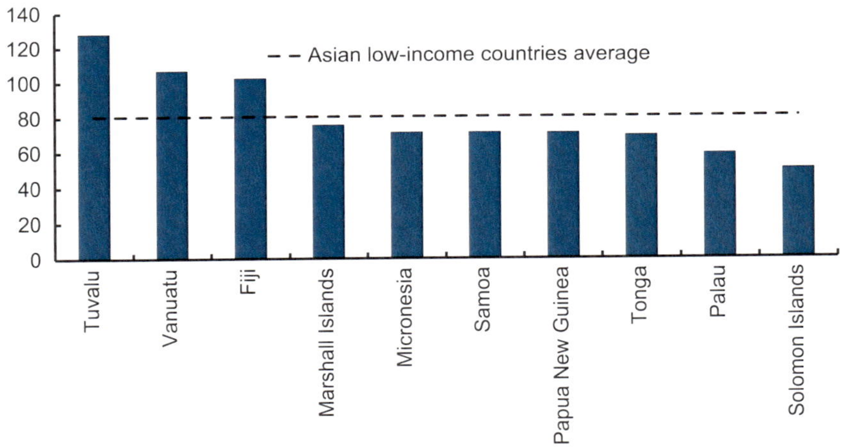

Figure 6.23 Banking Sector Total Assets (*Percent of GDP, 2014*)

Sources: Country authorities; and IMF staff estimates.

Note: The National Bank of Tuvalu performs some monetary functions, including the holding of government accounts and foreign assets.

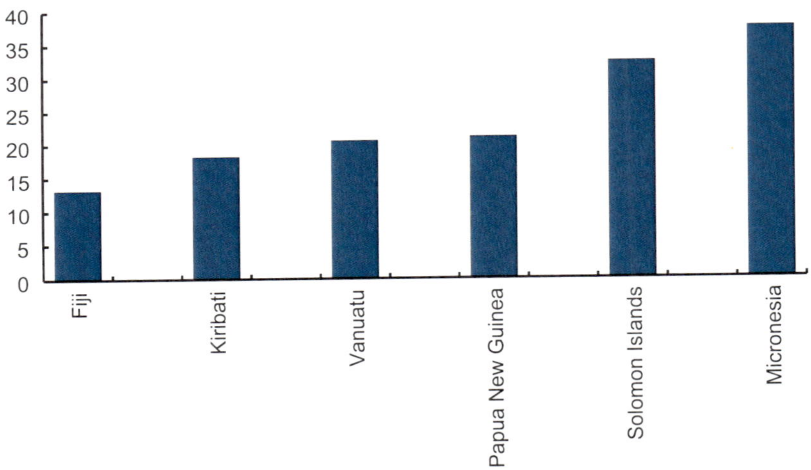

Figure 6.24 Banking Sector Total Capital Ratio (*Percent, 2013*)

Sources: Country authorities; and IMF staff estimates.

mining bank profitability in the region and is higher than in other regional comparators (Table 6.3).[11] Thus, a slowdown in tourism and remittances will put downward pressure on profits. Banks may attempt to make up for this lost revenue through higher interest rates, which could further stifle credit growth.

A prolonged slowdown in credit growth would hinder private sector development and lower prospects for inclusive growth. Both demand and supply factors are likely to lead to lower credit growth. Tighter credit standards, as occurred after the global financial crisis, will likely follow heightened global uncertainty and turmoil in global financial markets; and lower economic growth

[11] See Davies and Vaught (2011) for a more detailed discussion of bank profits in PICs.

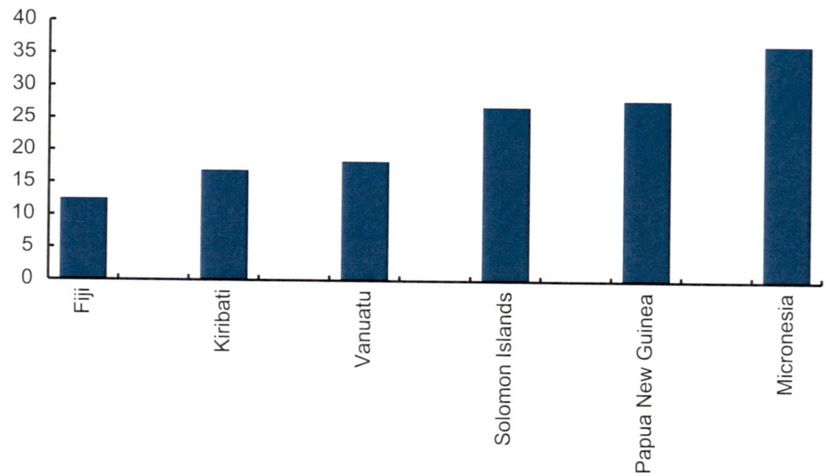

Figure 6.25 Banking Sector Tier 1 Capital Ratio (*Percent, 2013*)

Sources: Country authorities; and IMF staff estimates.

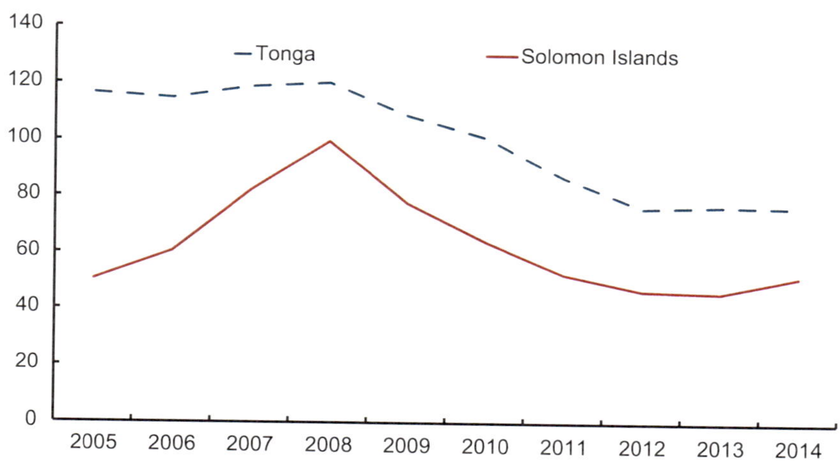

Figure 6.26 Banking Sector Loan-to-Deposit Ratios (*Percent*)

Sources: Country authorities; and IMF staff estimates.

coupled with potentially higher interest rates will reduce demand for credit. During 2008–09, credit growth fell across all PICs, with the largest declines—albeit from a high base—in commodity exporters. Since then, credit growth has remained anemic, with some mild signs of pickup in commodity exporters, but it has not yet recovered in commodity importers (Figures 6.29 and 6.30).[12]

A scenario where financial turmoil in the euro area leads to the deleveraging of European banks, for instance, could trigger a funding shock to Australian banks given their relatively high reliance on wholesale funding. But this risk is limited. Australian banks were highly resilient to the global financial crisis, mainly because of sound regulation and supervision. The government's Guarantee Scheme

[12] In the commodity exporters (Papua New Guinea, the Solomon Islands), favorable terms of trade continue to support growth. Investment in the commodity sector lately has been financed mainly offshore, through FDI.

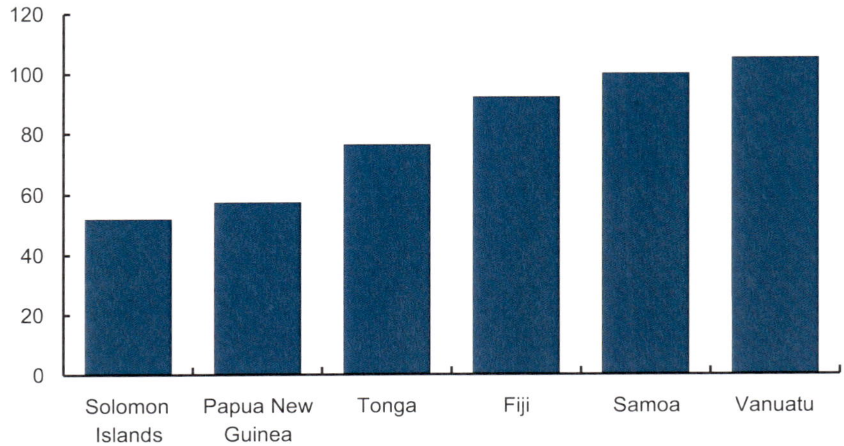

Figure 6.27 Banking Sector Loan-to-Deposit Ratios (*Percent, 2014*)

Sources: Country authorities; and IMF staff estimates.

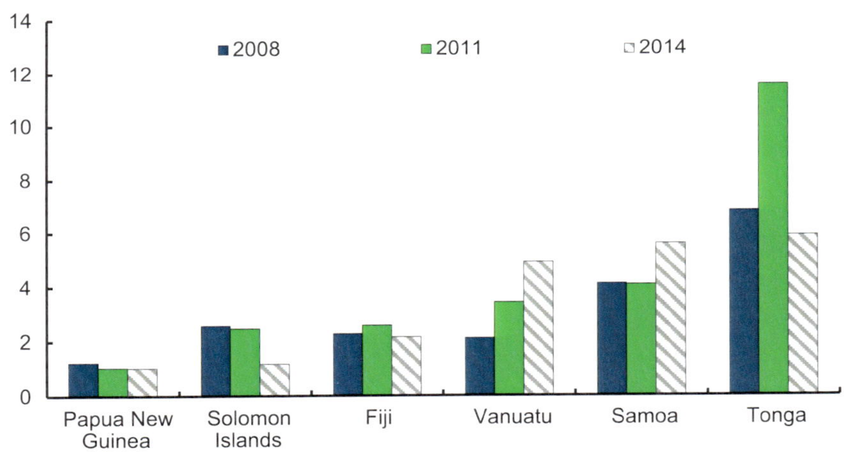

Figure 6.28 Banking Sector Ratios of Provision Expense to Gross Loans (*Percent*)

Sources: Country authorities; and IMF staff estimates.

for Large Deposits and Wholesale Funding for banks, begun in late 2008, also helped maintain access to funding, as did the swap arrangement between the Reserve Bank of Australia and the U.S. Federal Reserve. Indeed, an IMF study (Jauregui and Schule 2011) suggests that Australia is better placed to cope with shocks from the deterioration of the global outlook than any other country, because of its large policy space and flexible exchange rate (IMF 2014).

Our analysis suggests that the ratio of provisions to loans would increase by nearly 1 percent in the event of a downside scenario (Figure 6.31). To estimate the impact of negative spillovers on PIC banks from a global slowdown, we use the growth results generated by the previous vector error correction model analysis for PICs and previous IMF analysis (Jauregui and Schule 2011) to gauge the impact of the deterioration of the global outlook on Australia.[13] We then estimate the impact of the

[13] According to Jauregui and Schule (2011), Australia's growth rate drops by 1½ percentage points in the first year after the global negative shock and by 1 percentage point in the second year.

TABLE 6.1

Pacific Island Countries: Selected Sovereign Funds

Name	Country	Date Created	Estimated Value (Percent of GDP)			
			2007	2010	2012	2013
Trust Fund for the People of the Federated States of Micronesia (FSM Compact Trust Fund)	Micronesia	2004	48.0	60.4	78.9	102.7
Trust Fund for the People of the Republic of the Marshall Islands (RMI Compact Trust Fund)	Marshall Islands	2004	57.1	68.8	89.8	107.6
Revenue Equalization Reserve Fund (RERF)	Kiribati	1956	407.9	335.7	338.3	353.4
Tuvalu Trust Fund (TTF)	Tuvalu	1987	335.3	311.2	339.1	354.3
Petroleum Fund of Timor-Leste (Petroleum Fund)	Timor-Leste	2005	70.4	163.8	210.5	285.9
Fiji National Provident Fund (FNPF)	Fiji	1966	63.4	58.1	56.6	56.5
Nambawan Super (Nambawan)	Papua New Guinea	1961	12.0	11.7	11.7	12.3
Marshall Islands Social Security Trust Fund (MISSA)	Marshall Islands	1991	45.3	42.0	40.0	39.0
Palau Compact Trust Fund	Palau	1994	83.4	76.5	73.1	77.1

Sources: Annual Reports; and authors' estimates.

TABLE 6.2

Pacific Island Countries: Rates of Return on Sovereign Fund Assets *(Percent)*

	FY06	FY07	FY08	FY09	FY10	FY11	FY12	FY13
FSM Compact Fund	–10.0	18.4	–22.9	–1.8	17.4	–1.1	35.2	40.8
Fiji National Provident Fund	7.4	5.9	5.5	6.9	6.2	6.8	6.6	7.2
Kiribati RERF	7.4	3.7	–7.7	5.1	4.0	3.3	12.8	9.5
RMI Social Security Administration	9.1	11.6	–9.9	5.1	8.2	–2.3	10.9	. . .
RMI Compact Fund	14.6	20.4	–23.0	2.0	9.3	–2.6	20.4	14.8
Palau Compact Trust Fund	6.8	16.2	–13.2	1.9	9.0	0.9	21.5	14.0
PNG Nambawan	10.9	27.0	7.4	9.9	12.5	0.8	11.8	10.3
Timor Leste Petroleum Fund	4.3	5.4	10.7	0.7	4.1	3.2	4.3	3.2
Tuvalu Trust Fund (TTF)	4.6	5.1	–12.7	2.0	11.4	7.2	10.6	12.0

Source: Annual Reports.
Note: FSM = Federated States of Micronesia; RMI = Republic of the Marshall Islands.

TABLE 6.3

Interest and Noninterest Income in Pacific Island Countries and Selected Regional Comparators

	Net Interest Income (Percent of Total Assets, 2013)[1]	Noninterest Operations (Percent of Average Assets, 2013)[1]
Fiji	3.0	2.7
Papua New Guinea	3.8	2.0
Samoa	4.9	3.6
Solomon Islands	3.9	4.1
Tonga	4.0	4.3
Vanuatu	3.8	3.0
Australia	1.7	1.3
New Zealand	0.5	0.2
Indonesia	4.9	2.4
Malaysia	1.9	1.4
Philippines	2.7	2.2

Sources: Country authorities; IMF, Financial Soundness Indicators database; and IMF staff estimates.
[1] Papua New Guinea data are for 2012.

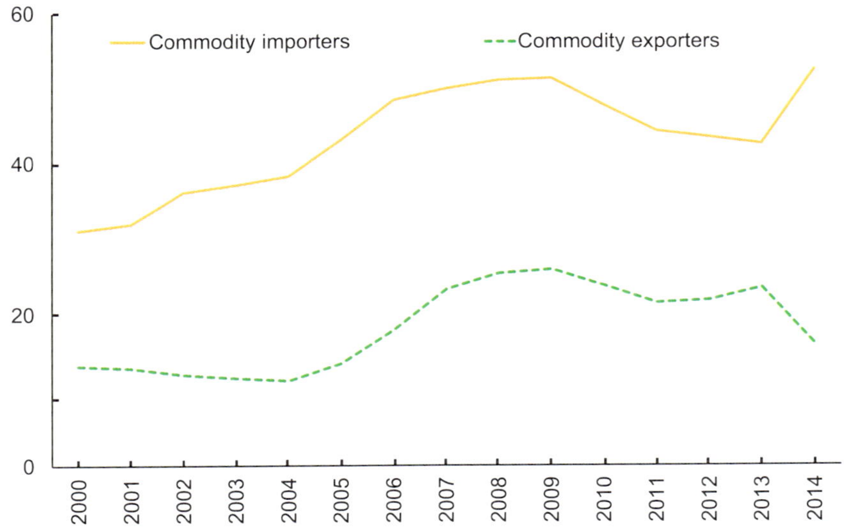

Figure 6.29 Pacific Island Countries: Credit to Private Sector (*Percent of GDP*)

Source: IMF staff estimates.

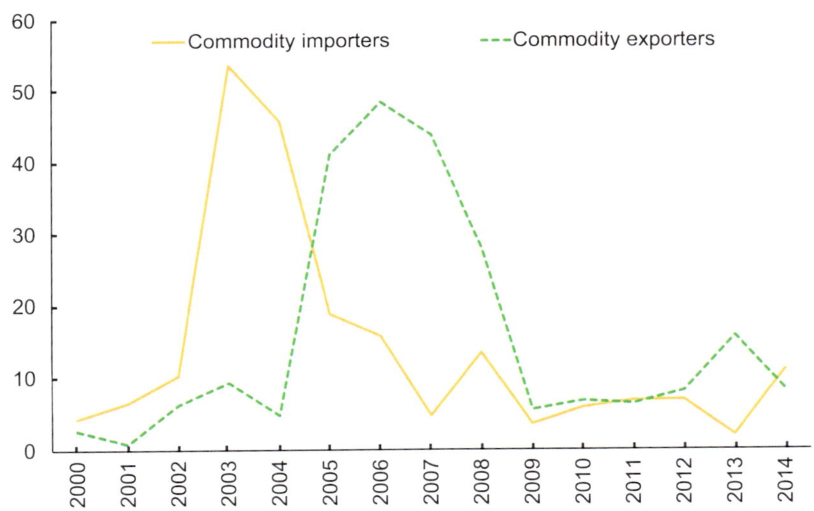

Figure 6.30 Pacific Island Countries: Change in Credit to Private Sector (*Percent, year-over-year*)

Source: IMF staff estimates.

slowdown on banks' provisioning. Simple econometric analysis suggests that the ratio of provisions to loans in PICs is linked to both the Australian and domestic business cycles, with all coefficients significant and with the expected sign.

WHAT ROLE FOR POLICIES? REBUILDING POLICY BUFFERS AND IMPLEMENTING STRUCTURAL REFORMS

The policy response to a downward economic scenario would vary across PICs depending on their policy space. Fiscal space is limited in countries with high public debt, narrowing the scope for countercyclical policies (Figure 6.32). In some countries with large trust funds, fiscal rules that

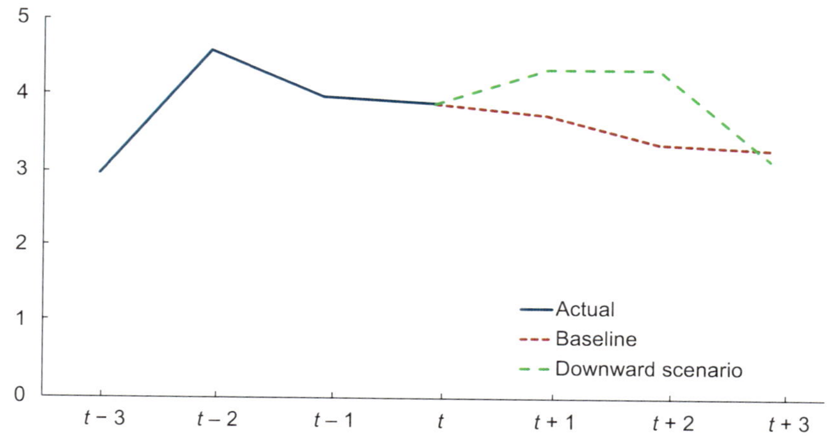

Figure 6.31 Pacific Island Countries: Impact of a Downward Scenario on the Financial Sector: Ratio of Provisions to Loans (*Percent*)

Source: IMF staff estimates.

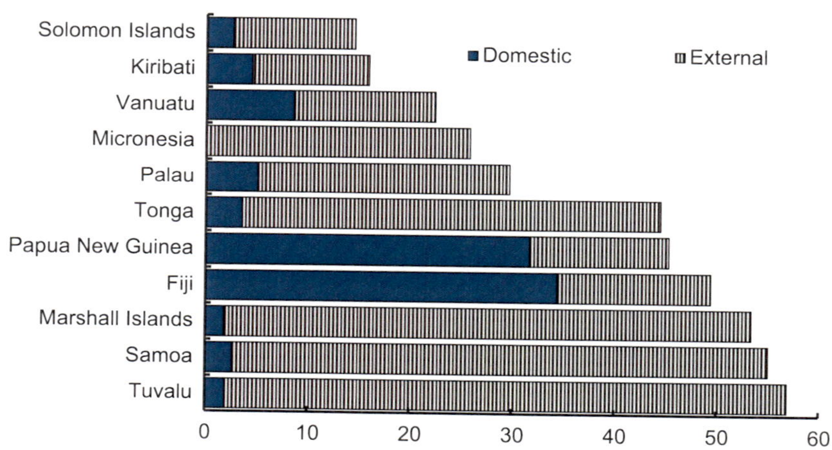

Figure 6.32 Public Debt, 2014 (*Percent of GDP*)

Sources: Country authorities; and IMF staff calculations.

prevent additional drawdowns to finance budget deficits in the face of a crisis could also lead to procyclical policies. Addressing fiscal rigidities by reducing recurrent spending could help make fiscal policy less procyclical (see Chapter 10 for further discussion). While fiscal space in some PICs (Kiribati, Marshall Islands, the Solomon Islands) has increased in recent years relative to the pre-crisis level, in others, fiscal space has diminished on account of lower underlying fiscal balances (Figure 6.33). All islands have accumulated comfortable levels of foreign exchange reserves, which could provide a temporary cushion. Greater exchange rate flexibility would be warranted in economies with relatively weak monetary transmission mechanisms. This is also the case in Papua New Guinea, where the exchange rate channel of monetary policy remains effective, but excess liquidity is currently weakening interest rates and credit channels. The onset of lower inflation pressure because of falling oil prices has also reduced the monetary policy trade-off, increasing policy space.

To strengthen their resilience to shocks, PICs need to step up the rebuilding of policy buffers. Most PICs have made progress on this front since the global financial crisis, especially on reserves.

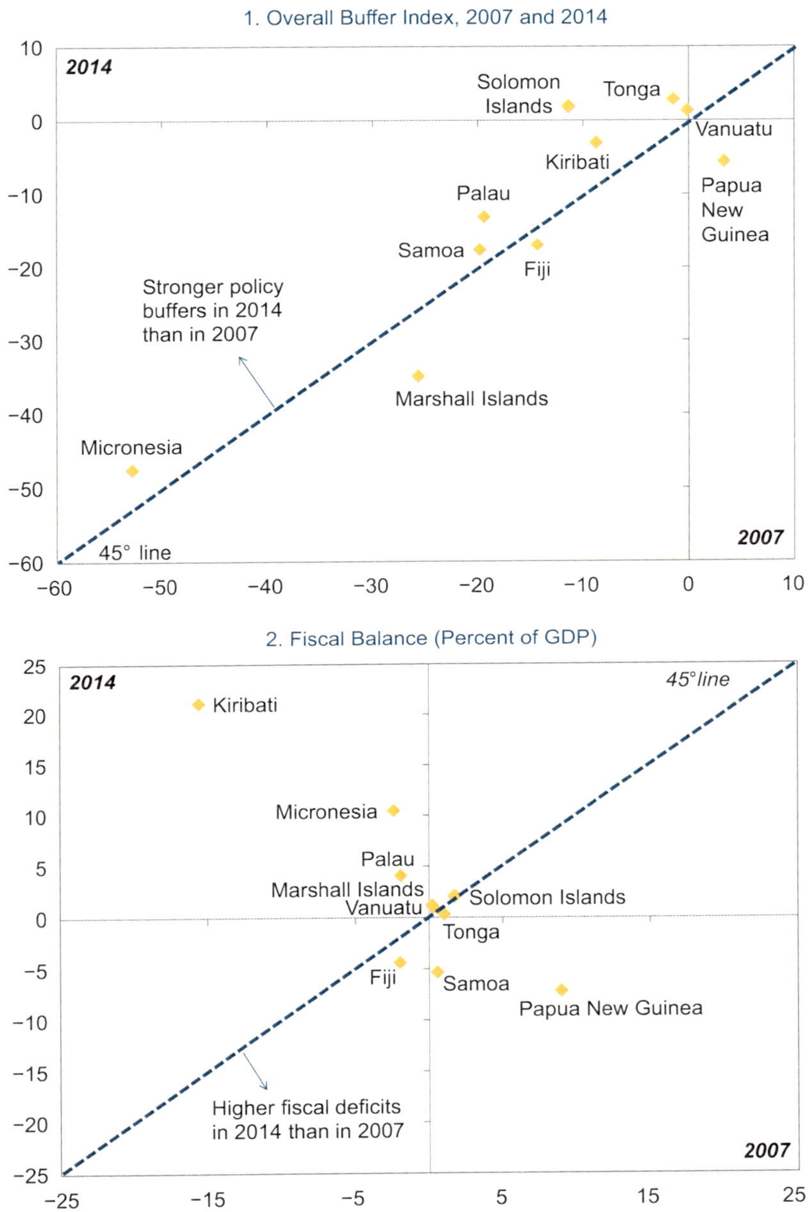

Figure 6.33 Rebuilding Policy Buffers

However, more than half of PICs emerged from the crisis with somewhat less comfortable fiscal buffers (higher debt and larger fiscal deficits). Implementing growth-oriented structural reforms would help boost investor confidence and ensure sustainable and inclusive growth. Savings from the windfall of lower oil prices should be used to rebuild buffers and cushion the effects of revenue volatility, as well as put PICs in better stead to deal with the threat of natural disasters. This is particularly critical given that aid flows are expected to slowly decline in the medium and long term. In addition, focusing on the quality of spending and improving the spending mix toward education, health, and infrastructure will be key in lifting long-term growth potential.

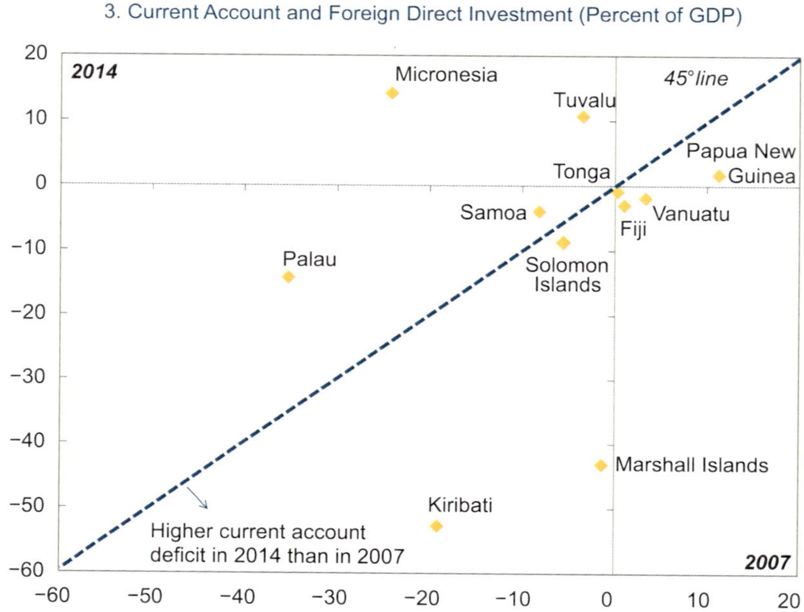

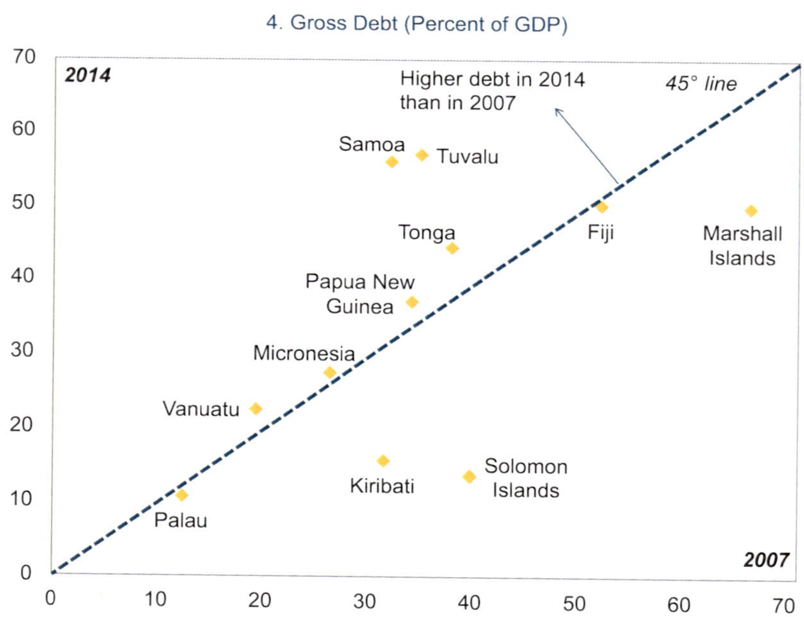

Figure 6.33 *(Continued)*

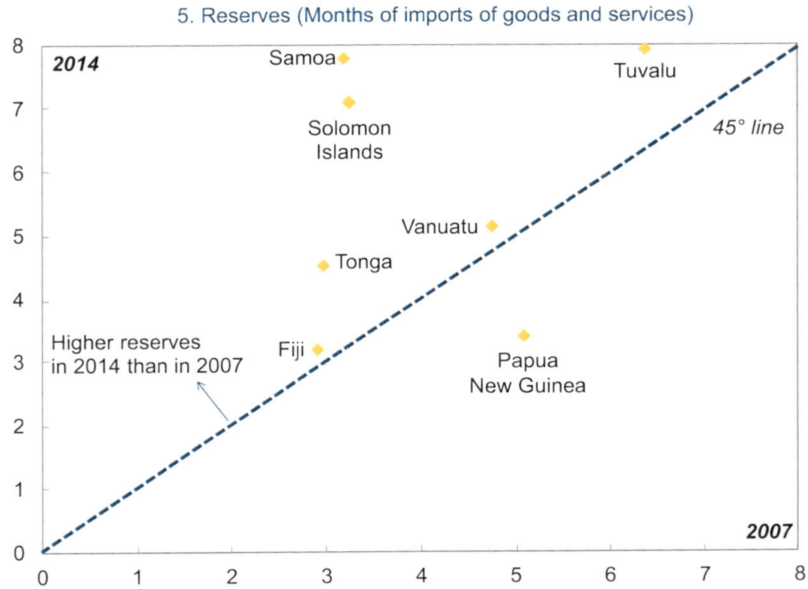

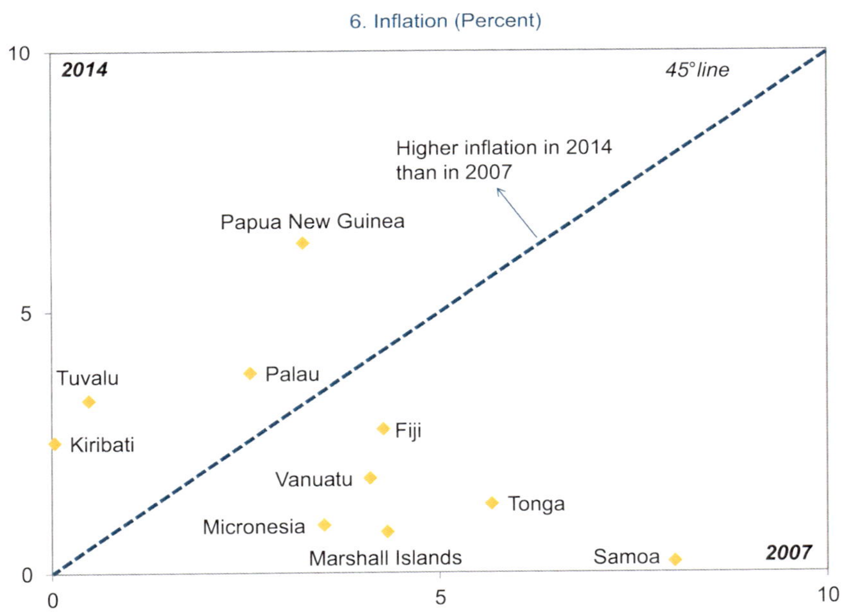

Figure 6.33 *(Continued)*

Sources: IMF, World Economic Outlook database; and IMF staff estimates.

ANNEX 6.1. TECHNICAL SUMMARY OF ECONOMETRIC METHODOLOGY AND RESULTS

Econometric Methodology

Econometric analysis has given us an understanding of the short- and long-term relationships between GDP in each of the Pacific island countries (PICs) and GDP in other countries or regions. The analysis has also enabled us to assess the relevance of commodity price shocks in PICs, using measures of real oil prices, real food prices, or real nonoil commodity prices. We also investigated country-specific factors, such as shocks to sugar output in Fiji, the role of aid and remittances, and the impact of changes in global equity prices.

We employed three methodologies to this end. First, we used a cointegration analysis to test and estimate long-term relationships using a vector error correction model. Second, within the model, we used the impulse response analysis to gauge the impact on each PIC's real GDP of a shock to the other variables in the model. And third, a structural version of the error correction model gave us estimates of the immediate impact of shocks and formed the basis of the scenario analysis.

Summary of Econometric Results for Each Country

Using the Johansen procedure, we found a cointegrating relationship for 10 of the 11 countries examined. For each country, we present the cointegrating relationship: the coefficient on the partner GDP variable is the long-term elasticity of growth in the PIC with respect to external partner GDP.

Details are provided of any restrictions on the long-term elasticities that were imposed and not rejected; for example, in some cases the coefficient estimate was close to one, suggesting that when a trading partner's GDP increases over the long term, GDP in the PIC under examination increases by an equal percentage. From this long-term equation, a variable is constructed that measures the deviation from long-term equilibrium.

This variable is then used in a structural equation for each country, together with other variables that could influence growth in the short term. The structural equation shows the immediate or within-the-same-period spillover to the PIC from external demand and the impact of other shocks (such as food and fuel prices or global equity prices). The parameter estimates from the long-term equation and the structural equation are then used as inputs into the scenario analysis. See Annex Figure 6.1.1 for a summary of our findings for selected countries.

Fiji

Long-term equation:

We found a long-term cointegrating relationship between log real GDP in Fiji and log real GDP in Australia.[14]

$$\ln(RGDP^{FJI}) = 0.8^{*} \ln(RGDP^{AUS}) + constant$$

Structural equation:

$$\begin{aligned} D(\ln(RGDP^{FJI})) = {} & 1^{*}D(\ln(RGDP^{AUS})) \\ & -0.77^{*}ECM(-1) \\ & -0.03^{*}\ln(real\ oil) + 0.10^{*}\ln(sugar\ output) + constant \end{aligned}$$

[14]The cointegration analysis suggests two long-term relationships at work (that is, two cointegrating vectors): one between Australia and New Zealand and one between Fiji and Australia. The relationship between Australia and New Zealand is 1 to 1 in the long term, consistent with previous IMF analyses; see Sun (2011) for the importance of growth spillovers from Australia to New Zealand. Direct growth spillovers from Australia to Fiji were found to be stronger than from New Zealand. In the long term, a 1 percent increase in GDP in Australia will raise GDP in Fiji by 0.8 percent.

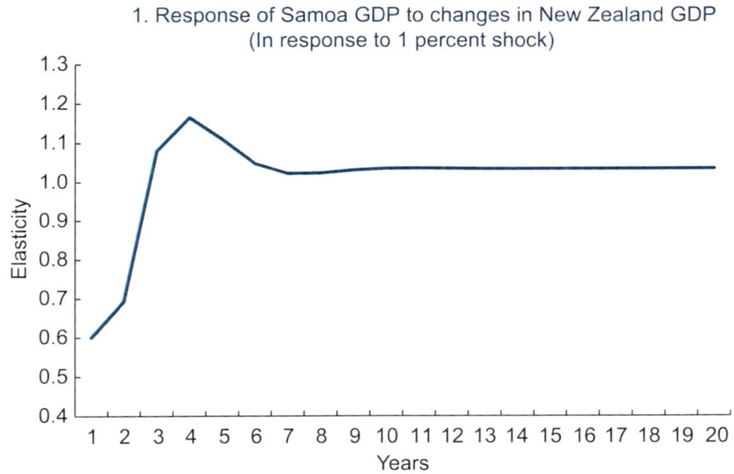

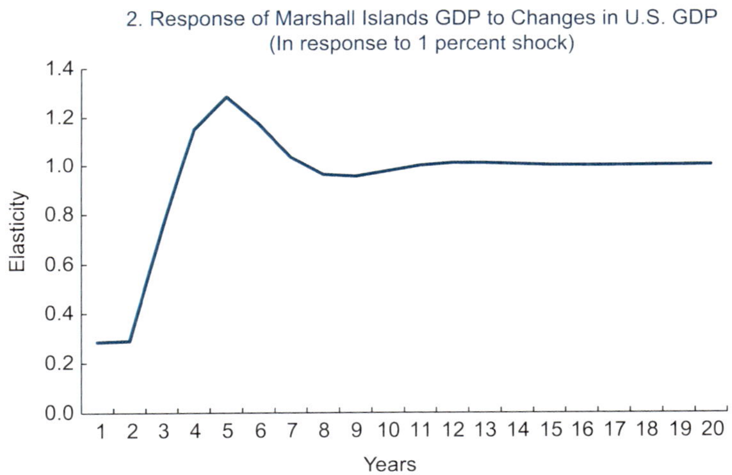

Annex Figure 6.1.1 Pacific Island Countries: Growth Spillovers

Source: IMF staff calculations.

In the short term, supply factors also matter in determining GDP in Fiji. On the domestic side, sugar output has a positive and significant coefficient, consistent with the importance of the sugar sector in the economy. A 1 percent increase in sugar production would boost GDP by 0.13 percent. As expected, higher international oil prices have a negative impact on output in Fiji.

Kiribati

Long-term equation:

A long-term cointegrating relationship was found between log real GDP in Kiribati and log real GDP in Australia.

$$\ln(RGDP^{KIR}) = 1 * \ln(RGDP^{AUS}) + constant$$

The restriction that the long-term elasticity was equal to one was not rejected (χ^2: 3.63, p-value 0.06).

Structural equation:

$$D(\ln(RGDP^{KIR})) = 0.43{*}D(\ln(RGDP^{AUS})) \\ -0.75{*}ECM(-1) \\ +0.05{*}\ln(\textit{world equity prices}) - 0.08{*}\ln(\textit{real oil}) + \textit{constant}$$

In the long term, growth in Australia spills over to Kiribati one for one. In the short term, fluctuations in Australian GDP affect Kiribati with an elasticity of 0.4. Real oil price shocks have a large impact on Kiribati GDP in the short term: a 10 percent increase in oil prices reduces GDP growth by 0.8 percentage point. World equity prices also influence Kiribati GDP in the short term, with a 10 percent rise in world equity prices boosting GDP by 0.5 percent.

Marshall Islands

Long-term equation:
We found a long-term cointegrating relationship between log real GDP in Marshall Islands and the United States.

$$\ln(RGDP^{MHL}) = 1{*}\ln(RGDP^{USA}) + \textit{constant}$$

The restriction that the long-term elasticity was equal to one was not rejected (χ^2: 5.68, p-value 0.06).
Structural equation:

$$D(\ln(RGDP^{MHL})) = 0.65{*}D(\ln(RGDP^{USA})) \\ -0.91{*}ECM(-1) \\ -0.03{*}\ln(\textit{real oil}) + \textit{constant}$$

In the long term, fluctuations in U.S. growth spill over to Marshall Islands one for one. In the short term, the impact is smaller but still large, with a short-term elasticity of 0.65. Real oil price shocks have a strong impact on the GDP of Marshall Islands in the short term, with a 10 percent increase in oil prices reducing GDP growth by 0.3 percent.

Micronesia

Long-term equation:
A long-term cointegrating relationship was found between log real GDP in Micronesia and the United States.

$$\ln(RGDP^{FSM}) = 1{*}\ln(RGDP^{USA}) + \textit{constant}$$

The restriction that the long-term elasticity was equal to one was not rejected (χ^2: 0.05, p-value 0.82).
Structural equation:

$$D(\ln(RGDP^{FSM})) = 0.84{*}D(\ln(RGDP^{USA})) \\ -0.58{*}ECM(-1) \\ -0.08{*}\ln(\textit{real oil}) + \textit{constant}$$

In the long term, fluctuations in U.S. growth spill over one for one to Micronesia, as in Marshall Islands. Most of this impact occurs quickly, with a short-term elasticity of 0.84. Real oil-price shocks have a large impact on Micronesia's GDP in the short term, with a 10 percent rise in oil prices lowering GDP growth by 0.8 percent.

Palau

Long-term equation:
A long-term cointegrating relationship was found between log real GDP in Palau and the United States.

$$\ln(RGDP^{PLW}) = 1*\ln(RGDP^{USA}) + constant$$

The restriction that the long-term elasticity was equal to one was not rejected (χ^2: 1.48, *p*-value 0.46).
Structural equation:

$$\begin{aligned} D(\ln(RGDP^{PLW})) = {} & 1.23*D(\ln(RGDP^{USA})) + 0.66*D(\ln(RGDP^{PLW}(-1))) \\ & -0.64*ECM(-1) \\ & -0.05*\ln(real\ oil) + constant \end{aligned}$$

In the long term, fluctuations in U.S. growth spill over one for one to Palau, as is the case in both Marshall Islands and Micronesia. In the short term, the impact is estimated to be greater than one, suggesting an overshooting in the near term. Real oil price shocks have a large impact on Palau GDP in the short term, with a 10 percent increase in oil prices reducing GDP growth by 0.5 percent.

Papua New Guinea

Long-term equation:
A long-term cointegrating relationship was found between log real GDP in Papua New Guinea and log real GDP in Australia and aid to Papua New Guinea.

$$\ln(RGDP^{PNG}) = 0.21*\ln(RGDP^{AUS}) + 0.29*\ln(Real\ AID^{PNG}) + constant$$

Structural equation:

$$\begin{aligned} D(\ln(RGDP^{PNG})) = {} & 0.55*D(\ln(RGDP^{AUS})) \\ & -0.07*ECM(-1) \\ & -0.02*\ln(real\ oil) + constant\ and\ dummy \end{aligned}$$

There is a long-term relationship between Papua New Guinean GDP, Australian GDP, and real aid to Papua New Guinea. Growth spillovers from Australia are large: holding the other variables constant, a 1 percent increase in Australian GDP would raise output in Papua New Guinea by 0.8 percent. Aid also appears to be important in the long term, but not in the short term. The coefficient on the real oil price is positive, consistent with Papua New Guinea being a commodity exporter.

Samoa

Long-term equation:
A long-term cointegrating relationship was found between log real GDP in Samoa and log real GDP in both Australia and New Zealand.

$$\ln(RGDP^{WSM}) = 0.16*\ln(RGDP^{AUS}) + 1*\ln(RGDP^{NZL}) + constant$$

The restriction that the long-term elasticity was equal to one was not rejected (χ^2: 0.67, *p*-value 0.41).

Structural equation:

$$D(\ln(RGDP^{WSM})) = 0.21{*}D(\ln(RGDP^{AUS})) + 0.50{*}D(\ln(RGDP^{NZL})) + 0.16{*}D(\ln(RGDP^{WSM}(-1))) \\ -0.85{*}ECM(-1) \\ +0.05{*}\ln(real\ commodity) + constant$$

Australia and New Zealand affect Samoa in both the short and long term, but the direct growth spillovers from New Zealand to Samoa are larger than from Australia. Over the long term, a 1 percent increase in GDP in New Zealand—holding other variables constant—will raise Samoan GDP by 1 percent, while the direct impact of Australia is much smaller. In the short term, the elasticity of Samoa's GDP with respect to that of New Zealand is 0.5.

The Solomon Islands

Long-term equation:
A long-term cointegrating relationship was found between log real GDP in the Solomon Islands and log real GDP in Australia.

$$\ln(RGDP^{SLB}) = 1{*}\ln(RGDP^{AUS}) + constant$$

The restriction that the long-term elasticity was equal to one was not rejected (χ^2: 3.16, p-value 0.02).
Structural equation:

$$D(\ln(RGDP^{SLB})) = 0.47{*}D(\ln(RGDP^{SLB}(-1))) \\ -0.25{*}ECM(-1) \\ +0.12{*}\ln(real\ commodity) -0.04{*}\ln(real\ oil) + constant$$

Australia is the main source of growth spillover, with a long-term elasticity of one. In the short term, however, there is no immediate impact on growth from Australia (but the impact begins to be felt after one year through the error correction term). GDP for the Solomon Islands is heavily influenced by international commodity prices, with nonoil commodity prices having a strong positive impact on growth, as might be expected for a commodity exporter. As an oil importer, however, higher oil prices are a drag on growth.

Tonga

Long-term equation:
A long-term cointegrating relationship was found between log real GDP in Tonga and New Zealand.

$$\ln(RGDP^{TON}) = 0.47{*}\ln(RGDP^{NZL}) + constant$$

Structural equation:

$$D(\ln(RGDP^{TON})) = 0.27{*}D(\ln(RGDP^{TON}(-1))) + 0.17{*}D(\ln(RGDP^{NZL})) \\ -0.71{*}ECM(-1) \\ -0.065{*}\ln(real\ commodity) + constant$$

New Zealand's growth spills over to Tonga in both the short and long term. In the short term, a 1 percent increase in New Zealand GDP boosts GDP in Tonga by 0.2 percent, other things being equal. However, over the long term the effect is twice as large. Commodity prices negatively affect the business cycle. Subsample analysis suggested the increasing importance of emerging Asia in generating growth spillovers in Tonga, but the above equation was preferred for the scenario analysis.

Tuvalu

Given the short data sample, long-term analysis was not feasible for Tuvalu, but the short-term dynamics (that is, using growth rates) suggest that the elasticity of Tuvalu with respect to world GDP is 0.5. Moreover, spillovers from regional economies would also occur through Tuvalu's trust fund, whose assets are invested offshore. The elasticity of Tuvalu GDP with respect to world equity prices is 0.05: a 10 percent increase in the world stock market will affect GDP growth in Tuvalu by ½ percentage point through wealth effects. For the scenario analysis, the elasticity of GDP in Tuvalu with respect to global oil prices is assumed to be 0.02, in line with other countries in the study.

Vanuatu

Long-term equation:
A long-term cointegrating relationship was found between log real GDP in Vanuatu and log real GDP in New Zealand and real tourism receipts.

$$\ln(RGDP^{VUT}) = 0.2^{*} \ln(RGDP^{AUS}) + 0.3^{*}\ln(\textit{real tourism receipts}) + \textit{constant}$$

Structural equation:

$$\begin{aligned} D(\ln(RGDP^{VUT})) = {} & 0.27^{*}D(\ln(RGDP^{AUS})) + 0.20^{*}\ D(\ln(RGDP^{VUT}(-1))) \\ & -0.69^{*}ECM(-1) \\ & +0.13^{*}D(\ln(\textit{real tourism receipts}) + \textit{constant and dummy} \end{aligned}$$

Australia is the main source of spillovers over both the short and long term. Subsample analysis suggests that Australia's importance has increased over time. Real tourism receipts are also relevant, both in the short and long term, consistent with the importance of tourism in the Vanuatu economy. Tourism receipts capture growth spillovers from economies other than Australia. The long-term elasticity of Australia and tourism with respect to Vanuatu GDP is 0.3.

ANNEX 6.2. COMMERCIAL BANKS

ANNEX TABLE 6.2.1

Commercial Banks in Small States of the Pacific and Papua New Guinea

Country	Australian Banks	U.S. Banks[1]	Other	Domestic Banks
Fiji	ANZ Westpac		Bank of Baroda (India) Bank South Pacific (Papua New Guinea) Bred Bank (Banque Populaire, France)	Home Finance Company
Kiribati	ANZ			
Marshall Islands		Bank of Guam		Bank of Marshall Islands
Micronesia		Bank of Guam		Bank of the FSM[1]
Palau		Bank of Guam Bank of Hawaii Bank Pacific		Asia Pacific Commercial Bank Palau Construction Bank
Papua New Guinea	ANZ Westpac			Bank South Pacific Kina Bank
Samoa	ANZ		Bank South Pacific (Papua New Guinea)	National Bank of Samoa Samoa Commercial Bank

(continued)

ANNEX TABLE 6.2.1 (*Continued*)

Commercial Banks in Pacific Island Countries

Country	Australian Banks	U.S. Banks[1]	Other	Domestic Banks
Solomon Islands	ANZ		Bank South Pacific (Papua New Guinea)	Pan Oceanic Bank
Timor-Leste	ANZ		Caixa (Portugal) Bank Mandiri (Indonesia)	National Commercial Bank of Timor-Leste
Tonga	ANZ		Bank South Pacific (Papua New Guinea) MBF Bank (Malaysia)	Tonga Development Bank Pacific International Commercial Bank
Tuvalu				National Bank of Tuvalu Development Bank of Tuvalu
Vanuatu	ANZ		Bred Bank (Banque Populaire, France) Bank South Pacific (Papua New Guinea)	National Bank of Vanuatu

Sources: Country authorities; and IMF staff compilation.
[1]Insured under the Federal Deposit Insurance Corporation scheme.

REFERENCES

Berg, A., C. Papageorgiou, C. Pattillo, and N. Spatafora. 2010. "The End of an Era? The Medium- and Long-Term Effects of the Global Crisis on Growth in Low-Income Countries." Working Paper 10/205, International Monetary Fund, Washington.

Davies, Matt, and John Vaught. 2011. "Interest Rates and Bank Profitability in the South Pacific." Regional Paper, Pacific Financial Technical Assistance Centre, Suva. http://www.pftac.org/page/resources/papers/.

International Monetary Fund (IMF). 2012a. "Growth Spillovers from the Global Economy." Box 1, in "Tonga: Staff Report for the 2012 Article IV Consultation," IMF Country Report 12/166, Washington.

———. 2012b. *World Economic Outlook: Growth Resuming, Dangers Remain.* World Economic and Financial Surveys, April. Washington.

———. 2014. "Australia: Staff Report for the 2013 Article IV Consultation." IMF Country Report No. 15/274, Washington.

———. 2015a. "Macroeconomic Developments and Selected Issues in Small Developing States." IMF Policy Paper, Washington, March.

———. 2015b. "Tonga: The Macroeconomic Impact of Lower Oil Prices." Box 1 in "Tonga: Staff Report for the 2015 Article IV Consultation," Washington, April.

———. 2015c. *World Economic Outlook: Adjusting to Lower Commodity Prices.* World Economic and Financial Surveys, October. Washington.

———. 2015d. "World Economic Outlook Update: Cross Currents." Washington, January.

Jauregui, Juan, and Werner Schule. 2011. "Policy Challenges for Emerging Asia and Australia from Rebalancing in China and Downside Risks in the Global Economy." In "Australia: Selected Issues." IMF Country Report 11/301, Washington.

Peiris, Shanaka Jayanath, and Ding Ding. 2012. "Global Commodity Prices, Monetary Transmission and Exchange Rate Pass-through in Pacific Islands." IMF Working Paper 12/176, International Monetary Fund, Washington.

Sheridan, Niamh, Patrizia Tumbarello, and Yiqun Wu. 2012. "Global and Regional Spillovers to Pacific Island Countries." IMF Working Paper 12/154, International Monetary Fund, Washington.

Sun, Yan. 2011. "From West to East: Estimating External Spillovers to Australia and New Zealand." IMF Working Paper 11/120, International Monetary Fund, Washington.

CHAPTER 7

Major Economic Shocks and Pacific Island Countries during the Global Economic Crisis

PATRICK COLMER AND RICHARD WOOD

Small island states are vulnerable to external shocks and generally experience greater instability in exports and agricultural production than other developing economies.[1] Pacific island countries (PICs) face the additional challenge of being highly vulnerable to natural disasters as well as to other economic shocks.[2] These economies are very small and have limited domestic and regional markets. They are remote from large international markets, they have high transportation costs, and they are not able to benefit from economies of large-scale production. PICs generally have narrow resource, production, and export bases, and many are dependent on primary commodities. Most PICs are heavily dependent on imports, particularly of food and fuel. Limited infrastructure, high import dependence, minimal export diversification, and an inability to rapidly increase exports make some PICs particularly vulnerable to shocks that have adverse effects on world trade. Even resource-rich PICs, as large commodity exporters, are vulnerable to global demand and international price shocks.

Economic shocks can arise from many sources, including major terms-of-trade adjustments, a sharp fall in external demand and other foreign economic developments, balance of payments difficulties, exchange rate misalignments, economic policy mistakes, debt explosions, political crises, business collapses, and corruption.

The global economic difficulties from 2007 to 2012 imposed a number of complex interrelated external shocks on PICs—the first food and fuel price shock, the global financial crisis, the global recession, the banking crisis, and, more recently, further food and fuel price shocks and public debt crises.

This chapter reviews available statistics and literature to shed light on the effects of these shocks on PICs, and discerns policy lessons from these experiences. As one can imagine, disentangling the various channels of causality and the different effects of these multiple, time-contiguous shocks is extremely difficult. Importantly, the effects of natural disasters are also reflected in the economic data and, consequently, care is needed to distinguish these from the impact of external economic shocks. We focus mainly on Fiji, Papua New Guinea, Samoa, the Solomon Islands, Tonga, and Vanuatu, referred to as "selected PICs," which were chosen on the basis of data availability. However, other PICs are included where reliable data are available. We assess the policy scope for increasing resilience to external shocks and offer policy recommendations.

This chapter benefited from the contributions and comments of Michael Anderson, Nicole Elsmore, Siddharth Shirodkar, Sarjit Singh, Millie Soei, Curtis Stewart, and Sharon Traucki. The views are those of the authors and do not necessarily reflect those of the Australian Treasury.

[1] See the United Nations Conference on Trade and Development (UNCTAD) webpage on Indicators Entering the Formulation of the Economic Vulnerability Index, http://unctad.org/sections/ldc_dir/docs/ldc_highlight001evi_en.pdf.

[2] For example, see Santos-Paulino (2011). UNCTAD estimates that small island developing states are 34 percent more economically vulnerable than other developing economies.

THE OVERALL EFFECTS OF GLOBAL ECONOMIC SHOCKS DURING 2007–11

Effects on GDP

As is well documented,[3] emerging market and developing economies generally fared better than industrialized countries during the global financial crisis, and this was also the case for the PICs. As Figure 7.1 shows, the economic slowdown in selected PICs owing to the global shocks arrived later and was shallower than the rate of slowdown experienced in the group of emerging market and developing economies. Compared to these economies, the recovery by selected PICs appears to have been slow in 2010, but it improved in the following year.

Figure 7.2 illustrates that the combined global economic shocks experienced during 2007–11 appear to have had no substantial negative impact on growth in Papua New Guinea, the Solomon Islands, and Vanuatu. During this period, output growth in Papua New Guinea was assisted by strong investment growth and fiscal spending. In the Solomon Islands, growth rebounded strongly in 2010 because of high demand for logging, strong logging prices, and increased copra production. Vanuatu was cushioned by strong tourism and investment growth and increased copra production. These countries reported relatively high average annual growth rates over the four years to 2011: 7.0 percent for Papua New Guinea, 4.2 percent for the Solomon Islands, and 3.9 percent for Vanuatu. In contrast, Fiji, Samoa, and Vanuatu experienced significant disruptions to their economic performance, going from annual average growth rates of 3.8 percent, 2.5 percent, and 8.5 percent, respectively, during 2000–07 to negligible growth or contraction in 2008–11.

The Pacific region is highly vulnerable to natural disasters and political disturbances.[4] Samoa, the Solomon Islands, and Tonga suffered from a major tsunami in 2009; the physical damage costs were estimated at more than 10 percent of GDP for Samoa alone (IMF 2010). Kiribati and Tuvalu continue to suffer from climate challenges, including Tuvalu's severe drought in September and October 2011, for which Australia and New Zealand provided freshwater and desalination units.

Fiji also suffered the effects of Cyclone Tomas in March 2010, with extensive damage to homes and infrastructure, and severe flooding in January 2012. Cane production losses from the same floods were 300,000 tons of raw sugar with a revenue worth F$27 million (ANZ 2012a).

The real output levels of a number of PICs were relatively resilient during the global crisis (Figure 7.2). In contrast, the smaller states, reviewed in Box 7.1, suffered greatly, experiencing substantial falls in real output.

---

[3] For example, see the IMF's September 2011 *World Economic Outlook* and Naudé (2011).

[4] Since the 1950s, PICs have experienced more than 200 disaster events, affecting 3.5 million people and costing in excess of US$6.5 billion. Natural disasters are believed to hit small island states, which are least able to cope, relatively hard. Natural disasters can substantially lower exports for up to three years (Andrade da Silva and Cernat 2012). The World Bank (2006) reports that in Samoa the average disaster costs 46 percent of GDP. During 1972–2004, Fiji suffered annual losses of F$20 million per year from cyclones and storms. The Asian Development Bank (2007) reports that the earthquake and accompanying tsunami that hit the Solomon Islands in 2007 cost about 90 percent of the recurrent budget estimate. In Niue, damage costs from Cyclone Heta in 2004 exceeded the value of the country's GDP by over five times. And in 1989 a series of cyclones in Vanuatu resulted in damage and economic losses amounting to twice the national income (Commonwealth Secretariat/World Bank 2000).

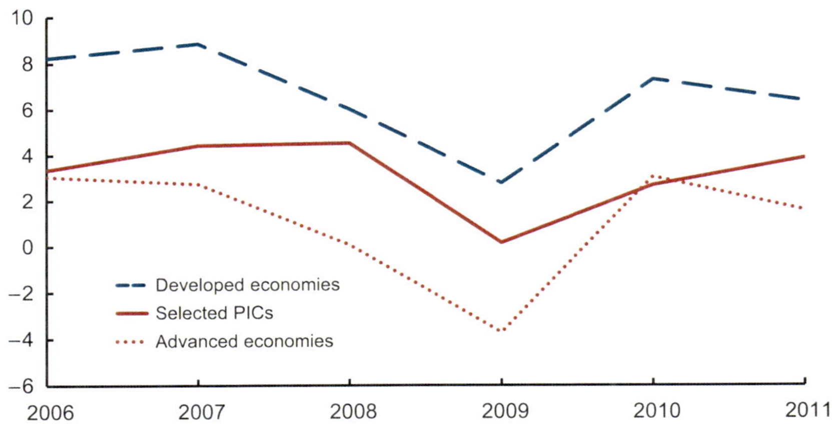

Figure 7.1 Real GDP in Developing and Advanced Economies and PICs, 2006–11 (*Percent change*)

Source: IMF, World Economic Outlook database.

Note: PICs = Pacific island countries. Selected PICs are Fiji, Papua New Guinea, Samoa, the Solomon Islands, Tonga, and Vanuatu.

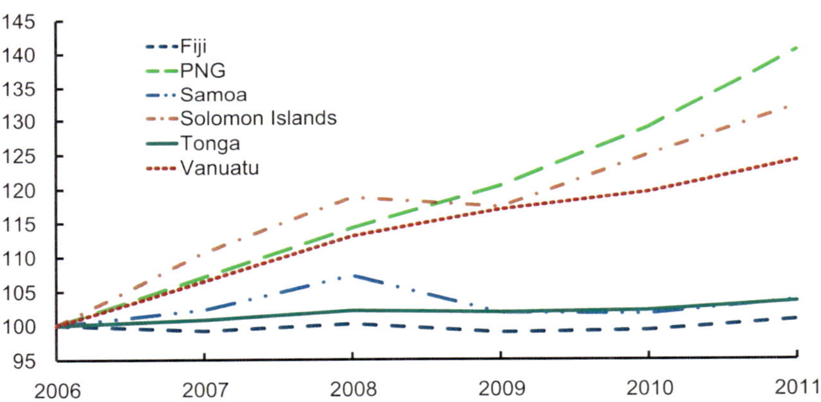

Figure 7.2 Real GDP in Selected PICs, 2006–11 (*Index, 2006 = 100*)

Source: IMF, World Economic Outlook database.

Note: PICs = Pacific island countries; PNG = Papua New Guinea.

Box 7.1. External Shocks and the Pacific Microstates

We examine how the Pacific microstates fared relative to Pacific island countries (PICs) as a whole during the global economic crisis. The selected microstates are the Cook Islands (population 15,529), Kiribati (100,835), Marshall Islands (54,439), Nauru (9,976), Niue (1,479), Palau (20,518), and Tuvalu (11,149).

These countries are identified later in this chapter as the PICs that are most vulnerable to external food and fuel price shocks, based largely on their high import dependency. International food prices rose 57 percent from January 2007 to January 2008, and international fuel prices by 145 percent in the same period. During the second international price shock, food prices rose 68 percent from February 2009 to April 2011, and international oil prices rose 195 percent. Much of these international price gains were passed through to domestic inflation.

Apart from Palau, which has a relatively large tourism sector, the microstates have very low levels of foreign-sourced income. Nauru has negligible tourism or remittance receipts, and Tuvalu has negligible tourism or export receipts. As a consequence, it is not surprising that, among PICs, the microstates are among those farthest from "external balance." And, in turn, they are the most heavily dependent on foreign aid.

Box 7.1. (*Continued*)

Table 7.1.1 shows real output changes during the global economic crisis. It is clear that the microstates experienced substantial contractions in real GDP levels during 2007–09. By comparison, real GDP for "other PICs" increased by 4.8 percent in the same period. The microstates suffered large terms-of-trade shocks during the crisis, and, as Table 7.1.1 shows, their fall in exports was far greater than the fall in in "other PICs." The case of Palau was made worse because of an "internal" shock—the failure of an airline company, which caused a contraction in the tourism sector. Palau's GDP also fell due to the completion of construction projects and the curtailment of foreign investment. Tuvalu, meanwhile, suffered lower offshore earnings, including from Tuvalu Trust Fund distributions.

TABLE 7.1.1

Percentage Change in Real GDP (*From peak to trough*)

	Between 2007 and 2009
Cook Islands	-7.0
Marshall Islands	-3.2
Kiribati	-1.8
Palau*	-10.4
Tuvalu	-2.2 (2008–10)
Nauru	-18.1 (2008–09)
"Other PICs"	+4.8

Sources: IMF data, except for Cook Islands and Nauru, which are based on data from the Asian Development Bank.
*Financial years from 2006/7 to 2008/9.

Inflation rates in the Pacific microstates were generally higher in 2008 than for "other PICs" (Figure 7.1.1), and averaged 12.4 percent in 2008. For "other PICs," the average inflation rate in the same year was 9.5 percent, with five out of six "other PICs" recording inflation rates of below 12 percent. The implication here is that, as a consequence of the global financial crisis, the first food and fuel price hike, and the global economic recession, the export, output, and inflation performances of Pacific microstates were generally worse than for "other PICs." This supports the supposition that these microstates are generally more vulnerable to external economic shocks than "other PICs."

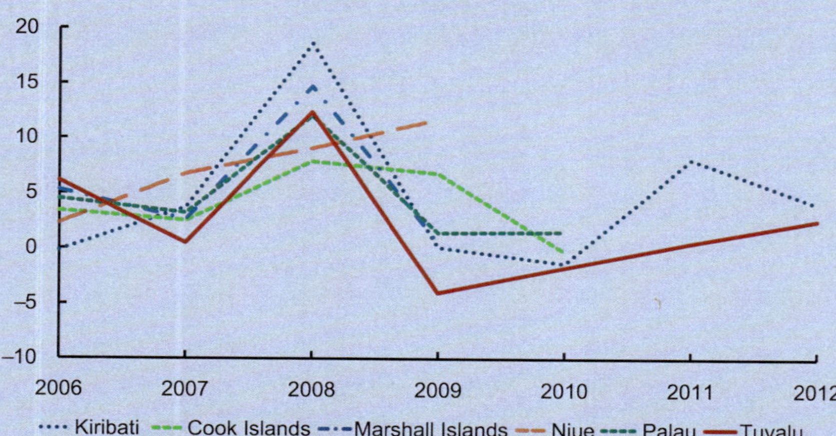

Figure 7.1.1 Annual Inflation Rates in Pacific Microstates (*Percent*)

Sources: Asian Development Bank (2011); and IMF, World Economic Outlook database.

Effects on Exports

The impact of weak global economic conditions on international trade was greater than the impact on global output. In 2009, real world output decreased by 0.7 percent, whereas real world trade flows fell by close to 11 percent (Bussiere, Ghironi, and Sestieri 2012). In light of this, it is not surprising that the major channel of disturbance to PICs has been through exports.[5]

Exports are very important to PICs, given their high dependence on imports, limited foreign capital inflows, and general balance of payments constraints. For the larger exporters (Papua New Guinea and the Solomon Islands), export receipts are a major source of budget revenues. In Papua New Guinea, revenues from mining and natural gas account for about 20 percent of government revenues. In the Solomon Islands, revenues from logging account for about 14 percent of government revenues.

Among the PICs, Fiji is a major exporter, with exports totalling 46 percent of GDP in 2009. The country has perhaps the region's most diversified export base in terms of products and markets,[6] and the country has benefited substantially from exporting over a long period. But exports are less than 15 percent of GDP in the smaller states of the Cook Islands, Kiribati, Marshall Islands, Micronesia, Palau, and Tuvalu.

Figure 7.3 shows that the value of exports for selected PICs fell by about 23 percent in 2009, recovering somewhat in 2010. For the microstates, export receipts fell about 25 percent between 2007 and 2010. In the advanced economies, export values contracted 20 percent between 2008 and 2009, but these declined only marginally in low-income countries as a group during the global financial crisis.

The region's largest commodity exporters (Papua New Guinea and the Solomon Islands) suffered substantial reductions in export values, driven by the decline in commodity prices in 2009. However, the strong rebound in prices in 2010 saw exports from Papua New Guinea returning to around 2008 levels, and exceeding previous highs in the Solomon Islands. The export performances of other PICs during the global financial crisis are shown in Table 7.1.

Table 7.2 indicates that, in 2010, Australia accounted for about 26 percent of exports from selected PICs. China and Japan together accounted for about 17 percent, while Europe accounted for about 4.5 percent of exports. The United States took only 2.5 percent of PIC exports. Figure 7.4 shows that PIC exports to Australia increased strongly over the past decade, while PIC exports to China and Japan increased far less rapidly.

The relatively strong economic expansion of Asia and Australia during the global recession provided direct demand for PIC exports, which partly cushioned the effects of the recession on the Pacific region. Australia's demand for PIC exports has, in part, been buoyed by the strong Asia-Australia trade link. Assuming that any renewed global recession is largely confined to Europe, the "shock" effect of a new recession abroad on PICs will be smaller than would be the case if the PICs had larger export markets in Europe, rather than in Australia and China.

Effects on Remittances

For a long time, remittances have been an important source of income and foreign exchange for some PICs. Indeed, the contribution of remittance flows to output growth in the Pacific has been more than double that of the remittance flows to small island developing states in the Caribbean (Santos-Paulino 2011).

---

[5] Care is required when assessing the impacts of falling recorded export volumes on individual PICs, as significant elements of export values (for instance, some significant part of mineral export earnings) may not always be received in these economies.

[6] Among PICs, Fiji and Papua New Guinea have increased export diversification over the past two decades. Prospective liquefied natural gas exports in Papua New Guinea and mining exports in the Solomon Islands will further contribute to their export diversification. There has been little export diversification in other PICs in recent decades, and in some, increased export concentration has occurred (ANZ 2012b).

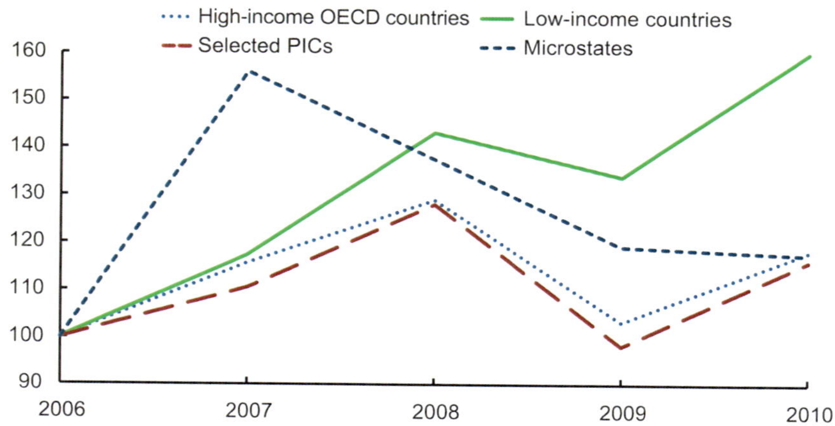

Figure 7.3 Exports in High- and Low-Income Countries, PICs, and Microstates (*Index, 2006 = 100*)

Sources: Asian Development Bank (2011); and World Bank, World Development Indicators database.
Note: OECD = Organisation for Economic Co-operation and Development; PICs = Pacific island countries. Selected PICs are Fiji, Papua New Guinea, Samoa, the Solomon Islands, Tonga, and Vanuatu.

TABLE 7.1

Decline in the Value of Exports during the Global Crisis

Country	Change in Exports (%) 2007–08	Change in Exports (%) 2008–09	Change in Exports (%) 2007–09
Cook Islands	−16	−25	−38
Fiji	22	−16	2
Kiribati	−23	−22	−39
Marshall Islands	15	6	21
Palau	4	0	4
Papua New Guinea	11	−23	−14
Samoa	−25	9	−19
Solomon Islands	30	−19	5
Tonga	−25	−4	−29
Vanuatu	12	8	21

Source: Asian Development Bank.

TABLE 7.2

Destination of Exports from Selected Pacific Island Countries (2010)

Destination	Exports from Selected PICs as Percent of Their Total Exports
Australia	25.8
China	8.3
European nations	4.4
Japan	8.5
United States	2.5

Source: Asian Development Bank.
Note: The Pacific island countries selected are Fiji, Papua New Guinea, Samoa, the Solomon Islands, and Tuvalu.

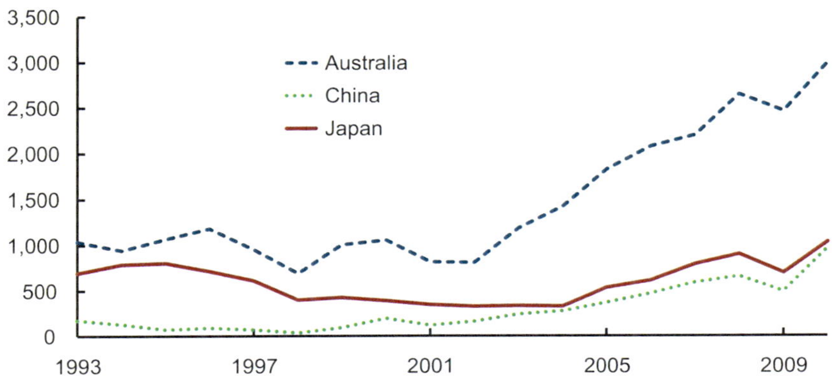

Figure 7.4 Three Largest Export Markets for Selected Pacific Island Countries (*Millions of U.S. dollars*)

Source: Asian Development Bank (2011).
Note: Selected Pacific island countries are Fiji, Papua New Guinea, Samoa, the Solomon Islands, Tonga, and Vanuatu.

But as Figures 7.5 and 7.6 show, remittance flows to individual PICs vary considerably. Remittance flows are particularly important for Tonga (24 percent of GDP in 2010) and Samoa (25 percent of GDP in 2010). However, for a number of states, including the Melanesian states (Papua New Guinea, the Solomon Islands, Vanuatu), remittance flows are very small, reflecting limited migration or foreign work opportunities.

The value of remittances for Fiji fell 33 percent between 2006 and 2008, due primarily to international and domestic difficulties, before staging a recovery. For Tonga, remittances fell 29.4 percent between 2007 and 2009, largely reflecting Tonga's heavy reliance on remittances from the United States, which went into recession in December 2007. For Samoa, remittances increased throughout the crisis. Papua New Guinea's strong growth was from an extremely low base.

During the global economic crisis, remittances as a percentage of GDP remained relatively stable in most PICs, except for Tonga, where they fell. The principal sources of remittances to the Pacific are Australia, New Zealand, and the United States (Browne and Mineshima 2007). For Samoa, 73 percent of remittances derive from Oceania and 27 percent from North America. For Tonga, 50 percent of remittances derive from Australia and 48 percent from the United States (Migration Policy Institute 2011a, 2011b). The relative buoyancy of the Australian economy during 2006–10 worked to partly cushion the effects on PICs from declining remittances during the

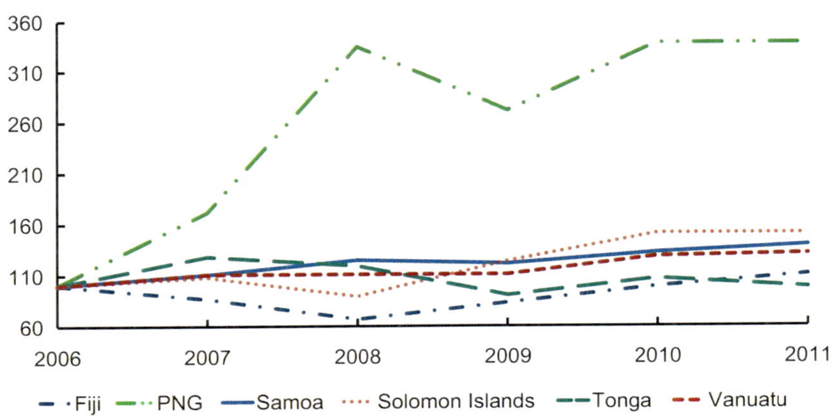

Figure 7.5 Remittances in Selected Pacific Island Countries, 2006–11 (*Index, 2006 = 100*)

Source: World Bank, Prospects, Annual Remittances data.
Note: PNG = Papua New Guinea.

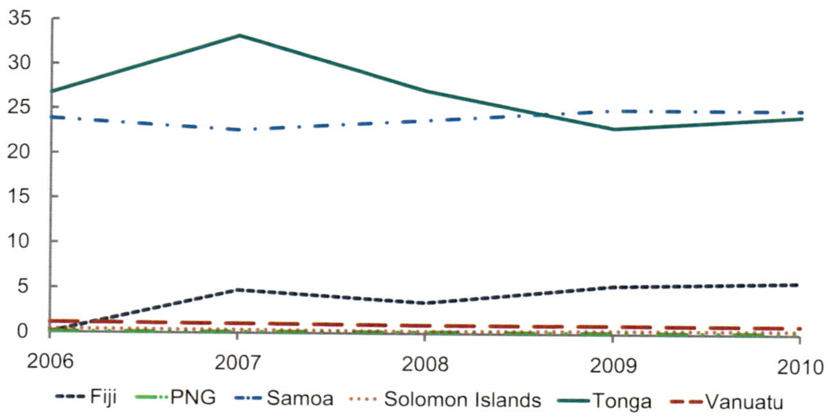

Figure 7.6 Remittances in Selected Pacific Island Countries, 2006–10 (*Percent of GDP*)

Source: World Bank, World Development Indicators database.
Note: PNG = Papua New Guinea.

global economic crisis. In contrast, the prolonged recession in the United States, and the weakening in New Zealand, likely led to lower remittance flows to a number of PICs.

Effects on Tourism

While trade in physical goods declined sharply in many PICs during the global economic crisis, tourist and business visitor arrivals generally increased across the region (Figure 7.7). Tourism provides formal employment, and tourism receipts are an important source of income and foreign exchange in a number of PICs.[7] Tourism receipts have historically accounted for about 60 percent of GDP in Palau and 50 percent in the Cook Islands. In Vanuatu, tourism accounts for almost 30 percent of GDP, and over 20 percent in Samoa and Fiji. Other small Pacific island states are more remote and have small tourism sectors.

Tourist and business arrivals in most PICs increased during the global economic crisis, though they were subdued in Fiji and Samoa. In Palau, tourism receipts fell 17 percentage points during 2008 and 2009, largely because of the bankruptcy of an airline from Taiwan Province of China. Civil unrest and extreme weather events can also have a substantial influence on tourism in the Pacific islands.

At face value, an increase in visitor arrivals during a global crisis may appear somewhat counterintuitive. However, about 36 percent of all tourist and business visitor arrivals in PICs come from Australia (Pacific Islands Trade and Investment Commission 2008), which experienced relatively strong growth during this period. Consequently, as Australia was quite buoyant during the global recession, and the Australian dollar was particularly strong,[8] tourist and business visitor arrivals to PICs were stronger than might otherwise have been the case.

Effects on Financial Systems

Many of the Pacific island microstates covered in this chapter were largely immune from the worst direct monetary transmission impacts of the global financial and debt crises. This reflected the fact that Pacific island financial markets and banks are small, largely domestically funded, and not strongly or directly integrated into or exposed to international financial markets.

However, Kiribati was affected by large falls in the value of its wealth and pension funds—the Revenue Equalization Reserve Fund and the Kiribati Provident Fund. The value of assets of the

[7] As with exports, care is required in interpreting the effects on PICs implied by tourism data. Significant elements of tourism receipts are held offshore, or are earned by foreign-owned hotels and airlines, and do not reach the island states.

[8] The Australian dollar fell 17.3 percent against the U.S. dollar from September 2008 to January 2009, at the outset of the global economic crisis.

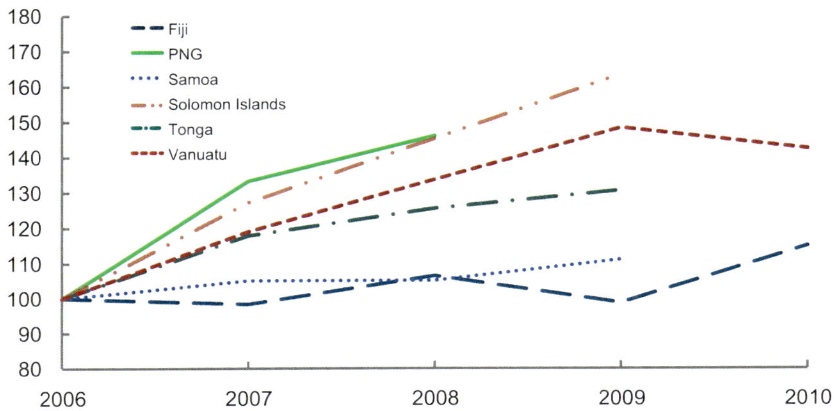

Figure 7.7 Tourism and Business in Selected Pacific Island Countries, 2006–10 (*Visitor arrivals; index, 2006 = 100*)

Source: World Bank, World Development Indicators database.
Note: PNG = Papua New Guinea. No 2010 data available for Samoa, the Solomon Islands, and Tonga; no 2009–10 data available for Papua New Guinea.

former fund fell 20 percent in 2008 due to the global financial crisis and drawdowns to finance the budget deficit. In Tuvalu, the value of its trust fund fell about 13 percent for the same reasons. Marshall Islands, Micronesia, and Palau also have trust funds with assets invested offshore, and were also negatively impacted, including through lower earnings flows.

Effects on Aid Flows to the Pacific

Aid flows into many PICs have historically been a more important source of finance than remittances and foreign direct investment. The small PICs are more dependent on aid flows than the small island developing states in Africa and the Caribbean (Santos-Paulino 2011). Aid in the form of grants represents 74 percent of GDP in Tuvalu, 69 percent in Kiribati, 45 percent in Marshall Islands, 34 percent in Micronesia, and 24 percent in Palau (Hezel 2012).

The global financial crisis, the global economic recession, and ongoing public debt problems in Europe, Japan, and the United States may have implications for the flow of foreign aid to developing economies and small island states.

Dabla-Norris, Minoiu, and Zanna (2010) conclude that severe economic downturns in donor countries have historically triggered persistent declines in aid disbursement, and that bilateral aid flows decline more sharply in the aftermath of large output contractions in donor countries when they have higher public debt burdens. In particular, the United States, Japan, and euro area countries have been experiencing output weakness and relatively high levels of public debt. Together, these countries account for about 32 percent of aid flows to the Pacific.

Australia is the major bilateral aid donor to the PICs, and the Pacific will continue to be a priority for the Australian aid program. As Figure 7.8 shows, Australia provided about 45 percent of all aid resources in the Pacific in 2010 and provides more than 60 percent of all donor assistance to Melanesia. Some 95 percent of official development assistance to the Pacific is in the form of grants, rather than loans.

Summary of Transmission Effects

Global economic difficulties hurt PICs mainly through a widespread decline in exports. Remittance flows fell substantially during 2006–09, and by about 30 percent in Fiji and Tonga. In some PICs, the difficulties reduced the values of trust funds. The global economic crisis hit output and the inflation performances of the smaller, fragile, and most vulnerable PICs in particular.

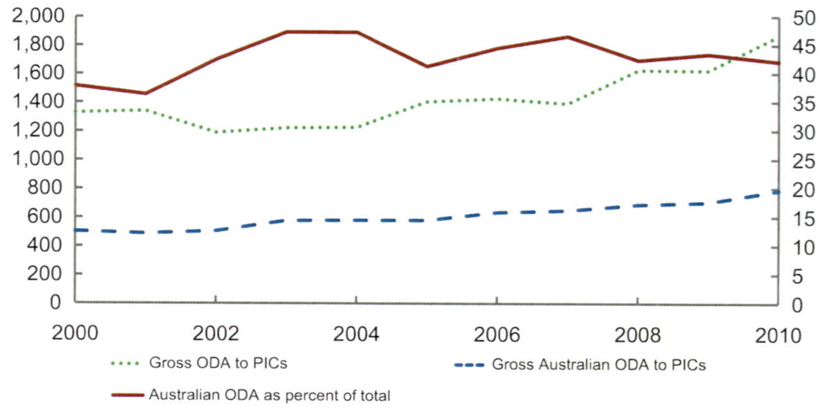

Figure 7.8 Gross Official Development Assistance to Pacific Island Countries, 2000–10 (*Millions of U.S. dollars, left scale; percent, right scale*)

Source: Organisation for Economic Co-operation and Development, aid statistics.
Note: ODA = official development assistance; PICs = Pacific island countries.

A BUFFER ROLE FOR RESERVE AND EXCHANGE RATES

Foreign Currency Reserves

Table 7.3 shows actual and target levels of foreign exchange reserves measured as months of import cover over recent years. Reserves declined in a number of PICs during 2008 and into 2009, suggesting that they played a cushioning role in the face of external shocks, particularly when nominal exchange rates generally remained fixed.

Reserves fell substantially below target levels in Fiji and less sharply in the Solomon Islands to cushion these economies in 2008. But the result was that both were threatened by balance of payments crises—and Fiji subsequently raised its reserve target from three months of import cover to five (the new target was reached in September 2011). Reserves in the Solomon Islands recovered comparatively quickly.

During August and September 2009, the IMF allocated new special drawing rights[9] to member countries, including the PICs, equivalent to some US$370 million,[10] effectively raising their holdings of foreign currency reserves. Import compression, higher remittances, and increased tourism receipts contributed to the buildup in reserves during 2009 in some PICs. Most of these countries continued to build foreign reserves after the global recession. The rebound in commodity prices assisted this in Papua New Guinea and the Solomon Islands, and substantial development assistance flows helped Samoa and Tonga in particular strengthen their reserves.

Fiji, Samoa, the Solomon Islands, and Tonga had a higher level of reserves in 2011 than at the end of 2007, and with these larger buffers they were better placed to withstand future economic shocks.

Exchange Rate Overvaluation

PICs use different exchange rate systems (Table 7.4), and the nature of these differences would have had some implications for the manner and extent to which the effects of the global crisis were transmitted to these countries.

[9]The special drawing right is an international reserve asset allocated by the IMF to its member countries. These are recorded as part of a country's official foreign currency reserves and are readily convertible into foreign currency held by another IMF member.
[10]Special drawing right allocations to PICs included Fiji (US$94 million), Kiribati (US$8.4 million), Marshall Islands (US$5.2 million), Micronesia (US$7.6 million), Palau (US$4.7 million), Papua New Guinea (US$183 million), Samoa (US$15.7 million), the Solomon Islands (US$14.6 million), Tonga (US$10.4 million), and Vanuatu (US$25.6 million).

TABLE 7.3

Official Foreign Currency Reserves (*Months of import cover*)

	Reserve Target at 2011	End-2007	End-2008	2009	2010	2011
Fiji	5	4.4	2.9	1.3 (Apr)	3.4 (Apr)	5.1 (Oct)
Papua New Guinea	No target	13.0	10.9	9.7 (Mar)	10.5 (Jun)	10.5 (Jun)
Samoa	4	4.7	4.4	5.1 (May)	7.0 (May)	6.1 (Aug)
Solomon Islands	3	3.7	2.5	3.2 (May)	6.2 (May)	8.5 (Sep)
Tonga	3–4	4.4	4.8	4.6 (May)	7.1 (Jun)	8.2 (Oct)
Vanuatu	4	7.0	5.8	5.2 (Mar)	5.9 (Feb)	6.5 (Oct)

Sources: ADB (2009b, 2009c, 2010, 2011); Central Bank of Samoa (2009); National Reserve Bank of Tonga, Monetary Policy Statement, 2009 and later; Reddy (2009); and Ministry of Finance and National Planning, Tonga (2009).

TABLE 7.4

Exchange Rate Regimes[1]

Fixed (peg)	Fiji, Samoa, Solomon Islands, Tonga, Vanuatu
Dollarization	
Australian dollar	Kiribati, Nauru, Tuvalu
New Zealand dollar	Cook Islands, Niue, Tokelau
U.S. dollar	Marshall Islands, Micronesia, Palau
Managed floating	Papua New Guinea

Sources: National authorities; and authors' compilation as of March 2012.

[1] For Samoa and Tonga there is a margin, a horizontal band, in the pegged arrangements that provides the opportunity for the authorities to move the exchange rate within the band. For Samoa, the margin is ±2 percent, while for Tonga the margin is ±5 percent per month around the central value.

Figure 7.9 shows that, as a result of the global financial crisis, the real effective exchange rates of a number of PICs became overvalued in 2009.[11] While this did not persist into 2010 in some countries, the overvaluation may nonetheless have damaged trade performance, particularly in 2009, when trade volumes collapsed. More recently, real exchange rates have appreciated in a number of countries, largely as a result of the higher inflation rates recorded in the Pacific than in major trading partner nations.[12] As a consequence, some exchange rates became overvalued once again.

One question that arises from the currency overvaluation in some PICs in 2009 and more recently, is whether those countries with fixed exchange rate regimes would have been better able to cope with the series of external economic shocks if they had a system that allowed for greater exchange rate flexibility—or had made greater use of the existing scope for flexibility within their adjustment bands. This issue—the use of the exchange rate as a shock absorber—may become relevant depending on the magnitude and nature of future economic shocks.

The international evidence appears to suggest that, generally, developing economies with flexible exchange rate regimes are better able to absorb economic shocks—for example, external demand shocks, negative terms-of-trade shocks (Berg, Borensztein, and Mauro 2003), and natural disasters—and deal more effectively with high current account deficits and exchange rate risk[13] than those with fixed exchange rates. However, empirical paradigms established by the

[11] Such assessments are based on information in IMF Article IV Staff Reports. Where no label is provided, the IMF does not appear to have expressed a concluded view on currency alignments.

[12] The rise in the nominal exchange rates of Papua New Guinea contributed to a real appreciation of the currency during 2011. Nonetheless, a tendency may develop toward currency undervaluation in Papua New Guinea, based on the current level of the real effective exchange rate and prospective exports of liquefied natural gas (IMF 2011).

[13] Floating exchange rate regimes force borrowers to confront the existence of exchange rate risk, thereby reducing unhedged foreign currency borrowing. See Cespedes, Chang, and Velasco (2004).

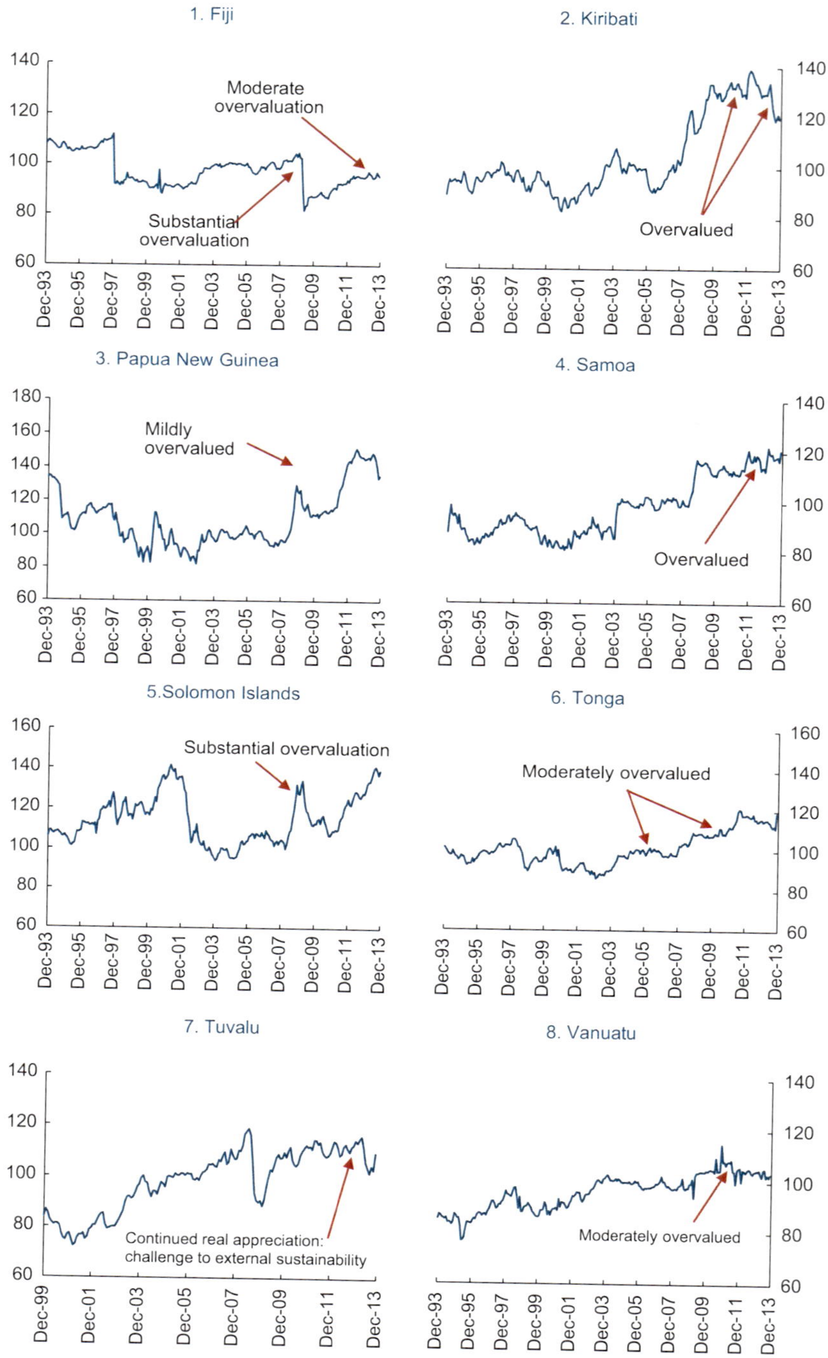

Figure 7.9 Real Effective Exchange Rates in Selected Pacific Island Countries (*Index*)

Sources: IMF, International Financial Statistics database; and Article IV Consultation Staff Reports.
Note: The descriptors for overvaluation are from the Article IV Consultation Staff Reports.

experience of developing economies as a whole may not necessarily be applicable to Pacific micro-states (Imam 2010).

Vulnerability to International Food and Fuel Price Surges and Exchange Rates

Small island states are generally characterized by low levels of diversification in production and exports, and are thought to be highly vulnerable to adverse external price shocks. Consequently, adverse terms-of-trade shocks, particularly long ones, can lead to a substantial deterioration in their current account balances, which, in turn, increases national indebtedness.

The PICs most vulnerable to international food price hikes are mainly smaller, remote, high-import-dependent states with low export bases—in contrast to Papua New Guinea and the Solomon Islands, which produce most of their own food. The smaller PICs also have a relatively high dependence on imported food (Figure 7.10). However, when consideration is also given to the ability of PICs to pay for food imports and to the vulnerability of children and women (UNICEF 2011), many other small PICs are also highly vulnerable to international food price hikes.

Most PICs are heavily dependent on oil for their energy needs, especially power generation and transportation. Intensity of oil use is more than 80 percent in the Pacific, with the Cook Islands, Kiribati, Nauru, the Solomon Islands, and Tonga relying almost exclusively on oil for their commercial energy requirements (ADB 2009a). The smaller PICs use more oil per citizen and are therefore generally more vulnerable to international fuel price hikes. The Asian Development Bank has noted that PICs are among the most vulnerable countries to fluctuations in crude oil prices (ADB 2009a). Figure 7.11 shows the vulnerability of various PICs to oil price movements.

It seems likely that Kiribati, the Marshall Islands, and Nauru are highly vulnerable both to food and fuel price shocks. In 2008 surging international food and fuel prices contributed to increased domestic inflation across the Pacific region, lifting inflation rates for PICs from 2.5 percent to about 12 percent per year.

Exchange rate arrangements, local exchange rate developments, and the currency used to pay for purchases of imported food and fuel can be important determinants of the severity of international price increases for PIC economies.[14] Generally those PICs with appreciating currencies during periods of global food and fuel price hikes have suffered less from rising domestic inflation than those with depreciating currencies. This pattern can be observed in Figures 7.12 and 7.13. Those countries with exchange rates tied to the depreciating U.S. dollar reported substantially higher imported fuel costs than those using the appreciating Australian and New Zealand dollars. However, the choice of exchange rate policies, anchors, and tying arrangements is, desirably, based on various longer-term considerations, including the pattern of trade and investment linkages, remittance and tourism sources, sources of aid, migration arrangements, and relative competitive advantages, rather than on shorter-term trends in exchange rates that may not be sustained and are unpredictable. It seems possible that the food and fuel price surge combined with exchange rate policies may have resulted in significant adverse effects on competitiveness and exports for some countries.

Exchange Rates and Shocks Resulting from the Global Economic Recession

The global recession directly contributed to falling global demand, which affected some exports of the PICs. In some small Pacific island states, capacity is likely to be limited for rapid import substitution or for substantially increased exports in the short term. This is because of their narrow production bases, high export concentration and inflexible economic structures, high import dependence, low short-term trade elasticities, constrained external demand, and slow supply-side responsiveness. To the extent this is the case, the ability of a more flexible exchange rate regime to act as a shock

[14] If a country is a net exporter of food and fuel (Papua New Guinea, for instance), some part of the observed rise in the real effective exchange rate during this period may not have reflected a loss of price competitiveness but, rather, an improvement in the terms of trade.

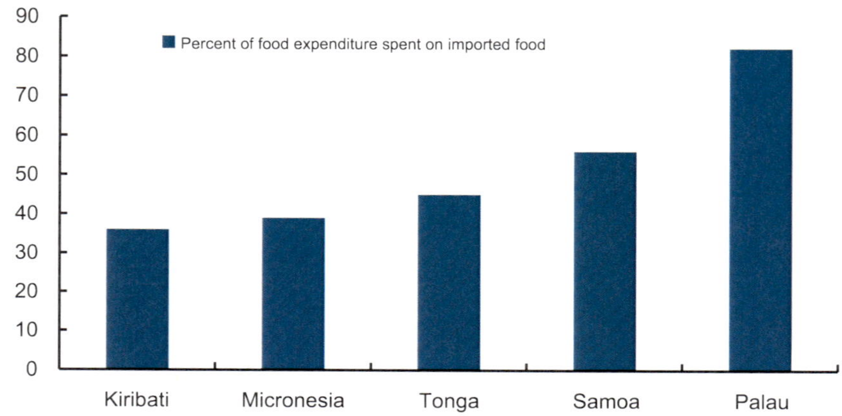

Figure 7.10 Proportion of Food Expenditure Accounted for by Imported Food (*Percent*)

Source: Pacific Island Ministers of Agriculture and Fisheries (2008).
Note: Data for Nauru are not available, but the country's dependence on imported food is high.

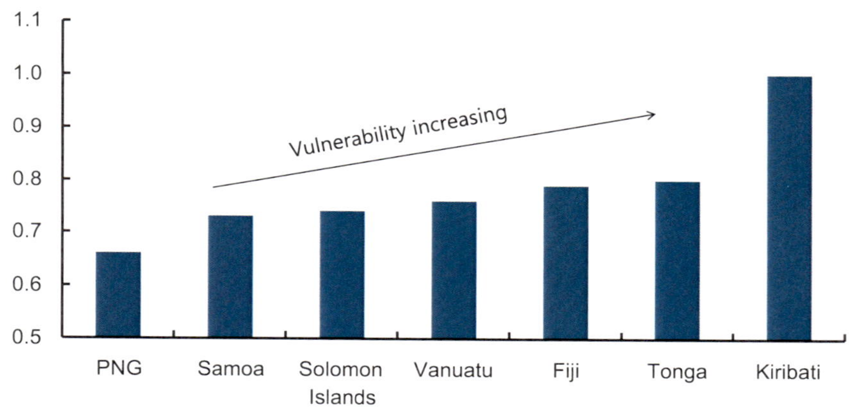

Figure 7.11 Oil Price Vulnerability, 2008 (*Index*)

Source: Asian Development Bank calculations.
Note: PNG = Papua New Guinea.

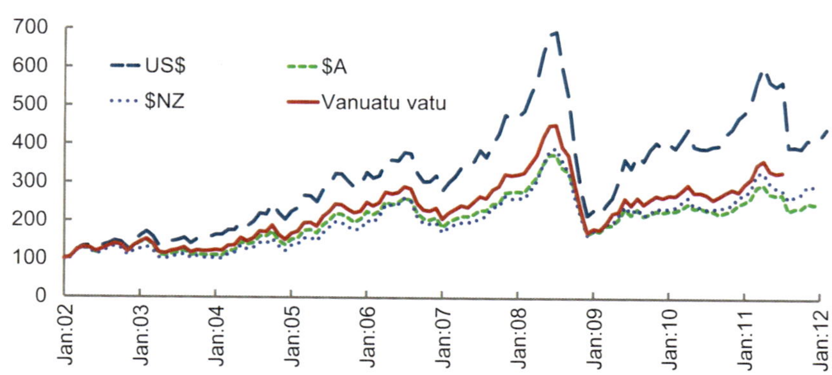

Figure 7.12 Oil Prices in Selected Pacific Island Countries, 2002–12 (*Index*)

Sources: IMF, World Economic Outlook database; and World Bank, World Development Indicators database.
Note: Oil prices in U.S. dollars for Marshall Islands, Micronesia, and Palau; local currency for Vanuatu; Australian dollars for Kiribati, Nauru, and Tuvalu; and New Zealand dollars for the Cook Islands and Niue.

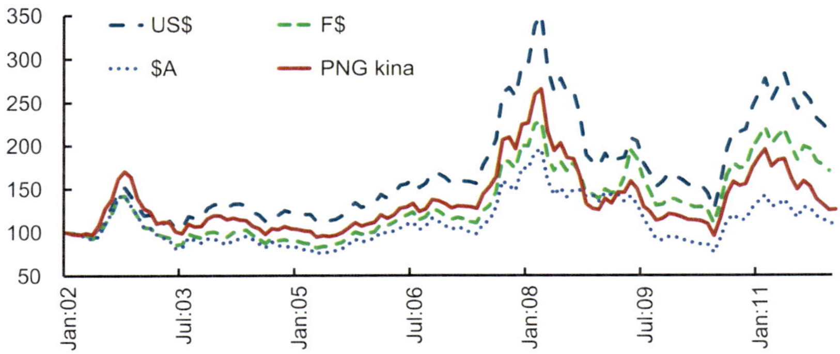

Figure 7.13 Wheat Prices in Selected Pacific Island Countries, 2002–11 (*Index*)

Sources: IMF, World Economic Outlook database; and World Bank, World Development Indicators database.
Note: PNG = Papua New Guinea. Wheat prices are in the local currencies of Fiji and PNG; Australian dollars for Kiribati, Nauru, and Tuvalu; and U.S. dollars for Marshall Islands, Micronesia, and Palau.

absorber, and to cause export and import substitution production to increase in the short term, is likely to be limited.

However, looking beyond the short term to a time when foreign demand will no longer be so volume constrained, and resource allocation can be adjusted to take advantage of relative price changes, the devaluation that would be permitted by a more flexible exchange rate arrangement is likely to be more effective[15] in raising foreign demand for exports from Pacific island states.[16] This assumes, however, that the real devaluation is maintained.

There were two major external economic shocks in quick succession: the food and fuel price shock and the global recession. To have addressed both of these shocks using the exchange rate could have created tensions between the objective of offsetting higher inflation due to rising food and fuel prices (by currency appreciation) and the objective of stimulating exports to address falling global demand (by currency depreciation).

MONETARY, FISCAL, AND RESOURCE ALLOCATION POLICY RESPONSE

Monetary Policy: Shocks and Responses

The monetary authorities in most PICs adopted a generally cautious approach to policy management during the global economic crisis. In line with the charters of PIC central banks, the principal objectives of monetary policy during much of this period were to maintain an adequate level of foreign currency reserves and to contain and lower inflation. The scope to attempt a countercyclical monetary stimulus to lift economic activity—an objective not usually listed in the central bank charters of these small island states—was largely precluded in 2008 and into 2009 by the need to address the higher-priority problems of declining reserves and high inflation.

During the global economic crisis, foreign currency receipts contracted and reserves fell in a number of PICs. As a result, the balances of exchange settlement accounts also fell and, in turn,

[15]The November 2009 IMF Article IV Staff Report for the Solomon Islands suggests that, while the authorities are concerned about the low elasticity of imports, the historical experience suggests that exports are more responsive than imports to a devaluation of the currency, and that devaluation could, therefore, be a useful adjustment instrument. Round logs, which account for 70 percent by value, are sold predominantly on the basis of contracts transacted in U.S. dollars, and are not affected by changes in the Solomon Islands exchange rate (which is de facto pegged to the U.S. dollar).

[16]There are few published studies on trade elasticities in PICs. In the case of Fiji, the long-term, own-price elasticity for export demand is estimated to lie between –1.25 and –1.49, suggesting devaluation improves export performance in the long term. See Narayan and Narayan (2004). In another article, the same authors (2007) find that a 10 percent devaluation in Fiji increases output by around 3.3 percent.

fewer funds were injected into the banking system and demand deposits, resulting in lower liquidity. Injecting liquidity when reserves fell, and draining off excess liquidity when it accumulated, proved to be a substantial function of monetary policy in PICs during the global economic crisis.

The management of interest rates also contributed to economic adjustment during the global economic crisis.[17] However, the relatively large gap between lending and borrowing interest rates in some PICs complicates the task of using a policy interest rate to impact inflation and smooth economic cycles, encourage saving, influence private investment, and address large current account deficits.

With constrained transmission mechanisms,[18] macroeconomic variables may not be strongly responsive to changes in monetary policy. It follows that the ability to quickly offset the effects of the global economic recession on economic activity with countercyclical monetary policy is likely to be limited, particularly as monetary policy was already busy addressing elevated inflation rates.

During 2011 headline inflation picked up as a result of the higher food and energy prices. Banking sector liquidity remained high across the region, reflecting healthy balance of payments outcomes and a more conservative approach to lending by commercial banks following the global financial crisis. Despite an increasingly strong case for the withdrawal of the stimulus of the past several years, several factors explain the cautious approach of PIC central banks toward tightening monetary policy. Headline inflation is not expected to rise much beyond current levels, with core inflation remaining within reasonable bounds, and private sector credit growth remains generally subdued. The healthy level of foreign exchange reserves in the region is also likely to have delayed the need to aggressively tighten monetary policy.

From a structural perspective, the PICs face enormous challenges in enhancing the effectiveness of monetary policy and the ability of monetary policy to deal with external economic shocks. Financial intermediation is low compared to other small island economies at a similar stage of economic development. Interbank lending is limited and secondary markets for government and central bank securities are mostly nonexistent. There is substantial banking sector liquidity, reflecting limited lending opportunities, though official interest rates remain quite low. Large subsistence sectors, shallow financial markets, limited private investment opportunities, sticky interest rates, limited financial arbitrage and oligopolistic commercial banking sectors also inhibit the effectiveness of monetary policy to respond to economic shocks.

Fiscal Policy: Shocks and Available Fiscal Space

At the beginning of the global economic crisis, public debt was already very high in Marshall Islands, Nauru, and the Solomon Islands, and for these countries there was judged to be no space for additional fiscal stimulus. By 2009 the Cook Islands, Kiribati, and Papua New Guinea had relaxed fiscal policy excessively in response to the global economic crisis (ADB 2009b).

From the beginning of the global economic crisis to 2011, fiscal balances have deteriorated in Samoa, Tonga, and Vanuatu. Figure 7.14 suggests that budget deficits in 2011 were clearly excessive in Kiribati and Samoa, and that public debt levels have deteriorated since the beginning of the global crisis. As of 2010 several countries had levels of public external debt that exceeded the IMF and World Bank threshold parameter of 30 percent of GDP (Table 7.5; IMF/World Bank 2004). And total public debt is excessive in some other PICs. The main implication from this is that the room for additional fiscal stimulus is currently limited in a number of countries.

---

[17] There is little evidence to suggest that interest rate policy was used proactively to directly reduce cross-border capital outflows and protect foreign currency reserves.

[18] A number of academic studies suggest that the existence of stable monetary demand functions and inadequately developed capital markets in some PICs provides a basis to use monetary aggregates rather than interest rates as an instrument of policy. See Jayaraman and Choong (2009), Jayaraman and Dahalan (2008), and Singh and Kumar (2009).

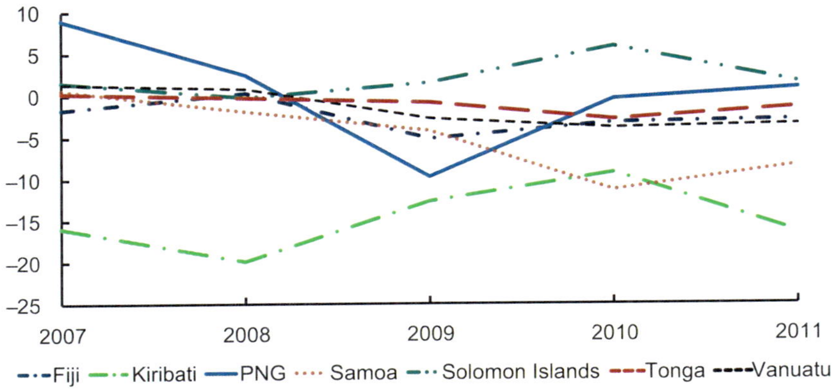

Figure 7.14 Net Government Lending and Borrowing, 2007–11 (*Percent of GDP*)

Source: IMF, World Economic Outlook database.
Note: PNG = Papua New Guinea.

TABLE 7.5

Debt in Pacific Island Countries, 2010

Country	External Public Debt (Percent of GDP)[1]	Total Gross Public Debt (Percent of GDP)[2]
Fiji	9	55.6
Kiribati	11.3	31.9
Papua New Guinea	10.7	26.5
Samoa	52.4	54.3
Solomon Islands	19.9	28.1
Tonga	36.6	42.8
Tuvalu	31	43.6
Vanuatu	16	20.2

Source: IMF Article IV Reports (2010–12).
[1] Fiji represents actuals; Tonga represents preliminaries; Papua New Guinea, the Solomon Islands, and Tuvalu represent estimates; and Kiribati and Samoa represent projections.
[2] Fiji and Tonga represent actuals; all others are estimates and projections.

Resource Allocation Policies

The food and fuel price hikes and the global economic recession have exposed resource allocation vulnerabilities in PICs. Clearly, broadening economic bases—where this is possible—would result in more diversified production and export structures, thereby creating potential for PICs to better withstand external economic and other shocks. Enhancing export capacity, and the diversification of exports and export markets, may therefore assist some countries to achieve greater internal stability during periods of economic shocks.

Some PICs are heavily dependent on imported food and fuel. Greater diversification in energy supplies and greater self-sufficiency in agriculture production could assist in reducing the adverse effects on domestic inflation and living standards created by surges in international food and fuel prices. Greater diversification of output and exports into service industries, including tourism, where feasible, may also assist PICs to become more resilient to external economic shocks.

Structural policies generally aimed at raising productivity are also likely to assist in generating scope for flexibility, lower production costs, improved competitiveness, and higher incomes. They also establish the basis for greater overall economic resilience in difficult times. Such policies would include addressing inefficiencies in state-owned enterprises, improving transport and communication links, progressively removing trade-distorting barriers, improving government service delivery, facilitating land reform and adopting improved agricultural techniques, greater deregulation, and encouraging greater domestic and overseas competition.

CONCLUSION

A number of PICs are experiencing relatively large macroeconomic imbalances, including excessive budget deficits, high public or external debt, and high current account deficits. Such macroeconomic imbalances may constrain the ability of these countries to respond to future economic shocks. Large budget deficits and high public debt constrain fiscal responses to shocks, and high current account deficits and high external debt imply greater vulnerability to adverse external shocks.

REFERENCES

Andrade da Silva, J., and L. Cernat. 2012. "Coping with Loss: The Impact of Natural Disasters on Developing Countries Trade Flows." *Vox Economics*, February 9.

Asian Development Bank (ADB). 2007. "Rehabilitation and Reconstruction Program for Disaster-affected Areas, Solomon Islands." Project document, Manila.

———. 2009a. *Taking Control of Oil: Managing Dependence on Petroleum Fuels in the Pacific.* Pacific Studies Series. Manila: ADB.

———. 2009b. *Taking the Helm: A Policy Brief on a Response to the Global Economic Crisis.* Pacific Studies Series. Manila: ADB.

———. 2009c. *Pacific Economic Monitor: August 2009,* Manila.

———. 2010. *Pacific Economic Monitor: July 2010,* Manila.

———. 2011. *Pacific Economic Monitor: December 2011,* Manila.

ANZ. 2012a. Asia Pacific Research, Pacific Monthly. March 15.

———. 2012b. "Pacific Export Diversification: Going the Wrong Way." Asia Pacific Research, Pacific Monthly, February.

Berg, A., E. Borensztein, and P. Mauro. 2003. "Monetary Regime Options for Latin America." *Finance and Development* 40 (3): 24–7.

Browne, C., and A. Mineshima. 2007. "Remittances in the Pacific Region." IMF Working Paper 07/35, International Monetary Fund, Washington.

Bussiere, M., F. Ghironi, and G. Sestieri. 2012. "Estimating Trade Elasticities: Demand Composition and the Trade Collapse of 2008–09." *Vox Economics*, February 14.

Central Bank of Samoa. 2009. "Monetary Policy Statement for the Financial Year 2009/2010." http://www.cbs.gov.ws/index.php/dmsdocument/242.

Cespedes, L., R. Chang, and A. Velasco. 2004. "Balance Sheets and Exchange Rate Policy." *American Economic Review* 94 (4): 1183–93.

Commonwealth Secretariat/World Bank. 2000. "Small States: Meeting Challenges in the Global Economy." Report of the Commonwealth Secretariat/World Bank Joint Task Force on Small States.

Dabla-Norris, E., C. Minoiu, and L. Zanna. 2010. "Business Cycle Fluctuations, Large Shocks, and Development Aid: New Evidence." IMF Working Paper 10/240, International Monetary Fund, Washington.

Hezel, F. 2012. "Pacific Island Nations: How Viable Are Their Economies?" *Pacific Islands Policy*, No. 7, EastWest Center.

Imam, P. 2010. "Exchange Rate Choices in Microstates." IMF Working Paper 10/12, International Monetary Fund, Washington.

International Monetary Fund (IMF). 2010. *Samoa: 2010 Article IV Consultation—Staff Report.* IMF Country Report 10/214, Washington.

———. 2011. *Papua New Guinea: 2011 Article IV Consultation—Staff Report.* IMF Country Report No. 11/117, Washington.

International Monetary Fund/World Bank. 2004. "Debt Sustainability in Low-Income Countries: Proposal for an Operational Framework and Policy Implications." Washington.

Jayaraman, T., and C. Choong. 2009. "How Does Monetary Policy Transmission Mechanism Work in Fiji?" *International Review of Economics* l (56): 145–61.

Jayaraman, T., and J. Dahalan. 2008. "Monetary Policy in an Undeveloped South Pacific Island Country: A Case Study of Samoa." *International Journal of Monetary Economics and Finance* 1 (4): 380–98.

Migration Policy Institute. 2011a. "Remittances Profile: Samoa."

———. 2011b. "Remittances Profile: Tonga." http://www.migrationpolicy.org/sites/default/files/publications/Tonga.pdf.

Ministry of Finance and National Planning, Tonga. 2009. *At a Glance*, June.

Narayan, S., and P. Narayan. 2004. "Determinants of Demand for Fiji's Exports: An Empirical Investigation." *Developing Economies* 42 (1): 95–112.

———. 2007. "Is Devaluation Expansionary or Contractionary? Empirical Evidence from Fiji." *Applied Economics* 39 (20): 2589–98.

Naudé, W. 2011. "The Global Financial Crisis and Development: Implications for the Entrepreneurial Economy." Working Papers 2011/01, Maastricht School of Management, Maastricht.

Pacific Island Ministers of Agriculture and Fisheries. 2008. "Pacific Island Food Security: Situation, Challenges, and Opportunities." Paper prepared for Pacific Island Ministers of Agriculture and Fisheries Meeting, Apia, Samoa, September.

Pacific Islands Trade and Investment Commission. 2008. "Australian Outbound Travel," Sydney.

Reddy, S. 2009. "Presentation to the Public and Private Sector Consultative Forum on the 2010 Budget." Suva Fiji, September 17.

Santos-Paulino. 2011. "Fragility and Vulnerability in Small Island Developing States: Issues and Challenges." UNCTAD, September. Paper presented at the First Meeting of the Caribbean Development Round Table, Economic Commission for Latin America and the Caribbean, Port of Spain, Trinidad, September 13.

Singh, R., and S. Kumar. 2009. "Some Empirical Evidence on the Demand for Money in the Pacific Island Countries." MPRA Paper 18703, Munich Personal RePEc Archive, Munich.

UNICEF. 2011. "Situation Monitoring: Food Price Increases in the Pacific. http://www.unicef.org/pacificislands/FINAL_SITUATION_REPORTING2.pdf.

World Bank. 2006. "Not If, but When: Adapting to Natural Hazards in the Pacific Islands Region." Policy Note, Washington.

CHAPTER 8

Drivers of Inflation in the Pacific Island Countries

XUEFEI BAI, PATRIZIA TUMBARELLO, AND YIQUN WU

The Pacific island countries (PICs) are highly exposed to commodity price shocks and exchange rate volatility. This is the result of the structure of these economies: narrow production and export bases and, hence, heavy reliance on imported food and fuel. This makes inflation volatile, posing a challenge for monetary policy. Some countries have also a de facto peg vis-à-vis the U.S. dollar, which makes the domestic currency volatile vis-à-vis the Australian dollar.

During 2000–14 average consumer price index (CPI) inflation in PICs was higher and more volatile than in other developing Asia and Pacific economies (Figure 8.1). Although more volatile, before 2007, average headline inflation in the Pacific region was nevertheless in single digits, in line with global inflation developments (Ciccarelli and Mojon 2010). The large increase in global food and fuel prices, a strong Australian dollar driven by high terms of trade in Australia, and several natural disasters drove headline inflation to a peak of almost 13 percent in the third quarter of 2008 (Figure 8.1). Since then, the global financial crisis put significant downward pressure on inflation through various channels, including lower commodity prices, and exchange rate depreciation exacerbated these pressures.[1]

As most PICs are low-income countries with relatively high weights of food and transportation in their CPI baskets (Annex Table 8.1.1) and large shares of food and oil in total imports (Figure 8.2), inflationary spillovers have been challenging for policymakers.[2] Although there is extensive literature on the effects of external factors on inflation, there are still few studies on the PICs. Research is needed to answer such questions as the extent to which recent inflation is attributable to changes in international commodity prices and to exchange rate volatility, and how commodity prices and exchange rate pass-through to inflation can be quantified.

To shed some light on these questions, this chapter uses two methodologies to study the inflation pass-through of international commodity prices and exchange rates. We first use fixed-effects panel regressions to examine the inflation dynamics from a regional point of view, and then estimate vector autoregression (VAR) models for each country, taking country-specific characteristics into account.

INFLATION PASS-THROUGH: PANEL REGRESSIONS

A cross-country dynamic panel model was estimated to cast light on the sources of inflation in the six countries in our sample. With the exception of Papua New Guinea, which has a de jure floating exchange rate regime and a de facto crawling-like arrangement since April 2014, five countries in

[1] In April 2009 Fiji devalued its currency by 20 percent to increase trade competitiveness and counter the rapid decline in its international reserves. The Solomon Islands operated a de facto peg against the U.S. dollar before 2009, and has gradually allowed greater exchange rate flexibility to safeguard reserves.

[2] The potential unfavorable effects of inflation on poverty and growth are well documented in the literature. Rising inflation can increase income inequality because it is essentially a regressive tax with an adverse impact on the poor. And rapid inflation can quickly erode the purchasing power of the poor because they have limited cash and bank deposits, and generally lack job security and financial assets to provide an adequate hedge against inflation (Tumbarello 2006). As a result, this could lead to severe economic and social problems.

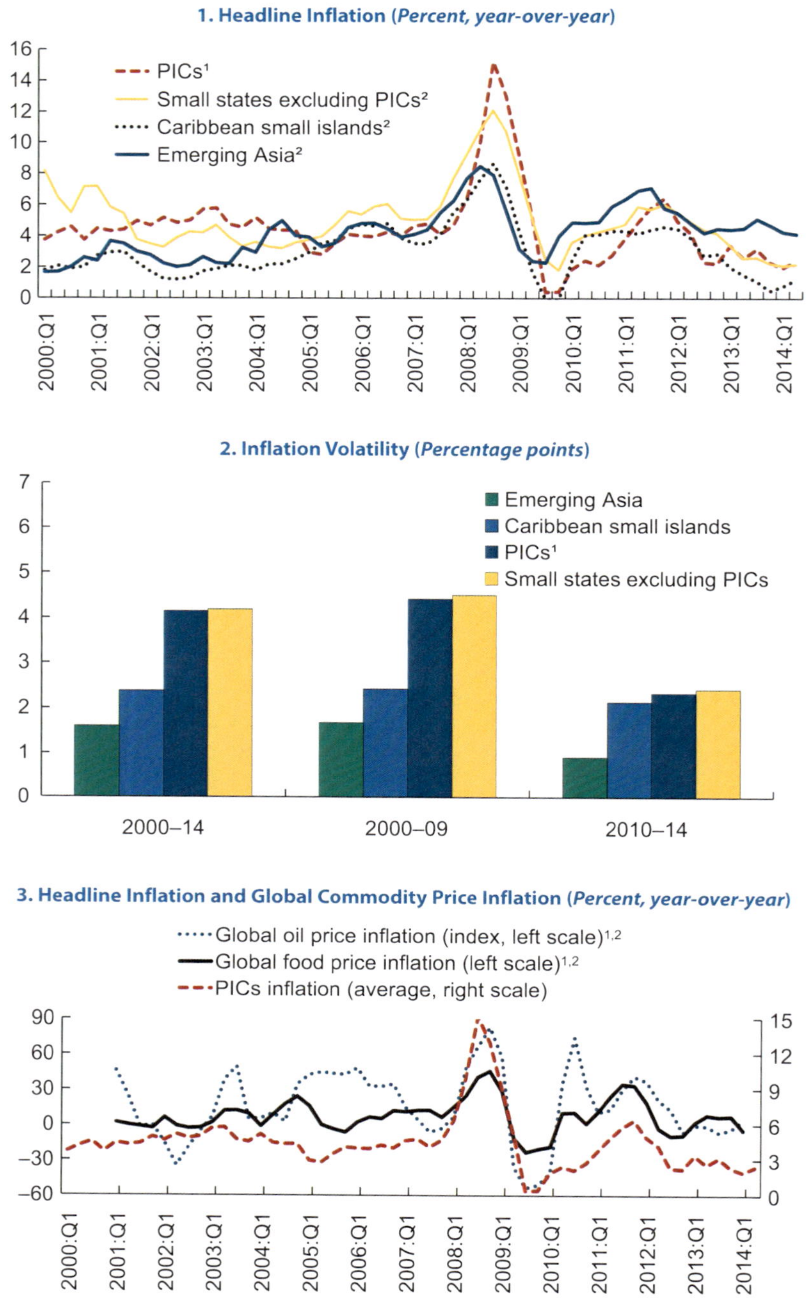

Figure 8.1 Inflation Development

our sample (Fiji, Samoa, Solomon Islands, Tonga, Vanuatu) peg their currencies to a basket of major trade partners' currencies, including the Australian dollar, U.S. dollar, Japanese yen, and others.

Our model incorporates the following variables: current CPI inflation (dependent variable); lagged inflation, which captures the inflation-inertia component; international food prices; international oil prices; current and lagged exchange rates against the Australian dollar (or the nominal effective exchange rate), which is intended to capture the degree of pass-through from the exchange rate to domestic prices; and output gap, as a measure of excess demand pressures. The output gap is

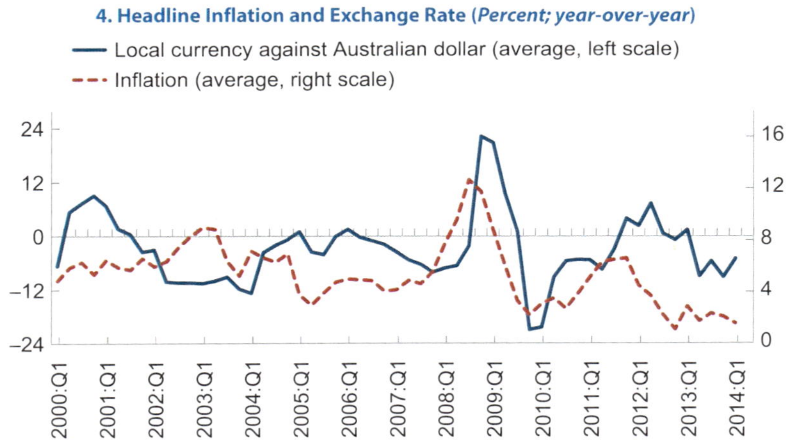

Figure 8.1 (*Continued*)

Sources: Country authorities; and IMF, International Financial Statistics database.
Note: PICs = Pacific island countries.
[1]Includes Fiji, Kiribati, Marshall Islands, Micronesia, Palau, Papua New Guinea, Samoa, the Solomon Islands, Timor-Leste, Tonga, Tuvalu, and Vanuatu.
[2]Average.

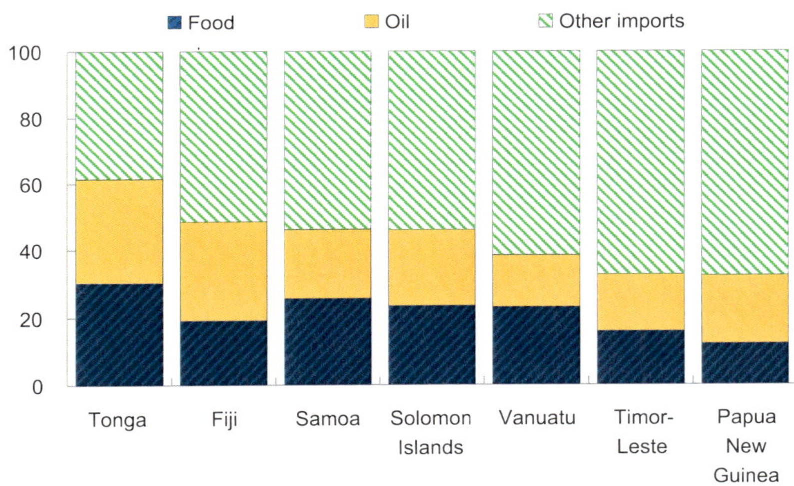

Figure 8.2 Pacific Island Countries: Import Composition, 2009–13 (*Percent*)

Source: IMF staff estimates.

measured as the deviation of actual output from potential output (defined as 1 – GDP/potential GDP). Potential output is estimated as a measure of the GDP trend using the Hodrick-Prescott filter. A positive output gap indicates that output is below trend. Our analysis focuses on the Australian dollar exchange rate. Australia remains the most important source of imports in the region,[3] and the nominal effective exchange rate of all six countries has moved closely with their nominal exchange rate against the Australian dollar, especially since the global financial crisis. We use quarterly data from the second quarter of 2003 to the first quarter of 2013. Annex Table 8.1.3 lists the details for data sources.

[3] It should also be noted that the import sources of PICs have become more diversified over time. In 2012 some 30 percent of import goods came from Australia, down from 43 percent in 1995.

Specifically, we estimate the following specification using a fixed-effects panel regression:

$$\Delta CPI_{i,t} = \alpha + \beta_1{}^*\Delta\log(CPI_{i,t-1}) + \beta_2{}^*\Delta\log(Fweight^*Pfood_{i,t-1}) + \beta_3{}^*\Delta\log(Poil_{i,t}) + \beta_4{}^*\Delta\log(AUD_{i,t}) + \beta_5{}^*\Delta\log(AUD_{i,t-1}) + \beta_6{}^*YGAP_{i,t-1} + \beta_7{}^*Credit_{i,t-1} + \varepsilon_{i,t}$$

where *CPI* is the consumer price index, *Pfood* is the international food price measured in the domestic currency, *Poil* is the international oil price measured in the domestic currency, *AUD* is the bilateral exchange rate against the Australian dollar (local currency per Australian dollar), *YGAP* is the output gap, and *Credit* is credit to the private sector measured in the local currency. We also run a separate set of models using the nominal effective exchange rate in the place of *AUD*. The model was estimated using a differenced generalized method-of-moments estimator that allows past actual values of the dependent variable (in this case, CPI inflation) to affect its current level without being subject to the problems of endogeneity present in dynamic panel analysis.

The econometric results are shown in Annex Table 8.1.2. Group 1 regressions use the base dynamic generalized method-of-moments model, while group 2 regressions estimate the same model but allow for cross-sectional fixed effects. The results show a high degree of persistence in inflation in PICs. In particular, 1 percentage point of past inflation is associated with an inflation increase in the current period in a range of 0.4 to 0.6 percentage point, depending on model specifications.

As expected, headline inflation depends on external factors, including international food prices, oil price inflation, and the Australian dollar exchange rate (or the nominal effective exchange rate). In general, an increase of 1 percentage point in international food price inflation, oil price inflation, and the Australian dollar exchange rate (depreciation) is associated with an increase in inflation of about 0.03, 0.01, and 0.10 percentage point, respectively. In a separate set of models, a 1 percentage point increase in the nominal effective exchange rate (appreciation) is roughly associated with a decrease in inflation of about 0.14 percentage point. Not surprisingly, the impact of international food prices is stronger than that for oil prices, since food is the largest category in the CPI basket for all six PICs.

As for domestic factors, the econometric results confirm that both output gap and credit to the private sector are important determinants of inflation. In general, a 1 percentage point increase in output gap (less demand) is associated with disinflation in a range of 0.02 to 0.07 percentage point, depending on model specifications. A 1 percentage point increase in private credit growth is associated with an inflation increase of about 0.04–0.05 percentage point.

VECTOR AUTOREGRESSION ESTIMATION

While the cross-country panel regression results have shed light on the inflation pass-through of global commodity prices and exchange rates in the region, it is also helpful to identify country-specific responses of headline inflation to external shocks. In this section, we conduct the VAR analysis for each of the six PICs, taking country-specific characteristics into account. The VAR system expresses current values of each series as a weighted average of the recent past of all the series, plus a term that contains all the other influences on the current values:

$$A_0 y_t = v + A_1 * y_{t-1} + \cdots + A_p * y_{t-p} + e_t$$

$$y_t = A_0^{-1}v + A_0^{-1}A_1 * y_{t-1} + \ldots + A_0^{-1}A_p * y_{t-p} + A_0^{-1}e_t$$

with $B_l = A_0^{-1}A_l$ and $\mu_t = A_0^{-1}e_t$

$$y_t = V + B_1 * y_{t-1} + \cdots + B_p * y_{t-p} + \mu_t$$

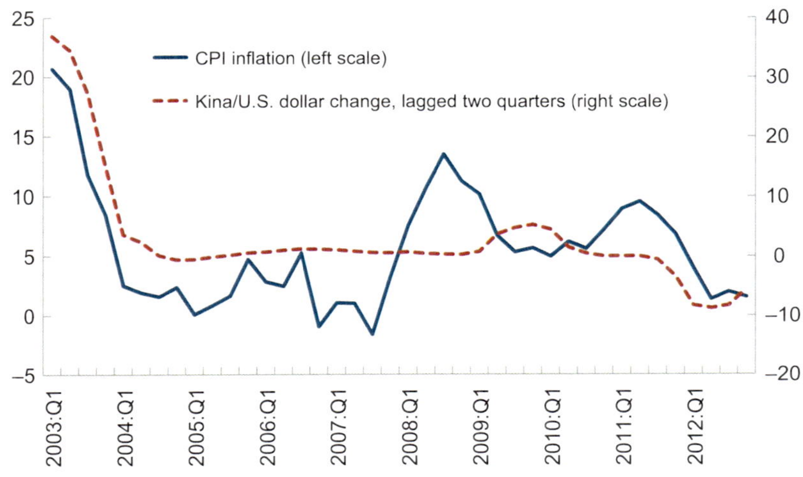

Figure 8.3 Papua New Guinea: CPI Inflation and the U.S. Dollar Exchange Rate (*Percent*)

Source: IMF staff estimates.
Note: CPI = consumer price index.

where y_t denotes the $m*1$ vector of variables included in the VAR for quarter t, and the error vector u_t measures the extent to which y_t cannot be determined exactly as a linear combination of the past values of y, with weights given by the constant coefficients v and B_l, $l = 1,2,\ldots,p$.

The selection of variables in the VAR models is based on the results of the panel regressions and country-specific ordinary least squares regressions. For each country, international oil price (Δlog (*Poil*)), international food price (Δlog (*Pfood*)), the Australian dollar exchange rate change against the local currency (Δlog (*AUD*)), headline inflation (Δlog (*CPI*)), output gap (*YGAP*), and credit to the private sector (Δlog (*Credit*)) are always included in the VAR system. Besides these common variables, we also consider country-specific factors.

For Fiji, since sugar is one of its main exports, and changes in sugar prices have a significant impact on headline inflation in our ordinary least squares regression for the country, we include Δlog (*Psugar*) in its VAR system. For Papua New Guinea, as Figure 8.3 shows, the inflation pass-through of the U.S. dollar exchange rate is more significant than that of the Australian dollar given the important role played by the U.S. dollar in the global oil market.

For this reason, Δlog (*USD*) is also included in its VAR system. The models are estimated from the first quarter of 2003 to the first quarter of 2013. The number of optimal lags in each VAR is determined by the Schwarz criteria. Based on VAR results, we plot the impulse responses of headline inflation to the shocks of global commodity prices and exchange rates on a two-year horizon.

The identification strategy assumes that shocks in food prices, oil prices, the Australian dollar exchange rate, and domestic credit growth affect inflation in the current and subsequent periods. This is implemented using a Choleski decomposition with the variables in the following order: Δlog(*Pfood*), Δlog(*Poil*), Δlog(*AUD*), *YGAP*, Δlog(*Credit*), and finally Δlog (*CPI*).[4] The relationship between reduced errors (μ_t) and structural errors (e_t) is presented in A_0^{-1}—an assumed matrix, whose coefficients are estimated.

$$E[\mu_t \mu_t'] = E[(A_0^{-1} e_t)(A_0^{-1} e_t)']$$

$$\mu_t = A_0^{-1} e_t$$

[4]The Fiji model includes the price of sugar; the Papua New Guinea model includes the U.S. dollar exchange rate.

$$\begin{bmatrix} \mu_{\Delta\log(Pfood),t} \\ \mu_{\Delta\log(Poil),t} \\ \mu_{\Delta\log(AUD),t} \\ \mu_{\Delta\log(Credit),t} \\ \mu_{YGAP,t} \\ \mu_{\Delta\log(CPI),t} \end{bmatrix} = \begin{bmatrix} * & 0 & 0 & 0 & 0 & 0 \\ * & * & 0 & 0 & 0 & 0 \\ * & * & * & 0 & 0 & 0 \\ * & * & * & * & 0 & 0 \\ * & * & * & * & * & 0 \\ * & * & * & * & * & * \end{bmatrix}^{-1} * \begin{bmatrix} e_{\Delta\log(Pfood),t} \\ e_{\Delta\log(Poil),t} \\ e_{\Delta\log(AUD),t} \\ e_{\Delta\log(Credit),t} \\ e_{YGAP,t} \\ e_{\Delta\log(CPI),t} \end{bmatrix}$$

Responses to International Commodity Price Shocks

The responses of headline inflation to the change in international food and oil prices for each country are presented in Annex Figures 8.1.1 and 8.1.2. The results suggest that the response of headline inflation to the international food price shocks is positive for all countries, as expected. Generally, the response peaks within one year, then tapers off and eventually disappears in two years. Take Fiji, for example: a positive shock to international food price increases inflation with a one-quarter lag and it lasts for two quarters. An increase of the international oil price also has a positive effect on inflation for all six countries.[5] Compared with the food price shock, the effect of the international oil price shock on inflation is overall smaller but lasts longer. As the only oil producer in our sample, Papua New Guinea has more resources to fight inflation when oil prices are rising. While the inflation effect of the oil price shock lasts in Papua New Guinea for almost one and a half years, the shock is mainly from the demand side, as more income with a high oil price leads to more consumption and investment. Among nonoil producers, the inflationary impact of the oil price shock lasts only two to three quarters in Fiji, Samoa, and the Solomon Islands, and one year or more in Tonga and Vanuatu.

Responses to the Exchange Rate Shocks

Annex Figure 8.1.3 presents the responses of headline inflation to the movement of the Australian dollar. In general, a depreciation of the currencies of the seven PICs against the Australian dollar does put pressure on headline inflation. However, Papua New Guinea appears to be an exception. There are two possible reasons. First, the country has a relatively flexible exchange rate regime, so the kina exchange rate has been more likely adjusted to accommodate the rising inflation pressure. Second, as the U.S. dollar is the primary oil currency, the inflation pass-through of the U.S. dollar exchange rate is more significant than that of the Australian dollar in Papua New Guinea. This point is supported by the synchronization between inflation and the U.S. dollar exchange rate change, as well as the VAR impulse response results (see Figure 8.3).

Besides the shocks from international commodity prices and exchange rates, credit to the private sector and output gap are also included in the VAR for each country. As expected, the response of headline inflation to a domestic credit shock is generally positive, while the response to an output gap shock is generally negative.

CONCLUSION

Given the relatively weak monetary transmission mechanism (see Chapter 12), the pass-through of international commodity prices (especially food prices) and exchange rates has been rapid and large in the PICs (see Chapter 13). However, our analysis indicates that these countries have been more resilient to external inflationary shocks since the global financial crisis. This is probably due to price controls and subsidies to food and transportation prices, the implementation of more prudential macroeconomic policies, and more diversified import sources.

[5] For the pass-through from the price of oil to inflation, see De Gregorio, Landerretche, and Neilson (2007) and Hooke (2002).

ANNEX 8.1. RESPONSES TO EXTERNAL SHOCKS IN PACIFIC ISLAND COUNTRIES

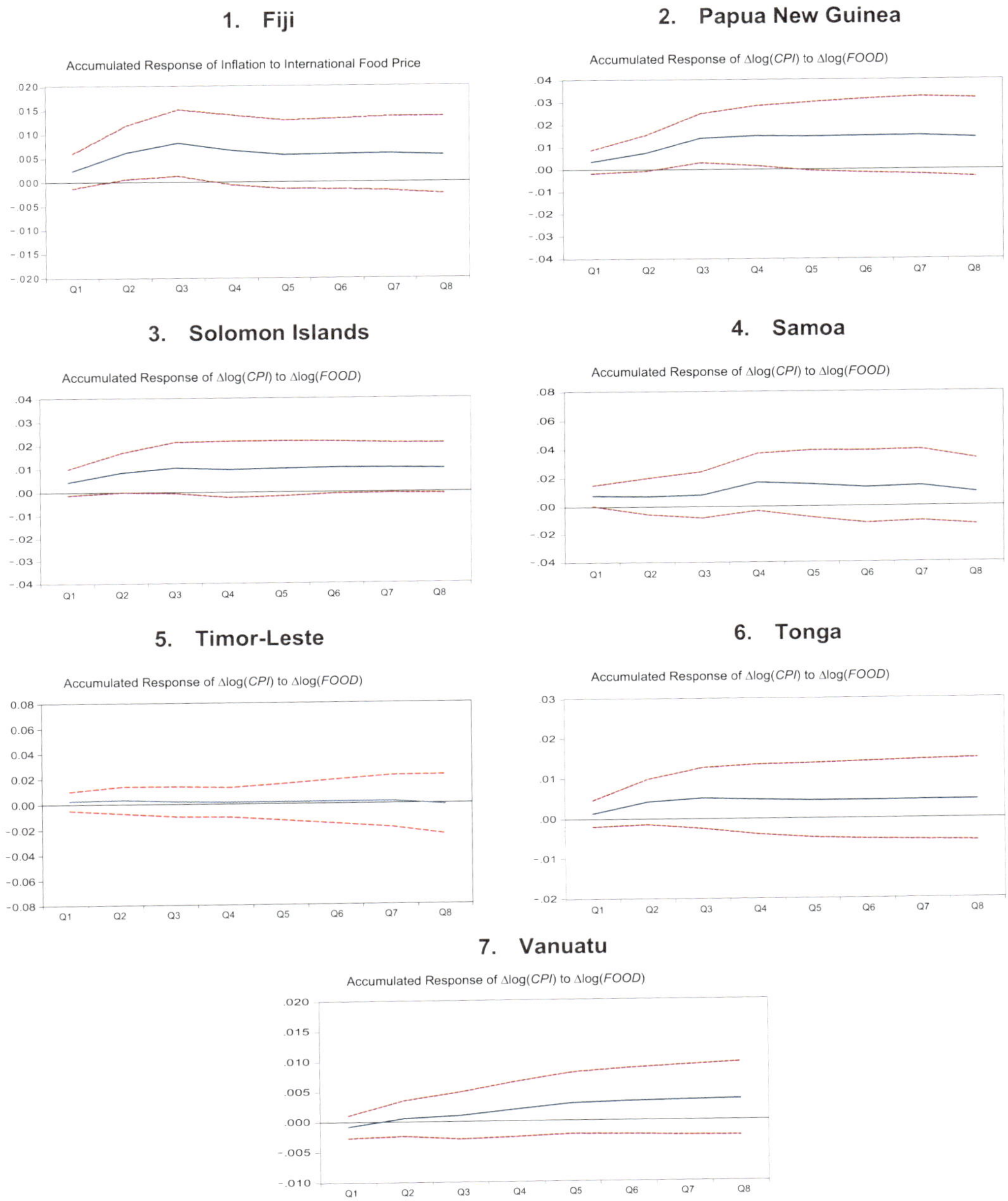

Annex Figure 8.1.1 CPI Response to One Standard Deviation Shock from International Food Price

Source: IMF staff estimates.

Note: CPI = consumer price index. Figure shows accumulated response of inflation to international food prices, measured as the ratio of Δlog(*CPI*) to Δlog(*FOOD*). The blue lines represent the impulse response function; red dotted lines the upper and lower bounds of the confidence interval.

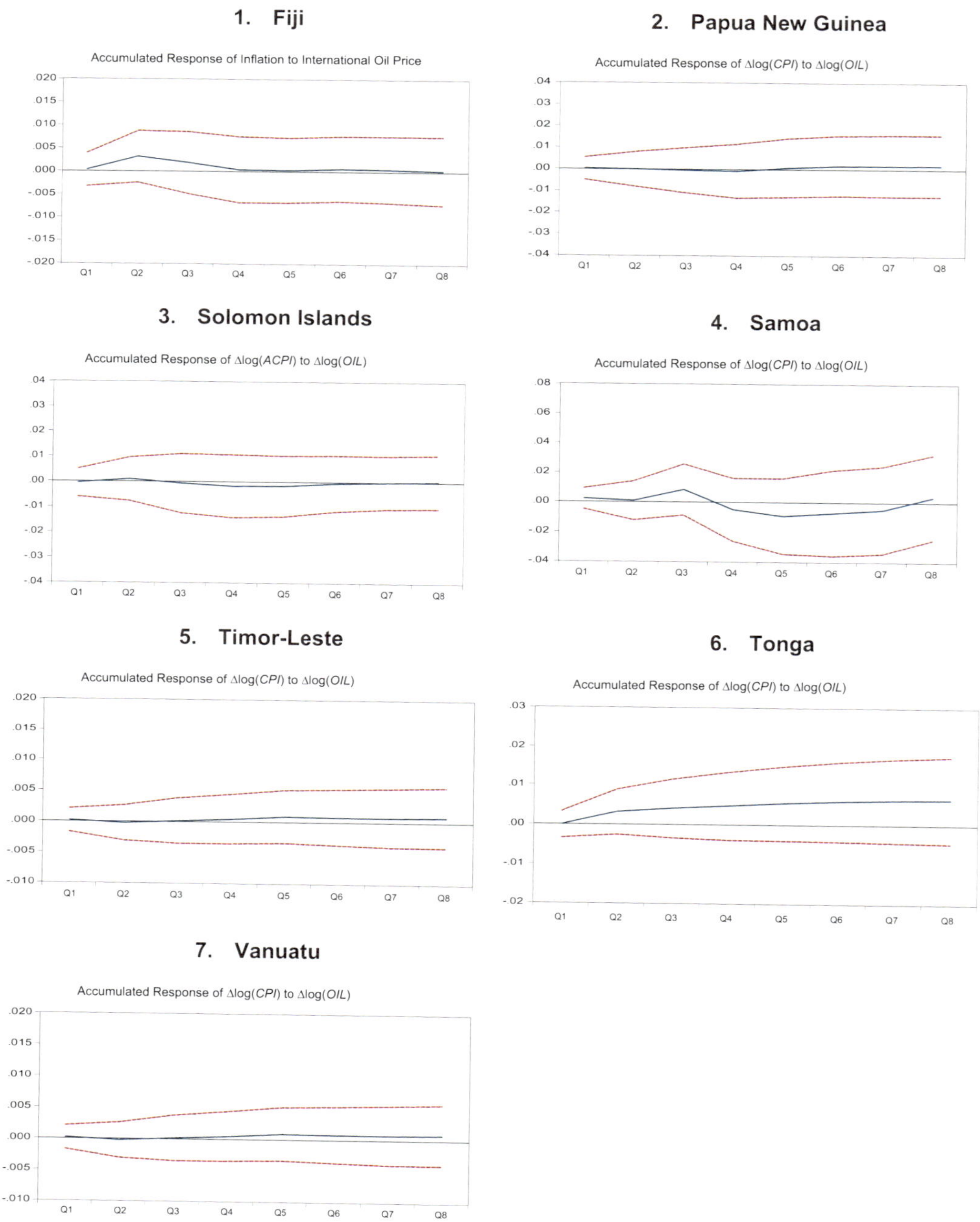

Annex Figure 8.1.2 CPI Response to One Standard Deviation Shock from International Oil Price

Source: IMF staff estimates.

Note: CPI = consumer price index. Figure shows accumulated response of inflation to international oil prices, measured as the ratio of $\Delta\log(CPI)$ to $\Delta\log(OIL)$. The blue lines represent the impulse response function; red dotted lines the upper and lower bounds of the confidence interval.

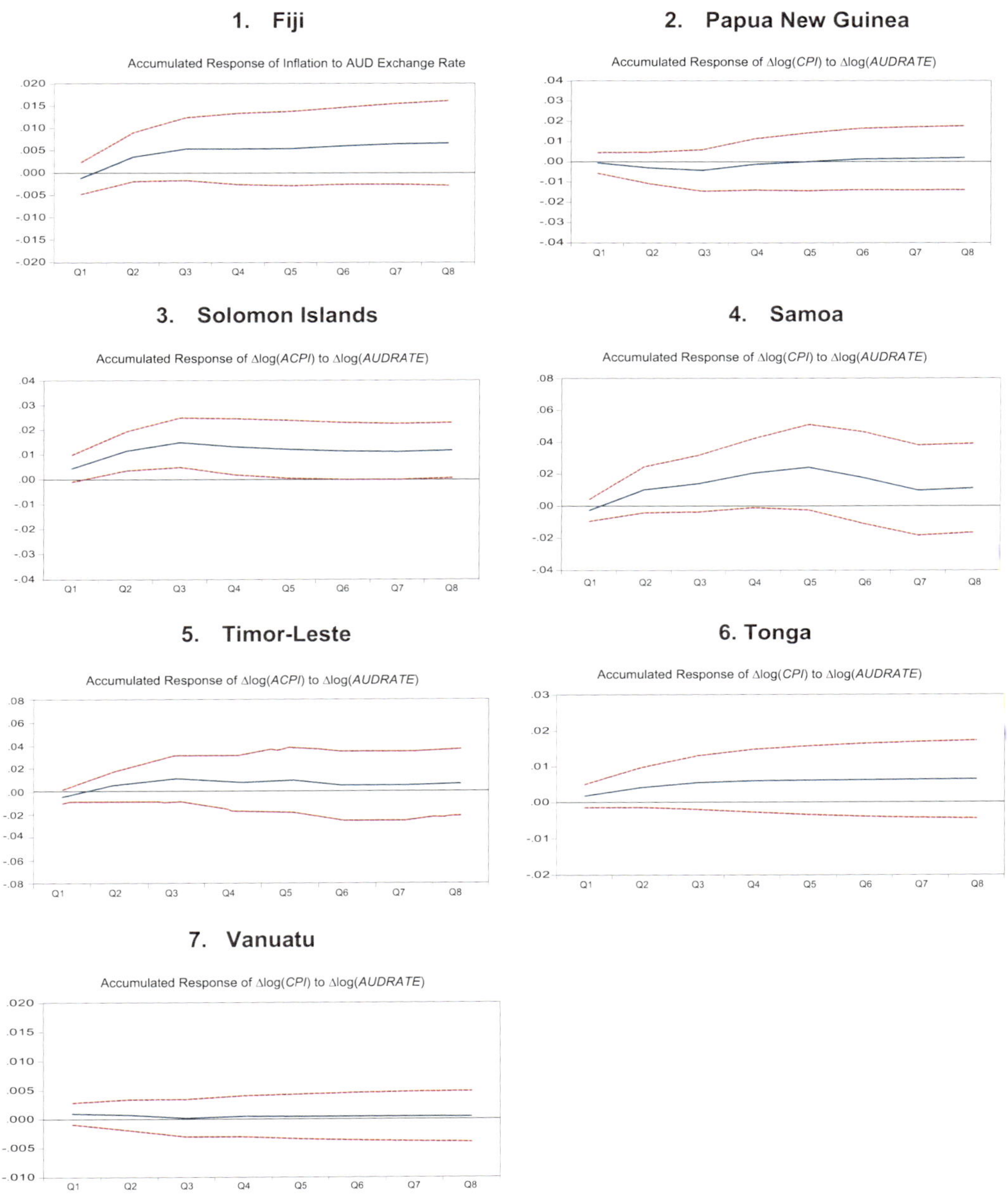

Annex Figure 8.1.3 CPI Response to One Standard Deviation Shock from Australian Dollar Exchange Rate

Source: IMF staff estimates.

Note: CPI = consumer price index. Figure shows accumulated response of inflation to Australian dollar (AUD) exchange rate, measured as the ratio of Δlog(*CPI*) to Δlog(*AUDRATE*). The blue lines represent the impulse response function; red dotted lines the upper and lower bounds of the confidence interval.

ANNEX TABLE 8.1.1

Selected Indicators in Pacific Island Countries

Country	Per Capita GDP (2012, US$)	Food's Weight in CPI Basket	Transportation's Weight in CPI Basket	CPI Inflation Central Bank Reference[1]
Fiji	4,578	40.3	16.2	3 percent
Kiribati	1,546	51.2	8.1	...
Marshall Islands	3,236	35.9	13.7	...
Micronesia	3,215	37.1	9.3	...
Palau	14,022	25.4	16.8	...
Papua New Guinea	2,098	40.9	13.0	5 percent
Samoa	4,165	50.3	9.3	3 percent
Solomon Islands	1,936	46.8	9.9	No specific reference value
Timor-Leste	4,142	64.3	6.4	No specific reference value
Tonga	4,572	45.7	11.9	6–8 percent
Tuvalu	3,575	42.0	8.8	...
Vanuatu	2,996	38.4	11.8	0–4 percent

Source: IMF staff estimates.
Note: ... = not applicable.
[1]All the Pacific island country central banks have price stability as one of their monetary policy objectives, and some set the inflation reference value. However, none of them has a formal inflation target.

ANNEX TABLE 8.1.2

Drivers of Inflation in Pacific Island Countries

	Basic GMM				GMM with Fixed Effects				Group 3 Regression			
	1	2	3	4	1	2	3	4	1	2	3	4
Constant	0.005***	0.004**	0.005***	0.004*	0.006***	0.005**	0.007***	0.004	0.006***	0.007***	0.006***	0.006***
Past inflation [$t-1$]	0.559***	0.495***	0.580***	0.544***	0.447***	0.411**	0.377***	0.514***	0.458***	0.398***	0.527***	0.482***
Global oil price inflation [$t-1$]	0.011**	0.005*	0.011**	0.010***	0.010**	0.005**	0.010**	0.01***	0.000	0.005	-0	0.003
Global food price inflation	0.027***	0.015**	0.024***	0.010	0.028***	0.016***	0.026***	0.011*	0.027***	0.025***	0.023***	0.022***
Depreciation against Australian dollar	0.038***				0.027***				0.045***	0.037***		
Depreciation against Australian dollar [$t-1$]	0.065***	0.093***			0.064**	0.090***			0.117***	0.117***		
NEER change			-0.046*				-0.028				-0.05	-0.04
NEER change [$t-1$]			-0.087***	-0.165***			-0.096***	-0.16***			-0.12***	-0.11***
								-0.07***				
Output gap	-0.021**	-0.061***	-0.015*	-0.071***	-0.027**	-0.054***	-0.024*			-0.04***		-0.03***
Credit growth		0.046**		0.037**		0.050**		0.04**				

Source: IMF staff estimates.
Note: GMM = generalized method of moments; NEER = nominal effective exchange rate.
[1] Includes Fiji, Papua New Guinea, Solomon Islands, Samoa, Tonga, and Vanuatu.
* $p < 0.1$, ** $p < 0.05$, *** $p < 0.01$.

ANNEX TABLE 8.1.3

List of Variables and Sources

Variable	Content	Source
CPI	Quarterly consumer price index	PICs authorities
Pfood	Average-quarter international food price by domestic currency	IMF IFS database and authors' calculation
Poil	Average-quarter international oil price by domestic currency	IMF IFS database and authors' calculation
AUD	Quarterly bilateral exchange rate against Australia dollar (local currency per AUD)	IMF IFS database
YGAP	Quarterly output gap, defined as 1-GDP/Potential GDP	GDP data is from PICs authorities, potential GDP is estimated by applying the HP filter to actual GDP
Credit	End-quarter level of credit to private sector (in local currency)	PICs authorities and authors' estimates
Fweight	Weight of food in CPI basket for each economy	PICs authorities
Imratio	Annual imports/GDP, which shows a country's reliance on imported goods, is used as a proxy for domestic production capacity (higher ratio means weaker capacity)	PICs authorities and authors' calculation

Note: CPI = consumer price index; IFS = IMF, International Financial Statistics; HP = Hodrick-Prescott; PICs = Pacific island countries.

REFERENCES

Ciccarelli, Matteo, and Benoit Mojon. 2010. "Global Inflation." *The Review of Economics and Statistics* 92 (3): 524–35.

De Gregorio, Jose, Oscar Landerretche, and Christopher Neilson. 2007. "Another Pass-Through Bites the Dust? Oil Prices and Inflation." Working Paper 417, Central Bank of Chile, Santiago.

Hooke, Mark. 2002. "Are Oil Shocks Inflationary? Asymmetric and Nonlinear Specifications versus Changes in Regime." *Journal of Money, Credit, and Banking* 34 (2): 540–61.

Tumbarello, Patrizia. 2006. "What Drives Inflation in Vietnam? A Regional Approach," Selected Issues Paper. IMF Country Report 06/422, International Monetary Fund, Washington.

CHAPTER 9

Vulnerabilities of Isolated Small Island States in the Pacific

CHRIS BECKER

This chapter considers features of small island states in the Pacific region as well as in Asia, and documents some of the key characteristics that set them apart from small states in other regions. The chapter restricts itself to a limited number of general indicators that are largely macro oriented. In particular, it considers population size, income per capita, the fertility of the land, and the ability to tap into economies of scale. It captures the degree of geographic isolation confronted by some countries. As a result, we leave aside equally important but more micro-oriented variables, such as telecommunications or electricity generation, as well as development indicators, such as literacy or infant mortality rates.

We show that small island states in the Pacific are typically different from small states in other regional groupings in that they are extremely geographically isolated and have limited scope to tap into economies of scale due to their small populations. The degree of smallness can complicate the interpretation of income per capita as a proxy for economic conditions, and the lack of fertile land constrains opportunities for some countries to diversify food sources away from imports. The cursory empirical evidence presented appears consistent with earlier evidence that most of these factors are important determinants of economic outcomes in small states.

Small states in other parts of the world have their own characteristics that lead to a somewhat different set of factors that might be associated with vulnerability to shocks. These may or may not have been taken into consideration in this chapter, which employs a far less than exhaustive set of potential indicators. So while the scope is purposely limited to the countries of principal interest for this study, it could provide a basis for more comprehensive future research.

The rest of the chapter discusses a number of key macro-related variables in the context of small states. These cover the definition of small states in terms of population size, constraints on the ability to take advantage of economies of scale, income per capita as a measure of poverty, the relationship between land fertility and import replacement through agriculture, and, perhaps most important, the degree of geographic isolation. These indicators are summarized by a simple and transparent ranking, and an attempt is made to relate the rankings to actual economic outcomes.

DEFINING SMALL STATES BY POPULATION

There is no universally accepted definition of what makes a country small. Relevant metrics include population, size of the land or territory (including maritime zones), and gross national income (GNI).[1] However, since population is usually correlated with other variables such as GNI in most countries, the number of residents is often used as the measure that defines smallness. The World

This chapter is a revised version of Becker (2012), and benefited from helpful comments by Hoseung Lee, Cynthia Rohan, John Rolle, Piers Merrick, Shanaka Peiris, Dominique Simard, Patrizia Tumbarello, and Yongzheng Yang. I thank Lucy Pan for discussions about the vulnerabilities of small island states in the Pacific while visiting Tuvalu. Data for the Environmental Vulnerability Index were gratefully received from Ursula Kaly at the South Pacific Applied Geoscience Commission.

[1] Given the importance of remittances and transfer payments as sources of income in many of these states, GNI is generally accepted as a more appropriate measure than the value added measured by GDP. See Annex 9.2 for metadata.

Bank defines a small state as one with a population of less than 1½ million people (World Bank 2007), but it also notes that no definition, whether it be population, geographic size, or income, is likely to be fully satisfactory. In practice, any threshold used has an arbitrary element, and larger states that lie outside this definition will share some of the characteristics or vulnerabilities of smaller countries.

Using World Bank data, we are able to derive a consistent data set for a preliminary analysis of a sample of 50 small states (see Annex 9.1).[2] The smallest of these is Tuvalu in the Asia and Pacific region, with a population of only about 10,000 people. The largest is Trinidad and Tobago in the Caribbean, with some 1.3 million people. Figure 9.1 ranks these countries by population. Those in the Asia and Pacific region are highlighted in a darker color.

Of the 10 smallest states, four are in Europe and central Asia, three are small island states in the Pacific (Marshall Islands, Palau, Tuvalu), and two are in Latin America and the Caribbean. Greenland represents an outlier not easily classified in any region.[3] The difficulty of defining aspects of smallness is usefully illustrated by examining these extremely small countries (sometimes referred to as microstates). While the number of people residing in them is indisputably small, they can be quite heterogeneous in terms of other economic indicators that make differentiation between small states important. For example, while the population of Monaco is about three times larger than that of Tuvalu, its GNI per capita is almost 40 times larger. Extremely small populations are therefore not always systematically related to income, but in some cases raise a number of other relevant idiosyncratic considerations. As a result, of the 10 smallest countries in this sample, fewer than half are eligible under the income criteria for both concessional borrowing from the International Development Association (IDA) (2001) and the IMF's Poverty Reduction and Growth Trust.[4]

LACKING ECONOMIES OF SCALE

Generally speaking, the relationship between population and total income appears to be positive. This is not surprising given that labor is a major input into the production process and a larger workforce can produce a greater number of goods and services for higher total income. Figure 9.2 shows this relationship for the small state sample and plots a simple trend line, which, admittedly, has only weak explanatory power. Asia and the Pacific is again highlighted by a darker color.

Since population is only one of many factors that determine income, the distribution of countries around the trend is relatively wide. Indeed, there appears to be a tendency to deviate further as population increases. Several outliers to the relationship are notable, with Luxembourg generating the largest GNI despite a relatively small population.[5] There is a confluence of attributes that makes some countries able to overcome the barriers of having a small resident workforce. In the case of Luxembourg, specialization in the provision of high-value-added financial services is possible due to a number of unique features, including very close proximity to highly skilled labor markets and infrastructure in neighboring countries, notably France and Germany. A significant share of the people employed in Luxembourg do not reside in the country itself, but commute daily from neighboring towns across the national border. Similarly, centers for trade and commerce such as Macao

[2] Fifteen states in the raw World Bank database were excluded from the initial sample of 65 on the basis that comparable data for other variables of interest, mainly GNI, were not available. These were American Samoa, Aruba, Bermuda, Cayman Islands, Curaçao, Faeroe Islands, French Polynesia, Guam, Mayotte, New Caledonia, Northern Mariana Islands, Sint Maarten, St. Martin, Turks and Caicos Islands, and the United States Virgin Islands.

[3] Groupings based on World Bank regional designations.

[4] Under the IDA framework, the exceptional circumstances of Marshall Islands and Tuvalu are recognized by an exemption from the income per capita threshold that allows them access to IDA loans. The IMF made some adjustments to the Poverty Reduction and Growth Trust eligibility criteria in view of the unique challenges they face (IMF 2013a, 2013b). See also IDA (2001) and IMF (2009, 2012) for background to the decisions.

[5] See Martins and Winters (2004) for a more detailed discussion of the economic factors that allow states such as Liechtenstein and Luxembourg to overcome the disadvantages of their smallness.

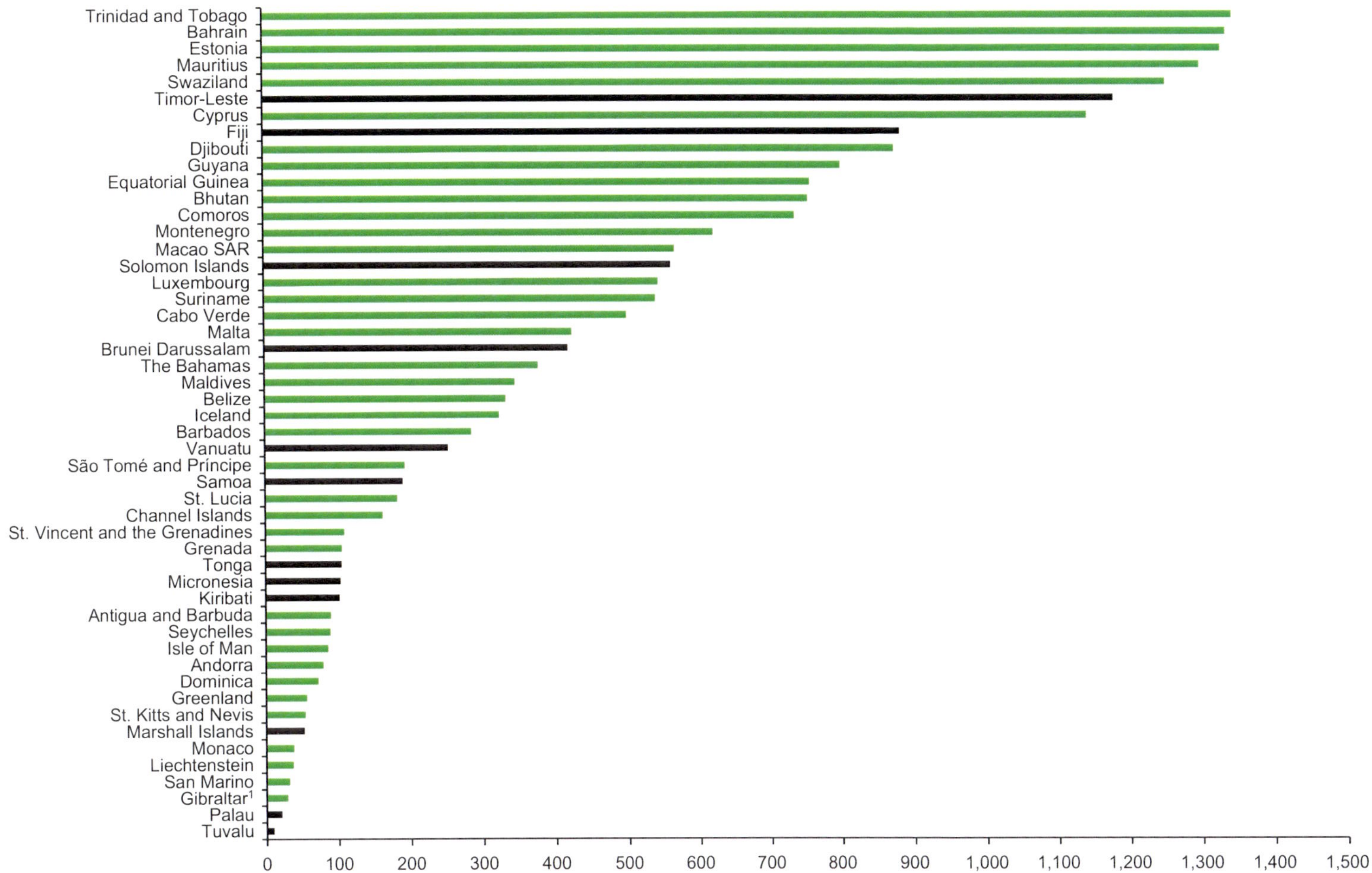

Figure 9.1 Small States with Populations of Less than 1.5 Million, 2013 *(Population, thousands)*

Source: World Bank, World Development Indicators database.
[1] The figure for Gibraltar is from 2012.

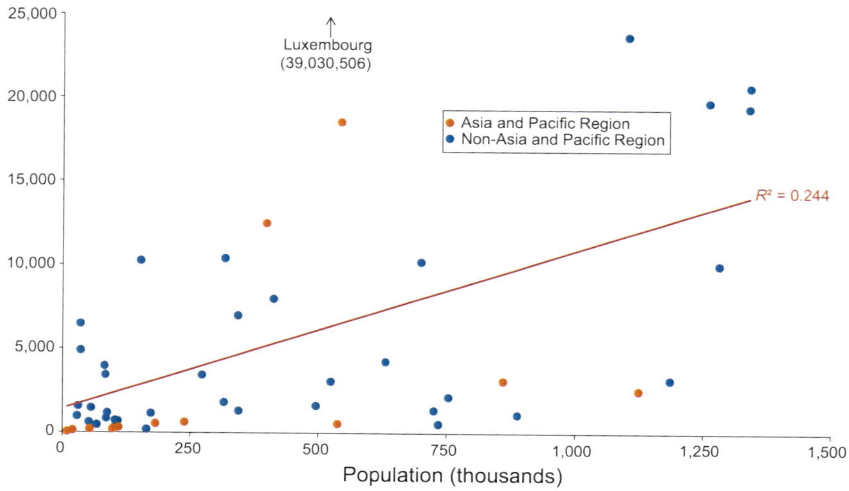

Figure 9.2 Relationship between Population and GNI (*GNI, millions of U.S. dollars*)

Sources: World Bank, World Development Indicators database; and author's calculations.
Note: GNI = gross national income.

Special Administrative Region are able to generate higher income than countries of similar size with less of this type of economic activity. The key feature of such trade hubs tends to be strategic location on major trade and shipping routes that act as gateways to major markets.

The small island states in the Pacific tend to lack the attributes enjoyed by financial centers and trade hubs. They are typically considerable distances from the major labor markets that are better equipped to supply a more skilled workforce, such as Australia and New Zealand (and this is discussed further later in the chapter). Geography also precludes sharing infrastructure with more developed neighbors. Indeed, basic infrastructure may need to be duplicated if populations are dispersed, as they are in countries comprising groups of islands. Furthermore, they are usually not on the routes of shipping lanes, which connect major producers with markets and are therefore unlikely candidates for establishing trade hubs. Nonetheless, there are certain types of financial services that are less closely linked to geographic location, such as business registration and the incorporation and registration of international cargo ships, which small Pacific islands are not precluded from pursuing.

Fixed Costs Spread over a Narrow Base

One implication of small population is that total income, and therefore the tax base, might be so small that the fixed costs associated with providing public goods and services have to be spread across a very narrow base. As a result, fixed costs may represent an unusually high share of national income. One consequence might be that there is insufficient tax revenue to secure the public provision of basic health services, transportation, and government administration. These constraints often result in small administrations that lack the capacity to function efficiently. The degree to which this is an issue varies among countries.

This is an argument related to economies of scale in that the provision of public goods and services might not be possible at the quantity necessary to minimize the average cost, giving rise to inefficient outcomes that are most difficult to successfully deal with in extremely small countries. Another consideration might be the expense incurred in building infrastructure resilient to frequent natural disasters and adverse weather conditions.

One simple way to make an assessment about the available opportunities to reap economies of scale is to calculate the percentage deviation of each country's GNI from the median of the small state sample.[6] This allows calibration of which states are the smallest and therefore the most likely to be lacking in the ability to exhaust economies of scale. The calculations are shown in Table 9.1. While very small states such as Palau and Tuvalu are more than 90 percent smaller than the sample median, others are considerably better placed. It is notable that of the small countries in the Pacific, almost all are so small that the scope to access economies of scale could be a significant issue. Only Fiji, Macao Special Administrative Region, and Timor-Leste were larger than the median income of $1.7 billion in 2010.

Scope for Regional Cooperation

Notwithstanding the country-specific constraints on accessing economies of scale, there may be scope to improve the position of small states through regional cooperation (see also Hausmann 2001). A number of small states could come together to form a larger common market for goods and services, or share access to certain types of infrastructure. Figure 9.3 sums the population of all countries in each region to derive a regional aggregate as an indication of the potential for cooperation.

In terms of the scope for cooperation in building scale based on the aggregate number of people in each region, the Pacific islands do not appear to be at a disadvantage relative to other regions. Instead, it would seem that small states in south Asia, as well as in the Middle East and North Africa, are the most limited in tapping into the benefits from cooperation—assuming that they are also somehow unable to cooperate with larger neighbors.[7] Greenland may be of less concern owing to its special relationship with Denmark.

Nonetheless, there may be many other obstacles to effective cooperation. Some of these might be related to culture, language, distance between countries, legal structure, and political and other forms of heterogeneity among neighboring states, which will differ according to region. However, there are regional forums that facilitate policy coordination and discussion, and this has certainly been the case for some time in the Pacific.[8]

GAUGING VULNERABILITY FROM INCOME PER CAPITA

Income per capita is an important variable, not least because it is often used as a proxy indicator for poverty and aid eligibility. For example, IDA eligibility is principally determined by a threshold related to GNI per capita, which is reviewed periodically. Eligibility for the IMF's Poverty Reduction and Growth Trust takes its cue from the IDA and is therefore similarly based on income per capita.

However, income per capita might also suffer from being an imperfect indicator, in the same way that the separate consideration of total income and population in relation to the possible inability of very small states to access economies of scale are imperfect indicators. Take, for example, an extremely small state. It might generate sufficient income from the sale of fishing licenses and remittances to rank relatively high on income per capita because the total income numerator is shared across a very small population denominator. Even so, this state might find itself in a situation in which total income is so small that it proves prohibitively expensive for the government to provide adequate health services domestically. If a substantial part of that higher income per capita has to be allocated toward expensive medical services in another country, the remaining disposable per capita amount available to households for consumption and saving might be significantly lower. In this simple example it is easy to recognize that assessments based on income per capita alone can be

[6] To investigate this issue more fully, factors such as different fixed costs arising from characteristics such as dispersion of the population and accessibility to service providers (for example, health care) would have to be considered.

[7] For small states in the Pacific, the scope for greater integration with Australia and New Zealand might hold the most promise.

[8] The main coordinating body in the region is the Pacific Islands Forum, which facilitates the Forum Economic Ministers' Meeting. This type of cooperation has resulted in the formulation of the Pacific Plan, the Pacific Agreement on Closer Economic Relations, several agreements on trade, and discussion about action on climate change. There is also coordination of technical assistance and training through the Pacific Financial Technical Assistance Center. See Browne (2006) for a concise summary of the Pacific Plan.

TABLE 9.1

Percentage Deviation from Small State Median Income

State	Percent Below	Percent Above
Tuvalu	–97.3	
Palau	–92.2	
Gibraltar	–43.6	
San Marino	–8.5	
Liechtenstein		185.3
Monaco		276.9
Marshall Islands	–88.6	
St. Kitts and Nevis	–64.2	
Greenland	–14.7	
Dominica	–73.3	
Andorra		100.6
Isle of Man		131.1
Seychelles	–50.8	
Antigua and Barbuda	–32.0	
Kiribati	–88.4	
Micronesia	–82.3	
Tonga	–80.1	
Grenada	–57.9	
St. Vincent and the Grenadines	–60.0	
Channel Islands		495.8
St. Lucia	–33.6	
Samoa	–68.1	
São Tomé and Príncipe	–88.4	
Vanuatu	–63.1	
Barbados		100.9
Iceland		503.9
Belize	–23.6	
Maldives		5.8
The Bahamas		305.7
Brunei Darussalam		624.9
Malta		363.0
Cabo Verde	–5.8	
Suriname		79.0
Luxembourg		2,170.6
Solomon Islands	–67.9	
Macao SAR		977.9
Montenegro		147.8
Comoros	–68.0	
Bhutan	–20.8	
Equatorial Guinea		492.3
Guyana		25.9
Djibouti	–35.7	
Fiji		81.7
Cyprus		1,276.2
Timor-Leste		45.0
Swaziland		81.5
Mauritius		477.4
Estonia		1,026.9
Bahrain		1,046.9
Trinidad and Tobago		1,099.9

Sources: World Bank, World Development Indicators database; and author's calculations.
Note: Median gross national income of small state sample was US$1,719 million, 2010. States are ordered by population.

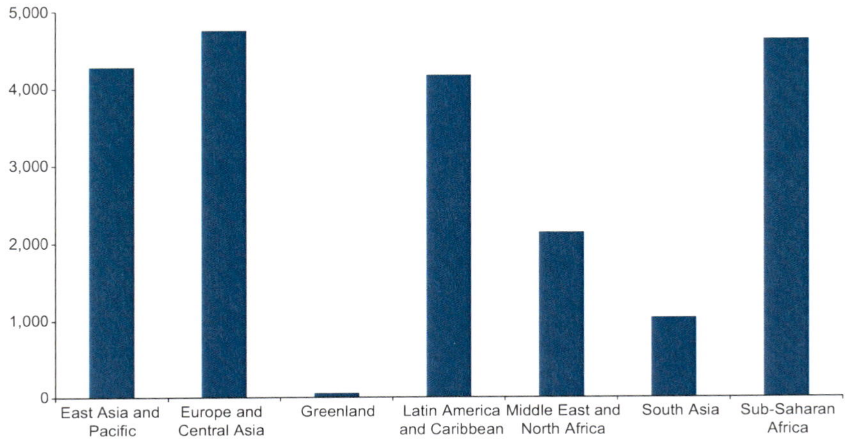

Figure 9.3 Small States: Population by Region

Source: World Bank, World Development Indicators database.
Note: Population measured as the sum of population in all states in the regions shown.

misleading.[9] This problem becomes more pronounced as the denominator in the calculation takes an extremely small value.

Figure 9.4 plots the income per capita for the sample of 50 small states. One consideration is that while this sample is restricted to small states, there are many countries with populations that exceed the 1½ million threshold but have income per capita that is much smaller than several of the countries depicted. This is typically attributable to a very small numerator relative to a very large denominator in the calculation. It therefore becomes important to understand the determinants of income per capita when making policy decisions.

The top decile of five small states with the highest GNI per capita is entirely composed of European countries (Channel Islands, Liechtenstein, Luxembourg, Monaco, San Marino). The proximity to neighboring countries—and access to their workforce, infrastructure, and the nearest continent—may well be important explanatory factors in the scope to overcome disadvantages associated with being small (Martins and Winters 2004). The proximity to neighboring countries also raises the need for consideration of multiple vulnerabilities for some small states. While it might be feasible to routinely overcome one or even two types of exposure, once countries are disadvantaged by several such factors, it becomes less likely that they can overcome all of them all the time and escape the adverse consequences of their vulnerabilities.

SCOPE FOR IMPORT SUBSTITUTION THROUGH AGRICULTURE

Another common feature of small states is that, despite sometimes very large overall land masses, they typically have very little fertile or arable land available for cultivation.[10] One reason why this might be considered an important macro-related indicator for countries is because it could be related to the ability to substitute for imports of foodstuffs. Countries may well be more exposed to balance of payments crises if they depend heavily on food imports because of inadequate conditions to foster domestic agriculture. The most striking example of this is Greenland, where an extremely large landmass is very sparsely populated and there is no arable land (Table 9.2). The vulnerabilities

[9] Given that income thresholds are used as a proxy for welfare, it might also be that in the presence of significant vulnerabilities and risk aversion, welfare is notably lower than implied by income per capita.

[10] This is not surprising given that if the land were very fertile and able to support a larger number of people, it would probably be more densely populated.

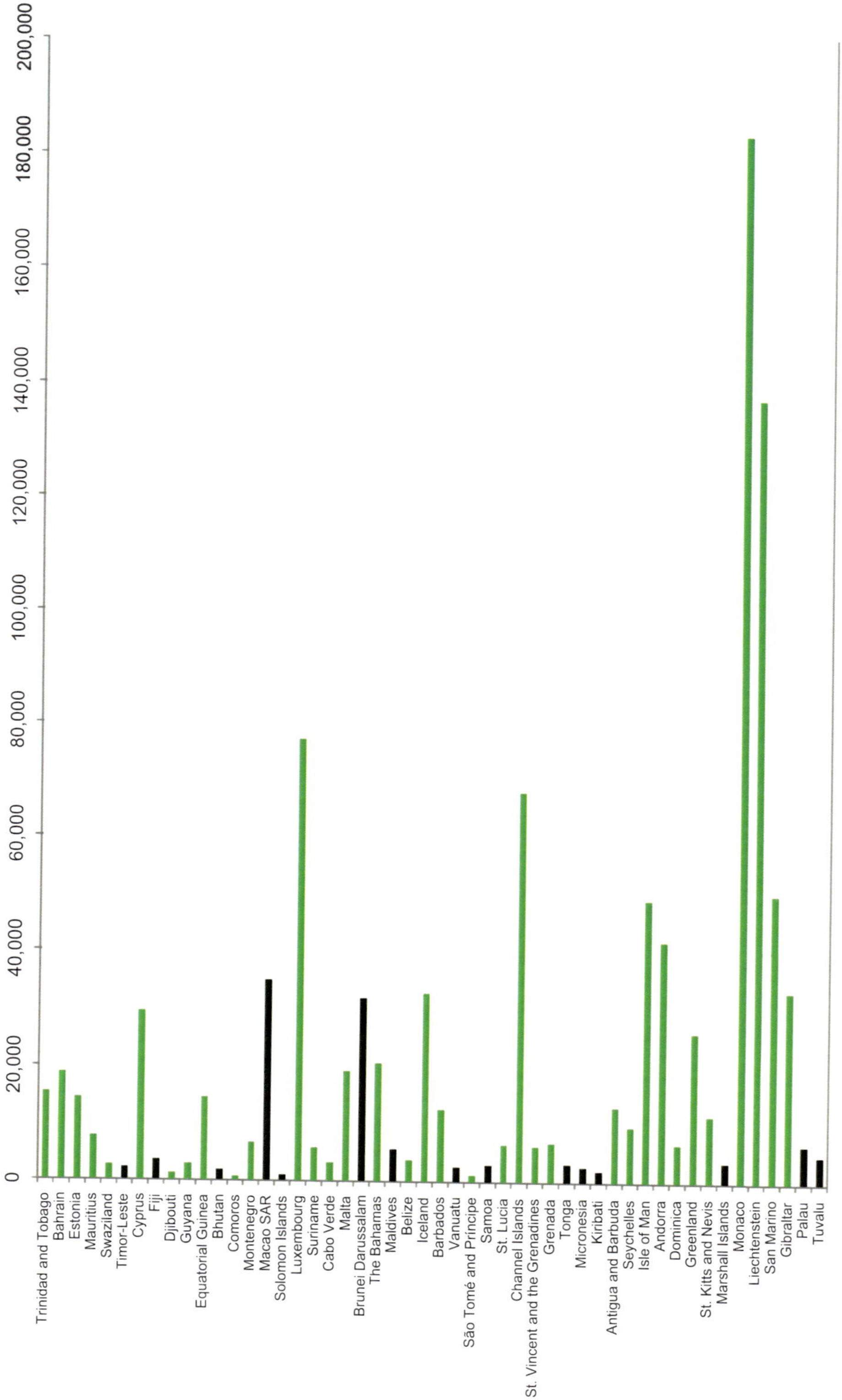

Figure 9.4 Small States: Gross National Income per Capita, 2010 *(Current U.S. dollars)*

Source: World Bank, World Development Indicators database.

TABLE 9.2

Scope for Agriculture

State	Total Landmass (km^2)	Nonarable Land (km^2)	Arable Land (km^2)	Arable Land (m^2 per Capita)
Tuvalu	30	30	0	0
Palau	460	450	10	478
Gibraltar	10	10	0	0
San Marino	60	50	10	318
Liechtenstein	160	130	30	812
Monaco	2	2	0	0
Marshall Islands	180	160	20	380
St. Kitts and Nevis	260	220	40	738
Greenland	410,450	410,450	0	0
Dominica	750	690	60	833
Andorra	470	460	10	126
Isle of Man	570	520	50	582
Seychelles	460	450	10	112
Antigua and Barbuda	440	360	80	889
Kiribati	810	790	20	195
Micronesia	700	680	20	193
Tonga	720	560	160	1519
Grenada	340	320	20	189
St. Vincent and the Grenadines	390	340	50	457
Channel Islands	190	150	40	247
St. Lucia	610	580	30	165
Samoa	2,830	2,580	250	1,313
São Tomé and Príncipe	960	860	100	518
Vanuatu	12,190	11,990	200	791
Barbados	430	270	160	562
Iceland	100,250	100,180	70	217
Belize	22,810	22,110	700	2,109
Maldives	300	260	40	116
The Bahamas	10,010	9,930	80	212
Brunei Darussalam	5,270	5,240	30	72
Malta	320	240	80	189
Cabo Verde	4,030	3,430	600	1,203
Suriname	156,000	155,420	580	1,076
Luxembourg	2,590	1,970	620	1,141
Solomon Islands	27,990	27,830	160	285
Macao SAR	28	28	0	0
Montenegro	13,450	11,720	1,730	2,784
Comoros	1,860	1,060	800	1,089
Bhutan	38,390	37,640	750	995
Equatorial Guinea	28,050	26,730	1320	1,744
Guyana	196,850	192,650	4,200	5,253
Djibouti	23,180	23,160	20	23
Fiji	18,270	16,670	1,600	1,816
Cyprus	9,240	8,370	870	762
Timor-Leste	14,870	13,220	1,650	1,400
Swaziland	17,200	15,450	1750	1,401

(Continued)

TABLE 9.2 (*Continued*)

Scope for Agriculture				
State	**Total Landmass (km^2)**	**Nonarable Land (km^2)**	**Arable Land (km^2)**	**Arable Land (m^2 per Capita)**
Mauritius	2,030	1,160	870	671
Estonia	42,390	36,430	5960	4,499
Bahrain	760	750	10	8
Trinidad and Tobago	5,130	4,880	250	186

Source: World Bank.

Note: Countries are ordered by population, as of 2013. Gibraltar's population data are for 2012; km^2 = square kilometer; m^2 = square meter.

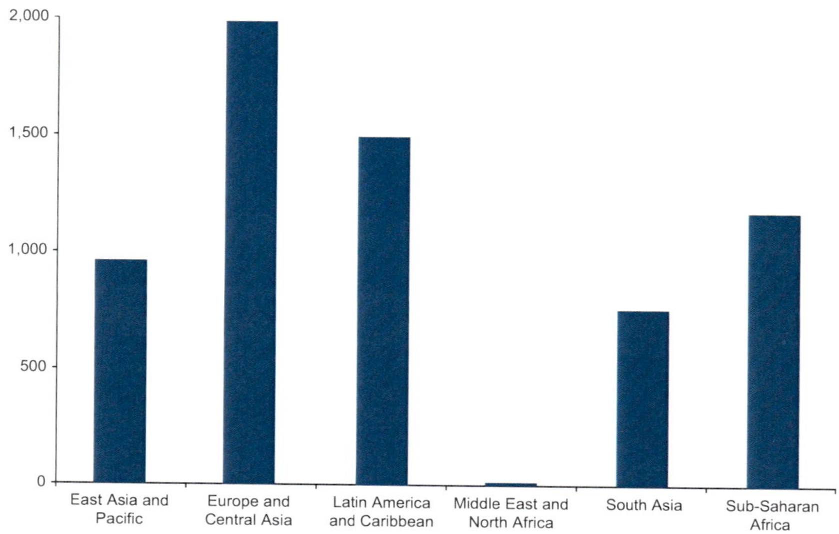

Figure 9.5 Small States: Fertility of Land by Region (*Average square meters per capita*)

Sources: World Bank, World Development Indicators database; and author's calculations.

resulting from excessive dependence on imports of foodstuffs were sharply underscored in recent years when food prices rose sharply (see Chapters 6 and 7).

In terms of the square meters per capita available for cultivation, some countries are in a considerably worse position than others. Five states in the sample countries have no arable land at all (Gibraltar, Greenland, Macao Special Administrative Region, Monaco, Tuvalu). Several Pacific islands suffer from very infertile soil or, in some cases, no soil at all. Many consist of nothing more than coral or sand, and Tuvalu stands out as being particularly infertile and unsuitable for agriculture. On the other hand, some of the larger Pacific islands, such as Fiji, Samoa, Timor-Leste, and Tonga, are relatively fertile, especially when compared to some states in Africa. On average, the states in the Pacific may not be as infertile as desert countries in the Middle East and North Africa or Greenland, but they are notably more infertile than small countries in Europe, Latin America, and the Caribbean (Figure 9.5).

The regional findings in Figure 9.5 are not surprising given the geographic location of states in the sample. European countries stand out as having the most arable land and, with the significant exceptions of India and Nigeria, the rest of the world has less agriculturally productive land (Figure 9.6).[11] There are, of course, several smaller exceptions to this.

[11] We acknowledge that while some states in the Northern Hemisphere may at face value appear to be quite arable, their proximity to the Arctic Circle severely curtails the ability to foster a productive agricultural sector.

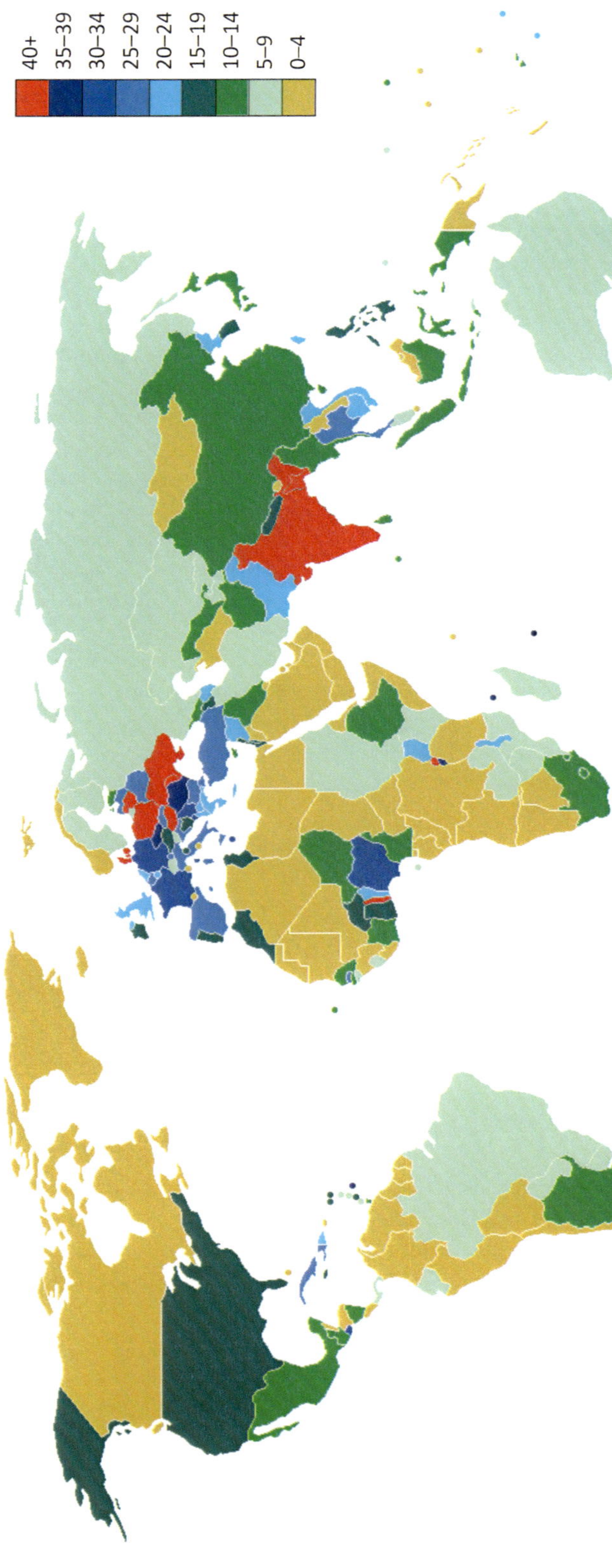

Figure 9.6 Arable Land (*Percent of total landmass*)

Source: U.S. Central Intelligence Agency, *The World Factbook.*

Trade with highly agriculturally productive countries is one way to overcome the domestic constraints that some small states face. Some of the important factors in determining that possibility are access to alternative resource endowments that can be traded and the proximity to trading partners. While Pacific island states might be able to trade fish stocks, or use the revenue from selling fishing rights, they remain disadvantaged by their geographic isolation, which raises transport costs and can even prove prohibitive to gaining market access.

GEOGRAPHIC ISOLATION

The most distinguishing characteristic of small Pacific islands is how remote they are, not only from the nearest continent, but also from neighboring countries. While technological progress has allowed countries to overcome barriers such as those related to effective communication, distance remains a key challenge to overcome when physical factors are important. The transportation costs associated with trade and commerce are therefore commensurately higher as distance increases (Commonwealth Secretariat and World Bank 2000; Zhu 2012).[12] This problem is compounded by import dependence, especially for foodstuffs, due to nonarable land, as discussed earlier. Martins and Winters (2004) show that small economies might not even be suitable locations for tourism unless they have specific comparative advantages that allow them to charge substantially higher prices to overcome cost disadvantages. Furthermore, since this geographic isolation is closely associated with the dispersion of many small islands in the Pacific Ocean, there is also a link to the susceptibility of these states to natural disasters such as tsunamis and hurricanes. The environmental challenges also extend to issues associated with rising sea levels and global warming, although some of these are in common with other regions. This is especially so in the Caribbean, where small states are vulnerable to similar environmental pressures. Annex 9.1 lists some relevant indicators on this issue, such as the distance to closest continent subindex of the Environmental Vulnerability Index calculated by the South Pacific Applied Geoscience Commission and the United Nations Environment Programme.

In the sample of small states, Kiribati, Marshall Islands, Samoa, Tonga, and Tuvalu are some of the most isolated states in the world (Figure 9.7). Each is more than 3,000 kilometers (1,900 miles) from the nearest continent, Australia.

The vulnerability represented by their geographic isolation therefore notably differentiates small islands in the Pacific from many of the other small states in the sample. The average distance to the nearest continent for Pacific islands is more than four to five times that applicable to the average country in the Caribbean or sub-Saharan Africa (Figure 9.8). On the other hand, small states in Europe, northern Africa, and the Middle East are considerably less isolated on the measure used here.[13]

When considering the issue of isolation, additional factors beyond the scope of this chapter are nevertheless worth mentioning briefly. Mayer and Zignago (2011) calculate a more comprehensive measure of remoteness by including not just the single distance between a country and the nearest continent, but by measuring the distance between each country and all other countries in their sample of 224 countries. This metric lends further support to the finding that small Pacific island states are particularly isolated. The main driving factor is that these states are not only far away from

---

[12] Many of the most remote states, for a variety of reasons, do not export any goods. As a consequence, container ships that deliver imports on the first leg of the journey have no cargo for the return leg. This raises the cost of delivering containers. Many smaller island countries also do not have sufficient infrastructure for the larger, more efficient, container ships to dock. Furthermore, since fuel is a major part of shipping costs, imports that require crossing substantial maritime distances expose the importing country even further to fluctuations in the price of fossil fuels.

[13] Once again caution is required when making inferences from the data. While the measure of distance used here is favored because it is simple and transparent, there are alternative ways to consider isolation. A country may be isolated not because of distance but because it is landlocked and surrounded by politically unstable neighbors that are subject to civil unrest. Financial isolation or connectivity to telecommunications might also be important variables.

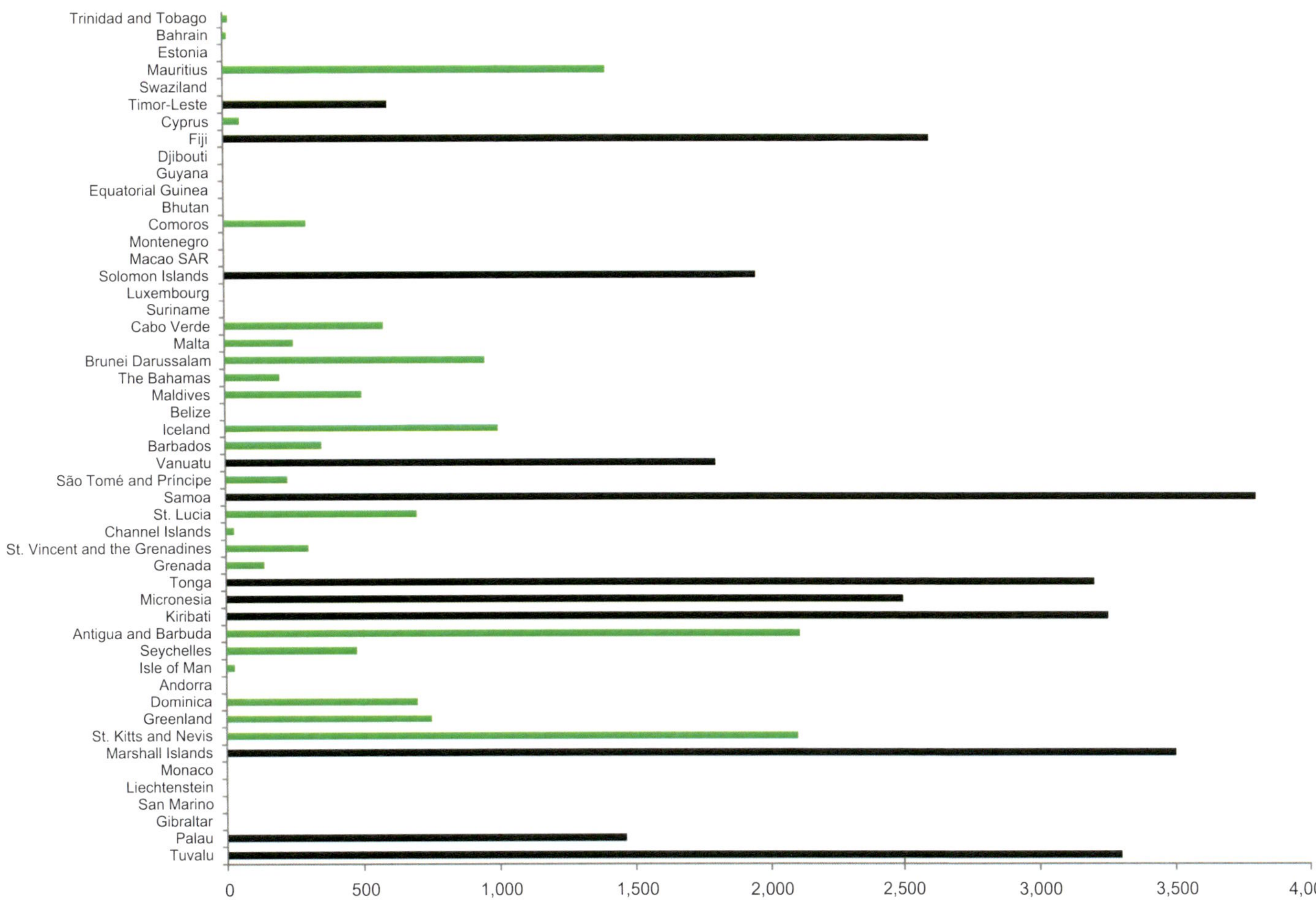

Figure 9.7 Small States: Distance to Nearest Continent (*Kilometers; countries ordered by population*)

Source: South Pacific Applied Geoscience Commission.

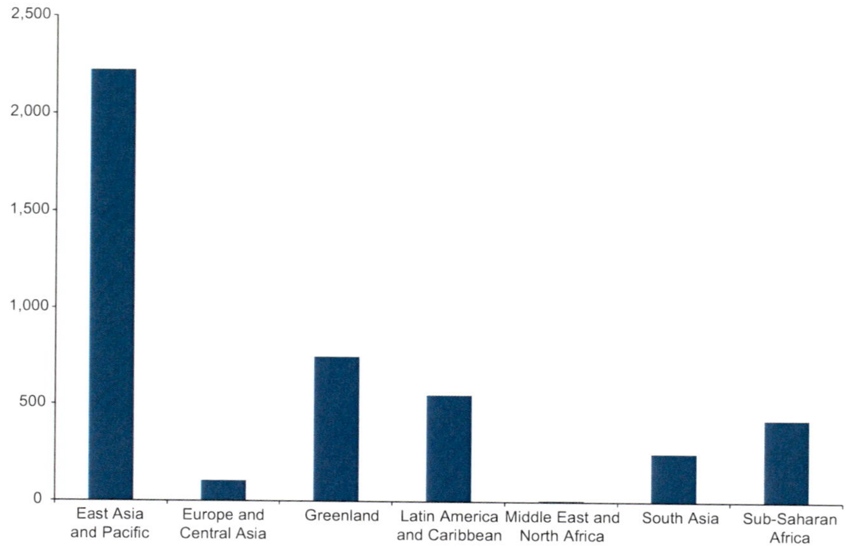

Figure 9.8 Small States: Distance to Nearest Continent by Region (*Average kilometers*)

Source: South Pacific Appled Geoscience Commission database.

the nearest continent, but are widely dispersed over a vast area of ocean and therefore also very far away from each other and all other countries.[14]

An interesting further augmentation of the data is to weight these distances by GDP to capture how physically far removed countries are from major world markets (see Chapter 4). Once again, this augmentation makes small states in the Pacific even worse off. Even though Australia has a very large landmass (the sixth largest state in the world), it has a relatively small population and therefore also represents a much smaller market than large neighbors, such as China, the euro area, or the United States, to some small states. This consideration of distance from major markets is also relevant to some countries in Africa even though the state might be on the actual continent, and could change some of the results just discussed.

VULNERABILITY RANKING

A simple way of summarizing this type of information is to rank states according to how they are positioned relative to other small states on the factors discussed in this chapter. The aim is to keep the summary indicator as simple and transparent as possible. We note the trade-offs involved from the outset. Mechanical indices can never fully reflect the complexities and changing dynamics involved in the interaction between these variables. Additionally, there are limitations that arise from the inputs into the calculations being far from exhaustive in their description of small states. Nevertheless, we hope to convey some of the key characteristics that set small Pacific islands apart from small states in other regions.

---

[14] On this measure even relatively heavily populated developed states can be considered remote from the rest of the world. New Zealand stands out as the single most distant state from all others in the world based on these calculations. Ranked at number 15, Australia is also very remote, but in part due to its size, resource endowments, and colonial ties to the Commonwealth, has been able to overcome this disadvantage more effectively than most small states. These data and the author's calculations are not shown in this chapter, but are in Mayer and Zignago (2011).

Ranking Small States

We use each variable discussed in the chapter and calculate how every small state ranks relative to all others. For example, if we rank the sample of 50 states according to population size, one might consider the smallest state as being the most vulnerable. The country with the smallest population, Tuvalu, is given an index ranking of 50 and the country with the largest population, Trinidad and Tobago, is given an index ranking of one. Larger numbers therefore indicate greater relative vulnerability on the indicator in question.[15] Similarly, countries with the least amount of arable land per capita might be vulnerable, as would be the countries that are the farthest away from the nearest continent and are the most isolated. Countries with the smallest absolute U.S. dollar level of GNI are probably less able to reap economies of scale in the provision of public goods and services and could be disadvantaged. Similarly, those with the lowest income per capita might typically be considered to be relatively poor and therefore exposed to adverse shocks that cannot be easily absorbed without assistance from the international community.

We try to capture vulnerability by synthesizing the measures just discussed into an index. An aggregate summary ranking is achieved by calculating the equally weighted average across the five individual indicator rankings used in this simple study.[16] The result is a broad reflection of which states in the sample are the most vulnerable. Table 9.3 provides the details of the calculations and ranking.

According to this metric, Tuvalu is the most vulnerable small state in the sample. It has a very small population, no arable land, is very isolated, and has little scope for accessing economies of scale in the provision of public goods and services, on account of its small GNI. These factors more than offset its more favorable ranking on income per capita.

Estonia is at the other extreme. In the context of small states, it has a relatively large population, its land is very fertile, it is surrounded by close European neighbors, and total GNI is quite high. These factors more than offset a fairly low ratio of income per capita. This outcome is not intended to imply that Estonia, or other states in the sample, do not face other substantial vulnerabilities. Instead, it is simply a reflection of how states compare based on just the five indicators chosen to illustrate the relative position of small states in the Pacific. Broadly speaking, some tentative conclusions can be reached about the average regional characteristics of small states (Figure 9.9).

Small states in the Pacific are the most vulnerable on a number of counts considered in this chapter. This is in part driven by several common vulnerabilities such as isolation, but also by the extreme exposure of some states in the region to several additional indicators of vulnerability. These states also lack the ability to reap economies of scale, generally have low income per capita, small populations, and little arable land. Compared with other regions, they rank worse than the average of 25.5 on all measures considered.[17] Small states in Latin America and the Caribbean, south Asia, and sub-Saharan Africa are probably somewhat less vulnerable to the factors considered here. These regions appear to have a common degree of overall exposure. Small countries in Europe appear to be the least disadvantaged in this sample—a result in large part driven by a number of outliers that are highly developed and rich countries that happen to have small populations but do not appear particularly disadvantaged by this characteristic. It is therefore worth keeping in mind that other small European countries are less fortunate, and that for the Caribbean, south Asia, and Africa we might need to improve our means of identifying and capturing other forms of vulnerability.

---

[15] There may also be advantages in dealing with some of the nonlinearities in the data by employing this ranking methodology.

[16] There is no reason to presume each of the five indicators discussed in this chapter is of equal importance as implied by the weighting employed. However, this chapter does not estimate the relevant preference function, as this would differ by region and state.

[17] However, there are some Pacific states that do not appear notably more exposed than those in other regions.

TABLE 9.3

Small States Ranked by Indicator

	Population	Arable Land	Distance	GNI	GNI per Capita	Average
Tuvalu	50	46	48	50	33	45.4
Marshall Islands	44	37	49	48	35	42.6
Kiribati	36	38	47	46	45	42.4
Palau	49	43	39	49	29	41.8
Micronesia	35	36	44	45	41	40.2
Tonga	34	19	46	44	37	36.0
Samoa	29	17	50	42	39	35.4
St. Kitts and Nevis	43	30	42	39	22	35.2
Dominica	41	27	33	43	26	34.0
São Tomé and Príncipe	28	22	24	47	48	33.8
Greenland	42	49	35	28	13	33.4
Seychelles	38	41	29	35	23	33.2
Solomon Islands	16	20	41	40	49	33.2
Vanuatu	27	18	40	38	42	33.0
St. Lucia	30	33	34	32	28	31.4
Gibraltar	48	50	15	34	9	31.2
Antigua and Barbuda	37	25	43	31	20	31.2
Grenada	33	39	22	36	25	31.0
St. Vincent and the Grenadines	32	28	27	37	30	30.8
Djibouti	9	40	13	33	47	28.4
Maldives	23	31	30	25	32	28.2
Comoros	13	10	26	41	50	28.0
San Marino	47	42	11	27	5	26.4
Cabo Verde	19	14	31	26	38	25.6
Andorra	40	45	12	19	7	24.6
Monaco	45	47	14	14	1	24.2
Fiji	8	6	45	20	36	23.0
Barbados	26	21	28	18	21	22.8
Brunei Darussalam	21	35	36	7	11	22.0
Isle of Man	39	29	19	17	6	22.0
Timor-Leste	6	5	32	23	44	22.0
Liechtenstein	46	34	10	15	2	21.4
Bhutan	12	11	9	29	46	21.4
Iceland	25	26	37	8	10	21.2
Belize	24	12	4	30	34	20.8
Channel Islands	31	32	20	9	4	19.2
The Bahamas	22	24	23	13	14	19.2
Malta	20	23	25	12	15	19.0
Suriname	18	15	8	22	31	18.8
Macao SAR	15	48	16	6	8	18.6
Mauritius	4	8	38	11	24	17.0
Bahrain	2	44	17	4	16	16.6
Swaziland	5	3	6	21	43	15.6
Guyana	10	2	1	24	40	15.4
Montenegro	14	4	3	16	27	12.8
Trinidad and Tobago	1	16	18	3	17	11.0
Cyprus	7	9	21	2	12	10.2
Equatorial Guinea	11	7	5	10	18	10.2
Luxembourg	17	13	7	1	3	8.2
Estonia	3	1	2	5	19	6.0

Source: Author's calculations.
Note: Vulnerability is ranked on a scale of 1 to 50. GNI = gross national income.

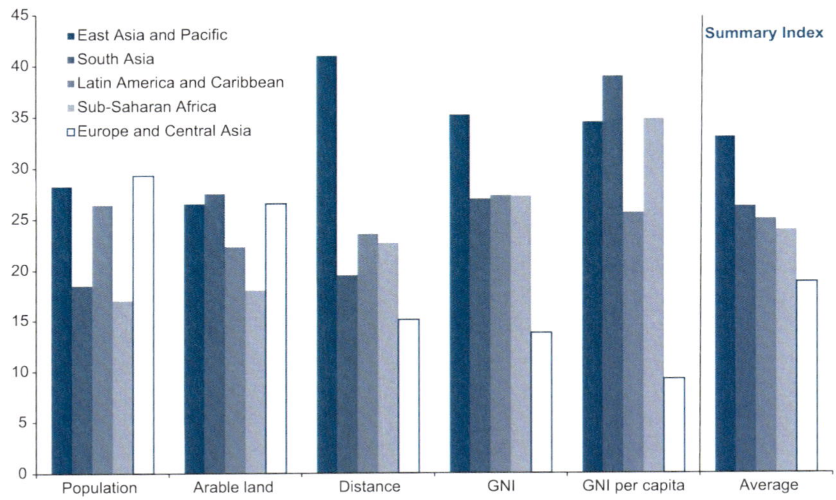

Figure 9.9 Regional Vulnerability by Indicator (*Index rank*)

Source: Author's calculations.
Note: GNI = gross national income.

Empirical Link to Real Economic Outcomes

A series of simple linear regressions are fitted to conduct a preliminary investigation of the relationship between the potential vulnerability indicators for small states and real economic outcomes. The growth rate in GNI is therefore the dependent variable we are trying to explain using indicators of vulnerability.

Economic outcomes are proxied by annualized nominal growth in GNI measured in U.S. dollar terms between 2001 and 2010. The data are annual and therefore only nine observations are available for most states. Three states (Montenegro, São Tomé and Príncipe, Timor-Leste) have fewer observations than this, and Gibraltar had to be dropped from the sample of 50 states because of a lack of time series data. We also note the high likelihood of cross-correlation between growth outcomes during the financial crisis, given that it represents a common shock to all countries in the sample, albeit with different intensities.

To investigate the usefulness of ranking countries by their degree of vulnerability, we fit separate regressions using each of the five vulnerability indicators shown in Table 9.3: population, arable land, distance, income, and income per capita (see also Gallup, Sachs, and Mellinger 1998; Kuznets 1960). Since states are ranked according to their relative degree of vulnerability in each of these indicators, we attempt to capture the relationship between growth and vulnerability. Our prior is to find a negative relationship between the relative degree of vulnerability exhibited by a state and the average growth rate it is able to achieve. For example, we would expect that a high ranking on distance—which by construction indicates that a state is relatively isolated—results in lower growth outcomes than for states that are less isolated.

A closer look at the regressions (Table 9.4) indicates that the slope coefficient for almost all individual indicators is consistent with the expected negative relationship between relative vulnerability and growth. A notable exception is income per capita, which indicates a weak positive relationship with growth. Possible explanations for why lower income per capita might be associated with faster growth could relate to structural factors such as developing economies typically being able to grow more rapidly than more developed economies (which would also tend to have higher income per capita). More realistically, the relationship between income per capita and growth is probably not a

TABLE 9.4

Relationship between Vulnerability Ranking and Growth

Ranking According to the *i*th Indicator of Vulnerability Number[1]	Slope Coefficient	*p*-value	RMSE(*i*th)	RMSE(*i*th)/RMSE(index)
Population	−0.19	0.0006**	5.15	1.0158
Arable land	−0.16	0.0063**	5.40	1.0651
Distance	−0.18	0.0015**	5.25	1.0355
Income	−0.14	0.0167*	5.50	1.0848
Income per capita	0.02	0.6899	5.84	1.1519
Index	−0.32	0.0003**	5.07	1.0000
Memorandum item:				
index-ex[2]	−0.23	0.0000**	2.96	0.5838

Source: Author's calculations.
Note: RMSE = root mean square error. * Denotes significance at the 5 percent level; ** significance at the 1 percent level.
[1] Sample excludes Gibraltar owing to data availability.
[2] Additional exclusions: (i) income per capita in the calculation of the Index, (ii) outliers (Timor-Leste and Equatorial Guinea).

very meaningful indicator, especially in the case of microstates, and this is reflected in a statistically insignificant relationship as indicated by the *p*-value on the variable.[18]

Among a number of other interesting findings is that the most statistically significant (*p*-value) explanatory variables for growth are size of the population, the degree of isolation measured by distance to the nearest continent, and fertility of the land.[19] As a result, the ratio of the root mean square error relative to the benchmark model fitted for the overall average index is lowest for these three core indicators. Furthermore, the combination of all indicators into the summary index yields the best fit. In part, this is because more variation and information are reflected by the index to explain the dependent variable, but we would also argue that the combination of vulnerabilities is important in influencing economic outcomes. It is clearly more difficult to register consistently good economic performance when exposed to a significantly larger number of sources for adverse shocks. This relationship is plotted in Figure 9.10. As in previous figures, states in Asia and the Pacific are depicted in a darker color.

The fitted relationship indicates the expected negative relationship between the degree of vulnerability and growth outcomes for small states, but it is significantly affected by two outliers on growth (Equatorial Guinea, Timor-Leste).[20] One interpretation of the clustering of Pacific states in the top-left quadrant of Figure 9.10 would be that their relatively high degree of vulnerability does indeed impede their economic performance by dragging average growth lower.

As a final illustration, we refit the equation using a recalculated average ranking index that excludes income per capita on the basis that its explanatory value was found to be statistically insignificant, and drop the two outliers from the sample.[21] The results are shown in Table 9.4 as *index-ex*. Not surprisingly, the fit improves dramatically. The root mean square error is significantly smaller and improves on the aggregate average *index* of vulnerability by more than 40 percent in explaining average growth outcomes.[22]

---

[18] Other considerations worth bearing in mind are whether one would necessarily expect a relationship between income per capita and average growth outcomes, or whether the relationship is significantly more complicated than the treatment afforded it in this chapter.

[19] Redding and Venables (2004) show that geography of access to markets is statistically significant and quantitatively important in explaining cross-state differences in income per capita.

[20] Both of these states enjoyed extraordinarily rapid income growth due to significant oil and gas exploration projects as well as rising fuel prices during 2001–10.

[21] Dropping the two outliers can also be justified on the grounds that they are almost 4 standard deviations away from the sample mean.

[22] An informative contrast to the findings presented here and in the literature more generally is Easterly and Kraay (2000), where the authors find no empirical evidence of such relationships and conclude that small states should receive the same policy advice as larger countries.

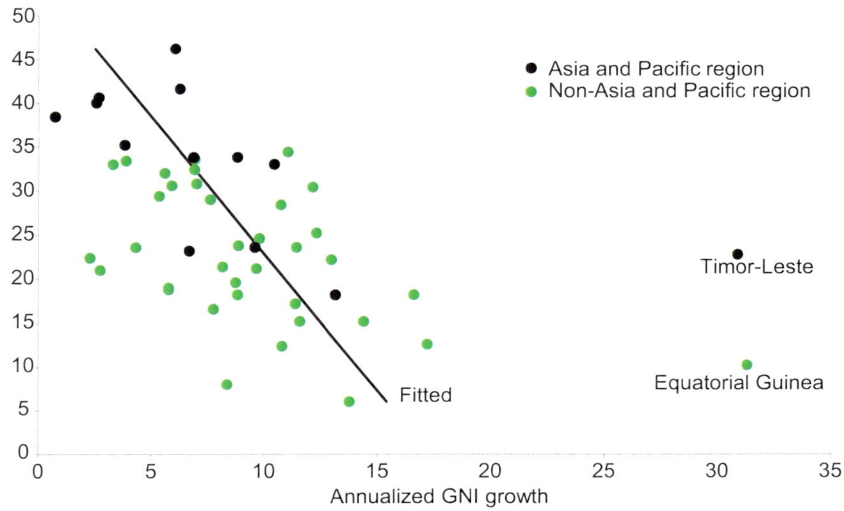

Figure 9.10 Vulnerability and Growth (*Index rank*)

Source: Author's calculations.
Note: GNI = gross national income.

CONCLUSIONS

This chapter does not definitively find that small states in the Pacific are absolutely more vulnerable than small states in other regions—the scope is simply too narrow to address this question adequately. It does, however, show that on the limited number of macro-oriented indicators considered, most small Pacific island countries rank as being particularly exposed to adverse shocks relative to their peers in other regions. We find that population size, distance from the nearest continent, arable land, and scope to exploit economies of scale are all statistically significant in explaining economic outcomes in small states. The combination of these vulnerabilities into an overall index lends support to the idea that a confluence of vulnerabilities is also important in determining growth outcomes.

Small island states in the Pacific are disadvantaged because they are sometimes extremely small in terms of population and, consequently, limited in being able to access economies of scale in the production of goods and services. The quality of soil is often not very good, and, as a result, they can be exposed to the disadvantages that follow from being heavily dependent on imports of foodstuffs.

It is, however, the extreme degree of isolation of most small states in the Pacific that is quite unique in defining their vulnerabilities on several facets. While technological progress has helped to bridge the communication chasm, when it comes to physical considerations in areas such as trade, commerce, and labor mobility, significant barriers with economic consequences are not only important, but also unlikely to be resolved in the foreseeable future. Furthermore, as a result of their geography, small states in the Pacific face a number of environmental challenges such as tsunamis, hurricanes, and rising sea levels. The tyranny of the sheer distances is therefore likely to remain a key challenge in the Pacific and will remain at the forefront on the minds of informed policymakers for some time.

ANNEX 9.1. STATE CLASSIFICATION DATA

ANNEX TABLE 9.1.1

Summary Statistics

Country Name	Regional Classification	Population as of 2013 (Thousands)	Arable Land as of 2013 (m^2 per Capita)	EVI-13 Isolation Index (1–7)	Distance to Closest Continent (km)	Closest Continent	GNI Current Prices as of 2010 (U.S.$ millions)	GNI/Capita Current Prices as of 2010 (U.S.$)	GNI/Capita PPP Basis as of 2010 (U.S.$)
Tuvalu	East Asia and Pacific	10	0	7	3,300	Australia	47	4,760	5,351
Palau	East Asia and Pacific	21	478	6	1,463	Australia	134	6,560	11,000
Gibraltar	Europe and Central Asia	29	0	1	0	Europe	969	33,151	33,151
San Marino	Europe and Central Asia	31	318	1	0	Europe	1,572	49,866	35,163
Liechtenstein	Europe and Central Asia	37	812	1	0	Europe	4,903	137,070	151,189
Monaco	Europe and Central Asia	38	–	1	0	Europe	6,479	183,150	182,990
Marshall Islands	East Asia and Pacific	53	380	7	3,500	Australia	197	3,640	3,003
St. Kitts and Nevis	Latin America and Caribbean	54	738	7	2,100	South America	615	11,740	15,850
Greenland	Greenland	56	–	5	750	North America	1,466	26,020	25,604
Dominica	Latin America and Caribbean	72	833	5	698	South America	458	6,760	11,990
Andorra	Europe and Central Asia	79	126	1	0	Europe	3,447	41,750	36,113
Isle of Man	Europe and Central Asia	86	582	2	30	Europe	3,972	48,910	47,926
Seychelles	Sub-Saharan Africa	89	112	5	475	Africa	845	9,760	21,210
Antigua and Barbuda	Latin America and Caribbean	90	889	7	2,110	South America	1,169	13,170	20,240
Kiribati	East Asia and Pacific	102	195	7	3,250	Australia	200	2,010	3,530
Micronesia	East Asia and Pacific	104	193	7	2,500	Australia	304	2,730	3,490
Tonga	East Asia and Pacific	105	1,519	7	3,200	Australia	342	3,280	4,580

Grenada	Latin America and Caribbean	106	189	4	140	South America	724	6,930	9,890
St. Vincent and the Grenadines	Latin America and Caribbean	109	457	4	300	South America	688	6,300	10,830
Channel Islands	Europe and Central Asia	162	247	2	30	Europe	10,241	67,960	66,781
St. Lucia	Latin America and Caribbean	182	165	5	698	South America	1,142	6,560	10,520
Samoa	East Asia and Pacific	190	1,313	7	3,800	Australia	549	3,000	4,270
São Tomé and Príncipe	Sub-Saharan Africa	193	518	4	225	Africa	199	1,200	1,920
Vanuatu	East Asia and Pacific	253	791	7	1,800	Australia	633	2,640	4,320
Barbados	Latin America and Caribbean	285	562	4	350	South America	3,454	12,660	19,000
Iceland	Europe and Central Asia	323	217	6	1,000	Europe	10,381	32,710	27,680
Belize	Latin America and Caribbean	332	2,109	1	0	North America	1,313	3,810	6,210
Maldives	South Asia	345	116	5	500	Asia	1,818	5,750	8,110
The Bahamas	Latin America and Caribbean	377	212	4	200	North America	6,973	20,610	24,800
Brunei Darussalam	East Asia and Pacific	418	72	6	950	Asia	12,461	31,800	50,180
Malta	Europe and Central Asia	423	189	4	250	Europe	7,958	19,270	24,840
Cabo Verde	Sub-Saharan Africa	499	1,203	5	580	Africa	1,620	3,270	3,820
Suriname	Latin America and Caribbean	539	1,076	1	0	South America	3,077	5,920	7,680
Luxembourg	Europe and Central Asia	543	1,141	1	0	Europe	39,030	77,160	61,790
Solomon Islands	East Asia and Pacific	561	285	7	1,950	Australia	552	1,030	2,210
Macao SAR	East Asia and Pacific	566	–	2	2	Asia	18,527	34,880	45,220
Montenegro	Europe and Central Asia	621	2,784	1	0	Europe	4,260	6,750	12,930
Comoros	Sub-Saharan Africa	735	1,089	4	300	Africa	550	750	1,090

(Continued)

ANNEX TABLE 9.1.1 (*Continued*)

Summary Statistics

Country Name	Regional Classification	Population as of 2013 (Thousands)	Arable Land as of 2013 (m^2 per Capita)	EVI-13 Isolation Index (1–7)	Distance to Closest Continent (km)	Closest Continent	GNI Current Prices as of 2010 (U.S.$ millions)	GNI/Capita Current Prices as of 2010 (U.S.$)	GNI/Capita PPP Basis as of 2010 (U.S.$)
Bhutan	South Asia	754	995	1	0	Asia	1,361	1,870	4,990
Equatorial Guinea	Sub-Saharan Africa	757	1,744	1	0	Africa	10,182	14,540	23,750
Guyana	Latin America and Caribbean	800	5,253	1	0	South America	2,164	2,870	3,450
Djibouti	Middle East and North Africa	873	23	1	0	Africa	1,105	1,270	2,460
Fiji	East Asia and Pacific	881	1,816	7	2,600	Australia	3,123	3,630	4,510
Cyprus	Europe and Central Asia	1,141	762	3	60	Asia	23,655	29,430	30,300
Timor-Leste	East Asia and Pacific	1,178	1,400	4	600	Australia	2,493	2,220	3,600
Swaziland	Sub-Saharan Africa	1,250	1,401	1	0	Africa	3,119	2,630	4,840
Mauritius	Sub-Saharan Africa	1,296	671	6	1,400	Africa	9,925	7,750	13,960
Estonia	Europe and Central Asia	1,325	4,499	1	0	Europe	19,371	14,460	19,760
Bahrain	Middle East and North Africa	1,332	8	2	15	Asia	19,714	18,730	24,710
Trinidad and Tobago	Latin America and Caribbean	1,341	186	2	20	South America	20,625	15,380	24,040

Sources: The South Pacific Applied Geoscience Commission; and World Bank.

Note: GNI = gross national income; km = kilometer; m^2 = square meter; PPP = purchasing power parity.

ANNEX 9.2. DATA SOURCES AND METADATA

- Arable land is sourced from data provided by the World Bank, as of 2010.
    - Arable land includes land defined by the United Nations Food and Agriculture Organization as land under temporary crops (double-cropped areas are counted once), temporary meadows for mowing or for pasture, land under market or kitchen gardens, and land temporarily fallow. Land abandoned as a result of shifting cultivation is excluded.
- Environmental Vulnerability Index, EVI-13, Distance to Closest Continent, is sourced from the South Pacific Applied Geoscience Commission and the United Nations Environment Programme (2005).
    - This indicator captures the proximity of a state to the nearest continent. Note that if a state is within a continent, this value is zero. Isolated states may have a greater risk of loss of ecosystem types and species during periods of stress if they are far away from refuges and sources of recolonization. Isolated states are also likely to support fewer species than those close to large continents or biogeographic centers of radiation. In addition, there is less chance of genetic interchange (part of genetic resilience) in isolated areas. The likelihood of isolation being an important part of a state's ecological resilience would be especially important if there are interactions with ongoing human impacts. States close to sources of recolonization are likely to be less at risk of permanent species losses, compared with those far away, particularly if they are small or fragmented.
- Gross national income (GNI), current U.S. dollars, is sourced from data provided by the World Bank, as of 2010.
    - GNI (formerly gross national product) is the sum of value added by all resident producers plus any product taxes (minus subsidies) not included in the valuation of output plus net receipts of primary income (compensation of employees and property income) from abroad. Data are in current U.S. dollars. GNI, calculated in national currency, is usually converted to U.S. dollars at official exchange rates for comparisons across economies, although an alternative rate is used when the official exchange rate is judged to diverge by an exceptionally large margin from the rate actually applied in international transactions. To smooth fluctuations in prices and exchange rates, a special Atlas method of conversion is used by the World Bank. This applies a conversion factor that averages the exchange rate for a given year and the two preceding years, adjusted for differences in rates of inflation between the state and, up to 2000, Group of Five states (France, Germany, Japan, United Kingdom, United States). Starting in 2001, these states include those in the euro area, Japan, the United Kingdom, and the United States.
- GNI per capita, current U.S. dollars, is sourced from data provided by the World Bank, as of 2010.
    - GNI per capita (formerly gross national product per capita) is the gross national income, converted to U.S. dollars using the World Bank Atlas method, divided by the midyear population.
- GNI per capita based on purchasing power parity is sourced from data provided by the World Bank, as of 2010.
    - This is GNI converted to international dollars using purchasing-power-parity rates. An international dollar has the same purchasing power over GNI as a U.S. dollar has in the United States.
- Some values estimated by the author using GDP and GDP per capita data are from the U.S. Central Intelligence Agency, *World Factbook*.
- Population is sourced from data provided by the World Bank, as of 2010.
    - Total population is based on the actual definition of population, which counts all residents regardless of legal status or citizenship—except for refugees not permanently settled in the

state of asylum, who are generally considered part of the population of their state of origin. The values shown are midyear estimates.

- Regional classification of states is sourced from data provided by the World Bank, as of April 2012.
  - Geographic classifications and data reported for geographic regions are only for low- and middle-income countries, sometimes referred to as developing economies. The use of the term is convenient and is not intended to imply that all economies in the group are experiencing similar development or that other economies have reached a preferred or advanced stage of development. Classification by income does not necessarily reflect development status.
- Land area is sourced from data provided by the World Bank, as of 2010.
  - Land area is a state's total area, excluding area under inland water bodies, national claims to continental shelf, and exclusive economic zones. In most cases the definition of inland water bodies includes major rivers and lakes.

REFERENCES

Becker, Chris. 2012. "Small Island States in the Pacific: The Tyranny of Distance?" IMF Working Paper 12/223, International Monetary Fund, Washington.

Browne, Christopher. 2006. *Pacific Island Economies.* Washington: International Monetary Fund.

Commonwealth Secretariat and World Bank, Joint Task Force on Small States. 2000. "Small States: Meeting Challenges in the Global Economy." http://siteresources.worldbank.org/PROJECTS/Resources/meetingchallengein globaleconomyl.pdf.

Easterly, William, and Aart Kraay. 2000. "Small States, Small Problems? Income, Growth, and Volatility in Small States." *World Development* (28) 11: 2013–27. http://papers.ssrn.com/sol3/papers.cfm?abstract_id=252873.

Gallup, John Luke, Jeffrey D. Sachs, and Andrew D. Mellinger. 1998. "Geography and Economic Development." Working Paper 6849, National Bureau of Economic Research, Cambridge, Massachusetts.

Hausmann, Ricardo. 2001. "Prisoners of Geography." *Foreign Policy* 122 (1): 44–53. http://www.hks.harvard.edu/fs/rhausma/editorial/fp01_prisoners_geog.htm.

International Development Association. 2001. "IDA Eligibility, Terms, and Graduation Policies." http://siteresources.worldbank.org/IDA/Resources/Seminar%20PDFs/ida%20eligibility.pdf.

International Monetary Fund (IMF). 2009. "IMF Reforms Financial Facilities for Low-Income States." Public Information Notice 09/94, Washington, July 29. http://www.imf.org/external/np/sec/pn/2009/pn0994.htm.

———. 2012. "Eligibility to Use the Fund's Facilities for Concessional Financing." Policy Paper, Washington. http://www.imf.org/external/np/pp/eng/2012/011312.pdf.

———. 2013a. "Macroeconomic Issues in Small States and Implications for Fund Engagement." Policy Paper, Washington. http://www.imf.org/external/np/pp/eng/2013/022013.pdf.

———. 2013b. "IMF Executive Board Reviews Facilities for Low-Income States and Eligibility for Using Concessional Financing." Public Information Notice 13/45, Washington. http://www.imf.org/external/np/sec/pn/2013/pn1345.htm.

Kuznets, Simon. 1960. "Economic Growth of Small Nations." In *Economic Consequences of the Size of Nations*, edited by E. A. G. Robinson. London: MacMillan.

Martins, Pedro M. G., and L. Alan Winters. 2004. "When Comparative Advantage Is Not Enough: Business Costs in Small Remote Economies." http://siteresources.worldbank.org/INTRES/Resources/WTR.pdf.

Mayer, Thierry, and Soledad Zignago. 2011. "Notes on CEPII's Distances Measures: The GeoDist Database." Working Paper 2011-25, Centre d' Études Prospectives et d'Informations Internationales, Paris. http://www.cepii.fr/anglaisgraph/bdd/distances.htm.

Redding, Stephen, and Anthony Venables. 2004. "Economic Geography and International Inequality." *Journal of International Economics* 62 (1): 53–82. www.princeton.edu/~reddings/pubchapters/WincJIE2004.pdf.

South Pacific Applied Geoscience Commission and United Nations Environment Programme. 2005. "Building Resilience in Small Island Developing States (SIDS): The Environmental Vulnerability Index." Paper presented at the Mauritius International Meeting, January 10–14. http://www.vulnerabilityindex.net/EVI_2005.htm.

World Bank. 2007. "Defining a Small Economy." http://go.worldbank.org/QLCDU7B8T0.

Zhu, Min. 2012. "Sheer Distance a Factor as Pacific Islands Seek to Boost Growth." *IMF Survey Magazine*, March 21. http://www.imf.org/external/pubs/ft/survey/so/2012/int032112a.htm.

PART III

Tailoring Macroeconomic Policies to the Small States of the Pacific

CHAPTER 10

Strengthening Fiscal Frameworks and Improving the Spending Mix in Small States

EZEQUIEL CABEZON, PATRIZIA TUMBARELLO, AND YIQUN WU

The unique characteristics of small developing states make fiscal management more challenging than elsewhere.[1] Most important, the indivisibility of the provision of public goods and public sectors, which are the main employers, introduces rigidities into budgets, tilting the composition of spending toward recurrent outlays. With limited fiscal resources, high recurrent spending can crowd out capital spending, leading to underinvestment in infrastructure and other growth-enhancing areas. At the same time, small states generally face greater revenue volatility than other country groups (IMF 2013; and see Chapter 2 in this volume) owing to their exposure to exogenous shocks and narrow production bases. This is particularly true for fragile states and commodity exporters. Small states often lack the capacity to weather revenue volatility for two reasons: they cannot finance temporary fiscal shocks because domestic banking systems are shallow, and they have limited access to international capital markets (Holden and Howell 2009).

Despite the lumpiness (relative to small GDPs) of capital projects, fiscal frameworks are not typically designed with a multiyear perspective, which would allow smoothing of expenditures over the business cycle. Although foreign assistance has provided some countercyclical support during downturns to aid-dependent small states, the volatility of revenue has generally resulted in volatile spending patterns and procyclical fiscal policy. Reflecting the recurrent spending rigidities, budget pressures typically, and primarily, affect capital spending. This means that already-strained capital budgets face further cuts in the event of external shocks, which further undermines longer-term growth prospects.

Assessing the fiscal stance of small states is complicated. Because of revenue volatility, especially in Pacific island countries, headline fiscal balances do not always accurately reflect underlying fiscal positions. However, data deficiencies, capacity constraints, and structural changes in the economy make it difficult to estimate meaningful cyclically adjusted or structural balances based on output gaps (IMF 2014a). Additional challenges include the existence of extrabudgetary funds not integrated into budget presentations, and the difficulty of measuring capital spending when projects are implemented outside the central government or controlled by planning ministries using different charts of accounts than those used by finance ministries.

Strengthening fiscal frameworks by isolating the budget from revenue volatility and shielding public spending (especially capital) could help increase small states' resilience to shocks and boost potential growth. This means using fiscal anchors to smooth the volatility of revenue and capital expenditure over the business cycle and creating policy space for spending on infrastructure, health, and education. It also means focusing fiscal policy more on the medium term, as it should not be formulated on a year-by-year basis only. In addition, public financial management (PFM) reforms to improve the quality of public spending is key to supporting growth.

However, policies need to be tailored to the special challenges of small states (Box 10.1). The design of fiscal anchors should be country specific and kept simple. Medium-term fiscal estimates

[1]Hereafter simply referred to as small states.

Box 10.1. From Best Practice to Best Fit: Lessons from Small States

Small states face extra challenges relative to comparators in strengthening fiscal frameworks and achieving the right mix of public spending, due to political economy considerations, capacity constraints, vulnerability to shocks, and data issues. However, many of these states have achieved progress in handling the challenges described in this chapter. Some examples are reported in the following.

- **Mauritius:** The new Public Financial Management (PFM) Act, which has yet to be adopted, looks to alleviate some of the budget execution difficulties, which led to the creation of special funds. The new government said it intends to eliminate the special funds and fully incorporate the related operations in the budget. Regarding the fiscal rule, authorities have adopted a liberal approach on its application, whereby (in principle legally binding) the debt target could be pushed out if it becomes difficult to achieve.
- **Jamaica:** Its rule-based fiscal framework has the following two distinct but complementary components:
    - *Macro-fiscal or quantitative*—The overall fiscal balance path is calibrated over a trailing three-year window to achieve a debt ceiling of 60 percent of GDP at the end of March 2026. The path is based on projections of, for example, real GDP growth, inflation, and the interest rate. This component kicks in only after the IMF Extended Fund Facility Arrangement, but the fiscal targets under the program aim to achieve the same policy goal and can be seen as a de facto fiscal rule. An exceptionally large adverse shock could require a temporary deviation from the debt reduction path, and for this purpose an escape clause was built into the fiscal rule. The clause is limited to natural disasters, severe economic contraction, banking or financial crises, and a state of emergency; it may only be activated if the estimated fiscal impact of such shocks exceeds 1½ percent of GDP.
    - *Institutional*—This component has four elements: (1) strengthened budgetary procedures (and in 2015 the budget will be presented to Parliament before the start of the fiscal year for the first time in many years); (2) exclusion criteria—the fiscal rule covers the public sector at large, except for the Bank of Jamaica and public entities deemed commercial; (3) bolstering capacity at the Office of the Auditor General, with the auditor general responsible for monitoring compliance with the fiscal rule (as such, the office must be appropriately staffed to fulfill its expanded mandate); and (4) sanctions for infringing the fiscal rule, with the authorities initiating dialogue with the IMF's Legal Department on the design of an enforcement mechanism.
- **Seychelles:** The country is the top performer in Africa on health, nutrition, and population outcomes. Its health indicators compare favorably with some Organisation for Economic Co-operation and Development countries, reflecting long-standing government commitment to providing universal free basic health care and access to education. Health spending accounts for only about 3½ percent of GDP.
- **The Solomon Islands:** The new Public Financial Management Act passed in December 2013 and the accompanying public financial management road map (2014–17) provide a coherent platform to anchor fiscal reforms; in particular by improving the quality of spending and enhancing budget planning.
- **Swaziland:** During the country's 2014 Article IV consultation, authorities agreed with anchoring the fiscal policy with a medium-term international reserve target of 5–7 months of imports, while exploring the options of a fiscal rule or a stabilization fund to help address the high volatility of fiscal revenues.
- **Timor-Leste:** The estimated sustainable income rule has worked well to minimize the effects of revenue volatility, and it has also allowed Timor-Leste's Petroleum Fund to grow to the equivalent of three times GDP.

should focus only on main aggregates to facilitate the adoption of a multiyear budget framework. Using such a framework could, from a political point of view, also help contain spending pressure by better sequencing the implementation of capital projects. Such spending pressure is particularly acute in small states given their development needs.

IMPROVING THE MIX OF PUBLIC SPENDING

Current spending rigidity is a key issue in small states, which results from the large share of current spending in GDP in these countries relative to others (Figure 10.1). In providing public services, small states face higher government costs per capita than other country groups, because public goods are indivisible and broad public services must be provided despite small populations, which creates diseconomies of scale. Indeed, the relationship between the size of the country and current spending is

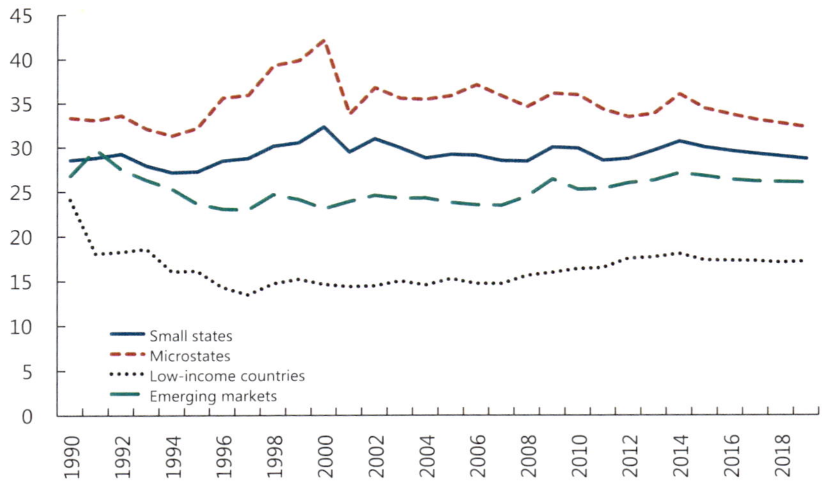

Figure 10.1 Current Government Expenditure (*Percent of GDP*)

Sources: IMF, World Economic Outlook database; and IMF staff estimates.

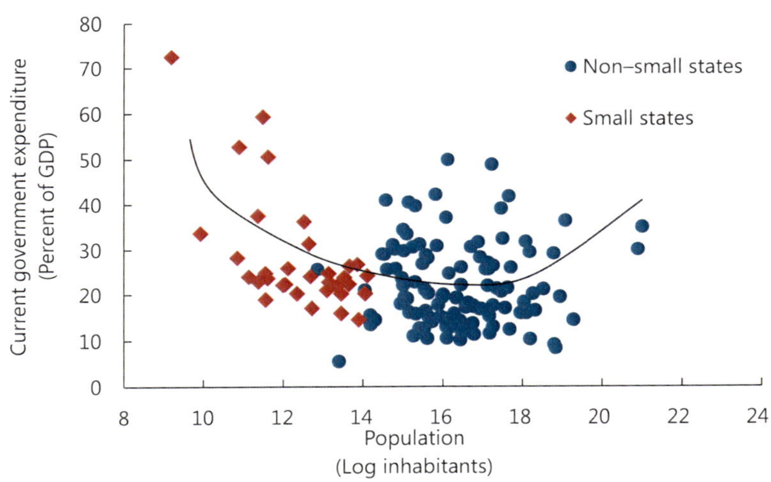

Figure 10.2 Current Expenditure and Population, 2003–13

Source: IMF staff estimates.

U-shaped; that is, the smaller the country, the bigger is its current government spending (Figure 10.2). Distance from key markets also raises import transport costs. All of these effects are worsened in microstates, while extreme remoteness and population dispersion compound the challenges in Pacific island countries (Figure 10.3).

The spending mix in small states is tilted toward current spending, despite infrastructure bottlenecks, which could impede higher real GDP per capita growth (Figure 10.4). The resultant underinvestment impedes sustainable growth. Despite large development and infrastructure gaps over the last 10 years, capital spending in the small states accounted for less than 20 percent of government spending, well below the average of 32 percent in low-income countries. An exception is Cabo Verde, off Africa's west coast, which embarked on a large investment program in the past decade at the cost of recurrent spending.

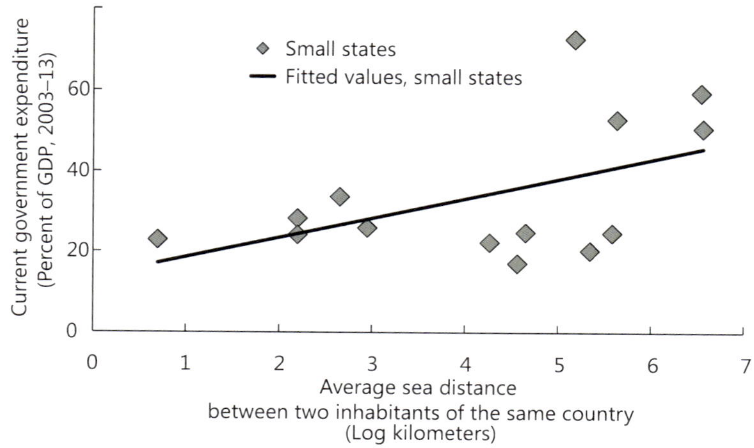

Figure 10.3 Small States: Current Government Expenditure and Geographic Dispersion

Source: IMF staff estimates.

Note: Includes Antigua and Barbuda, The Bahamas, Fiji, Kiribati, Marshall Islands, Micronesia, Palau, Samoa, the Solomon Islands, St. Kitts and Nevis, Tonga, Trinidad and Tobago, Tuvalu, and Vanuatu.

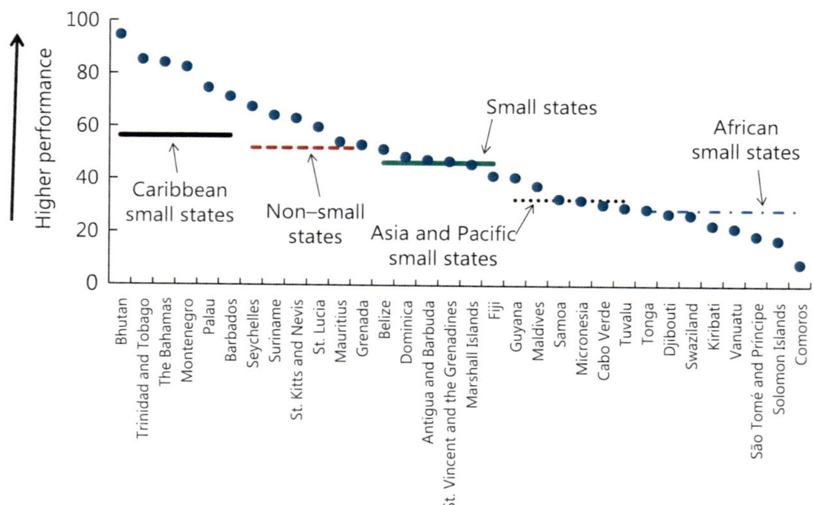

Figure 10.4 Infrastructure Quality: Electricity Generation per Capita, 2010 (*Percentile ranks*)

Sources: World Bank, World Development Indicators; and IMF staff estimates.

The composition of public spending matters in determining the impact of fiscal policy on growth in small states (Figures 10.5 and 10.6). Econometric results suggest that the higher the share of public investment for a given amount of public spending, the higher the per capita growth (Annex Table 10.1.1). Moreover, the impact of capital spending on growth is stronger in small states than in other country groups. The effect is even stronger in Asia and Pacific small states, consistent with their large development needs, both in terms of capital and human infrastructure. The IMF staff econometric analysis also suggests that increasing the share of capital investment will boost per capita growth, but expanding the deficit and increasing public debt after a certain threshold does not support growth. The threshold derived within the model, after which debt harms growth, is 30 percent of GDP for the Asia and Pacific small states, well below the 50 percent threshold that

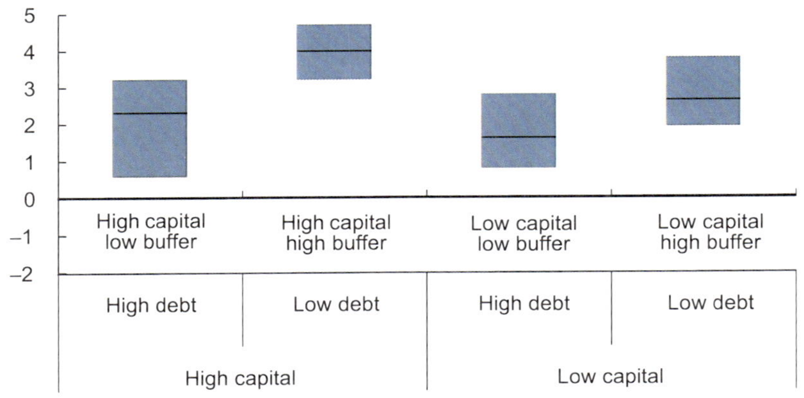

Figure 10.5 Relationship between Real GDP per Capita Growth, Composition of Spending, and Public Debt (*Percent*)

Source: IMF staff estimates.
Note: Data are for 1990–2012. High (low) capital means the share of capital spending is above (below) the median. High (low) deficit means the fiscal deficit in percent of GDP is above (below) the median.

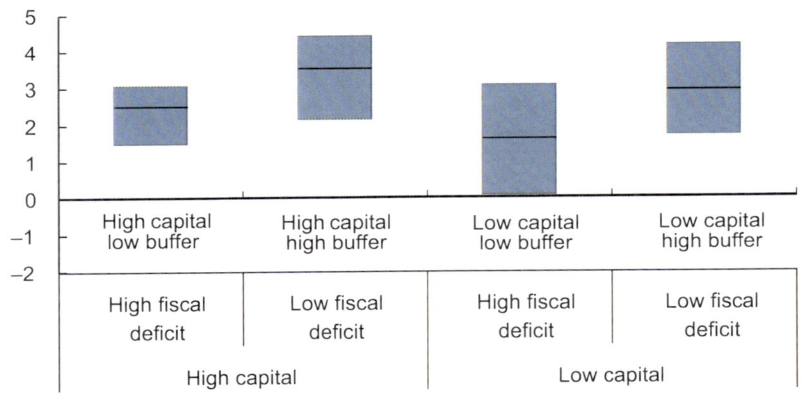

Figure 10.6 Relationship between Real GDP per Capita Growth, Composition of Spending, and Public Deficit (*Percent*)

Source: IMF staff estimates.
Note: Data are for 1990–2012. High (low) capital means the share of capital spending is above (below) the median. High (low) deficit means the fiscal deficit in percent of GDP is above (below) the median.

applies to the full sample. This calls for building buffers (keeping debt at manageable levels and having low fiscal deficits) and tilting the composition of spending toward capital outlays.

Indeed, the statistical analysis presented below supports the view that such buffers (that is, keeping deficits or debt low) are good for growth—and even more so when spending is tilted toward capital investment. Nonetheless, although higher capital spending is good for growth, it is less so when it expands deficits too much and raises debt unduly. This calls for preserving fiscal space for growth-enhancing investment, including infrastructure spending.

Additional IMF staff findings based on an event analysis (Figures 10.7 and 10.8) show that, in small states, an expansion in government spending led by capital spending results in higher real GDP per capita and lower public-debt-to-GDP ratios than expansions led by current spending. In small

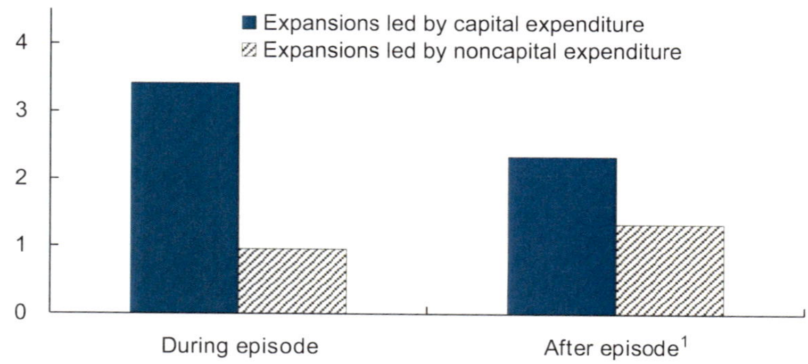

Figure 10.7 Small States: Real GDP per Capita during Episodes of Government Expenditure Expansion (*Year-over-year percent change*)

Source: IMF staff estimates.

Note: Data are for 1990–2012. Includes only public expenditure episodes that resulted in higher fiscal deficits.

[1]Three-year average after the episode.

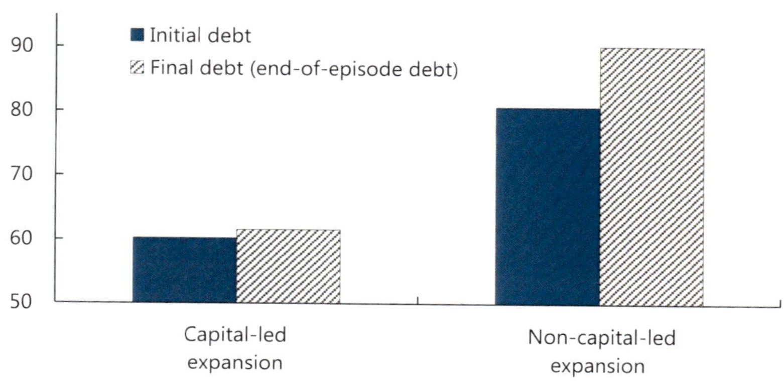

Figure 10.8 Small States: Public Debt during Episodes of Government Expenditure Expansion (*Percent of GDP*)

Source: IMF staff estimates.

Note: Data are for 1990–2012. Includes only public expenditure episodes that resulted in higher fiscal deficits.

states, government spending expansions driven by capital lead to a minimum increment in public-debt-to-GDP ratios of about 2 percent, but this soars by about 10 percentage points of GDP in government spending expansions led by current spending. The impact on growth of government expansion led by capital is also much higher during and after the episode than the impact on growth led by increased current spending.[2] One important caveat is that event analysis does not determine causality, because it does not control for the endogeneity of the variables and it should therefore not be interpreted as such. The endogeneity issues are solved within the econometric analysis presented in Annex Table 10.2.1 by using the generalized method of moments.[3] These results are in line with

[2]Specifically, an episode of expenditure expansion is defined as an increment in the ratio of government expenditure to GDP for at least two consecutive years. Government expansion is assumed to be led by capital expenditure if capital expenditure explains at least two-thirds of the government expenditure growth.

[3]Ongoing debate on the impact of public spending policies on growth shows that the growth dividend of public capital spending also hinges on the return on investment (see Box 10.2), the sources of financing (Gemmell, Misch, and Moreno-Dodson 2012; Romp and de Haan 2007), and the quality of the investment processes in project selection and implementation (Gupta and others 2014).

the analysis of the IMF's October 2014 *World Economic Outlook*, which found that public investment raises output in a wide range of countries. However, relative to the *World Economic Outlook*, this chapter finds that, for small states, the impact of public investment on real GDP growth is somewhat lower than for larger states. This could be due to lower fiscal multipliers in small, open economies whose capital inputs are mainly imported, as well as weaker PFM frameworks that could prevent efficient public investment.

Public spending efficiency in small Pacific states is lower than in other small states (Figure 10.9). In the Pacific island countries, a large share of government spending (current and capital) is allocated to health and education, relative to other small states, which is consistent with their large development needs (Figure 10.10). However, the relatively poor outcomes on human development indicators, despite such spending, can be explained by the high cost of providing these services in small remote islands. By looking at the relationship between population dispersion and efficiency in public expenditure (proxied by the ratio between education and health outcomes and the share of health and education spending as a percent of GDP), we find a positive relationship between population density and efficiency indicators in public expenditure (Figure 10.9). High population dispersion is associated with less efficient education and health expenditure (that is, positive slopes) with a correlation of 0.3–0.4. While remoteness and dispersion matter, recent analysis (Haque, Knight, and Jayasuriya 2012) points to the need to improve the quality of public spending by accelerating PFM reforms.

Box 10.2. Quantifying the Opportunity Cost of Building Fiscal Buffers in Pacific Island Countries

Policymakers in small developing states face a key fiscal policy choice: building fiscal buffers to enhance resilience to shocks—including natural disasters—or funding development spending. When a government expands fiscal space by accumulating public savings instead of financing spending for development needs, it forgoes the rate of return on the associated public investment. The opportunity cost of building fiscal buffers can be used to assess the optimal mix between building fiscal space and capital spending.

IMF staff estimated the social return on public investment assuming that it equals the marginal productivity of capital for a group of Pacific island countries. Following Caselli (2007), they calibrated a Cobb-Douglas production function for the group using data on output and investment from the Penn World Table and World Economic Outlook database for 1970–2010.

The results suggest that several Pacific island countries enjoy a high rate of return on capital. And as such they would benefit from capital spending, which is consistent with these countries' large infrastructure needs (proxied by the Human Development Index). The social return on capital in these countries is also in line with the return in low-income countries.

The IMF staff also estimated two measures of fiscal space: one based on the IMF/World Bank debt sustainability analysis (that is, a fiscal liquidity indicator is derived by measuring the average gap over the medium term between the debt-service-to-revenue ratio of public and publicly guaranteed debt and an indicative threshold after which the debt becomes unsustainable), and a second measure calculated as the difference between the actual debt relative to GDP and an estimated sustainable debt (as in Ostry and others 2010) implied by each country's historical record of fiscal adjustment.

Figures 10.2.1 to 10.2.3 shed light on the room for fiscal maneuvering in Pacific island countries. A plot of the estimated cost of building buffers against the Human Development Index—a proxy for infrastructure needs—suggests that some countries stand to gain the most from increasing the share of their budget devoted to capital spending. When plotting the three different measures of fiscal space against the index, even though they are different, the measures provide a similar ordering of countries across methodologies in the size of the fiscal space or the opportunity costs of building buffers.

Box 10.2. (*Continued*)

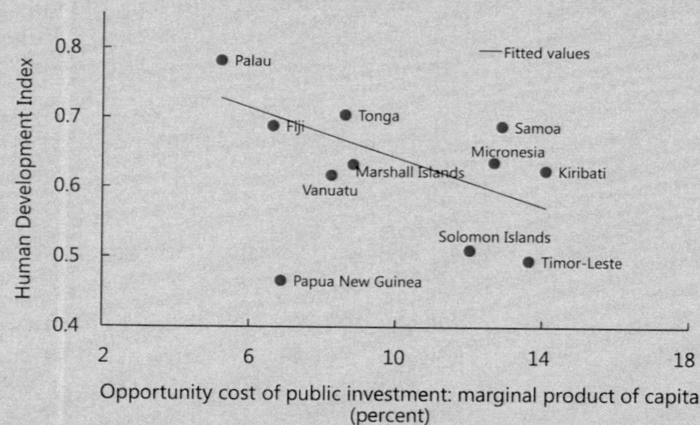

Figure 10.2.1 Opportunity Cost of Building Fiscal Buffers and Human Development Index

Source: IMF staff estimates.

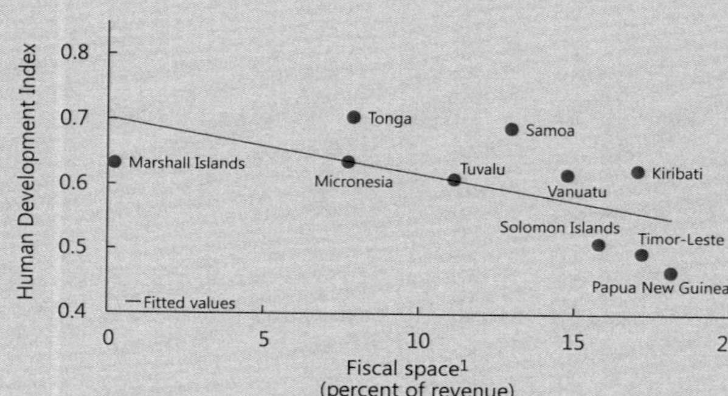

Figure 10.2.2 Fiscal Space and Human Development Index

Source: IMF staff estimates.

[1]Fiscal space measured by the gap in the IMF-World Bank Group's debt sustainability analyses between the threshold of the public and publicly guaranteed external debt-service-to-revenue ratio and the forecasted baseline path of the same ratio.

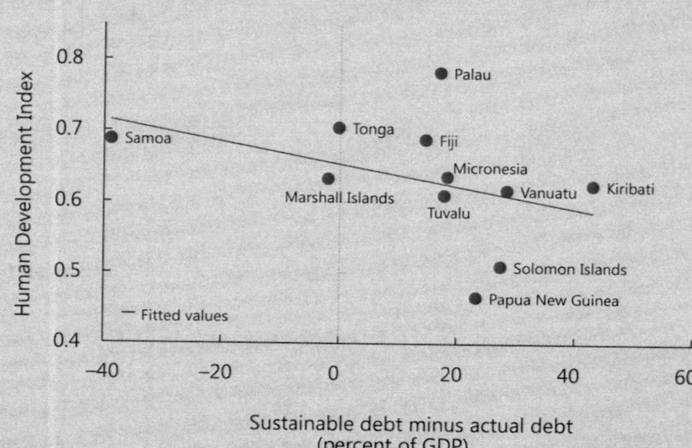

Figure 10.2.3 Fiscal Distress and Human Development Index

Source: IMF staff estimates.

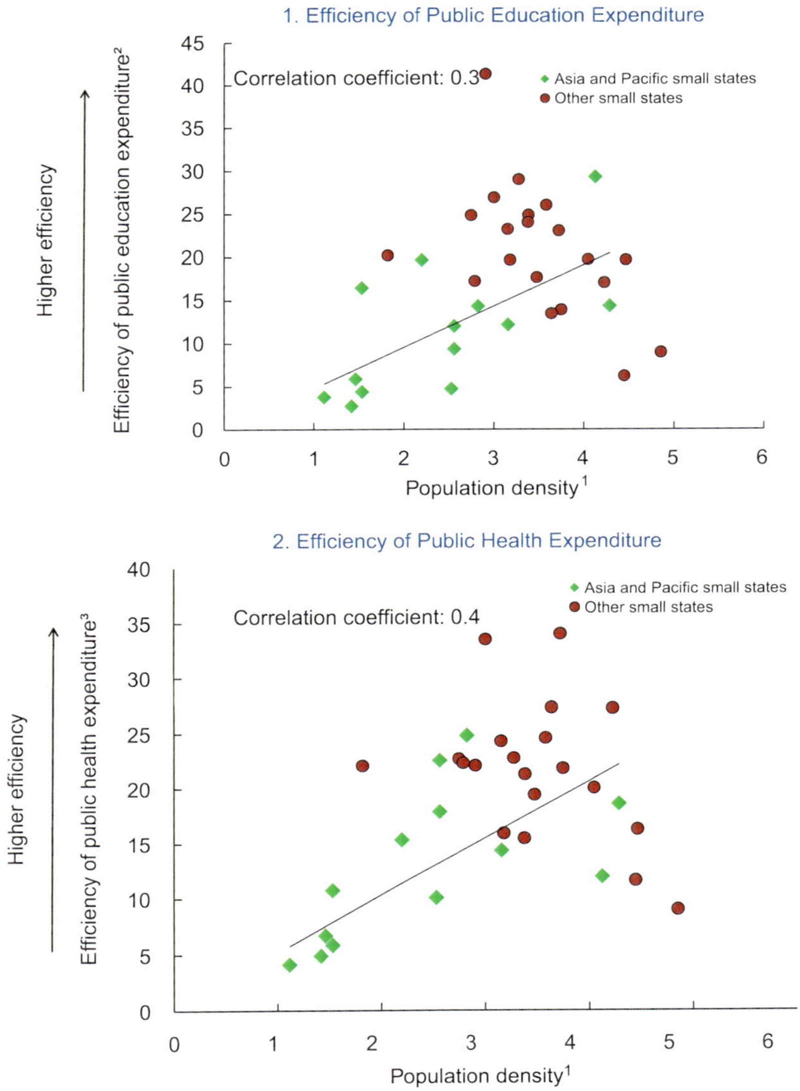

Figure 10.9 Measures of Efficiency of Public Spending and Population Dispersion, 1990–2012

Source: IMF staff estimates.

[1] Density computed as inhabitants per square kilometer. The variable was rescaled by taking the log of the density multiplied by 1,000.

[2] Efficiency measured as secondary school enrollment rate divided by public education expenditure-to-GDP ratio.

[3] Efficiency measured as life expectancy divided by public health expenditure-to-GDP ratio.

COPING WITH REVENUE VOLATILITY

Revenue volatility in small states is larger than in developing non–small states, because the revenue base is narrow and subject to several exogenous shocks, and this is expected to continue due to the recent large drop in oil prices.

The sources of volatility vary across small states and depend on cyclical and noncyclical factors (Figure 10.11 and Annex Table 10.1.2). On average, revenue shows strong procyclicality, especially in net

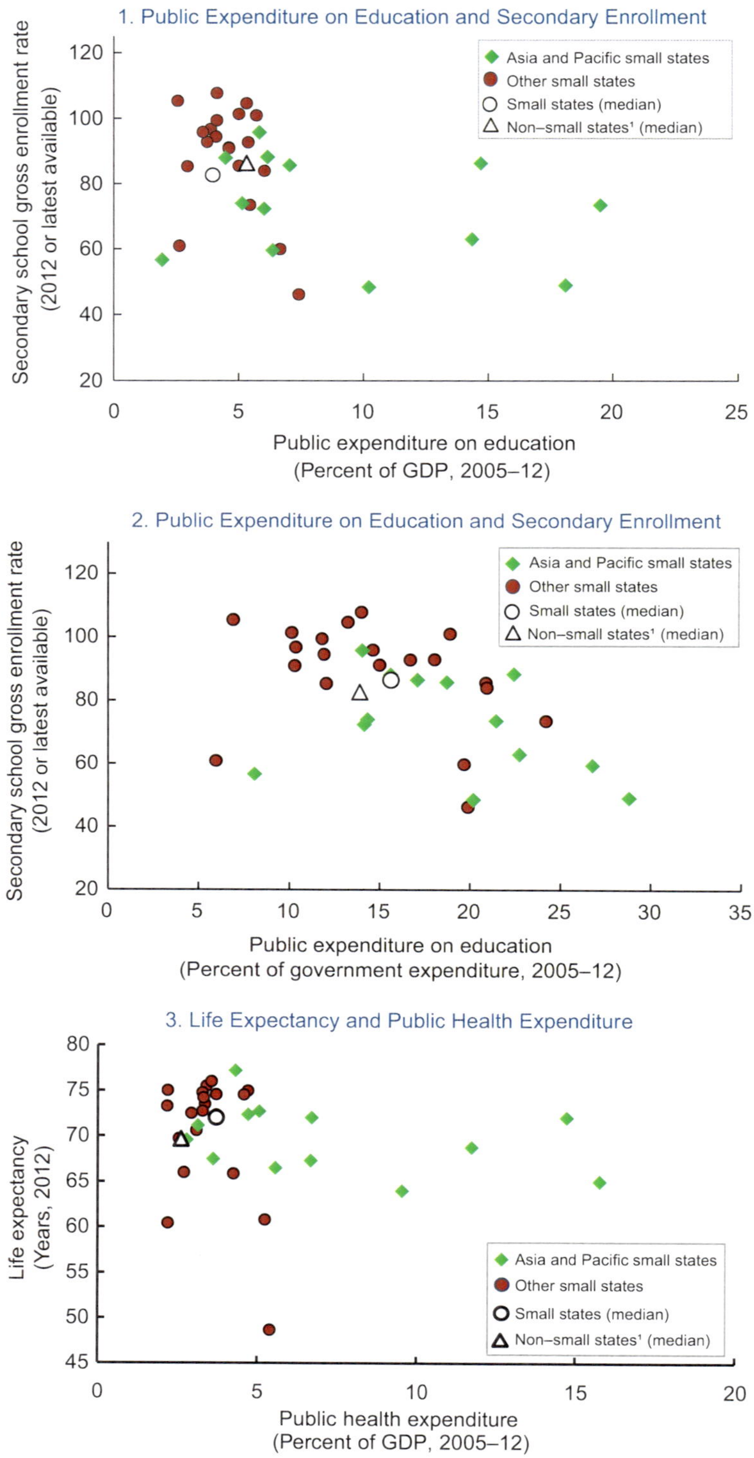

Figure 10.10 Health, Education Expenditure, and Selected Human Development Indicators

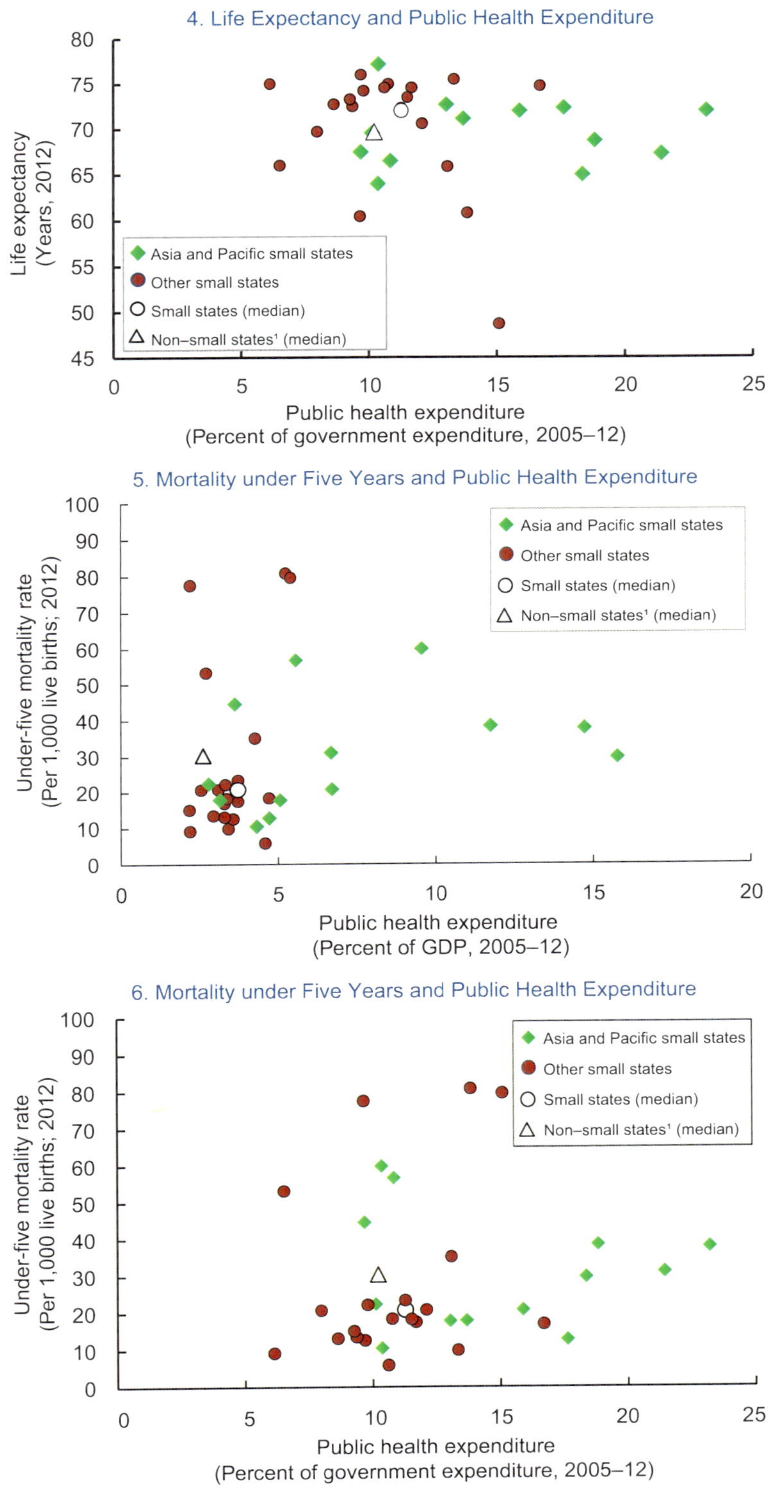

Figure 10.10 *(Continued)*

Sources: World Bank, World Development Indicators; and IMF staff estimates.
[1] Excludes advanced economies.

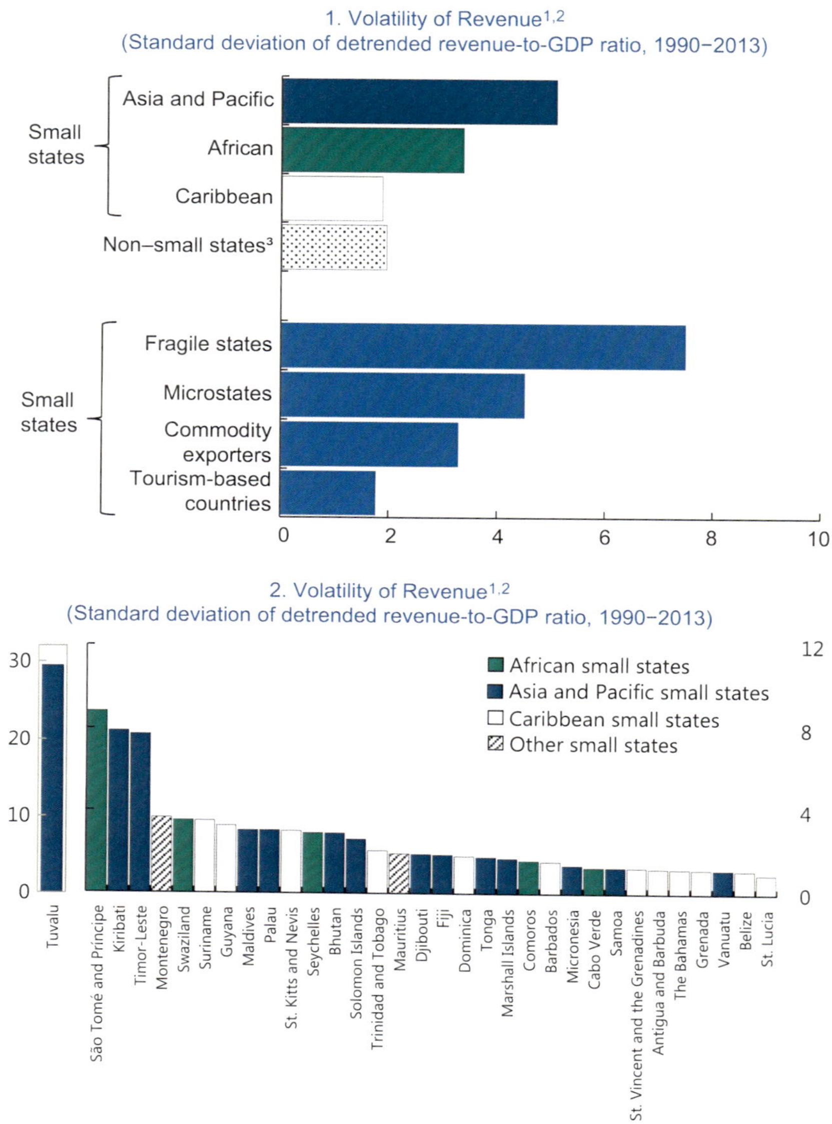

Figure 10.11 Revenue Volatility across Different Groups in Small States

commodity importers. Revenue volatility in small states also results from terms-of-trade shocks attributable to a lack of diversification and narrow production bases. The elasticity of revenue to terms of trade, after controlling for GDP, is much higher in resource-rich small states than in comparators. Furthermore, revenue in small states depends on vulnerability to natural disasters. The IMF staff analysis suggests that a natural disaster that affects 1 percent of the population causes a drop in real revenue of 0.2 percentage point in small states and 0.4 percentage point in the Pacific islands small states. Further analysis of the small states of the Pacific points to a contraction in tax revenue of 0.2 percentage point of GDP in the year of the disaster, followed by a revenue rebound in the following year (Annex Figure 10.1.1). After controlling for GDP, the volatility of trade flows (including tourism) and remittances also affects revenue

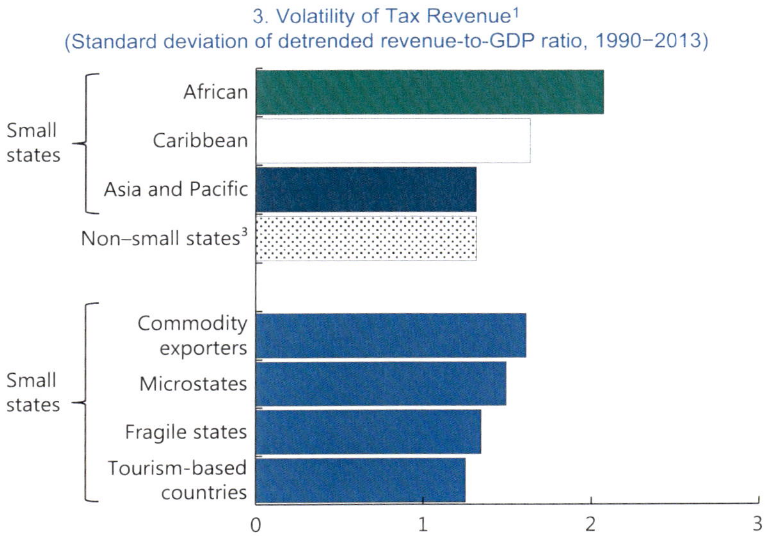

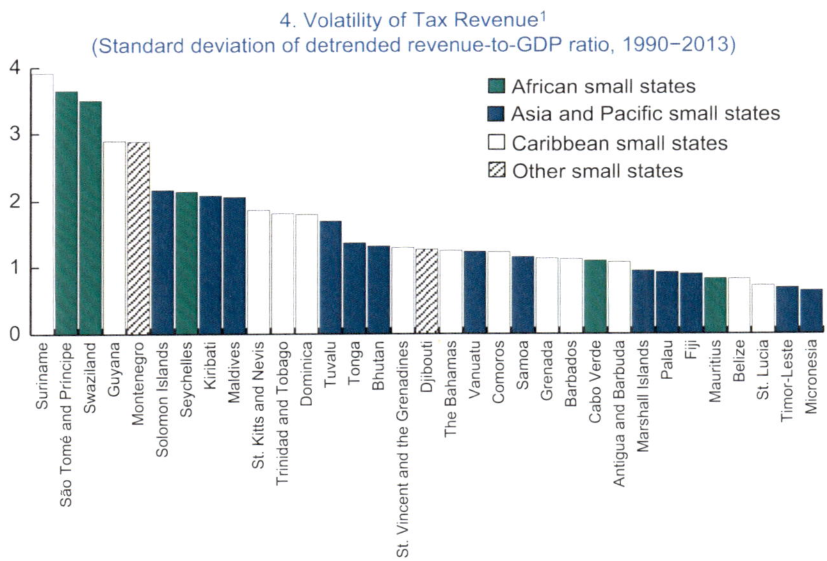

Figure 10.11 *(Continued)*

volatility. In Asia and Pacific small states, most of the volatility is caused by fishing license fees, which are independent of the economic cycle.

The degree of revenue volatility differs across small states, with fragile states, commodity exporters, and microstates affected most. The volatility of tax revenue is highest among resource-rich countries (Guyana, the Solomon Islands, Suriname, Trinidad and Tobago) as a result of commodity price shocks, as well as uncertainty about the size and exhaustibility of resources. The volatility of nontax revenues is extremely high, especially in Asia and Pacific microstates that rely on fishing license fees, such as Kiribati and Tuvalu, where these fees represent about 50 percent of revenues. This is also true in such resource-rich countries as Bhutan, São Tomé and Príncipe, and Timor-Leste, owing to the volatility of royalties associated with natural resources.

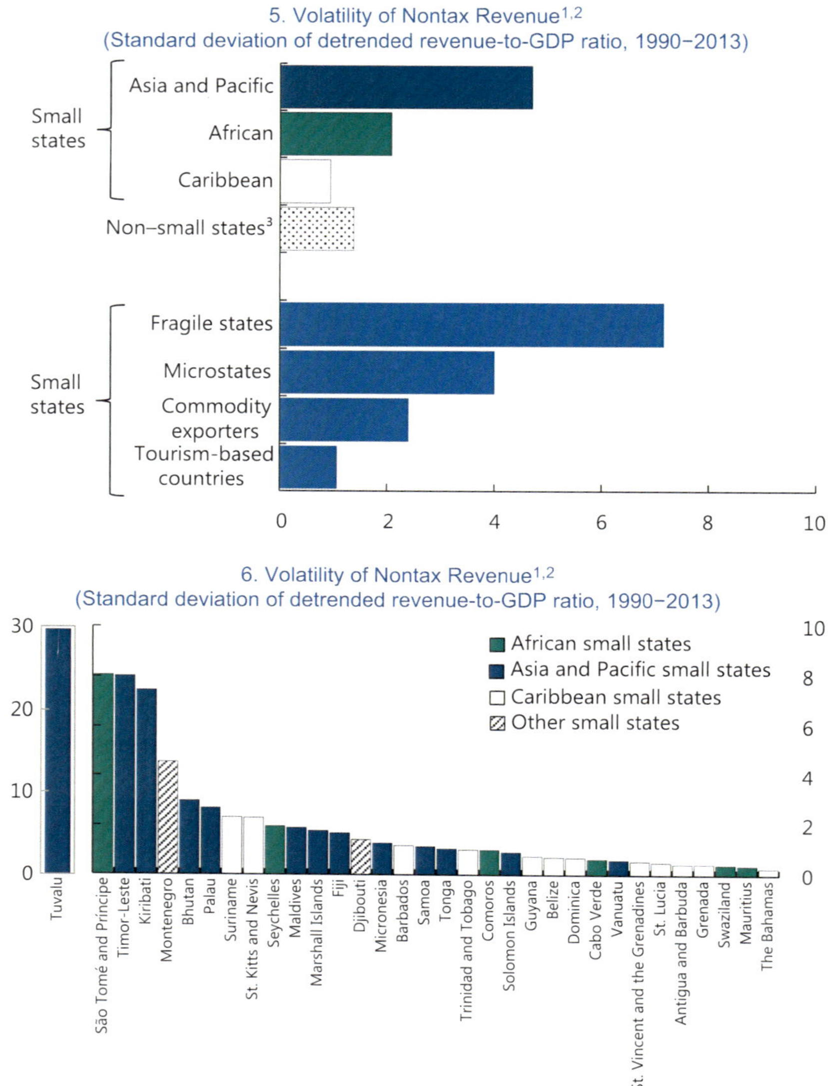

Figure 10.11 *(Continued)*

Sources: IMF World Economic Outlook database; and IMF staff estimates.
[1] Volatility after excluding time trend in the underlying ratios to remove structural factors.
[2] Excluding grants.
[3] Excluding advanced economies.

Revenue volatility is also a potential source of vulnerability. High volatility may lead to significant output volatility and undermine overall fiscal performance in the absence of a stabilization fund (IMF 2012).

Addressing Procyclical Fiscal Policy

The combination of revenue volatility and current spending rigidities, compounded by the low access to finance of small states, has prevented expenditure smoothing over the business cycle and has thus fostered fiscal procyclicality (namely, spending went up together with revenues during upturns and vice versa during recessions; Figure 10.12). Revenue volatility has generally translated into spending volatility, especially capital spending. The IMF staff analysis suggests that revenue

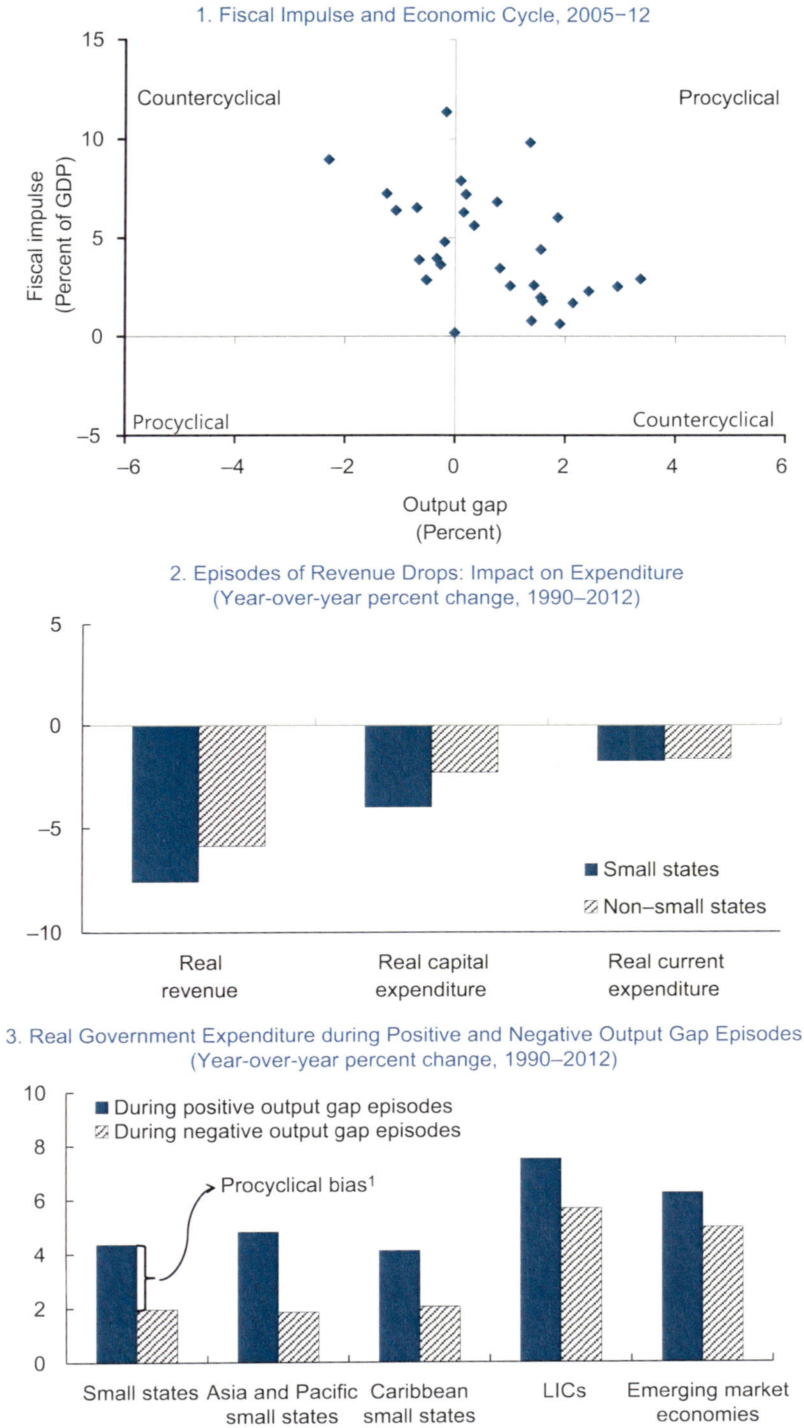

Figure 10.12 Procyclical Bias in Fiscal Policy in Small States

Sources: IMF, World Economic Outlook database; and IMF staff estimates.

Note: LICs = low-income countries. Bars in panel 2 show the change in the variables when revenue drops by at least 2 percent of GDP after removing the cyclical impact; all variables are corrected for GDP cycle. Panel 3 shows primary government spending.

[1]The procyclical bias is measured by the difference between the bars within each group. For each country output gaps are estimated using Hodrick-Prescott filters.

shortages have resulted in cuts to capital spending. Econometric results also confirm the procyclicality of capital spending (Annex Table 10.1.3).

Building Fiscal Buffers to Enhance Resilience: The Role of Fiscal Anchors

Policies that manage revenue volatility and avoid procyclical fiscal bias could foster resilience in small states. Given their vulnerability to shocks, enhancing resilience requires building adequate fiscal buffers for rainy-day countercyclical support and creating policy space for spending on infrastructure to boost potential output. Indeed, some small states have made progress in rebuilding fiscal buffers after the global financial crisis (Figures 10.13 and 10.14), but more than half still have less comfortable buffers (higher debt and lower fiscal balances) than before the crisis (Figure 10.15).

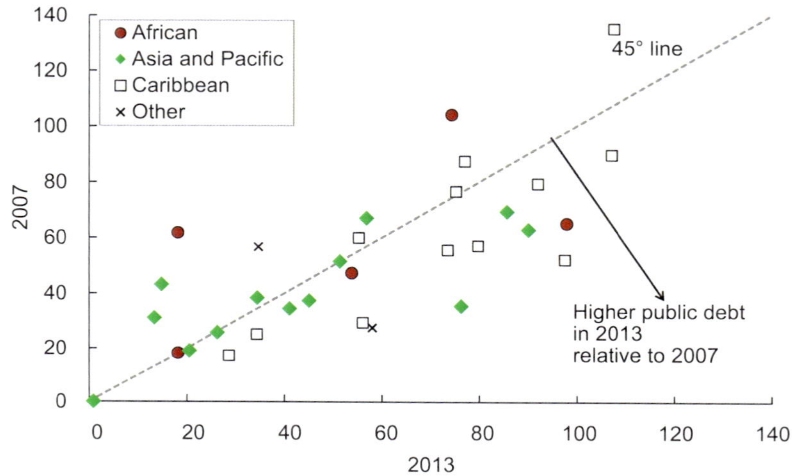

Figure 10.13 Small States: Gross Public Debt (*Percent of GDP*)

Sources: IMF, World Economic Outlook database; and IMF staff estimates.

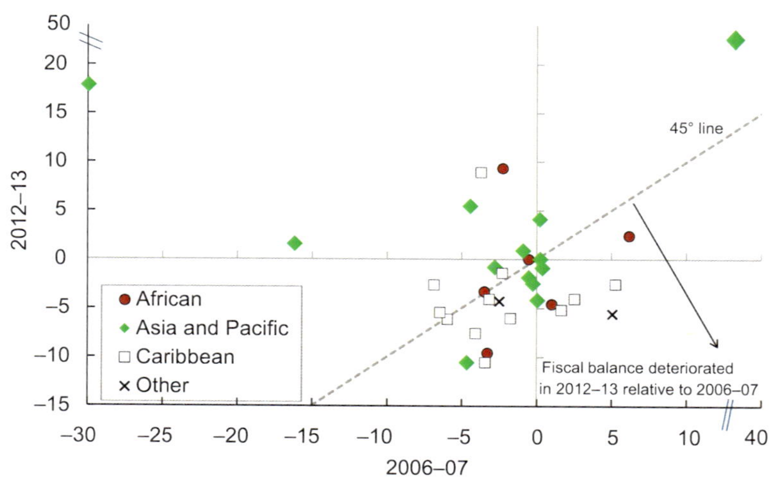

Figure 10.14 Small States: Overall Fiscal Balance (*Percent of GDP*)

Source: IMF staff estimates.

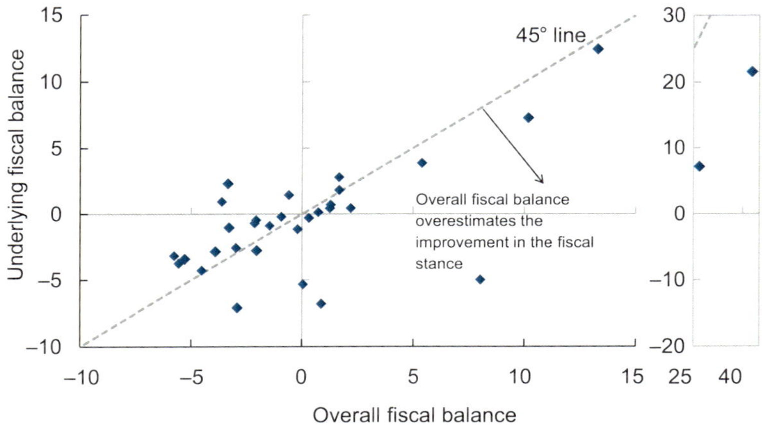

Figure 10.15 Fiscal Balance and Underlying Fiscal Balance, 2013 (*Deviation from 2010–11; percentage points of GDP*)

Source: IMF staff estimates.

Because of revenue volatility, small states' headline fiscal balances do not always accurately reflect their underlying fiscal position. The improvement in the fiscal position of small states, defined by the change in the underlying fiscal balance, appears to be smaller than the change in the overall balance suggests in a quarter of the small states.

Strengthening fiscal frameworks by using fiscal anchors to insulate the budget from revenue volatility is essential. A country-specific fiscal anchor helps illustrate that fiscal policy reflects both short-term cyclical and medium-term sustainability goals. It also helps properly assess a country's underlying fiscal position, which is sometimes masked by headline fiscal balances. Stronger fiscal frameworks will avoid fiscal procyclicality by saving windfall revenue during an "up" cycle and vice versa. The use of a fiscal anchor to smooth spending over the cycle would also go hand in hand with strengthening the medium-term orientation of fiscal policy, replacing the year-by-year formulation based on volatile and uncertain revenue.

The design of fiscal frameworks by using anchors that help manage revenue volatility and ensure debt sustainability in small states should be kept simple. Moreover, a fiscal-rule framework should set both a fiscal anchor target and an operational target. While the former is the final objective to preserve fiscal sustainability, the latter is an intermediate target under the direct control of governments, with a close link to debt dynamics. Since the final objective of the framework is to preserve fiscal sustainability, a natural anchor for expectations is the debt ratio, which creates an upper limit to repeated (cumulative) fiscal slippage. In addition to the anchor, the framework should include an operational target, which would be under the direct control of governments, while also having a close link to debt dynamics.

As IMF (2014c) reports, the choice of the operational target is more difficult and controversial. Public debt cannot play this role, as factors other than policy decisions affect public debt changes, including below-the-line operations and valuation effects. Available options include a revenue rule, an expenditure rule, a nominal balance, a structural balance target (in level or in first difference), or a combination of these options. Actual capacity constraint and, importantly, structural changes in the economy imply that meaningful, cyclically adjusted balances are difficult to calculate. In this context, the output gap is not only difficult to estimate, but is also erratic in nature. This is because it depends less on the dynamics of domestic economies and more on external and unpredictable developments (for example, trends in activity in trade partners, terms of trade, and commodity prices, including the recent drop in oil prices) given undiversified export bases. The underlying fiscal balance could be designed using a *normal* level of revenue (that is, backward-looking averages) or, for commodity exporters, by removing the direct and indirect effect of commodity revenue.[4]

Fiscal anchors are not a panacea. Moreover, they need to be accompanied by a more broad-based fiscal reform strategy. Political economy considerations suggest that moving away from a budget balance rule without strengthening fiscal institutions could create a fiscal deficit bias. While a country will find it easy to run a deficit during downturns, building fiscal buffers during upturns by saving revenue windfalls could be difficult because of political pressure to spend to meet large development and infrastructure needs. Appropriate fiscal institutions need to support fiscal framework reforms, including institutions that facilitate the formulation of long-term revenue forecasts, the implementation of quality public investment projects, and the sound management of rainy-day funds.

POLICY REFORM OPTIONS

Small states need to strengthen their fiscal frameworks to sustain economic growth. This requires an appropriate balance between fiscal buffers for rainy days and fiscal space for investment in infrastructure and human capital (see Box 10.2 for a quantification of the trade-off between building buffers and investing). Strengthening the fiscal framework is important for growth because it:

- Enhances resilience by minimizing fiscal risks, which are particularly high in microstates and arise from volatile revenue and budget-spending rigidities.
- Creates fiscal space for growth-enhancing and poverty-reducing investment, including infrastructure spending.
- Builds fiscal buffers to enhance macroeconomic management and uses countercyclical spending during more difficult times.
- Allows nonrenewable resource revenue in resource-rich small states to be used wisely and ensure long-term fiscal sustainability.

But strengthening fiscal frameworks is particularly challenging in small states. This is because of their budget rigidities, extreme revenue volatility, spending procyclicality, and limited capacity. Tackling these challenges thus requires a comprehensive macro and fiscal reform strategy, including spending and revenue reforms. This strategy should include several pillars:

- *Preserving strong fiscal fundamentals*—Over the fiscal cycle, deficits should be kept low, on average, to avoid accumulating rising debt burdens. Low deficits and moderate debt burdens are correlated with stronger GDP growth.
- *Minimizing fiscal rigidity and lowering recurrent spending to create fiscal space for capital spending*—Typical sources of rigidities are high spending on public wages, large entitlement programs for civil servants, and revenues earmarked for large capital projects. Reform of wage bills, public servants' benefits, and revenue administration should thus be included in the fiscal package. Countries should also seek to deliver public goods and services at the lowest possible recurrent cost, avoiding the use of public resources to support loss-making, inefficient public sector enterprises. To this end, exploring opportunities to outsource service delivery to the private sector is warranted, where possible. This will create scope to finance growth-enhancing capital spending (see Figures 10.5 and 10.6).
- *Improving the spending mix toward investment in human and physical capital*—This will require spending reforms in the form of spending reviews and medium-term expenditure frameworks. Their goal should be to reallocate resources toward priority spending, especially infrastructure

[4]The indirect component of resource revenue is estimated by running a regression of the nonresource revenue on the resource revenue. This provides an estimation of the comovements of the two components of revenues. The indirect effect of resource revenue is estimated by projecting the nonresource revenue based on the resource revenue.

investment, including climate-proofing infrastructure and strengthening health and education sectors. This will also improve the business environment and attract private investors from abroad.

- *Adopting budget and investment practices that can foster high returns on capital investments*—Because resources for capital spending will remain tight, countries need to adopt investment practices that maximize value for money. This will involve identifying, prioritizing, and implementing public investment projects. At the same time, strengthening the medium-term orientation of fiscal policy by adopting a multiyear budget framework can help clarify which projects should be financed and over what timeframe. Developing a multiyear budget framework should also help, politically, to deal with spending pressures arising from large development needs. This could help build consensus on the appropriate sequencing of development projects and better calibrate the pace of development spending. Such a framework, however, needs to take into account capacity constraints, which is a pressing issue in small states.
- *Identifying resources to help weather revenue volatility*—These could include contingency funds within the budget, sovereign wealth funds for resource-rich economies, and/or insurance policies. Contingency funds can also be used to manage shocks. Natural disaster funds or general budget contingency reserves can be used to save resources to deal with natural disasters. From a PFM perspective, access to these funds and reporting on their use should be clearly defined, and budget allocations transparent. The Solomon Islands' National Transport Fund is a case in point.
- *Using fiscal anchors to help smooth spending and isolate budgets from revenue volatility*—Where resources can be identified, budgets should allow for spending to be smoothed in the face of revenue shocks. In commodity-resource-rich countries, targeting the noncommodity fiscal balance and using sovereign wealth funds to enhance the management of natural resources will also ensure the long-term sustainable use of exhaustible resources. Rather than focusing on the current fiscal deficit, the budget should provide for spending in line with underlying revenues. The caveat is that countries will need to distinguish between temporary and more sustained revenue shocks. In the latter case, there may be no alternative to adjusting spending, and here the focus should be on the pace of adjustment and on achieving a balanced adjustment between recurrent and capital spending.
- *Strengthening domestic revenue mobilization to support the rebuilding of policy buffers*—Mobilizing revenues by bolstering administration capacity and reforming the domestic tax system is also needed to increase fiscal space to meet critical development spending needs while improving the business environment. In practice, these reforms need to be tailored according to country circumstances. For example, realistically enforcing customs compliance in very large and scattered territories, as are many Pacific island countries, is extremely challenging and costly. There is also a need to focus on large taxpayers, who account for 70–80 percent of revenue, by creating a special unit in tax administration offices, while using a simplified tax system and simplified compliance rules for medium-sized and small taxpayers. Developing a proper mix of income and consumption taxation (value-added and sales tax) would raise additional revenues.[5] Lower oil prices also offer an opportunity to reform energy subsidies and taxes in both oil exporters and importers. Oil-importing small states should use savings from the removal of energy subsidies to strengthen fiscal buffers or to increase public infrastructure if conditions allow.
- *Enhancing regional cooperation on nontax revenue to increase revenue mobilization*—The small Pacific states need to strengthen regional economic, institutional, and technological networks to compensate for geographical isolation and dispersion and create a more attractive business

[5]Kiribati has experienced a significant improvement in tax collection with the introduction of a withholding tax at source in March 2009. It also introduced value-added tax in 2014.

environment for foreign investors. Key sectors for this are fisheries and information and communication technology. Adopting regional agreements and cooperative subregional measures to strengthen the bargaining power of license-issuing countries could improve fishing sector productivity. The Nauru agreement, a regional pact on fisheries among Kiribati, Marshall Islands, Micronesia, Nauru, Palau, Papua New Guinea, the Solomon Islands, and Tuvalu, is a success story in using regional cooperation to mobilize revenues (IMF 2014b).

These fiscal reforms need to be accompanied by measures to strengthen fiscal institutions and fiscal governance. The reform measures should aim at improving transparency (by enhancing budget planning, internal auditing on the use of public funds, monitoring, reporting, and evaluation systems to improve accountability), cash management, and project management capacity. Developing institutional frameworks will help better identify, quantify, monitor, and mitigate fiscal risks. And fiscal frameworks should be integrated with a debt management strategy to manage cash flows effectively and reduce sovereign financing risks. A successful case of this was the introduction in the Solomon Islands in May 2012 of a strategy to strengthen debt management and debt sustainability, which superseded the Honiara Club Agreement, which prevented the country from contracting external borrowing.

The IMF, for its part, has been assisting small states through capacity development in strengthening fiscal frameworks. This has involved both IMF headquarters and regional technical assistance centers providing technical assistance and training. In this respect, the work by the IMF Fiscal Affairs Department could be further leveraged to reduce the procyclicality of fiscal policy (through the appropriate design of fiscal rules, for example), create fiscal space (by energy subsidy reforms and revenue enhancing measures), and strengthen revenue and PFM.

ANNEX 10.1. ECONOMETRIC ANALYSIS

Determinants of Real per Capita GDP Growth

To assess the effects of fiscal policy on per capita output (Annex Table 10.1.1), we use dynamic panel regressions where real per capita GDP growth (that is, the dependent variable) is regressed on a fiscal balance indicator on the share of government capital spending over total public spending and on the ratio of public debt, as in Baldacci, Hillman, and Kojo (2004). The model controls for external conditions by including an indicator of trade openness. The signs and the significance of the model's coefficients suggest that for a given amount of public spending, expanding the share of capital investment helps boost per capita growth but expanding the deficit does not.

The impact of capital spending on growth is stronger in Asia and Pacific small states than in other small states, consistent with their larger development needs. The model also suggests there is a nonlinear relationship between debt and growth in line with previous results (IMF 2012); that is, while low levels of debt are good for growth, high levels are not.

Determinants of Real Revenue

Separate dynamic panel regressions were run for different groups (small states, Pacific island small states, low-income countries, emerging markets, resource-rich small states, and non-resource-rich small states) to identify the variables that explain real revenue (Annex Table 10.1.2). The dependent variable (real revenue) is regressed on GDP (and its lag), weighted terms of trade (and its lag), a variable on natural disasters, lagged real revenues, and fishing license fees. Revenue shows strong procyclicality, especially in small states that are net commodity importers. And revenue procyclicality is a source of revenue volatility. Coefficients on real GDP growth variables higher than 1 suggest revenue procyclicality (that is, revenue is growing faster than GDP during upturns and slower than GDP during downturns). For small states, the sum of the coefficients on real GDP growth (current period and one period lagged)—a proxy for cyclical components of revenues—is equal to 1.7. After controlling for GDP, revenue depends on terms-of-trade shocks, especially in resource-rich small

ANNEX TABLE 10.1.1

Determinants of Real per Capita GDP Growth

	Asia and Pacific Small States	African Small States	Caribbean Small States	Small States	Emerging Market and Developing Economies[1]
Overall fiscal-balance-to-GDP ratio	0.227***	0.135	0.0664	0.226***	–0.0237
Ratio of government capital expenditure to total government expenditure	0.124***	0.154***	0.0299	0.0878***	0.0160
Debt-to-GDP ratio (lagged)	0.249***	–0.00147	0.00169	0.0380**	–0.00466
Lag (debt-to-GDP ratio)^2	–0.00214***	–4.79e–05	–0.000103	–0.000218***	–2.26e–05
Trade openness	0.0384***	0.00121	0.00620	0.0274***	0.0422***
World GDP growth, percent	0.610***	0.490*	0.849***	0.641***	0.697***
Five-year lag of log (real GDP per capita, purchasing power parity)	0.720	1.739*	–1.503**	0.535*	–0.0982
Constant	–19.31*	–17.41**	11.95	–10.90***	4.204*
Observations	192	77	194	482	1,325
Number of countries	13	6	12	33	102

Source: IMF staff estimates.
Note: Panel regressions, 1990–2013.
* $p < 0.1$; ** $p < 0.05$; *** $p < 0.01$.
[1] Excludes small states.

ANNEX TABLE 10.1.2

Determinants of Real Revenue (*Year-over-year percent change*)

	Small States	Pacific Island Small States[1]	Low-Income Countries	Emerging Markets	Resource-Rich Small States	Non-Resource-Rich Small States
Real GDP growth	1.093***	1.672***	1.622***	1.41***	0.933***	1.249***
Real GDP growth (lagged)	0.607*	0.568	0.236	−0.124	0.512	0.556*
Weighted terms-of-trade growth	0.390**	0.659**	0.468***	0.821**	1.401**	0.120**
Weighted terms-of-trade growth (lagged)	0.227	0.352	0.130	−0.180	0.260	0.136
Intensity of natural disasters (lagged)	−0.248**	−0.429***	0.039	−0.189	−0.294	−0.239**
Real revenue growth (lagged)	−0.410	−0.375	−0.181	0.024	−0.237	−0.545
Fishing license fees		0.206***				
Constant	0.009	−1.667	−1.223	−0.895	2.498	−0.684
Observations	591	92	730	745	100	466
Number of countries	33	6	49	49	6	27

Source: IMF staff estimates.

Note: Panel regressions, 1990–2013. Combined coefficients higher than 1 on real GDP growth and lagged GDP growth imply revenue procyclicality.

* $p < 0.1$; ** $p < 0.05$; *** $p < 0.01$.

[1] Includes countries dependent on fishing license fees.

states. Natural disasters also raise revenue volatility. The IMF staff analysis suggests that a natural disaster that affects 1 percent of the population causes a drop in real revenue of 0.2 percentage point.

Impact of Natural Disasters on Tax Revenue

The IMF staff analysis in Chapter 5, using a panel vector autoregression, suggests that a natural disaster that affects 1 percent of the population in Pacific island small states leads to a contraction in tax revenue of 0.2 percentage point of GDP in the year of the disaster, followed by a revenue rebound the next year (Annex Figure 10.1.1). The model focuses on the impact of natural disasters on real GDP and fiscal variables. The specification includes the following variables: natural disaster intensity, real GDP growth, change in total government expenditure as a percent of GDP, change in

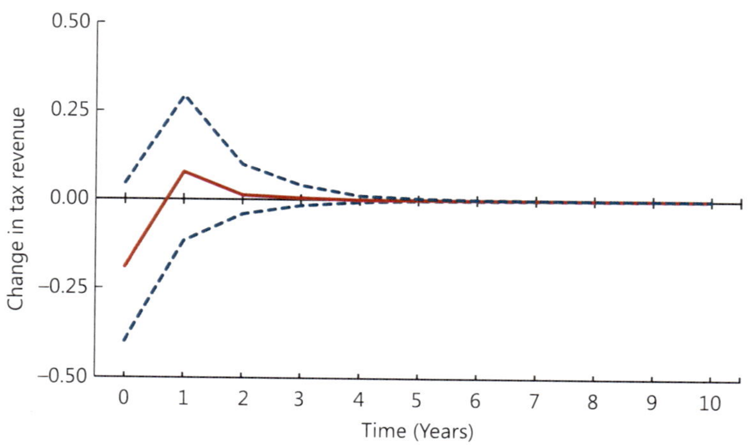

Annex Figure 10.1.1 Response of Tax Revenue to Natural Disasters (*Percentage points of GDP*)

Source: IMF staff estimates.

ANNEX TABLE 10.1.3

Degree of Spending Procyclicality

	Real Current Government Expenditure (Year-over-Year Percent Change)						Real Capital Government Expenditure (Year-over-Year Percent Change)					
	Small States	African small States	Asia and Pacific Small States	Caribbean Small States	Low-Income Countries	Emerging Markets	Small States	African Small States	Asia and Pacific Small States	Caribbean Small States	Low-Income Countries	Emerging Markets
Real GDP growth	0.523***	0.756	0.623**	0.223	0.633***	0.413***	2.346***	2.560	2.058**	2.412**	2.634***	1.476***
Constant	1.522**	0.683	0.922	2.528**	1.751	1.949**	–5.323**	–6.682	–6.921*	–3.474	–6.342	–2.120
Observations	679	126	264	253	830	1,872	679	126	264	253	830	1,872
Number of countries	33	6	13	12	44	101	33	6	13	12	44	101

Source: IMF staff estimates.

Note: Panel regressions, 1990–2013. Spending is procyclical if the coefficient on real GDP growth is higher than 1.

* $p < .10$; ** $p < .05$; *** $p < .01$.

tax revenue as a percent of GDP, and change in the overall fiscal balance as a percent of GDP. The variable on natural disaster intensity is measured by the number of fatalities and others hurt by the disaster as a share of total population, in line with Fomby, Ikeda, and Loayza (2013).

Degree of Spending Procyclicality

This model assesses the degree of spending procyclicality; that is, capital spending increasing during good times and declining during recessions (Annex Table 10.1.3). The change in real government spending is regressed on changes in real growth. The elasticity of real current government spending is lower than 1, suggesting that current spending is not procyclical. The elasticity of capital is much.

REFERENCES

Baldacci, Emanuele, Arye L. Hillman, and Naoko C. Kojo. 2004. "Growth, Governance, and Fiscal Policy Transmission Channels in Low-Income Countries." *European Journal of Political Economy* 20 (3): 517–49.

Caselli, Francesco. 2007. "The Marginal Product of Capital." *The Quarterly Journal of Economics* 122 (2): 535–68.

Fomby, Thomas, Yuki Ikeda, and Norman V. Loayza. 2013. "The Growth Aftermath of Natural Disasters." *Journal of Applied Econometrics* 28 (3): 412–34.

Gemmell, N., F. Misch, and B. Moreno-Dodson. 2012. "Public Spending for Long-Run Growth: A Practitioners' View." Economic Premise 99, World Bank, Washington.

Gupta, S., A. Kangur, C. Papageorgiou, and A. Wane. 2014. "Efficiency-Adjusted Public Capital and Growth." *World Development* 57: 164–74.

Haque, Tobias, David Knight, and Dinuk Jayasuriya. 2012. "Capacity Constraints and Public Financial Management in Small Pacific Island Countries." Policy Research Working Paper 6297, World Bank, Washington.

Holden, Paul, and Hunt Howell. 2009. "Enhancing Access to Finance in the Caribbean." Private Sector Development Discussion Paper 4, Inter-American Development Bank, Washington.

International Monetary Fund (IMF). 2012. "Macroeconomic Policy Frameworks for Resource-Rich Developing Countries." Policy Paper, Washington.

———. 2013. "Macroeconomic Issues in Small States and Implications for Fund Engagement." Washington.

———. 2014a. "Staff Guidance Note on the Fund's Engagement with Small Developing States." Staff Guidance Note, Washington.

———. 2014b. "Leveraging Marine Fisheries Resources: Implication of Fiscal Policy." Asia & Pacific: Small States Monitor, April 2014. Washington.

———. 2014c. "Fiscal Governance in the Euro Area: Progress and Challenges." Selected Issues Papers, Euro Area Policies, Country Report No. 14/199, Washington.

———. 2014d. *World Economic Outlook.* World Economic and Financial Survey. Washington, October.

Ostry, J. D., A. R. Ghosh, J. I. Kim, and M. S. Qureshi. 2010. "Fiscal Space." IMF Staff Position Note SPN/10/11, International Monetary Fund, Washington.

Romp, W., and J. de Haan. 2007. "Public Capital and Economic Growth: A Critical Survey." *Perspektiven der Wirtschaftspolitik* 8 (S1): 6–52.

CHAPTER 11

Estimating Fiscal Multipliers Using a Simplified General Equilibrium Model of Small States, with Application to Kiribati and Palau

SERGEI DODZIN AND XUEFEI BAI

The aim of this chapter is to help policymakers and economists better comprehend the link between fiscal policies and growth and to use this understanding operationally to design better macroeconomic policies. The links between fiscal policy and growth are highly significant in small states, where the government sector plays a major role in the economy (Figure 11.1). The importance of the government sector is even greater in the most remote and dispersed Pacific island countries. Moreover, for some Pacific islands (Kiribati, Marshall Islands, Micronesia, Palau, Tuvalu) fiscal policy is a single main economic policy instrument, as they do not have a central bank, and some could face a significant loss of fiscal resources (Marshall Islands, Micronesia, Palau) when grants from their Compacts of Free Association with the United States expire after 2023/24. This makes assessing the impact of fiscal policy on growth critical for helping governments design fiscal policies that take into account output dynamics and ensure long-term fiscal sustainability.

Designing such policies requires a thorough understanding of the major contribution that government taxation, spending, and labor demand make to GDP growth. In particular, the design of fiscal adjustment policies needs to take into account the impact of adjustment on growth and to what extent and how fast private sector demand can offset the decline in government demand. To fully understand the impact of changes in government fiscal policies on growth and the overall economy, economists and policymakers need to understand the two-way linkages between government spending and taxation on one side and GDP growth on the other.

In general, however, these two-way linkages are not modeled explicitly in current practical frameworks. The common approach is to make the growth assumption and estimate the deficit, revenue, and expenditure aggregates without linking these aggregates or their changes explicitly to growth. The absence of these linkages makes it difficult to answer critical questions on the impact of changes in fiscal policies on the real sector, such as what the impact of a proposed fiscal adjustment would be on growth.

This chapter presents an operational and practical framework that incorporates these two-way linkages between the government sector and the overall economy that can be used by economists and policymakers to better answer such questions. The framework is based on a general equilibrium model that connects government spending, taxation, government employment, and wage setting with foreign demand, private sector production and employment, and demand for domestic and foreign goods. It is calibrated and linked to country economic sectoral accounts and other country data, rather than based on estimates from cross-country regressions. The framework—which this chapter applies to two Pacific island countries, Kiribati and Palau—allows specific policy questions to be addressed. These include the growth impact of a change in public wages versus a change in other government expenditures, and the size of private sector growth needed to offset the impact of fiscal consolidation. Such questions are answered through the differential treatment of different components of government spending and their changes, such as a change in the wage bill and

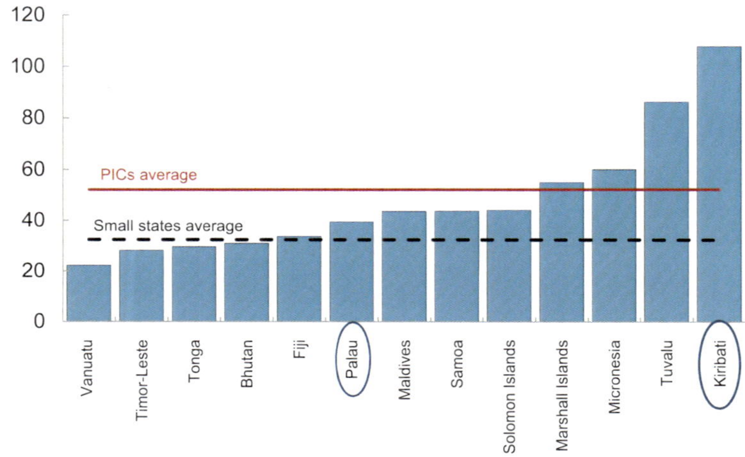

Figure 11.1 Government Expenditure in Pacific Island Countries (PICs), 2014 (*Percent of GDP*)

Sources: Country authorities; and authors' estimates.

changes in other components of public spending. The framework also allows estimation of separate fiscal multipliers for separate components, which are demonstrated in the application section of this chapter.

The model and framework rely on explicit integration and links between the fiscal sector and other sectoral accounts and projections. The most relevant literature is from those approaches that evaluate fiscal policy and fiscal multipliers in the general equilibrium calibrated models. Baxter and King (1993), Gali, Lopez-Salido, and Valles (2007), and Uhlig (2010) analyze fiscal multipliers in the general equilibrium nonstochastic framework. However, these works do not incorporate the impact of differential government spending on imports and domestic demand, and they do not explicitly model employment by government sector. Another strand of the literature is the Global Integrated Monetary and Fiscal model type of global equilibrium model (Kumhof and others 2010) in multicountry settings. This model, however, does not explicitly incorporate government sector employment, and a global setting is not needed given the size of the Pacific economies considered. The other extension is the calibrated dynamic stochastic general equilibrium type models, as observed by Baksa, Benk, and Jakab (2010). Similarly, the models of this type that we are aware of do not explicitly model government employment and are too complex for the types of economies examined in this chapter. Galstyan and Lane (2009) consider the effects of composition of government spending on the real exchange rate in the open economy model with tradable and nontradable goods; however, they do not investigate fiscal multipliers or separate the public and private sectors.

THE FRAMEWORK: LINKING THE GOVERNMENT SECTOR AND GROWTH

The framework is based on a model that links government spending, taxation, government employment, and wage setting with foreign demand, private sector production and employment, and demand for domestic and foreign goods. This allows the relationships between economic growth and government spending, taxation, as well as other factors such as external demand, to be estimated. These estimates can then be used to assess the impact of fiscal policy on the economy, including evaluating fiscal multipliers. The framework can also be used to directly evaluate the implications for fiscal sustainability.

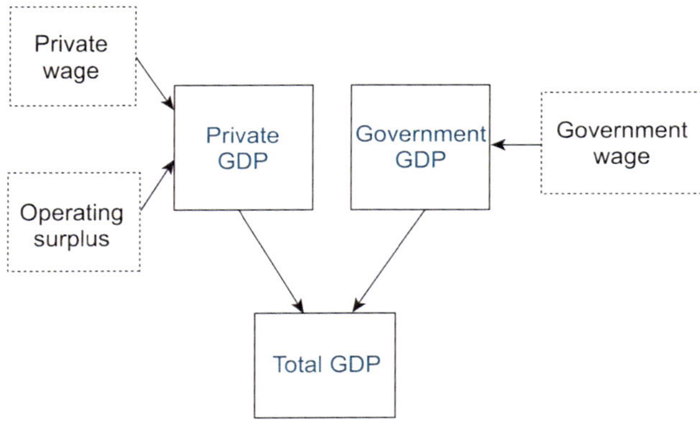

Figure 11.2 GDP on the Production Side

Source: Authors' representation.

Our main approach is to estimate the demand for domestic output from government, domestic residents, and foreigners, and then link it to domestic output and GDP on the production side. This is conceptually divided into government and private GDP. Government GDP mainly consists of wages of public employees, which the government determines. Private GDP is the remaining GDP corresponding to private output, which is modeled as a Cobb-Douglas production function (Figure 11.2).

This underlying model is the general equilibrium model in which markets for goods, labor, and financial assets clear (detailed specifications are provided in Annex 11.1). At the same time some elements, such as household saving decisions, are modeled on the reduced form specified by economists, rather than within the fully optimizing framework used, for example, by the dynamic stochastic general equilibrium model. The specifications can vary depending on the circumstances of a particular country, but we believe this approach increases the framework's applicability and flexibility.

Demand for private output critically depends on consumption; saving and investment decisions by government, domestic residents, and foreigners; and on the share of spending on domestic versus imported goods. Private sector wages and employment are determined by demand for the domestic product. The private wage w_{pt} is set with some discount compared to the government wage, consistent with the observed practices in the countries considered in the example (Kiribati and Palau). Private employment is determined by the optimization of production given demand for private sector output.[1]

Government consumption, saving, and investment are determined by fiscal policy and the government budget. Government is also responsible for decisions on public sector hiring. Public and private employees pay taxes and allocate income between consumption and saving. Saving decisions are significantly affected by pension rules that are prevalent in a particular country. Taking into account the economy of the countries considered and to enhance tractability, nonpension-related saving is determined in the reduced form specified by economists and teams applying the framework rather than in the full optimization setting.

Businesses invest in the local economy after paying taxes to the government, wages to domestic employees, and interest obligations and dividends to domestic and foreign investors.

Foreign consumption and investment form a portion of spending on private output (Figure 11.3). Foreign investment in a small country normally occurs through foreign direct investment and bank

[1]The wage setting function considered in this chapter is consistent with countries' circumstances where the private unemployment rate is high enough to incorporate an increase in demand for domestic products. The framework flexibility allows the modeler to incorporate different employment functions.

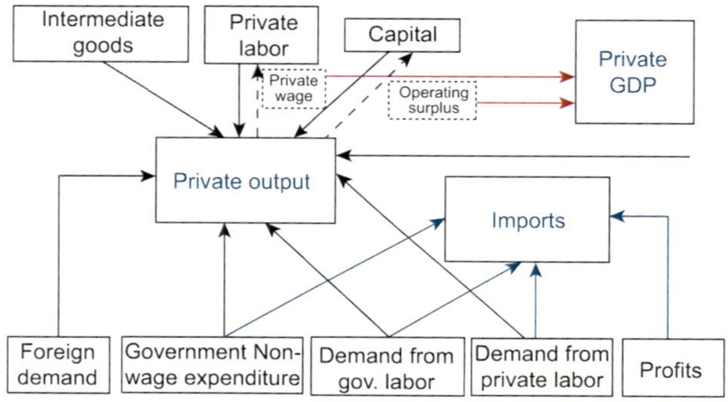

Figure 11.3 Private Output and GDP

Source: Authors' representation.

loans. Foreign investors decide on the share of dividends that is reinvested as well as on new investments. The share of imports in consumption and investment spending is determined by individual preferences and an economy's production capacity. For example, in an economy with abundant agricultural resources and significant agricultural production, the share of spending on domestic agriculture will be higher.

The parameters of the model are calibrated and depend on a country's particular circumstances as well as data availability. For example, in some countries, where input-output statistics are available, the share of spending on domestic versus imported products can be found directly from these data. When such data are not available, shares can be estimated, to the extent possible, using income and expenditure surveys, weights of imported and domestic goods in the consumer price index, and other sources. If data are unavailable, the shares will be based on those of other economies that are similar in structure. For example, to the extent data are available, future extensions of the model beyond current limitations could include modeling of the real sector in multi-output settings and the extension of modeling for monetary-fiscal interactions.

After the model is calibrated, it can be applied to estimate the government's impact on economic dynamics, such as the calculation of fiscal multipliers. This estimation can be made by comparing changes in simulated economic outcomes to changes in government policy, such as spending or taxation.

APPLICATIONS OF THE FRAMEWORK: KIRIBATI AND PALAU

We now apply the framework to Kiribati and Palau, and calibrate the model and conduct simulations in each case (Annex Table 11.1 shows the parameters used in our simulation). These countries are representative of small states: they are constrained by small size, limited economic scale, and geographic remoteness. According to 2013 data, Palau's population was 20,918 and Kiribati's 102,531. Because of these constraints, they suffer narrow production bases, limited opportunities for diversification, and high transportation costs.

At the same time, the two differ in income, economic structure, and level of development. Palau is a high-income country (GDP per capita was US$14,086 in 2013), with the government having a relatively smaller share in the economy than in Kiribati. In 2012, government spending in Palau was about 30.9 percent of GDP, with the central and local government accounting for about 20 percent of the total. In low-income Kiribati (GDP per capita was US$1,583 in 2013), the government plays a more significant role. In 2012 government spending accounted for 56.4 percent of GDP and the government sector for 28.1 percent of total GDP (Figure 11.4). In Palau, tourism is the most important source of external earnings and foreign exchange, while in Kiribati fishing license fees and

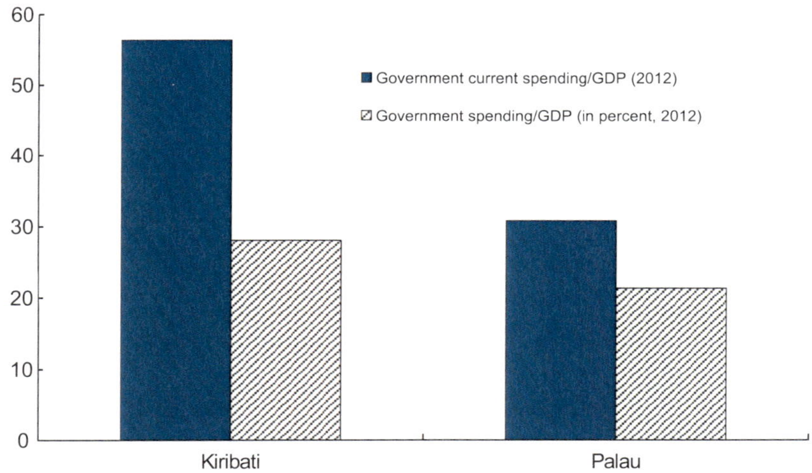

Figure 11.4 Kiribati and Palau: Government Spending and Share of Government Spending in GDP (*Percent of GDP*)

Sources: Kiribati and Palau authorities; and authors' estimates.

remittances are the major sources of external income. The two governments also differ in how they finance fiscal deficits: Palau mainly relies on external debt for fiscal financing, while Kiribati draws down the Revenue Equalization Reserve Fund, its sovereign wealth fund.[2]

The conclusions and suggestions from our case studies could shed light on a variety of small state cases, including other Pacific island countries as well as nonregional, low-income states and small states with large tourism sectors in the Caribbean and Africa.

The calibration of the framework covers the main sectors of economies and key channels of interaction between them (Figure 11.5), taking into account all relevant components of investment and consumption demand, public and private outputs, GDP, and production inputs. Using parameters and actual public wage and expenditure data since 2006, we can conduct a simulation of the model for both Kiribati and Palau.

Because of data limitations, we had to estimate and calibrate some of the key parameters based on the data available. For example, Kiribati and Palau do not compile input-output tables, so the shares of domestic goods and services in government spending, public and workers' consumption, and total investment were estimated based on historical fiscal statistics, household spending statistics, national account statistics, and balance of payments data. Since Kiribati's agricultural sector is significantly larger than Palau's, its shares of domestic goods and services in consumption and investment are generally higher. For example, the share of domestic goods and services in government workers' expenditure in Kiribati is 50–60 percent, while in Palau it ranges from 20–30 percent.[3] For public workers, the saving rate is mainly determined by the provident contribution; for private workers, it is estimated based on financial statistics due to the data limitation.

Another key aspect of the calibration is to estimate the share of wages, profits, and intermediate goods in private output.[4] Detailed data on intermediate goods, which allow the direct calculation of shares, are only available for Palau. For Kiribati we assumed that the share of intermediate goods in

[2]There is no formal target for the Revenue Equalization Reserve Fund balance. An informal target for the fund authorities used in the past was to maintain the real per capita value of the fund at or above the level in 1996; that is, $A4,700.

[3]The different economic structure may explain the difference between these two ranges. For example, the share of the agricultural sector in Palau's total GDP was 2.1 percent (in 2012) and 17.5 percent in Kiribati's (2009).

[4]These shares are parameters α, β, and γ in our augmented Cobb-Douglas production function.

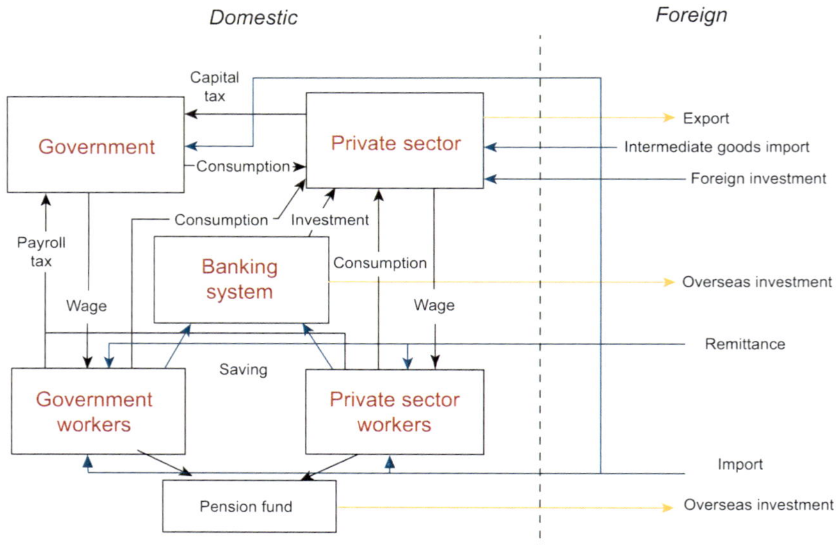

Figure 11.5 Interactions in the Simulation System

Source: Authors' representation.

each detailed industry is similar to that of Palau. We confirmed that the estimates are reasonable by fitting them to historical data.

Once historical parameters have been calibrated, parameters for future years can be projected based on the historical parameters and available forward-looking information. We assume the government sets the public wage and other expenditure levels, while external demand is also exogenous. The model then endogenously determines private output and workers compensation. Future public expenditure and the external demand path under the baseline scenario are in line with IMF fiscal and balance of payments projections, and GDP growth is simulated based on the calibrated model. In our baseline scenario, real GDP growth in the medium term is about 2 percent for both Palau and Kiribati.

Calculating the Fiscal Multipliers

To examine the interaction between fiscal adjustment and GDP growth, we simulated different scenarios, including public wage spending shock (both nominal wage increases and real or additional public hiring);[5] public expenditure shock scenarios (using expenditure other than wages, including current expenditure and development expenditure); and compound public spending shock scenarios. We then calculated the corresponding fiscal multipliers under each scenario. Fiscal multipliers can be measured in several ways. They are defined here as the ratio of a change in GDP output (ΔY) to a discretionary change in government spending (ΔG) (see IMF 2013a for more details). Here GDP is in real terms, so the multiplier means the effect of a US$1 increase in spending on the real GDP level. Depending on the time frame, two types of fiscal multipliers are considered:

$$Impact\ Multiplier = \frac{\Delta Y(t)}{\Delta G(t)}$$

[5]For nominal wage shocks, public wages increase only because the government decides to raise the average wage per employee. For real wage shocks, the payroll bills grow purely as the government decides to hire more people. Under both types of shock, we assume the public wage shocks are permanent.

$$Cumulative\ Multiplier = \frac{\sum_{j=0}^{N} \Delta Y(t+j)}{\sum_{j=0}^{N} \Delta G(t+j)}$$

It is worth noting that different kinds of public wage expenditure shocks have different impacts on real GDP. If the government increases public wages without changing public employment levels, the impact on real output is indirect, mainly transmitting through consumption and investment channels. In contrast, under the real public wage shock, the wage bill increases because the government sector employed more workers. In addition, real public GDP will increase. The magnitude of the increase will depend on the degree of crowding out of private sector employment. If the crowding-out effect is low (in cases in which unemployment is high), the corresponding fiscal multiplier would be close to or larger than 1. In the case of high crowding out, the multiplier will be significantly less than 1. We examined multipliers in both cases.

The simulation results show that different spending shocks have different multipliers (Figure 11.6). In line with the above discussion, values of impact multipliers under real wage shocks are close to 1 (assuming a low crowding-out effect). In contrast, as the shares of imported goods and services in household consumption and government expenditure are high in both countries, the stimulus effects of fiscal policy on domestic GDP are limited, and fiscal multipliers under these shocks are relatively small compared with bigger states and economies with more developed and larger domestic industries (IMF 2013a).

Under a positive real public wage shock, the impact multiplier is 1.25 for Kiribati and 0.98 for Palau, while the multiplier under a positive nominal public wage shock is 0.44 and 0.14, respectively. Under a public expenditure (other than wage) shock, impact multipliers are also relatively small (0.47 for Kiribati and 0.16 for Palau), which means that the effect of expansionary fiscal policy stimulus on GDP growth is limited in these two countries.

Moreover, the stimulus effect of expansionary public spending (both wage and other expenditure) on private GDP in Kiribati is higher than in Palau. As already noted, the rationale behind this phenomenon is that in Kiribati, more domestic goods and services are used by households and the government for consumption and investment.

In our results, the wage shocks have higher fiscal multipliers than the nominal wage shocks and the public expenditure shocks, under the assumption of low crowding out. However, hiring more public workers may not be an effective way to increase growth. First, there may not be enough skilled workers in these countries and that can lead to a crowding-out effect that would negatively impact private GDP growth. Simply hiring more public workers may lead to low efficiency and a waste of resources if the scope of hiring exceeds capacity. Furthermore, the spending increases may not sustainable, a point that applies to various types of expansionary public expenditure as the fiscal multipliers under public expenditure shocks are smaller.[6]

The fiscal sustainability of government policy is an essential component of analysis. As noted earlier, to finance its public deficit, Palau mainly relies on external debt, while Kiribati draws down its sovereign wealth fund. The nominal fund per capita dynamic in Kiribati and the public debt dynamic in Palau under expansionary fiscal policy shocks are shown in Figures 11.7 and 11.8, respectively. These indicate that, if other conditions are kept unchanged, expansionary fiscal policy can worsen fiscal sustainability. So fiscal sustainability should be taken into account when designing fiscal policies.[7]

---

[6]However, the impact of government expenditure on productivity is not fully taken into account here. If public expenditure increases productivity, namely, "A" in our production function, the actual fiscal multiplier would be higher.

[7]The model assumes yields on the Revenue Equalization Reserve Fund and public debt consistent with the observed actual rates.

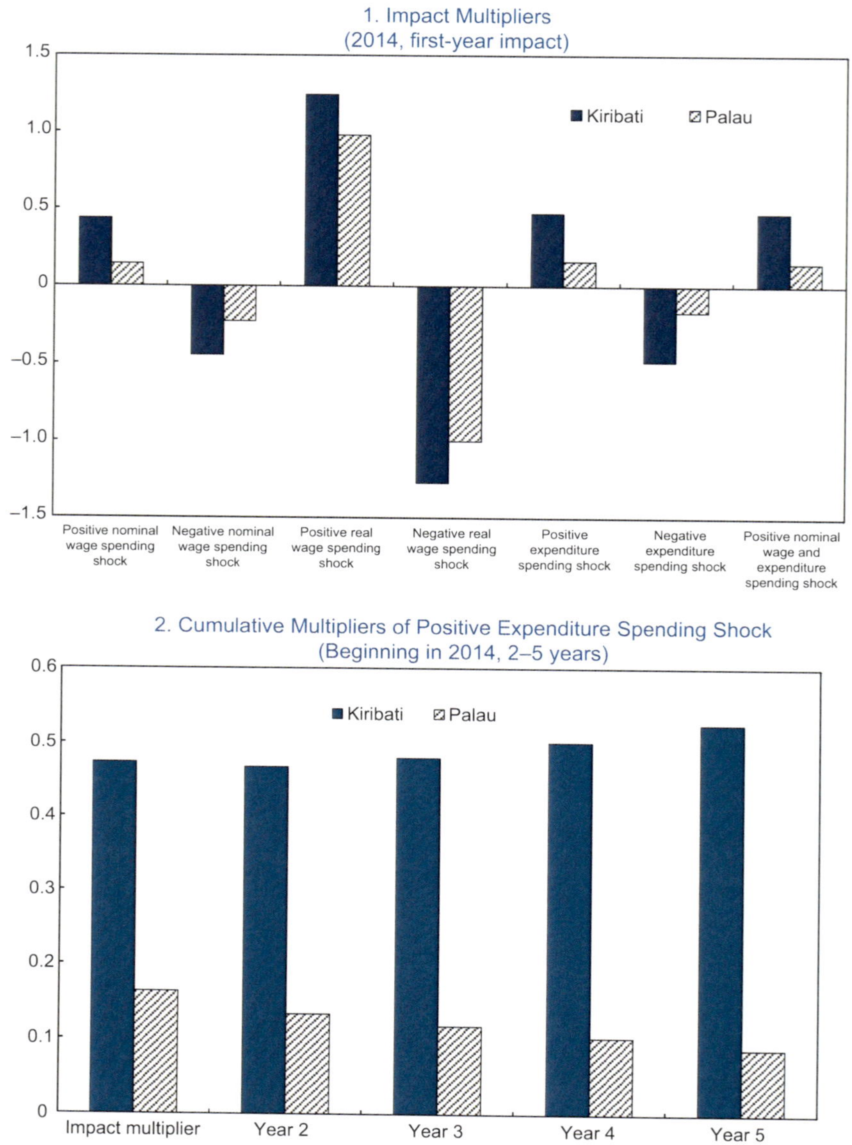

Figure 11.6 Simulation Results: Impact Multipliers and Cumulative Multipliers

Sources: Kiribati and Palau authorities; and authors' estimates.

HOW TO OFFSET THE NEGATIVE GROWTH IMPACT OF FISCAL CONSOLIDATION

The framework allows us to analyze various related aspects of economic dynamics in addition to building up the two-way link between the fiscal and real sectors and investigating the fiscal impact. For example, we look at the question of the extent to which an economy should improve productivity and external demand in order to offset the possible negative effects of fiscal consolidation. Because productivity is difficult to measure for small states, the analysis in the following section mainly focuses on external demand. It calculates the external demand gap that is needed to offset the negative impact of fiscal contraction on private output based on our model.

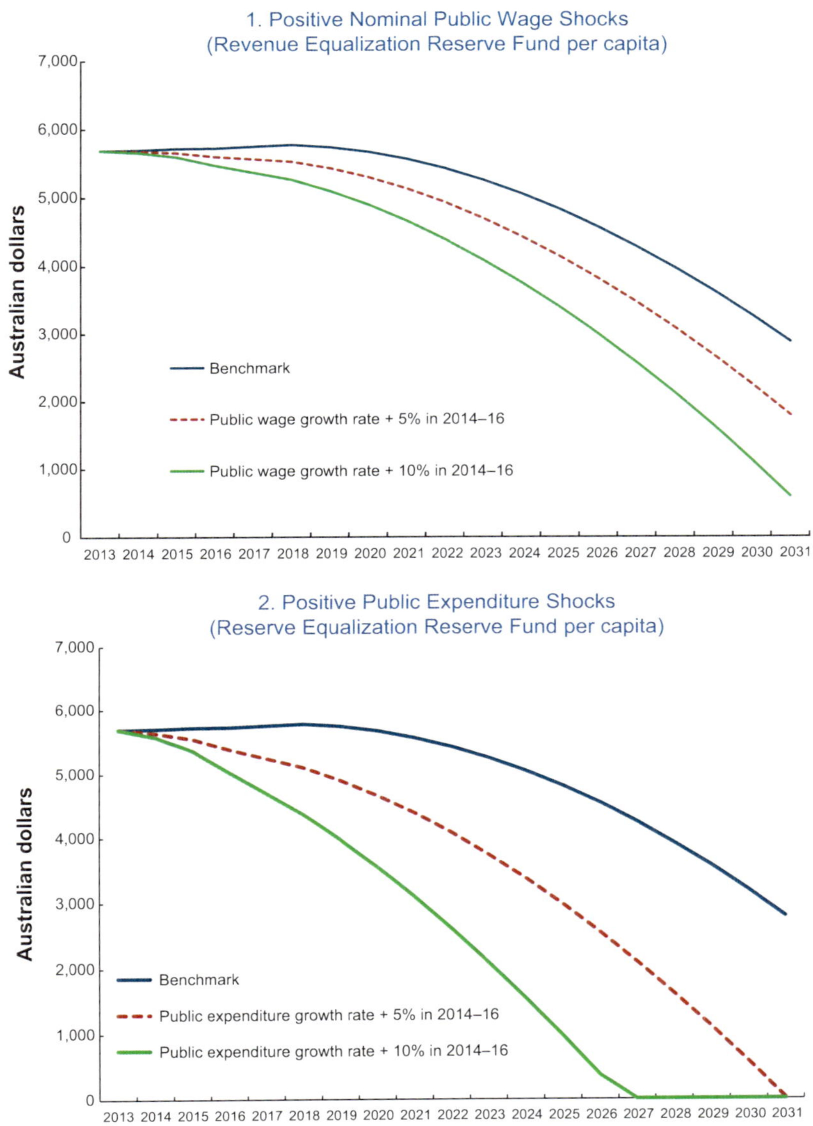

Figure 11.7 Kiribati: Sovereign Wealth Fund Dynamic under Positive Spending Shocks

Sources: Kiribati authorities; and authors' estimates and projections.

The results suggest that the necessary increase in external demand may be significant (Figure 11.9). In Kiribati, to offset the negative impact of a US$1 reduction in the deficit, external demand for domestic goods and services needs to increase by about US$0.60 if the fiscal contraction is from declining nominal public wages and by US$0.55 if the consolidation is achieved by cutting public expenditure. In Palau, external demand needs to rise by US$0.56 and US$0.32, respectively, to maintain the same scale of consolidation.

These results are in line with the estimated fiscal multipliers. First, for Kiribati, in which the government sector plays a larger role in the economy and fiscal multipliers are higher than those in Palau, a larger increase in external demand is needed to maintain private GDP growth when facing fiscal consolidation. Second, as the shares of domestic goods are higher in the consumption basket of households, more external demand is required when public spending consolidation is undertaken by cutting public wages.

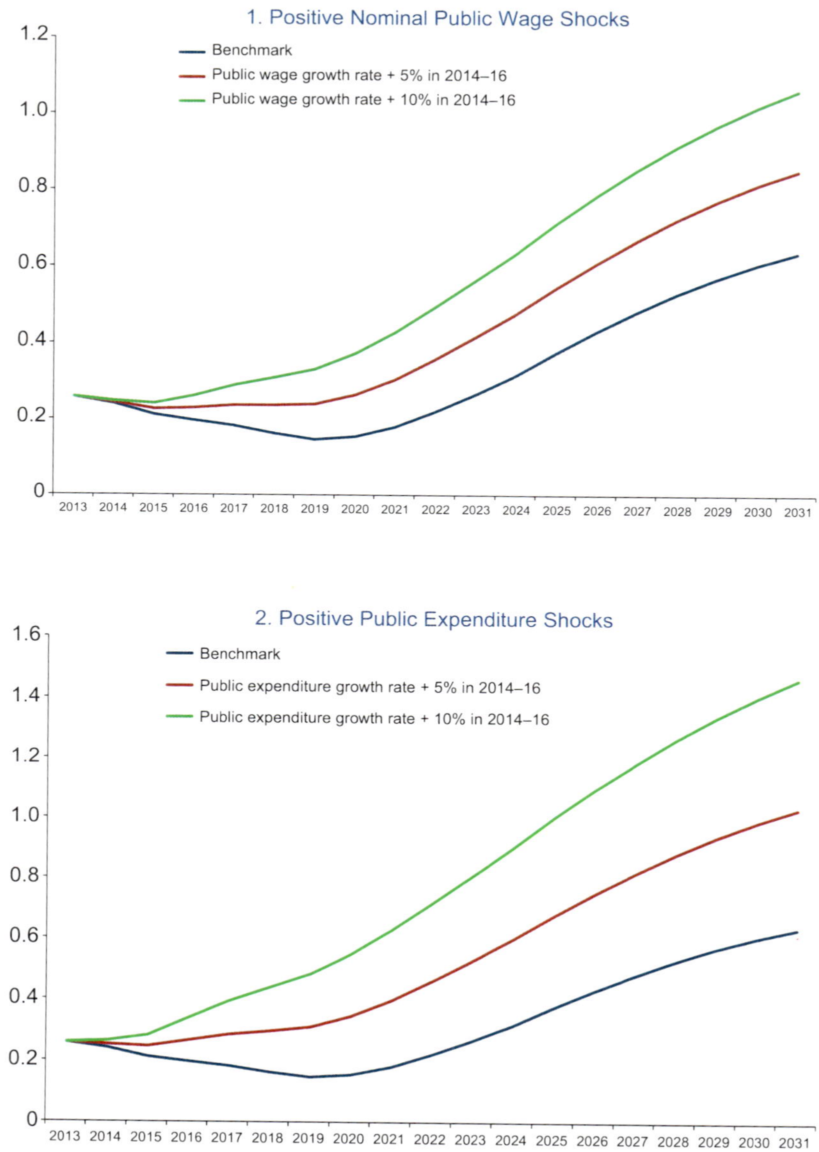

Figure 11.8 Palau: Public-Debt-to-GDP Ratio under Positive Public Spending Shocks

Sources: Palau authorities; and authors' estimates and projections.

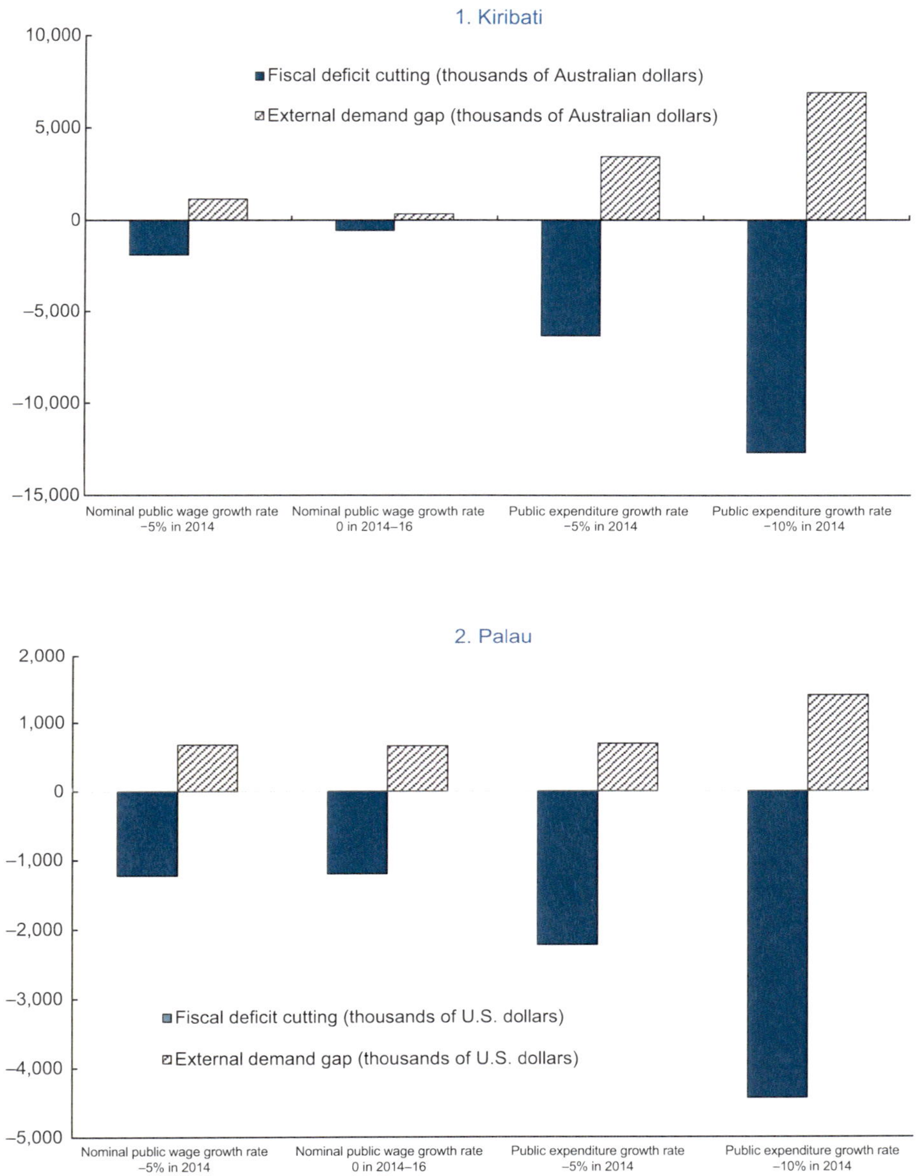

Figure 11.9 Increases in External Demand to Offset the Impact of Fiscal Contraction

Source: Authors' calculations.

ANNEX 11.1. MODEL OF FISCAL IMPACT ON GDP AND THE OVERALL OUTPUT ECONOMY: ANALYTICAL DETAILS

Private Sector Output

Private sector output is produced with three factors: capital, labor, and intermediate goods (intermediate goods are assumed to be partly domestically produced and partially imported).

The production function in the private sector is a Cobb-Douglas production function:

$$Y_t = A_t K_t^{\alpha} L_{pt}^{\beta} Q_t^{\gamma}, \alpha+\beta+\gamma=1$$

It can be shown from the standard cost minimization that the minimum cost of the given amount of output is then:

$$C(Y) = \frac{1}{A\alpha^{\alpha}\beta^{\beta}\gamma^{\gamma}} r^{\alpha} w_p^{\beta} p_I^{\gamma} Y$$

where r denotes return to capital, w_p private wages, and p_I price of intermediate goods. Under the assumption that the price is equal to minimum costs, the price deflator for the output can be approximated as:

$$p = \frac{1}{A\alpha^{\alpha}\beta^{\beta}\gamma^{\gamma}} r^{\alpha} w_p^{\beta} p_I^{\gamma}$$

Government

The government levies tax τ_L on labor (private and public), τ_K on capital, and hires labor L_G at the wage w_G and also gets and spends on nonwage expenditure E. It also can finance the deficit with the change of net debt, as $\Delta F_t = \Delta D_t - \Delta A_t$, where D is gross debt and A is assets. The budget constraint of the government therefore is:

$$\tau L w_{pt} L_{pt} + \tau_L w_G L_{Gt} + \tau_K r_K K_t - w_G L_{Gt} - E_t = -\Delta F_t = \Delta D_t - \Delta A_t$$

Public Workers

Wage w_{gt} and the number L_{pt} of public workers are set by the government. Public workers receive wages from the government and private sector, respectively. The wage of government worker w_{gt} is set by the government. In addition to wage income, government workers receive other noninterest income oi_{Lgt} and also receive income on investments in the form of interest and dividends.[8]

Denote C_{Lgt}, S_{Lgt} as total consumption and saving of government workers, and sr_{Lgt}, sr_{Lpt} corresponding saving rates. Then, total consumption and total saving by domestic workers are:

$$C_{Lgt} = (1-sr_{glt})((1-\tau_L)w_{Lgt} + oi_{Lgt} + r_{ft}NA_{Lg\_ft} + r_{dt}NA_{Lg\_dt})$$

$$S_{Lgt} = sr_{glt}((1-\tau_L)w_{gt} + oi_{Lgt} + r_t NA_{Lgt})$$

where $r_{ft}NA_{Lg\_ft}$, $r_{dt}NA_{Lg\_dt}$ is interest received on (net) assets invested abroad and domestically.

---

[8]The other income includes remittances, which are an important source of income.

Private Sector Workers

Private sector wages and employment are determined by the demand for the domestic product. In the model it is assumed that the private wage w_{pt} is set with some discount compared to the government wage. The private employment is determined by the production optimization given demand for private sector output. As with government workers, private workers receive other noninterest income and interest and dividends on their investments. Total consumption and spending of private workers can be written as:

$$C_{Lpt} = (1 - sr_{plt})((1 - \tau_L)w_{Lpt} + oi_{Lpt} + r_{ft}NA_{Lp\_ft} + r_{dt}NA_{Lp\_dt})$$

$$S_{Lpt} = sr_{plt}((1 - \tau_L)w_{pt} + oi_{Lpt} + r_t NA_{Lpt})$$

Domestic Private Firms and Entrepreneurs

Domestic firms and entrepreneurs receive their share of output (after paying for intermediate goods) and then pay for:

$$C_{Bt} = (1 - sr_{Bt})((1 - \tau_L)r_{Kt}K_t + r_t NA_{Bt})$$

$$S_{Bt} = sr_{Bt}((1 - \tau_L)r_{Kt}K_t + r_t NA_{Bt})$$

Foreigners

Foreigners' demand for domestic output consists of consumption C_{Ft} of domestic goods and services and foreign savings I_{Ft} invested in the country. Foreigners receive dividends and interest r_t on their investment NA_{Ft} and decide on the rate of reinvestment, $rinv_t$. In addition, they decide on new investments, nI_{Ft}. Therefore, total foreign investment demand I_{Ft} is determined as $I_{Ft} = rinv_t * r_t NA_{Ft} + nI_{Ft}$.

Intermediate Demand for Domestic Products

Intermediate demand for domestic products depends on the distribution between imports. If the share of domestic goods in intermediate goods is δ_d, then from a Cobb-Douglas production function the share of spending on intermediate goods is $\delta_d\gamma$, and equating final and intermediate demand to the total demand to output, $PY = D_{Fin} + \delta_d\gamma PY$. Therefore:

$$(1 - \delta_d\gamma)PY = D_{Fin} \text{ and } \frac{1}{(1-\delta_d\gamma)} D_{Fin} = \mu D_{Fin}, \text{ where } \mu = \frac{1}{(1-\delta_d\gamma)} \text{ is a multiplier.}$$

Total Demand for Domestic Output

The demand for domestic output consists of (1) the share of government nonwage expenditure on domestic output, (2) the share of total consumption spent by domestic public and private workers on domestic output, (3) the share of investment goods in the total investment demanded by domestic residents, (4) foreign final demand for domestic output, and (5) intermediate demand for domestic output.

Where C_{Lgt}, C_{Lpt} denote total consumption by the government and private workers, respectively, S_{Lgt}, S_{Lpt} represent corresponding saving.

Let φ_E be the share of other government expenditure falling on consumption of domestic product, φ_{Lg} the share of government workers' expenditure falling on consumption of domestic product,

ANNEX TABLE 11.1

Selected Parameters Used in Simulation

	Kiribati	Palau
Share of domestic goods in government expenditure (%)	40–50	20–30
Share of domestic goods in government workers' consumption (%)	50–60	20–30
Share of domestic goods in private sector workers' consumption (%)	55–65	30–40
Share of domestic goods in total domestic investment (%)	35–45	20–30
Government workers' saving rate (%)	15–20	15–20
Private sector workers' saving rate (%)	3–10	10–15
Government workers' average wage/private workers' average wage	2.1	1.7

Sources: Kiribati and Palau authorities; and authors' estimates.

φ_{Lp} the share of private workers' expenditure falling on consumption of domestic product, and φ_I the share of investment expenditure falling on domestic product.

Let ψ_{Lg}, ψ_{Lp}, and ψ_{Lk} denote shares of savings invested domestically by government workers, private workers, and private firms and entrepreneurs, respectively.

The total demand for domestic output therefore must be equal to output produced:

$$\varphi_E E_t + \varphi_{Lg} C_{Lgt} + \varphi_{Lp} C_{Lpt} + \varphi_B C_{Bt} + \varphi_i I_t + X_t = C(Y) = p_t Y_t$$

Using the discussion of multipliers above, this equation can be rewritten as:

$$\mu(\varphi_E E_t + \varphi_{Lg} C_{Lgt} + \varphi_{Lp} C_{Lpt} + \varphi_B C_{Bt} + \varphi_i I_t) = p_t Y_t$$

Taking into account that the total amount of savings invested in the domestic sector is equal to total investment.

$$\psi_{Lg} S_{Lgt} + \psi_{Lp} S_{Lpt} + \psi_{LB} S_{LBt} + S_{LFt} = I_t$$

Substituting into the first equation above, we obtain:

$$\mu(\varphi_E E_t + \varphi_{Lg} C_{Lgt} + \varphi_{Lp} C_{Lpt} + \varphi_B C_{Bt} + C_{Ft} + \psi_{Lg} S_{Lgt} + \psi_{Lp} S_{Lpt} + \psi_{LB} S_{LBt} + S_{LFt}) = p_t Y_t$$

Substituting consumption and saving calculations for public workers, private workers, and foreigners, and noting that $w_{Lpt} L_{Lpt} = \beta p_t Y_{pt}$, $r_k K_t = \alpha p_t Y_t$, and simplifying, we get the expression for $p_t Y_t$:

$$p_t Y_{pt} = \frac{(\varphi_E E_t + \theta_{Lg} w_{gt} L_{gt} + C_{Ft} + nI_{Ft})}{(1 - \mu(\alpha \vartheta_K + \beta \theta_{Lp}))}$$

where coefficients θ_{Lg}, θ_{Lp}, ϑ_K are derived from the parameters of the model and correspond to the shares of domestic spending on consumption and investment by government workers, private workers, and private firms and entrepreneurs, respectively.

REFERENCES

Baksa, D., S. Benk, and M. Z. Jakab. 2010. "Does 'The' Fiscal Multiplier Exist? Fiscal and Monetary Reactions, Credibility and Fiscal Multipliers in Hungary." Office of the Fiscal Council, Bangko Sentral ng Pilipinas, Manila.

Baxter, Marianne, and Robert G. King. 1993. "Fiscal Policy in General Equilibrium." *American Economic Review* 8 (3): 315–34.

Gali, Jordi, J. David Lopez-Salido, and Javier Valles. 2007. "Understanding the Effects of Government Spending on Consumption." *Journal of the European Economic Association* 5 (1): 227–70.

Galstyan, Vahagn, and Philip Lane. 2009. "The Composition of Government Spending and the Real Exchange Rate." *Journal of Money, Credit and Banking* 41 (6): 1233–49.
International Monetary Fund (IMF). 2013a. "Guidance Note on Fiscal Multipliers." Unpublished, Washington.
———. 2013b. "Macroeconomic Issues in the Small States and Implications for Fund Engagement." Washington. http://www.imf.org/external/np/pp/eng/2013/022013.pdf.
Kumhof, M., D. Laxton, D. Muir, and S. Mursula. 2010. "The Global Integrated Monetary Fiscal Model (GIMF)—Theoretical Structure." IMF Working Paper 10/34, International Monetary Fund, Washington.
Uhlig, Harald. 2010. "Some Fiscal Calculus." *American Economic Review* 100 (2): 30–34.

CHAPTER 12

Monetary Policy Transmission Mechanisms in Pacific Island Countries

YONGZHENG YANG, MATT DAVIES, SHENGZU WANG, JONATHAN DUNN, AND YIQUN WU

The global financial crisis tested the effectiveness of monetary policy transmission mechanisms in Pacific island countries (PICs).[1] At the onset of the crisis, monetary policy remained tight in a number of these countries, reflecting the overriding priority of protecting foreign reserves and keeping inflation under control in the wake of the global food and fuel price shocks. However, as the effects of the crisis intensified, central banks began to loosen policy to maintain a flow of credit to productive sectors and ease pressures on existing borrowers, with an explicit objective of lowering interest rates. The policy stance was eased by lowering policy rates (Fiji, Samoa), ceasing the sale of government and central bank paper to the market (Samoa, Tonga), lowering reserve requirements (Fiji, Tonga, Vanuatu), and devaluing or depreciating exchange rates (Fiji, the Solomon Islands). Despite these efforts, reductions of lending rates by banks have been limited and the growth of private credit has been anemic in some countries. The sluggish response raised a key question about the effectiveness of monetary policy transmission mechanisms in PICs.

PICs are susceptible to external shocks, and effective monetary policy is vital to maintaining macroeconomic stability. As most countries in the region maintain fixed exchange rate regimes, the burden of addressing the impact of exogenous shocks falls most heavily on monetary and fiscal policies. Because of limited capital flows, monetary policy enjoys a certain degree of freedom despite fixed exchange rate regimes. However, if monetary policy transmission is indeed muted, and the prospects for improvement in the short term limited, effective macroeconomic management will require an appropriate mix of monetary, fiscal, and exchange rate policies. In particular, monetary policy should be closely coordinated with fiscal policy to achieve the desired impact. Fixed exchange rate regimes should not preclude some flexibility to increase the role of the exchange rate in absorbing external shocks and to provide additional freedom for monetary policy.

This chapter assesses monetary policy transmission mechanisms in PICs and explores options for an appropriate mix of macroeconomic policies. We review the main objectives of monetary policy and how it is conducted in PICs, and provide an empirical assessment of monetary policy transmission mechanisms, focusing on the responses of market interest rates and private sector credit growth to policy rates (or their proxies). We then examine the structural constraints on monetary policy transmission and identify areas of reform that could foster long-term financial market development. This is followed by a discussion on the role of monetary and fiscal policy coordination, and exchange rate flexibility. We close with some policy implications.

This chapter was originally prepared as a paper for the 25th Meeting of South Pacific Central Bank Governors in Wellington, New Zealand, December 2–3, 2010. The authors thank the central bank governors and other participants for their helpful comments. Ray Brooks, Tubagus Feridhanusetyawan, Tarhan Feyzioglu, Simon Gray, Joji Ide, Papa N'Diaye, Runchana Pongsaparn, and Daranee Saeju provided valuable comments on an earlier version, published in *Asian-Pacific Economic Literature*.

[1]The chapter covers the six PICs with their own currencies: Fiji, Papua New Guinea, Samoa, the Solomon Islands, Tonga, and Vanuatu.

TABLE 12.1

Monetary Policy Frameworks in Pacific Island Countries

Country	Monetary Objectives	Main Monetary Instruments	Exchange Rate Regime
Fiji	Promote monetary stability and a sound financial structure; foster credit and exchange conditions conducive to orderly and balanced economic development.	Open market operations; discount windows; policy rate	Pegged to a basket
Papua New Guinea	Achieve and maintain price stability and financial system stability, and promote macroeconomic stability and economic growth.	Open market operations; policy rate; cash reserve requirement	De facto crawl-like arrangement (effective April 2014)
Samoa	Promote sustainable real economic growth by maintaining price stability and international reserves viability.	Open market operations; discount rate; reserve requirements	Pegged to a basket within a ±2 percent band (New Zealand dollar, Australian dollar, U.S. dollar, euro)
Solomon Islands	Achieve and maintain domestic price stability, foster and maintain a stable financial system, and support the general economic policies of the government.	Open market operations; short-term securities (Bokolo bills) issued by the central bank; cash reserve requirement	Pegged to a basket
Tonga	Maintain internal and external monetary stability; promote a sound and efficient financial system; support macroeconomic stability and economic growth.	Open market operations; statutory reserve deposit; credit ceilings	Pegged to a basket within horizontal bands
Vanuatu	Maintain low and stable inflation rate and maintain a sufficient level of official foreign exchange reserves.	Statutory reserve deposit; Open market operations; rediscount rate	De facto other managed arrangement

Source: Authors' compilation.

MONETARY POLICY OBJECTIVES AND OPERATIONS

Monetary policy in most PICs aims primarily to maintain international reserves in the context of fixed exchange rates (Table 12.1). The small, open economies of the region are subject to frequent internal and external shocks, and adequate foreign reserves are essential to weathering them. A fixed exchange rate provides a nominal anchor, and many in the region believe that exchange rate movements have limited effect on exports, which tend to be dominated by commodities. Yet tourism and other industries do seem to respond strongly to exchange rate movements, as evidenced by Fiji's tourism boom following the 20 percent devaluation of the Fiji dollar in April 2009. There is also a concern that more flexible exchange rates would create considerable volatility in currencies and domestic prices, given relatively small foreign exchange markets.

With narrow export bases and the need to import most manufactured goods, food, and fuel, PIC trade balances are generally in deficit.[2] Although most countries enjoy a surplus in their services and income accounts due to tourism and remittances, current account deficits are often very high (Figure 12.1). Capital inflows—both private and official—that are needed to offset the current account deficits are volatile. Monetary policy therefore needs to be vigilant to contain import demand. Speculative capital inflows are not a significant issue in PICs at the moment, but could become one given ample global liquidity.

[2] Papua New Guinea is an exception. Its exports are dominated by minerals and petroleum, and the country's current account deficit in 2009/10 was driven by large imports of goods and services for the construction of a large liquefied natural gas project.

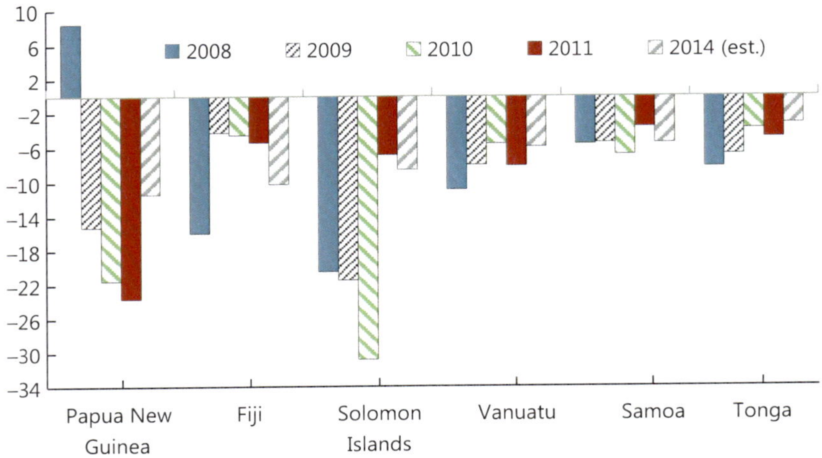

Figure 12.1 Current Account Balance (*Percent of GDP*)

Sources: IMF World Economic Outlook database; and IMF staff estimates.

Maintaining price stability is a key objective in PICs, and some place similar emphasis on financial sector stability. While managing aggregate demand is the main focus in maintaining price stability, movements in world commodity prices and domestic supply conditions, mainly in agriculture, often play a dominant role in determining inflation outcomes in PICs. This highlights the importance of monetary policy not only in mitigating the direct impact of exogenous shocks, but also in preventing their second-round effects on inflation with support of other policies (for example, through restraint on public sector wage bills). Information and analysis of these effects are often lacking. Policymakers therefore have to make decisions with the knowledge that monetary policy actions to influence domestic demand often have a limited impact on headline inflation—and that the longer-term impact of monetary policy actions is subject to considerable uncertainty. The role of monetary policy in maintaining financial sector stability is mainly reflected in combating high inflation and nonperforming loans by avoiding excessive money and credit expansion. Other policy tools that central banks use to ensure financial sector stability are prudential regulation and supervision.[3]

Most central banks in the region explicitly include promotion of economic growth in their monetary policy objectives. Indeed, most react to threats to growth by loosening monetary policy, as shown during the global financial crisis. It is widely recognized that with a small and narrow base of domestic production, the effects of monetary policy on domestic supply are generally weak (tourism is probably an exception), and credit growth often translates largely into raising import demand with limited pass-through into the domestic economy. Thus, the effectiveness of monetary policy in managing domestic supply and aggregate demand is often diminished by the limited capacity of domestic industries and large external leakages.

As in any other region, it is difficult for PICs to achieve these multiple objectives using monetary policy alone even if transmission is strong. This difficulty was made abundantly clear during the 2007–08 global food and fuel crisis. To arrest rapid depletion of foreign reserves as import costs rose and to prevent inflation from getting out of control, countries needed to tighten monetary policy. Yet doing this would have exacerbated falling liquidity and rising production costs in these economies. The limitation of monetary policy was also evident at the onset of the global financial crisis. Despite declining external demand for exports (including tourism) and falling growth, some PICs were reluctant to ease monetary policy, as inflation remained high (Figure 12.2) and international

[3] Recent research has highlighted the importance of effective prudential supervision—as well as better regulation—in maintaining financial sector stability. In drawing lessons from the global financial crisis, Viñals and Fiechter (2010) argue that good supervision is "intrusive, skeptical, proactive, comprehensive, adaptive, and conclusive."

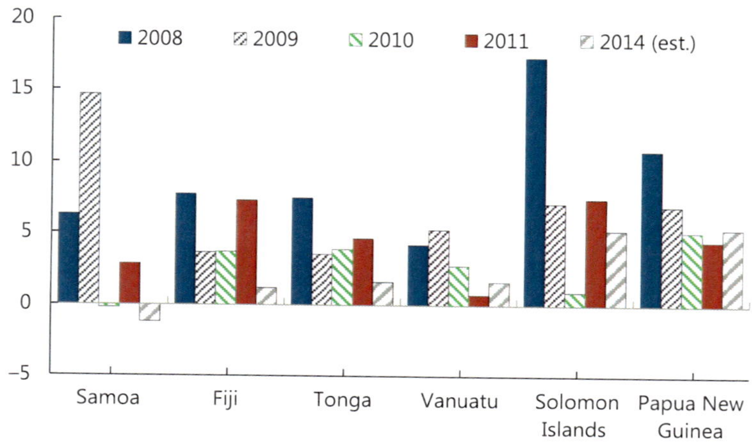

Figure 12.2 Consumer Price Inflation (*Percent*)

Sources: IMF World Economic Outlook database; and IMF staff estimates.

reserves were low. Exchange rate depreciation—which was not considered an option for most PICs because of their fixed exchange rates—would have helped cushion the demand shock and contain import growth. But it would also have had an adverse effect on inflation.[4] Fiscal expansion—again not a viable option for some countries that entered the crisis with high public debt—would also have exacerbated inflation pressure, though it could at least have been targeted at those most affected by the crisis. The point here is that in many circumstances monetary policy cannot achieve one objective—for example, stimulating growth—without undermining other objectives, such as controlling inflation and preserving reserves.

All six PICs covered in this chapter conduct their monetary policy through various money-targeting frameworks (described in Table 12.1). Central banks in the region typically target some broad money aggregates such as M2 to ensure adequate credit growth and healthy foreign reserves. Policy instruments for achieving money targets include policy rates, open market operations, central bank discount windows, reserve requirements, moral suasion, and, sometimes, administrative measures such as interest rate/spread and credit controls. PICs are trying to move away from administrative measures to market-based instruments, and making these instruments more effective in the broad macroeconomic policy context is a major challenge. This is discussed in the following section.

EMPIRICAL EVIDENCE ON MONETARY PASS-THROUGH

Interest rate movements are used as the main indicator to gauge the effectiveness of monetary policy transmission in PICs. As noted earlier, the lack of response of market interest rates to central bank policy changes during the global financial crisis was a major source of frustration among policymakers. It was hoped that changes in policy rates would translate into commensurate movements in the lending and deposit rates of commercial banks, resulting in increased credit to the private sector, thereby boosting economic activity. Against this backdrop, our assessment of monetary policy transmission begins with a look at the role of policy rates.

The pass-through of policy rates to commercial bank interest rates appears to be indeed low, though this varies across PICs (Figure 12.3). In Papua New Guinea, Samoa, and Vanuatu, commercial banks' deposit and lending rates do seem to respond to changes in policy rates, but this response is barely discernible in Fiji, the Solomon Islands, and Tonga. The low response in the latter countries is hardly surprising as their policy rates do not change very often, indicating either an inactive interest

[4] Nevertheless, Fiji did decide to devalue its currency by 20 percent in April 2009 to arrest the decline of foreign reserves.

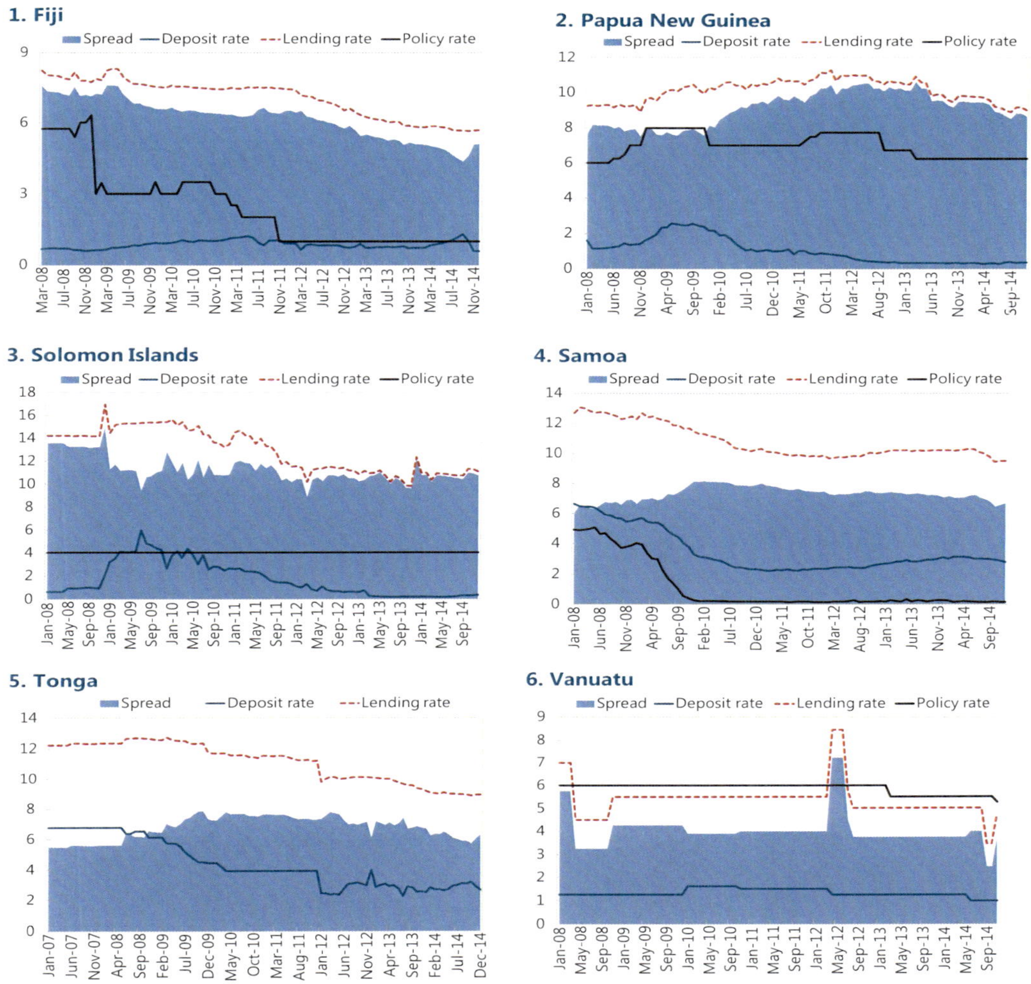

Figure 12.3 Interest Rates and Their Spreads in Pacific Island Countries

Sources: Country authorities; IMF, *Monetary and Financial Statistics*; and IMF staff calculations.

rate policy or the presence of some other policy measures that may have been taken as substitutes for interest rate policies. Indeed, in Fiji in 2009, the central bank lowered lending rates by setting an interest rate ceiling at the level prevailing at the end of 2008 and by imposing an allowable interest rate spread of 4 percent. While interest rate spreads have fallen somewhat in Fiji and Vanuatu, they have not changed much or have even increased in other PICs. It is worth noting that interest rate spreads in PICs are broadly comparable to those observed in Caribbean countries, and their recent developments have followed a similar path (PFTAC 2010).[5]

Econometric analysis confirms that interest rate pass-through in PICs is generally low (see Annex 12.1). Based on an autoregressive distributed lags model using monthly data over 2001–10, the estimated long-term interest rate pass-through—defined as the percentage point change in commercial banks' lending rates divided by the percentage point change in central bank policy rates—ranges

[5] PFTAC (2010) also shows that the profitability of PIC banks' interest operations, based on prudential data, appears to be in line with international norms, though overall profitability is higher than in comparable regions when all sources of bank income (not just interest income) are considered.

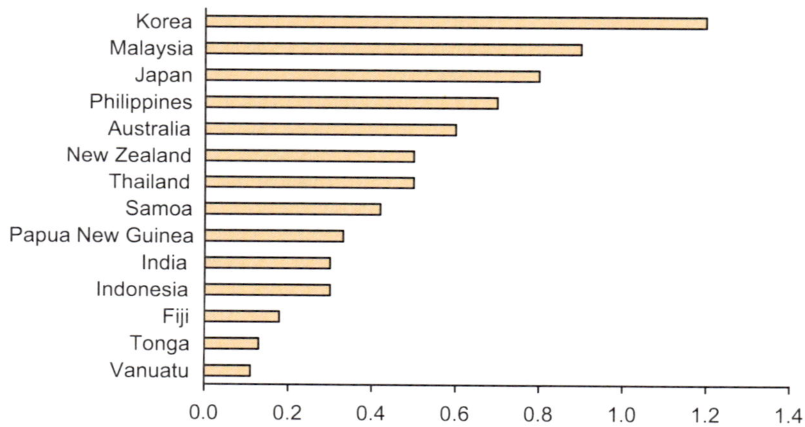

Figure 12.4 Long-Term Interest Rate Pass-Through

Source: IMF staff calculations.
Note: Data not available for the Solomon Islands.

from 0.1 in Vanuatu to 0.5 in Samoa (Figure 12.4).[6] Although it is not surprising that the pass-through in PICs is lower than in larger countries in Asia and the Pacific, its absolute levels indicate limited influence of central bank policy rates over commercial bank lending rates in some PICs.[7] The analysis also shows that Papua New Guinea and Samoa have much higher pass-through than Fiji, Tonga, and Vanuatu. This is primarily because policy rates in Papua New Guinea and Samoa are more directly linked to money market rates (rates on central bank securities and government paper), and are more actively used to signal the policy stance, as measured by the frequency of change in policy rates (see Figure 12.3).[8] This highlights the importance of a well-developed money market through which policy rates can directly affect liquidity.

Compared with interest rate pass-through, the response of private sector credit to policy rate changes is more significant. A similar econometric analysis (see Annex 12.1) shows that for each percentage point change in policy rates, the growth of private sector credit responds by a change of 4–5 percentage points in Fiji, Papua New Guinea, and Vanuatu, 1½ percentage points in Tonga, and only half a percentage point in Samoa (Figure 12.5). Such large variation may reflect different underlying economic circumstances (data could also be an issue). In Samoa, the limited response of credit growth could result from higher interest rate pass-through. This is because competition forces commercial banks to lower lending rates, but they are reluctant to increase lending when responding to lower policy rates, perhaps due to limited low-risk lending opportunities. In Fiji and Vanuatu, on the other hand, commercial banks respond primarily by increasing credit rather than lowering lending rates, whereas banks in Papua New Guinea seem to respond by both reducing lending rates and increasing credit. In Tonga, both interest rate and credit responses are relatively weak. One possible reason that credit is generally more responsive than lending rates is that banks target risk-adjusted

[6]To the extent that other policy moves accompany policy rate changes, such as changes in reserve requirements, the estimated pass-though would reflect the combined effects of all simultaneous policy changes. This also applies to the estimates of pass-through from policy rates to private sector credit. For Tonga, the repo rate was used as a proxy for the policy rate. Pass-through rates could not be estimated for the Solomon Islands because there were no changes in the policy rate over time.

[7]The results for Fiji seem to be consistent with the findings of Jayaraman and Choong (2009) that money supply is the most effective channel of monetary policy transmission. The low interest rate pass-through found here is also consistent with findings for developing economies in other regions. Dabla-Norris and Floerkemeier (2006), for instance, show that the interest channel of monetary policy transmission in Armenia is weak.

[8]Given that short-term money market rates are probably more indicative of the monetary policy stance in PICs, it would have been useful to estimate their pass-through to bank lending rates and credit growth. However, data limitations precluded such estimation.

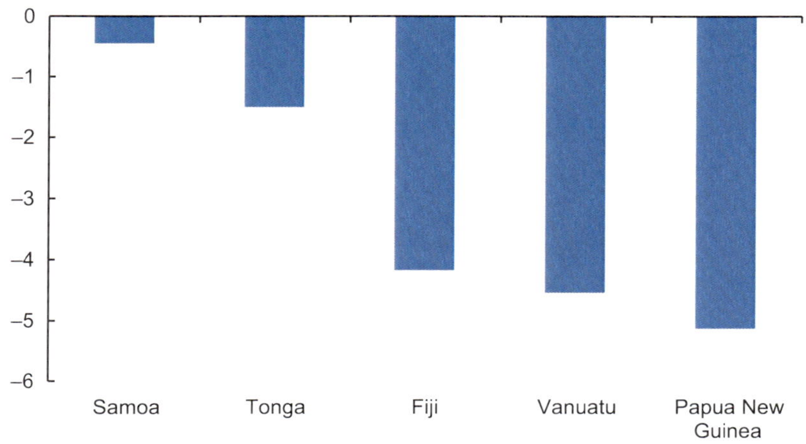

Figure 12.5 Private Credit Long-Term Pass-Through (*Percent*)

Source: IMF staff estimates.

returns on their lending. For example, when funding costs are reduced as a result of policy easing, banks may be more willing to extend credit to customers with higher credit risk without lowering interest rates.[9]

Monetary policy transmission appears to have been even weaker during the global financial crisis than these long-term responses would suggest. Not only has the interest rate pass-through been generally low, but the response of private sector credit appears to have deviated from its long-term behavior. As panel 1 of Figure 12.6 shows, despite the easing of the policy stance, growth of private sector credit slowed sharply in the wake of the global financial crisis—and even turned negative in the Solomon Islands and Tonga in 2009. Slow credit growth was also reflected in the rising levels of excess reserves held by commercial banks and their falling loan-to-deposit ratios in some PICs. Nevertheless, the rising level of excess reserves and falling loan-to-deposit ratios do indicate that monetary policy in PICs achieved the important objective of ensuring sufficient liquidity when economic activity is weak.

The poor interest and credit responses to monetary policy during the global financial crisis seem to reflect the weak state of regional economies as well as the broader international environment. The sharp slowdown in economic growth undoubtedly reduced opportunities for profitable investments. On the supply side, even though central banks signaled an easing of the monetary policy stance, commercial banks were reluctant to lower lending rates or increase lending. This appears to have been the case even in Samoa, where long-term interest pass-though is relatively high (Pongsaparn 2010). The global financial crisis made banks more risk averse, resulting in tighter lending standards. This occurred even though most banks in the region (mostly owned by Australian parent banks) weathered the crisis well.[10] Other factors also played a role. In Tonga, slower credit expansion was a reaction to high nonperforming loans arising from a previous lending boom. In Fiji, exchange restrictions and intensified price controls in the wake of the crisis may have dampened the appetite for new investment and hence demand for credit. On the other hand, Vanuatu's strong credit expansion in 2008 and 2009 resulted from BRED Bank opening a branch there and the ensuing competition in the banking sector.

[9] An examination of the effective lending rates or distribution of lending rates could shed light on this hypothesis, but data limitations preclude such an analysis.

[10] Parent banks in Australia also experienced slower credit growth after the crisis, especially to the corporate sector for similar reasons—tighter credit standards and some corporate deleveraging.

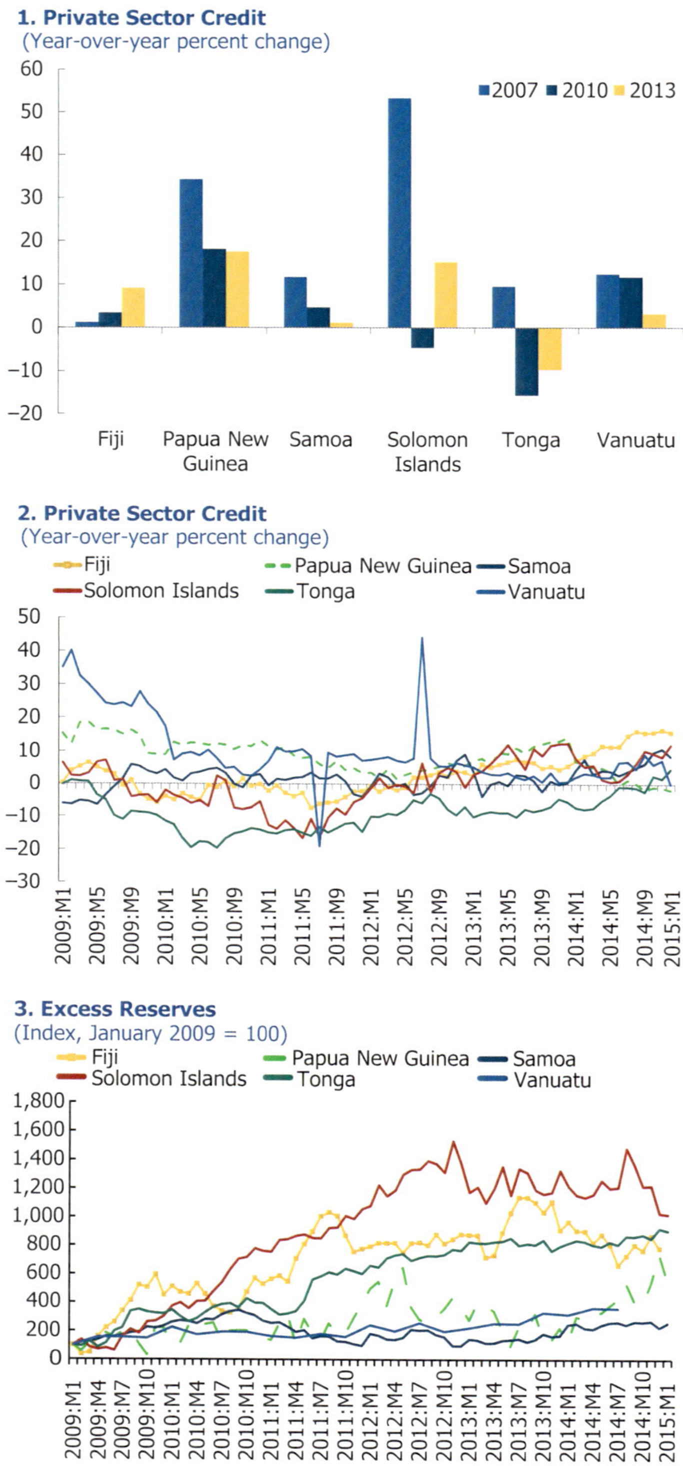

Figure 12.6 Credit and Liquidity Indicators

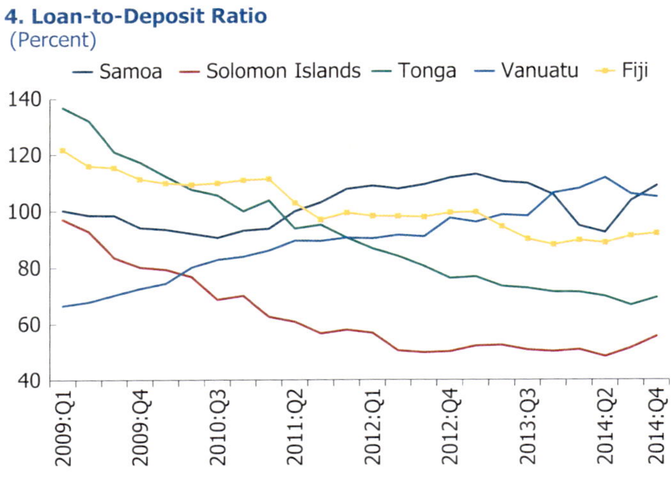

Figure 12.6 *(Continued)*

Sources: Country authorities; and IMF staff calculations.

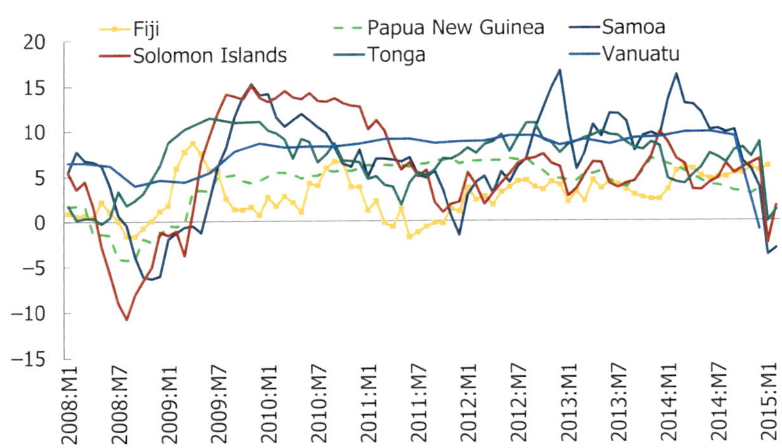

Figure 12.7 Real Lending Rate *(Percent)*

Sources: IMF, Information Notice System database; and IMF staff calculations.

Developments in real interest rates may have also dampened credit demand during the crisis. As world food and fuel prices began to retreat in the second half of 2008, inflation rates fell quickly in most PICs, leading to sharp, sustained increases in real lending rates in most countries (Figure 12.7).[11] The sharp fall in Fiji's real lending rates in 2009–10 reflected the one-off increases of domestic prices following the April 2009 devaluation. Overall, real borrowing costs for business increased considerably during the crisis, and this likely contributed to the slow credit growth.

Real exchange rate appreciation during the crisis may have also contributed to weak credit demand, as all PICs except Papua New Guinea maintain a pegged exchange rate. Although there were some movements over time, nominal effective exchange rates at the end of 2010 for most PICs remained roughly at their 2005 levels (Fiji and the Solomon Islands were the exceptions, as shown in Figure 12.8). Higher inflation than in trading partners, largely reflecting the pass-through to domestic markets of higher world food and fuel prices, led to real exchange rate appreciation during the global financial crisis in five of the six PICs covered in this chapter (Fiji was the exception). In

[11] Real lending rates were obtained by deflating nominal rates by the headline consumer price index. Ideally, a core inflation index should have been used, but these data are not available.

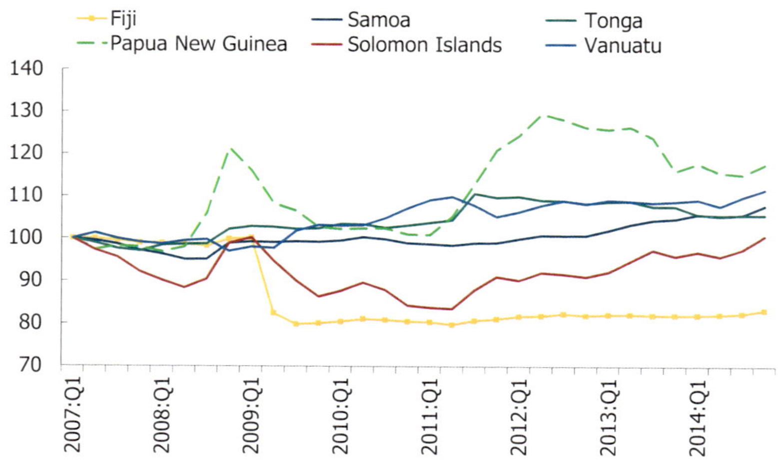

Figure 12.8 Nominal Effective Exchange Rate (*Percent*)

Source: IMF, Information Notice System database.

the Solomon Islands, the real exchange rate was on an appreciating trend well before world prices began to rise (Figure 12.9). The decline in world prices since mid-2008 did not bring real exchange rates back to their precrisis levels. The monetary easing to boost economic activity has therefore not been supported by real exchange rate movements, with the exception of Fiji. Its April 2009 devaluation led to a sharp real depreciation of the Fiji dollar since the second quarter of that year, which boosted tourism amid weak overall economic activity.

Most PICs eased fiscal policy during the crisis to support economic activity. Vanuatu kept the policy stance neutral and the Solomon Islands tightened, while Fiji, Papua New Guinea, Samoa, and Tonga loosened fiscal policy in 2009, and Tonga and Samoa continued to loosen in 2010 (largely due to post-tsunami reconstruction in the latter; Figure 12.10). At least part of the fiscal expansion was financed domestically, but given weak private sector activity, there was little risk of crowding out and hence the fiscal expansion most likely did not contribute to slow private sector credit growth.

Macroeconomic policy developments during the global financial crisis highlight the limitations of monetary policy in economic stabilization without the support of other macroeconomic policies. To be sure, the crisis experience does not prove that monetary policy easing was totally ineffective. One could argue that even though interest and credit responses appear to be weak, the credit situation

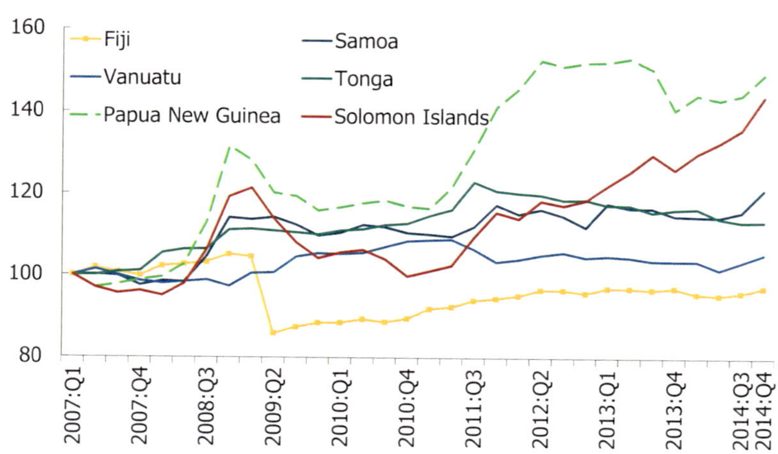

Figure 12.9 Real Effective Exchange Rate (*Percent*)

Source: IMF, Information Notice System database.

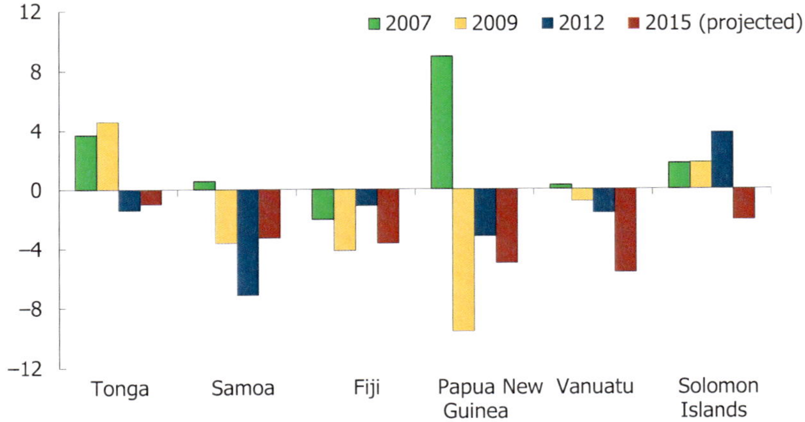

Figure 12.10 Fiscal Balance (*Percent of GDP*)

Source: IMF staff estimates.

facing the private sector could have been worse had there been no policy action. Nevertheless, the experience does suggest inconsistency between exchange rate and monetary policies, which is difficult to avoid when a fixed exchange rate regime is faced with an adverse terms-of-trade shock such as rising international prices.

CONSTRAINTS ON MONETARY POLICY TRANSMISSION

At the broadest level, the effectiveness of monetary policy transmission depends on the macroeconomic policy framework it operates in. In particular, since most PICs have a fixed exchange rate regime one way or another, monetary policy is subordinate to the maintenance of the exchange rate regime. However, because of limited capital flows across their borders, monetary policy does enjoy a certain degree of autonomy. Namely, higher domestic interest rates in response to monetary policy may not attract rapid capital inflows and bring interest rates back to where they were, thereby largely avoiding increased liquidity and inflation pressures. It is not clear, however, how some private transfers, particularly remittances, respond to domestic interest rates. The literature suggests that remittances respond mainly to the needs of families in migrants' home countries rather than to returns on investments or exchange rates (Chami and others 2008). Nevertheless, given large remittance volumes in some PICs (Australia and New Zealand Governments 2010), their response to interest rates and exchange rates could make a major difference to domestic liquidity and, hence, the effectiveness of monetary policy transmission.[12]

Underdeveloped domestic financial markets appear to be the main constraints on monetary policy transmission in PICs. Measured by the ratio of broad money (M2) to GDP, domestic money markets are quite shallow and on average compare unfavorably with Caribbean countries (Figure 12.11).[13] Collateralized interbank lending is not widely available, and secondary markets for government and central bank paper are virtually nonexistent. Markets for commercial paper, corporate bonds, and foreign exchange products are also underdeveloped, while equity markets are in their

[12] This subject may be worth a separate examination.

[13] Of course, in making such comparisons one has to be mindful that, despite their smaller populations, Caribbean countries have high income per capita and are more integrated among themselves and with North American goods and financial markets because of greater geographic proximity.

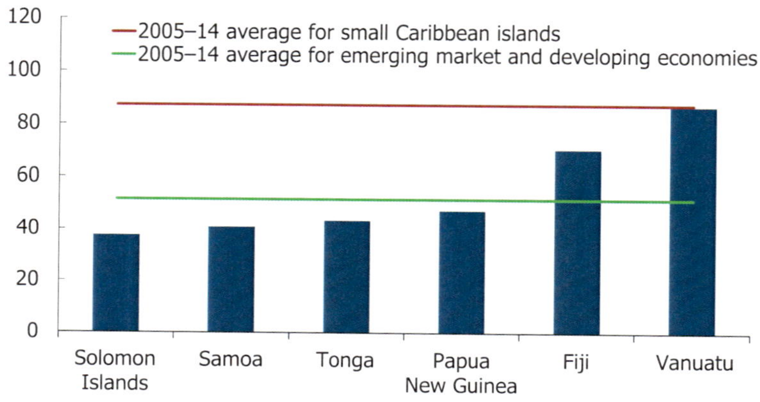

Figure 12.11 Pacific Islands: Broad Money, 2005–14 Average (*Percent of GDP*)

Sources: IMF International Financial Statistics database; and IMF staff calculations.
Note: Small Caribbean islands are Antigua and Barbuda, Dominica, Grenada, St. Kitts and Nevis, St. Lucia, St. Vincent and the Grenadines, and Trinidad and Tobago. The definition for emerging market and developing economies accords with the IMF's World Economic Outlook database.

TABLE 12.2

Structure of the Banking Sector in PICs, 2000–14

	Number of Commercial Banks			
	2000	**2005**	**2009**	**2014**
Fiji	5	5	5	6
Papua New Guinea	6	4	4	4
Samoa	3	4	4	4
Solomon Islands	3	3	3	4
Tonga	3	3	3	4
Vanuatu	4	3	4	4

Sources: Central banks; and IMF staff reports.
Note: PICs = Pacific island countries.

infancy.[14] This not only affects interest rate and credit pass-through, but also all other channels of monetary policy transmission, particularly those through asset prices and exchange rates.[15]

Lack of vigorous competition in the domestic banking sector may also be partly responsible for the weak monetary policy transmission. Reflecting the small size of domestic markets, only a few commercial banks operate in each of the PICs (Table 12.2). These banks, together with provident funds and a few insurance companies, are also major players in domestic money and credit markets. Provident funds account for a large share of total domestic financial assets in PICs. Because opportunities for long-term investment and restrictions on overseas investment are lacking, provident funds often hold large volumes of their assets in bank deposits and government paper. Given their size, actions by provident funds often have a large influence on domestic liquidity and hence on the effectiveness of monetary policy transmission (Box 12.1).

Domestic financial markets require continued reforms to reduce risk to investors, who see broader country risk and economic risk as high in PICs (PFTAC 2010). Such risks find their way into higher interest rates and impede the expansion and deepening of financial markets, as investors require higher returns. While some risk factors (vulnerability to cyclones, for example) are

[14] The lack of foreign exchange products is predictable given the fixed exchange rates in most countries.
[15] For an overview of various channels of monetary policy transmission, see Bank of England (2010) and Loayza and Schmidt-Hebbel (2002).

Box 12.1. Provident Funds in Pacific Island Countries

Provident funds are the largest financial sector institutions in Pacific island countries (PICs) and account for the bulk of private savings in many of them. Provident fund assets average 36 percent of total banking sector assets and reach over 60 percent in Fiji (Figure 12.1.1). These assets are normally held in a mixture of long-term investments, government paper, and bank deposits. Very few funds hold assets overseas, in part due to concerns over the impact this may have on official reserve positions.

Provident funds complicate the transmission of monetary policy in a number of ways:

- *Deposit rates*—Because provident funds often control much of the liquidity in the banking system, banks compete vigorously for their deposits, which are often made available in lumpy amounts. This can drive up the cost of funding for banks even when there is ample liquidity in the system, thereby frustrating central bank attempts to ease monetary policy.
- *Lending rates*—Provident funds are significant sources of private sector credit in some PICs. This can diminish the influence of monetary policy on credit growth and aggregate demand, as actions designed to tighten the credit environment have limited impact on the credit made available by provident funds.
- *Dampening price signals*—Provident funds can come under pressure to provide finance at lower than true market rates if they are government owned and represent a key source of domestic finance for the budget deficit. Some funds also have considerable lending to quasi-government bodies and state-owned enterprises, and this lending is not always on a fully commercial basis.

Some central banks have taken action to moderate the impact of provident funds on the domestic money market. For instance, the Reserve Bank of Vanuatu placed a temporary ceiling on deposit rates when provident fund offerings began pushing up interest rates as it was trying to loosen policies.

Provident funds are likely to continue to complicate monetary policy transmission in PICs. While markets are still relatively shallow and investment opportunities limited, provident funds are likely to remain one of the main providers of liquidity to the banking system. There are, however, a number of measures that could increase their sensitivity to market interest rates and therefore strengthen the transmission of monetary policy. These include ensuring open and transparent price auctions for the deposits that the funds place in the banking system, holding market-based variable-rate auctions for government securities, increasing the range of financial products available to provident funds for investment, and, contingent on the external position, allowing greater levels of investment overseas.

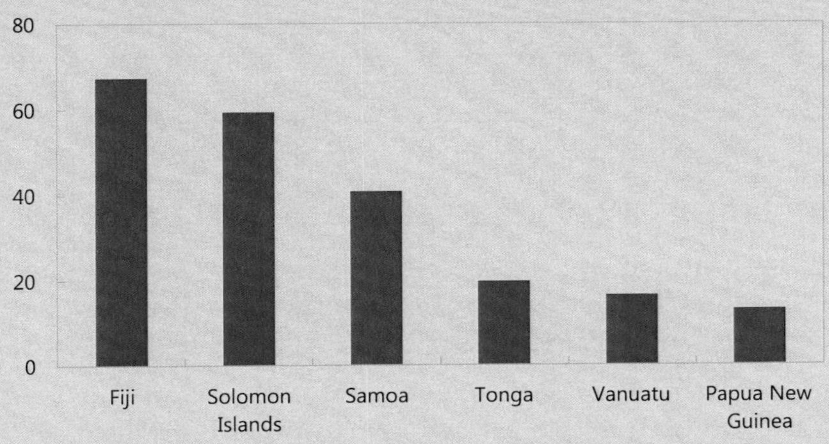

Figure 12.1.1 Ratio of Provident Fund Assets to Total Banking Assets (*Percent*)

Source: IMF staff compilations based on official websites.
Note: 2011 data for Vanuatu, 2012 data for Tonga, and 2013 data for other countries.

beyond the control of governments, much can be done to improve market infrastructure for financial development. In many PICs, measures could include establishing credit reporting bureaus, secured transactions laws, and collateral registries. Moreover, the enforcement of credit contracts needs to be strengthened to ensure reliable and rapid resolution of defaults, bankruptcies, and disputes.

Policy consistency can also help market development and strengthen signals for monetary policy transmission, as market expectations can play an important role in monetary policy transmission. Central bank independence, policy consistency, and effective communication help build expectations in line with policy intentions. For instance, when fiscal and monetary policies are moving in the same direction, it increases the credibility of monetary policy and the strength of transmission. In contrast, if the fiscal policy stance does not support a monetary easing it is likely to mute the effect on market interest rates or result in interest rates moving in unintended directions. Similarly, restrictions and controls on interest rates inconsistent with market conditions are unlikely to help long-term monetary policy transmission as market players see greater uncertainty and risk to their future activities.

MACROECONOMIC POLICY COORDINATION

The ultimate objective of macroeconomic policies is to achieve high economic growth and low and stable inflation. But, as noted earlier, it is difficult to rely on a single policy to accomplish this objective, be it fiscal, monetary, or exchange rate policy. Given the rather weak transmission of monetary policy in PICs, it is particularly important that it is employed in a macroeconomic policy framework in which all policies are geared toward the same objectives.

Despite fixed exchange rate regimes in most PICs, exchange rate policy can still be useful in economic stabilization. Under a flexible regime, the exchange rate itself is the first absorber of external shocks. Although a fixed exchange rate regime precludes such an automatic role, some flexibility—either through a one-off devaluation when facing a negative external shock or permitting the exchange rate to move within a narrow band—could still have significant stabilizing effects. Fiji, for instance, devalued its dollar when its balance of payments was under considerable pressure, as foreign reserves were running very low. The devaluation helped rebuild reserves quickly, with few second-round effects on inflation. One could argue that had Fiji relied on monetary tightening alone, the domestic price level would have had to fall substantially to restore the external balance, possibly with significant output losses. More generally, Wood (2010) argues that greater downward exchange rate flexibility could be expected to have favorable impacts on competitiveness over the medium to longer term, though it may not be able to counter a recession-induced decline in exports in the short term. Similarly, when a country faces increasing capital inflows, such as Papua New Guinea experienced during 2010–11 as a result of a large liquefied natural gas project, upward exchange rate flexibility would help reduce inflation pressure.

The expenditure-switching effects of exchange rate policy can be powerful in PICs. Even though real exchange rate depreciation through devaluation may have a limited impact on the supply of domestic goods, tourism seems to respond well to real exchange rate movements. Moreover, imports, which often consist of a high proportion of manufactured goods, tend to be more elastic, and devaluations can quickly reduce import demand. At the same time, because of high dependency on imports, devaluations can put considerable upward pressure on domestic prices, rendering policy-makers reluctant to take such actions. However, an increase in the price of imports is a necessary part of expenditure-switching adjustment, a key reason why the exchange rate can be effective in monetary policy transmission.[16] A critical step in preventing second-round effects of higher import prices, as Fiji took in 2009, is to have supportive monetary and fiscal policies to stamp out further inflation pressure.

Fiscal policy is particularly important in maintaining macroeconomic stability in PICs. As discussed earlier, a core objective of monetary policy under the mostly fixed exchange rate regimes in

[16] Jayaraman and Dahalan (2009) show that in Samoa, M1 and exchange rate channels are important in transmitting monetary impulses to output. In its exchange rate assessment of Fiji, IMF (2010) reports that a 1 percent real depreciation leads to a 4 percent increase in gross reserves. This suggests that most of the increase in reserves—excluding the special drawing rights allocation and the repatriation by Fiji National Provident Fund assets—since April 2009 was due to the devaluation.

PICs is to protect foreign reserves by keeping inflation in line with the levels of major trading partners. But they can only achieve this if fiscal policy is prudent and aimed at keeping aggregate demand at an appropriate level. Moreover, when countries need to stimulate domestic demand, such as when an external shock weakens domestic economic activity, fiscal policy is more powerful under a fixed exchange rate regime. To take advantage of it, countries need to build adequate fiscal space during good times to serve as a policy buffer during bad times.

A prudent fiscal policy can also help ensure adequate credit to the private sector and promote long-term growth and stability. It is now less common for governments to borrow directly from central banks, which, in turn, finance such borrowing by printing money. Unless private activity is depressed, even a fiscal expansion financed in a noninflationary manner (by issuing government paper, for example) will ultimately require a tightening of credit to the private sector to keep overall inflationary pressure under control. This is particularly important in PICs, as public sectors tend to be large and government borrowing can crowd out the private sector, undermining the objective in the region of private sector–led growth.

At an operational level, fiscal, and monetary authorities need to coordinate closely to maintain appropriate liquidity. While central bank operations should aim to maintain money supply at a level consistent with inflation objectives, fiscal authorities should provide central banks with forecasts of borrowing needs to ensure the availability of adequate liquidity. At the same time, there is considerable scope for PIC central banks to strengthen monetary projections and liquidity forecasts. Such projections can be challenging, however, given frequent exogenous shocks in the region. Actions by the large provident funds also have a significant effect on domestic liquidity, as noted earlier.

Experience in the region demonstrates the importance of prudent fiscal policy in maintaining price stability and promoting growth. Figure 12.12 shows that smaller fiscal deficits and lower public

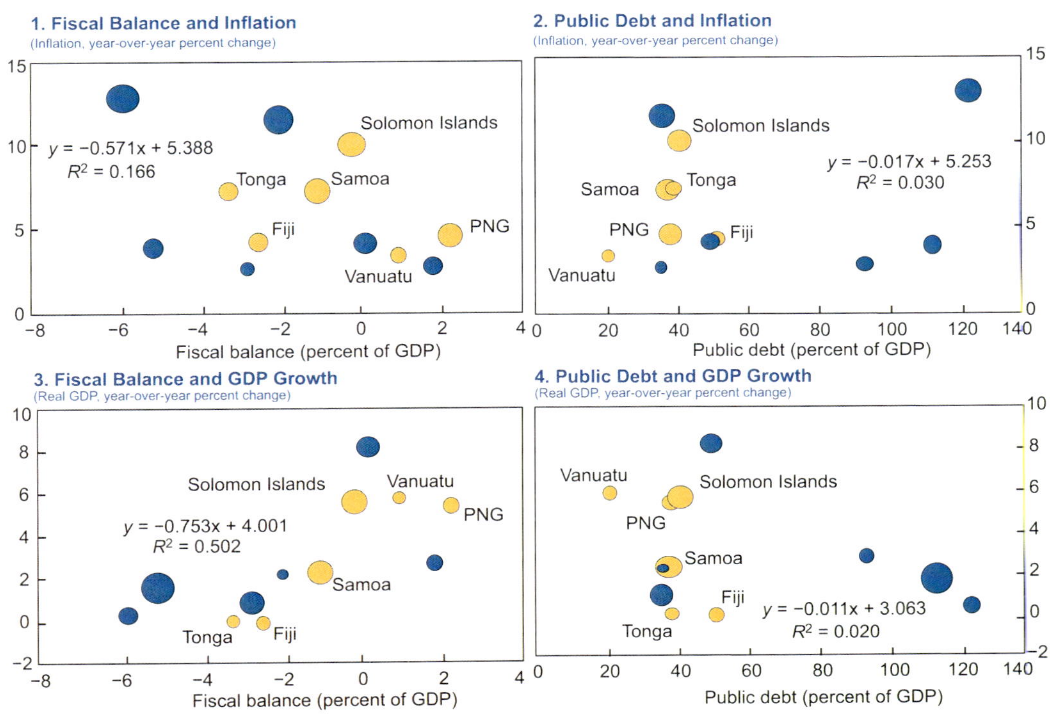

Figure 12.12 Fiscal Balance and Inflation, 2005–09

Source: IMF staff estimates.

Note: Blue bubbles indicate the following Caribbean countries: The Bahamas, Dominica, Grenada, Haiti, Jamaica, and Panama. PNG = Papua New Guinea. Bubble size indicates standard deviation of inflation.

debt are generally associated with lower inflation among PICs and Caribbean countries. Moreover, inflation seems to vary less in countries with lower inflation, generating greater certainty for economic agents, as the smaller bubbles in Figure 12.12 show. Similarly, both lower fiscal deficits and public debt appear to be associated with higher economic growth.

SUMMARY AND POLICY IMPLICATIONS

Recent experience in the global financial crisis highlighted the weakness of monetary policy transmission in PICs. In particular, interest rate pass-through—a channel to lower borrowing costs to boost economic activity—seems quite limited in some countries. On the other hand, the credit channel of monetary policy transmission appears to be stronger in some countries. That said, weak interest rate pass-through should not be interpreted as the total ineffectiveness of monetary policy in influencing commercial interest rates. This is because other factors could also offset the effects of monetary policy on commercial interest rates and credit growth.[17]

Nevertheless, cross-country variations in pass-through suggest that policy rates are poorly connected to money markets in some PICs. The inactive use of policy rates weakens their signaling effects and exacerbates the problem. Relatively weak monetary policy transmission through the interest rate channel is therefore unsurprising, especially given the region's shallow money markets. During the global financial crisis, monetary easing in PICs was not supported by real exchange rate movements because domestic inflation was higher than in trading partners, and nominal exchange rate adjustments were avoided due to concerns about rapid inflation pass-through. This diminished the power of monetary policy to stimulate economic activity.

Development of the domestic financial markets should focus on strengthening monetary policy transmission in PICs. Measured by standard indicators, such as the ratio of broad money to GDP and the availability of financial products, domestic financial markets in PICs are relatively shallow compared with Caribbean countries. A deeper financial market would strengthen monetary policy transmission, not only through interest rate and credit channels, but also through other channels that are now likely very weak, such as those through asset prices and balance sheets that are effective only in sophisticated financial markets.

Better market infrastructure is critical to stronger monetary transmission. In many PICs, specific measures could include establishing credit reporting bureaus, secured transactions laws, and collateral registries. Countries need to strengthen the enforcement of credit contracts to ensure reliable and rapid resolution of defaults, bankruptcies, and disputes. And as market infrastructure improves, they can accelerate the development of financial products, such as commercial paper, corporate bonds, equities, and foreign exchange products.

While focusing on the development of domestic financial markets in the long term, policymakers need to expand the use of their toolkit in macroeconomic management. The ultimate objective of monetary policy—and those of other macroeconomic policies—is to achieve low and stable inflation and high economic growth. Achieving this, along with intermediate objectives such as protecting foreign reserves, calls for using all macroeconomic tools available and closely coordinating them, especially when monetary policy transmission is weak.

Exchange rate policy remains powerful for macroeconomic stabilization in PICs. Fixed exchange rates have provided a useful nominal anchor and policymakers should recognize this benefit. However, some exchange rate flexibility (that is, a band around a central rate) would help countries absorb the impact of frequent external shocks in the region. Monetary and fiscal policy adjustment without the support of exchange rate flexibility would require larger changes in domestic prices to restore external balances and could result in larger output losses. This flexibility could be extended

[17] For example, changes in risk premiums, including risk arising from policy interventions such as controls and restrictions, and the availability of investment opportunities.

to one-off devaluations of the central parity when inconsistent fiscal and monetary policies have made the fixed exchange rate untenable at its set level. Of course, each country should examine such considerations carefully for their feasibility and appropriateness.

Prudent fiscal policy is vital to macroeconomic stability in PICs. To maintain a credible fixed exchange rate, fiscal policy must ensure that government spending does not lead to higher inflation than in trading partners. Even when governments finance spending in a noninflationary manner, they still need to be mindful of crowding out private sector credit. Experience in PICs and the Caribbean shows that prudent fiscal policy pays off: lower fiscal deficits and lower public debt seem to be associated with lower average inflation and higher GDP growth. Moreover, lower fiscal deficits and lower public debt are associated with lower variability of inflation.

ANNEX 12.1. ESTIMATING INTEREST RATE AND CREDIT PASS-THROUGH

We used an autoregressive distributed lags (ADL) model to estimate interest rate and credit pass-through. The model postulates the relationship between the policy rate and lending (deposit) rate as follows:

$$l_t = \alpha_0 + \alpha_1 \cdot m_t + \alpha_2 \cdot p_t + \alpha_3 \cdot l_{t-1} + \alpha_4 \cdot p_{t-1} + \varepsilon_t \qquad (12.1.1)$$

where l_t = lending rate;
m_t = time trend
p_t = policy rate
ε_t = error term
α = parameters to be estimated

The long-term interest pass-through is measured by $(\alpha_2 + \alpha_4)/(1 - \alpha_3)$.

Empirical studies use this type of ADL model widely to compare interest rate pass-through across countries (Cottarelli and Kourelis 1994; Moazzami 1999; Espinosa-Vega and Rebucci 2003; Guimarães-Filho and Ruiz-Arranz 2009; Pongsaparn 2010). Vector autoregression (VAR) is another popular model for the analysis of monetary policy transmission. However, the multivariable-VAR approach requires much more information and determination of the optimal lag length for each variable. Moreover, a VAR model with long lag structures would reduce estimation efficiency in small samples. The two-variable ADL model used here can be reparameterized as a VAR-type error-correction model without altering the estimated residuals.

The ADL model for estimating credit pass-through follows a similar structure by essentially replacing the lending rate with credit growth in equation (12.1.1).

Data used for the estimation were compiled from various internal IMF sources, which are often supplied by country authorities. For easy reference, the sources are as follows:

Fiji

Deposit rate (savings deposit rate): IMF, International Financial Statistics (IFS) database.
Lending rate (maximum commercial bank lending rate): IMF, IFS database.
Policy rate (bank rate, end of period): IMF, IFS database.
Private sector credit (monthly): IMF, Monetary and Financial Statistics database.
Private sector credit (annual): IMF staff estimates.
Excess reserves: IMF staff estimates.
Loan-to-deposit ratio: IMF, Monetary and Financial Statistics database.
Overall fiscal balance: IMF staff estimates.
Total government debt: IMF staff estimates.

Papua New Guinea

Deposit rate (weighted average): Country authority.
Lending rate (weighted average): Country authority.
Policy rate (bank rate, end of period): Country authority.
Private sector credit (monthly): Country authority.
Private sector credit (annual): IMF staff estimates.
Excess reserves: Country authority and IMF staff estimates.
Loan-to-deposit ratio: Country authority and IMF staff estimates.
Overall fiscal balance: IMF staff estimates.
Total government debt: IMF staff estimates.

Samoa

Deposit rate (weighted average): Central Bank of Samoa.
Lending rate (weighted average): Central Bank of Samoa.
Policy rate (bank rate, end of period): Central Bank of Samoa.
Private sector credit (monthly): Central Bank of Samoa.
Private sector credit (annual): IMF staff estimates.
Excess reserves: Central Bank of Samoa.
Loan-to-deposit ratio: Central Bank of Samoa.
Overall fiscal balance: IMF staff estimates.
Total government debt: IMF staff estimates.

Solomon Islands

Deposit rate: Central Bank of Solomon Islands.
Lending rate: Central Bank of Solomon Islands.
Private sector credit (monthly): Central Bank of Solomon Islands.
Private sector credit (annual): IMF staff estimates.
Excess reserves: Central Bank of Solomon Islands and IMF staff estimates.
Loan-to-deposit ratio: Central Bank of Solomon Islands and IMF staff estimates.
Overall fiscal balance: IMF staff estimates.
Total government debt: IMF staff estimates.

Tonga

Deposit rate (six months): National Reserve Bank of Tonga.
Lending rate (weighted average): National Reserve Bank of Tonga.
Private sector credit (monthly): National Reserve Bank of Tonga.
Private sector credit (annual): IMF staff estimates.
Excess reserves: National Reserve Bank of Tonga and IMF staff estimates.
Loan-to-deposit ratio: National Reserve Bank of Tonga and IMF staff estimates.
Overall fiscal balance: IMF staff estimates.
Total government debt: IMF staff estimates.

Vanuatu

Deposit rate (three months, representative): IMF, IFS database.
Lending rate (commercial advances, representative): IMF, IFS database.
Policy rate (discount rate, end of period): IMF, IFS database.
Private sector credit (monthly): IMF, Monetary and Financial Statistics database.
Private sector credit (annual): IMF staff estimates.
Excess reserves: IMF, Monetary and Financial Statistics database.
Loan-to-deposit ratio: IMF, Monetary and Financial Statistics database.
Overall fiscal balance: IMF staff estimates.
Total government debt: IMF staff estimates.

REFERENCES

Australia and New Zealand Governments. 2010. "Trends in Remittance Fees and Charges." Paper prepared for the Forum Economic Ministers' Meeting, Niue, October 26–29.

Bank of England. 2010. "The Transmission Mechanism of Monetary Policy." http://www.bankofengland.co.uk/publications/Documents/other/monetary/montrans.pdfw.

Chami, Ralph, Adolfo Baraja, Thomas F. Cosimano, Connel Fullenkamp, Michael T. Gapen, and Peter Montiel. 2008. *Macroeconomic Consequences of Remittances*. IMF Occasional Paper 259. Washington: International Monetary Fund.

Cottarelli, C., and A. Kourelis. 1994. "Financial Structure, Bank Lending Rates, and the Transmission Mechanism of Monetary Policy." *IMF Staff Papers* 41 (4): 587–623.

Dabla-Norris, Era, and Holger Floerkemeier. 2006. "Transmission Mechanisms of Monetary Policy in Armenia: Evidence from VAR Analysis." Working Paper. 06/248, International Monetary Fund, Washington.

Espinosa-Vega, Marco, and Alessandro Rebucci. 2003. "Retail Bank Interest Rate Pass-Through: Is Chile Atypical?" Working Paper 03/112, International Monetary Fund, Washington.

Guimarães-Filho, Roberto, and Marta Ruiz-Arranz. 2009. "Monetary Transmission in Asia: Is It Working? Box 1.3 in *Regional Economic Outlook: Asia and the Pacific*, October, International Monetary Fund, Washington.

International Monetary Fund (IMF). 2010. "Fiji: 2009 Article IV Consultation—Staff Report." IMF Country Report, May, Washington.

Jayaraman, T. K., and Chee-Keong Choong. 2009. "How Does Monetary Policy Transmission Work in Fiji?" *International Review of Economics* 56 (2): 145–61.

Jayaraman, T. K., and J. Dahalan. 2009. "Monetary Policy Transmission in an Undeveloped South Pacific Island Country: A Case Study of Samoa." *International Journal of Monetary Economics and Finance* 1 (4): 380–98.

Loayza, Norman, and Klaus Schmidt-Hebbel. 2002. "Monetary Policy Functions and Transmission Mechanisms: An Overview." In *Monetary Policy: Rules and Transmission Mechanisms*, edited by Norman Loayza and Klaus Schmidt-Hebbel. Santiago: Central Bank of Chile.

Moazzami, B. 1999. "Lending Rate Stickiness and Monetary Transmission Mechanism: The Case of Canada and the United States." *Applied Financial Economics* 9 (6): 533–38.

Pacific Financial Technical Assistance Centre (PFTAC). 2010. "Interest Rates and Bank Profitability in the South Pacific." Paper prepared for the Pacific Forum Economic Ministers' Meeting, Niue, October 26–29.

Pongsaparn, Runchana. 2010. "Samoa: Impediments to Bank Intermediation and Monetary Transmission." Selected Issues Papers, International Monetary Fund, Washington.

Viñals, Jose, and Jonathan Fiechter. 2010. "The Making of Good Supervision: Learning to Say 'No'." IMF Staff Position Note 10/08, International Monetary Fund, Washington.

Wood, Richard. 2010. "Monetary and Exchange Rate Policy Issues in Pacific Island Countries." Treasury Working Paper 2010-05, Australian Government, Canberra.

CHAPTER 13

Global Commodity Prices, Monetary Transmission, and Exchange Rate Pass-Through

SHANAKA J. PEIRIS AND DING DING

Pacific island countries (PICs) are vulnerable to commodity price shocks and this poses challenges for monetary policy. The spike in global commodity prices in 2007–08 led to a rise in headline inflation, while the global financial crisis that intensified in September 2008 put downward pressure on imported and domestic inflation through lower commodity prices and weak demand (Figure 13.1). Authorities loosened monetary policy, but reductions in bank lending rates have been limited and private credit growth anemic. These sluggish responses raise key questions about the effectiveness of monetary policy transmission mechanisms in PICs and the appropriate nominal anchor, given the high volatility in global commodity prices.

The exchange rate could be used to cushion against exogenous shocks.[1] With a conventional exchange rate peg, the burden of addressing the impact of exogenous shocks falls on monetary and fiscal policies. Given limited capital mobility in PICs, monetary policy enjoys a certain degree of freedom despite the pegged exchange rate regime. However, if monetary policy transmission is weak and the prospects for improving its effectiveness are limited in the short term, countercyclical policies will require an appropriate mix of monetary, fiscal, and exchange rate policies.[2] Monetary policy could be closely coordinated with fiscal policy to achieve the desired impact, but that is often constrained by the lack of fiscal buffers. Therefore, pegged exchange rate regimes should not preclude considerations to introduce some flexibility to increase the role of the exchange rate in absorbing external shocks and to provide additional freedom for monetary policy.

This chapter assesses the impact of international commodity price shocks and monetary and exchange rate transmission in PICs to explore whether the exchange rate can help absorb exogenous shocks. The chapter reviews the key objectives of monetary policy and how it is conducted in PICs. This is followed by an empirical assessment of monetary and exchange transmission mechanisms in these countries, focusing on the responses of real GDP and headline inflation to external shocks, exchange rate changes, and monetary aggregates or interest rates. We then more formally consider the appropriate nominal anchor to maintain macroeconomic stability in a small island country using a model-based approach applied to Tonga. The chapter concludes with some policy implications.

This chapter is based on IMF Working Paper 12/176. We thank Patrizia Tumbarello, Hoe Ee Khor, Subir Lall, and Joyce Mafi, the former governor of the National Reserve Bank of Tonga, and members of the IMF's Small Islands Club for their helpful comments.

[1]De jure exchange rate regimes in Fiji, Samoa, the Solomon Islands, and Vanuatu are adjustable pegs or bands to a basket of currencies. Papua New Guinea has a de jure floating exchange rate regime. Marshall Islands, Micronesia, and Palau use the U.S. dollar as legal tender, while Kiribati and Tuvalu use the Australian dollar.

[2]Chapter 12 shows that the monetary transmission mechanism in PICs is weak.

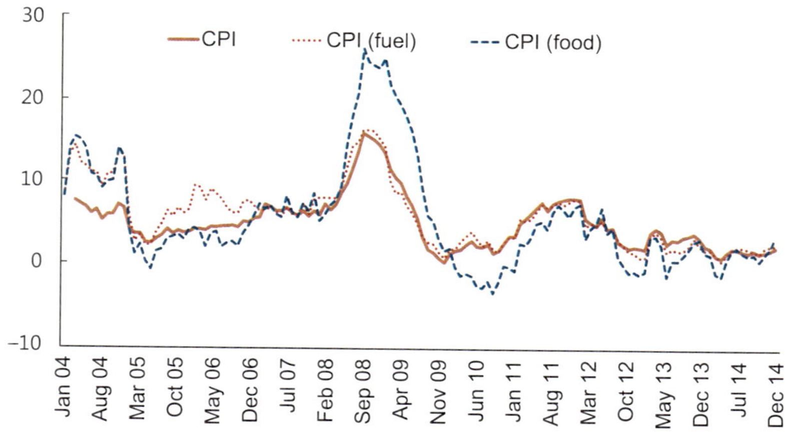

Figure 13.1 Pacific Island Countries: Average Fuel, Food, and Headline Inflation

Sources: Country authorities; and IMF staff estimates.
Note: CPI = consumer price index.

THE CHOICE OF A NOMINAL ANCHOR

To ensure price stability, central banks around the world must choose between strategies that target a monetary indicator or the exchange rate.[3] Analyses based on the dynamic stochastic general equilibrium (DSGE) model generally find interest rate based inflation targeting performs better than exchange rate targeting in maximizing social welfare and minimizing macroeconomic volatility (Stone and others 2009). However, McCallum (2006) compares the performances of Taylor-type interest rate rules and exchange rate based approaches to inflation targeting in an economy with varying degrees of openness. The key finding is that, as the degree of openness increases, an exchange rate based approach to inflation targeting does much better than the standard interest rate based approach in stabilizing output, with no adverse consequences for inflation variability. This is because in an interest rate based approach the variability of the interest rate is low, while that of the exchange rate based approach is high. The results suggest that in an economy with a high exchange rate pass-through to imported goods prices and low interest rate sensitivity of aggregate expenditures, smoothing the exchange rate rather than interest rates may help control inflation and reduce output volatility. Parrado (2004) shows that a trade-weighted exchange rate index explained a significant share of the variation in consumer price index (CPI) inflation in Singapore and that the Monetary Authority of Singapore has used the index to target inflation.

The high pass-through of global commodity prices and import propensity in PICs suggest a greater role for exchange rate flexibility in controlling inflation (Figure 13.2). There is a large weight of fuel and food items in the CPI basket in PICs, and thus a high pass-through of global commodity prices to headline inflation (Figures 13.3 and 13.4). More generally, the import propensity (or share of imported items in consumption and investment) is high in most PICs given the region's small domestic manufacturing base.[4] One would therefore expect the exchange rate to be an effective tool to control imported inflation without significant output costs. In fact, it appears that during 2010–11 PIC central banks appreciated their currencies in nominal and real effective terms to cushion the impact of higher global food and fuel prices. This exchange rate adjustment could be based

[3]Exchange rate flexibility is also important to maintain external stability and thus may not be available to target domestic stability objectives. Therefore, this discussion presupposes a comfortable level of international reserves, but does not preclude the possibility of the exchange rate being subordinate to external stability concerns.

[4]For example, the share of imported items in the CPI basket is more than 40 percent in the Solomon Islands and Tonga, two countries that disaggregate the CPI basket between domestic and imported goods.

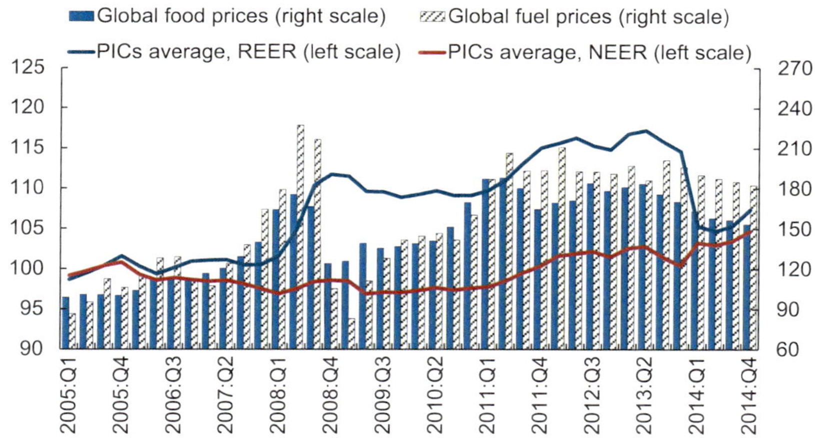

Figure 13.2 Effective Exchange Rate (*Index, 2005 = 100*)

Source: IMF staff estimates.

Note: NEER = nominal effective exchange rate; PICs = Pacific island countries; REER = real effective exchange rate. Includes Marshall Islands, Papua New Guinea, Samoa, the Solomon Islands, Tonga, and Vanuatu.

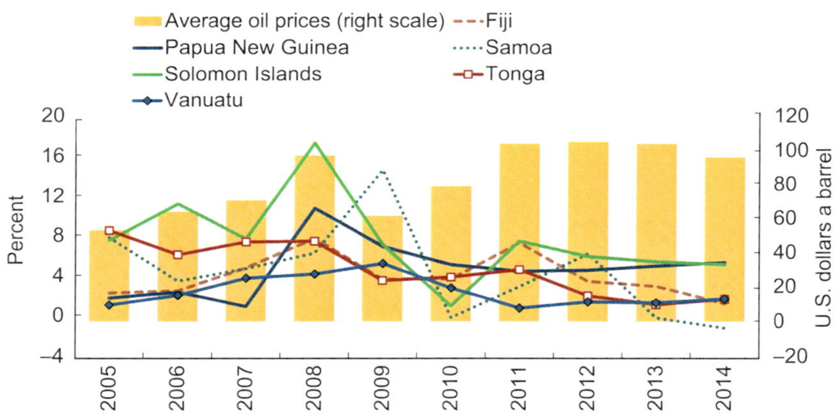

Figure 13.3 Pass-Through of Oil Prices to Inflation

Source: IMF staff calculations.

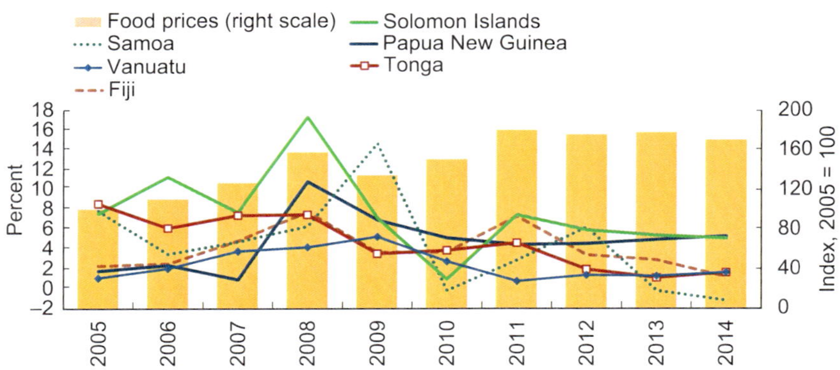

Figure 13.4 Pass-Through of Food Prices to Inflation

Source: IMF staff calculations.

Note: Food-only consumer price inflation for Papua New Guinea, Samoa, the Solomon Islands, Tonga, and Vanuatu; and overall consumer price inflation for Fiji.

on a view of the greater efficacy of exchange rate flexibility in managing inflation or evidence of the limited effectiveness of monetary policy transmission to commercial bank interest rates and private sector credit documented in Chapter 12.

MONETARY AND EXCHANGE RATE TRANSMISSION MECHANISMS

The literature on the transmission mechanism of monetary policy in advanced economies and emerging markets is burgeoning, but there is a dearth of studies on the Pacific islands. Typically, this strand of research has been conducted in the context of a vector autoregression (VAR) framework pioneered by Sims (1980). Notable examples using VAR to identify the transmission of monetary policy for advanced economies include Christiano, Eichenbaum, and Evans (1999) for the United States and Kim and Roubini (2000) for the Group of Seven economies. However, there has been little analysis of the monetary transmission mechanism in the Pacific island economies, leaving a number of unanswered questions and somewhat of a vacuum of knowledge in this area.[5]

Chapter 12 uses single-equation econometric techniques to assess the pass-through of policy rates to lending rates and private credit growth; the authors conclude that the monetary transmission mechanism is relatively weak in the Pacific islands. However, Jayaraman and Choong (2009), using a simple VAR approach, show that money supply is the most effective channel of monetary policy transmission in Fiji. Jayaraman and Dahalan (2008) suggest that the money and exchange rate channels are important in transmitting monetary impulses to Samoa's output, while monetary aggregates matter more for inflation. We follow a similar approach but attempt to account for the pass-through of international commodity prices and alternative channels of monetary and exchange transmission by using a more comprehensive set of external and macro-financial variables for six PICs, while controlling for endogeneity in a panel VAR framework.[6]

A panel VAR model is estimated for PICs to reflect the pass-through of global commodity prices and monetary and exchange rate transmission mechanisms to the real economy.[7] The ordering of variables in the recursive VAR is the following: the global exogenous factors (global fuel and food prices) come first followed by the assumption that the exchange rate and monetary indicators (interest rates or monetary aggregates) respond to demand conditions (real GDP). These factors can impact headline inflation with no immediate effects and vice versa. The VAR models are estimated using annual data from 1995 to 2011 for all countries to minimize structural breaks. All variables are in log-differences, except interest rates. Standard information criteria are used to select the lag lengths of the VAR, which turn out to be two years. Results of Granger causality tests lend support for a transmission of external shocks and the exchange rate to the domestic economy.

RESULTS

The results of the baseline panel VAR model are shown in Figures 13.5 and 13.6. The graphs display the impact on headline inflation, as measured by the impulse response, of a one standard deviation shock to global fuel prices, global food prices, output, the bilateral exchange rate against the U.S. dollar, domestic interest rates, and the headline price index itself. The exchange rate pass-through is calculated as the impact of a shock on the exchange rate (defined as an exogenous, unexpected, temporary rise at $t = 0$) on the headline inflation index over a specific time interval. The relative importance of the exogenous and monetary shocks for fluctuations in headline inflation and the output gap at different forecast horizons can be gauged through the forecast error variance decompositions.

---

[5]This has been partly related to data limitations, particularly a lack of quarterly real sector aggregates.
[6]The six countries are Fiji, Papua New Guinea, Samoa, the Solomon Islands, Tonga, and Vanuatu.
[7]See Annex 13.1 for more details on the VAR modeling approach.

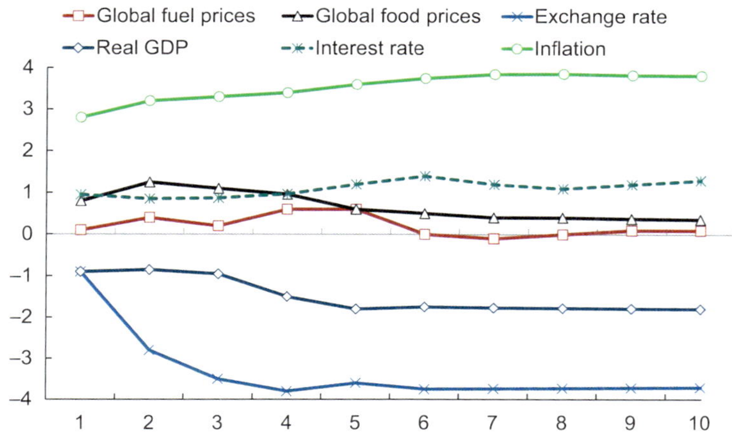

Figure 13.5 Impulse Response of Inflation to Shocks

Source: IMF staff estimates.

Note: Figure shows accumulated response of inflation to Cholesky one standard deviation innovations.

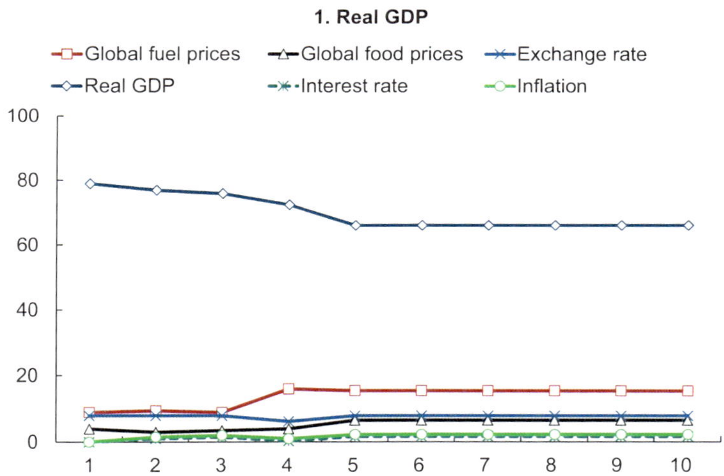

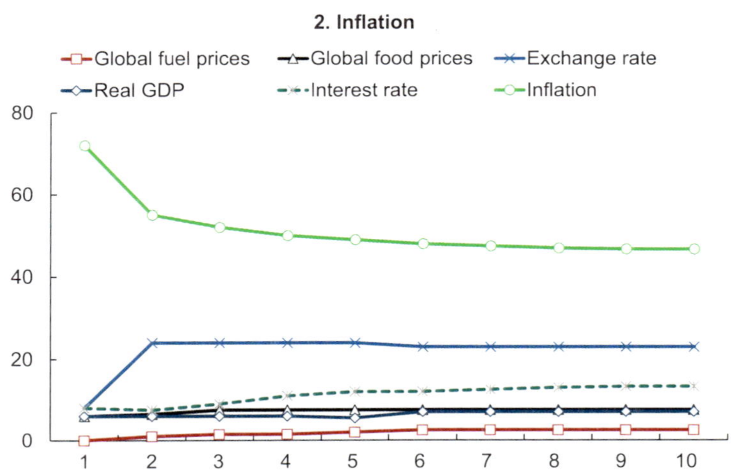

Figure 13.6 Variance Decomposition of Real GDP and Inflation

Source: IMF staff estimates.

The transmission of external and monetary shocks provides little scope for PICs to influence the real economy through monetary management alone. The key insights are:

- As expected, higher global food and fuel prices raise headline inflation. The impact of global food prices is larger and more persistent than global fuel prices given the greater weight of food items in the CPI basket.
- The impact of monetary impulses on headline inflation is not as significant as the impact of exchange rate fluctuations. The pass-through of the exchange rate to headline inflation is 60 percent within one year, with a complete pass-through within the second year. On the other hand, the impact on and variation of headline inflation explained by monetary impulses is relatively small whether one considers broad money, domestic credit, reserve money, or interest rates, as in the baseline model. In fact, higher interest rates are associated with greater inflation, possibly indicating reverse causation, where exchange rate changes and inflation determine the level of interest rates.
- Real GDP is not well explained by the shocks considered, except its own innovations. This probably reflects the importance of supply-side factors and policy variables not captured, such as fiscal policy. Interestingly, global commodity prices appear to affect economic activity more than global GDP, indicating a relatively weak impact of external demand compared to terms of trade, although none of these effects is statistically significant.[8]

A FORECASTING AND POLICY ANALYSIS SYSTEM MODEL FOR SMALL ISLAND COUNTRIES

While the high exchange rate pass-through and weak monetary transmission mechanism provide greater scope to use the exchange rate for controlling inflation, the appropriateness of using it as a tool of macroeconomic stabilization largely depends on the size and nature of shocks as well as the country's economic structure. The panel VAR analysis shed light on the relative efficacy of monetary and exchange rate transmission controlling for exogenous shocks, but it did not take into account the distribution of shocks and structural economic relationships in the economy. In particular, linkages to real economic activity were not well identified, possibly owing to data limitations and country heterogeneity in the transmission of shocks. To better identify the shocks and overcome some of these limitations, we estimate and simulate a small macroeconomic model for Tonga as an illustrative PIC and small island economy using quarterly data from 1995 to 2011.

The monetary policy analysis is conducted by extending the small New Keynesian macroeconomic model of Berg, Karam, and Laxton (2006a, 2006b) to better capture factors specific to Tonga. The model is a stripped down version of a DSGE model with rational expectations. In recent years, the macroeconomic literature has used DSGE models and small New Keynesian models to analyze economic behavior and to forecast developments. The DSGE models are based on theoretical underpinnings and have been found to be useful for analyzing the effects of structural changes in the economy, as well as the effects of longer-term developments such as persistent fiscal and current account deficits. By virtue of their relatively simple structure, small New Keynesian models have also been used for forecasting and policy analysis purposes in central banks and by IMF country desks. A number of inflation-targeting central banks have used similar models as an integral part of their policy analysis (see Laxton, Rose, and Scott 2009).

Global commodity prices and the possible use of the exchange rate for domestic stabilization are incorporated in work by Carabenciov and others (2008) and Parrado (2004), respectively. To capture the commodity price dependence of Tonga and that of PICs more generally, the baseline model is extended to incorporate global oil and food prices. Moreover, to better understand the dynamics of

[8]The panel VAR with global GDP instead of global commodity prices was statistically insignificant and not reported here.

inflation, we estimate two Phillips curves—headline inflation and domestic price inflation (rather than core inflation)—like Berg, Karam, and Laxton (2006b). Estimating domestic price inflation provides insights into the potential role of intermediate imports emphasized by McCallum (2006) for very open economies. As Tonga is a small island country, we incorporate external demand shocks from the rest of the world captured by partner country GDP growth. Output developments in the rest of the world feed directly into the small economy as they influence foreign demand for Tongan products and services (for example, remittances and tourism). To allow for the possibility of using the exchange rate as the tool of macroeconomic stabilization, we consider two closure rules to the model: a standard Taylor rule and a modified exchange rate targeting rule following Parrado (2004). Changes in foreign inflation and interest rates affect the interest rate or exchange rate depending on the closure of the model and, subsequently, demand and inflation in Tonga.

The extended Forecasting and Policy Analysis System model has four behavioral equations: (1) an aggregate demand or IS curve that relates the level of real activity to expected and past real activity, the real interest rate, the real exchange rate, foreign demand, the fiscal stance, and financial conditions; (2) a price setting or Phillips curve that relates inflation to past and expected inflation, the output gap, fuel prices, and the exchange rate; (3) an uncovered interest parity condition for the exchange rate or interest rate, with some allowance for backward-looking expectations; and (4) a modified Taylor rule for setting the policy interest rate or exchange rate as a function of the output gap and expected inflation.

The aggregate demand equation is as follows:

$$\begin{aligned} ygap_t &= \beta_{ld}\, ygap_{t+1} + \beta_{lag}\, ygap_{t-1} - \beta_{RRgap} RRgap_{t-1} \\ &\quad + \beta_{Zgap} zgap_{t-1} + \beta_{RWygap}\, ygap_t^{RW} + \beta_{BL}\eta_t + \varepsilon_t^{ygap} \end{aligned} \tag{13.1}$$

where $ygap$ is the output gap; $RRgap$ the real interest rate gap; $zgap$ the real exchange rate gap; $ygap^{RW}$ the output gap in the United States; η is a measure of lending conditions specified in the aggregate demand equation, as in Carabenciov and others (2008); β a series of parameters attached to these variables; and ε^{ygap} an error term that captures other temporary exogenous demand shocks. Lending conditions are proxied by real credit growth.

The Phillips curve equation is as follows:

$$\begin{aligned} \pi_t &= \alpha_{\pi ld}\pi 4_{t+1} + (1-\alpha_{\pi ld})\pi 4_{t-1} + \alpha_{ygap}\, ygap_{t-1} + \alpha_{zgap}(z_t - z_{t-1}) + \alpha_o(\pi_t^o - \pi^o) \\ &\quad + \alpha_{olag}(\pi_{t-1}^o - \pi^o) + \alpha_f(\pi_t^f - \pi^f) + \alpha_{flag}(\pi_{t-1}^f - \pi^f) + \varepsilon_t^{\pi} \end{aligned} \tag{13.2}$$

where $\pi 4_{t+1}$ is the four-quarter-ahead inflation rate (year over year), $\pi 4_{t-1}$ the four-quarter lagged inflation rate, $ygap$ the output gap, $z_t - z_{t-1}$ the real depreciation, α the parameters, π_t^o international fuel price inflation, π_t^f international food price inflation, and ε_t^{π} an error term. Note that international fuel and food price inflation is in terms of domestic prices. For example, international fuel price inflation is expressed as:

$$\pi_t^o = \pi_t^{RWo} + 4*(z_t - z_{t-1}) \tag{13.3}$$

where π_t^{RWo} is the global (Brent) oil price inflation.

As an extension, we add the following equation for domestic core inflation:

$$\begin{aligned} \pi_{c,t} &= \alpha_{c,\pi ld}\pi 4_{c,t+1} + (1-\alpha_{c,\pi ld})\pi 4_{c,t+1} + \alpha_{c,ygap}\, ygap_{t-1} + \alpha_{c,zgap}(z_t - z_{t-1}) \\ &\quad + \alpha_c(\pi 4_{t-1} - \pi 4_{c,t-1}) + \varepsilon_{c,t}^{\pi} \end{aligned} \tag{13.4}$$

where the term $\pi 4_{t-1} - \pi 4_{c,t-1}$ has been added to the simple canonical inflation equation to allow for the possibility that imported goods are an important input into the production costs of many domestic goods, or if workers resist the reduction in their real wages in response to an increase in headline inflation related to higher imported prices.

The uncovered interest parity equation (UIP) is as follows:

$$z_t = \delta_z z_{t+1} + (1-\delta_z) z_{t-1} - (RR_t - RR_t^{RW} - \rho^*)/4 + \varepsilon_t^z \tag{13.5}$$

where z_t is the log of the real exchange rate (an increase represents a depreciation), RR_t the real interest rate, RR_t^{RW} the U.S. real interest rate, ρ^* the historical average risk premium on the domestic currency, δ_z the smoothness parameter, and ε_t^z an error term. This equation, an uncovered interest rate parity condition, posits that the real exchange rate is a function of the expected real exchange rate (the first two terms), the real interest rate differential (the currency risk premium), and a disturbance term. Note that the above equation is equivalent to the conventional UIP condition, which is usually expressed in nominal terms. Denote the log of the nominal exchange rate as N_t, then the change of the nominal exchange rate is:

$$\Delta e_t = N_{t+1}^e - N_t = z_{t+1}^e - z_t + \pi_t - \pi_t^* \tag{13.6}$$

Substituting this in the conventional UIP condition will derive the UIP condition in real terms. In the case of exchange rate targeting, the UIP condition is written in terms of the domestic interest rate instead.

The Taylor rule is as follows:

$$\begin{aligned} RS_t = {} & \gamma_{RSlag} RS_{t-1} + (1-\gamma_{RSlag}) \\ & *(RR_t^* + \pi 4_t + \gamma_\pi(\pi 4_{t+4} - \pi_{t+4}^*) + \gamma_{ygap} ygap + \gamma_{zgap} zgap_t) + \varepsilon_t^{RS} \end{aligned} \tag{13.7}$$

The Taylor rule can be modified by inverting the equation in terms of the exchange rate, as in Parrado (2004).

In the case of the exchange rate targeting regime, we replace the Taylor rule and the uncovered interest parity equation with the following equations. We follow the exchange rate targeting framework in Khor, Robinson, and Lee (2004) and Parrado (2004) in which the change of nominal effective exchange rate is a function of the inflation gap and output gap

$$\Delta e_t = \Delta e + \gamma_{e1}(\pi_t - \pi^*) + \gamma_{e2}(y_t - y^*) + \varepsilon_t^N \tag{13.8}$$

where Δe is the long-term equilibrium change in the nominal effective exchange rate.

Exchange rate targeting follows:

$$zgap_t = \delta_z zgap_{t-1} + (1-\delta_z)[\delta_\pi(\pi 4_{t+4} - \pi_{t+4}^*) + \delta_y ygap_t] + \varepsilon_t^z \tag{13.9}$$

where the real exchange rate gap is a function of the inflation gap and output gap. It is easy to show that the above function is equivalent to the nominal exchange rate targeting rule in Khor, Robinson, and Lee (2004), as the nominal exchange rate gap depends on the real exchange rate gap and the inflation rates. For model consistency and estimation, we express the nominal exchange rate targeting rule in terms of an equivalent real exchange rate targeting rule.

Correspondingly, the real interest rate is determined by the UIP equation as:

$$RR_t = \gamma_{RRlag} RR_{t-1} + (1-\gamma_{RRlag}) * \left(RR_t^* + \rho^* - 4(z_t - z_{t-1} - \pi_t + \pi_t^*) \right) + \varepsilon_t^{RS} \tag{13.10}$$

where ρ^* is the historical average risk premium on the domestic currency.

The model is estimated using Bayesian techniques based on prior distributions for the parameters from cross-country work and assumptions about the Tongan economy. Bayesian estimation in a situation of a relatively small sample size (which is almost always the case for macro time series data) helps ameliorate the problems of classical econometric estimation, which often gives macro model results that are inconsistent and faces simultaneity challenges. This is a particularly important aspect for Tonga and other PICs where data are extremely limited and other cross-country studies could help pin down structural parameters. However, to avoid imposing too much structure, we use diffused priors. All variables are seasonally adjusted using the X12 filter, with the exception of the interest rate and the exchange rate, and expressed in "gap" terms, defined as deviations from a Hodrick-Prescott time trend.

The trade-off between targeting interest rates and the exchange rate is assessed based on the historical distribution of shocks. Using the estimated parameters and distributions for the stochastic shocks, solutions are derived for the variability in inflation and the output gap under alternative policy reaction functions where the interest rate or exchange rate is the target variable in the modified Taylor rule. The rule that minimizes a loss function of inflation and output variability of a standard quadratic form given by the following equation can be used to gauge the "optimal" policy rule in terms of minimizing macroeconomic volatility:

$$L = \sum_{t=0}^{\infty} \lambda_{\pi}(\pi_t - \pi^T)^2 + \lambda_y \, ygap_t^2 \quad (13.11)$$

where λ_{π} and λ_y are the relative weights on inflation and output-gap variability and π^T is the inflation target.

The impulse responses and variance decomposition of all stochastic shocks suggest that demand and supply shocks are nearly equally important in accounting for inflation dynamics. As far as the impulse response functions are concerned, the model shows reasonable and expected patterns. Global commodity price and demand shocks have a significant impact on output and inflation dynamics, requiring a policy response to help stabilize the economy. Exchange rate changes have a greater influence on inflation while interest rates affect aggregate demand more than exchange rate changes, albeit having a small impact. This contrasts somewhat with the perceived dominance of supply-side factors based on the results of a pure empirical panel VAR approach, highlighting the need for more systematic and country-specific analyses to better identify and interpret shocks.

An exchange rate based targeting approach is better at achieving macroeconomic stability (see Table 13.1). An exchange rate based targeting rule does much better at stabilizing both output and inflation in Tonga. The variance decompositions suggest that this result is a consequence of the greater importance of global commodity prices and external demand shocks that could be more effectively insulated through the exchange rate. The spillover of imported inflation to domestic consumption goods prices through the use of intermediate imports or wage indexation in terms of headline inflation likely makes the exchange rate a more powerful channel in controlling inflation. Moreover, the low interest rate sensitivity of aggregate demand leads to less macroeconomic volatility under an exchange rate based targeting approach than in advanced economies. The preference for targeting interest rates over exchange rates in PICs and other small island countries is thus not as clear-cut as in advanced inflation targeting economies, as suggested by McCallum (2006). Our result is also consistent with the fact that nearly all PICs except Fiji appreciated the exchange rate in response to the surge in headline inflation in 2010–11, mainly driven by higher commodity prices.

POLICY IMPLICATIONS

Exchange rate flexibility could be a useful tool for macroeconomic stabilization in PICs. External shocks—particularly global commodity shocks—have a significant impact on headline inflation, both directly and indirectly through intermediate imports. The high degree of exchange rate pass-through

TABLE 13.1

Macroeconomic Volatility under Alternative Policy Rules

	GDP Gap	Headline Inflation
Exchange rate targeting	0.34	1.01
Interest rate targeting	1.09	4.76

Source: IMF staff estimates.

to headline inflation in PICs and the weak monetary transmission mechanism suggest a greater efficacy of exchange rate changes, as opposed to monetary policy, in affecting inflation. The impact of monetary impulses on headline inflation is weak, whether one considers broad money, reserve money, interest rates, or domestic credit. This probably reflects the excess liquidity in the banking system and structural impediments to lending such as weak contract enforcement and bankruptcy procedures.

In terms of the trade-off between exchange rate and monetary policy in macroeconomic stabilization, the empirical evidence of the model-based approach tilts in favor of exchange rate policy. This is because of the close relationship between exchange rate changes and headline inflation, and the low interest rate sensitivity of aggregate demand. That said, the use of exchange rate flexibility for short-term domestic stability objectives in the context of the de jure exchange rate basket regime will only be possible in a situation of comfortable international reserves, and should avoid significant deviation of the exchange rate from its medium-term fundamentals.

Greater exchange rate flexibility and structural reforms may help strengthen the effectiveness of the monetary transmission mechanism. While monetary policy is unlikely to be subordinate to the exchange rate regime because of limited interest-sensitive, cross-border capital flows, some private transfers such as remittances and nonresident bank deposits may respond to changes in domestic interest rates. Thus, greater exchange rate flexibility may provide greater independence to monetary policy. More important, the monetary transmission could be strengthened by enhancing the interest rate pass-through to lending rates and by addressing the excess liquidity and structural problems, such as by introducing greater competition in the financial system. The underdeveloped state of PIC financial markets also affects the interest rate and credit channel of monetary policy. Collateralized interbank lending is not widely available, and secondary markets for government and central bank paper are virtually nonexistent.

ANNEX 13.1. IDENTIFICATION OF VECTOR AUTOREGRESSION (VAR)

Structural VAR Modeling

Following Kim and Roubini (2000) and Sims and Zha (2006), we assume the economy is described by a structural-form equation:

$$G(L)\,Yt = C(L)\,X_t + \varepsilon_t$$

where $G(L)$ is an $n \times n$ matrix polynomial in the lag operator; $C(L)$ is an $n \times k$ matrix polynomial in the lag operator; Y_t is an $n \times 1$ vector of endogenous variables; and X_t is a $k \times 1$ vector of exogenous foreign variables; ε_t is an $n \times 1$ vector of structural disturbances, with var(ε_t) = Λ, where Λ is a diagonal matrix and the diagonal elements are the variances of structural disturbances. Therefore, structural disturbances are assumed to be mutually uncorrelated.

Corresponding with this structural model we can estimate a reduced-form VAR:

$$Y_t = A(L)\,Y_t + B(L)X_t + \mu_t$$

where $A(L)$ and $B(L)$ are matrices polynomials; μ_t is a vector of reduced-form disturbances, with var(μ_t) = Σ.

We assume the exogenous vector X_t contains IMF *World Economic Outlook* global fuel prices (*Fuel*) and food prices (*Food*):

$$X_t' = [Fuel\ Food]$$

These variables are included to control for changes in overall global economic conditions and fluctuations in the prices of PICs' main imported commodities. The other endogenous variables include the real GDP (Y), exchange rate (E), a monetary aggregate or interest rate (M), and headline consumer price index ($HCPI$).

$$Y_t' = [Y\ E\ M\ HCPI]$$

In the baseline model, the money policy variable is chosen to be interest rates, but other monetary aggregates are tested, and domestic credit to the private sector has the largest explanatory power, albeit still relatively small compared to the exchange rate impact on inflation.

Identification Scheme: Recursive VAR

There are many ways of recovering the parameters in the structural-form equations from the estimated parameters in the reduced form equation. A popular and convenient method is to orthogonalize reduced-form disturbances by Cholesky decomposition using a simple recursive VAR, as in Sims (1980).

REFERENCES

Berg, Andrew, Philippe Karam, and Douglas Laxton. 2006a. "A Practical Model-Based Approach to Monetary Policy Analysis: Overview." IMF Working Paper 06/80, International Monetary Fund, Washington.

———. 2006b. "Practical Model-Based Monetary Policy Analysis: A How-to Guide." IMF Working Paper 06/81, International Monetary Fund, Washington.

Carabenciov, Ioan, Igor Ermolaev, Charles Freedman, Michael Juillard, Ondra Kamenik, Dmitry Korshunov, Douglas Laxton, and Jared Laxton. 2008. "A Small Quarterly Multi-Country Projection Model with Financial-Real Linkages and Oil Prices." IMF Working Paper 08/280, International Monetary Fund, Washington.

Christiano, Lawrence J., Martin Eichenbaum, and Charles L. Evans. 1999. "Monetary Policy Shocks: What Have We Learned and to What End?" In *Handbook of Macroeconomics*, Edition 1, edited by J. Taylor and M. Woodford. Amsterdam: North-Holland.

Jayaraman, T. K., and Chee-Keong Choong. 2009. "How Does Monetary Policy Transmission Work in Fiji?" *International Review of Economics*, 56 (2): 145–61.

Jayaraman, T. K., and Jauhari Dahalan. 2008. "Monetary Policy Transmission in an Undeveloped South Pacific Island Country: A Case Study of Samoa." *International Journal of Monetary Economics and Finance*, 1 (4): 380–98.

Khor, Hoe Ee, Edward Robinson, and Jason Lee. 2004. "Managed Floating and Intermediate Exchange Rate Systems: The Singapore Experience." Staff Paper 37, Monetary Authority of Singapore.

Kim, Soyoung, and Nouriel Roubini. 2000. "Exchange Rate Anomalies in the Industrial Countries: A Solution with a Structural VAR Approach." *Journal of Monetary Economics*, 45 (3): 561–86.

Laxton, Douglas, David Rose, and Alasdair M. Scott. 2009. "Developing a Structured Forecasting and Policy Analysis System to Support Inflation-Forecast Targeting (IFT)." IMF Working Paper 09/65, International Monetary Fund, Washington.

McCallum, Bennett T. 2006. "Singapore's Exchange Rate-Centered Monetary Policy Regime and Its Relevance for China." Staff Paper 43, Monetary Authority of Singapore.

Parrado, Eric. 2004. "Singapore's Unique Monetary Policy: How Does It Work?" IMF Working Paper 04/10, International Monetary Fund, Washington.

Peiris, Shanaka J., and Ding Ding. 2012. "Global Commodity Prices, Monetary Transmission, and Exchange Rate Pass-Through in the Pacific Islands." IMF Working Paper 12/176, International Monetary Fund, Washington.

Sims, Christopher. 1980. "Macroeconomics and Reality." *Econometrica*, 48 (1): 1–48.

Sims, Christopher, and Tao Zha. 2006. "Does Monetary Policy Generate Recessions?" *Macroeconomic Dynamics*, 10 (2): 231–72.

Stone, Mark, Scott Roger, Anna Nordstrom, Seiichi Shimizu, Turgut Kisinbay, and Jorge Restrepo. 2009. *The Role of the Exchange Rate in Inflation-Targeting Emerging Economies*. IMF Occasional Paper 267. Washington: International Monetary Fund.

CHAPTER 14

The Role of Excess Liquidity and Interest Rate Pass-Through for the Monetary Transmission Mechanism in the Pacific

JAN GOTTSCHALK

Monetary transmission in the Pacific is complicated by the absence of a number of channels that are available to central banks in advanced economies. This leaves monetary policy dependent on interest rate pass-through, which has been ineffective in the region, largely because of the nature of its financial markets rather than issues with the monetary policy frameworks. Very little can be done in the short term to improve the functioning of the interest rate channel. In the long term, however, the available policy options could considerably improve the functioning of the banking sector, improving both competition and market infrastructure.

This chapter revisits discussions during the Sixth Seminar on Monetary Transmission Channels, Liquidity Conditions, and Determinants of Inflation, a regional central banking seminar cohosted by the Bank of England's Centre for Central Banking Studies and the Pacific Financial Technical Assistance Centre. The chapter focuses on issues of excess liquidity and limited interest rate pass-through in Pacific island economies.

It does not provide a complete summary, but highlights selected points that help to better understand the role of these factors for the monetary transmission mechanism in the Pacific island economies. The focus is on the aftermath of the global financial crisis when the transmission mechanism was perceived to be weak, with excess liquidity and limited interest rate pass-through seen as signs of this weakness. The chapter seeks to recapitulate the discussion in an informal manner, adding literature references where needed for depth, especially with respect to interest rate pass-through.

EXCESS LIQUIDITY

Defining Excess Liquidity

Commercial bank reserves held with the central bank can be decomposed into required reserves and free reserves.[1] Central banks typically require commercial banks to hold a portion of their deposit liabilities with them for monetary policy purposes. These required reserves are sometimes, but not always, remunerated. Free reserves are the remaining reserves held by commercial banks with the central bank that do not contribute to fulfilling reserve requirements. In other words, they constitute the difference between total and required reserves.

Free reserves can be decomposed further into voluntary reserve holdings to meet a bank's liquidity requirements and excess reserves.[2] Voluntary reserves are additional reserves that commercial

This chapter is based on discussions at and subsequent to the Sixth Seminar on Monetary Transmission Channels, Liquidity Conditions, and Determinants of Inflation held at Honiara, Solomon Islands, July 18–23, 2012. Given the informal nature of the seminar, no specific attributions are made, but the central contribution of Garreth Rule (Bank of England's Centre for Central Banking Studies) should nevertheless be highlighted. Thanks are also due to Ole Rummel (Centre for Central Banking Studies), Adam Gorajek (National Reserve Bank of Tonga), and John Vaught (Pacific Financial Technical Assistance Centre financial sector supervision advisor at the time of the seminar) for their valuable contributions.

[1]The discussion draws on Rule (2012a).

[2]The following discussion is based on Rule (2012b).

banks hold for precautionary motives; the demand for voluntary reserves arises from a desire to self-insure and can vary depending on the uncertainty of payment flows. Reserves in general are a highly liquid and safe asset, and the lack of financial investment instruments in the Pacific island economies can imply that banks may be holding reserves voluntarily, simply due to the lack of other liquid and safe investment opportunities that are readily convertible into cash without undue loss. From a monetary policy viewpoint, an increase in voluntary reserve holdings is not problematic as such (even though it could signal a rise in uncertainty). But monetary policy tends to be concerned about the level of excess reserves; that is, reserves that are likely to be in excess of what banks are holding voluntarily. The rest of this section reviews the extent to which excess liquidity is present in selected Pacific countries and what it implies for the monetary policy stance and transmission mechanism.

Measuring Excess Liquidity

Liquidity has risen significantly in the Pacific islands since the global economic crisis. Table 14.1 shows significant increases in liquidity since 2008 in countries with data on liquidity indicators. In 2013 banks in Fiji, Papua New Guinea, the Solomon Islands, and Tonga were holding reserves significantly above the regulatory level, and most held high proportions of their assets in liquid form.

The extent to which there is clear evidence of excess liquidity differs across countries. As already noted, identifying excess liquidity requires attention to prudential as well as monetary policy considerations. The appropriate level of voluntary reserves depends on the level of risk, the predictability of deposit withdrawals, and the ease of liquidating nonreserve assets. As many recent papers note, the situation in Pacific financial markets suggests that, on most of these dimensions, banks should aim to hold voluntary reserves well in excess of required levels. The exact margin required, however, is hard to quantify as it depends in part on the perception of risk and the risk aversion of individual banks. With that in mind, the following provides an initial assessment of the presence of excess reserves for the four countries (Table 14.1):

- In Papua New Guinea, loan-to-deposit ratios were low, indicating plenty of room to expand lending from a supervisory perspective. However, banks did not hold a large proportion of their nonlending assets in central bank reserves as they invested them in securities, largely central bank and Treasury bills, which are not marketable. Free reserves were about 30 percent above the level of required reserves, and overall liquid assets were about 20 percent of deposits and short-term liabilities. This was at the low end of what would be expected given market conditions in Papua New Guinea.
- In Fiji, the loan-to-deposit ratio, the highest in the region on average during 2009–13, is at a comfortable level from a supervisory perspective, but significant increases in the ratio would require close prudential attention. Banks hold most of their nonlending assets as reserves and thus have adequate liquidity to manage short-term liabilities and shocks. But such liquidity does not appear excessive.
- In 2013, the loan-to-deposit ratio in Tonga was higher than the ratio in Fiji, Papua New Guinea, and the Solomon Islands, and only slightly below that of Fiji on average during 2009–13. Banks held significant levels of free reserves with the National Reserve Bank of Tonga and had more than adequate liquidity to manage short-term liabilities. However, given the continued high level of nonperforming loans in Tonga, supervisors would expect banks to hold higher-than-normal ratios of liquid assets, and any sharp decreases in liquidity ratios or increase in lending volume should be monitored closely.
- In the Solomon Islands, loan-to-deposit ratios are low, and banks hold large amounts of free reserves with the Central Bank of Solomon Islands. Liquidity is well above that needed to manage short-term liabilities, and so there is plenty of room to expand lending from a supervisory perspective.

Excess Liquidity and the Monetary Policy Stance

Interest rate issues arise when excess liquidity leads to an undesired easing of the monetary policy stance. This has been the situation in Papua New Guinea, where the interest rate on central bank

TABLE 14.1

Liquidity Indicators for Selected Pacific Islands 2005–13 (*Percent*)

	2005	2006	2007	2008	2009	2010	2011	2012	2013
Liquid-Assets-to-Total-Deposits Ratio[1]									
Fiji	17	15	22	16	22	25	28	28	27
Papua New Guinea	76	76	78	70	73	71	75	71	71
Solomon Islands	48	36	21	22	35	56	60	77	74
Tonga	21	23	24	24	28	34	44	50	54
Liquid-Assets-to-Short-Term Liabilities Ratio[1]									
Fiji	21	19	25	20	28	32	39	38	39
Papua New Guinea	26	16	18	15	18	19	20	...	...
Solomon Islands	...	...	...	...	...	73	87	80	80
Tonga	...	...	...	...	...	...	...	...	...
Loan-to-Deposit Ratio									
Fiji	77	82	75	87	82	85	76	77	75
Papua New Guinea	38	37	36	46	47	50	46	47	50
Solomon Islands	49	59	80	97	74	58	49	44	43
Tonga	97	95	96	94	79	75	68	71	76
Liquid-Assets-to-Total-Assets Ratio									
Fiji	15	13	19	14	18	20	24	24	23
Papua New Guinea	63	64	65	58	58	57	59	57	55
Solomon Islands	39	30	17	16	27	43	45	61	59
Tonga	16	18	18	18	23	26	34	36	31
Liquid-Assets-to-Required-Reserves Ratio									
Fiji	365	230	375	282	350	265	297	281	282
Papua New Guinea	750	848	829	520	646	553	628	579	480
Solomon Islands	645	488	278	297	472	767	824	838	1,062
Tonga	173	223	289	285	655	763	952	962	979
Free-Reserves-to-Required-Reserves Ratio									
Fiji	60	54	171	29	130	104	132	122	120
Papua New Guinea	171	125	50	153	119	58	82	54	27
Solomon Islands	1,963	984	258	117	809	3,443	4,036	4,360	554
Tonga	9	30	84	43	358	442	629	771	790

Sources: Central bank prudential data; and IMF, Pacific Financial Technical Assistance Center.
[1] Liquid assets exclude nonmarketable securities.

bills has declined since around mid-2011, even though the Bank of Papua New Guinea preferred a tightening in its monetary policy stance, as indicated by subsequent increases in the Kina Facility Rate. This situation arises because of large foreign exchange inflows—in the case of Papua New Guinea, due to the commodity boom and foreign direct investment inflows to the mining and petroleum sectors—that lead to a substantial increase in liquidity unless they are fully sterilized. When the Bank of Papua New Guinea scaled back the volume of sterilization around mid-2011 (not least because of the sizable fiscal costs of these operations), this led to a sizable increase in commercial bank reserves with the central bank. The increase probably corresponded to a buildup of excess liquidity and a bidding down of rates on central bank bills as banks tried to invest at least part of their reserves in these instruments. The result was, in effect, an easing of the monetary policy stance.

In other countries in the Pacific, central banks desire a loose monetary policy stance, but perceive the presence of excess liquidity as a sign that monetary policy is ineffective because it does not lead to the desired increase in lending, which would absorb excess liquidity. In short, the conclusions are as follows:

- The underlying concern that the monetary policy transmission mechanism is weak or ineffective is well founded. However, the main culprit is not excess liquidity in itself but a weak interest rate transmission channel that largely reflects structural characteristics of financial markets in the Pacific—for example, the absence of institutions such as credit bureaus that facilitate bank lending, and the small size of these markets.
- The notion that excess liquidity would be eliminated if banks increased lending is true (and intuitive) for individual banks, but much less likely to be operative at the systemic level. The issue is that an increase in lending by one bank tends to create deposits—and therefore reserves—at another. This suggests that the level of excess reserves does not constitute a reliable summary statistic of whether monetary policy is effective. Lending volumes and interest rates are better indicators for this purpose.

The Role of Excess Liquidity in Monetary Policy Transmission

The clearest case for a strong role of liquidity emerges when banks are liquidity constrained. Injecting liquidity in such a situation will affect lending substantially by easing liquidity constraints. However, the institutional setup of monetary policy operations in advanced economies such as the United Kingdom or the United States ensures that such a situation practically never arises. That is, if banks are reluctant to lend in these countries it is not because they are liquidity constrained, but because the risk-adjusted return on lending is not high enough compared to the risk-adjusted return on other investments (including simply holding reserves). A different institutional setup in the Pacific could imply that banks may at times be liquidity constrained, and the absence of liquid interbank markets is a factor here. But it is safe to say that this is not the case when central banks are concerned with excess liquidity. Clearly, the current issue is that banks do not lend out their excess liquidity and not because they might be liquidity constrained.

Taking as a starting point a situation in which banks are not liquidity constrained, what effect would the injection of liquidity have? First, if it is meant to accomplish a monetary easing, it would need to create excess liquidity. This is because if banks were to hold on voluntarily to the extra liquidity, the macroeconomic effects of the injection are likely to be negligible. Next, assuming that the injection of liquidity creates excess liquidity, the key steps of the transmission mechanism are:

- *Open market operations*—For simplicity, it is assumed that the central bank injects liquidity via an open market operation; that is, it purchases central bank bills or short-term government securities from market participants. This operation simultaneously injects liquidity and lowers the interest rate on these instruments, which is the hallmark of a successful monetary easing.
- *Reducing the interest rate on short-term securities*—This means that these instruments have become less attractive compared to longer-term securities or lending activities (provided that the relative riskiness of these investments has not changed). Moreover, assuming that excess reserves are not remunerated, banks would now be less motivated to hold more reserves that earn them no return. Both factors give banks more incentive to invest in longer-term securities and expand lending.
- *Reducing the lending rate*—Assuming a competitive lending market with little friction (for example, banks are well able to judge the creditworthiness of their potential customers), expanding lending will require a reduction in lending rates. Hence, lending volumes should increase and lending rates decline.

The transmission mechanism just outlined corresponds to a standard interest rate transmission channel in which the injection of liquidity leads to a decline in interest rates across maturities and activities and stimulates lending. There are three points to note when applying this transmission mechanism to the Pacific island economies and specifically to the question of the implications of excess reserves at the systemwide level:

- *An increase in lending will not necessarily absorb all excess liquidity*—As Garreth Rule noted: "For the system as a whole the quantity of reserves is determined by the balance sheet of the central bank. This means that once reserves are in the system there are few places for them to go. Some could seep into cash in circulation or into government balances. But, if a bank buys an asset (even in foreign currency) or makes a loan then reserves will return to the central bank at another bank" (Rule 2012a, 15). Hence, the existence of excess reserves at the systemwide level does not necessarily imply that the monetary transmission mechanism has been ineffective; rather, changes in lending volumes and interest rates are much more relevant here.
- *The transmission mechanism hinges crucially on the assumption of a competitive lending market with little friction*—This is key for interest rate pass-through and for a related rise in lending volumes. However, this assumption may not fully apply to the Pacific, as discussed later. In a nutshell this is because of a low level of competition, high costs of screening customers and loan proposals to identify bankable projects, and the use of lending as a gateway to other profitable banking activities such as foreign exchange trading, under certain circumstances, limiting interest rate pass-through. As a result, lending volumes may not increase by much in response to a monetary easing.
- *Effective interest rate transmission in advanced economies is supported by a number of channels that are mostly absent in the Pacific*—Specifically, in advanced economies deep financial markets ensure that short-term interest rates under the control of the central bank have influence over a wide range of interest rates, especially long-term rates. Key elements of the transmission mechanism are expectations over the future path of short-term interest rates—that is, expectations regarding the future monetary policy stance—as well as term and risk premiums. This is an important part of the interest rate channel given that long-term interest rates should be more important for investment, durable consumption, and housing decisions, which are highly interest rate sensitive. In Pacific island economies, underdeveloped financial markets imply that this part of the interest rate channel is likely to be very weak. Likewise, in advanced economies the interest rate channel is reinforced by the effect of interest rates on asset prices, which leads to the asset price channel. In what is known as the balance sheet channel, asset prices also affect the value of collateral and the balance sheet of households and companies more generally, which affects their access to loans. Both channels are likely to be weak in the Pacific islands.

Another question is the source of excess reserves in recent years. A key factor is probably the negative effect of the global financial crisis on aggregate demand due to declining export earnings and general uncertainty about economic prospects. The reduction in aggregate demand would have lowered import demand sufficiently to lead to a buildup of foreign exchange, which did indeed happen in the region. Central banks chose for the most part not to sterilize the foreign exchange buildup—probably in the hope of easing the monetary policy stance and stimulating lending, which would account for the rise in excess reserves. The effect on lending was probably quite limited owing to the weaknesses in the transmission mechanism already outlined, and generally soft demand conditions.

The upshot of this discussion is that concerns about the effectiveness of the monetary transmission mechanism are well justified, but the issue is mainly the interest rate channel. Given the importance of bank lending as the main transmission mechanism, the next section takes a closer look at interest rate pass-through in the banking sector. The other main result is that the existence of excess liquidity in itself is not sufficient to show that monetary policy has been ineffective. To the extent that excess reserves were built up in the few years following the global financial crisis, these can likely be attributed to a rise in foreign exchange inflows that were not sterilized by the central bank. The increase in excess reserves probably did not stimulate lending much but, even if it had, this would have been only a secondary factor for the systemwide level of excess reserves, which is ultimately controlled by central banks and not by the lending decisions of banks.

INTEREST RATE PASS-THROUGH IN THE PACIFIC

The market for the supply and demand of credit is not like a "normal" market in which a large number of firms (banks) intermediate this supply and demand, and low barriers for the entry and exit for firms ensure a high degree of competition. If this were the case, the pass-through of changes in the cost of funds should be immediate and complete. But banking is not a market with low barriers for entry and exit: banking requires trust, because savers need to trust banks to return savings they deposit, and trust is not easily acquired. For the same reason regulatory barriers for entry and exit are high. Hence, competition in the banking sector is limited.

Another characteristic of banking is that financial intermediation is inherently plagued by credit market frictions such as asymmetric information problems and costly contract enforcement. These make lending a costly activity and justify the existence of banks in the first place (Mishra, Montiel, and Spilimbergo 2010). Both factors—limited competition and credit market frictions—tend to reduce interest rate pass-through, and this section looks at the underlying channels.

Limited Competition

Limited competition in the banking sector has an impact on markups, the degree of pass-through, and, in conjunction with adjustment costs, it can make interest rates sticky. We now take a closer look at these impacts:

- *Markup*—Imperfect competition in the banking sector implies that individual banks have market power in both the lending and deposit markets. This implies that banks set lending rates as a markup over the marginal cost of loanable funds given by the forgone return on government securities plus marginal intermediation costs. The less competitive the banking sector, the higher the markup (Mishra, Montiel, and Spilimbergo 2010).
- *Pass-through*—In a world of perfect competition with complete information, price equals marginal cost and pass-through is immediate; that is, prices adjust instantly and fully to changes in marginal costs.[3] As the degree of competition decreases—and leaving aside for the moment the possibility of collusion—the degree of pass-through tends to diminish. For example, for a monopolist facing a linear demand curve, only half of the change in marginal costs is passed through to prices. However, the degree of pass-through does not necessarily decline with the degree of competition; instead, this depends on the functional form of the demand curve.[4] Limited competition by itself will not affect the timing of pass-through—that is, to the extent that pass-through occurs—as this is instantaneous. For interest rates to become sticky, another ingredient is needed in the form of adjustment costs.
- *Adjustment costs*—Similar to the introduction of sticky prices in New Keynesian macroeconomic models,[5] for lending rates to be sticky it is necessary to combine a limited degree of competition with fixed adjustment costs of changing lending rates (Cottarelli and Kourelis 1994). The latter, for instance, could take the form of costs of printing promotional materials to reflect new lending rates, costs of adjustments to the information technology systems, and

[3]This discussion draws on Lowe and Rohling (1992).
[4]For a detailed discussion, see Cottarelli and Kourelis (1994).
[5]These stem from the assumption of monopolistic competition combined with so-called menu costs that represent price adjustment costs.

> changing loan manuals. These adjustment costs matter if, for example, the cost of funding falls due to an easing in the monetary policy stance. In this case, banks have to determine whether incurring the adjustment costs of lowering lending rates to pass through lower costs to customers outweighs the cost of not doing so—and therefore risk losing customers, as banks that lower their lending rates gain a price advantage. Lending rates will generally be sticky if banks find it optimal in the presence of adjustment costs to keep lending rates unchanged.

A key factor for the stickiness is the elasticity of loan demand with respect to lending rates. Low elasticity implies that customers are less likely to leave a bank in response to better lending rates on offer elsewhere; in other words, loan customers are relatively insensitive to the lending rates on offer when the loan-demand elasticity is low. In this case, banks have little incentive to reduce lending rates to pass through lower costs of funding after an easing of the monetary policy stance because they run little risk that their customers will go elsewhere. This raises the question of under what circumstances the loan-demand elasticity is low, leaving loan customers insensitive to lending rates. A major factor is a lack of choice: customers may be forced to stick with a bank that does not pass through lower funding costs if they have few alternatives to turn to. Lack of choice is likely to arise from limited competition—there are not many banks to choose from—and from underdeveloped financial markets that offer few alternatives to bank loans as a source of funding. In both situations, lending rates are likely to be sticky.

Short-term elasticities are likely to be lower than long-term elasticities. This is because in the long term it may be possible to access alternative forms of financing such as bond or equity issuance. Hence, lending rates are more likely to be sticky in the short rather than in the long run. Cottarelli and Kourelis (1994, 6) summarize this situation as follows: "The demand for loans of each bank will indeed be less elastic in markets with fewer competitors, barriers to entry, or in the absence of sources of finance alternative to bank loans (e.g., other financial intermediaries, foreign capital markets, commercial paper or bankers' acceptances markets). In these markets lending rates may show a limited response to changes in money market rates."

The discussion so far has abstracted from the possibility of collusion. In oligopolistic markets, price stickiness may emerge because maintaining collusion is more difficult when prices change frequently; hence, the colluding banks would tend to keep lending and deposit rates stable (Cottarelli and Kourelis 1994). It should be noted, however, that there is not necessarily a monotonic link between the degree of stickiness and the concentration of the banking sector. What matters is whether oligopolistic collusion arises or not, which can be the case for different degrees of concentration in the banking market. That said, the small number of players in the Pacific banking market may indeed make it easier to maintain an effective degree of collusion. The rapid increase in private sector credit following the entry of BRED Bank shows how a new entry can shake up the market and further its development. Finally, collusion could lead to an asymmetric pass-through in the sense that colluding banks are more likely to pass through an increase in funding costs than a reduction.

A related issue to monopolistic behavior of banks is the presence of switching costs.[6] For customers, switching costs come in the form of, for example, costs related to learning about lending rates and conditions at other banks and the paperwork for new loan applications. For banks, switching costs are incurred when they screen new customers. The effect of these switching costs is to segment the market, making it possible for banks to act as quasi-monopolists toward the customers they already have. Given that monopolistic practices can lower the degree of interest rate pass-through, this is a possible side effect of switching costs.

The factors discussed here are especially relevant for the Pacific island economies. Being small inherently limits the size of their banking sector. Besides favoring collusion, the small number of banks operating in these economies tends to lower the elasticities for loan demand, making it more

[6]This discussion draws on Lowe and Rohling (1992).

likely that sticky lending rates are an optimal business strategy. A contributing factor is that underdeveloped financial markets mean there are few alternatives to bank loans. Switching costs are another factor relevant for the Pacific because the absence of credit bureaus and limited use of financial tools such as credit cards and bank accounts imply that it is difficult for banks to screen new customers who may not have an extensive financial history that can be easily tracked. Hence, for many customers it may not be easy to obtain loans from other banks, which hardens the quasi-monopolistic behavior of their current bank.

Credit Market Frictions

Asymmetric Information

Asymmetric information in the context of bank lending means that a bank knows less about the projects it has been asked to finance than borrowers do. Specifically, it does not know how risky these projects are. If a bank-financed project fails, the borrower is likely to default, leading to losses for the bank. Charging a high interest rate to compensate for this risk can be a self-defeating strategy: potential borrowers with safe projects that have a relatively low rate of return will withdraw from the market, leaving only those with high-risk projects (adverse selection). Alternatively, borrowers that obtained loans for a relatively safe project may use the money to pursue riskier projects with a higher rate of return instead (moral hazard). In either case, the bank ends up financing a high-risk project instead of the low-risk one it would rather finance. To avoid this, banks can pursue an alternative strategy that Lowe and Rohling (1992, 4) summarize as follows: "Faced with this situation, the bank will elect not to increase its lending rate even if its cost of funds increase. In such an equilibrium, the bank will set the loan rate below the market clearing rate and ration credit. The interest rate will exhibit upward stickiness."

Major banks operating in most countries tend to be foreign owned, which means their lending rates need to incorporate country risk premiums set by their headquarters. As a result, there is likely to be a lower bound for how much lending rates can fall, making them both upwardly and downwardly sticky.

Critically, credit rationing implies that setting the lending rate and the loan amount are two different decisions. With the lending rate set low enough to make safe but low-return projects viable, there will also be a large number of high-risk projects seeking loans at this rate. Banks will decline to extend loans to high-risk projects to the extent they can identify them, which implies that the decision on whether to finance a project and how much to lend is indeed separate from the interest rate decision. To be able to discriminate against high-risk projects, banks need instruments other than the interest rate; these will likely include an extensive screening of borrowers and collateral requirements as well as limiting bank exposure by requiring borrowers to put equity into their projects.

The need to screen borrowers suggests that the problem of asymmetric information is likely to be more acute in the Pacific than in advanced economies because the necessary instruments, such as credit histories and credit scores, are less available. Hence, it is more difficult (and costly) for banks in the Pacific to determine whether potential borrowers have a track record of implementing low-risk projects and living up to their loan obligations. Other potential remedies such as collateral requirements are hampered by an absence of suitable collateral and asset registries, and costly enforcement of collateral claims. As a result, the strategy outlined of charging relatively low lending rates compared to the risk environment, while rationing credit, is likely to be more prevalent in the Pacific than in advanced economies. This has a number of policy implications:

- Interest rate pass-through is likely to be limited. This is shown formally in Mishra, Montiel, and Spilimbergo (2010), where the pass-through coefficient is a decreasing function of the slope of the marginal intermediation-cost curve. As they explain: "What this means is that if a deficient institutional environment causes problems of asymmetric information and costly contract enforcement to generate a steeply rising cost of financial intermediation when banks try to expand their lending, banks are less likely to adjust their lending rates in response to changes in the central bank's policy rate" (Mishra, Montiel, and Spilimbergo 2010, 21).

- Even if the central bank manages through moral suasion, for example, to lower lending rates, this is unlikely to affect the volume of lending, because the latter is a separate decision. Hence, relatively little is gained from solely lowering lending rates from the viewpoint of providing a monetary stimulus to the economy.
- In advanced economies, a lowering of policy interest rates tends to boost asset prices and therefore raises the value of collateral and equity, which in turn facilitates bank lending. This is the balance sheet channel already mentioned that reinforces the interest rate channel. In principle, collateral and equity could be especially important for bank lending in the Pacific because these are among the few instruments banks potentially have to discriminate against high-risk projects. Hence, a balance sheet channel could have important effects in the Pacific on the volume of lending, but unfortunately it is likely to be weak, if it exists at all, because of the region's underdeveloped financial markets.

Relationship Banking

Building a close relationship with customers is a way for banks to overcome the asymmetric information problem. This may give rise to an implicit contract where banks with close ties to their customers offer relatively stable retail interest rates to insulate customers from volatile market rates (Kwapil and Scharler 2006). For risk-averse customers, such interest rate smoothing provides a valuable insurance service, and banks might be willing to provide this if they can charge a higher average rate or see the lending business as a way to open doors to other business transactions.[7] In a literature survey for the euro area, where relationship banking is common, Kwapil and Scharler (2006) find that the immediate pass-through from money market rates to retail interest rates is only 0.55 and the long-run pass-through remains mostly below 1. They interpret these results as indicating that banks indeed insulate their customers from volatile money market rates by absorbing part of the changes in money market rates. For the United States, where banking plays a less central role in financial intermediation than in the euro area, they find that interest rate pass-through is higher and mostly complete in the long term.

The Pacific has much more in common with the euro area than the United States in terms of the importance of banking for financial intermediation. With banks in the Pacific dominating financial intermediation, it also makes sense for them to build up close relationships with their customers to overcome the asymmetric information problem. Indeed, doing so may be their best option, given the relative dearth of other tools such as the availability of credit scores or easily enforceable collateral claims. The opportunity to cross-sell other products, especially foreign exchange services, provides banks in the Pacific with another incentive to smooth interest rates to preserve customer relationships.

CONCLUSION

The concern with excess liquidity significantly reflects a frustration with ineffective monetary policy transmission mechanisms. This chapter shows that the issue is not excess liquidity in itself, but a weak interest rate channel. Before discussing policy implications, it is useful to outline conditions in the aftermath of the global financial crisis as background:

- The crisis damaged the balance sheets of many international banks, and this typically leads to a curtailment of lending until capital is rebuilt. To the extent that this affected banks operating in the Pacific (ANZ and Westpac, for example), this would have dampened lending activity in the years following the crisis because rebuilding balance sheets often takes considerable time. Businesses and private households that borrowed heavily during the boom years may also need to repair their balance sheets and will curtail borrowing in the interim.

[7] For the risk-sharing argument, see Lowe and Rohling (1992).

- Banks became considerably more risk averse following the global financial crisis and tightened lending standards. This change in attitude is likely to have affected all banks operating in the Pacific. For international banks such as ANZ and Westpac it is possible that their headquarters imposed higher country and lending risk premiums on their Pacific operations in the period following the crisis.
- The global financial crisis led to a reduction in demand and left the economic outlook clouded for years as elements of the crisis such as the European debt situation had not yet been resolved. This reduces private sector demand for credit and raises lending risk.

In sum, without central bank intervention, these factors combine into a tightening of credit conditions, driven both by the supply and demand side. The task for monetary policy is to offset these factors by easing the monetary policy stance; that is, a reduction in policy interest rates. As discussed, central banks in advanced economies can draw on mechanisms such as the asset and bank lending channels to reinforce the effect of lower interest rates. In the Pacific, however, central banks have to rely on the interest rate channel alone without these "boosters." In addition, the degree of interest rate pass-through is likely to be limited, leaving monetary policy potentially ineffective. And some central banks in the Pacific have also reached the "lower-zero-bound" constraint for policy interest rates that is also hampering advanced economies.

For central banks in the Pacific, a higher degree of interest rate pass-through in the current situation would be desirable to make the monetary transmission mechanism more effective. The type of policy measures—if any—for achieving this will depend on the source of lending rate stickiness and will be affected by:

- *Monopolistic behavior of banks*—This chapter has shown that sticky interest rates can emerge naturally from the monopolistic behavior of banks even without collusion, especially if loan demand elasticities are low. If this is the main source of sticky lending rates, the introduction of more competition and regulatory interventions that mitigate monopolistic behavior are the most obvious policy responses, even though these would take effect only over the long term. But is monopolistic behavior really the main source of sticky lending rates? If so, one would expect bank lending to be a profitable business, but Chapter 18 shows that lending operations in the Pacific although profitable are not extraordinarily so. Another argument is that the downward stickiness of lending rates in the aftermath of the global financial crisis reflects collusion. It is, however, also possible that lending rates did not decline by much in the years immediately following the crisis because of higher country and lending risk premiums, and the setting of low lending rates during normal times to avoid adverse selection and moral hazard problems. In both cases, lending rates could not significantly decline because they were already close to their lower bound. Hence, it is by no means clear that the stickiness of lending rates in recent years reflected "untoward" behavior of banks either in the form of collusion or monopolistic behavior.
- *Asymmetric information*—From a policy perspective, stickiness of lending rates that stems from asymmetric information has two implications. First, as noted, lending rates may have reached their lower bound already as they were set low to begin with. A further reduction in lending rates would only be possible if risk premiums decline, but this is outside the control of central banks. Second, even if it were possible to lower lending rates through administrative measures or moral suasion, this would not increase the amount of lending because setting interest rates and determining the amount of lending are two separate decisions. The only promising policy intervention is to improve the functioning of the banking sector by making it easier to expand lending through lowering the cost for screening borrowers. That is, the asymmetric information problem itself needs to be addressed through the introduction of credit bureaus and other institutions that facilitate bank lending. Obviously, this can be successful only in the long term, but it would have benefits that go well beyond improving the effectiveness of the interest rate channel by making the advantages of financial intermediation available to a larger part of the population.

- *Relationship banking*—The implications here are similar to those for asymmetric information in that lowering lending rates through administrative measures or moral suasion would not necessarily achieve an increase in the amount of lending. Lower "headline" lending rates achieved by such an intervention would not automatically benefit customers that are in a close relationship with their banks. This is because they would not expect to benefit from the best rates during periods of low interest rates, just as they would not expect to be charged the highest rates during other times. The policy options in this case are very limited.

The bottom line is that there is very little that can be done in the short term to improve the functioning of the interest rate channel in Pacific island economies. However, in the long term, policy options are available to improve considerably the functioning of the banking sector, especially if it is currently hampered by monopolistic behavior or asymmetric information.

REFERENCES

Cottarelli, Carlo, and Angeliki Kourelis. 1994. "Financial Structure, Bank Lending Rates, and the Transmission Mechanism of Monetary Policy." IMF Working Paper 94/39, International Monetary Fund, Washington.

Kwapil, Claudia, and Johann Scharler. 2006. "Limited Pass-Through from Policy to Retail Interest Rates: Empirical Evidence and Macroeconomic Implications." *Monetary Policy & the Economy*, Quarter 4: 26–36.

Lowe, Philip, and Thomas Rohling. 1992. "Loan Rate Stickiness: Theory and Evidence." Research Discussion Paper 9206, Reserve Bank of Australia, Sydney.

Mishra, Prachi, Peter J. Montiel, and Antonio Spilimbergo. 2010. "Monetary Transmission in Low Income Countries." IMF Working Paper 10/223, International Monetary Fund, Washington.

Rule, Garreth. 2012a. "Introduction to the Central Bank's Balance Sheet." CCBS-PFTAC course on Monetary Transmission Channels, Liquidity Conditions, and Determinants of Inflation, Bank of England, London.

———. 2012b. "The Impact of Surplus Liquidity." CCBS-PFTAC Course on Monetary Transmission Channels, Liquidity Conditions, and Determinants of Inflation, Bank of England, London.

PART IV

Removing Structural Impediments to Growth

CHAPTER 15

Planning Public Financial Management Reforms in Pacific Island Countries

TOBIAS HAQUE, RICHARD BONTJER, MARY BETLEY, AND RON HACKETT

Weaknesses in public financial management (PFM) compound economic vulnerabilities in many Pacific island countries (PICs). These countries face challenges in small domestic markets, high transport costs, and exposure to a wide range of shocks such as natural disasters and volatility in the terms of trade. Yet their weak PFM systems—and government processes for raising public revenues, implementing macroeconomic policy, and ensuring the efficiency and effectiveness of spending programs—often limit their abilities to respond effectively. Accordingly, many PICs are prioritizing PFM reforms to build revenue bases, better align government spending programs and social and economic objectives, and bolster resilience to economic volatility and natural disasters.

PFM reforms face unique constraints in PICs. In addition to the challenges larger countries face in implementing PFM reforms, most PICs must also grapple with the constraints particular to small populations (Haque, Knight, and Jayasuriya 2012). With limited human resources, civil servants, and secondary and tertiary educational institutions crucial to development, PIC labor markets often lack the skills for some specialized PFM functions. Frequently, there are simply too few people to complete all of the functions required in a full PFM system, with available staff stretched across a wide range of functions. PIC public sectors also face strong competition for human resources from the local private sector, donors, and nongovernment organizations, both locally and overseas. Capacity building is often disrupted, as staff with newly acquired skills and qualifications move to new roles in and outside of the public service.

Capacity constraints have not always been adequately reflected in the design of PFM reforms in the Pacific. It is common practice to develop PFM reform plans or "road maps" based on the weaknesses identified in standardized assessments of PFM systems under the Public Expenditure and Financial Accountability (PEFA) framework, rather than setting priorities for reform.[1] It is therefore important that PICs identify these objectives when a PEFA assessment lists more PFM weaknesses than they can realistically address. Broad and ambitious reforms often not only provide ineffective support for sustainably improved PFM performance, but can actually harm PFM systems by diverting scarce capacity away from areas that are more important for service delivery and macroeconomic stability.

PFM reform needs to fit Pacific realities. This chapter suggests ways reforms can do so and better match the development priorities of PICs. Taking account of the inevitable resource and capacity constraints in these countries, there should be an emphasis on:

- *Tight prioritization of reforms*—Capacity constraints mean that PICs cannot implement all of the functions assessed under the PEFA framework or expected of PFM systems in larger countries. PICs therefore need to target available capacity to improve PFM functions that are likely to have the greatest development impact, even if this means poor PEFA scores in lower priority areas.

This chapter is adapted from a guidance note prepared by a joint World Bank and IMF/Pacific Financial Technical Assistance Centre team.

[1]The PEFA assessment has become a standard mechanism for assessing the quality of PFM systems globally and in the region.

- *"Good enough" rather than "best practice" solutions*—In specific priority areas for individual PICs, establishing processes that achieve goals and address key risks is more important than implementing processes that resemble those used in larger countries. One example of an often repeated failure is the approach tried in some PICs to move toward "outcome budgeting." Sometimes, this has been tried in a rather abstract and remote way from the activities that service-providing departments are conducting on a day-to-day basis. These approaches have often ignored a basic building block of any good approach to budgeting—getting the divisions or units of a ministry or line department to first prepare budget narratives that clearly state what they do, what they think they should do, the issues they face, and how public services will change if their funding request is granted.
- *A broad range of approaches to addressing capacity constraints*—Capacity-building efforts have been the standard solution to capacity constraints in PICs for many years. These approaches have met with uneven success, however, because of high staff rotation, emigration of skilled staff, and fundamental constraints to the number of specialized tasks that a small number of public servants can perform. Alternative approaches to meeting capacity gaps include drawing on regional facilities for capacity supplementation in vital areas, and contracting certain specialized PFM functions to private sector or nongovernment providers. If appropriately designed and implemented, these approaches—in some circumstances—can be more sustainable than attempts to build local capacity.

The rest of this chapter outlines good practice in planning PFM reforms, presents a framework for prioritizing PFM reforms for best possible use of available capacity, and suggests ways PICs can ameliorate capacity constraints. The chapter complements, and is consistent with, extensive previous work by other organizations supporting improved PFM globally and across the Pacific, including the Pacific Financial Technical Assistance Centre, the PEFA Secretariat, the IMF, and the European Commission.[2]

PLANNING PUBLIC FINANCIAL MANAGEMENT REFORMS

There is no single blueprint for designing and implementing PFM reforms. Suitable approaches will vary by country and circumstance. The experience in the Pacific region shows that careful planning of reforms is vital to sustainable gains given the importance of making the best possible use of scarce capacity. Development of "PFM road maps" has emerged as a common approach to planning and sequencing these reforms in PICs, and one regional agencies and PIC governments have endorsed as good practice.

Functions of a Public Financial Management Road Map

PFM road maps are used to convert a PEFA assessment and other analytical inputs into a reform process. They outline a realistic list of specific, prioritized, and sequenced PFM activities to be undertaken over a given period. They identify expected improvements and assign responsibility for undertaking these reforms to specific teams or agencies within government. A good road map will provide a framework for monitoring progress and a tool with which to communicate and build consensus around PFM reform plans.

PEFA assessments, generally undertaken by teams of government officials and donor-financed technical advisors, are often the starting point for PFM reform programs in PICs. But such assessments, alone, do not provide an adequate basis for planning PFM reforms. In particular, the PEFA assessment does not provide information on (1) priorities for PFM reforms, when there may be

[2]See Pacific Islands Forum Secretariat and Pacific Financial Technical Assistance Centre (2010, 2012), Welham, Krause, and Hedger (2013), Diamond (2013a, 2013b), and Tommasi (2012).

many "low" PEFA scores (that is, C, D, or NR [not rated] scores against particular dimensions and indicators); (2) appropriate sequencing of PFM reforms, given that progress in one area of PFM is often dependent on progress in another; (3) specific actions to address underlying causes of PFM weaknesses, including capacity development or supplementation requirements; and (4) limits to the extent of possible reform arising from capacity and resource constraints. Attempting to simultaneously address every low score in a PEFA assessment is unlikely to be feasible, or represent an effective use of scarce resources. Countries need to carefully consider which weaknesses to address, how to address them, and in which order to address them.

Good Practices in Public Financial Management Road Map Development

The process used to develop a PFM reform road map is critical. Experience in PICs has demonstrated the importance of the following factors:

- *Taking account of the political context*—Planning PFM reforms is not just a technical process. Planning PFM reform involves the allocation of resources, work, and responsibility, which may have impacts not in the narrow interests of all parties. Planning PFM reform is therefore, inevitably, political. Plans that do not take account of the interests of key stakeholders are unlikely to be implemented. At all stages, planning processes should take account of potential sources of political opposition, allow space for discussion and debate over reform priorities, and build broad ownership and political support for planned reforms.
- *Allocating sufficient time and resources*—The same capacity constraints that impede PFM systems and reforms can also impede the planning of PFM reforms. Investing the time and effort of available staff in road map development can have high opportunity costs. But such investment is, ultimately, likely to be worthwhile given the potential inefficiency that can arise from a poorly designed PFM reform process. Allocation of adequate time from finance ministry officials is vital, but it is also important to ensure that sufficient staff time is available within other central and line ministries affected or involved in reforms.
- *Government leadership*—A PFM road map is ultimately a government document, although it may also serve some purpose in communicating with donors or external stakeholders. Government resources will be used to implement reforms, and the actions of government employees will determine their success. Government leadership of the PFM road map development process is therefore vital, with government staff both making the required decisions and leading the drafting of the document. While technical assistance can be a useful input to this process, required levels of ownership can only be achieved if officials, in close contact with ministers, lead the process.
- *Ensuring extensive consultation*—Consultation is required with technical staff working in different PFM areas, senior managers overseeing these areas, and representatives at the political level. Consultation with donors, while not always necessary, can help build support for the PFM priorities identified by the government and facilitate the provision of required resources and technical assistance. Civil society organizations and the private sector could also be involved in consultations. While potentially time consuming, this can help build ownership and consensus around the road map and ensure that it incorporates the government's priorities for reform. If external consultants are used to develop a PFM road map, terms of reference should emphasize the need for close coordination with the government to ensure the road map is consistent with government objectives and priorities and well understood by all key government actors.
- *Taking a medium-term focus*—PFM reforms take time to implement. If the time frame for the road map is too short, goals are unlikely to be achievable. But time frames for implementing reforms also need to be short enough to ensure that progress can be regularly assessed to ensure accountability and demonstrate results. In PICs, a time frame of three to four years for the reform action plan is generally appropriate.

Box 15.1. New Approaches to Road Map Development

The Pacific Financial Technical Assistance Centre (PFTAC) in 2012 began changing the legacy approach used to develop road maps. Instead of continuing the earlier practice of allowing them to be prepared just by external consultants, the new approach provided a mentor to teams of officials from the country preparing a road map. The Public Expenditure and Financial Accountability (PEFA) framework's "self-assessment workbooks" were used to ensure that team participants understood the PEFA rating criteria used to evaluate their systems. Participants were then encouraged to discuss public financial management shortcomings identified by their PEFA assessments and prioritize changes that in their view were most critical to their county's development. They were also asked to write the road map themselves to improve ownership. The mentor was available for advice and guidance during the preparation process if needed, but the goal was for country officials to develop their own improvement plan. The process has been successfully implemented in almost all of the countries covered by PFTAC.

- *Building in adequate flexibility*—While planning is important to build political support and achieve efficient resource allocation, PFM priorities will change with broader economic and political circumstances. Building flexibility into plans can be important, particularly when plans span political cycles.

Methodology for Road Map Development

Approaches to developing a PFM road map will vary (Box 15.1). The methodology needs to be tailored to take account of available capacity and resources, existing analysis and background material, political interest, and the role to be played by technical assistance or other external stakeholders. While individual approaches will be country specific, all should lead to an output based on the government's own priorities and be realistic in terms of the resources available.

PRIORITIZING PUBLIC FINANCIAL MANAGEMENT REFORMS

One of the most important functions of a PFM road map is to identify the relative priorities for reform when a PEFA assessment identifies more weaknesses than can realistically be addressed. PFM reforms, especially those involving changes to established processes and systems, are notoriously effort intensive and time-consuming. Limited resources and capacity mean that the scope of achievable reforms will be constrained and prioritization of possible PFM reforms is necessary. Owing to resource constraints, not all areas of the PFM system can be improved at the same time (Box 15.2).

A wide range of factors will inevitably determine the prioritization of PFM reforms. These include political imperatives, the capacities of staff, development partner requirements for budget support or project assistance, and windows of opportunity arising from particular pressures or needs. Prioritization, however, should also be guided by identifying the PFM reforms likely to have the greatest impact. This section can help trace the common elements linking the common PFM challenges that undermine macroeconomic management and service delivery in PICs and the most important reforms for addressing them.

Figure 15.1 shows four such PFM challenges. The following subsections outline a process for determining how to prioritize scarce PFM capacity to address the challenges. In developing a PFM road map, countries can use this process to identify which of the challenges is most relevant to achieving improved development outcomes in their particular country context (Haque and others 2013). From here, countries can identify (1) the PFM reforms that could be prioritized, (2) the specific PEFA dimensions that relate to a particular challenge and might be identified as priorities for improvement, and (3) gaps in the PEFA framework where reform steps may be required to address a particular challenge but are not measured by PEFA assessments.

Box 15.2. Progress in Addressing Public Financial Management Constraints

Many Pacific island countries have acknowledged some of the problems discussed in this chapter and have taken steps to improve public financial management recently. Some of the changes implemented or being started in different Pacific island countries include:

- Redesigning budget documentation to provide a more strategic medium-term focus (Cook Islands, Fiji, Papua New Guinea, Samoa, the Solomon Islands, Tuvalu).
- Using professional procurement agents to supervise government procurement (Nauru).
- Activating commitment control features in financial management information systems and improving financial reporting to line agencies to help them understand and control their spending commitments (Samoa).
- Combining staff from previously separate planning, budgeting, or aid management units into one integrated division and reorganizing staff into sector groups (for example: education, health, and natural resources) with each staff member in the sector groups performing integrated budgeting, planning, and aid management tasks (Kiribati).
- Consolidation of previously separate corporate plans, annual plans, and budget documents into one integrated policy and service focused budget document (Niue, Tonga).
- Integration of previously separate recurrent and development budgets into one unified document (Papua New Guinea).
- Adding a narrative that is focused on medium-term issues to budget documents at the program and activity levels (Fiji).

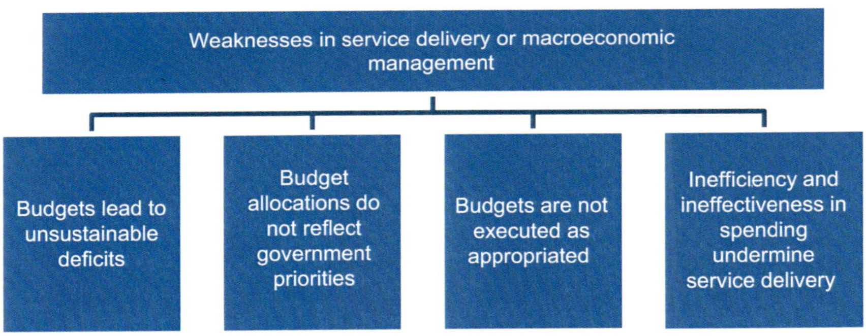

Figure 15.1 Weaknesses in Service Delivery or Macroeconomic Management

This framework is intended to guide prioritization and is not prescriptive. Countries may face public finance challenges not described in this section. In other situations, the solutions suggested here may be impractical or unsuitable. The framework should therefore be applied selectively and carefully. The underlying logic of the approach, however, is generally applicable when developing PFM road maps. Prioritizing PFM capacity to address the challenges most relevant to development outcomes can avoid the risk of overstretching available capacity and maximize the probability of sustainably overcoming them.

Budgets Lead to Unsustainable Deficits

PICs often face problems of macro-fiscal stability, with aggregate expenditure exceeding sustainable levels. Expenditure beyond sustainable levels leads to the accumulation of debt or the depletion of investments, such as sovereign wealth funds. These problems can often be driven by revenue inflows falling short of budgeted levels or expenditure exceeding budgeted levels (Figure 15.2).[3]

[3]We include budget support grants as a source of revenue in this framework, given the importance of such inflows for several PICs.

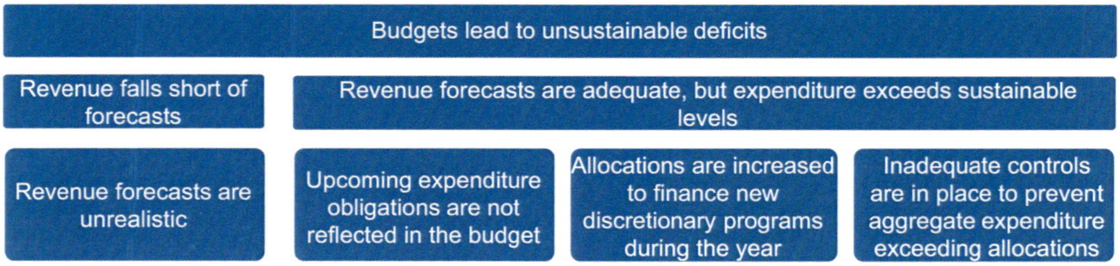

Figure 15.2 Budgets Lead to Unsustainable Deficits

Revenue can fall short of forecasts because:

- *Revenue forecasts are unrealistic*—Revenue projections provide a foundation for budgeting, but budgeting in PICs is often undermined by unrealistic revenue forecasts. If macro-fiscal sustainability is suffering due to unrealistic revenue projections, countries can prioritize improvements in revenue forecasting. Sophisticated modelling is seldom needed to achieve reasonable revenue estimates. Because PIC economies with narrow export bases and high reliance on imports are more vulnerable to economic and other shocks, uncertainty is inevitable, and a conservative approach to revenue forecasting is generally appropriate.

Expenditure may exceed sustainable levels because:

- *Upcoming expenditure obligations are not reflected in the budget*—PIC governments must often deal with nondiscretionary expenditure pressures during the fiscal year. These could sometimes be foreseen if better systems were in place to record expenditure obligations and fiscal risks. Clearly foreseeable costs for utilities and other essential items are sometimes underestimated to comply with expenditure ceilings at the ministry level. Close oversight by the finance ministry and comparison with previous-year spending patterns can help eliminate deliberate underestimation. Furthermore, spending obligations can arise from debt-servicing requirements, the realization of unrecorded contingent liabilities, the need to meet accumulated arrears, failure to consider in advance the needed future costs to operate donor-funded infrastructure projects upon completion, inadequate recognition of the effects of demographic flows, failure by cabinets to request or consider fiscal reviews of policy or project proposals before taking a decision, or the ongoing costs of policy decisions. If macro-fiscal planning is undermined by inadequate allocations for expenditure pressures and obligations, countries can prioritize improvements in systems to record and monitor these pressures and ensure they are reflected in budgets. Genuinely unforeseeable spending pressures can also arise from natural disasters or other shocks. Ensuring adequate contingency allocations in the budget is the most appropriate means of dealing with these risks, but—with inevitably limited resources—in-year reallocation may still be needed in the case of major shocks.
- *Allocations are increased to finance new discretionary programs*—Expenditure pressures can sometimes arise from decisions to fund new, discretionary programs outside of the regular annual budget process. The scope to manage such pressures through PFM reforms is limited. If macroeconomic sustainability is undermined by pressure from new discretionary spending, countries can prioritize systems to ensure that such decisions are made transparently, and that the budget process allows sufficient opportunity for priority programs to be adequately financed during regular annual budget formulation. Training for parliamentarians and cabinet members can augment their understanding of the budgetary process, including their role in setting ceilings and the consequences of approving additional between-budget expenditures.
- *Controls are inadequate to prevent aggregate expenditure exceeding allocations*—Even with good revenue forecasts and systems to record spending obligations, macro-fiscal sustainability in PICs is sometimes undermined simply because governments end up spending more than was

intended. This can occur through inadequate controls on expenditure and commitments and inexact tracking of expenditures during the year. If macro-fiscal sustainability is impaired because aggregate expenditure exceeds allocations, countries can prioritize systems to exert expenditure control. Priorities for reform will depend on whether overspending is driven by payroll or other expenditure. Systems should be improved to address the cause of the overspending. For example, payroll expenditure may exceed limits because of outdated and inaccurate personnel and payroll data or because of the illegitimate alteration of payroll and personnel information during the year. Other spending may exceed limits because commitment rules are inadequate or unclear, or because rules are not complied with.

Budget Allocations Do Not Reflect Government Priorities

Mismatches between government policy objectives and budget allocations often reduce the effectiveness of public expenditure in PICs (Figure 15.3). Ministries' budgets do not reflect what they are expected to deliver during the year, disrupting implementation, and making it more difficult to hold ministries accountable for delivering on policy objectives. Resources are expended in ways that do not align with development goals, slowing development progress. Inadequate planning and failure to take account of plans when budgets are developed are two PFM weaknesses often driving these problems.

Plans may be inadequate to inform budget development because:

- *Plans are not prepared or do not provide a realistic basis for prioritizing resources*—National development strategies, sector strategies, or ministries' corporate plans in PICs are often inconsistently prepared or contain insufficient information to inform or justify the allocation of resources through the budget. Clarity concerning agency deliverables and expected costs is often lacking. Plans often include unrealistic and unaffordable objectives. Where plans cannot inform the allocation of resources, better plans that can guide prioritization under realistic resource constraints are a clear priority. But preparing exhaustive plans with realistic cost estimates at the national, sector, and ministry levels can be a major drain on limited human resources. Instead, line ministries can prepare simple, short written explanations in their annual budget documents relatively easily, outlining the activities to be undertaken, links to national development plans, and trade-offs between activities that would have to be made under different, realistic resource envelopes. These documents can be used to meet both corporate planning and budget process requirements. High-level national strategies with a focus on the country's most significant government sectors can be incorporated into annual medium-term fiscal strategy statements developed prior to, and to inform, annual budgets. Annual corporate plans with a medium-term outlook, however, can and should be developed as part of budget documentation to ensure consistency and integration between budgets and objectives for service delivery. In all cases, it is vital to ensure that planning and budgeting are aligned and consistent, and that plans take account of the availability of resources. Central agencies

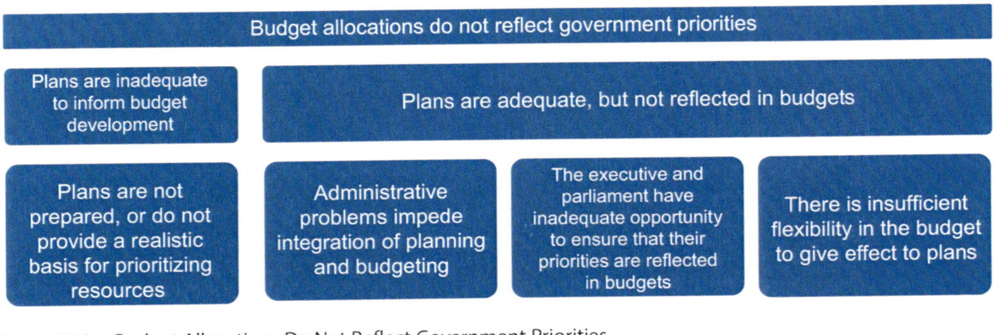

Figure 15.3 Budget Allocations Do Not Reflect Government Priorities

have an important role to play in assisting ministries in the development of plans, including avoiding overlaps and gaps in activities and ensuring affordability within aggregate fiscal resources. This process can be facilitated if the responsibility for planning and budgeting is not separated between different staff members in different teams within central and line agencies.

Even if adequate plans are developed budgets may not reflect plans because:

- *Administrative problems prevent the integration of planning and budgeting*—Budgets and plans are often inconsistent in PICs because different staff at different times prepare documents, with insufficient contact and coordination. Plans and budgets need to be well integrated and should be prepared at the same time by finance ministry staff involved in both processes, closely liaising with line ministries. Institutional divisions between budget and planning divisions in finance ministries are sometimes an important constraint on this integration. The introduction of a single calendar for budgeting and planning processes, improved coordination among staff, joint responsibility for planning and budgeting within the same teams in central and line agencies, and combining budgeting and planning information into single ministry documents can help address these problems.
- *The executive and parliament have insufficient opportunity to ensure budgets reflect government priorities*—In PICs, budget allocations are often weakly linked to development objectives because cabinet and parliament have limited engagement in relevant stages of the budgetary process. Without strong executive and parliamentary involvement, budgeting sometimes becomes a technocratic exercise involving consideration only of the cost of programs and inputs, and not linked to government priorities. Budget preparation and reporting processes can be strengthened to ensure that the cabinet sets budget ceilings, proposes a budget within this framework that reflects policy priorities, and monitors execution throughout the year. Processes can be improved to ensure that parliament has the opportunity to review the proposed budget for how closely it links to policy objectives.
- *Insufficient flexibility in the budget to implement government priorities*—In small PICs, governments are often hindered in carrying out policy priorities through the budget because a large proportion of spending is considered already committed to ongoing activities and programs and meeting payroll or other cost increases. Ensuring that plans list ministry activities and options for changing the mix of these activities within a range of realistic expenditure envelopes would allow the executive to consider prioritization options across all expenditure, rather than focusing on the allocation of often small amounts of marginal additional expenditure during the budget.

Budgets Are Not Executed as Appropriated

The effectiveness of public expenditure in PICs is often reduced by large differences between the planned budget and actual resource use (Figure 15.4). Reallocation of resources leads to disruptions in service

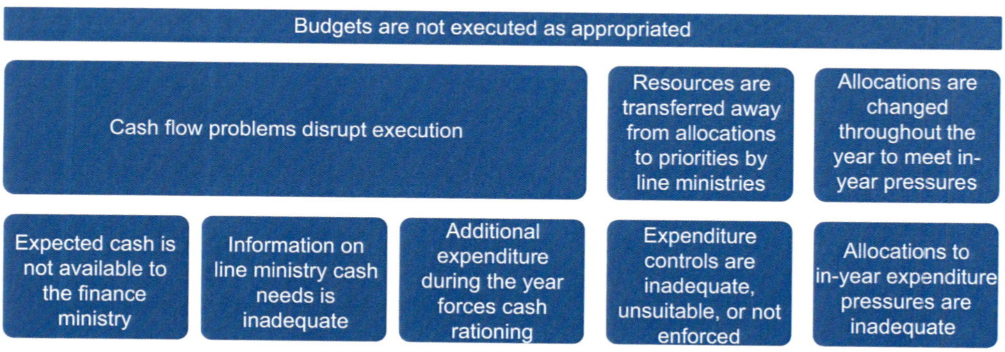

Figure 15.4 Budgets Are Not Executed as Appropriated

delivery. It also impedes the usefulness of the budget as a planning tool and makes it difficult to implement policies and achieve development objectives. PFM weaknesses that often drive these problems include (1) weak cash management systems, (2) the transfer of resources away from allocated areas by line ministries, and (3) changes to expenditure allocations during the year to meet in-year pressures. Cash-flow problems can disrupt execution if:

- *Expected cash is not available to the finance ministry*—Shortages of cash held by Pacific island finance ministries often force cash rationing, which can cause serious disruptions to service delivery. Shortfalls in expected cash to the finance ministry may occur because overall revenue forecasts are inaccurate, inadequate account has been taken of unevenness in revenue receipts throughout the year, expected donor funds have not been forthcoming, or because revenue flows have been disrupted by economic or other shocks. If cash flow problems arise because expected cash is not available to the finance ministry, countries can prioritize improving revenue forecasts—including monthly cash revenue forecasting at the level of revenue items—and building up sufficient cash reserves to deal with external shocks.
- *Information on the cash needs of the line ministry is inadequate or incomplete*—Even if revenue flows to the finance ministry as expected, cash rationing may be necessary because the cash needs of ministries have not been adequately taken into account. This problem often arises because line ministries do not prepare, regularly update, or submit proper cash-flow forecasts to the finance ministry. If cash-flow problems arise from inadequate forecasting of cash needs by spending ministries, countries can prioritize improvements in the processes for (1) preparing annual cash flow disaggregated monthly forecasts (going beyond the common practice of assuming an equal amount of cash is needed in each month of the year) and submitting these to the finance ministry; (2) recording in-year expenditure by line ministries, so that actual cash needs can be monitored; and (3) reviewing cash flow needs throughout the year, and communicating changes to the finance ministry as necessary.
- *Available cash is exhausted because of additional expenditure or changed priorities during the fiscal year*—In some PICs, cash rationing has been required because additional expenditure has been authorized during the fiscal year without regard to available cash. In this situation, countries can prioritize processes to ensure that (1) clear rules and transparent processes exist for new in-year spending (including clear processes and criteria for accessing the contingency fund), (2) funding sources are identified for all new spending proposals, and (3) availability of cash is taken into consideration.

Ministry expenditure may not be aligned with budgeted allocations if:

- *Controls to ensure appropriate spending are inadequate, unsuitable, or not enforced*—Budget execution is undermined in some PICs because there are inadequate controls to ensure that resources are used in ways that align with budgets. In these cases, budget allocations may reflect government priorities, but actual expenditure does not reflect allocations. Large variances between budgeted allocations and actual spending at the level of inputs and functions can disrupt the implementation of government priorities and the usefulness of the budget as a planning tool. Problems can arise because formal controls do not exist, appropriate controls are in place but not enforced, or controls are excessively burdensome or poorly matched to available capacity. If budget execution is weakened by problems with expenditure controls, countries can prioritize the development or revision of expenditure control systems. Reforms should be aimed at ensuring expenditure is aligned with the budget without imposing unrealistic burdens on available capacity or preventing flexibility when it is necessary and appropriate.

Allocations may be changed throughout the year to meet expenditure pressures because of:

- *Insufficient allocations to address expenditure pressure*—Budget execution in PICs is often disrupted by the reallocation of expenditure during the year as foreseeable and unforeseeable priorities emerge. Many pressures could be foreseen and budgeted for if better systems were in place to record medium-term expenditure obligations. These spending obligations can arise from inadequately budgeted debt-servicing requirements, insufficient provisioning for contingent liabilities, the need to meet accumulated arrears, the effects of demographic flows that have not been recognized earlier, or ongoing costs of policy decisions. If budget execution is undermined by the need to meet foreseeable in-year expenditure pressures, countries can prioritize improvements in systems to record and monitor these pressures. Genuinely unforeseeable spending pressures can also arise from natural disasters or other shocks. Ensuring adequate contingency allocations in the budget is the most appropriate means of dealing with these risks, but, with inevitably limited resources, in-year reallocation may still be needed for major shocks.

Inefficiency and Ineffectiveness in Spending Undermine Service Delivery

Service delivery in PICs is sometimes undermined by poor-quality spending (Figure 15.5). Public funds are often used to purchase poor-quality inputs. Here, inputs are purchased in combinations inappropriate to policy priorities. PFM weaknesses that often drive these problems include inadequate control measures to ensure good-quality spending and a lack of transparency and oversight of spending decisions. However, such weaknesses are often also caused by weaknesses at the line level that are not assessed in the PEFA framework and are not fully amenable to being addressed through the reform of central PFM systems. Policymakers concerned about the impact of inefficiency and ineffectiveness of spending at the line level should consider improvements in government-wide PFM systems as only one tool in a range of reform solutions.

Systems may be inadequate to ensure good-quality spending if:

- *Weak internal controls lead to low-quality inputs*—The efficiency and effectiveness of expenditure is sometimes undermined in PICs because of inappropriate controls. Control systems in procurement and payroll play an important role in preventing inappropriate spending or deliberate misuse of funds, as well as improving public perceptions regarding the integrity of systems. These systems, however, will only be effective if compliance is enforced. Spending quality can also be harmed if very tight expenditure control systems cause bottlenecks and impede the appropriate input mix at the line level. If expenditure quality is undermined by weak control systems, countries can prioritize improvements in these systems to achieve a more appropriate balance between control and flexibility.
- *Systems provide excessive or inadequate flexibility to line ministries in determining what they spend money on*—Efficiency and effectiveness in public expenditure are sometimes undermined in PICs by either excessive or insufficient management discretion over the input mix. Inflexibility in the inputs available to ministries—such as staff, equipment, or contracted services—can lead to inefficiency, with managers often having too much of a particular input or not enough. Discretion over inputs can provide important benefits by allowing those with direct accountability and good

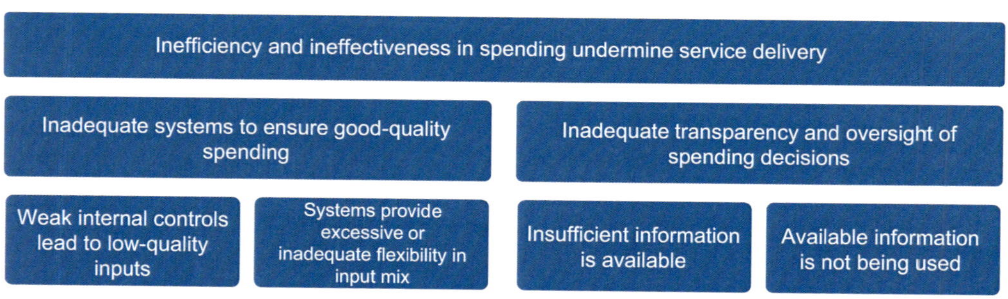

Figure 15.5 Inefficiency and Ineffectiveness in Spending Undermine Service Delivery

information to decide what is needed to deliver programs and achieve objectives. But, if excessive, such discretion can lead to poor outcomes. Discretion will only lead to better spending if there are strong incentives for delivery, good accountability systems, mechanisms for monitoring outputs or outcomes, and a performance culture. If expenditure quality is being harmed by excessive or insufficient flexibility in the input mix, countries can prioritize reforms of systems to achieve a more appropriate level of flexibility, taking account of the broader context and the extent to which managers can and will be held accountable for resource use and delivery. In most PICs, granting some discretion to line ministries over the use of inputs may be appropriate. But few countries have the accountability systems in place to grant full discretion over inputs.

There may be inadequate transparency and oversight over expenditure decisions if:

- *Insufficient information is available*—Transparency can be an important driver of efficiency and effectiveness in the use of public resources. Limited access to high-quality fiscal information may be impeding the efficient use of public resources in some PICs. Accountability to the public, parliament, and the executive relies on the availability of information, including information on policy priorities, budget allocations, debt, cash flows, future liabilities, and procurement decisions. If the efficiency and effectiveness of expenditure are undermined by a lack of information, countries can prioritize (1) the collection of key fiscal information by the finance ministry, (2) analysis of relevant information to identify trends and patterns that may be of interest to the public or decision makers, and (3) dissemination of information in an accessible format to relevant audiences (including the executive, parliament, the public, development partners, and civil society organizations).
- *Available information is not being used*—The collection and dissemination of information will not lead to improved efficiency and effectiveness unless that information is used by decision makers to make better decisions, reward good performance, and address underperformance. In PICs, as in other countries, action sometimes does not occur even when the right information is collected. While resolving this problem may be beyond the scope of a PFM reform process, countries may wish to prioritize broader engagement between the finance ministry, the cabinet, parliament, and the public accounts committee on budget formation and execution and various review processes (including audit). Options for direct public engagement, including through outreach to nongovernment organizations and civil society groups, could also be considered.

ACCESSING CAPACITY FOR PUBLIC FINANCIAL MANAGEMENT REFORM

The process of implementing PFM reforms can be difficult and resource intensive, and PFM road maps must also address how capacity gaps can be filled. The design and introduction of new processes, systems, and structures may not only place temporary additional demands on capacity, but may lead to permanent changes in the skills required. PFM reforms should involve explicit consideration of and planning for changed capacity needs. Different approaches to addressing capacity gaps might be needed in countries in which capacity constraints are particularly pressing. Along with traditional capacity-building approaches, attention should also be given to accessing capacity from alternative sources, such as regional institutions or long-term arrangements with development partners, private firms, and individuals with required skills.

There is no single solution to capacity needs. Rather, consideration should be given to what will work best in the circumstances. The following section provides an overview of options available to meet capacity gaps when implementing PFM reforms and a framework for choosing among these options.

Options for Meeting Capacity Gaps

Countries with small populations face particular challenges in building local capacity, even over a longer time frame. Thought should be given to the full range of possible approaches to addressing capacity needs, including capacity building, capacity supplementation, and capacity substitution. These options include (1) training and education, with staff acquiring new skills to undertake a broader range of PFM functions, (2) supporting PFM improvements by external advice and assistance (but responsibility for delivery remains with local agencies and staff), and (3) outsourcing responsibility for the delivery of improved PFM functions to external providers.

Deciding among Options

Governments need to consider which approach, or combination of approaches, is most appropriate to address identified capacity needs. There are a number of practical issues that need to be weighed when deciding on capacity options, including:

- *Complexity of specific functions*—More demanding technical and specialized PFM skills are difficult to establish and costly (or difficult) to retain. These skills might include specialist accounting, fiscal policy, modeling, and forecasting. In these instances it may be more economical and less risky over time to use pooled regional resources or outsourced arrangements to establish formal contractual arrangements.
- *Efficient scale for providing specific functions*—A feature of the Pacific region is the prominence of many small island states that cannot take advantage of scale, but are still expected to provide certain PFM functions. This comes at a high cost. It is therefore in the interests of PICs to undertake some of these functions on a regional scale to reduce this cost burden without compromising sovereignty or national interests. A regional approach is one way to lower costs through the sharing of skilled resources or knowledge. Outsourcing can realize similar advantages, particularly if done in collaboration with other PICs. Regional approaches can also support the development and deployment of capacity with relevant regional experience, leading to higher-quality advice and reducing the amount of investment required in familiarization. Furthermore, regional approaches can encourage the adoption of similar systems, standards, and policies across countries, allowing further economies of scale and facilitating the transfer of specific capacities and skills. For example, the use of common revenue and customs systems allows economies of scale in training. Regional approaches can be used to support all approaches to addressing capacity gaps, including capacity building, capacity supplementation, and capacity substitution. Existing regional approaches involved in addressing PFM capacity gaps include (1) shared training facilities and courses (University of the South Pacific and the Pacific Islands Centre for Public Administration); (2) pools of skilled and specialist resources that can be shared across countries (Pacific Financial Technical Assistance Centre, Pacific Islands Forum Secretariat, and the Pacific Islands Centre for Public Administration); and (3) opportunities for networks of information sharing (the Pacific Islands Financial Managers' Association and the Pacific Islands Tax Administrators Association).
- *Funding constraints and options*—The appropriateness of outsourcing will depend on affordability.
- *Capacity for managing external providers*—Contracting out requires specific capacities, ranging from procurement to legal framework and contract management skills.

Decisions also need to be made regarding the appropriate duration for various approaches. Different models for accessing specific capacities can be used in different ways over time, with assorted approaches applied over the short, medium, and longer term. Externally sourced capacity is often viewed as a short-term option to be provided only until local capacity can be developed. But the permanent external provision of certain functions has often proved cheaper, more sustainable, and less risky in some PICs, owing to a limited availability of specialized local staff to take on all required functions, even over an extended time frame.

Lessons from International Experience

There is extensive international experience to learn from. Many reviews have now been completed of capacity-building projects undertaken around the world.[4] These highlight that improving capacity is difficult and outcomes often fall short of objectives. Lessons from the extensive regional and international experience with accessing PFM capacity include the following:

- Strong ownership and political leadership are required.
- Extensive planning and long time frames are necessary. Capacity-building efforts in PICs have often been fragmented, sporadic, and inadequately planned. The amount of time necessary to build capacity has often been underestimated, and frequent changes in the involvement of donors, in the scope and coverage of capacity-building projects, and in the advisors who are financed by such projects have led to duplication and gaps.
- Role clarity and appropriate accountability arrangements are important. In PICs, capacity substitution is frequently used, but its use is sometimes not explicitly acknowledged due to common expectations that technical assistance should always be intended to build local capacity. This is problematic, as capacity-substitution goals are not reflected in project monitoring and evaluation arrangements, leading to a lack of accountability. Advisors contracted to build capacity but fulfilling in-line roles typically report to donor agencies rather than to the government, impeding ownership and management. And funding for advisors is usually available only for a fixed period, generating risks for sustainability when in-line roles are performed without an exit strategy.
- Sustainability can be achieved in different ways in different contexts. Claims that long-term capacity supplementation and capacity substitution are less sustainable need to be carefully tested. Capacity supplementation and capacity substitution can be delivered sustainably if costs are acknowledged and planned for. At the same time, experience in the PICs shows that specialized technical skills may be costly to develop locally and difficult to retain; regional or outsourced approaches may sometimes be more economical and longer lasting. Furthermore, there is an opportunity cost in dedicating scarce skills in areas that are not critical (for example, resourcing administrative functions can divert capacity away from policy development, where local staff might be better utilized). It is important to recognize that advanced economies take advantage of outsourced service provision to enable civil servants to focus on core government roles and responsibilities.

CONCLUSION

Sound public financial management provides a vital foundation for efficient service delivery and macroeconomic management. PICs must deal with particularly severe capacity constraints when designing and implementing PFM systems. It is essential to take explicit account of the importance of capacity constraints through (1) ensuring public financial management reforms are well planned and have political support, (2) prioritizing available capacity toward reforms that are likely to have the greatest impact in achieving development objectives and policy goals, and (3) considering the full range of possible approaches to addressing capacity needs, including capacity building, capacity supplementation, and capacity substitution.

---

[4]See Wescott (2008) for a useful example.

REFERENCES

Diamond, Jack. 2013a. "Good Practice Note on Sequencing PFM Reforms." Public Expenditure and Financial Accountability Secretariat, Washington.

———. 2013b. "Background Paper 1: Sequencing PFM Reforms." Public Expenditure and Financial Accountability Secretariat, Washington.

Haque, Tobias, David S. Knight, and Dinuk S. Jayasuriya. 2012. "Capacity Constraints and Public Financial Management in Small Pacific Island Countries." Policy Research Working Paper 6297, World Bank, Washington.

Haque, Tobias, Richard Bontjer, Mary Betley, Ron Hackett, Vivek Suri, and Franz Dress-Gross. 2013. "Pacific Islands—PFM Design under Capacity Constraints: Planning Public Financial Management Reforms in Pacific Island Countries." Guidance Note, World Bank, Washington.

Pacific Islands Forum Secretariat and Pacific Financial Technical Assistance Centre (PFTAC). 2010. "A Public Financial Management Roadmap for Forum Island Countries." Regional Papers, Pacific Finanacial Technical Assistance Center, Suva.

———. 2012. "Update on Public Finance Management Roadmap Implementation." Briefing paper prepared for the Forum Economic Ministers' Meeting, Tarawa, Kiribati, July 2–4.

Tommasi, Daniel. 2012. "Background Paper 2: The Core PFM Functions and PEFA Performance Indicators." Public Expenditure and Financial Accountability Secretariat, Washington.

Welham, Bryn, Philipp Krause, and Edward Hedger. 2013. "Linking PFM Dimensions to Development Priorities." Working Paper 380, Overseas Development Institute, London.

Wescott, Clay. 2008. "World Bank Support for Public Financial Management: Conceptual Roots and Evidence of Impact." Internal Evaluation Group Working Paper, World Bank, Washington.

CHAPTER 16

Pacific Island Countries: Trade Integration in a Changing Global Economy

HONG CHEN, LANIETA RAUQEUQE, SHIU RAJ SINGH, YIQUN WU, AND YONGZHENG YANG

Trade integration is widely considered to be essential for economic development and prosperity in Pacific island countries (PICs).[1] This thinking is not without theoretical or empirical foundations. It is well known that domestic markets in PICs are too small to allow them to exploit economies of scale, a disadvantage exacerbated by their geographic remoteness from major global economic centers. Small size and remoteness reinforce each other, leading to high costs of production and trading, and hence contribute to the lower competitiveness of PIC exports. It is thought that, through trade integration, producers in PICs can effectively enlarge their markets and reduce those costs. Historically, a number of relatively small developing economies, such as Hong Kong Special Administrative Region, Mauritius, and Singapore, have managed to develop manufacturing industries that spearheaded industrialization and enabled significant increases in incomes per capita through trade integration with larger markets.

Two key questions PIC policymakers face is what needs to be done to facilitate trade integration with the rest of world and what industries can spearhead this process. Most observers doubt that PICs can or should try to replicate the use of manufacturing as the main platform for trade integration. Given the size and geographic disadvantages of these countries, their comparative advantage lies in industries other than manufacturing, and most likely in a combination of tourism, agriculture, fisheries, and minerals, depending on each country's circumstances. All PICs seem to have potential in tourism, and, for those with abundant and fertile land, also in agriculture. PICs with large fishery resources can extract more economic benefits from these resources through better management and regional cooperation. Papua New Guinea and the Solomon Islands have significant commodity resources for production and export, while other PICs are engaged in onshore and offshore exploration. The export of labor services is another area with great potential for several of these countries. With small populations, PICs export labor services, which generate inbound remittances in a significant proportion to total output, without a large impact on the labor importing countries.

This chapter focuses on trade in goods and tourism in PICs and explores the potential for tourism to drive trade integration and inclusive economic growth. The analysis is made in the context of the eastward shift of global economic gravity, focusing on emerging Asia as an increasingly important source of demand for resource-based goods and services. This is particularly so for tourism and agricultural products, the latter both directly and indirectly (that is, by supplying the local tourism industry). It should be noted from the outset that the PICs' traditional markets will remain important for a long time and should be further developed for deeper economic development beyond trade

This chapter is based on Chen and others (2014).

[1] In this chapter, PICs include Fiji, Kiribati, Marshall Islands, Micronesia, Palau, Papua New Guinea, Samoa, the Solomon Islands, Tonga, Tuvalu, and Vanuatu.

in goods and services. Nevertheless, PICs should continue to position themselves to tap into Asian markets for long-term benefits.

We begin by reviewing the current institutions for trade integration and trade performance in PICs, and examining the determinants of merchandise trade and tourism in PICs using gravity models. We then explore growth potential in tourism in the context of the shifting global economic gravity to Asia, and how a booming tourism industry in PICs can help revive agriculture and support more broad-based growth. We conclude with policy implications.

TRADE INTEGRATION: THE INSTITUTIONS

The trade integration of PICs began late in the global context and has followed two tracks: intraregional and interregional integration.[2] Figure 16.1 summarizes the institutions that support trade integration in the region. The Pacific Island Countries Trade Agreement (PICTA) of 2001 is the key agreement promoting intraregional trade.[3] In 2004, PICTA members agreed to extend the agreement to trade in services. Twelve of the 14 Pacific Islands Forum countries have signed PICTA and, apart from Micronesia, all 11 PICs that have signed PICTA have ratified the agreement. But only six have announced a readiness to implement it. Tariff reductions have long phase-in periods, up to 10 years for the least developed members and 13 years for the three PICs under the Compacts of Free Association with the United States (Marshall Islands, Micronesia, Palau). While PICTA has yet to be fully implemented, a subregional free trade agreement of the Melanesian Spearhead Group—effective in 1993 and comprising Fiji, New Caledonia's Kanak and Socialist National Liberation Front, Papua New Guinea, the Solomon Islands, and Vanuatu—has moved ahead. Fiji, Papua New Guinea, and Vanuatu are trading duty free, with the exception of sugar, salt, and mackerel for Papua New Guinea. However, contingency measures have often been invoked to protect certain domestic industries (Duncan 2008). In 2012 the Melanesian Spearhead Group countries signed a memorandum of understanding on a scheme to facilitate the movement of skilled nationals within countries in the group for employment purposes.[4]

The late start and slow progress in intraregional trade integration are reflected in relatively low trade volumes among PICs (Figure 16.2).[5] But the main reason for this, rather than trade policy, seems to be that PICs, while geographical neighbors with many common features, are not "natural" trade partners. Trade complementarity is low because of the similarity of export and import products among PICs, particularly for smaller PICs with fewer goods and services to offer. Moreover, PICs are distant from each other and scattered over an area about one-third of the Pacific. Fiji is farther from Papua New Guinea than from Australia, for example, and Palau is much closer to Asia than to most other PICs.

PICs' interregional trade integration has largely focused on the Australian and New Zealand markets given their geographic proximity and historical ties. The South Pacific Regional Trade and Economic Cooperation Agreement (SPARTECA) is the main accord promoting trade between PICs and Australia and New Zealand, providing nonreciprocal duty and quota free entry for PIC goods exports to both countries. Since its inception in 1981, SPARTECA appears to have played an important role in facilitating some exports from PICs to Australia and New Zealand, with Fiji's textile,

[2] Chand (2010) looks at the history of regional integration in PICs, and Chand (2005) gives a comprehensive account of various aspects of regional integration and governance.

[3] PICTA members include the 14 developing Pacific Islands Forum countries: Cook Islands, Fiji, Kiribati, Marshall Islands, Micronesia, Nauru, Niue, Palau, Papua New Guinea, Samoa, the Solomon Islands, Tonga, Tuvalu, and Vanuatu.

[4] Temporary workers are typically employed one to three years, often extendable for another one to three years.

[5] Fiji and Vanuatu are the only PICs that have a significant portion of their exports destined for other PICs. Some of Fiji's manufactured goods, such as processed food and cement, are quite competitive in some other PICs, and a large portion of Vanuatu's beef and kava exports goes to other PICs.

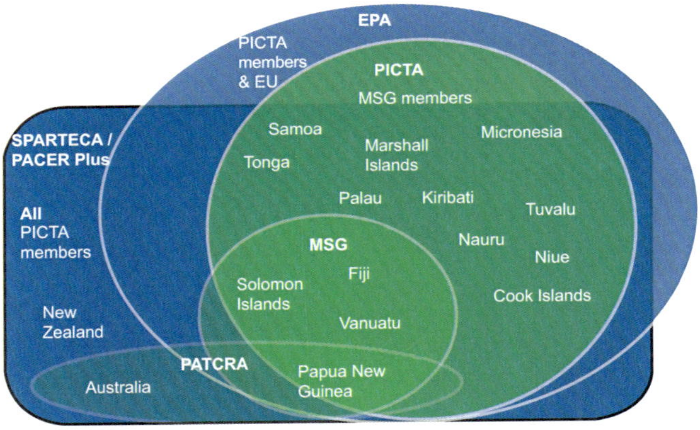

Figure 16.1 Trade Agreements among Pacific Island Countries

Sources: Compiled by IMF staff, with information from ministries of foreign affairs.
Note: EPA = Economic Partnership Agreement; EU = European Union; MSG = Melanesian Spearhead Group; PACER = Pacific Agreement on Closer Economic Relations; PATCRA = Papua New Guinea and Australia Trade and Commercial Relations Agreement; PICTA = Pacific Island Countries Trade Agreement; SPARTECA = South Pacific Regional Trade and Economic Cooperation Agreement.

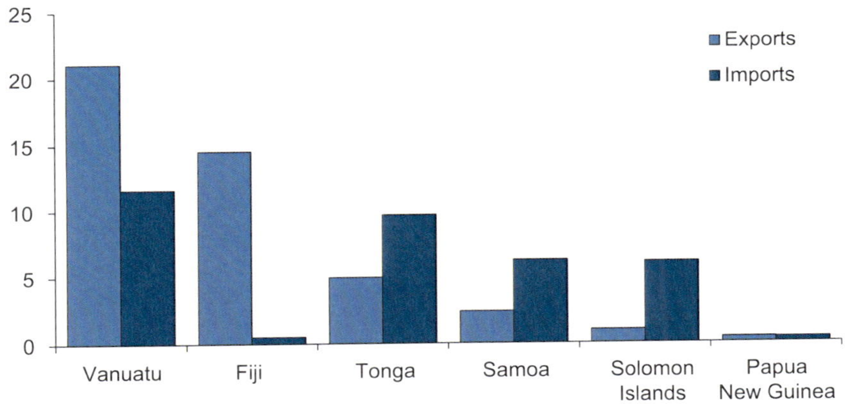

Figure 16.2 Intraregional Trade (*Percent of GDP*)

Source: IMF staff calculations.

clothing, and footwear industry and Samoa's auto wire harness assembly industry being the primary beneficiaries. However, SPARTECA's effect has waned as preference margins on textile, clothing, and footwear have fallen with the removal of quotas and reductions in most-favored-nation tariffs on these goods. In Samoa, the decline of Australia's automobile manufacturing industry in recent years has substantially reduced the demand for wire harnesses assembled there.[6]

The Pacific Agreement on Closer Economic Relations Plus (PACER Plus) is being negotiated to broaden PICs' intraregional trade integration to include Australia and New Zealand on a reciprocal basis. Given that Australia and New Zealand already provide relatively easy access for most PIC goods, PACER Plus is likely to bring the largest benefits in three areas. The first is more secure access

[6] Before the global financial crisis, the wire harness plant in Samoa employed over 2,000 people and was the single largest private employer in the formal sector. Employment fell to less than 1,000 in 2012.

to the Australian and New Zealand agricultural markets by binding the two countries to more science-based quarantine restrictions. The second is development assistance from Australia and New Zealand to improve domestic supply capacity. And the third is temporary migration in the context of Mode 4 of the World Trade Organization General Agreement on Trade in Services (Braxton 2009). Both Australia and New Zealand already offer seasonal workers schemes, but PICs are seeking to expand these and to have them formalized in PACER Plus. At least in the short term, the focus on temporary migration as a driver of future growth is unsurprising given that some of the smaller PICs have limited capacity to export goods and services (even in tourism) to Australia and New Zealand (Box 16.1).

Another strand of PICs' interregional trade integration has been their long-standing preferential trade agreement with the European Union (EU). As part of the African, Caribbean and Pacific group, PICs have benefited from the Lomé Convention and its successor, the Cotonou Agreement. Negotiations have moved slowly on a regional Economic Partnership Agreement to replace the trade-related sections of the Cotonou Agreement. Fiji and Papua New Guinea have signed an interim Economic Partnership Agreement with the EU to avoid interruptions of trade with Europe. This was done to protect Papua New Guinea's market access for tuna exports to the EU, and Fiji's sugar exports at preferential prices. For other PICs, exports to the EU are very limited and there

Box 16.1. Remittances and Pacific Seasonal Worker Programs

Remittances have long been a dependable source of foreign exchange and income for Pacific island countries (PICs). Limited domestic growth and special relationships with host countries have ensured continual emigration to developed economies, making PICs some of the most remittance-dependent countries in the world. During 2010–15 remittances averaged 20 percent of GDP in Tonga, 22 percent in Samoa, and 5 percent in Fiji. At the household level, remittances supplement incomes and help obtain education, health, and housing services, in addition to smoothing highly variable incomes and providing funds for investment and entrepreneurial activities without indebtedness. For many PIC households, remittances are an insurance against income loss and other financial difficulties. At the macro level, remittances have been critical for financing large trade deficits. In Fiji, remittances proved to be largely countercyclical amid political instability until recent years, which led to declines in official development assistance up to 2014.

Regional policymakers recognize that because of the remoteness, smallness, and resulting limited economic opportunities in PICs, greater access to labor markets in larger neighbors is important for regional economic integration, and is mutually beneficial for host and origin countries. While the three Compact of Free Association countries—the Marshall Islands, Micronesia, and Palau—have free access to the U.S. labor market, other Pacific island countries rely on seasonal worker programs in Australia and New Zealand for certain types of labor. These programs are quite attractive for Pacific workers skilled in agriculture and fisheries. New Zealand introduced the Recognised Seasonal Employer program in 2007. The current program includes workers from Fiji, Kiribati, Marshall Islands, Micronesia, Nauru, Palau, Papua New Guinea, Samoa, Solomon Islands, Tonga, Tuvalu, and Vanuatu.

Australia established the Pacific Seasonal Worker Pilot Scheme in 2008 and converted it into a permanent Seasonal Worker Programme in December 2011. The Seasonal Worker Programme offers seasonal labor to employers in the agricultural industry, and employers in selected locations in the accommodation industry who cannot meet their seasonal labor needs with local jobseekers. Participating countries include Fiji, Kiribati, Nauru, Papua New Guinea, Samoa, Solomon Islands, Timor-Leste, Tonga, Tuvalu, and Vanuatu.

Remittances from seasonal worker schemes are a beneficial link between migration and development. As with other remittance-dependent countries, efforts to reduce the cost of remitting have boosted flows. Seasonal worker programs will need to be further enhanced to sustain and increase remittances in the long term as an alternative or supplement to official development assistance.

appears to be little incentive for them to negotiate a regional Economic Partnership Agreement with the EU.

Most PICs have been left out of economic integration in Asia. Papua New Guinea is the only PIC member of the Asia Pacific Economic Cooperation, and no PICs are members of the other groupings of Asian preferential trade agreements. This exclusion stems from their remoteness and smallness, which give them less influence and attraction to Asian countries. In the past, this arguably did not matter much as there was little trade between PICs and Asian countries (including trade in services such as tourism); Australia, New Zealand, North America, and Europe mattered more, especially given the trade preferences they offered. However, low trade integration with Asia will increasingly disadvantage PICs in a world of growing regionalism and given Asia's emergence as a global center of economic activity.[7] Deepening regional trade integration will be a particular challenge for PICs without mineral resources.

TRADE INTEGRATION: THE PERFORMANCE

Trade performance has diverged between resource-rich and resource-poor PICs during 2006–10 and converged more recently. Export growth in the two resource-rich PICs, Papua New Guinea and the Solomon Islands, was very strong during 2011–14 (Figure 16.3), stemming from commodity booms.[8] Micro and other PICs[9] have also seen strong export growth since then after very slow growth in the previous decade. On the import side, growth largely mirrored export performance (Figure 16.4).

PICs have a high degree of trade openness because of their small size and hence need to trade to meet domestic demand. Openness has not changed significantly over the past two decades as measured by the trade-to-GDP ratio (Figure 16.5), except for Papua New Guinea and the Solomon Islands, whose openness has been boosted by commodity booms which lasted until 2014. Among non-resource-rich exporters, micro PICs tend to have higher openness, and other PICs lower openness relative to small states outside the region.

However, the high trade openness masks large trade deficits for most PICs, particularly among non-resource-rich exporters. In micro PICs, exports are often a small fraction of imports, but even in some of the larger ones (for example, Samoa and Tonga) trade deficits are large and compare unfavorably with small states outside the region (Figure 16.6).[10] The sources for financing these deficits vary considerably, but in most PICs, including Fiji, Samoa, and Tonga, remittances and aid are major sources (Box 16.1). Most remittances in Kiribati and Tuvalu come from seafarers, but seafaring has been under pressure in recent years (Box 16.2). Income from industrial fishing access licenses is also important for some countries, especially for PICs with large exclusive economic zones, such as Kiribati, Papua New Guinea, and the Solomon Islands (Box 16.3).

PICs' exports are highly concentrated, reflecting their narrow economic bases. Approximately two-thirds of merchandise exports are primary products, predominantly agricultural products and natural resources (Figure 16.7). In non-commodity-rich economies (Kiribati, Fiji, Marshall Islands, Micronesia, Palau, Samoa, Tonga, Tuvalu, and Vanuatu) agriculture alone accounts for over 60 percent of total merchandise exports, and even in resource-rich countries agricultural exports are larger than resource exports. Manufactured exports are significant in non-resource-rich countries, but they

[7] Armstrong and Read (1998) discuss the challenges facing small states in a globalizing world economy.

[8] It is difficult to assess trade growth in PICs, because of the lack of export price statistics suitable for deflating the nominal values of their exports. In Figures 16.3 and 16.4, the nominal exports and imports of PICs are deflated using the U.S. import and export price indices, respectively.

[9] Micro PICs include Kiribati, Marshall Islands, Micronesia, Palau, and Tuvalu. Other PICs include Fiji, Samoa, Tonga, and Vanuatu.

[10] Chapter 4 finds that lower export openness in PICs has contributed to slow growth compared with other small states.

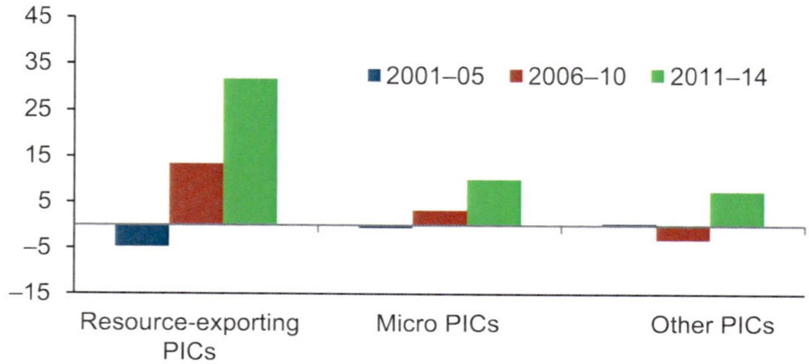

Figure 16.3 Real Export Growth (*Percent*)

Sources: IMF APDLISC database; and IMF staff calculations.
Note: PICs = Pacific island countries.

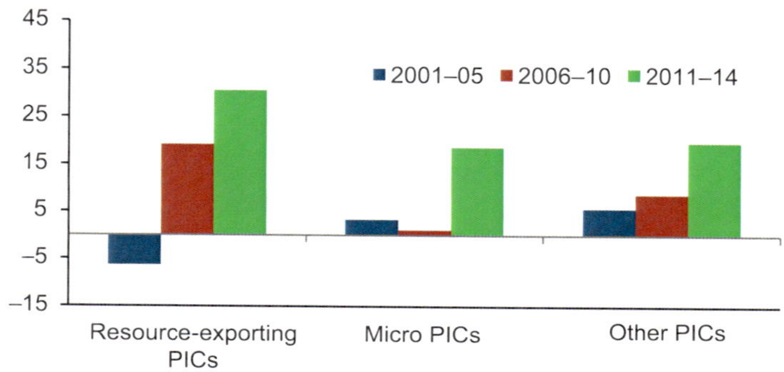

Figure 16.4 Real Import Growth (*Percent*)

Sources: IMF APDLISC database; and IMF staff calculations.
Note: PICs = Pacific island countries.

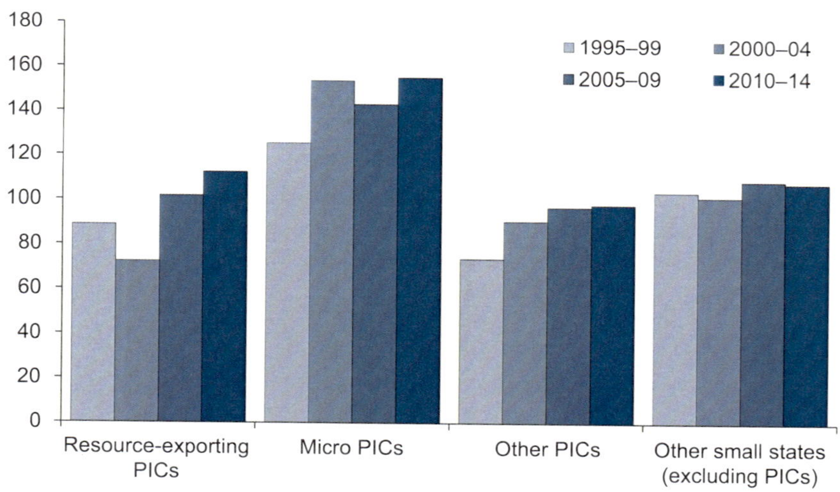

Figure 16.5 Openness Comparisons, 1995–2014 (*Goods and services trade; percent of GDP*)

Source: IMF, World Economic Outlook database.
Note: PICs = Pacific island countries.

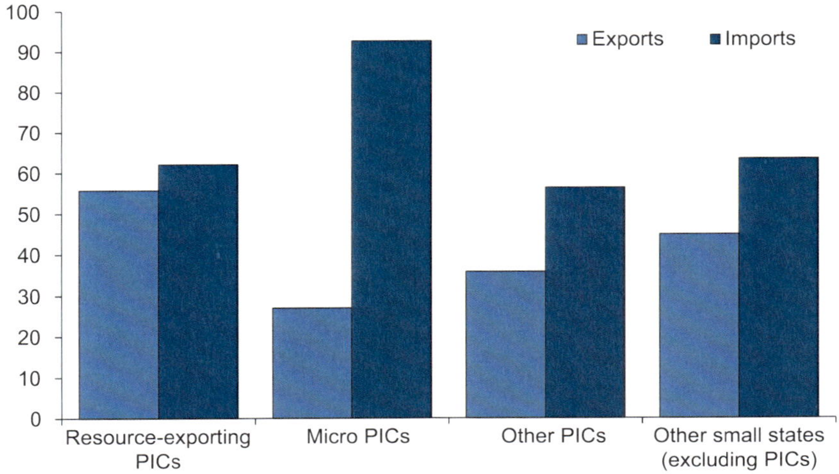

Figure 16.6 Trade Balance, Goods and Services, 2003–14 (*Percent of GDP*)

Sources: IMF APDLISC database; and IMF staff calculations.
Note: PICs = Pacific island countries.

Box 16.2. Seafarers' Employment in Kiribati and Tuvalu

For Kiribati and Tuvalu, seafaring is an important source of employment and remittances, but both have clearly trended downward in recent years.

While remaining sizable, employment in seafaring fell sharply during the global financial crisis. As of October 2013 about 1,008 Kiribati and 112 Tuvalu seafarers had jobs on vessels, compared to 1,452 and 361, respectively, in 2006. Over the same period, seafarer remittances fell by 5 percent of GDP for Kiribati and 36 percent for Tuvalu. The depreciation of the U.S. dollar until 2013 had also significantly reduced the Australian dollar value of seafarer remittances (Figure 16.2.1).

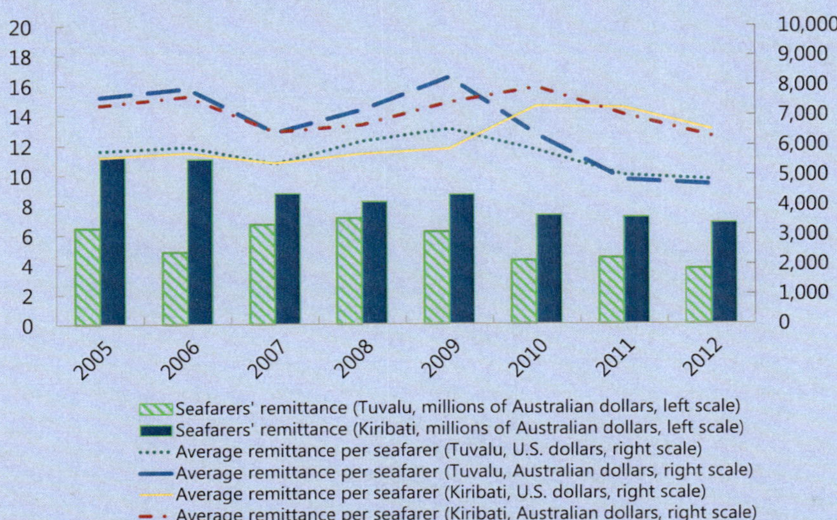

Figure 16.2.1 Seafarers' Remittances: Kiribati and Tuvalu

Sources: Country authorities; and IMF staff calculations.

Box 16.2. (*Continued*)

The recovery in world trade from the global financial crisis did not produce a corresponding recovery in seafarer employment for a number of structural reasons. The shipping industry still suffers from low profitability and overcapacity, and the increasing automation of ship operations has reduced demand for seafarers. Moreover, seafarers from Kiribati and Tuvalu have become less competitive compared with those from south and southeast Asian countries as transportation costs for Kiribati and Tuvalu seafarers traveling to their ships have become relatively high.

While the Kiribati Marine Training Center is considered one of the best vocational training institutes in the region, the Tuvalu Maritime Training Institute's training programs are generally for traditional merchant vessels and have become inadequate for ships equipped with modern technology. And while the close connection with German merchant ships has traditionally provided stable employment and income, this concentration has reduced options to diversify into ships operated by other countries.

The difficulties facing seafarers in Kiribati and Tuvalu highlight the unique challenges facing small Pacific island countries, which have few options for earning foreign exchange other than maximizing ocean resources and manpower. Compared with some larger Pacific island countries, Kiribati and Tuvalu have little agricultural land, and their prospects for developing tourism are less favorable because they are poorly connected with the rest of the world. Both countries should therefore aim to diversify into seasonal worker programs in Australia and New Zealand, and make the most of ocean resources for job creation and government revenue (see Box 16.3).

This box was prepared by Xuefei Bai, Sergei Dodzin, and Jiangyan Yu.

Box 16.3. Fisheries in Pacific Island Countries

Pacific islands in the western and central Pacific Ocean hold one-third of the world's tuna stocks. Industrial tuna fishing, mainly by international fishing fleets is a vital source of government revenue for several of these countries. In Kiribati, Micronesia, and Tuvalu, fishing license fees account for about 30 percent of total government revenue. Coastal fisheries help sustain rural livelihoods, and fish exports provide the largest source of foreign exchange earnings in several Pacific island countries (PICs), including Fiji, Kiribati, Samoa, and Tonga.

If properly managed, fishery resources can be an important source of sustainable economic growth and income. A key challenge, however, is how to extract more economic rents and value added from industrial fishing by ensuring the sustainability of ocean resources and improving regional cooperation in industrial fishing arrangements.

The Parties to the Nauru Agreement represents a major achievement in regional cooperation in managing PICs' tuna resources. Under this initiative, Kiribati, the Marshall Islands, Micronesia, Nauru, Palau, Papua New Guinea, the Solomon Islands, and Tuvalu established a regional vessel register and subsequently a vessel monitoring system, enabling them to operate a so-called Vessel Day Scheme. By limiting the number of days for purse seine fishing by each member and allowing members to trade their approved days (quotas), the scheme has led to almost a tripling of license revenues, from US$70 million to US$230 million a year. To maintain and improve regional cooperation, PICs need to create greater scarcity of tuna resources by (1) expanding the scheme to nonmembers to increase leverage over international fishing fleets, (2) avoiding bilateral fishing agreements with countries outside the region, and (3) enforcing compliance with quota allocation by existing agreement members.

PICs have also made progress in the sustainable management of ocean resources. Pacific Islands Forum leaders have endorsed a regional Oceanscape Program to better manage ocean resources, recognizing that the current and potential economic benefits of these resources depend on their underlying

Box 16.3. (*Continued*)

health and environmental status. In supporting this initiative, the World Bank has provided a series of overlapping grants and credits to participating countries to enhance the natural capital embodied in the ocean resources.

Several PICs have made considerable effort to create jobs and increase local value added through downstream processing, but significant challenges remain. As with other manufacturing activities, small market size and remoteness, and inadequate infrastructure, technology, and capital, are major constraints. Many countries have tried to overcome them by initiating joint ventures with foreign companies. While some processing plants (such as those in Papua New Guinea) are doing reasonably well, many others, particularly in smaller PICs, are struggling for survival or have gone bankrupt. Countries need to examine their own circumstances to determine whether they should focus on maximizing fishing license fees or also venture into downstream activities, which may not be commercially viable or increase national economic welfare if processing plants cannot be run efficiently.

This box draws partly on material from a World Bank workshop on fisheries at the 2013 IMF/World Bank Annual Meetings.

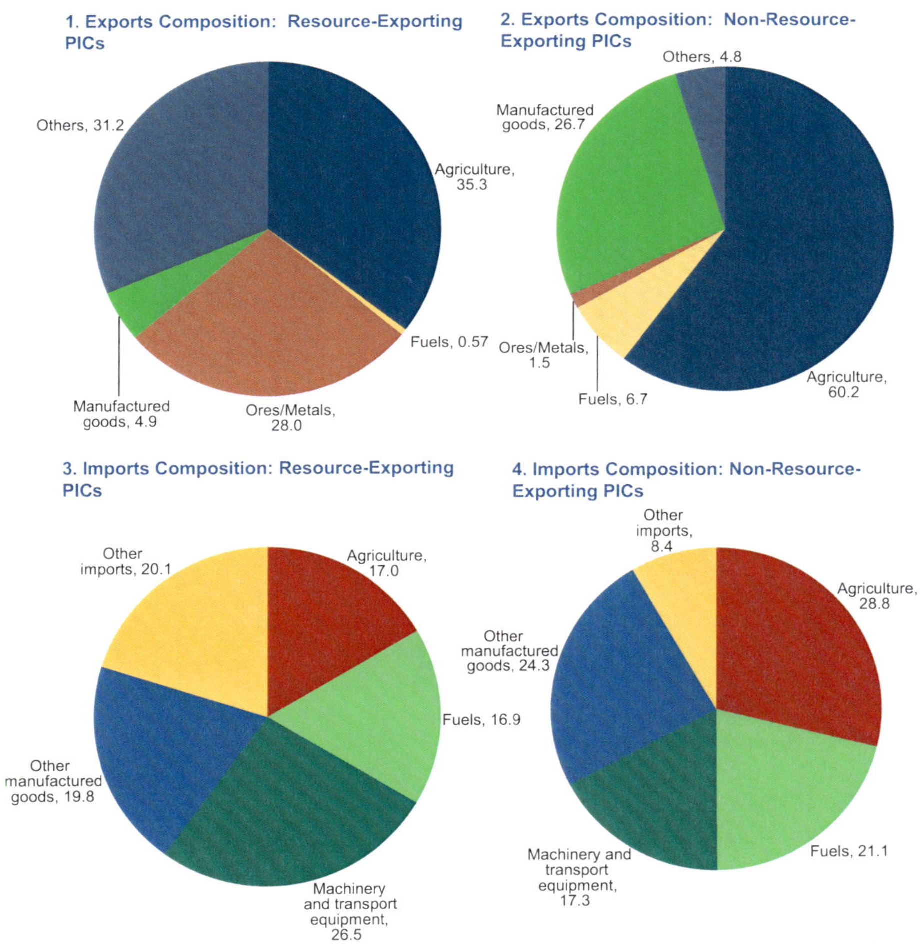

Figure 16.7 Trade Composition in Pacific Island Countries (*Percent*)

Source: World Integrated Trade Statistics, recent year averages.
Note: PICs = Pacific island countries.

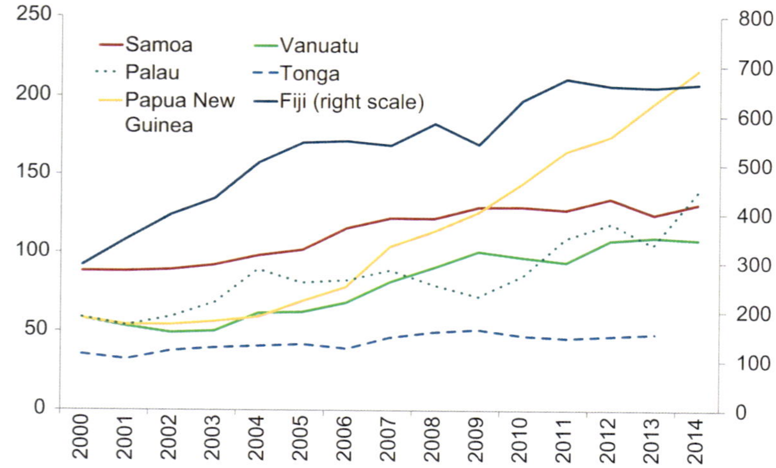

Figure 16.8 Annual Visitor Arrivals

Source: National tourism and statistics authorities.

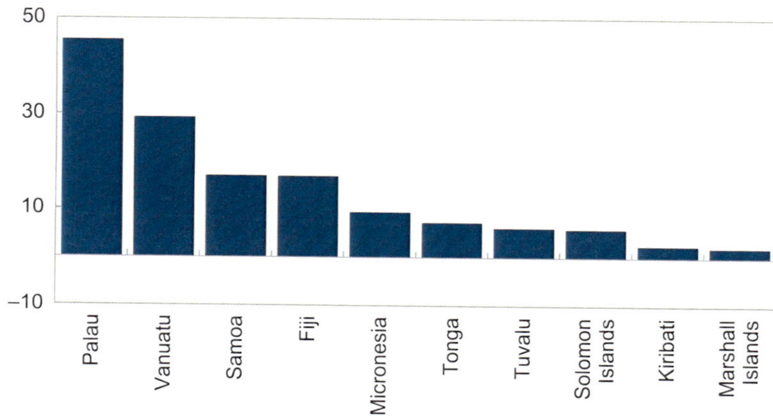

Figure 16.9 Tourism in the Pacific Islands (*Percent of GDP, 2005–14 average*)

Sources: Country authorities; and IMF staff calculations.

are very small in resource-rich ones.[11] On the import side, agriculture (including food) is important, although this is more so in non-resource-rich countries, where it accounts for nearly 30 percent of total imports. Fuel imports are also important, again more so in non-resource-rich countries than in others. Agriculture and fuel combined account for nearly half of total imports in non-resource-rich PICs, and over one-third in resource-rich PICs. It is worth noting that resource-rich countries also import more machinery and equipment as a result of their relatively large investment in the resource sector.

PICs' merchandise export destinations are quite concentrated on Australia and New Zealand. But the Australian and New Zealand markets have shrunk significantly, as have the North American[12] and European markets in favor of emerging Asia, including China (Chapter 4). Turning to trade in services, inbound tourism has gained in importance for several PICs (Figure 16.8), and this is a bright spot in their trade integration with the rest of the world. The growth of tourist arrivals has

[11] There may be classification issues with regard to the size of manufactured exports. Compared with non-resource-rich countries, the "others" category is very large and may include some manufactured products.

[12] In this case, North America includes the United States and Canada.

averaged 6 percent a year since 2000—and it is not just Fiji that has done well. Tourist receipts now make an important contribution to several PIC economies (Figure 16.9). Australia, New Zealand, and the United States account for the bulk of tourist arrivals in most PICs, but the main sources of tourists for Palau have been the Asian economies, notably Japan, Korea, and Taiwan Province of China.[13]

GRAVITY MODELS FOR PACIFIC GOODS AND TOURISM

To examine what drives the growth of goods trade and tourism in PICs, we employ two gravity models—one for goods exports and imports and the other for tourism—to aid our analysis. These are standard gravity models tailored to the circumstances in PICs. Our model for goods trade is based on a three-way error components model:[14]

$$\ln T_{ijt} = \alpha_i + \alpha_j + \alpha_1 \ln Y_{it} + \alpha_2 \ln Y_{jt} + \alpha_3 \ln D_{ij} + \alpha_4 F_{ij} + \alpha_5 C_{ij} + \mu_{ijt} \quad (16.1)$$

where T_{ijt} stands for trade flows from Pacific island country i to partner country j in period t (in the export equation T_{ij} stands for exports, X_{ij}, and in the import equation it stands for imports, M_{ij}); Y_{it} is the GDP of exporting country i and Y_{jt} is the GDP of importing country j; D_{ij} stands for distance between country i and country j; F_{ij} is a dummy variable indicating if countries i and j are both signatories to the same preferential trade agreement ($F_{ij} = 1$ if both countries are signatories and $F_{ij} = 0$ if they are not); and C_{ij} indicates if countries i and j share colonial ties, with binary values 1 and 0 indicating the existence and absence of such ties, respectively. α_i and α_j are export country and import country fixed effects; values for α (1 to 5) are the coefficients of corresponding variables, and μ_{ijt} is the error term.

The equation is estimated using data for 1990–2012 covering six PICs as exporting countries[15] and 100 countries as importing countries (Annex 16.1). The above three-way error component equation is estimated with two high-dimensional fixed effects estimators, such as the fixed effects least squares dummy variable estimator (FELSDV) and the two-stage FELSDV estimator (Annex 16.2 details the estimation methods and Annex 16.3 provides more information on the data). All estimated coefficients have the expected signs, and the equation has reasonably good explanatory power with $R^2 = 0.64$ from the FELSDV estimator (Table 16.1).

A striking result from the regression is the very low elasticity of PIC exports with respect to their own GDP. The estimated coefficient indicates that, on average, with each percentage increase in the GDP of the exporting country, exports rise only by 0.27 percent. Thus, there is a tendency for export growth to lag behind output growth in PICs, indicating a strong inward orientation of economic activity. The elasticity of PIC exports with respect to importing country GDP is also low, but considerably higher than the elasticity with respect to PICs' own GDP. This low elasticity may reflect the fact that PIC exports are primarily commodities, such as agricultural products and minerals.[16] For agricultural products, lack of product differentiation or processing could also be associated with low income elasticities of demand. Even with this low elasticity, income growth in importing countries should have helped PICs narrow their trade deficits. This is because in recent years their trading partners have grown much more rapidly (Papua New Guinea and the Solomon Islands being exceptions).

[13] Palau's total tourist arrivals in recent years have increased rapidly, helped by more chartered flights from Asia.

[14] Prasad (2008) examines the trade impact of PACER Plus using a gravity model. His analysis focuses on trade turnover rather than evaluating the impact on exports and imports separately.

[15] These are Fiji, Papua New Guinea, Samoa, the Solomon Islands, Tonga, and Vanuatu.

[16] We tried the real exchange rate as an explanatory variable in the equation, but it turned out to be statistically insignificant. Thus, the low income elasticity does not seem to reflect effects other than income.

TABLE 16.1

Estimation Results of the Gravity Model for Pacific Island Countries' Merchandise Exports

Independent Variable	Estimated Coefficient
Exporting country real GDP (in logs)	0.27
Importing country real GDP (in logs)	0.44
Distance (in logs)	−2.32
Preferential trade agreement (existence = 1)	0.39
Colonial ties (existence = 1)	1.31

Source: IMF staff calculations.
Note: The dependent variable is real bilateral exports in logs; all coefficients are statistically significant at the 99 percent confidence level.

Remoteness is a major barrier to export growth in PICs. Based on the estimated coefficient on distance,[17] for each percentage increase in distance to an export market, PICs' exports decline by about 2.3 percent. Take Fiji and Tonga for illustrative purposes. Since Tonga's distance to Australia (3,585 kilometers) is 11 percent greater than Fiji's (3,224 kilometers), all else equal,[18] Tonga's exports to Australia would be 25 percent lower than Fiji's.

The regression results also show that preferential trade agreements generally have a positive impact on bilateral trade. However, this impact varies across individual agreements, with the Melanesian Spearhead Group and SPARTECA showing positive effects, but the Lomé Convention, Cotonou Agreement, and the Economic Partnership Agreement having no significant effects. The impact of being a member of a preferential trade agreement on the bilateral trade of PICs is quite large. In the case of the Melanesian Spearhead Group, for instance, bilateral exports could be nearly 50 percent higher, while bilateral exports for SPARTECA could be 115 percent higher. It should be noted, however, that bilateral trade among most PICs is mostly very low, so even a large percentage increase in this trade would translate into only a small impact on overall trade.

Additionally, the welfare implications of the Melanesian Spearhead Group and SPARTECA can be very different despite both having a positive impact on exports. As a nonreciprocal agreement, SPARTECA essentially allows PICs to reap rents generated by tariffs and quotas imposed on Australia's and New Zealand's imports from non-PICs. Thus, there is little doubt that increased exports under SPARTECA translate into a welfare improvement for PICs. On the other hand, the Melanesian Spearhead Group Trade Agreement is reciprocal, and any increase in bilateral trade is a result of reciprocal tariff reductions among Melanesian Spearhead Group members. It is well known that such agreements can result in trade diversion as well as trade creation, and that the trade diversion effect is more likely to dominate the trade creation effect in free trade agreements that involve only small trading partners, a point emphasized by Duncan (2008).[19]

Colonial ties also seem to have a positive impact on PICs' exports to their former colonial powers. On average, and other things being equal, a PIC exports 134 percent more to its former colonial power than to other countries. Such a positive impact on exports reflects the cultural (including language), political, and business ties that bind countries with their former colonial powers. However, it should be noted that the estimated effects of colonial ties are based on historical experience, and it is possible that such effects will diminish over time as trade preferences accorded to former colonies are gradually eroded or phased out.

Results from a similar import equation show that PICs have a tendency toward a deteriorating trade balance. The elasticity of their imports with respect to their GDP is estimated to be 0.91,

---

[17] Distance is measured in kilometers between the capital cities of the exporting and importing countries.

[18] That is, even if Tonga had the same income level and its country size was the same as Fiji's.

[19] Put differently, if Melanesian Spearhead Group countries were dominant trading partners of each other, trade liberalization under the group's trade agreement would have effects similar to unilateral liberalization, and, hence, the trade diversion effect would be limited.

substantially higher than the elasticity of exports to their GDP (Table 16.2). This suggests that as these economies expand, import growth tends to outpace export growth, and hence nontrade accounts (namely, services, income, and financial accounts) will need to generate a sufficient surplus to maintain the initial balance of payments position. This in turn will require either structural adjustment to increase goods and services exports and/or reduce imports unless external inflows (aid, remittances, and capital) continue to increase.

Other dependent variables have similar and expected impacts as those for the estimation of exports. The elasticity of imports with respect to trading partner GDP is positive but very low. This reflects the fact that, on average, PIC economies have been growing more slowly than their major trading partners and have not been able to absorb their exports at the same pace as the growth in their trading partners. This implies that PICs have become less important export destinations for their trading partners and increasingly marginalized in international trade. Another significant result is that distance seems to have a smaller negative impact on the imports of these countries than their exports. This may suggest that import consignments are larger and, therefore, their cost of shipping is lower. Preferential trade agreements have a magnitude of impact on the imports of PICs that is similar to that on their exports, but the colonial ties seem to be less important for imports than for exports. This result probably points to the wider range of options available for sourcing imports than diversifying export destinations.

The tourism equation has a structure similar to the goods model but with an expanded set of explanatory variables.

$$\ln V_{ijt} = \beta_0 + \beta_1 \ln N_{jt} + \beta_2 \ln YPC_{jt} + \beta_3 \ln D_{ij} + \beta_4 L_{ij} + \beta_5 S_i + \beta_6 U_{it} + \varepsilon_{ijt} \quad (16.2)$$

where V_{ijt} stands for the number of tourist arrivals in PIC i from source country j in period t; N_{jt} is the population of source country j; YPC_{jt} is the GDP per capita of source country j; D_{ij} is the distance between PIC destination i and source country j; L_{ij} is a dummy variable indicating if countries i and j share a common language ($L_{ij} = 1$ if both countries share a common language and $L_{ij} = 0$ if they do not); S_i denotes land surface area of PIC destination i, and U_{it} is the share of urban population in PIC destination i, a proxy for domestic connectivity for tourist travel. βs are the coefficients of corresponding variables, and ε_{ijt} is the error term. The tourism equation is estimated with the ordinary least squares estimator. Similar to the goods equations, the estimated coefficients are statistically highly significant and have the expected signs, as well as a relatively high level of overall explanatory power ($R^2 = 0.76$).

The regression results highlight the importance of establishing tourism links with large and fast-growing source countries and increasing destination awareness (Table 16.3). For each percentage increase in source-country population, tourist arrivals rise by about 0.2 percent. This means that, all else being equal, only a small fraction of population growth translates into tourism growth in PICs. However, the same percentage increase from a large source country means a larger number of tourist arrivals than from a small source country. Given that this result is based on panel data, the low elasticity

TABLE 16.2

Estimation Results of the Gravity Model for Pacific Island Countries' Merchandise Imports

Independent Variable	Estimated Coefficient
Importing country real GDP (in logs)	0.91
Exporting country real GDP (in logs)	0.21
Distance (in logs)	–1.74
Preferential trade agreement (existence = 1)	0.36
Colonial ties (existence = 1)	0.81

Source: IMF staff calculations.
Note: The dependent variable is real bilateral imports in logs; all coefficients are statistically significant at the 99 percent confidence level.

TABLE 16.3

Estimation Results of the Gravity Model for Pacific Island Countries' Tourist Arrivals

Independent Variable	Estimated Coefficient
Log (source population)	0.20
Log (source-country real GDP)	0.95
Log (distance)	–1.43
Common language (dummy = 1 if exists)	1.48
Log (land surface of destination country)	0.17
Degree of urbanization	0.08
Constant	8.67

Source: IMF staff calculations.
Note: The dependent variable is tourist arrivals in logs; all coefficients are significant at the 99 percent confidence level. Destinations include Fiji, Palau, Samoa, Tonga, and Vanuatu. Source countries are listed in Annex Table 16.1.2.

could also mean that the awareness of PICs as tourist destinations is lower in large source countries than in small ones. Such facts could hamper the long-term growth of tourism in PICs, but they also suggest that there is greater potential to attract tourists from large countries. On the other hand, distance has a smaller negative impact on tourism than on goods exports. For each percentage increase in distance from a destination country, tourist arrivals decline by 1.4 percent (compared with 2.3 percent for goods exports), reflecting distance-induced increases in travel costs. Clearly, this relationship may be nonlinear and only holds up to a certain distance.

Income is the most important force driving tourist arrivals from a source country. The results indicate an income elasticity of close to unity with respect to source-country income. This is more than twice that for the import-country income elasticity for goods exports. Nevertheless, the estimate indicates that, on average, tourism in PICs is not a luxury service.[20] This seems to be consistent with anecdotal evidence that Australian tourists tend to go to North America, Europe, and Asia when they have more disposable income, whereas the Pacific is more likely to be regarded as a budget holiday destination. However, it is quite possible that the income elasticity varies among income groups and age cohorts and source countries. Information on such variations can be useful for tourism marketing and should be examined in country-specific research.

The results also indicate that a common language shared with a source country helps raise tourist arrivals. A PIC can expect 148 percent more tourist arrivals from a source country that shares its language than from a country that does not. Underlying the role of common languages could also be familiarity with destinations, and hence the availability of information about PICs in source-country languages could play an important role in attracting tourists. Training tour operators and local tourist guides to speak source-country languages could also help. Larger land surface in destination countries is also found to help attract more tourists, probably reflecting the higher capacity of larger countries to receive tourists and the greater diversity of their destinations. However, the role of land surface may also reflect the attraction of a greater range of tourism products and point to the possibility of the gains of collectively marketing a wider range of tourism products and attractions in PICs. Domestic connectivity, as measured by the degree of urbanization, also helps increase tourist arrivals, confirming the importance of general infrastructure for tourism development, although the estimated impact appears to be relatively small.

[20] Song and Li (2008) provide an extensive survey of estimated elasticities of demand for tourism. Most estimates surveyed are greater than one. Eilat and Einav (2004) suggest that income elasticities for tourism in high-income countries tend to be higher than in lower-income countries. Their estimate indicates that the elasticity for high-income countries ranges between 1.29 and 1.55, and between 0.41 and 1.48 for lower-income countries.

TAKING ADVANTAGE OF THE SHIFTING GRAVITY

The results of the gravity model analysis suggest that tourism in PICs is likely to face more favorable conditions for growth than goods exports. The estimated demand elasticity of close to unity with respect to source-country income means that demand for PIC tourist arrivals can expand over time at a similar rate of income growth in source countries, and the smaller negative impact of distance on tourist arrivals helps moderate the disadvantage of remoteness. The common English language and political ties with traditional source countries such as Australia and New Zealand will remain a positive factor for tourist arrivals from these countries. Moreover, the wide use of English in PICs also helps minimize language barriers among Asian tourists, for whom English is the most common second language.[21]

However, it is the shifting global economic gravity that is likely to bring the greatest opportunities for tourism in PICs. Asia's emergence as a global economic center has changed international tourism over the past two decades. Traditionally, Europe and the Americas dominated the global tourism market, both as sources and destinations for international tourism. According to United Nations World Tourism Organization statistics, while Europe remains the largest source of tourists globally, Asia and the Pacific has emerged as the second largest source, overtaking the United States. The region accounted for 23 percent of global tourist departures in 2012, an increase of 10 percentage points from 1990 (Figure 16.10). Tourists from China have increased particularly rapidly, with close to 100 million of its citizens traveling overseas in 2013, the largest country group in the world. The World Tourism Organization (2013) projects that world tourist arrivals will continue to grow robustly over the next two decades, at 3.3 percent per year and reaching 1.8 billion by 2030. International tourist arrivals in emerging markets are projected to grow twice as fast (4.4 percent) as in advanced economies (2.2 percent). Although there is no forecast by source country or region, departures from emerging markets are likely to outpace those from advanced economies, driven by higher populations and income growth.

Emerging markets in Asia could become a major source of tourists in PICs if the right conditions are created there, with China deserving special attention for its large population and rapid income growth. Since 1995, China's travel departures have increased at an annual rate of 15½ percent. Song (2013) forecasts that travel departures could reach 345 million by 2020. Song's implied 19½ percent average annual growth appears to be overly optimistic given the recent economic slowdown. But it is quite likely that the number of tourists from China will still grow rapidly over the medium term, and potentially by about 6.5 percent a year, matching the average forecast of China's GDP growth (based on IMF October 2015 *World Economic Outlook* forecasts). However, household spending is likely to grow significantly faster than GDP as China rebalances growth toward greater reliance on domestic consumption, which would also lead to real exchange rate appreciation over time and therefore more affordable overseas travel.

Tourists from China have come in waves, and one appears to have just arrived in the Pacific. The first wave tended to concentrate on neighboring countries, particularly in northeast and southeast Asia. Over time and as the households grew richer, more tourists traveled to North America and Europe, and the next wave is likely to reach farther afield as nontraditional destinations are explored. Starting from an admittedly low base, tourist arrivals in the Pacific have surged over the past few years (Figure 16.11). The challenge for PICs is to sustain strong growth into the future. In this regard, Maldives provides a benchmark for PICs. Since 2005, Maldives has attracted tourists from China at an astonishing growth rate of 53 percent a year, surpassing 350,000 arrivals in 2014, according to Maldives government data. This represents more than a quarter of total tourist arrivals, with China now the country's biggest source of tourist arrivals. High-end tourist facilities, diversification, and improvements in service, innovation, and marketing to cater to tourist demand have allowed Maldives to create a niche market that is now central to the success of its tourism industry.

---

[21] Bolton (2008) discusses the exponential increase in Asians knowing and speaking English in recent years.

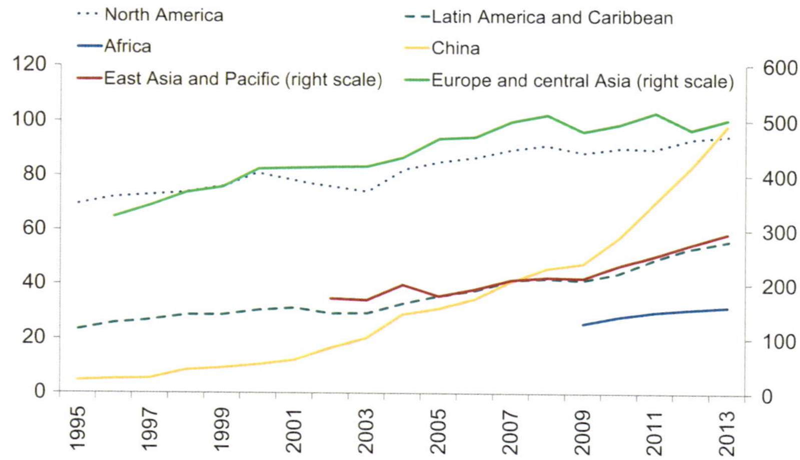

Figure 16.10 International Departures (*Millions*)

Sources: World Bank database; and UN World Tourism Organization.

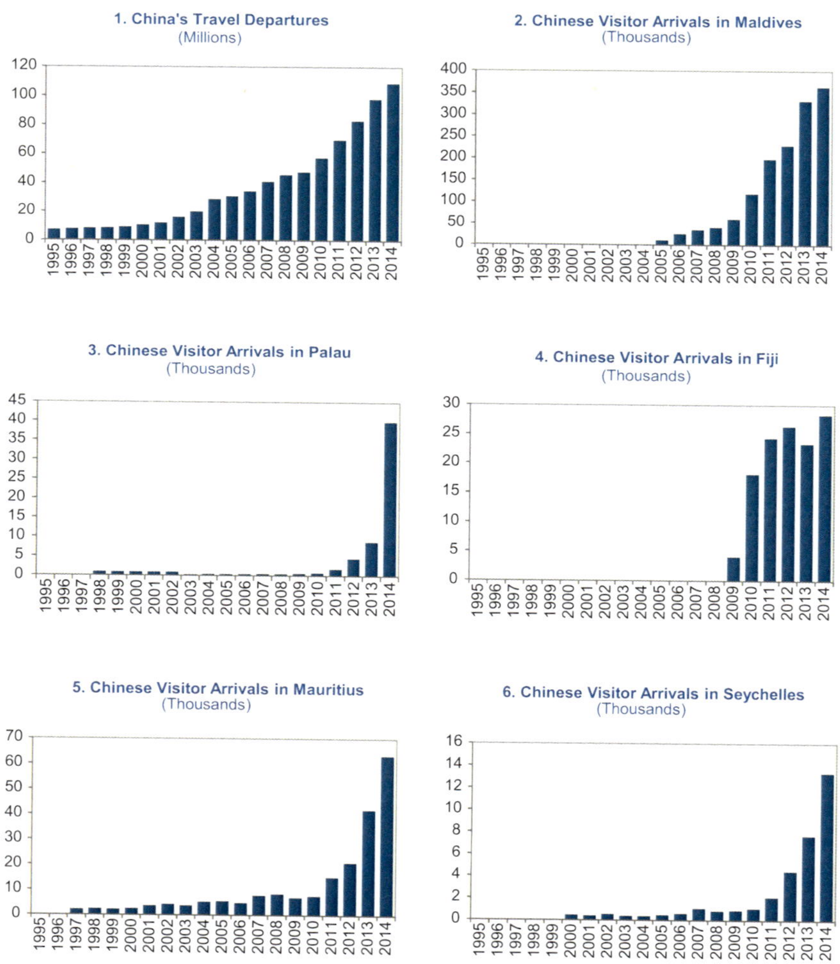

Figure 16.11 Visitors from China, 1995–2014

Source: National statistical agencies.

PICs need to create similar conditions to grow tourism from China and Asia in general. These include raising awareness of the Pacific as a tourism destination through marketing and other forms of information dissemination; more frequent and affordable flights; improved tourism infrastructure and services (for example, hotels and restaurants); and a greater variety and quality of tourist products. Obviously, the starting point varies considerably across PICs, and bottlenecks differ from country to country. Smaller and more remote PICs have a lower starting point and face tougher challenges. A small market makes it difficult to attract frequent and affordable flights and yet without such flights investment in tourist infrastructure will not be viable and tourist products will not develop. As such, an integrated approach to developing tourism with a concerted effort by public and private sectors may be warranted. In particular, the government needs to create the necessary conditions for domestic and foreign investment, including facilitating land leases for tourist infrastructure development. Scope also exists for intergovernmental or regional cooperation to overcome diseconomies of scale, such as through joint marketing and improved cooperation in aviation.

Securing a share of the Asian tourism boom is critical to the future of tourism in PICs. Figure 16.12 shows how tourist arrivals in Fiji could evolve with different degrees of success in attracting tourists just from China. Such rapid tourism growth, in turn, could significantly boost the agricultural sector in PICs, especially if synergies between tourism and agriculture can be exploited. PICs have long recognized the benefits of these synergies, but have been slow to exploit them. The linkage is particularly important for small states, as agricultural exporters face high transportation costs in selling their products to overseas markets, and tropical produce often faces more stringent sanitary and phytosanitary restrictions. By supplying the domestic tourism industry, producers could avoid the disadvantages of long distance and sanitary and phytosanitary restrictions. And those close to tourism sites could save significantly on domestic transportation costs, which are often high.

The linkage between tourism and agriculture is important because it not only offers a way to reduce export costs and barriers, but also serves as a critical strategy to foster inclusive growth. Despite weak performance over the past decade, agriculture is by far the largest sector of most PIC economies and provides employment and income for more households than any other sector. Thus, linking agriculture to tourism can help revive agriculture and broaden the base for economic growth.

While there is little information about the current state of agricultural supply to the tourism industry, anecdotal evidence suggests significant potential. A study based on a "farm to table" project by the University of the South Pacific reports that 70 percent of food for the tourism industry in the

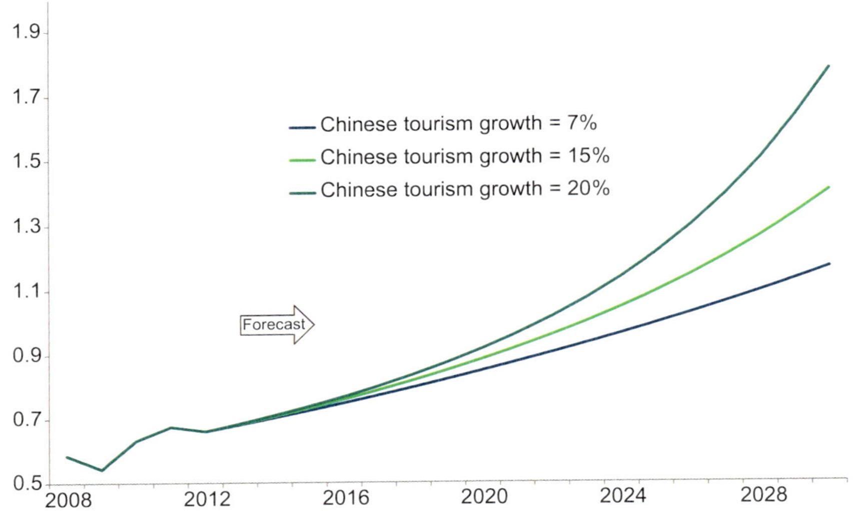

Figure 16.12 Projection of Chinese Visitor Arrivals in Fiji (*Millions*)

Sources: Fiji Bureau of Statistics; and authors' projections.

Pacific is imported (Gibson 2013). The overall retention rate for tourist expenditure is about 44 percent in Fiji; that is, for each dollar a tourist spends, 56 cents leaks out of Fiji through spending on imported goods and services, a large portion of which is food and agricultural products. The Food and Agriculture Organization (2012) notes that with the exception of pork, virtually all meats are imported in Tonga and Samoa, particularly for high-end hotels and restaurants because local producers cannot supply these products in required volumes with consistent quality. Similarly, hotels and restaurants often rely on imported vegetables and fruits. Imports of food products are inevitable in PICs and help reduce costs given the undiversified production base and climate conditions in the region. Even so, there seems to be considerable scope to supply produce suitable for cultivation in the tropical climates of these countries. What has prevented the development of a supply chain to meet this local demand and consistently supply quality needs to be examined.

Once domestic producers can supply local hospitality industries with adequate volumes and consistent quality, local producers will be in a stronger position to export. The larger volumes and higher quality would effectively reduce the cost of agricultural exports and make PICs more competitive in overseas markets. In fact, overseas markets and domestic hospitality markets can be highly complementary. The seasonality of certain vegetables and fruits has been a major issue for local hotels and restaurants, but this is because small production volumes make it economically unviable to develop local storage facilities. Once production volumes reach critical mass, it will become more cost effective to develop such logistics to facilitate exports.

Agricultural development can also help enhance the tourism industry. As Rogers (2012) points out for Samoa and Tonga, agricultural systems are an integral part of the natural environment that provides the aesthetic context for a tourist destination. Thus, it is important to preserve the essential features of Pacific agricultural systems to ensure ecological sustainability and commercial value for tourism. Greater use of agricultural systems can enhance the tourist experience as well as increase local value added. However, care should be taken in developing tourism infrastructure to protect the agricultural environment. Similarly, agricultural development should minimize pollution and avoid damage to tourist attractions. Organic farming has often been advocated both as a way to produce higher-value-added products by product differentiation as well as to better preserve the natural environment. This requires a holistic approach to development planning and coordinated efforts between agriculture and tourism authorities.

CONCLUSIONS

PICs have made considerable effort—albeit with mixed success—to advance trade integration, both within and outside the region. Large preference margins offered by former colonial powers in earlier years appear to have helped boost certain exports, such as sugar; textile, clothing, and footwear products; and automobile parts. But as preference margins have fallen and Australia's automobile manufacturing industry declines, PICs' exports have suffered. Meanwhile, weak domestic supply capacity and rigorous quarantine requirements continue to hamper agricultural exports. PICs have increasingly turned to intraregional trade integration to boost export demand, but the lack of trade complementarity among PICs and the slow implementation of trade agreements mean that benefits may be limited, and their impact may not even be welfare improving because of trade diversion. Furthermore, the likely uneven distribution of trade expansion in favor of larger countries in the region may lead to tensions that continue to hinder trade liberalization.

Asia's economic emergence globally further reinforces the rationale for unilateral trade liberalization in PICs. Australia and New Zealand will remain major sources of imports for these countries for a long time, but the rapidly growing importance of Asian imports has increased the chance of trade diversion from PACER Plus. Some of the major benefits for PICs from this are likely to be in the area of development assistance to improve their domestic supply capacity. This is especially so in agriculture and tourism, as well as in a scientifically based relaxation of quarantine restrictions on Pacific produce. Perhaps the largest benefits lie in an expanded and more institutionalized temporary migration scheme that would allow PICs to export labor services, especially the small countries with limited capacity, at least in the short to medium term, to export goods and services. All these measures should be included in the final PACER Plus agreement, but PICs should at the same time pursue unilateral liberalization to avoid trade diversion.

While continuing to expand trade, temporary migration schemes, and other forms of economic cooperation with traditional trading partners, PICs should make a greater effort to diversify trade into Asian markets. This will not be easy, as shown by the limited progress of non-resource-rich PICs in tapping the Chinese market. Apart from domestic supply constraints, this is partly because of ever-closer trade integration in Asia that has enabled southeast Asian countries to supply increasing quantities of tropical produce to northeast Asian countries. To improve competitiveness, PICs will need to make significant progress on two fronts. The first is to improve agricultural productivity. At the micro level, this requires, among other things, supporting infrastructure and services, such as extension services and efficient marketing arrangements, and land systems that provide secure access to land for productive purposes. At the macro level, PICs need to maintain exchange rates at appropriate levels through macroeconomic policies that keep inflation low and make greater use of aid and remittances for productive investment and minimizing the potential for Dutch disease. And second, PICs should negotiate a more level playing field in Asian countries, perhaps collectively, through freer market access and the extension of existing preferential access in some markets, such as China.

The prospects for diversification into Asian markets are much more promising in tourism, and here policies should focus on creating conditions for private business to thrive. PICs have comparative advantage in tourism, despite their remoteness from major global economic centers. As global economic momentum moves eastward, it presents PICs with an unprecedented opportunity to develop tourism. Surging outbound tourists from China and other Asian countries have already begun to benefit PICs, and this could be the beginning of a long boom. To seize the opportunity, PICs must market themselves proactively. Countries need to attract foreign investment and know-how in building and upgrading tourism infrastructure, and provide secure access to land leases. Regional cooperation in marketing and trade-related infrastructure could help overcome diseconomies of scale. Governments could help reduce barriers for entering the tourism market faced by local businesses, particularly small and medium-size ones; and help promote Pacific cultures as a tourist attraction, which would benefit local communities.

Strong tourism growth could also provide much-needed support to agriculture in PICs, and policies should actively support the establishment of agriculture-tourism linkages. But strong linkages need to be made between the two sectors; otherwise a tourism boom could increase pressure on the agriculture sector. In the past, some PICs may have experienced competition between agriculture and tourism, particularly in use of land and labor. Furthermore, strong exchange rates that are supported by tourism earnings may have had a negative impact on agricultural production and exports. Yet if the linkages are made, a tourism boom could generate demand for local food and other products, as there are considerable synergies to be exploited that would benefit both sectors. Government policies should therefore encourage initiatives to build supply chains to ensure a sufficient supply of food and agricultural products to the tourism industry with consistent quality, and unique Pacific agricultural systems should be integrated into local tourism products. Strong growth of both tourism and agriculture would provide a sound basis for inclusive growth.

ANNEX 16.1. LIST OF GOODS-IMPORTING COUNTRIES AND TOURIST SOURCE COUNTRIES

ANNEX TABLE 16.1.1

Importers of Goods from Pacific Island Countries, 1992–2014 (100 Countries in Total)

Algeria	Côte d'Ivoire	Ireland	Netherlands	Solomon Islands
Australia	Denmark	Israel	New Zealand	South Africa
Austria	Dominica	Italy	Nigeria	Spain
Bahrain	Dominican Republic	Jamaica	Norway	Sri Lanka
Bangladesh	Ecuador	Japan	Oman	Sweden
Barbados	Egypt	Jordan	Pakistan	Switzerland
Belarus	Estonia	Kenya	Panama	Tanzania
Belgium	Fiji	Kiribati	Papua New Guinea	Thailand
Brazil	Finland	Korea	Peru	Tonga
Brunei Darussalam	France	Kuwait	Philippines	Trinidad and Tobago
Bulgaria	Gabon	Lao P. D. R.	Poland	Tunisia
Cambodia	Germany	Latvia	Portugal	Turkey
Canada	Greece	Lebanon	Qatar	Tuvalu
Chile	Guatemala	Lithuania	Romania	Ukraine
China	Haiti	Former Yugoslav Republic of Macedonia	Russia	United Kingdom
Colombia	Honduras	Malaysia	Samoa	United States
Costa Rica	Hungary	Malta	Saudi Arabia	Vanuatu
Croatia	Iceland	Mauritius	Singapore	Venezuela
Cyprus	India	Mongolia	Slovak Republic	Vietnam
Czech Republic	Indonesia	Morocco	Slovenia	Yemen

Source: Authors' compilation.

ANNEX TABLE 16.1.2

Major Source Countries of Tourist Arrivals, 2000–14

Australia	Japan	Philippines
China	Malaysia	United Kingdom
India	New Zealand	United States

Source: Authors' compilation.

ANNEX 16.2. MODEL, METHODOLOGY, AND DATA DESCRIPTIONS

Both goods and tourism analyses are based on a modified gravity model as follows:

$$T_{ijt} = A_0 e^{\Sigma \delta W} \cdot \frac{Y_{it}^{\beta_1} Y_{jt}^{\beta_2}}{D_{ij}^{\beta_3}} \tag{16.2.1}$$

where subscript i represents individual PICs; j represents PICs' trading partners in the analysis of goods and source country of tourist arrivals in the analysis of tourism; and t, year. T is trade flow in the analysis of goods and tourist arrivals in the analysis of tourism. T varies with i, j, and t. A_0 is the constant term. Y_{it} is individual PICs' real GDP, which varies with i and t. Y_{jt} is PICs' trading partners' real GDP in the analysis of goods and source countries' real GDP per capita in the analysis of tourism. It varies with j and t. D_{ij} is distance between capitals of pairwise trading partners. It is time-invariant, and varies with i and j. W is a matrix of other factors affecting trade flows and tourist arrivals. They will be defined in detail in models explaining trade flows and tourism arrivals, respectively. β and δ are parameters.

Note that among the above relationships between trade flow/tourism arrivals T and control factors, the linkage between T and PICs' GDP Y_{it} may be bidirectional, which may therefore lead to an endogeneity problem. An instrumental variables estimator should therefore be employed to yield unbiased estimates if endogeneity exists.

Modeling PICs' Exports and Imports

Logarithmic transformation of equation (16.2.1) and taking into account other relevant factors X give an econometric model for modeling trade flows (exports and imports, respectively) for PICs:

$$\ln T_{ijt} = \alpha_i + \alpha_j + \alpha_1 \ln Y_{it} + \alpha_2 \ln Y_{jt} + \alpha_3 \ln D_{ij} + \alpha_4 F_{ij} + \alpha_5 C_{ij} + \mu_{ijt} \tag{16.2.2}$$

where T_{ijt} stands for trade flows of PICs, and we use X to denote exports and M imports; Y_{it} is the GDP of export country i, and Y_{jt} is the GDP of importing country j; D_{ij} is the distance between capitals of pairwise trading countries; F_{ij} is a dummy variable indicating if countries i and j are both signatories of the same preferential trade agreement ($F_{ij} = 1$ if both countries are signatories, and $F_{ij} = 0$ if they are not); and C_{ij} indicates if countries i and j share colonial ties, with binary values 1 and 0 indicating existence and absence of such ties, respectively. F and C are the additional factors composing W in equation (16.2.1), which are found significant in explaining PICs' trade flows.[22] Furthermore, α_i and α_j are the exporting country's and importing country's fixed effects, α is the vector of control factors' coefficients, and μ_{ijt} is the white noise error term.

Data for the trade flows (goods) cover six PICs and their 100 trading partners over 1990–2012.[23] Equation (16.2.2) is estimated with the fixed effects least squares dummy variables estimator (henceforth FELSDV, also referred to as the two high-dimensional fixed effects estimator) and two-stage FELSDV (henceforth TSFELSDV) to control for the endogenous effect of PICs' real GDP if it exists, for exports and imports respectively. The null hypothesis of no fixed effects of exporting countries and importing countries is rejected at the 1 percent level with the p-value of zero for F critical statistic greater than the observed F statistic. This points to the necessary employment of the FELSDV estimator. In the TSFELSDV estimation, gross fixed capital formation (investment) is the external instrumental

[22] We also considered the relative price index $RELRER_X^j = RER_X^j \Big/ \sum_{k \neq X} \alpha_k RER_k^j$, where j is importer, X is exporter, $RER = \frac{CPI_X}{CPI^j} \Big/ \frac{\$_X / \$_{US}}{\$^j / \$_{US}}$, and α_k is the share of exports to country j from country k. The estimated coefficient of this relative price index turns out to be negative but highly insignificant.

[23] Note that the two high-dimensional panel is not a balanced panel.

ANNEX TABLE 16.2.1

Estimation Results of the Gravity Model for Pacific Island Countries' Merchandise Exports and Imports

	Dependent: ln(exports)		Dependent: ln(imports)	
Independent Variable	**FELSDV**	**TSFELSDV**	**FELSDV**	**TSFELSDV**
PIC's real GDP, $\ln Y_{it}$	0.27 (2.95)	0.19 (1.62)	0.81 (12.93)	0.91 (11.23)
Trading partners' real GDP, $\ln Y_{jt}$	0.44 (10.78)	0.44 (9.96)	0.28 (9.69)	0.29 (8.92)
Distance, $\ln D_{ij}$	−2.32 (−15.90)	−2.36 (−15.47)	−1.65 (−15.27)	−1.74 (−15.17)
Preferential trade agreement, F_{ij}	0.39 (3.40)	0.35 (2.67)	0.40 (5.67)	0.36 (4.43)
Colonial ties, C_{ij}	1.31 (8.89)	1.28 (7.73)	0.90 (7.73)	0.81 (6.38)
Sample size	3028	2585	4104	3493
Instrumented variable	–	$\ln Y_{it}$	–	$\ln Y_{it}$
External instruments	–	Investment	–	Investment
F-statistic for instruments' significance	–	5554.57	–	5554.57
F (H_0: $\alpha_i = \alpha_j = 0$)	13.15	–	42.38	–
R^2	0.640	0.650	0.763	0.768

Source: IMF staff calculations.
Note: *t*-statistics are in brackets. FELSDV = fixed effects least squares dummy variable estimator; PIC = Pacific island country; TSFELSDV = two-stage FELSDV.

variable to control randomness of $\ln Y_{it}$ in the first stage of estimation, which is found to be a strong instrument since the Wald test yields an F statistic of more than the threshold value of 10.

Since there is no significant difference between the FELSDV and TSFELSDV estimates, the null hypothesis of exogeneity is not rejected; namely, $\ln Y_{it}$ is not endogenous in models explaining PICs' exports and imports. This leads to the conclusion that the FELSDV estimates are unbiased and consistent. Estimation results for goods exports and imports are summarized in Annex Table 16.2.1.

Modeling Tourist Arrivals

Similar to the model explaining merchandise exports and imports in PICs, an econometric model for modeling tourist arrivals in PICs is developed as follows:

$$\ln V_{ijt} = \beta_0 + \beta_1 \ln N_{jt} + \beta_2 \ln YPC_{jt} + \beta_3 \ln D_{ij} + \beta_4 L_{ij} + \beta_5 S_i + \beta_6 U_{it} + \varepsilon_{ijt} \quad (16.2.3)$$

where V_{ijt} stands for the number of tourist arrivals in country i from country j; N_{jt} is the population of source country j; YPC_{jt} is the GDP per capita of source country j; D_{ij} is the distance between destination country i and source country j; L_{ij} is a dummy variable indicating if countries i and j share a common language ($L_{ij} = 1$ if both countries share a common language, and $L_{ij} = 0$ if they do not); and S_i stands for land surface area of country i. U_{it} is the share of urban population in destination country i, a proxy for domestic connectivity for tourist travel. βs are the coefficients of corresponding variables, and ε_{ijt} is the white noise error term.

In equation (16.2.3), a destination country's urban population ratio, U_{it}, which to a great extent reflects a country's urbanization level, may be endogenous because development of the tourism industry may in turn speed up the country's urbanization progress. If this is the case an instrumental variables estimator should be used.

Data for the analysis of tourist arrivals are based on a strongly balanced panel covering five PICs and nine source countries over 2000–14. Equation (16.2.3) is estimated with the ordinary least squares (henceforth OLS), two-stage least squares estimator (henceforth TSLS) and the FELSDV estimator. The TSFELSDV estimator was also tried, and it yielded the same result as the FELSDV: that U_{it} is not significant.

Estimation results for PICs' tourist arrivals are summarized in Annex Table 16.2.2, which shows that the FELSDV estimator is more appropriate than the least squares (LS) estimators since the null

ANNEX TABLE 16.2.2

Estimation Results of the Gravity Model for Tourist Arrivals, ln(tourist arrivals)

Independent Variable	OLS	TSLS	FELSDV
Source country's total population, $\ln N_{jt}$	0.20 (3.41)	0.22 (3.29)	1.92 (1.82)
Source country's per capita GDP, $\ln YPC_{jt}$	0.95 (9.86)	0.77 (6.30)	1.38 (5.15)
Destination country's urban population ratio, U_{it}	0.08 (20.00)	0.11 (9.87)	−0.005 (−0.74)
Distance, $\ln D_{ij}$	−1.43 (−8.98)	−1.68 (−8.60)	−2.81 (−12.59)
Destination country's land surface, $\ln S_{it}$	0.17 (5.83)	0.21 (6.02)	–
Common language, L_{ij}	1.48 (10.04)	1.60 (9.34)	–
Sample size	273	273	273
Instrumented variable	–	U_{it}	–
External instruments	–	Destination country's per capita GDP	–
F-statistic for instruments' significance		45.62	–
Hausman *F*-statistic (*p*-value)		16.38 (0.000)	
F (H_0: $\alpha_i = \alpha_j = 0$)	–	–	65.62
Adjusted/centered R^2	0.7601	0.6885	0.9424

Source: IMF staff calculations.

Note: *t*-statistics are in parentheses. FELSDV = fixed effects least squares dummy variable estimator; OLS = ordinary least squares; TSLS = two-stage least squares estimator.

hypothesis of no fixed effects is rejected at the 1 percent level. Although LS estimators provide more information about determinants of tourist arrivals in PICs, the FELSDV has a better goodness of fit, which means that heterogeneities of destination countries and source countries are more than the additional three factors identified in the LS estimates; namely, the destination country's urban population ratio, the destination country's land surface, and common language.

ANNEX 16.3. DATA SOURCES AND DESCRIPTIONS

ANNEX TABLE 16.3.1

Series and Data Sources

Abbreviation	Series	Source of Data
X_{ijt}	PICs' exports (deflated by U.S. import price index, U.S. dollars)	IMF
M_{ijt}	PICs' imports (deflated by U.S. export price index, U.S. dollars)	IMF
P_{it}	PICs' population (persons)	IMF
P_{jt}	Trading partners' population (persons)	IMF
Y_{it}	PICs' real GDP	IMF
Y_{jt}	Trading partners' real GDP	IMF
D_{ij}	Distance between capitals of pairwise trading partners (kilometers)	CEPII – French Research Center in International Economics
F_{ij}	Trade agreement between trading countries (binary series)	Country authorities
C_{ij}	Exporter and importer share colonial ties (binary series)	Issue Correlates of War Colonial History Data–Paul Hensel
V_{ijt}	Tourist arrivals in PICs (persons)	Country authorities
U_{it}	PICs' urban population ratio (percent)	World Bank, World Development Indicators database
YPC_{jt}	Source countries' real GDP per capita (U.S. dollars)	IMF
N_{jt}	Source countries' population (persons)	World Bank
L_{ij}	Common language (binary series)	InfoPlease database–Pearson Education Inc.
S_i	PICs' land surface area (square kilometers)	World Bank

Source: IMF staff compilation.
Note: PICs = Pacific island countries.

ANNEX TABLE 16.3.2

Summary Statistics: Exports from Pacific Island Countries (based on 3,028 observations)

	PICs' Exports (millions of U.S. dollars)	PICs' Population (million persons)	Trading Partners' Population (million persons)	PICs' Real GDP (billions of U.S. dollars)	Trading Partners' Real GDP (billions of U.S. dollars)	Distance (thousand kilometers)	Trade Agreement between Trading Countries	Exporter and Importer Share Colonial Ties
Mean	32.30	1.95	124.75	2.80	1334.33	9.96	0.38	0.06
Standard deviation	153.02	2.45	290.24	3.09	2631.85	5.28	0.49	0.24
Maximum	3,260.00	7.17	1,354.04	15.03	14,937.56	19.39	1.00	1.00
Minimum	0.10	0.10	0.00	0.21	0.01	0.75	0.00	0.00

Source: IMF staff calculations.
Note: PICs = Pacific island countries.

ANNEX TABLE 16.3.3

Summary Statistics: Imports of Pacific Island Countries (based on 4,104 observations)

	PICs' Imports (millions of U.S. dollars)	PICs' Population (million persons)	Trading Partners' Population (million persons)	PICs' Real GDP (billions of U.S. dollars)	Trading Partners' Real GDP (billions of U.S. dollars)	Distance (thousand kilometers)	Trade Agreement between Trading Countries	Exporter and Importer Share Colonial Ties
Mean	23.72	1.79	112.61	2.65	1,106.55	10.96	0.34	0.05
Standard deviation	110.20	2.37	270.73	3.01	2,321.52	4.97	0.47	0.22
Maximum	2,856.60	7.17	1,354.04	15.03	14,937.56	19.12	1.00	1.00
Minimum	0.03	0.10	0.00	0.21	0.01	0.75	0.00	0.00

Source: IMF staff calculations.
Note: PICs = Pacific island countries.

REFERENCES

Armstrong, Harvey W., and Robert Read. 1998. "Trade and Growth in Small States: The Impact of Global Trade Liberalization." *The World Economy* 21 (4): 563–85.

Bolton, Kingsley. 2008. "English in Asia, Asian Englishes, and the Issue of Proficiency." *English Today* 24 (02): 3–12.

Braxton, Nick. 2009. *PACER Plus and Its Alternatives: Which Way for Trade and Development in the Pacific?* Auckland: Oxfam New Zealand.

Chand, Satish, editor. 2005. *Pacific Islands Regional Integration and Governance*. Canberra: Asia Pacific Press.

———. 2010. "Shaping New Regionalism in the Pacific Islands: Back to the Future?" Working Paper Series on Regional Economic Integration 61, Asian Development Bank, Manila.

Chen, Hong, Lanieta Rauqueque, Shiu Raj Singh, Yiqun Wu, and Yongzheng Yang. 2014. "Pacific Island Countries: In Search of a Trade Strategy." IMF Working Paper 14/158, International Monetary Fund, Washington.

Duncan, Ron. 2008. *Pacific Trade Issues*. Pacific Studies Series. Manila: Asian Development Bank.

Eilat, Yair, and Liran Einav. 2004. "Determinants of International Tourism: A Three-Dimensional Panel Data Analysis." *Applied Economics* 36 (12): 1315–27.

Food and Agriculture Organization. 2012. "Report on a Scoping Mission in Samoa and Tonga: Agriculture and Tourism Linkages in Pacific Island Countries." Food and Agriculture Organization Sub-regional Office for the Pacific Islands.

Gibson, Dawn. 2013. "Farm to Table: Celebrating Local Produce and Cuisine." Unpublished. University of the South Pacific, Suva.

Prasad, Biman. 2008. "A Quantitative Analysis of the Potential Benefit and Cost of a PACER-Plus Agreement." In *Research Study on the Benefits, Challenges and Ways Forward for PACER-Plus*. Adelaide: Institute for International Trade, University of Adelaide.

Rogers, Tuifa'asisina S. 2012. "Agriculture and Tourism Linkages in Pacific Island Countries." Food and Agriculture Organization, Rome.

Song, Haiyan. 2013. "China Outbound Tourism: Trends and Prospects." Presentation for Hong Kong Polytechnic University, Hong Kong Special Administrative Region.

———, and Gang Li. 2008. "Tourism Demand Modeling and Forecasting—A Review of Recent Research." *Tourism Management* 29 (2): 203–220.

World Tourism Organization. 2013. *Tourism towards 2030: Global Overview*. Madrid: World Tourism Organization.

CHAPTER 17

Determinants of Interest Rate Spreads in the Solomon Islands

NOOMAN REBEI

Deposit-lending rate spreads are large in the Solomon Islands compared with the rest of the Pacific island countries, despite their recent decline. Several studies have looked at the causes and implications of high spreads in other regions. However, few have addressed the banking sector in the Pacific islands, and almost none have considered the case of the Solomon Islands. This chapter, which examines the determinants of interest rate spreads in the Solomon Islands, aims to address this gap. Interest rate spreads are very heterogeneous in the region, and finding common lessons from a panel analysis can be misleading (Figure 17.1). Unlike previous empirical studies, this chapter focuses on local banks by using detailed quarterly bank and macroeconomic data.

High bank spreads, among other factors, hinder the private sector's access to credit, which is an impediment to inclusive growth (Figure 17.2). It is therefore important to identify the sources of high spreads in the Solomon Islands to formulate potential reforms that can be implemented.

This chapter begins by providing the background and theory on interest rate spreads and their determinants. It then describes the empirical methodology and discusses the estimation results. This is followed by an examination of the structure of the banking sector in the Solomon Islands and an investigation into potential collusion in the sector. Finally, policy recommendations are offered.

FACTORS BEHIND HIGH INTEREST RATE SPREADS

To capture the different aspects of the banking sector in the Solomon Islands, bank-level data collected and published on a quarterly basis by the Central Bank of Solomon Islands (CBSI) are used. Our panel data set contains quarterly balance sheet and income statement data on every commercial bank from the first quarter of 2009 to the third quarter of 2013. Data from the IMF's World Economic Outlook and International Financial Statistics databases were used to identify other macroeconomic aggregates.

Bank spreads measure the gap between the amounts a bank pays the providers of funds and what it receives from users of bank credit. The literature distinguishes among different definitions of bank spreads. The most common are a narrow definition, which is described as the difference between interest income over loans and the interest expense over deposits; and a broad definition, which corresponds to a bank's total interest income minus total interest expense, divided by total interest-bearing assets.[1]

Figures 17.3 and 17.4 show that from the first quarter of 2009 to the third quarter of 2013 bank-specific interest rate spreads in the Solomon Islands remained high regardless of the adopted methodology to measure them. Figure 17.3 shows some persistence of bank spreads, which may indicate low competition in the banking industry. This raises concerns about the effectiveness of the credit channel for monetary policy transmission and would influence the appropriate policy stance for the

This work would not have been possible without the generous cooperation and hospitality of the authorities in the Solomon Islands. The author also thanks Ezequiel Cabezon for excellent research assistance; Sami Ben Naceur, Luis Breuer, Ray Brooks, Reda Cherif, Fuad Hasanov, Hoe Ee Khor, Roger Kronenberg, Vicki Plater, Patrizia Tumbarello, Moez Souissi, and the staff of the Central Bank of Solomon Islands for their helpful comments.

[1] See Brock and Rojas-Suarez (2000) for a detailed discussion of the definitions of interest rate margins.

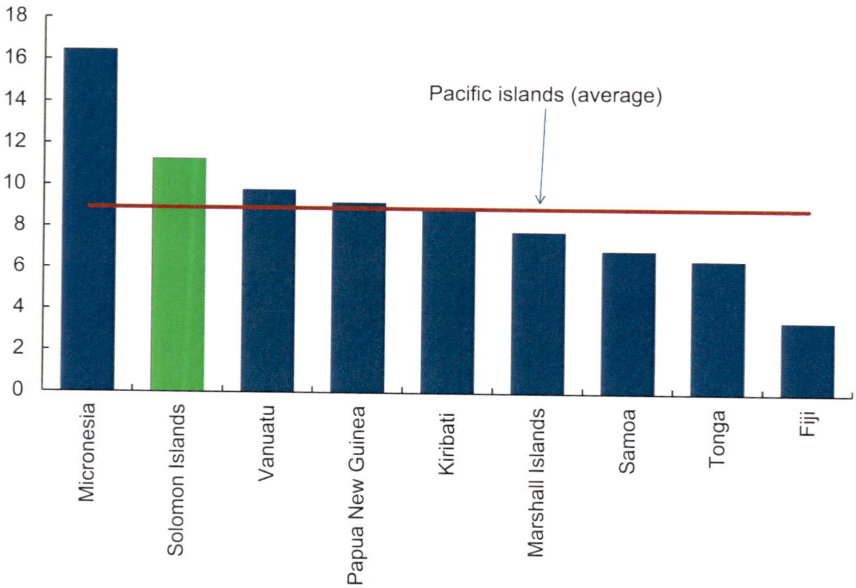

Figure 17.1 Interest Rate Spreads of Commercial Banks, 2014 (*Annualized spreads*)

Sources: Country authorities; IMF, Monetary and Financial Statistics and International Financial Statistics databases; and IMF staff calculations.

Note: Annualized interest rates. For Kiribati and Marshall Islands data are for 2011.

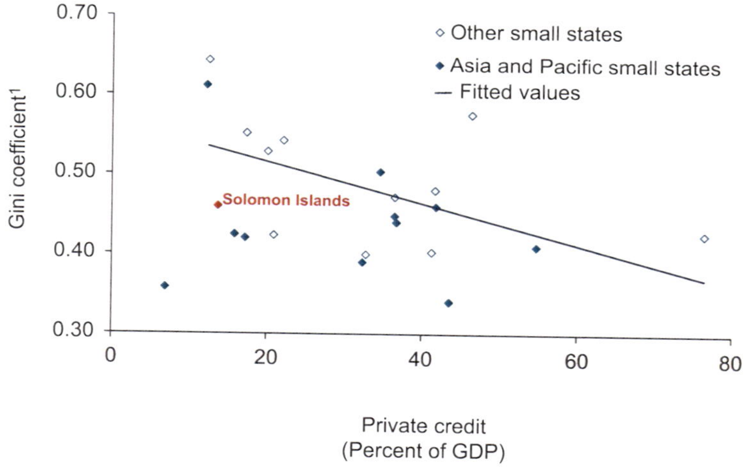

Figure 17.2 Financial Development and Inequality, Average 1990–2013

Sources: Asian Development Bank, *Key Indicators for Asia and the Pacific*; IMF, Financial Access Survey; World Bank, World Development Indicators; and IMF staff calculations.

[1]A value of 1 indicates maximum inequality.

monetary authorities.[2] It may also raise concerns about financial stability because investors tend to undertake risky projects to compensate for high lending rates, leading to increased default risks. This is the "concentration-fragility" view of the relationship between market power and bank soundness, which holds that a concentrated market weakens stability. Another view—the "concentration-stability" view—argues that larger banks in concentrated banking sectors reduce financial fragility because,

[2]The spread is widely considered an indicator of the efficiency of financial intermediation. High spreads can alter financial intermediation, because they discourage potential savers owing to low returns and increase financing costs for borrowers, reducing investment and growth opportunities (Mirzaei, Moore, and Liu 2013).

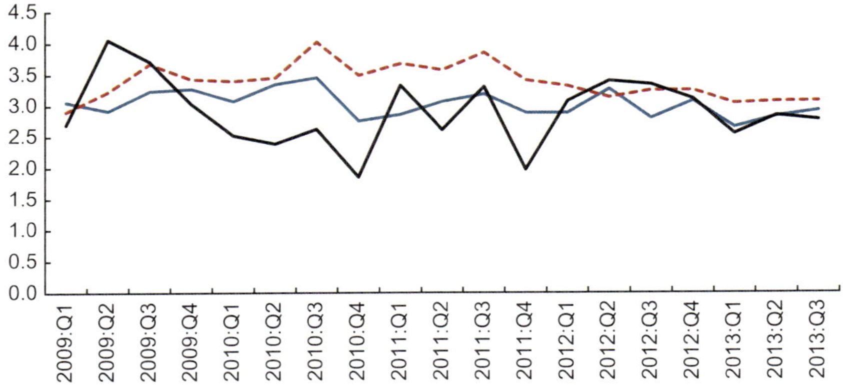

Figure 17.3 Commercial Bank Spreads, Narrow Definition

Sources: Central Bank of the Solomon Islands; and IMF staff calculations.
Note: The interest rate spreads for the three banks, Australia and New Zealand Banking Group Limited (ANZ), Bank South Pacific (BSP), and Westpac Banking Corporation (WBC), are calculated by taking the total interest received by banks on loans during one quarter divided by the total loans for that period and subtracting from the result the total interest paid on deposits throughout the quarter divided by total deposits. Numbers are displayed as quarterly percentages.

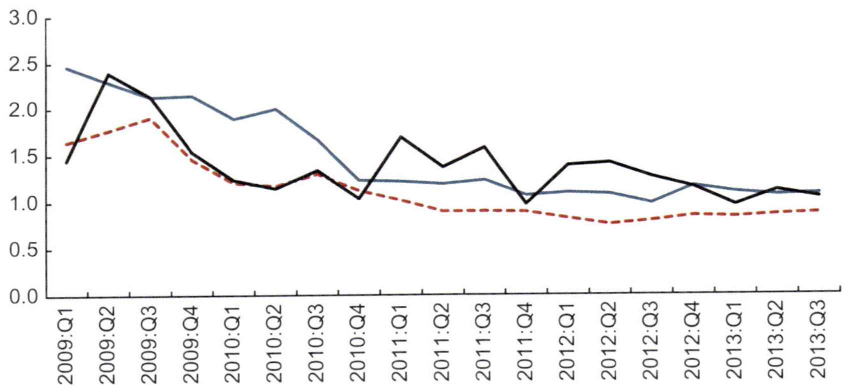

Figure 17.4 Commercial Bank Spreads, Broad Definition

Sources: Central Bank of the Solomon Islands; and IMF staff calculations.
Note: The interest rate spreads for the three banks in the graph are defined as the difference between the quarterly interest income and quarterly interest expense divided by the total amount of assets during the same period.

among other reasons, they tend to increase profits and build up high capital buffers. This makes them less prone to liquidity and macroeconomic shocks (see, for example, Berger 1995; Uhde and Heimeshoff 2009; and Mirzaei, Moore, and Liu 2013).

The key determinants of interest rate spreads of banks in the Solomon Islands are now examined using a set of bank-specific variables, the main banking industry characteristics, and macroeconomic conditions. Different authors use the same classification of variable categories, including Gelos (2006) for Latin America, Crowley (2007) for the English-speaking African countries, and Samuel and Valderrama (2006) for Caribbean countries. The selection of variables was guided by the abundant existing literature, but data availability for banks in the Solomon Islands is taken into consideration.

Characteristics of Banks in the Solomon Islands and the South Pacific Region

Before focusing on bank-specific indicators, we start with comparing selected indicators of banks in the Solomon Islands with those in the region (Chapter 2 provides additional cross-country comparisons). Although, this is not reflected in the empirical analysis—where we consider only time

TABLE 17.1

Selected Bank Indicators

	Number of Commercial Banks	Return on Average Assets	Ratio of Equity to Average Assets	Ratio of Loan Loss Reserves to Gross Loans	Ratio of Gross Noninterest Expense to Average Assets	Ratio of Nonsalary, Noninterest Expense to Average Assets
Samoa	4	5.4	18.3	3.9	5.6	3.2
Solomon Islands	3	7.0	17.8	3.5	6.3	3.4
Tonga	4	3.5	16.7	7.2	5.5	3.1
Vanuatu	4	3.4	11.8	4.3	3.0	1.7
Average, small island states	**3.7**	**4.9**	**16.0**	**4.7**	**5.1**	**2.9**
Fiji	6	3.4	9.3	2.3	4.0	1.7
Papua New Guinea	4	4.1	13.8	4.0	3.5	2.5

Sources: Country authorities' central bank prudential data; and IMF staff estimates.
Note: All numbers, unless otherwise mentioned, are percentages calculated based on average yearly data covering the period 2000–13. Papua New Guinea's numbers are from 2000–12. The number of commercial banks is as of end-2014.

series for the domestic banks—this should shed some light on the general characteristics of banks in the Solomon Islands and the major variables that should be identified as potential sources of high interest rate spreads.

These banks show clear evidence of high profitability compared with regional and international standards. They also show a higher degree of risk aversion owing to the excessive accumulated levels of equity to average assets. Credit risk, as measured by loan loss to gross loans, is moderate compared with the South Pacific region in recent years. Moreover, banks in the Solomon Islands exhibit relatively prominent salary and other noninterest expenses to average assets compared with other island countries in the South Pacific (Table 17.1). More disaggregated quarterly bank-specific data are used in the following sections to better understand the determinants of bank spreads in the Solomon Islands.

Bank-Specific Variables

In this section, we use the broad definition of interest rate spreads; that is, the quarterly net interest income as a percentage of total interest-bearing assets (called interest margins hereafter). Relationships between bank spreads and a set of selected bank-specific variables are examined. As a start, these relationships are explored visually using scatter plots, and the mechanism and intuition through which each variable could affect spreads are discussed.[3]

Several empirical studies find a positive relationship between operating costs and interest margins. Many banking studies, including Park and Weber (2006), Claeys and Vander Vennet (2008), Tregenna (2009), and Mirzaei, Moore, and Liu (2013), found that low operational efficiency is reflected in high bank margins. These results provide support for the structure-conduct-performance paradigm, which posits that banks can pass high operating costs almost fully on to customers in highly concentrated markets. One way to account for this is to include an index for management quality—generally measured with the ratio of noninterest expenses to total assets—as an explanatory variable. This analysis uses three disaggregated measures of operating costs: (1) salaries and wages, which are scaled by total assets and are expected to have a positive effect on spreads; (2) depreciation and occupancy costs as a ratio of net fixed assets, which are expected to have a negative

[3] All scatter plots reflect the relationship between average spreads and the averages of the selected explanatory variables. The observations in Figures 17.5 to 17.12 represent combinations of average observations for each quarter; and therefore could be interpreted as time series.

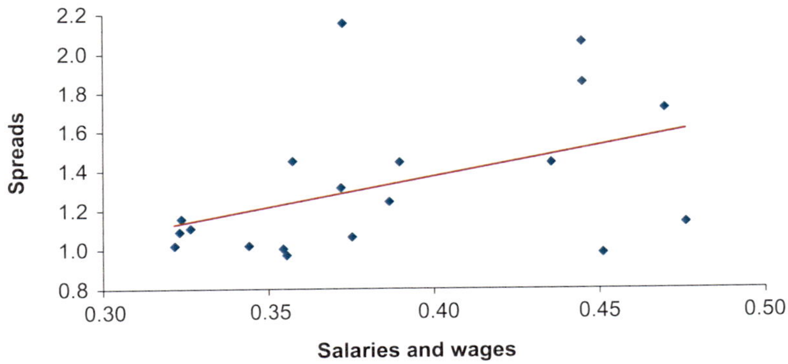

Figure 17.5 Average Spreads and Staff Costs

Sources: Central Bank of the Solomon Islands; and IMF staff calculations.

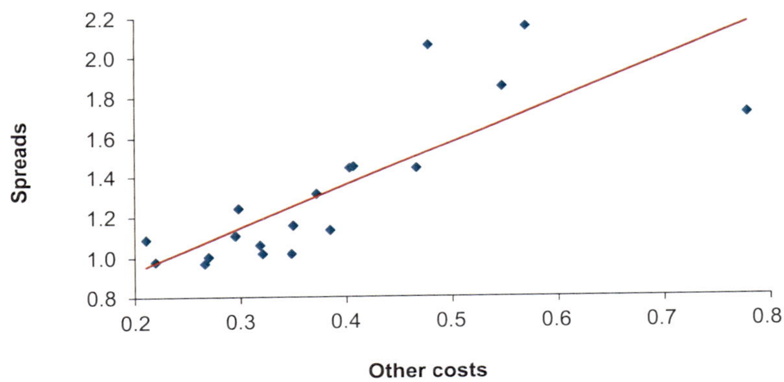

Figure 17.6 Average Spreads and Other Costs

Sources: Central Bank of the Solomon Islands; and IMF staff calculations.

impact because they may contribute to improving banks' productivity; and (3) other costs as a ratio of total assets, which are expected to have a positive effect.[4]

In principle, the higher the overhead costs in the banking sector the larger the required spreads to compensate for the additional costs. Figures 17.5 and 17.6 confirm the presence of this relationship for salaries and wages and other costs. This result is consistent with the findings of Berger, Hanweck, and Humphrey (1987), who argue for the positive correlation between the relative scale of banks and agency costs. Surprisingly, spreads exhibit the same positive relationship for capital costs (see Figure 17.7); however, some period outliers seem to drive this result, which can be mitigated in the formal empirical analyses.

Another important determinant of a bank's interest margins is the scale of operations. However, the relationship between these two variables is ambiguous. On one hand, increasing the scale of operations may lead to lower average costs, which in turn can translate into smaller spreads when a bank faces competitive pressures to pass on cost savings to customers. On the other hand, a bank's costs are, in part, affected by the risk-taking behavior of its managers. Deficient risk management functions and poor asset quality feed into higher nonperforming loans (NPLs), and borrowers can

[4]The main reason behind disaggregating overhead costs is that their components may have a heterogeneous impact on the interest charged to borrowers (for example, staff costs versus capital costs).

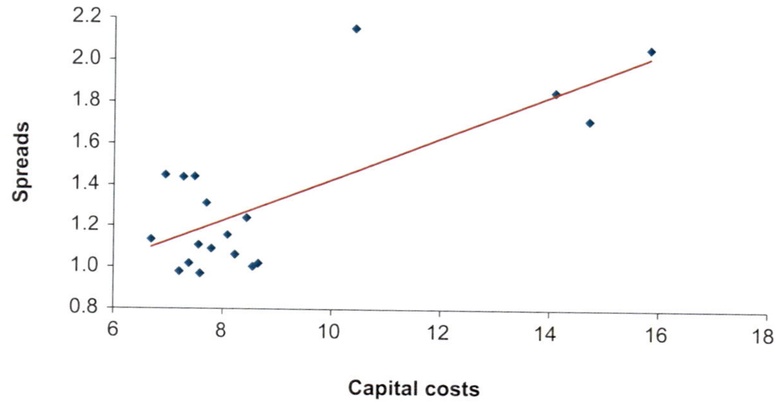

Figure 17.7 Average Spreads and Physical Capital Costs

Sources: Central Bank of the Solomon Islands; and IMF staff calculations.

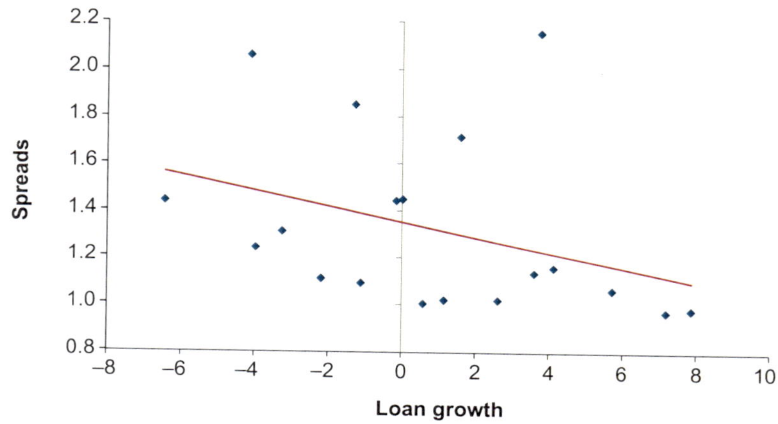

Figure 17.8 Average Spreads and Scale of Operations

Sources: Central Bank of the Solomon Islands; and IMF staff calculations.

then face higher spreads. Using the growth rate of loans as a proxy of this variable, Figure 17.8 shows a negative correlation, which is consistent with the low share of loans in total assets and the moderate financial inclusion in the Solomon Islands.[5]

An additional bank-specific variable that should be considered in the analysis of bank spreads is the extent of risk aversion. A more risk-averse bank will hold more equity in its capital structure, and, to lower profit variability, its managers will tend to secure their deposit base by offering higher deposit rates. Accordingly, risk aversion is proxied by the ratio of equity to total assets. Figure 17.9 shows a positive correlation between bank averages of interest spreads and the risk aversion index.[6]

---

[5]The effect of a growing bank loan portfolio (and therefore size) on margins has been proved to be positive by Goddard and others (2011). They argue that banks with larger growth of loan portfolios benefit from economies of scale and, to some extent, benefit from increased market powers generating abnormally large margins. We believe that this should not happen in an economy with low financial inclusion—a very low level of bank loans to the private sector—as shown in Figure 17.8. Focusing on the time aspect justifies using growth rates of loans. In fact, all the variables in the regression, as described in the following section, are stationary.

[6]Mirzaei, Moore, and Liu (2013) propose another explanation in which the ratio of equity to total assets is employed as a measure of capital strength. Capitalization is seen as the main source to cover loan losses. Well-capitalized banks increase their creditworthiness, which reduces their costs of funding, lowers the risk of bankruptcy, and increases their margins.

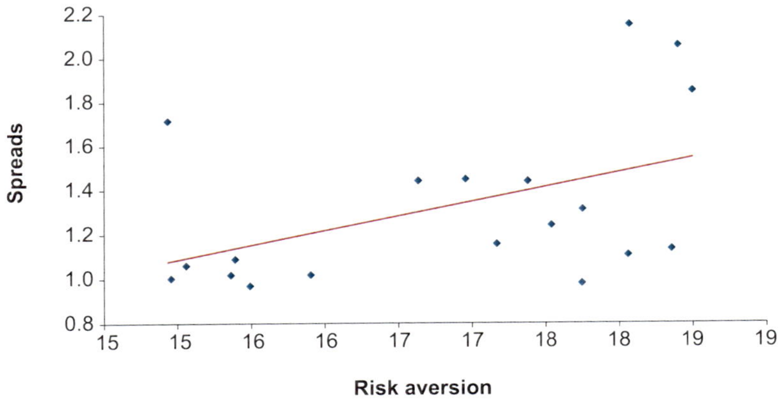

Figure 17.9 Average Spreads and Risk Aversion

Sources: Central Bank of the Solomon Islands; and IMF staff calculations.

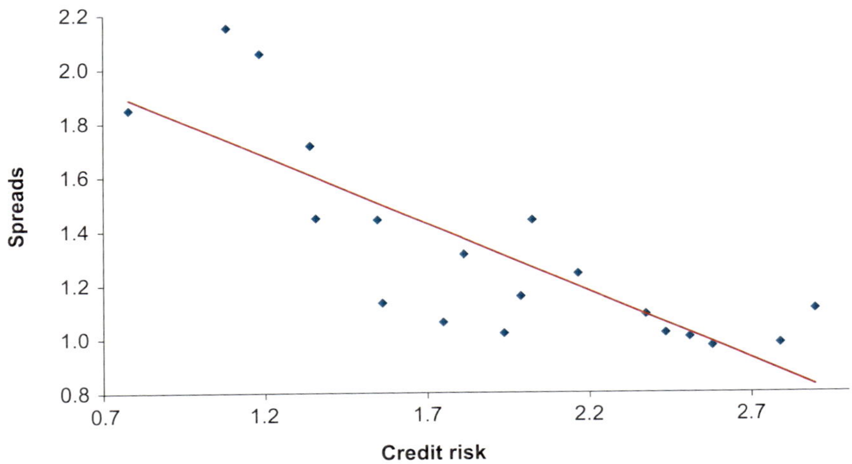

Figure 17.10 Average Spreads and Credit Risk

Sources: Central Bank of the Solomon Islands; and IMF staff calculations.

Empirical research clearly finds a positive relationship between bank interest spreads and interest credit risk, which influences margins positively, suggesting that banks add a default risk premium to loan rates. The default risk is captured through the ratio of NPLs to total loans. Intuitively, the ability to pass on the costs of NPLs to borrowers via increased margins allows commercial banks to maintain positive returns. Surprisingly, this relationship does not seem to be supported by a simple relationship between historical averages of spreads and credit risk (Figure 17.10).

SECTOR-SPECIFIC VARIABLES

The Herfindahl-Hirschman index (HH index) is viewed in the literature as a measure of concentration—the extent to which a few banks dominate market shares with respect to total assets, loans, or deposits. The HH index is a standard measure of consolidation in any industry and it is defined as the sum of the squared deposit, asset, or loan shares of all the banks in the market. By construction, the HH index has an upper value of 10,000 in the case of a monopolistic firm with a 100 percent share of the market; the index tends to zero in the case of a large number of firms with very small market shares.

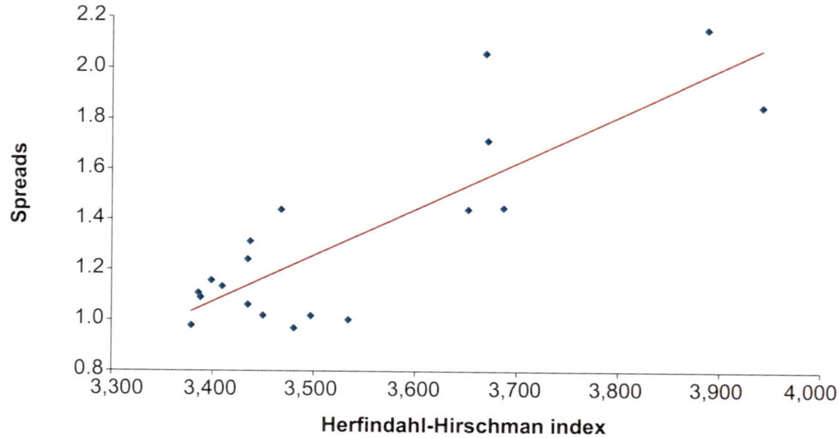

Figure 17.11 Average Spreads and Market Concentration

Sources: Central Bank of the Solomon Islands; and IMF staff calculations.

In the present context, the HH index is measured as the sum of squares of banks' market shares of the banking industry's total assets, total deposits, or total loans. Generally, banks in highly concentrated markets earn monopoly rents, because they tend to collude. Collusion may result in higher rates being charged on loans and lower interest rates being paid on deposits. As in many studies presented in banking literature (for instance Goddard and others 2011), we find a positive relationship between concentration and bank spreads (Figure 17.11).

Macroeconomic Variables

Clearly, an unstable and unfavorable macroeconomic and policy environment is perceived as more risky, and banks may compensate for it by requiring wider margins. To test for this assumption three main indicators are used, which are commonly employed in the literature to assess the impact of macroeconomic conditions on the interest rate spreads (Bolt and others 2012).

The first indicator is expected inflation. In an inflationary environment, bank costs generally rise, leading to higher borrowing costs for the private sector. Furthermore, high inflation is generally associated with an unstable and unpredictable economic environment. In other words, higher inflation is expected to lead to higher inflation-adjusted spreads if it causes banks to charge a risk premium. Actual inflation is used as a proxy for expected inflation in this chapter.

The second indicator is policy interest rates. Commercial banks usually use short-term deposits to finance long-term loans. This maturity transformation is an important function of commercial banks and is an important influence on pricing decisions for loans. The effect of an increase in the regulated interest rate—on central bank "Bokolo" bills—is twofold. First, this should increase the interest requested on loans, and deposit interest rates would react following the specificities of the banking market. Second, a second-round effect can take place through the reaction of the real sector: lower growth and high risks on loans. One should expect that the first-order effect will dominate. As a proxy we use the three-month Bokolo bill interest rate.

The third factor is real GDP growth. A larger economy might be expected to allow for economies of scale and greater competition, which drives down interest rate spreads. At the same time, if real GDP growth slows, banks are confronted with increased credit risk and they charge higher interest to borrowers. However, it is possible that a larger economy allows for greater specialization and deeper financial markets, in which riskier borrowers have better access to funds. The latest scenario is only expected to occur if the economy is already at high levels of private sector access to financial products, which is not the case in the Solomon Islands.

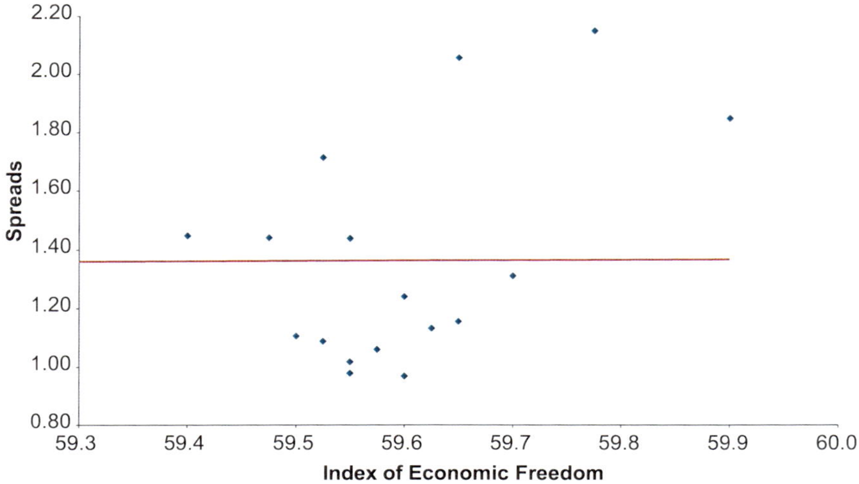

Figure 17.12 Average Spreads and Economic Freedom

Sources: Central Bank of the Solomon Islands; and IMF staff calculations.

Legal and Empirical Results

Experts generally agree that the main barriers limiting credit supply in the Solomon Islands include insufficient investor protection in addition to family land tenure—which makes property rights unclear and limits the ability to use land as collateral—as well as bottlenecks in land registration. The Index of Economic Freedom is used to reflect this feature in the empirical analysis; this is very tractable since it covers 10 elements of economic freedom, some of which are particularly relevant in this framework, such as property rights, entrepreneurship, and, most important, the evolution of land ownership.[7] Moreover, the strength of legal rights, which the index also captures, can measure the degree to which collateral and bankruptcy laws protect the rights of borrowers and lenders and thus facilitate lending. Figure 17.12 shows an ambiguous relationship between spreads and the Index of Economic Freedom, which is slightly positive and clearly led by some outliers in the sample.

EMPIRICAL FINDINGS FROM A POOLED REGRESSION

Methodology

The length and size of the sample pose challenges in data handling when the analysis is conducted on an individual bank. In that regard, the analysis of panel data brings additional information, reduces the phenomenon of multicollinearity of the variables, and increases the number of degrees of freedom. The latter would enhance the power of the tests and thus the degree of trust in their results.[8]

[7] The index is published annually by the Heritage Foundation in partnership with the *Wall Street Journal* and measured based on 10 quantitative and qualitative factors, grouped into four broad categories, or pillars, of economic freedom: (1) rule of law (property rights, freedom from corruption); (2) limited government (fiscal freedom, government spending); (3) regulatory efficiency (business freedom, labor freedom, monetary freedom); and (4) open markets (trade freedom, investment freedom, financial freedom). Each of the 10 economic freedoms within these categories is graded on a scale of 0 to 100. A country's overall score is derived by averaging these 10 economic freedoms, with equal weight given to each.

[8] We run alternative bank-specific time series estimations, and the regressions seem to suffer from several problems, mainly owing to the small sample of the individual bank data.

In what follows we estimate four versions of the model specified as:

$$SPREAD_{i,t} = f\,(X_{i,t}, HHindex_t, Macro_t, Legal_t, \varepsilon_{i,t}) \tag{17.1}$$

In this equation *i* denotes bank *i* and *t* denotes a quarter *t*. The vector of bank-specific variables, $X_{i,t}$, contains COST_STAFF, COST_PCAPITAL, COST_OTHER, LOANS_GROWTH, RISK_AVERSION, and CREDIT_RISK.

SPREAD is defined as net interest income as a percentage of total assets or (interest income – interest expense)/total assets. COST_STAFF stands for the cost related to salaries and wages and measured as salary and wages/total assets. COST_PCAPITAL denotes the cost of implementing new physical capital and identified as costs of occupancy and depreciation expenses/total assets. COST_OTHER corresponds to other costs/total assets. LOANS_GROWTH is a measure of the scale of operation identified as the quarterly growth rate of loans and advances. RISK_AVERSION captures the degree of bank risk aversion measured as equity/total assets. CREDIT_RISK is defined as net NPLs to total loans. *HHindex* stands for the Herfindahl-Hirschman index and is defined as the sum of the squared bank loans/total loans. *Macro* comprises variables measuring the macroeconomic environment; specifically, we use inflation (INFLATION), Bokolo bill interest rates (INTEREST RATE), and real GDP growth (GROWTH). *Legal* denotes the Index of Economic Freedom (LEGAL).

In Table 17.2, model (1) exhibits only the bank-specific variables, $X_{i,t}$. Model (2) encompasses bank-specific and sectoral variables. Model (3) displays the macroeconomic variables, in addition to the others. Finally, model (4) extends model (3) by considering the legal and economic environment index as an additional explanatory variable.

Using pooled estimated generalized least squares to take into account cross-sectional heterogeneity, the alternative specifications of the model are estimated using the seemingly unrelated regression method. Standard errors and covariances are calculated with (panel-corrected) cross-section weights to obtain a robust estimate of the cross-section residual covariance matrix.

Empirical Results

A negative relationship was found between spreads and the scale of operations, which is statistically significant through the alternative specifications of the regression. This result suggests that banks in the Solomon Islands would pass on lower rates to borrowers assuming a surge in the volume of lending. In particular, an increase of 10 percent in total loans generates about a 1 percent decline in bank spreads.

The first regression results highlight the role of bank-level factors in determining banking spreads. The results shown in column 1 of Table 17.2 suggest that the main drivers of the fluctuations of spreads are related to the quality of management, proxied by the operating costs and, more particularly, to capital and other costs. The results are statistically and economically significant. And they are largely robust to the inclusion of banking sector, macro, and legal variables. Furthermore, salary and wages become more significant in explaining interest rate spreads, as suggested in columns 1, 3, and 4. According to the results of regressions, a fall in salary and wages (other) costs of 1 percentage point would be associated with a drop in interest spreads by 0.5–0.7 (0.6–0.7) percentage point. This result is robust to the model specification and remains significant regardless of the version of estimated equation.

To support the empirical result showing the high correlation between overhead costs and banking spreads, we compare the magnitude of these costs in the Solomon Islands to other countries during 2011. Figure 17.13 contrasts the overhead costs to total assets in 166 countries classified based on their income per capita adjusted by purchasing power parity. The figure shows a clear negative relationship between banks' overhead costs and income. In addition, the Solomon Islands is among the top quintile with the highest banking costs in the sample (also higher than the average for the world, east Asia, and Pacific low-income countries).

The finding on the effect of risk aversion is consistent with the theoretical interpretation in the sense that it positively affects spreads. For instance, an increase in the ratio of equity to total assets

TABLE 17.2

Factors Explaining Interest Spreads

	(1)	(2)	(3)	(4)
		Bank-Specific Variables		
Loan growth	−0.008	−0.014***	−0.010***	−0.010***
	(0.006)	(0.004)	(0.004)	(0.004)
Cost of staff	0.582	0.762**	0.531*	0.557*
	(0.451)	(0.334)	(0.284)	(0.304)
Cost of physical capital	0.020*	0.001	−0.002	−0.002
	(0.011)	(0.010)	(0.011)	(0.011)
Other costs	0.730***	0.659***	0.560***	0.558***
	(0.177)	(0.152)	(0.151)	(0.152)
Credit risk	0.009	0.007	−0.009	−0.008
	(0.014)	(0.010)	(0.011)	(0.012)
Risk aversion	0.022	0.020	0.021*	0.022*
	(0.016)	(0.013)	(0.012)	(0.012)
		Industry Characteristics		
HH index	...	1.58E−03***	8.10E−04***	8.31E−04***
		(1.72e−4)	(1.99e−4)	(2.38e−4)
		Macroeconomic Variables		
Inflation	...	...	−0.008	−0.006
			(0.017)	(0.018)
Interest rate	...	...	0.090***	0.086***
			(0.024)	(0.030)
Growth	...	...	−0.049**	−0.051**
			(0.023)	(0.024)
		Legal Aspect		
Legal	...	...	...	−0.046
				(0.180)
Intercept	0.226	−5.198***	−2.410*	0.207
	(0.339)	(0.680)	(0.744)	(10.238)
R-squared	0.561	0.853	0.914	0.913
Adjusted *R*-squared	0.509	0.832	0.895	0.892
Durbin-Watson statistic	1.218	1.696	1.742	1.749

Source: IMF staff calculations.
Note: HHI = Herfindahl-Hirschman index.
$^{*}p = .10$; $^{**}p = .05$; $^{***}p = .01$.

of 10 percent generates an increase in interest spreads by 2 percent. This result becomes significant at the 10 percent level in models (3) and (4) of Table 17.2. On the other hand, NPLs have an insignificant impact on the interest rate spread in all versions of the estimated models.

The HH index gauges the degree of market concentration and might show the opportunity to earn excess rates of return via collusion. Table 17.2 unambiguously shows that changes in the concentration of the respective banking sector are positively correlated with bank spreads. The elasticity is statistically significant in the different specifications. This result is somewhat expected given the small number of banks in the Solomon Islands.

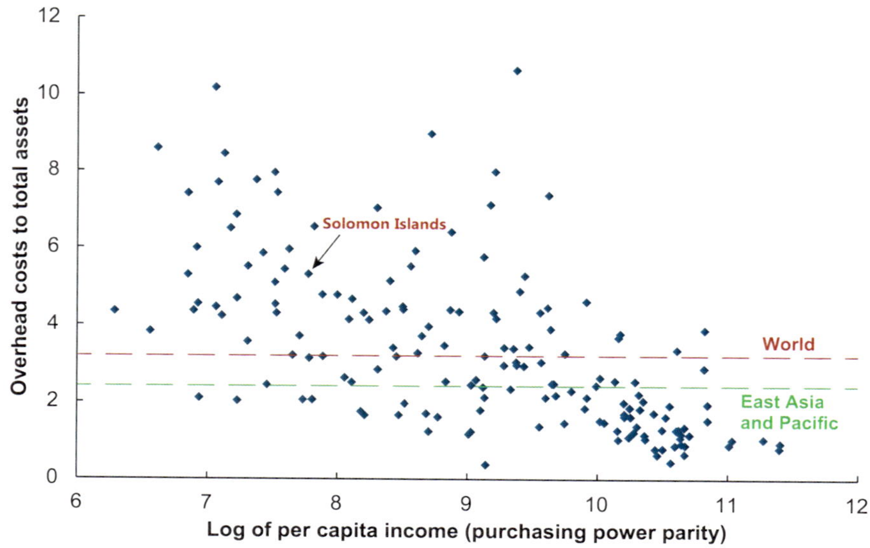

Figure 17.13 Relationship between Banks' Overhead Costs and Income

Source: IMF staff calculations.

In a highly inflationary environment this variable is predicted to be a significant determinant of profitability.[9] Inflation in the Solomon Islands remained relatively low and stable during the period covered in this study, partly owing to the stability of exchange rates. Hence, the different versions of the regression do not show any evidence in favor of a close relationship between spreads and inflation.

The relatively high policy interest rates significantly explain bank spreads. According to the results of regressions, a fall in the central bank interest rates of 1 percentage point would be associated with a decline of spreads by roughly 8 basis points. It is fairly normal for a country using sterilization through issuing central bank bills—Bokolo bills in the Solomon Islands—to have high interest rates. Greater exchange rate flexibility could reduce the cost of sterilization, keep interest rates low, and hence reduce the spreads in the medium term—and Bokolo bill rates were already low at the end of the sample period.

In line with the existing literature, a strong negative elasticity is expected between overall economic activity and spreads in the banking sector. During booms, business opportunities are more available and the perceived risk is lower for commercial banks; therefore, spreads are expected to contract if growth increases. Growth is negatively affecting spreads with a statistically significant estimated elasticity of –0.06 in our sample.

The quality of the regulatory regime and economic environment, proxied by the Index of Economic Freedom, was found to have a positive effect on lowering spreads in the regression; however, the coefficient is not statistically significant; see model (4) in Table 17.2.

The impact of noninterest income on spreads is identified by introducing an additional bank-specific variable in the regression—the ratio of total noninterest income to total assets, which is highly related to foreign exchange operations in the Solomon Islands. This variable is expected to illustrate the implementation of the new Central Bank of Solomon Islands regulation in 2011 aiming to narrow the foreign exchange margin, which should force banks to engage more in the lending market and lower spreads. Although not reported in Table 17.2, the sensitivity of interest spreads to noninterest income is found to be weak and statistically not significant.[10]

[9] Various studies find a positive correlation between spreads and inflation (see Honohan 2003 and Gelos 2006).

[10] Alternatively, the coefficient of a dummy variable that captures the new policy implementation in 2011 was tested, and the result remains the same.

A FURTHER LOOK AT MARKET STRUCTURE

In this section the structure of the banking sector is evaluated by identifying the impact of a change in the interest rate spread in one bank on the other banks. Formally, we estimate a vector autoregression model of the form:

$$SPREAD_t = A(L) \times SPREAD_t + \mu_t, \tag{17.2a}$$

where

$$SPREAD_t = [SPREAD_t^{Bank\,1}, SPREAD_t^{Bank\,2}, SPREAD_t^{Bank\,3}]' \tag{17.2b}$$

and $A(L)$ is a lag matrix.

A Cholesky identification scheme is used assuming that the biggest bank (in terms of total assets)—Bank 1—is the one that affects the two other banks contemporaneously. Then Bank 2 is ranked second; so its decisions would affect Bank 3's spreads immediately and those of Bank 1 with a one-quarter lag. Finally, Bank 3 would influence the two other banks only during the next quarter.

The impulse response functions of bank-specific spreads to idiosyncratic shocks, as well as the confidence intervals, are reported in Figure 17.14. The results show that the different banks change spreads in a coordinated fashion. In particular, following the first scenario (an unexpected increase of spreads by Bank 1), the two other banks react immediately through a mild but significant increase in interest spreads. It is worth noting that, following the same shock, Bank 3 decides to change interest spreads by virtually the same amount as in Bank 1. The same thing happens following a shock originating from Bank 2. On the other hand, the biggest bank does not seem to be significantly responsive to shocks in other banks' spreads.

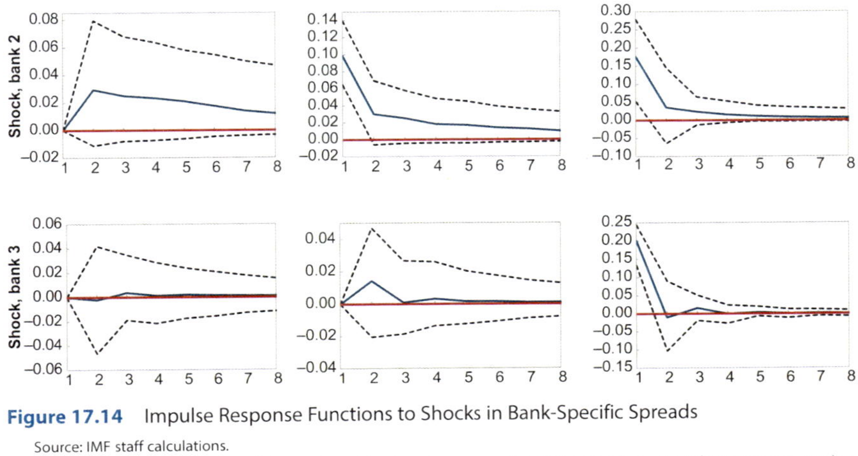

Figure 17.14 Impulse Response Functions to Shocks in Bank-Specific Spreads

Source: IMF staff calculations.
Note: We construct bootstrap confidence intervals for impulse response functions from the structural vector autoregression. Solid blue lines correspond to 50th percentiles, and the dashed lines identify 90 percent confidence intervals.

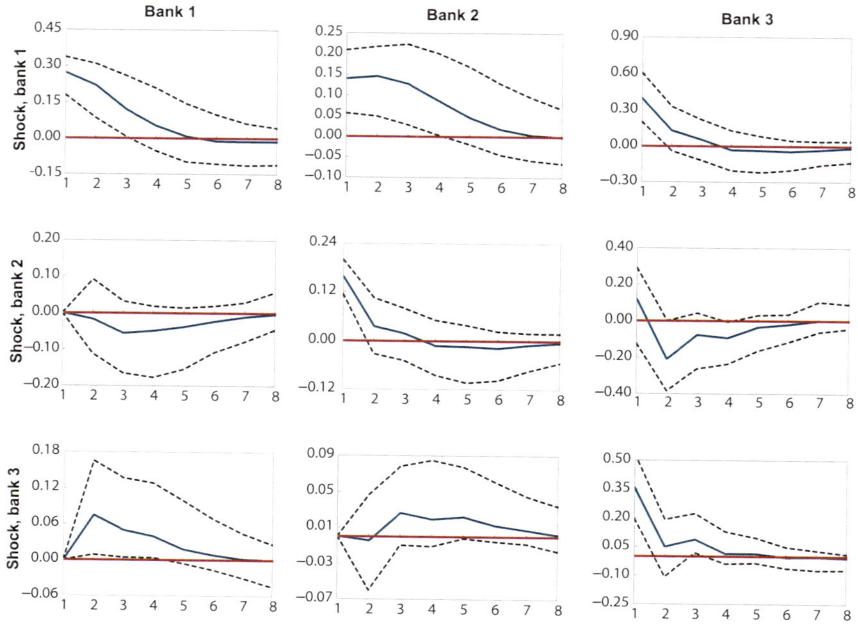

Figure 17.15 Impulse Response Functions to Shocks on Bank-Specific Lending Rates

Source: IMF staff calculations.

To test the robustness of these findings, the same exercise is repeated using shocks on lending rates. Figure 17.15 shows the same pattern as in Figure 17.14, with highly correlated bank reactions to lending rate adjustments by their pairs.

As the identification strategy cannot be empirically tested, a final exercise is conducted where the arrangement of variables is alternated and the robustness of the presence of collusion is assessed. The results are not reported here, but the impulse response functions are very similar, especially following the period where an idiosyncratic shock on spreads materializes. Consequently, we see this result as additional evidence of the significant influence of high banking market concentration on spreads, as reported in the previous section.

CONCLUSION

Bank spreads and overhead costs are significantly and positively correlated. The scale of operations is another impediment to lowering the cost of borrowing from banks in the Solomon Islands. Besides, the results reported in this chapter also suggest that high market power and bank concentration tend to increase the possibility of collusion.

Some scope exists for increasing competition in the banking sector in the Solomon Islands, but financial deepening also requires the development of nonbank institutions. These include finance companies, foreign exchange dealers, and microcredit institutions, which have the potential to be competitive, apart from the main commercial banks. Financial inclusion initiatives, such as lowering the cost of remittances and mobile phone banking, could also help foster private sector development.

Another policy issue is the central bank lending rate. The empirical findings suggest that increases in the central bank lending rate are likely to increase net interest margins. Furthermore, a less supportive legal and economic environment in the Solomon Islands contributes to larger intermediation costs, although the result is not statistically significant. This argument is very often used to explain the limited access to bank loans. Although the empirical result is insignificant, this does not mean that policymakers should ignore potential reforms in this area.

REFERENCES

Berger, Allen N. 1995. "The Profit-Structure Relationship in Banking: Tests of Market-Power and Efficient-Structure Hypotheses." *Journal of Money, Credit and Banking* 27 (2): 404–31.

Berger, Allen N., Gerald Hanweck, and David Humphrey. 1987. "Competitive Viability in Banking: Scale, Scope, and Product Mix Economies." *Journal of Monetary Economics* 20 (3): 501–20.

Bolt, Wilko, Leo de Haan, Marco Hoeberichts, Maarten van Oordt, and Job Swank. 2012. "Bank Profitability during Recessions." *Journal of Banking and Finance* 36 (9): 2552–64.

Brock, Philip, and Liliana Rojas-Suarez. 2000. "Understanding the Behavior of Bank Spreads in Latin America." *Journal of Development Economics* 63 (1): 113–34.

Claeys, Sophie, and Rudi Vander Vennet. 2008. "Determinants of Bank Interest Margins in Central and Eastern Europe: A Comparison with the West." *Economic Systems* 32 (2): 197–216.

Crowley, Joe. 2007. "Interest Rate Spreads in English-Speaking African Countries." IMF Working Paper 07/101, International Monetary Fund, Washington.

Gelos, R. Gaston. 2006. "Banking Spreads in Latin America." IMF Working Paper 06/44, International Monetary Fund, Washington.

Goddard, John, Hong Liu, Philip Molyneux, and John Wilson. 2011. "The Persistence of Bank Profit." *Journal of Banking and Finance* 35 (11): 2881–90.

Honohan, Patrick. 2003. "The Accidental Tax: Inflation and the Financial Sector." In *Taxation of Financial Intermediation: Theory and Practice for Emerging Economies,* edited by Patrick Honohan. Washington: World Bank; New York: Oxford University Press.

Mirzaei, Ali, Tomoe Moore, and Guy Liu. 2013. "Does Market Structure Matter on Banks' Profitability and Stability? Emerging vs. Advanced Economies." *Journal of Banking and Finance* 37 (8): 2920–37.

Park, Kang H., and William L. Weber. 2006. "Profitability of Korean Banks: Test of Market Structure versus Efficient Structure." *Journal of Economics and Business* 58 (3): 222–39.

Samuel, Wendell, and Laura Valderrama. 2006. "The Monetary Policy Regime and Banking Spreads in Barbados." IMF Working Paper 06/211, International Monetary Fund, Washington.

Tregenna, Fiona. 2009. "The Fat Years: The Structure and Profitability of the U.S. Banking Sector in the Pre-Crisis Period." *Cambridge Journal of Economics* 33 (4): 609–32.

Uhde, André, and Ulrich Heimeshoff. 2009. "Consolidation in Banking and Financial Stability in Europe: Empirical Evidence." *Journal of Banking and Finance* 33 (7): 1299–1311.

CHAPTER 18

Interest Rates, Bank Profitability, and Capital Adequacy in the South Pacific

MATT DAVIES, JOHN VAUGHT, AND EZEQUIEL CABEZON

The structure of the banking sector in the South Pacific remained relatively stable over the last decade. The banking sector in most countries in the region is limited to about three to five commercial banks (Table 18.1), dominated by two large Australian-owned banks (ANZ and Westpac), either in the form of branches or wholly owned subsidiaries. Local banks generally hold low market shares. In recent years, however, a new regional player has emerged—Bank of the South Pacific, a Papua New Guinea bank, which has operations in three Pacific island countries. In July 2015 Westpac sold its banking operations in the Cook Islands, Samoa, the Solomon Islands, Tonga, and Vanuatu to the Bank of South Pacific. In addition, in 2012 BRED Bank, a French-owned bank with a previous presence in French Pacific jurisdictions, started operations in Fiji and Vanuatu.[1]

This chapter provides comparative information on interest rate levels, profitability indicators, and capital adequacy among banks in the South Pacific. It was motivated by inquiries from central bank governors and ministers of finance at the Forum Economic Ministers' Meeting in 2009 and the South Pacific Central Bank Governors' Meetings in 2009 and 2011 on the cost of financial services to the public in the Pacific. Our analysis focuses on the six South Pacific countries with central banks—Fiji, Papua New Guinea, Samoa, the Solomon Islands, Tonga, and Vanuatu—and uses data they provided to compare their financial sectors to those of other countries and regions following Davies and Vaught (2009). Data availability and reliability are major constraints in cross-country analysis of this type. To ensure comparability, the analysis works wherever possible from disaggregated prudential data so that ratios can be derived on a similar basis.

The analysis draws regional conclusions where possible. However, banking experiences in the six countries have ranged broadly over the last decade, despite the similarity in their banking systems. Regional averages can obscure as much as inform, and so results for individual countries are the main focus of discussion.

The chapter begins with a brief review of the key determinants of interest rates in the Pacific, and a survey of interest rates across the region, which allows a broad cross-country analysis (though these rates are difficult to compare on a like-for-like basis). We then compare interest rates in the South Pacific and other regions using data derived from disaggregated prudential sources. The following sections examine bank profitability in the Pacific, the contribution of noninterest operations to bank profitability, and capital adequacy in the region. We close with a discussion on policy implications, regulatory responses, and the scope for regional coordination to support financial sector deepening.

INTEREST RATE DETERMINANTS

As is the case elsewhere, interest rates in the South Pacific reflect a wide range of factors. Interest rates are the centerpiece of commercial banks' core business of financial intermediation; they are the key price in the financial sector, the foremost transmission mechanism of monetary policy, the main vehicle for matching supply and demand of funds and, normally, the key determinant of profitability.

[1]See Chapter 6 for a cross-country discussion of the banking sector in the Pacific islands.

TABLE 18.1

Structure of the Banking Sector in the South Pacific, 2001–14

	2001		2005		2009		2014	
	Number of Commercial Banks	Broad Money as Percent of GDP	Number of Commercial Banks	Broad Money as Percent of GDP	Number of Commercial Banks	Broad Money as Percent of GDP	Number of Commercial Banks	Broad Money as Percent of GDP
Fiji	5	45	5	60	5	70	6	80
Papua New Guinea	6	32	4	34	4	53	4	47
Samoa	3	33	4	36	4	43	4	44
Solomon Islands	3	21	3	29	3	38	4	43
Tonga	3	37	3	45	3	43	4	48
Vanuatu	4	95	3	99	4	92	4	73

Sources: IMF, International Financial Statistics database; and IMF staff estimates.

Interest rate levels reflect banks' perceptions of risk (country and creditor), market liquidity conditions, and the depth of financial markets, which affect the ability of banks to spread their risk, the cost of doing business, and the level of competition in the financial sector.

Economic risk is quite high in the Pacific. This is the case for many small, open economies. South Pacific economies have relatively low and volatile growth and are vulnerable to shocks on both the growth and inflation fronts. Inflation is a particularly important risk to the financial sector, and exchange rate risks are also significant. Although most countries in the South Pacific have fixed exchange rate regimes, their vulnerability to external shocks is high, which can rapidly impact market liquidity. Periodic devaluations are a risk to overseas investors, as happened in Fiji in 2009 and the Solomon Islands in 1997. There is also vulnerability to movements in cross-rates, such as abrupt movements of the Australian and U.S. dollars. Capital and exchange controls also add to economic risk.

Broader country risk is also perceived to be elevated in the Pacific. This can come from a number of sources, including political instability, the potential for social unrest and violence, and vulnerability to natural disasters. South Pacific countries are perceived to be vulnerable to all of these to a greater or lesser degree, which affects the way in which international banks price products in the region. As an illustration, Table 18.2 provides comparisons from one risk index to other countries.[2] It shows that internationally the Pacific is perceived to have considerably higher country risk than emerging market countries, but somewhat lower risk than the countries listed in Table 18.2 in south Asia, the Caribbean, and Africa.

The depth of financial markets and the cost of complying with prudential regulations also affect interest rate levels. The more financial products available, the easier it is for banks to diversify their risk. However, in the markets of the South Pacific, where products such as foreign exchange futures, corporate bonds, leasing, and collateralized interbank lending are not widely available, banks' assets tend to be concentrated in lending products. The lack of high-quality, readily marketable instruments (that is, government and corporate bonds) also means that liquid assets are often placed in non- or low-earning deposit accounts or even held in cash, thereby requiring higher lending rates or spreads and increasing the costs of banking services. There are few opportunities for diversification.

Credit risk is a key determinant of interest rate levels. When setting interest rates, banks need to take into account the likelihood of interest and principal payments being received, and the ability to access and liquidate collateral in a timely manner when loans go bad. A number of factors that can moderate credit risk are not present in many South Pacific economies. Among them are secured transactions laws, collateral registries, rapid and reliable contract enforcement through the legal

[2]The source is Delcredere/Ducroire, Belgium's public credit insurer, which provides one of the most comprehensive publicly available listings of country risk. The ratings are highly regarded internationally and broadly reflect Organisation for Economic Co-operation and Development consensus. They do not reflect the views of the IMF, but are provided as an illustration of outside perceptions of the region as they affect investors.

TABLE 18.2

Perception of Country Risk

	Export Transactions				Direct Investments	
	Political Risk					
	Short Term	Medium Term	Special Transactions	Commercial Risk[1]	War Risk	Transfer Risk
Fiji	5	5	5	C	4	4
Papua New Guinea	3	5	3	C	3	4
Samoa	2	6	4	C	2	6
Solomon Islands	3	5	4	B	4	5
Tonga	3	5	4	C	3	5
Vanuatu	3	4	3	B	4	4
Australia	1	1	1	B	1	1
New Zealand	1	1	1	B	1	1
Brazil	2	3	2	C	2	3
Indonesia	2	3	2	C	2	3
Kazakhstan	2	5	3	B	3	5
Malaysia	1	2	1	A	2	2
Mexico	1	3	2	B	2	3
Philippines	1	3	2	B	3	3
Uruguay	3	3	3	A	1	1
Pakistan	5	7	5	C	6	6
Bangladesh	3	6	3	B	5	4
Sri Lanka	3	6	4	B	3	5
Grenada	5	6	5	C	2	6
Guyana	4	6	5	C	3	6
Barbados	3	4	3	B	1	4
Jamaica	2	7	5	C	2	6
The Bahamas	3	3	3	B	1	3
Dominica	4	6	5	B	2	6
St. Kitts and Nevis	4	6	5	C	1	6
Seychelles	5	7	6	B	2	7
Rwanda	4	7	5	C	5	6
Tanzania	3	6	4	C	3	5

Source: ONDD Belgian Export Credit Agency, 2013.
Note: Values are on a seven-point scale, with 1 being the lowest risk.
[1] A = lowest risk.

system, credit reporting bureaus, and bankruptcy laws. Moreover, there are inadequate markets in many jurisdictions to liquidate collateral in a timely manner or without significant loss.

INTEREST RATES COMPARED WITH OTHER REGIONS

Headline Rates

The IMF's International Financial Statistics database allows for broad international comparison. All IMF members report headline interest rates to the IMF on a regular basis, at varying levels of disaggregation. This allows comparisons between the Pacific and a broad range of other countries. However, the data are vulnerable to mistakes in reporting, and reported interest rates are not always directly comparable. The illustrative results that follow select relevant countries with available comparable data between 2003 and 2014.

Lending rates in the Pacific vary widely both in level and trend. Figure 18.1 shows interest rates in the Pacific as reported to the IMF, and the rates are, wherever possible, weighted average lending

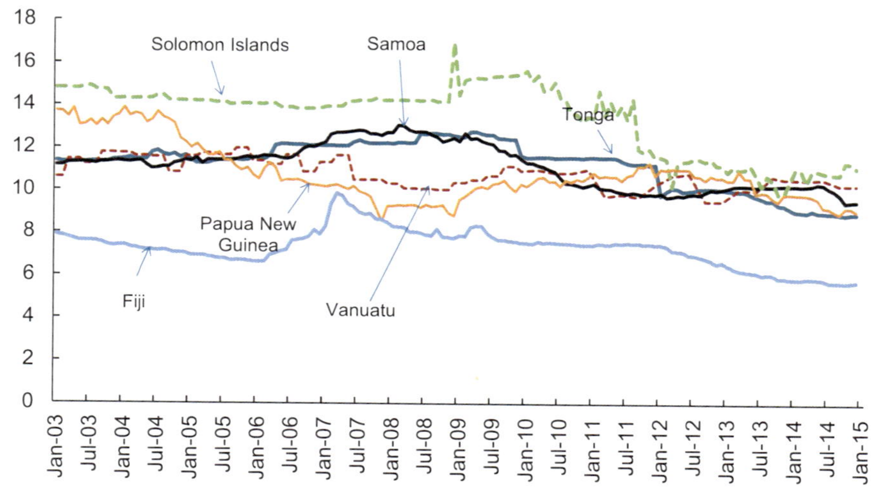

Figure 18.1 Lending Rates in the Pacific (*Percent*)

Source: IMF, International Financial Statistics database.

rates. The range is wide, with the Solomon Islands consistently having the highest rates, at above 12 percent, and Fiji the lowest, averaging 8 percent. Other countries consistently lie between these two extremes, with some declines in the lending rates since 2009 (for example, Fiji, Samoa, and the Solomon Islands).

On average, lending rates in the Pacific appear in line with comparator economies. Figure 18.2 shows that while rates are higher than those in Australia, they lie, on average, below countries in Africa and South Asia and are broadly in line with the Caribbean. African lending rates were broadly at the level of the Solomon Islands until 2011, while south Asian rates have climbed from broadly comparable with Samoa, Tonga, and Vanuatu at the start of the period covered in Table 18.2 (2003) to levels similar to those in the Solomon Islands in recent years. Lending rates in the Caribbean—in many ways the most pertinent comparison—are on average below the rates in the Solomon Islands, but in line with other Pacific island countries.

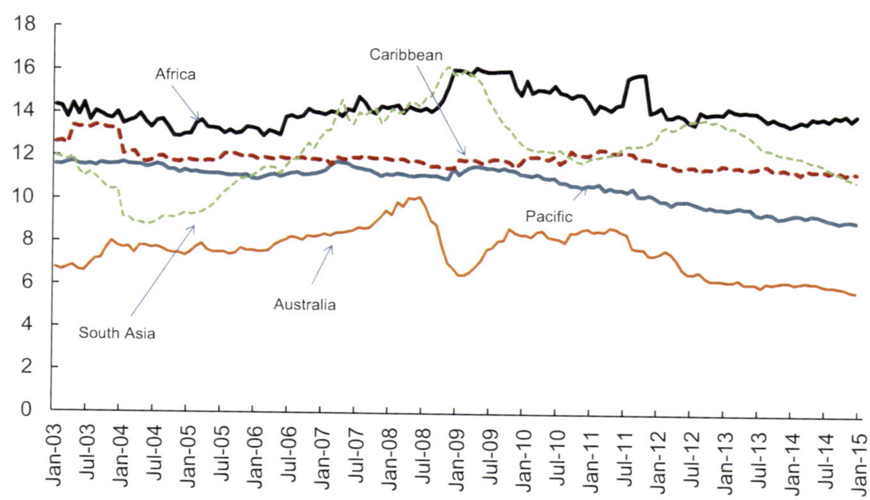

Figure 18.2 Lending Rates for Selected Regions (*Percent*)

Source: IMF, International Financial Statistics database.

Note: Africa shows data for Rwanda, Seychelles, and Tanzania; south Asia, data for Bangladesh, Pakistan, and Sri Lanka; Caribbean, data for The Bahamas, Barbados, Dominica, Grenada, Guyana, Jamaica, and St. Kitts and Nevis.

Spreads follow a similar pattern. Figures 18.3 and 18.4 show that average spreads—weighted average lending rates minus the standard savings deposit rate—in the South Pacific are in the mid-range of the Caribbean countries and somewhat higher than average spreads in south Asia. Interest rate spreads should be considered in the context of investment options. Limited investment options in the South Pacific require higher interest spreads to compensate for higher nonearning asset levels. In the South Pacific's small financial sectors, large institutions, such as publicly owned provident funds that hold large lumpy deposits, can introduce distortions into the level of deposit rates.

Analysis from Prudential Data

Prudential data allow a more rigorous comparison of interest rates. The data used in the previous section allow for a broad international comparison, but distortions in deposit rates, as noted earlier, and reporting issues may hamper comparisons. They also do not provide a full picture of implicit interest rates and other operations, including actual flows of interest income and expenses. This

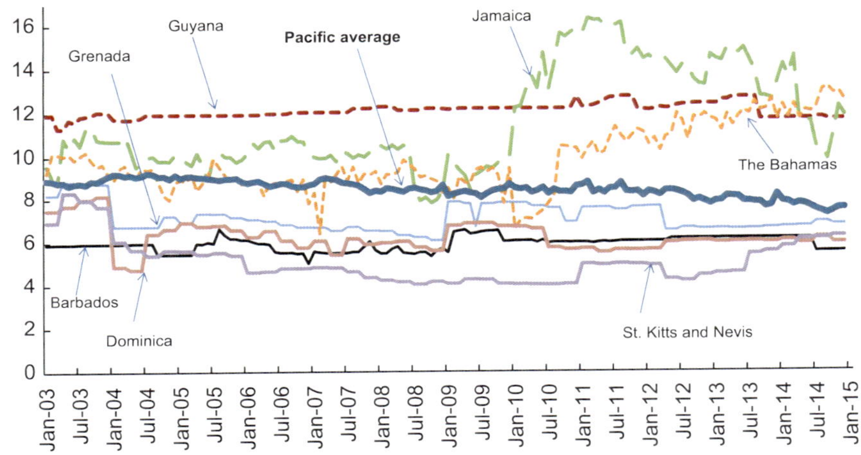

Figure 18.3 Interest Rate Spreads in the Caribbean and the Pacific (*Percent*)

Source: IMF, International Financial Statistics database.

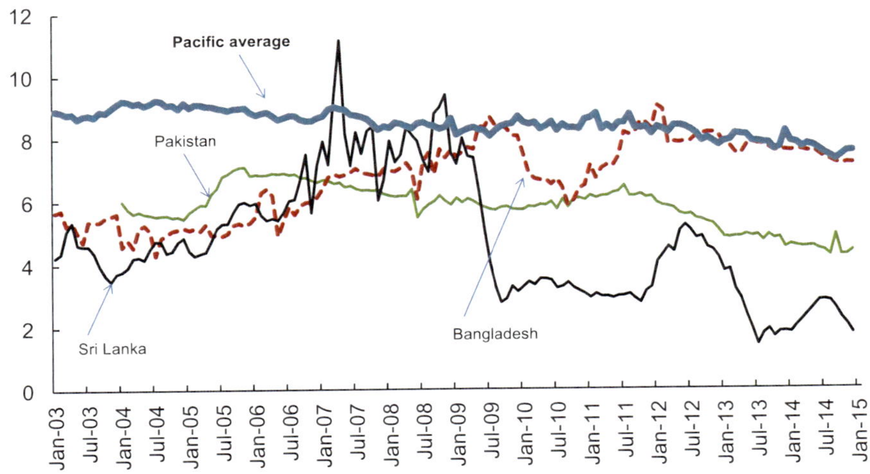

Figure 18.4 Interest Rate Spreads in South Asia and the Pacific (*Percent*)

Source: IMF, International Financial Statistics database.

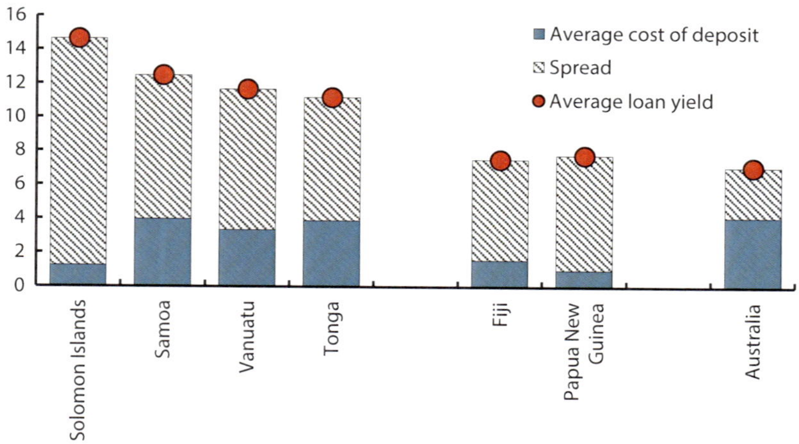

Figure 18.5 Loan Yields and Cost of Deposits (*Percent, 2000–13*)

Sources: Country authorities; and IMF staff estimates.

section therefore uses prudential data provided by South Pacific central banks to build up a more complete picture of income and expense.

The comparative analysis uses Australia as the main reference point. Many of the large banks in the region are branches or subsidiaries of Australian banks so there is a clear relevance in this comparison. New Zealand is also used for comparison. But because market conditions are very different in Australia and New Zealand than in the South Pacific, comparisons are also drawn from the IMF's Financial Soundness Indicators.[3] This database has a far more restricted coverage than the International Financial Statistics database—it focuses on advanced and emerging markets—but allows comparison on a broader set of analytical ratios derived from commercial banks' balance sheets. This chapter uses emerging market countries from Latin America (Brazil, Colombia, Mexico, Uruguay), Asia (Indonesia, Malaysia, Philippines, Sri Lanka) and central Asia (Georgia, Kazakhstan).

Prudential data are broadly in line with interest rate data provided to the IMF (Figure 18.5, Annex Tables 18.1.1 and 18.1.9). Loan yields in the region are highest in the smaller countries, with the Solomon Islands consistently having the highest yield (averaging around 15 percent, although falling recently) and Fiji and Papua New Guinea the lowest.[4] Australian loan yields are broadly in line with those in Fiji and Papua New Guinea but consistently below other South Pacific countries. Despite inflation volatility, loan yields have remained quite stable over the past decade in many South Pacific economies, particularly the smaller ones. The cost of deposits, broadly equivalent to the weighted average deposit rate, is generally very low, particularly in Fiji and Papua New Guinea. They are on average below Australian levels in nominal terms, and much lower in real terms given the lower inflation in Australia. As a result, spreads—the difference between yield and cost of deposits—are two to three times the levels in Australia.

Net interest income is a conventional indicator of the contribution of core bank services to profitability. The simple spreads just discussed are analogous to the public understanding of interest rates, but do not reflect the profits that banks derive from their core lending operations. Net interest income takes into account the fact that banks cannot hold all of their assets in loans, which are

[3]IMF Financial Soundness Indicators data for Australia and New Zealand were supplemented with Australian Prudential Regulation Authority and Reserve Bank of New Zealand data.

[4]The loan yield is total interest income for a calendar year divided by the average stock of outstanding loans for that year net of specific provisions for bad loans. It should, in the absence of large nonperforming loans, be equivalent to the reported weighted average interest rate.

TABLE 18.3

Net Interest Income (*Percent of average assets, 2013*)	
Samoa	5.5
Solomon Islands	4.4
Tonga	4.5
Vanuatu	4.1
Average selected small islands	**4.6**
Fiji	3.4
Papua New Guinea[1]	3.5
Australia	1.7
New Zealand	2.0
Average selected emerging markets	**3.4**
Brazil	5.3
Colombia	2.8
Georgia	1.5
Indonesia	5.4
Kazakhstan	2.2
Malaysia	1.3
Mexico	5.2
Philippines	1.6
Sri Lanka	3.0
Uruguay	5.1

Sources: Country authorities' central banks; IMF, Financial Soundness Indicators; and World Bank (2013).

[1] Latest available 2012.

typically the highest-yielding asset category. Regulatory and prudential operating requirements mean that banks must also hold lower or nonearning assets such as statutory reserve deposits, deposits with other banks, and cash in addition to fixed assets. Using this measure, South Pacific spreads in 2013 range between 3 percent in Papua New Guinea and about 6 percent in Samoa (Table 18.3 and Annex Table 18.1.2).

Net interest income in the South Pacific is, as expected, generally higher than in emerging markets. Australia, New Zealand, and some emerging markets, with net interest income between 1 and 3 percent, are considerably below the South Pacific average. Although it is hard to quantify exactly, these differentials are broadly in line with what one might expect given the country risks discussed earlier and the greater size of these risks, sophistication, and depth of financial markets in these emerging economies.

NONINTEREST OPERATIONS

Interest rates are not the only source of bank profitability, however, even in the relatively shallow markets of the South Pacific. Fees, charges, and foreign exchange activities are significant contributors to bank income and profitability. The high level of income from foreign exchange activities is not surprising given the highly open nature of the Pacific island economies, leading to a large volume of international trade transactions supplemented by tourism payments and remittances. A number of central banks in the South Pacific have become increasingly focused on these issues, in part because of the cost of sending remittances in the Pacific, which is extremely high by international standards.

Noninterest income in the Pacific is higher than in most other regions. As a proportion of total assets, it was on average around four times more than in Australia in 2013 and well above emerging market comparators (Table 18.4). There is a reasonably wide range, however, with Tonga being the

TABLE 18.4

Noninterest Operations *(Percent of average assets, 2013)*

	Noninterest Income	Gross Noninterest Expenses	Net Noninterest Income
Samoa	3.6	5.6	−2.0
Solomon Islands	4.1	4.7	−0.6
Tonga	4.3	5.4	−1.1
Vanuatu	3.0	4.0	−1.0
Average selected small island states	**3.8**	**4.9**	**−1.2**
Fiji	2.7	3.7	−0.9
Papua New Guinea[1]	2.0	2.5	−0.5
Australia	0.9	1.3	−0.4
New Zealand	0.7	1.2	−0.5
Average selected emerging markets	**1.7**	**2.6**	**−0.9**
Brazil	1.7	3.9	−2.2
Colombia	1.9	2.2	−0.3
Georgia	0.8	1.2	−0.4
Indonesia	2.4	3.8	−1.4
Kazakhstan	1.6	1.4	0.3
Malaysia	1.1	1.2	−0.1
Mexico	2.3	3.8	−1.5
Philippines	1.7	1.9	−0.2
Sri Lanka	1.3	1.6	−0.3
Uruguay	1.8	5.1	−3.3

Sources: Country authorities' central bank data; IMF, Financial Soundness Indicators; and IMF staff estimates.
[1] Latest available 2012.

highest at about 4⅓ percent and Papua New Guinea the lowest at about 2 percent—though still significantly higher than Australia's 1 percent (Annex Tables 18.1.6, 18.1.7, and 18.1.8).

Foreign exchange operations are the largest source of noninterest income in the South Pacific, accounting for roughly two-thirds of noninterest income in many jurisdictions. For jurisdictions that allow for the disaggregation of this income source, profits from foreign exchange activities are, on average, equally split between revaluation profits and losses and service charges and fees on foreign exchange transactions. Using data provided on these spreads by central banks, which are subject to the quality of reporting by commercial banks, the average spread in the Pacific is about 8 percent.

Data constraints hamper further analysis of noninterest income. It is possible, however, that fees and charges on loans, such as commitment and transaction fees, could make up much of the remaining noninterest income. This has certainly been a concern in a number of countries. Work in Tonga has suggested that when fees and charges are consolidated into an effective interest rate, the rate increases by large amounts, particularly for small loans.

Noninterest expenses are also high in the Pacific island countries. It is not clear why this is the case, as labor and building costs, although high, are still lower than in Australia and other emerging market economies. In this regard, it is notable that "other" noninterest expenses—expenses other than salary and depreciation—reported by banks are, on average, more than half of total noninterest expenses. More disaggregated data are required to better understand the operating expenses of South Pacific banks.

BANK PROFITABILITY

At first glance, overall bank profitability in the South Pacific appears very high. Return on assets (ROA)—total pretax profit as a proportion of average assets—is a standard measure for comparing

TABLE 18.5

Profitability Indicators of the Banking System *(Percent, 2013)*

	Return on Assets[1]	Return on Equity[2]	Provision Expenses[3]	Leverage[4]
Samoa	4.0	21.1	−0.6	19.0
Solomon Islands	3.8	23.7	0.2	15.8
Tonga	3.2	14.0	0.4	22.5
Vanuatu	2.6	17.9	0.8	14.4
Average selected small island states	**3.4**	**19.2**	**0.2**	**18.0**
Fiji	2.2	23.6	0.3	9.4
Papua New Guinea[5]	2.7	19.3	3.5	13.8
Australia	1.2	20.9	0.3	5.7
New Zealand	1.5	19.6	0.1	7.4
Average selected emerging markets	**2.1**	**18.1**	**2.9**	**11.5**
Brazil	1.4	13.1	4.7	10.6
Colombia	3.1	21.7	4.0	14.5
Georgia	2.5	14.4	1.8	17.3
Indonesia	3.1	24.5	0.6	12.5
Kazakhstan	1.5	14.8	10.8	10.3
Malaysia	1.4	15.5	0.7	9.3
Mexico	2.1	19.3	3.8	10.8
Philippines	2.5	22.3	1.5	11.4
Sri Lanka	1.6	19.4	0.6	8.4
Uruguay	1.6	16.0	0.7	9.8

Sources: Country authorities' central bank data; IMF, Financial Soundness Indicators database; and IMF staff estimates.
[1] Net income before taxes as proportion of average assets.
[2] Net income before taxes as proportion of average equity.
[3] As proportion of average total loans.
[4] Equity-to-average-assets ratio.
[5] Latest available 2012.

not only individual bank profitability, but also bank profitability across countries. ROA in the South Pacific ranged between 2¼ and 4 percent in 2013 (Table 18.5), and averaged around 3¼ percent, which is high by international standards.[5] Advanced banking systems generally yield ROAs of about 1–2 percent, as seen in Australia. ROAs in the Pacific island countries generally exceed averages in other regions and in some cases—Samoa and the Solomon Islands in particular—are well in excess of levels observed in other regions. Returns remained broadly at these levels over the last decade, but have been on a declining trend in most countries (see Annex Table 18.1.4).

However, profits from interest operations are broadly in line with international norms. To analyze the contribution of interest operations to overall profitability, Table 18.6 illustrates the ROA of South Pacific banking systems, excluding the contribution of the very high foreign exchange earnings already identified. The table clearly shows that foreign exchange activities contribute significantly to the income and profits of commercial banks, and that without them, ROA would be more in line with international comparators. However, it is not possible from current data sources to identify whether foreign exchange income is a significant element in profitability regions other than those identified in Table 18.6.

Profits from foreign exchange operations account for at least half of total profits; they are particularly high in the Solomon Islands. Data on noninterest expenses are not sufficiently disaggregated

[5]Profits are averages across all commercial banks in a country and may have wide variation. Banks that have large branch networks in rural areas tend to have lower profitability.

TABLE 18.6

Return on Average Assets *(Percent)*

		2007	2008	2009	2010	2011	2012	2013
South Pacific	Median	4.6	4.1	3.2	3.1	3.1	3.0	3.2
	High	8.6	10.5	9.3	8.0	5.1	4.8	4.0
	Low	2.9	-2.5	-4.6	0.5	2.6	2.5	2.2
South Pacific	Median	2.0	2.5	1.8	1.7	1.3	1.1	1.0
(excluding foreign exchange income)	High	3.1	3.9	3.3	2.4	2.1	1.3	2.1
	Low	1.2	-6.6	-7.2	-2.0	-0.4	0.8	0.6
Australia		1.4	0.7	0.9	1.1	1.1	1.0	1.2
New Zealand		1.5	1.3	0.8	1.0	1.4	1.2	1.5
Latin America	Median	2.0	2.0	1.7	1.8	1.7	1.8	1.9
	High	3.1	3.9	3.6	4.0	3.9	4.3	5.0
	Low	1.1	0.9	0.1	0.6	1.1	1.3	1.1
Sub-Saharan Africa	Median	2.7	3.2	2.3	2.8	3.2	3.2	2.7
	High	3.8	4.9	3.9	4.6	5.2	5.4	6.2
	Low	1.4	1.4	-8.8	0.5	0.3	1.4	1.2
Middle East and Central Asia	Median	2.0	1.4	1.2	1.5	1.8	1.5	1.7
	High	3.9	3.8	2.6	2.8	3.2	3.0	2.9
	Low	0.9	-2.5	-5.5	-1.4	-0.6	0.2	0.2
Emerging Europe	Median	1.7	1.4	0.6	0.8	0.5	0.6	0.6
	High	2.6	3.4	3.3	3.1	2.2	2.4	2.0
	Low	0.7	-0.6	-4.5	-2.7	-1.1	-2.0	-0.2

Sources: Country authorities' central bank data; Autralian Prudential Regulatory Authority; Reserve Bank of New Zealand; and IMF, *Global Financial Stability Report*, Financial Soundness Indicators table, April 2015.

to identify expenses associated with foreign exchange activities which may overstate the returns slightly. But expenses for conducting foreign exchange activities are not believed to be significant. This is because foreign exchange operations do not require separate fixed asset investments or significant additional personnel, though an exception is perhaps foreign exchange traders whose services may be outsourced to a parent or subsidiary bank.

Credit risk does not appear to have been excessively high in the Pacific island countries in recent years. Banks' provision expenses—the precautionary expenses banks make against loans that are not performing as expected or that are believed to pose more than a normal degree of credit risk—have remained at about 1 percent of average gross loans (Annex Table 18.1.3). The ratio has been much higher in Tonga in recent years,[6] however, demonstrating the impact of high credit risk manifesting itself in a sharp increase in nonperforming loans. Even excepting Tonga's recent experience, the provision expenses of banks in the Pacific island countries are significantly above those in Australia and in some emerging markets. They are lower, however, than in Brazil and Mexico. A similar conclusion comes from the proportion of total loan-loss reserves—the amount banks have over a number of years put aside to cover bad loans—to total loans.

[6]Tonga's banking system has gone through a prolonged period of balance sheet repair since the third quarter of 2008. During 2004–08, the stock of private credit doubled. The credit boom ended in the third quarter of 2008, driven by sharp deterioration of debt servicing capacities and moderating asset prices during the global financial crisis.

Significant losses in Tonga demonstrate the downside risk. These have been well in excess of those observed in other regions in recent years—and demonstrate both the potential credit risk in the Pacific island countries and that profits in good years can protect against such risks.

CAPITAL REQUIREMENTS AND HOLDINGS

This section reviews capital requirements and holdings in the South Pacific. It assesses the extent to which capital requirements in the Pacific island countries may be contributing to high interest rates. Holding capital is expensive, and thus if banks are forced to hold more they tend to increase interest rates to retain profitability.

Headline risk-based capital (RBC) requirements for South Pacific central bank jurisdictions are either 12 percent (Fiji, Papua New Guinea, Vanuatu) or 15 percent (Samoa, the Solomon Islands, Tonga). These generally apply to all banks, including branches that are required to retain assigned capital in order to protect local depositors and creditors.

RBC requirements in the Pacific are higher than international minimum standards. Basel II requires a minimum RBC requirement of 8 percent for sound, well-managed internationally active banks. But this requirement is primarily aimed at developed markets with lower risk and more developed market infrastructure. Many emerging and developing markets set RBC requirements above the international minimum to reflect the higher risks in their markets and to provide suitable protection for depositors and creditors.

Risk is perceived to be elevated in the Pacific, so RBC requirements above minimum international standards are to be expected. Capital requirements are usually higher where risk is higher, where legal frameworks are weak, and where supervisory challenges are greater. The aim of RBC is to set an adequate cushion to protect depositors from risk. However, there is no clear formula for determining just how much capital should be maintained above the minimum international standard. Comparisons with other countries and regions may be useful since they show how other regulators facing similar market conditions have reacted.

RBC requirements in the Pacific are higher than in comparable regions, as Figure 18.6 shows. In Caribbean countries, the RBC requirement is, for the most part, significantly lower than in the Pacific, averaging 8.7 percent and only marginally higher than in Australia. However, the banking system in the Caribbean is larger and deeper than in the Pacific, so lower RBC requirements may be

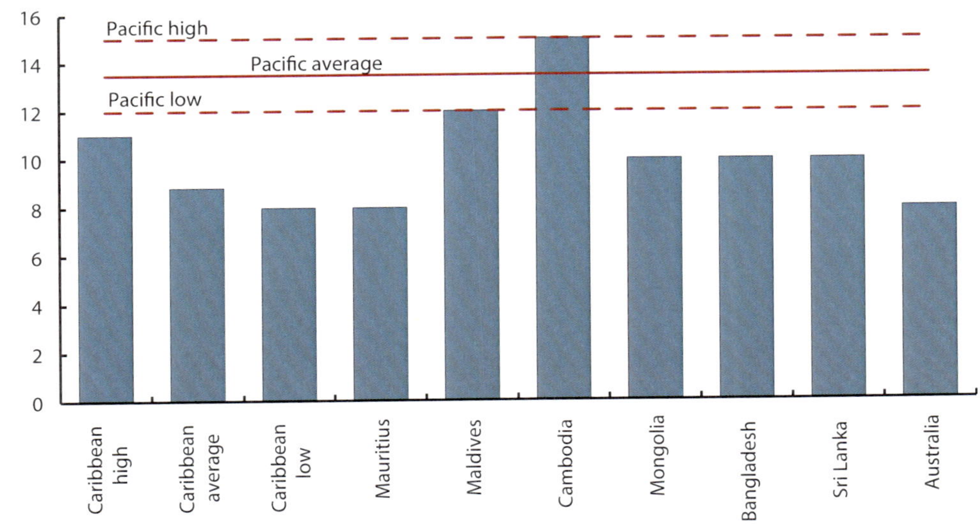

Figure 18.6 Risk-Based Capital Requirements (*Percent, 2013*)

Sources: Country authorities' central bank data; and IMF staff estimates.

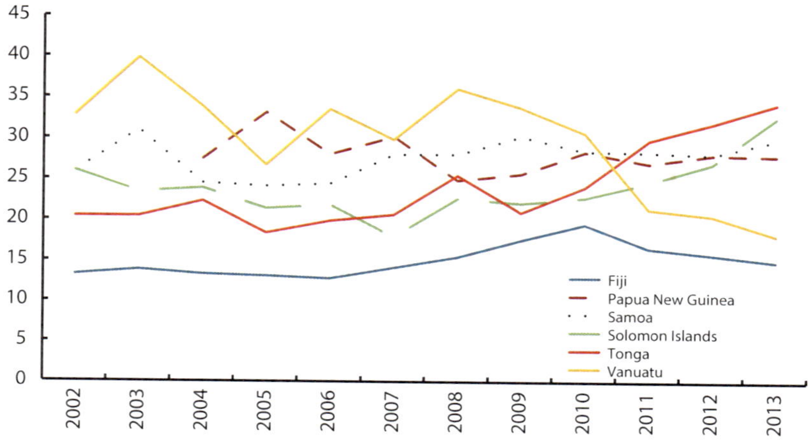

Figure 18.7 Total Risk-Based Capital *(Percent)*

Sources: Country authorities' central bank data; and IMF staff estimates.

justified. Low-income countries in Asia tend to have RBC requirements of about 10 percent, with the exception of Cambodia at 15 percent, which is consistent with the high end of the Pacific. Maldives, whose banking system is dominated by foreign banks, has an RBC requirement of 12 percent, and in Mauritius it is 8 percent.

Commercial banks in the Pacific also hold significantly more capital than required. Consolidated RBC holdings at the end of 2013 were approximately 26 percent compared with the regional average minimum requirement of about 14 percent. Only in Fiji did banks maintain RBC close to the prudential minimum; in all other jurisdictions reported RBC was nearly double the minimum prudential requirement. This pattern was much the same for the previous decade. RBC holdings in most South Pacific countries have remained within the 20–35 percent range, with only Fiji consistently below this level—averaging about 14 percent (Figure 18.7). These holdings are high by international standards—average holdings in the Pacific island countries are higher than in most other regions covered by the IMF's Financial Soundness Indicators (Table 18.7).

In some Pacific island countries the actual capital at risk is well below reported capital holdings. Branches and subsidiaries of regionally active foreign banks often have significant net balances due from their head office.[7] Deposits placed with the foreign bank home or head office effectively represent a withdrawal of capital since the funds are not at risk in the Pacific island countries, and may not be available to repay local depositors and creditors if the home or head office experiences a crisis. For this reason, many countries require assigned capital to be maintained in the country in which the foreign bank branch is operating. Adjusting headline RBC to exclude funds placed back with the home or head office reduces "excess" capital holdings. Even after adjusting for this, capital remains well above minimum prudential requirements in most South Pacific countries. Foreign banks may also impose capital charges on their Pacific operations, which would imply that return on assets and other performance indicators for the Pacific are understated.

RBC holdings do have to be carefully interpreted. Commercial banks in the Pacific island countries have been holding large balances due from other banks (including their head or parent office and the central bank). These and other liquid asset holdings attract low risk weightings. RBC ratios would likely fall if lending volume picked up as these lower-risk-weighted liquid assets were invested in higher-risk-weighted loans.[8] This would be moderated, however, if banks chose to hold more

[7] In the Pacific, foreign bank branches in their books maintain a separate assigned capital account, while also reflecting separate due-from (nostro) and due-to (vostro) balances with their head office.

[8] Basel III provides guidance on the minimum risk weights on claims (assets) according to the underlying counterparty. These are adapted for the needs of individual countries.

TABLE 18.7

Bank Risk-Based Capital by Region, 2013

	Median	Minimum	Maximum
Advanced economies	15.4	11.8	18.9
Emerging market and developing economies			
Central and Eastern Europe	17.2	14.4	20.9
Developing Asia	16.7	12.2	26.2
Middle East and Central Asia	18.1	13.3	25.0
Sub-Saharan Africa	17.9	11.6	30.1
Western Hemisphere	15.6	12.7	17.7
Pacific (unadjusted)	28.8	14.9	34.2

Sources: Country authorities' central bank data; IMF, Financial Soundness Indicators; and IMF staff estimates.

capital owing to the increased risk profile of their assets. These movements would not occur using a simple leverage capital ratio (capital to total assets), which uses total assets as a proxy for the relative risks in the balance sheet. Tables 18.8 and 18.9, and Annex Table 18.1.5, show that, in the Pacific island countries, these ratios have been increasing over time and are high by international standards. On an unadjusted basis, leverage ratios in the Pacific exceed those in all the regions in the Financial Soundness Indicators database. That said, care should be taken when considering leverage capital

TABLE 18.8

Trends in Consolidated Leverage Capital Positions *(Percent)*

	2007	2008	2009	2010	2011	2012	2013
Fiji	6.4	8.6	9.6	11.3	8.4	7.7	7.6
Fiji adjusted[1]	4.4	6.5	9.6	11.3	6.5	...	...
Papua New Guinea	11.3	12.6	11.9	13.2	12.5	13.3	14.7
Samoa	7.6	18.4	18.1	17.0	18.6	18.6	19.7
Samoa adjusted[1]	17.6	18.2	18.0	16.7	18.4	...	...
Solomon Islands	12.7	17.5	15.2	18.7	17.8	14.6	14.0
Solomon Islands adjusted[1]	12.7	17.5	15.2	13.6	13.2	...	...
Tonga	18.0	19.8	15.6	18.8	20.3	24.2	25.0
Tonga adjusted[1]	17.9	17.6	14.8	17.2	18.3	...	...
Vanuatu	11.2	14.5	14.3	14.3	15.1	16.3	16.2
Vanuatu adjusted[1]	–57.6	–37.4	–12.8	–5.4	1.3	...	...

Source: IMF staff calculations based on country authorities' central bank data.

[1] Excludes net balances due from head/home office when calculating total capital and total assets.

TABLE 18.9

Bank Leverage Ratios by Region, 2013 *(Percent)*

	Median	Minimum	Maximum
Advanced economies	7.0	4.8	24.0
Emerging market and developing economies			
Central and Eastern Europe	11.3	8.0	21.1
Developing Asia	9.6	6.7	17.5
Middle East and Central Asia	13.2	7.1	19.8
Sub-Saharan Africa	11.0	7.9	20.0
Western Hemisphere	10.0	6.9	14.8
Pacific (unadjusted)	15.4	7.6	25.0

Sources: Country authorities' central bank data; and IMF, Financial Soundness Indicators bank data.

positions since they do not consider off-balance-sheet business and risks or the relative risks of different types of assets.

POLICY IMPLICATIONS

Banks in the Pacific are sound and profitable. This critically important outcome from a financial sector stability perspective enabled the Pacific to withstand the global financial crisis without significant shocks to its financial systems or significant government intervention and financial support. The dominance of Australian banks in the region's banking sectors, which were able to withstand the crisis better than most international banks, contributed to this outcome. In cases in which banks made losses and capital fell below required levels, the strong position of parent institutions enabled swift and appropriate recapitalization.

However, although interest operations are in line with expectations, in some cases banks do make very high profits. This is because:

- Lending rates and spreads do not appear to be out of line with comparable economies after taking into account likely determinants of interest rates such as country and credit risk and shallow financial markets. Over time, lending rates have stayed broadly constant with a slight downward trend. These findings are consistent with the findings from an International Finance Corporation study that assessed interest rate levels from a microeconomic perspective (IFC 2010).
- Foreign exchange income and other noninterest flows add substantially to profits, reflecting the high level of international trade in goods and services.
- Banks generally remained highly profitable over the last decade, with an average ROA of 4.9 percent since 2001, the majority of which is based on income received from foreign exchange activities. The healthy profits may also reflect the limited competition in South Pacific financial systems.

The hypothesis that high minimum capital requirements in the Pacific cause elevated lending rates does not appear to be borne out by reality. If banks genuinely believed that RBC requirements were excessive for the amount of risk they faced, it would be expected that they aim to hold capital closer to prudential requirements with only a small buffer to avoid breaches of the limit. This is not the case, however, in most South Pacific countries, even after deducting net balances due from their home or head offices.

High capital holdings are likely to be driven by risk perception. The main reason for high capital holdings in most countries is likely to be commercial bank management's high risk perception in a given market. Given this, banks hold additional capital to protect against the risk eventuating. Exchange control requirements making it difficult to remit profits to the head or home office are another potential cause for high capital holdings. However, these restrictions have been eased in recent years and so are unlikely to be playing a large role.

REGULATORY RESPONSES

During the global financial crisis, South Pacific policymakers considered whether a policy response was required, particularly given the economic pressures. At that time, some central banks took policy action and others examined whether their regulatory frameworks provided an appropriate framework to allow interventions. After the crisis, central banks in the region took the following measures:

- Fiji, in early 2009, imposed restrictions on the growth of lending rates (constraining them to levels at the end of 2008 for each commercial bank), and a ceiling on the interest rate spread of 4 percent for all banks. These formal restrictions were lifted in late 2009, but banks are still strongly encouraged to keep spreads within the 4 percent guideline.

- Tonga, in mid-2009, gained voluntary agreements from banks to reduce exchange rate spreads charged to customers and, through regulation, required banks to disclose effective interest rates (including all fees and charges) to customers. The agreements came alongside reducing reserve requirements as part of a monetary policy move to encourage credit growth.
- Samoa, in the context of revising its central bank act, introduced a provision for the central bank to have a more active role in regulating fees and charges of commercial banks.

The need for a response depends on the ultimate policy objective. There are a number of possible objectives that policymakers in the South Pacific may have, including increasing access to affordable credit for domestic businesses, moderating bank profitability, and enhancing consumer protection. These are not exclusive to one another, and many policy objectives can and should be addressed through institutions other than central banks.

In central banking terms, the long-term means to achieve these objectives are clear and are already being pursued by all South Pacific countries. These include:

- *A credible and effective monetary policy framework*—This is vital for providing central banks tools to address interest rates. But it will require better transmission mechanisms than currently exist in most Pacific economies.
- *Well-functioning financial markets*—Deeper financial markets will improve transmission mechanisms and increase the efficiency of the financial sector. Priorities include the development of securities markets, foreign exchange trading, and other financial products. This will require building better market infrastructure, such as credit bureaus, secured transactions laws, and collateral access.
- *Competitive financial markets*—Maintaining space for new market entrants and monitoring actions through high-quality supervision within an appropriate prudential framework and effective competition policy will boost competition.
- *Reduced country risk*—This requires maintaining a stable macroeconomic and political environment, and continuing progress on structural reforms to improve the business environment.
- *Improved consumer protection and financial literacy*—Consumer protection bodies such as financial ombudspersons can help protect customers from predatory practices. However, the vital requirement is a population that is financially competent, which requires progress on a number of fronts, in particular building financial literacy and developing clear business guidelines that protect the interests of both consumers and banks.

Taking additional short-term measures to control interest rates or profitability is risky and requires careful consideration of the costs and benefits. A particular risk is the potential for these measures to act against progress on the long-term agenda already outlined. Short-term regulatory measures that control bank profitability or interest rates can frustrate market development, and the short-term benefits need to be substantial to justify them.

Interest rate regulation can influence rates in the short term, but it throws up many challenges and can lead to unintended outcomes. Direct regulation of rates can achieve the immediate aim of ensuring banks charge interest rates at the required level. However, this may not achieve longer-term policy objectives and can undermine the effectiveness of the banking sector. Some possible outcomes are:

- *Reduced efficiency*—The financial sector is particularly reliant on price signals, and restricting the ability of banks to price their services to include risk is likely to lead to other, less efficient, means of allocation such as rationing.
- *Increased charges in other areas*—For instance, loans can be priced at the same effective rate through fees and charges rather than using interest.
- *Contractions in credit*—Banks may achieve reductions in interest rates by reducing credit to higher-risk customers rather than by reducing the interest rates across the board. Higher-risk sectors such as small and medium-sized enterprises are particularly sensitive to this.

- *Slower market development*—Current market participants are less likely to invest in new products and services if they are unable to control their prices. Similarly, potential new entrants will have less incentive to invest.
- *Pressure on supervision services*—Supervision departments, which in the Pacific island countries are already stretched, are put under additional strain by having to monitor interest rate practices.

Regulation and/or increased taxation of profits is less damaging to market development but remains challenging. Regulating profits and/or taxing profits at higher levels has the advantage of not interfering with the pricing mechanism and therefore has less damaging impacts on efficiency. But it can share the problems of interest rate regulation in terms of discouraging market development and deterring new investors. It also has significant challenges for identifying targets or maximum levels of profits and monitoring compliance. This is particularly relevant given the limited capacity in many supervision departments in the South Pacific and the absence of well-formed competition policies and supporting institutions.

Stepped-up action on the longer-term agenda may yield better and more sustainable short-term outcomes. Given the policy and administrative challenges inherent in the short-term regulatory actions available to address price and profit levels, scarce resources may be better devoted to more aggressive actions to build deep and competitive financial markets.

Holding excess capital is costly to banks and elevates lending rates, but central banks can do little to reduce holdings in the short term. Because capital is well in excess of minimum requirements in most South Pacific countries, it is not obvious that if central banks lower their RBC requirements to reduce borrowing costs that it would lead to lower capital holdings by commercial banks or to lower lending rates. Capital requirements are generally set with regard to prudential concerns rather than to influence interest rates. Any move toward lowering capital requirements should therefore be taken with great caution to ensure that commercial banks are obligated to retain adequate risk protection in the country in which they operate.

Actions to reduce commercial banks' perception of risk could help lower capital buffers closer to minimum prudential requirements. But this will only yield results in the medium term.

REGIONAL ACTIONS TO SUPPORT FINANCIAL SECTOR DEVELOPMENT

While the focus of efforts must necessarily be at the national level, coordinated regional action may also be able to contribute to financial sector development. The underlying regulatory system is very similar across the South Pacific, as are the main actors in the banking system. This provides scope for adding to national policies through regional coordination. To conclude the chapter, we identify a number of areas that could be considered, mostly building on activities already taking place.

Regular and frank dialogue between central and commercial banks can lead to improvements in market functions and outcomes. Commercial banks are likely to be willing to discuss amending their pricing structures in a cooperative environment that takes account of their own constraints. Ultimately, financial deepening, which is the underlying aim of many of the measures proposed in this chapter, is to the benefit of the banking industry, and banks themselves should be keen to engage in discussions to achieve this. These will predominately be at the national level, but regional forums can also be used. Given the strong regional network of the main banks in the Pacific, it may be valuable to establish a regular dialogue between regional managers and governors attached to the annual meeting of central bank governors.

Transparency and disclosure provide important support and accountability. Measures such as ensuring banks disclose effective interest rates (as implemented in Tonga), allow customers to better determine and compare the cost of borrowing. Dissemination of financial data, including interest rates and financial soundness indicators, can also contribute to accountability. There has been some movement toward this, nationally and regionally, through the websites of central banks and the Association of Financial Supervisors of Pacific Countries. Improving the breadth and timeliness of published data could build on these initiatives.

Enhanced supervision is also critical. Effective supervision not only helps monitor and assess the health and condition of the banking industry, but also provides vital information to policymakers, including financial soundness data and indicators. Supervisors need to understand the risks that banks face and to be able to identify what is driving banks' costs and profits. Significant progress has been made in improving supervision and regulation in the South Pacific, but many improvements can still be made. Priorities include updating prudential regulations, enhancing and automating bank reporting to allow easier and more comprehensive analysis, improving on-site inspection techniques, and deepening capacity in supervision departments. Given the similarity of the regulatory environment and the main players in the banking system in the region, formal and informal interaction in the context of the Association of Financial Supervisors of Pacific Countries should continue to benefit supervisors in the South Pacific. Harmonizing returns and systems across jurisdictions could yield economies of scale to regional banks and help reduce the cost of banking. Enhanced cooperation with the Australian Prudential Regulation Authority may also yield benefits given the dominance of Australian-supervised banks in the South Pacific.

Governors of South Pacific central banks could also consider harmonizing RBC requirements (minimum levels, risk weightings, and the definition of assigned capital) across the region. This would reduce the regulatory burden on regionally active banks and allow central banks to compare regionwide financial sector behavior more easily, including implications on interest rates for loans.

Increased competition is also likely to lead to lower consumer costs. However, prospective entrants into South Pacific banking markets have to consider competing with established players with the advantages of a regional network, with accompanying efficiencies of scale and large market shares. The available returns, while potentially high in proportionate terms, will be low in absolute terms given the smallness of the individual national markets. This could deter additional large regional-level players from entering these markets. However, addressing this issue at a regional level is difficult and will be limited to information sharing and cooperation on effective competition frameworks while efforts to encourage and foster private, local bank ownership continue at the national level. Competition can come from outside the banking sector, particularly given the influence of noncore banking operations on banks' profits. The promotion of efficient foreign exchange markets and nonbank financial institutions can also broaden consumer choice and lower costs.

Strengthened consumer protection will still be required. While this will primarily be an issue to be taken forward at the national level, central banks and other consumer protection bodies can cooperate regionally with the aim of having broadly similar regimes. This would facilitate low-cost compliance by banks with a large regional presence. For example, regulators could require that loan and deposit contracts clearly specify the frequency and basis of any adjustments to the interest rate and any fees. To prevent predatory practices, adjustments to loan interest rates and fees should be required to be calculated against an independent index specified in loan contracts—and these should clearly specify how and when adjustments (both increases and decreases) are to be calculated. Loan contracts should also require repayments to be increased or decreased to reflect any adjustment in interest rates or fees, and ensure that loans amortize within the contract period.

Building financial competence and inclusion is fundamental to long-term financial sector development. South Pacific central bank governors and finance ministries have already recognized regional and national initiatives to improve competition. In addition, increased investment in physical and technological infrastructure will be required to bring the unbanked into the financial sector in a cost-effective manner. The challenge is to ensure that the regional coordination of these many initiatives is manageable and does not cause unsustainable demands on financial sector managers.

ANNEX 18.1. SOUTH PACIFIC BANKING INDICATORS

ANNEX TABLE 18.1.1

Simple Interest Ratios *(Percent)*

	2000	2001	2002	2003	2004	2005	2006	2007	2008	2009	2010	2011	2012	Average
							Average Loan Yields							
Samoa	24.8	12.3	12.4	11.7	11.9	12.3	12.5	12.9	12.7	11.1	10.4	10.0	9.4	12.7
Solomon Islands	14.5	13.8	14.8	15.7	17.8	15.3	15.1	13.7	13.7	16.1	14.5	14.0	13.3	14.8
Tonga	10.5	11.9	10.7	10.4	12.8	10.6	11.4	11.6	12.5	10.9	10.9	10.3	11.5	11.2
Vanuatu	19.2	7.8	12.4	12.7	12.0	12.3	13.4	12.3	11.8	11.0	10.5	9.7	9.2	11.9
Average small island states	**14.7**	**11.2**	**12.6**	**12.9**	**14.2**	**12.8**	**13.3**	**12.5**	**12.6**	**12.7**	**12.0**	**11.3**	**11.3**	**12.6**
Fiji	...	...	7.9	7.6	7.2	6.9	8.1	9.3	8.1	7.8	7.3	7.2	6.7	7.6
Papua New Guinea	...	6.5	8.8	10.2	8.2	7.7	6.7	6.6	6.8	7.0	9.8	6.9	...	7.7
Australia	...	...	...	...	...	7.3	7.7	8.0	8.4	6.0	6.8	7.2	6.4	7.2
							Average Cost of Deposits							
Samoa	7.9	3.4	3.8	4.0	4.0	3.8	4.6	6.2	5.0	3.7	2.2	2.1	2.1	4.1
Solomon Islands	2.7	1.4	0.9	1.2	1.5	0.7	0.5	0.6	1.1	3.2	2.0	1.1	0.4	1.3
Tonga	3.9	4.7	3.2	3.2	3.8	3.7	5.0	5.2	6.5	4.5	3.5	2.9	2.4	4.0
Vanuatu	3.4	2.8	3.4	3.3	3.6	3.8	4.3	4.3	4.3	3.3	2.5	2.6	2.6	3.4
Average small island states	**4.4**	**3.1**	**2.8**	**2.9**	**3.2**	**3.0**	**3.6**	**4.1**	**4.2**	**3.7**	**2.6**	**2.2**	**1.9**	**3.2**
Fiji	...	...	0.9	0.8	0.8	0.8	2.5	3.3	1.1	2.3	2.5	1.8	1.2	1.6
Papua New Guinea	...	1.4	1.8	1.8	1.2	0.5	0.6	0.5	0.8	1.1	1.0	0.7	0.4	1.0
Australia	...	...	...	...	...	4.3	4.6	5.0	5.7	3.1	3.8	4.1	3.6	4.3
							Simple Spread							
Samoa	16.9	8.9	8.6	7.8	7.9	8.5	7.9	6.7	7.7	7.4	8.2	7.9	7.3	8.6
Solomon Islands	11.8	12.5	13.9	14.5	16.3	14.6	14.6	13.1	12.6	13.0	12.5	12.8	12.9	13.5
Tonga	6.6	7.2	7.5	7.2	9.0	7.0	6.4	6.4	6.0	6.4	7.4	7.4	9.1	7.2
Vanuatu	15.8	5.1	9.0	9.4	8.4	8.6	9.1	8.0	7.5	7.7	8.0	7.1	6.6	8.5
Average small island states	**12.8**	**8.4**	**9.8**	**9.7**	**10.4**	**9.7**	**9.5**	**8.6**	**8.4**	**8.6**	**9.0**	**8.8**	**9.0**	**9.4**
Fiji	...	...	7.0	6.8	6.5	6.1	5.6	6.0	7.0	5.5	4.7	5.3	5.5	6.0
Papua New Guinea	...	5.1	7.0	8.4	7.0	7.1	6.1	6.1	6.0	5.9	8.8	6.2	...	6.7
Australia	...	...	...	...	...	3.0	3.1	3.0	2.8	2.9	3.0	3.1	2.9	3.0

Sources: Country authorities' central bank prudential data; and IMF staff estimates.

ANNEX TABLE 18.1.2

Net Interest Income *(Percent)*

	2000	2001	2002	2003	2004	2005	2006	2007	2008	2009	2010	2011	2012	Average
Samoa	9.5	5.6	5.7	5.4	5.6	5.9	6.6	6.0	6.1	5.5	5.8	6.0	5.6	6.1
Solomon Islands	6.8	6.7	6.8	6.4	5.7	5.2	6.8	7.6	8.6	8.5	6.1	5.2	4.5	6.5
Tonga	5.2	6.1	5.6	6.0	6.0	7.0	5.7	4.7	–2.5	–4.6	0.5	2.6	3.2	3.5
Vanuatu	5.8	2.6	3.5	3.2	3.1	3.5	3.9	3.6	3.6	3.6	3.9	4.1	4.2	3.7
Average small island states	**6.8**	**5.2**	**5.4**	**5.3**	**5.1**	**5.4**	**5.7**	**5.5**	**3.9**	**3.3**	**4.1**	**4.5**	**4.4**	**5.0**
Fiji	8.3	4.5	4.6	4.5	4.5	4.6	4.5	4.6	5.2	4.2	3.3	3.6	3.6	4.6
Papua New Guinea	0.0	4.8	6.5	7.0	4.6	4.1	3.7	3.6	3.8	3.6	4.7	3.3	3.5	4.1
Australia	...	...	...	...	...	1.8	1.8	1.6	1.6	1.7	1.7	1.8	1.7	1.7

Sources: Country authorities' central bank prudential data; and IMF staff estimates.

ANNEX TABLE 18.1.3

Credit Risk Indicators *(Percent)*

	2000	2001	2002	2003	2004	2005	2006	2007	2008	2009	2010	2011	2012	Average
						Provision Expense to Gross Loans								
Samoa	0.0	0.0	0.0	0.0	0.0	0.8	0.2	0.4	1.0	0.5	0.3	1.1	0.9	0.4
Solomon Islands	1.2	0.5	1.3	0.0	0.1	0.3	0.7	1.5	1.2	1.2	0.3	1.8	−0.0	0.8
Tonga	1.1	0.5	1.2	1.1	1.6	0.4	1.1	3.2	10.4	10.2	3.8	1.1	0.9	2.8
Vanuatu	0.5	0.5	0.8	1.3	0.8	0.1	0.4	0.5	0.6	0.0	0.2	0.1	0.1	0.5
Average small island states	**0.7**	**0.4**	**0.9**	**0.6**	**0.6**	**0.4**	**0.6**	**1.4**	**3.3**	**3.0**	**1.1**	**1.0**	**0.5**	**1.1**
Fiji	2.4	0.7	0.5	0.6	0.5	0.4	−0.1	1.0	0.2	1.1	−0.2	0.2	0.1	0.6
Papua New Guinea	0.0	0.0	0.0	0.0	0.0	0.0	0.0	0.2	0.6	0.0	0.0	0.0	...	0.1
Australia	...	...	...	...	...	0.2	0.2	0.2	0.8	0.8	0.5	0.3	0.4	0.4
						Loan Loss Reserves to Gross Loans								
Samoa	3.4	3.4	3.4	3.7	4.1	3.3	2.8	3.3	4.1	5.1	3.7	4.1	5.5	3.8
Solomon Islands	3.9	5.1	5.6	3.5	3.9	1.1	1.1	2.0	2.3	3.9	4.0	5.1	4.3	3.5
Tonga	4.7	4.5	4.5	4.6	4.8	2.5	2.4	3.6	6.4	14.3	15.1	12.8	11.5	7.1
Vanuatu	3.0	2.4	3.5	4.0	5.0	4.6	5.1	4.4	4.5	4.0	3.1	5.2	5.4	4.2
Average small island states	**3.7**	**3.8**	**4.2**	**4.0**	**4.4**	**2.9**	**2.9**	**3.3**	**4.3**	**6.8**	**6.5**	**6.8**	**6.7**	**4.7**
Fiji	3.3	3.8	3.9	3.5	2.6	1.6	1.9	2.7	2.2	1.5	1.3	1.4	1.3	2.4
Papua New Guinea	5.7	4.6	7.6	5.9	4.8	3.2	2.6	2.3	2.0	2.6	3.3	3.5	3.9	4.0
Australia	...	...	...	...	...	0.8	0.7	0.6	1.0	1.2	1.3	1.2	1.1	1.0

Sources: Country authorities' central bank prudential data; and IMF staff estimates.

ANNEX TABLE 18.1.4

Profitability Indicators *(Percent)*

	2000	2001	2002	2003	2004	2005	2006	2007	2008	2009	2010	2011	2012	Average
						Return on Average Assets (Pretax)								
Samoa	10.5	6.2	6.2	5.0	4.6	5.6	6.3	5.0	5.5	4.3	4.6	4.4	3.1	5.5
Solomon Islands	4.6	5.0	7.2	8.7	7.7	6.6	7.7	8.6	10.5	9.3	8.0	5.1	4.8	7.2
Tonga	5.2	6.1	5.6	6.0	6.0	7.0	5.7	4.7	−2.5	−4.6	0.5	2.6	3.2	3.5
Vanuatu	5.0	2.8	3.5	3.5	3.8	3.8	4.0	3.5	2.3	2.9	2.8	3.5	3.0	3.4
Average small island states	**6.3**	**5.0**	**5.6**	**5.8**	**5.5**	**5.8**	**6.0**	**5.5**	**3.9**	**3.0**	**4.0**	**3.9**	**3.5**	**4.9**
Fiji	5.2	3.3	3.7	3.6	3.8	4.0	3.9	2.9	4.3	2.8	2.6	2.6	2.5	3.5
Papua New Guinea	0.0	5.7	7.5	8.0	3.9	4.7	3.5	4.4	3.9	3.5	3.4	2.6	2.6	4.1
Australia	...	...	...	...	...	1.6	1.5	1.4	0.7	0.9	1.1	1.1	1.0	1.2
						Return on Equity (Pretax)								
Samoa	68.2	39.4	34.9	27.7	26.5	33.6	37.5	28.1	31.1	23.3	26.6	24.5	16.3	32.1
Solomon Islands	30.0	28.4	35.4	48.7	48.0	41.5	50.8	65.1	66.8	52.6	45.1	28.1	28.2	43.8
Tonga	36.1	41.9	34.4	37.6	40.5	52.7	42.2	35.0	−16.8	−30.2	3.7	14.4	15.5	23.6
Vanuatu	64.3	30.1	42.1	37.1	34.0	36.3	38.8	36.0	19.9	21.7	21.8	26.6	21.4	33.1
Average small island states	**49.7**	**35.0**	**36.7**	**37.8**	**37.3**	**41.0**	**42.3**	**41.1**	**25.3**	**16.8**	**24.3**	**23.4**	**20.3**	**33.2**
Fiji	78.1	43.4	49.0	51.0	54.4	58.5	51.7	37.7	49.4	24.4	20.7	22.3	25.6	43.6
Papua New Guinea	0.0	56.7	74.7	68.8	30.3	37.5	30.0	39.5	32.3	28.5	25.8	19.5	30.0	36.4
Australia	...	...	...	...	...	23.9	25.8	25.9	14.8	17.4	18.3	20.5	18.3	20.6

(Continued)

ANNEX TABLE 18.1.4 (*Continued*)

Profitability Indicators *(Percent)*

	2000	2001	2002	2003	2004	2005	2006	2007	2008	2009	2010	2011	2012	Average
							Return on Equity (Post-Tax)							
Samoa	48.0	27.5	24.3	19.4	18.7	23.5	26.3	20.2	22.6	16.7	19.2	17.8	14.8	23.0
Solomon Islands	19.0	18.6	23.9	32.7	30.5	27.2	33.2	42.1	43.0	34.4	28.5	17.8	19.1	28.5
Tonga	24.7	29.4	23.7	26.8	26.4	32.4	28.3	24.3	−16.8	−29.7	3.4	12.9	11.4	15.2
Vanuatu	64.3	30.1	42.1	37.1	34.0	36.3	38.8	36.0	19.9	21.7	21.8	26.6	21.4	33.1
Average small island states	**39.0**	**26.4**	**28.5**	**29.0**	**27.4**	**29.9**	**31.6**	**30.7**	**17.2**	**10.8**	**18.2**	**18.8**	**16.7**	**24.9**
Fiji	47.3	30.2	34.7	38.2	37.9	41.4	36.4	26.4	34.8	17.4	15.3	15.9	19.8	30.4
Papua New Guinea	0.0	39.9	52.7	49.6	23.3	39.2	20.6	27.4	22.3	19.6	18.7	14.2	...	27.3
Australia	...	...	...	...	...	15.8	16.9	18.0	13.2	10.6	13.2	15.2	12.4	14.4

Sources: Country authorities' central bank prudential data; and IMF staff estimates.

ANNEX TABLE 18.1.5

Ratio of Equity to Average Assets *(Percent)*

	2000	2001	2002	2003	2004	2005	2006	2007	2008	2009	2010	2011	2012	Average
Samoa	16.3	16.5	18.7	18.9	17.9	17.3	18.9	19.0	19.4	19.3	17.3	18.6	18.6	18.2
Solomon Islands	15.3	19.0	21.0	18.5	17.5	18.5	16.5	13.9	19.1	16.5	20.2	20.3	17.1	17.9
Tonga	13.6	16.5	16.4	16.9	13.0	14.1	13.5	15.6	17.7	13.0	17.5	19.1	23.0	16.1
Vanuatu	8.8	10.0	9.7	10.6	11.9	10.3	11.1	10.0	14.3	13.3	12.2	13.4	14.7	11.6
Average small island states	**13.5**	**15.5**	**16.4**	**16.2**	**15.1**	**15.1**	**15.0**	**14.6**	**17.6**	**15.5**	**16.8**	**17.9**	**18.3**	**16.0**
Fiji	7.0	8.5	7.9	8.5	7.9	8.3	8.1	8.2	10.2	12.7	12.9	10.7	10.0	9.3
Papua New Guinea	18.6	11.4	11.9	13.3	13.4	14.4	13.0	13.4	13.4	13.8	14.0	13.7	14.4	13.8
Australia	...	...	...	...	...	6.8	5.6	5.6	5.3	5.7	5.9	5.8	5.9	5.8

Sources: Country authorities' central bank prudential data; and IMF staff estimates.

ANNEX TABLE 18.1.6

Noninterest Income *(Percent)*

	2000	2001	2002	2003	2004	2005	2006	2007	2008	2009	2010	2011	2012	Average
							Noninterest Income to Average Assets							
Samoa	10.1	5.8	6.0	6.3	5.0	5.6	5.1	4.4	4.9	3.6	3.9	4.0	3.7	5.3
Solomon Islands	4.4	5.2	8.8	10.1	9.7	8.0	7.6	8.5	8.6	7.6	7.9	6.2	5.2	7.5
Tonga	4.5	5.1	4.6	5.7	6.0	5.6	5.2	6.7	6.3	3.8	3.8	4.8	4.6	5.1
Vanuatu	1.7	1.8	2.3	3.0	3.1	3.2	3.0	3.2	2.9	2.9	3.0	3.2	3.0	2.8
Average small island states	**5.2**	**4.5**	**5.4**	**6.3**	**6.0**	**5.6**	**5.2**	**5.7**	**5.7**	**4.5**	**4.6**	**4.5**	**4.1**	**5.2**
Fiji	5.2	3.3	3.7	3.5	3.5	3.5	2.9	2.5	2.6	2.9	2.8	3.0	2.9	3.3
Papua New Guinea	0.0	4.9	6.5	7.1	4.2	4.6	3.0	3.4	3.0	2.4	2.6	2.1	2.0	3.5
Australia	...	...	...	...	...	2.0	1.7	1.7	1.3	1.2	1.2	0.9	0.8	1.3

(Continued)

ANNEX TABLE 18.1.6 (*Continued*)

Noninterest Income *(Percent)*

	2000	2001	2002	2003	2004	2005	2006	2007	2008	2009	2010	2011	2012	Average
							Foreign Exchange Income to Average Assets							
Samoa	4.9	2.9	2.6	2.7	2.6	3.3	2.8	1.9	2.3	2.3	2.2	2.2	2.1	2.7
Solomon Islands	3.4	3.9	7.0	8.2	7.9	6.2	5.5	6.4	6.6	6.0	5.7	4.5	4.0	5.8
Tonga	3.6	4.2	3.6	3.9	3.7	3.1	3.2	3.5	4.0	2.6	2.5	3.0	2.4	3.3
Vanuatu	0.7	0.7	1.0	1.8	1.7	1.9	1.6	1.6	1.6	1.7	1.8	2.0	1.8	1.5
Average small island states	**3.2**	**2.9**	**3.5**	**4.2**	**4.0**	**3.6**	**3.3**	**3.4**	**3.6**	**3.1**	**3.1**	**2.9**	**2.6**	**3.3**
Fiji	2.1	1.3	1.6	1.4	1.3	1.2	1.2	1.1	1.2	1.1	1.3	1.5	1.3	1.4
Papua New Guinea	0.0	4.1	5.2	5.7	3.1	2.8	1.5	2.2	2.0	1.3	1.3	1.1	1.4	2.4
							Other Noninterest Income to Average Assets							
Samoa	5.2	2.8	3.4	3.6	2.4	2.3	2.3	2.5	2.6	1.3	1.6	1.8	1.6	2.6
Solomon Islands	1.0	1.2	1.8	2.0	1.8	1.8	2.0	2.1	2.0	1.6	2.1	1.7	1.3	1.7
Tonga	0.9	1.0	1.0	1.7	2.3	2.5	2.0	3.2	2.3	1.3	1.3	1.8	2.2	1.8
Vanuatu	1.0	1.0	1.3	1.2	1.4	1.3	1.3	1.5	1.4	1.2	1.1	1.2	1.2	1.2
Average small island states	**2.0**	**1.5**	**1.9**	**2.1**	**2.0**	**2.0**	**1.9**	**2.3**	**2.1**	**1.3**	**1.5**	**1.6**	**1.5**	**1.8**
Fiji	3.1	2.0	2.1	2.1	2.2	2.2	1.7	1.4	1.4	1.7	1.6	1.6	1.6	1.9
Papua New Guinea	0.0	0.8	1.2	1.4	1.1	1.7	1.5	1.2	1.1	1.1	1.3	1.0	0.6	1.1

Sources: Country authorities' central bank prudential data; and IMF staff estimates.

ANNEX TABLE 18.1.7

Noninterest Expenses *(Percent)*

	2000	2001	2002	2003	2004	2005	2006	2007	2008	2009	2010	2011	2012	Average
							Gross Noninterest Expense to Average Assets							
Samoa	9.1	5.2	5.5	6.7	5.9	5.4	5.2	5.1	4.8	4.4	4.8	4.8	5.5	5.6
Solomon Islands	6.0	6.6	7.9	7.8	7.7	6.5	6.3	6.6	5.9	6.1	5.9	5.5	4.9	6.4
Tonga	4.4	4.9	4.6	5.3	6.2	4.7	4.7	5.5	6.4	5.9	6.4	6.6	6.0	5.5
Vanuatu	2.4	1.4	2.0	2.3	2.2	2.9	2.6	3.1	4.0	3.6	3.9	3.7	4.1	2.9
Average small island states	**5.5**	**4.5**	**5.0**	**5.5**	**5.5**	**4.9**	**4.7**	**5.1**	**5.2**	**5.0**	**5.3**	**5.1**	**5.1**	**5.1**
Fiji	6.8	4.0	4.2	4.0	3.9	3.8	3.5	3.6	3.4	3.5	3.7	3.9	3.9	4.0
Papua New Guinea	0.0	4.1	5.5	6.1	4.8	4.0	3.2	2.5	2.7	2.5	3.9	2.8	2.5	3.4
Australia	...	...	...	...	...	2.1	1.9	1.9	1.7	1.5	1.6	1.3	1.3	1.7
							Nonsalary, Noninterest Expense to Average Assets							
Samoa	4.7	3.2	3.4	4.1	3.5	2.7	2.8	2.7	2.7	2.5	2.9	2.8	3.2	3.2
Solomon Islands	2.8	2.9	3.9	4.0	4.2	3.2	3.3	3.3	3.6	3.7	3.5	3.4	3.0	3.5
Tonga	2.0	2.3	2.5	2.7	3.7	2.6	2.6	3.2	3.8	3.8	3.8	3.9	3.9	3.1
Vanuatu	1.4	1.2	1.5	1.5	1.4	1.6	1.4	1.6	2.2	1.7	2.0	1.7	2.1	1.6
Average small island states	**2.7**	**2.4**	**2.8**	**3.1**	**3.2**	**2.5**	**2.5**	**2.7**	**3.1**	**2.9**	**3.0**	**3.0**	**3.1**	**2.8**
Fiji	2.1	1.2	1.8	1.7	1.6	1.6	1.5	1.7	1.5	1.6	1.8	1.8	1.8	1.7
Papua New Guinea	0.0	3.0	3.4	4.0	3.0	3.7	3.0	1.6	1.8	1.6	2.6	1.8	...	2.5
Australia	...	...	...	...	...	1.1	0.9	0.9	0.9	0.8	0.9	0.6	0.6	0.9

Sources: Country authorities' central bank prudential data; and IMF staff estimates.

ANNEX TABLE 18.1.8

Ratio of Net Noninterest Income to Average Assets *(Percent)*

	2000	2001	2002	2003	2004	2005	2006	2007	2008	2009	2010	2011	2012	Average
Samoa	1.0	0.6	0.5	–0.4	–0.9	0.3	–0.1	–0.7	0.2	–0.8	–1.0	–0.8	–1.8	–0.3
Solomon Islands	–1.6	–1.5	0.9	2.3	2.0	1.5	1.2	1.9	2.7	1.6	2.0	0.7	0.3	1.1
Tonga	0.1	0.2	–0.0	0.3	–0.2	0.9	0.6	1.2	–0.1	–2.1	–2.6	–1.8	–1.4	–0.4
Vanuatu	–0.7	0.3	0.2	0.7	0.9	0.3	0.3	0.0	–1.0	–0.7	–1.0	–0.5	–1.1	–0.2
Average small island states	**–0.3**	**–0.1**	**0.4**	**0.8**	**0.4**	**0.7**	**0.5**	**0.6**	**0.4**	**–0.5**	**–0.6**	**–0.6**	**–1.0**	**0.1**
Fiji	–1.6	–0.7	–0.5	–0.5	–0.4	–0.4	–0.6	–1.0	–0.8	–0.6	–0.9	–0.8	–1.0	–0.8
Papua New Guinea	0.0	0.8	1.0	1.0	–0.7	0.6	–0.2	0.9	0.3	–0.1	–1.3	–0.7	–0.5	0.1
Australia	...	...	...	...	...	–0.1	–0.2	–0.2	–0.4	–0.3	–0.4	–0.5	–0.5	–0.3

Sources: Country authorities' central bank prudential data; and IMF staff estimates.

ANNEX TABLE 18.1.9

Return on Assets: Composition and Trends *(Percent)*

Solomon Islands	2000	2001	2002	2003	2004	2005	2006	2007	2008	2009	2010	2011	2012	2013	Average
ROA, deposit and lending activities	**1.2**	**1.1**	**0.2**	**0.6**	**−0.3**	**0.4**	**2.2**	**2.2**	**3.9**	**3.3**	**2.2**	**0.7**	**0.8**	**0.6**	**1.4**
Net interest	6.8	6.7	6.8	6.4	5.7	5.2	6.8	7.6	8.6	8.5	6.1	5.2	4.5	4.4	6.5
Minus loan loss provision expense	0.5	0.2	0.5	0.0	0.0	0.1	0.3	0.8	0.8	0.8	0.2	0.8	0.0	0.1	0.4
Plus noninterest income															
Service charges and fees on deposit accounts	0.9	1.0	1.3	1.1	1.1	1.1	1.0	0.9	0.9	0.9	0.7	0.8	0.6	0.6	0.9
Other noninterest income	0.1	0.2	0.5	0.8	0.7	0.8	1.0	1.2	1.1	0.7	1.4	1.0	0.6	0.4	0.8
Minus noninterest expenses															
Salary and benefits	2.8	3.3	3.2	3.2	2.8	2.5	2.2	2.5	1.8	1.8	1.8	1.6	1.4	1.5	2.4
Other expenses	3.2	3.4	4.6	4.6	5.0	4.0	4.1	4.1	4.1	4.2	4.1	3.8	3.5	3.2	4.1
ROA, foreign exchange activities	**3.4**	**3.9**	**7.0**	**8.2**	**7.9**	**6.2**	**5.5**	**6.4**	**6.6**	**6.0**	**5.7**	**4.5**	**4.0**	**3.1**	**5.8**
ROA, all activities	**4.6**	**5.0**	**7.2**	**8.7**	**7.7**	**6.6**	**7.7**	**8.6**	**10.5**	**9.3**	**8.0**	**5.1**	**4.8**	**3.8**	**7.2**
Noninterest income/gross income	**39.5**	**43.6**	**56.4**	**61.3**	**62.8**	**60.7**	**52.8**	**52.7**	**49.8**	**47.4**	**56.1**	**54.3**	**54.0**	**48.2**	**53.2**
Foreign exchange income/gross income	**30.5**	**33.3**	**45.1**	**49.5**	**51.3**	**46.7**	**38.6**	**39.6**	**38.3**	**37.3**	**40.9**	**39.2**	**41.0**	**36.7**	**40.9**
Samoa	**2000**	**2001**	**2002**	**2003**	**2004**	**2005**	**2006**	**2007**	**2008**	**2009**	**2010**	**2011**	**2012**	**2013**	**Average**
ROA, deposit and lending activities	**5.6**	**3.3**	**3.6**	**2.3**	**2.1**	**2.2**	**3.5**	**3.1**	**3.2**	**2.1**	**2.4**	**2.1**	**1.0**	**2.1**	**2.8**
Net interest	9.5	5.6	5.7	5.4	5.6	5.9	6.6	6.0	6.1	5.5	5.8	6.0	5.6	5.5	6.1
Minus loan loss provision expense	...	...	...	...	...	0.5	0.1	0.3	0.8	0.4	0.2	0.9	0.7	−0.5	0.5
Plus noninterest income															
Service charges and fees on deposit accounts	4.9	2.6	2.6	2.8	2.2	2.3	2.2	2.5	2.6	1.3	1.5	1.7	1.5	1.7	2.4
Other noninterest income	0.4	0.2	0.8	0.8	0.3	0.0	0.1	0.1	0.1	0.0	0.1	0.0	0.0	0.0	0.2
Minus noninterest expenses															
Salary and benefits	3.2	1.6	1.7	2.1	1.9	2.2	1.9	1.9	1.6	1.4	1.5	1.5	1.8	1.7	1.9
Other expenses	5.9	3.5	3.8	4.7	4.1	3.2	3.3	3.2	3.1	3.0	3.3	3.3	3.7	3.9	3.7
ROA, foreign exchange activities	**4.9**	**2.9**	**2.6**	**2.7**	**2.6**	**3.3**	**2.8**	**1.9**	**2.3**	**2.3**	**2.2**	**2.2**	**2.1**	**1.9**	**2.7**
ROA, all activities	**10.5**	**6.2**	**6.2**	**5.0**	**4.6**	**5.6**	**6.3**	**5.0**	**5.5**	**4.3**	**4.6**	**4.4**	**3.1**	**4.0**	**5.5**
Noninterest income/gross income	**51.6**	**50.7**	**51.1**	**53.8**	**47.5**	**49.1**	**43.6**	**42.4**	**44.7**	**39.2**	**39.9**	**39.7**	**39.5**	**39.5**	**45.6**
Foreign exchange income/gross income	**24.9**	**25.8**	**22.2**	**23.3**	**24.4**	**29.0**	**24.2**	**18.4**	**21.0**	**24.8**	**23.3**	**22.1**	**22.3**	**20.7**	**23.5**

(Continued)

ANNEX TABLE 18.1.9 (*Continued*)

Return on Assets: Composition and Trends *(Percent)*

Vanuatu	2000	2001	2002	2003	2004	2005	2006	2007	2008	2009	2010	2011	2012	2013	Average
ROA, deposit and lending activities	**4.3**	**2.0**	**2.5**	**1.7**	**2.0**	**1.9**	**2.4**	**1.8**	**0.8**	**1.3**	**1.0**	**1.5**	**1.2**	**0.7**	**1.9**
Net Interest	5.8	2.6	3.5	3.2	3.1	3.5	3.9	3.6	3.6	3.6	3.9	4.1	4.2	4.1	3.7
Less loan loss provision expense	0.2	0.2	0.2	0.4	0.2	0.0	0.1	0.2	0.2	0.0	0.1	0.0	0.1	0.6	0.2
Plus noninterest income															
Service charges and fees on deposit accounts	1.0	1.0	1.2	1.0	0.6	0.6	0.6	0.9	0.6	0.6	0.6	0.6	0.6	0.6	0.8
Other noninterest income	0.0	0.0	0.1	0.2	0.8	0.7	0.7	0.7	0.7	0.6	0.6	0.5	0.6	0.6	0.5
Less noninterest expenses															
Salary and benefits	0.8	0.3	0.5	0.6	0.7	1.0	1.0	1.2	1.5	1.5	1.6	1.6	1.7	1.7	1.1
Other expenses	1.6	1.1	1.6	1.6	1.5	1.9	1.6	1.9	2.5	2.1	2.3	2.1	2.4	2.4	1.9
ROA, foreign exchange activities	**0.7**	**0.7**	**1.0**	**1.8**	**1.7**	**1.9**	**1.6**	**1.6**	**1.6**	**1.7**	**1.8**	**2.0**	**1.8**	**1.9**	**1.5**
ROA, all activities	**5.0**	**2.8**	**3.5**	**3.5**	**3.8**	**3.8**	**4.0**	**3.5**	**2.3**	**2.9**	**2.8**	**3.5**	**3.0**	**2.6**	**3.4**
Noninterest income/gross income	**22.7**	**41.0**	**39.4**	**48.6**	**49.9**	**47.7**	**43.4**	**46.8**	**44.9**	**44.4**	**43.1**	**43.9**	**41.5**	**42.2**	**42.9**
Foreign exchange income/gross income	**9.7**	**16.9**	**17.4**	**29.2**	**28.1**	**28.2**	**23.9**	**24.2**	**24.0**	**25.8**	**26.5**	**27.8**	**25.2**	**26.0**	**23.6**
Tonga	**2000**	**2001**	**2002**	**2003**	**2004**	**2005**	**2006**	**2007**	**2008**	**2009**	**2010**	**2011**	**2012**	**2013**	**Average**
ROA, deposit and lending activities	**1.6**	**1.9**	**2.0**	**2.1**	**2.2**	**4.0**	**2.5**	**1.2**	**−6.6**	**−7.2**	**−2.0**	**−0.4**	**0.8**	**1.0**	**0.2**
Net interest	5.8	6.1	6.5	6.5	7.3	6.5	6.1	6.0	5.8	5.2	5.9	5.1	5.1	4.5	6.0
Less loan loss provision expense	0.7	0.3	0.8	0.8	1.1	0.3	0.9	2.5	8.2	7.7	2.7	0.7	0.5	0.2	2.1
Plus noninterest income															
Service charges and fees on deposit accounts	0.8	1.0	1.0	1.7	2.2	2.3	1.9	2.0	2.2	1.3	1.3	1.8	0.9	1.0	1.6
Other noninterest income	0.1	0.0	0.1	0.0	0.1	0.2	0.1	1.1	0.1	0.0	0.0	0.0	1.3	1.1	0.2
Less noninterest expenses															
Salary and benefits	1.9	1.9	1.8	1.9	1.9	1.7	1.6	1.7	2.2	1.6	2.1	2.2	1.5	1.8	1.8
Other expenses	2.5	3.0	2.8	3.4	4.3	3.0	3.0	3.8	4.2	4.3	4.3	4.4	4.5	3.6	3.7
ROA, foreign exchange activities	**3.6**	**4.2**	**3.6**	**3.9**	**3.7**	**3.1**	**3.2**	**3.5**	**4.0**	**2.6**	**2.5**	**3.0**	**2.4**	**2.2**	**3.3**
ROA, all activities	**5.2**	**6.1**	**5.6**	**6.0**	**6.0**	**7.0**	**5.7**	**4.7**	**−2.5**	**−4.6**	**0.5**	**2.6**	**3.2**	**3.2**	**3.5**
Noninterest income/gross income	**43.9**	**45.6**	**41.5**	**46.4**	**45.3**	**46.2**	**46.3**	**52.7**	**52.1**	**42.4**	**39.5**	**48.5**	**47.4**	**49.0**	**46.0**
Foreign exchange income/gross income	**35.2**	**36.8**	**32.3**	**32.3**	**28.2**	**25.6**	**28.3**	**27.7**	**33.4**	**28.5**	**26.1**	**30.2**	**25.1**	**25.1**	**30.0**

Papua New Guinea	2000	2001	2002	2003	2004	2005	2006	2007	2008	2009	2010	2011	2012	2013	Average
ROA, deposit and lending activities	...	**1.6**	**2.3**	**2.3**	**0.9**	**1.9**	**2.0**	**2.2**	**1.9**	**2.2**	**2.1**	**1.6**	**...**	**...**	**1.9**
Net interest	...	4.8	6.5	7.0	4.6	4.1	3.7	3.6	3.8	3.6	4.7	3.3	3.5	3.9	4.4
Less loan loss provision expense	...	0.0	0.0	0.0	0.0	0.0	0.0	0.1	0.2	0.0	0.0	0.0	...	...	0.0
Plus noninterest income	...														
Service charges and fees on deposit accounts	...	0.7	1.2	1.3	1.0	1.6	1.2	0.8	0.8	0.8	1.0	0.8	...	...	1.0
Other noninterest income	...	0.1	0.1	0.1	0.2	0.1	0.3	0.3	0.3	0.3	0.3	0.2	...	...	0.2
Less noninterest expenses	...														
Salary and benefits	...	1.1	2.1	2.1	1.8	0.3	0.2	0.9	1.0	0.9	1.4	1.0	...	...	1.2
Other expenses	...	3.0	3.4	4.0	3.0	3.7	3.0	1.6	1.8	1.6	2.6	1.8	...	...	2.7
ROA, foreign exchange activities	...	**4.1**	**5.2**	**5.7**	**3.1**	**2.8**	**1.5**	**2.2**	**2.0**	**1.3**	**1.3**	**1.1**	**1.4**	...	**2.6**
ROA, all activities	...	**5.7**	**7.5**	**8.0**	**3.9**	**4.7**	**3.5**	**4.4**	**3.9**	**3.9**	**3.4**	**2.6**	**2.7**	...	**4.5**
Noninterest income/gross income	...	**50.5**	**49.8**	**50.4**	**47.7**	**52.5**	**44.6**	**48.3**	**44.6**	**39.7**	**36.0**	**38.9**	**...**	**...**	**45.7**
Foreign exchange income/gross income	...	**42.1**	**40.2**	**40.3**	**34.9**	**32.6**	**22.4**	**31.8**	**28.7**	**21.5**	**18.0**	**19.8**	**...**	**...**	**30.2**
Fiji	**2000**	**2001**	**2002**	**2003**	**2004**	**2005**	**2006**	**2007**	**2008**	**2009**	**2010**	**2011**	**2012**	**2013**	**Average**
ROA, deposit and lending activities	**3.1**	**2.0**	**2.1**	**2.2**	**2.5**	**2.7**	**2.7**	**1.7**	**3.1**	**1.6**	**1.3**	**1.1**	**1.2**	**1.2**	**2.1**
Net interest	8.3	4.5	4.6	4.5	4.5	4.6	4.5	4.6	5.2	4.2	3.3	3.6	3.6	3.4	4.6
Less loan loss provision expense	1.5	0.5	0.3	0.4	0.3	0.3	0.0	0.7	0.1	0.8	−0.1	0.2	0.1	0.2	0.4
Plus noninterest income															
Service charges and fees on deposit accounts	0.0	0.0	0.6	0.7	0.6	0.6	0.5	0.5	0.5	0.5	0.4	0.5	0.5	0.4	0.4
Other noninterest income	3.1	2.0	1.4	1.4	1.6	1.6	1.2	1.0	0.9	1.3	1.1	1.1	1.1	1.3	1.5
Less noninterest expenses															
Salary and benefits	4.0	2.4	2.0	1.9	1.8	1.8	1.7	1.7	1.6	1.6	1.6	1.7	1.8	1.6	2.0
Other expenses	2.7	1.6	2.2	2.2	2.1	2.0	1.8	1.9	1.8	1.9	2.1	2.1	2.1	2.1	2.0
ROA, foreign exchange activities	**2.1**	**1.3**	**1.6**	**1.4**	**1.3**	**1.2**	**1.2**	**1.1**	**1.2**	**1.1**	**1.3**	**1.5**	**1.3**	**1.0**	**1.4**
ROA, all activities	**5.2**	**3.3**	**3.7**	**3.6**	**3.8**	**4.0**	**3.9**	**2.9**	**4.3**	**2.8**	**2.6**	**2.6**	**2.5**	**2.2**	**3.5**
Noninterest income/gross income	**38.6**	**42.4**	**44.4**	**44.0**	**43.7**	**42.6**	**38.9**	**35.7**	**33.3**	**40.7**	**45.9**	**46.1**	**44.8**	**44.9**	**41.6**
Foreign exchange income/gross income	**15.6**	**16.7**	**19.5**	**17.4**	**16.5**	**15.4**	**15.7**	**15.7**	**15.4**	**16.0**	**20.4**	**22.4**	**20.2**	**17.2**	**17.5**

Sources: Country authorities' central banks; and IMF staff estimates.
Note: ROA = return on assets.

REFERENCES

Davies, M., and J. Vaught. 2009. "Interest Rates and Bank Profitability in the South Pacific." Regional Papers, Pacific Financial Technical Assistance Centre, Suva.

———. 2011. "Capital Requirements and Holdings in the South Pacific." Unpublished, Pacific Financial Technical Assistance Centre, Suva.

International Finance Corporation (IFC). 2010. "Credit Markets in the Pacific: A Review of Loan Pricing in Four Pacific Countries." Unpublished, Washington.

World Bank. 2013. *Global Financial Development Report*. Washington: World Bank.

Appendix 1. Fiji

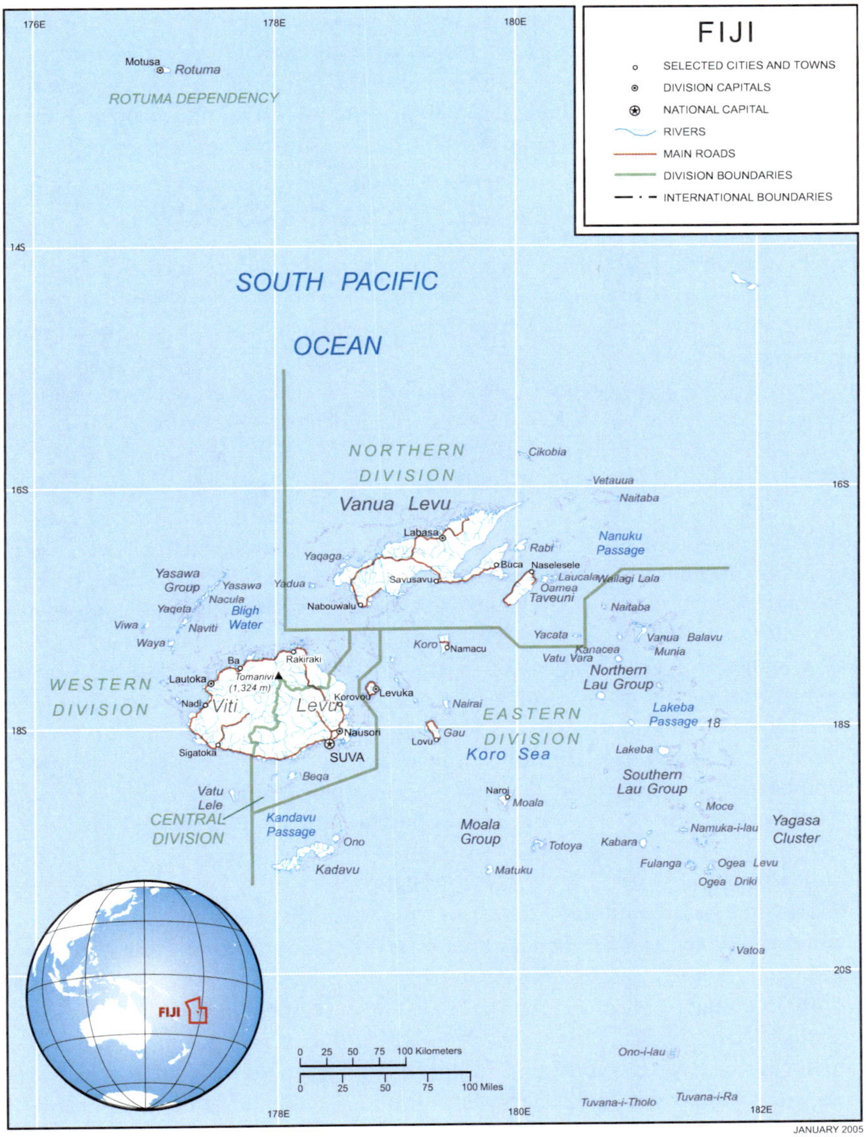

Fiji, located in the South Pacific, has a territory of 18,274 square kilometers spread over 332 islands, of which about one-third are inhabited. Most of Fiji's population of nearly 900,000 live on Viti Levu and Vanua Levu, the two largest islands.

Several coups since 1987 have made political stability elusive. But with a landmark election in September 2014, Fiji took a decisive stride toward democratic government for the first time since a 2006 military coup. This has improved relationships with traditional development partners, access to concessional development finance, and overall confidence. The comfortable parliamentary majority

Prepared by Roberto Guimarães-Filho and Leni Hunter.

for the former interim prime minister's Fiji First Party is expected to maintain the momentum of economic reform.

Fiji, like other Pacific island countries, is prone to natural disasters. On February 20, 2016, Cyclone Winston hit Fiji with unprecedented force, claiming over 40 lives and causing over 5 percent of the population to take shelter in evacuation centers. The authorities' preliminary assessment of the damage and losses was US$940 million (about 20 percent of GDP). Foreign aid and remittances are expected to increase and help finance the rebuilding.

SOURCES OF GROWTH AND ECONOMIC PROFILE

Main sources of growth. Fiji's economy has become increasingly diversified, although it relies considerably on tourism, and the sugar sector remains important. Lower political uncertainty has boosted business confidence and investment, and underpinned a robust pickup in growth that is currently underway.

Production, employment, exports, and imports. Fiji is a middle-income country with an income per capita of about US$5,000. The share of agriculture (particularly sugar), forestry, and fisheries in GDP has declined over the past decade, while services account for more than half of GDP, driven by tourism, finance, communications, wholesale and retail trade, and public services. Fiji's main exports are sugar, gold, garments, mineral water, fish, timber, coconut oil, fruit, and vegetables. Major imports include foodstuffs, mineral fuel, manufactured goods, machinery, and transport equipment. Fiji's trade deficit is large and has widened over time, contributing to sizable current account deficits in the past decade. Unemployment has remained persistently high at approximately 9 percent, with youth and underemployment rates significantly higher.

Sources of external income. Large trade balance deficits have been partly offset by surpluses in the services account, owing to positive net earnings from tourism and remittances. Remittance inflows have increased in recent years, reaching about 5 percent of GDP in 2015. In the capital account, Fiji has relied on foreign direct investment inflows, primarily into the tourism sector.

Development aid. Fiji's traditional development partners (Australia, Japan, New Zealand, and the Asian Development Bank and World Bank) limited new projects and aid following the 2006 coup. To finance increased infrastructure investment, the government tapped nontraditional sources, such as the export-import banks of China and Malaysia, for financing. With the return of democracy, relations with a broader group of development partners have improved.

Government finance. Fiji's fiscal policy continues to balance the competing needs for a stronger fiscal position and increased public investment to enhance growth. Fiscal policy has been generally prudent, with an emphasis on increasing the share of capital spending in total expenditure and an estimated budget deficit of 3.2 percent of GDP in 2015. The ratio of government debt to GDP has declined to approximately 46 percent of GDP, down from 56 percent in 2010. The Medium Term Fiscal Framework projects smaller deficits over time and associated declines in debt-to-GDP levels.

Financial sector. The banking sector consists of five foreign-owned banks and one domestic bank. Most banks remain well capitalized, with average capital adequacy ratios above regulatory levels, and have low nonperforming loans and adequate loan-loss provisioning. Access to credit needs broadening, particularly in the agricultural sector and for small- and medium-sized enterprises, where the lack of adequate collateral and credit history often impedes access to credit. The Reserve Bank of Fiji has introduced a small- and medium-sized enterprise loan guarantee scheme, established sector lending ratios for banks, and encouraged microfinance operations.

Business climate and investment. The return of democracy boosted business and consumer confidence, and expectations of continued economic reform have created a favorable overall business climate. Sector-specific structural reforms are now needed to improve the investment climate. This will require faster implementation of reforms in land use and the sugarcane sector, relaxing price controls, and continued improvements in infrastructure, among other measures. A reliable energy supply is essential to meet the increasing demands of the economy and crucial to improve the investment environment.

Monetary policy. Accommodative monetary policy has stimulated economic activity over the past few years, with the policy rate nearing the zero lower bound. Monetary policy is focused on maintaining price stability, a comfortable foreign reserve position, and a stable exchange rate. The monetary transmission mechanism remains weak, and structural excess liquidity remains. The Reserve Bank of Fiji's current policy stance has contributed to low lending rates, while positive economic sentiment has led to a strong pickup in credit growth in 2013 and 2014, though this has moderated more recently.

Exchange rate and competitiveness. Fiji maintains a basket peg. The competitive boost from the April 2009 devaluation was largely eroded by creeping real exchange rate appreciation, driven by partner-country inflation differentials. The real exchange rate is now slightly higher than a level consistent with medium-term macroeconomic fundamentals, while in nominal terms, the Fijian dollar has appreciated against the Australian dollar since 2013. The current stable macroeconomic environment provides a good opportunity to lay the foundation for a more flexible exchange rate regime.

GROWTH CHALLENGES, VULNERABILITIES, AND SPILLOVERS

Main growth challenges. Fiji is a richly endowed country, but average growth has remained slow over the past decades owing to political instability, susceptibility to external shocks, and slow progress on structural reform. While the authorities have accelerated reforms in recent years, raising potential growth and increasing resilience remain major policy challenges.

Main vulnerabilities. Domestic risks stem from the slowing reform momentum, which could impact investment. Planned large-scale privatizations may not materialize, jeopardizing the authorities' medium-term debt and deficit targets unless offsetting expenditure and revenue measures are undertaken. Fiji is also susceptible to natural disasters, requiring significant fiscal buffers. Given rapid credit growth, particularly over 2014, authorities need to be vigilant to avoid overheating amid strong import growth and relatively shallow markets for skilled labor and capital.

Regional and global economic spillovers. Fiji remains vulnerable to international commodity price shocks, as higher import prices would lead to higher current account deficits and lower reserve coverage. Even so, the recent decline in oil prices provided a significant windfall.

APPENDIX TABLE 1.1

Fiji: Selected Economic Indicators, 2010–15

Nominal GDP (2014): US$4,532 million
Main export products: Sugar, Mineral water, Gold
Remoteness (GDP-weighted distance): 9,234 km
GDP per capita (2014): US$5,118
Population (2014): 885,470 (est.)

	1991–2000 Average	2001–09 Average	2010–15 Average	2010	2011	2012	2013	2014	2015 Estimate
GDP, GDP growth, employment, and prices									
Real GDP (at constant factor cost, percent change)	2.7	1.6	3.6	3.0	2.7	1.4	4.7	5.3	4.3
Real GDP per capita (percent change)	1.6	1.1	2.8	2.0	1.8	0.6	4.0	4.8	3.8
Unemployment (percent)	. . .	7.5	8.8	8.9	9.0	8.6	8.7	8.8	8.8
Consumer prices (percent change, average)	. . .	2.1	3.4	3.7	7.3	3.4	2.9	0.5	2.8
Shares in nominal GDP (percent)									
Largest sector (services)	44.8	50.4	48.4	54.7	49.6	48.0	46.4	44.1	47.6
Transport and communications	7.9	9.2	9.7	10.4	9.6	9.6	9.5	9.4	10.0
Wholesale and retail trade	10.6	11.0	8.5	9.9	8.7	8.5	8.0	7.4	8.2
Real estate and business services	5.5	7.0	7.2	8.2	7.5	7.4	6.9	6.5	6.9
Second largest sector (manufacturing)	12.4	12.7	10.1	11.7	10.7	10.2	9.7	9.2	9.3

(continued)

APPENDIX TABLE 1.1

Fiji: Selected Economic Indicators, 2010–15 (*Continued*)

Nominal GDP (2014): US$4,532 million | **GDP per capita (2014): US$5,118**
Main export products: Sugar, Mineral water, Gold | **Population (2014): 885,470 (est.)**
Remoteness (GDP-weighted distance): 9,234 km

	1991–2000 Average	2001–09 Average	2010–15 Average	2010	2011	2012	2013	2014	2015 Estimate
Third largest sector (agriculture, forestry, and fishing)	12.1	10.6	8.2	8.9	8.6	8.5	8.0	7.6	7.5
Tourism	...	14.8	18.1	19.8	19.0	18.3	17.4	16.9	17.0
Contributions to nominal GDP growth (percent)									
Largest sector (services)	2.7	3.6	2.6	1.7	1.1	0.9	2.3	2.4	7.2
Transport and communications	0.6	0.7	0.8	0.7	0.4	0.5	0.7	0.9	1.4
Wholesale and retail trade	0.4	0.5	0.3	0.1	–0.1	0.2	0.3	0.1	1.5
Real estate and business services	0.6	0.5	0.4	0.3	0.3	0.3	0.1	0.3	1.0
Second largest sector (manufacturing)	0.8	0.6	0.4	0.6	0.3	0.0	0.3	0.5	0.8
Third largest sector (agriculture, forestry, and fishing)	0.9	0.2	0.3	–0.3	0.7	0.3	0.2	0.4	0.5
Share in nominal GDP (percent)[1]									
Private consumption	...	...	...	...	...	...	...	...	...
Private investment	...	...	...	...	...	...	...	...	...
Public consumption	...	...	...	...	...	...	...	...	...
Public investment	...	...	...	...	...	...	...	...	...
Exports minus imports	...	...	...	...	...	...	...	...	...
Contributions to nominal GDP growth (percent)[1]									
Private consumption	...	...	...	...	...	...	...	...	...
Private investment	...	...	...	...	...	...	...	...	...
Public consumption	...	...	...	...	...	...	...	...	...
Public investment	...	...	...	...	...	...	...	...	...
Exports minus imports	...	...	...	...	...	...	...	...	...
Public finances									
Central government finance (percent of GDP)									
Revenue and grants	26.8	24.9	26.9	25.5	26.7	26.5	27.0	27.6	28.2
Total domestic revenue	26.8	24.9	26.7	25.4	26.6	26.3	26.8	27.3	27.9
Grants	...	...	0.2	0.1	0.1	0.2	0.2	0.3	0.3
Expenditure and net lending	29.0	28.7	29.2	27.7	28.0	28.9	27.6	31.8	31.4
Current (excluding grants)	24.1	23.9	20.8	22.1	20.7	20.8	20.0	21.0	20.3
Of which: wages and salaries	11.6	11.0	8.7	9.4	8.4	8.4	8.1	8.9	9.0
Development (capital)	4.9	4.8	8.0	5.0	5.7	7.5	7.6	10.9	11.1
Current balance[2]	2.7	1.0	5.9	3.3	5.9	5.5	6.8	6.3	7.6
Overall balance	–2.2	–3.7	–2.3	–2.2	–1.4	–2.4	–0.6	–4.3	–3.2
Financing	...	...	2.3	2.2	1.4	2.4	0.6	4.3	3.2
Assets (sinking fund)	...	...	–0.2	–0.2	–0.5	–0.7	–0.9	0.3	0.6
Debt	...	...	2.5	2.5	2.4	3.7	2.4	3.5	0.9
Of which: external	...	...	1.5	0.7	4.2	1.8	1.0	1.1	0.0
Of which: concessional	...	...	1.4	0.8	1.7	1.9	1.3	1.8	1.1
Other	...	...	0.2	0.0	0.0	0.0	0.1	0.1	1.1

(continued)

APPENDIX TABLE 1.1

Fiji: Selected Economic Indicators, 2010–15 (*Continued*)

Nominal GDP (2014): US$4,532 million
Main export products: Sugar, Mineral water, Gold
Remoteness (GDP-weighted distance): 9,234 km

GDP per capita (2014): US$5,118
Population (2014): 885,470 (est.)

	1991–2000 Average	2001–09 Average	2010–15 Average	2010	2011	2012	2013	2014	2015 Estimate
Public-debt-to-GDP ratio (percent)	47.3	50.1	50.6	56.2	52.6	51.7	49.5	47.7	45.1
Sinking fund: closing balance (percent of GDP)	...	...	2.0	1.4	1.8	2.4	3.1	2.5	0.8
Balance of payments (percent of GDP, unless otherwise indicated)									
Current account including official transfers	2.0	−8.5	−5.4	−4.1	−4.9	−1.3	−9.8	−7.2	−5.4
Current account excluding official transfers	0.7	−8.5	−5.5	−4.2	−4.9	−1.4	−9.9	−7.3	−5.4
Overall balance	...	...	−1.1	−4.8	−3.0	−2.1	1.8	0.4	1.1
External debt service (percent of exports of goods and services)	0.3	0.4	0.3	0.4	0.3	0.3	0.3	0.2	0.2
Foreign direct investment	...	...	8.2	11.1	10.7	9.5	6.3	7.3	7.6
External debt	14.8	12.5	18.0	14.0	16.4	16.9	21.7	21.8	20.7
Total external income	...	...	8.6	8.9	8.0	8.9	8.7	8.1	8.8
Investment income	...	...	1.9	2.5	2.6	1.9	2.1	1.3	1.3
Remittances	...	...	4.6	4.9	4.3	4.3	4.4	4.5	5.0
Other	...	...	2.1	1.5	1.1	2.7	2.2	2.3	2.6
Contributions to external income growth (percent)									
External income growth	...	...	6.5	−4.9	0.4	16.9	6.8	2.5	17.3
Investment income	...	...	0.0	5.3	5.0	−7.8	4.3	−7.5	0.7
Remittances	...	...	6.8	15.9	−0.9	2.9	5.3	6.5	11.0
Other	...	...	−0.3	−26.1	−3.8	21.9	−2.7	3.6	5.7
Exchange rate (Fiji dollar to U.S. dollar period average)	1.6	1.9	1.9	1.9	1.8	1.8	1.8	1.9	1.9
Real effective exchange rate (period average)[3]	118.5	112.4	104.8	100.0	103.4	106.6	107.6	106.6	...
(percent change)	−0.9	0.1	0.4	−4.6	3.4	3.1	1.0	−0.9	...
Money, credit, and financial sector									
Broad money (percent change)	...	11.6	3.6	3.5	11.5	5.9	19.0	10.4	13.9
Credit to private sector (percent of GDP)	...	51.7	57.0	62.7	58.0	58.6	59.0	61.5	65.3
(percent change)	...	17.2	2.0	3.5	3.9	6.3	9.2	15.5	14.2
Bank assets (percent of GDP)	...	54.7	61.6	62.8	61.9	62.1	69.0	68.9	72.3
Short-term treasury bill interest rate (three-month)	...	2.8	1.4	3.9	1.0	0.3	0.1	2.5	0.8
Nonperforming loan ratio	...	1.8	1.0	1.4	...	0.8	0.7	0.7	0.7
Foreign bank market share (percent)[4]	...	...	...	...	...	...	...	...	...

(continued)

APPENDIX TABLE 1.1

Fiji: Selected Economic Indicators, 2010–15 (*Continued*)

Nominal GDP (2014): US$4,532 million
Main export products: Sugar, Mineral water, Gold
Remoteness (GDP-weighted distance): 9,234 km

GDP per capita (2014): US$5,118
Population (2014): 885,470 (est.)

	1991–2000 Average	2001–09 Average	2010–15 Average	2010	2011	2012	2013	2014	2015 Estimate
Business climate indicators									
Business environment rankings[5]									
Doing business (overall)	...	...	60.7	38	42	51	59	86	88
Construction permits	...	...	75.0	50	55	59	66	109	111
Getting electricity	...	...	69.2	61	64	67	70	75	78
Enforcing contracts	...	...	66.0	53	53	55	59	88	88
Getting credit	...	...	53.5	38	39	42	52	71	79
Human development index[5]	...	...	...	0.7	0.7	0.7	0.7	0.7	...
Memorandum:									
Nominal GDP (F$ million)	2,902.2	4,899.4	7,566.4	6,024.4	6,768.5	7,119.6	7,726.7	8,552.9	9,206.1
Nominal GDP (US$ million)	1,785.3	2,717.2	4,067.1	3,140.5	3,774.5	3,977.7	4,196.1	4,531.5	4,782.0

Sources: Fiji authorities; IMF, World Economic Outlook database (April 2016); and IMF staff estimates.
Note: ... = data not available; SDR = special drawing rights.
[1] GDP expenditure shares are IMF staff estimates.
[2] Current balance excludes grants and development (capital expenditure).
[3] Index, 2005 = 100.
[4] Share in total loans; does not include small loan scheme.
[5] World Bank, *Doing Business* reports.
[6] United Nations Development Programme.

Appendix 2. Kiribati

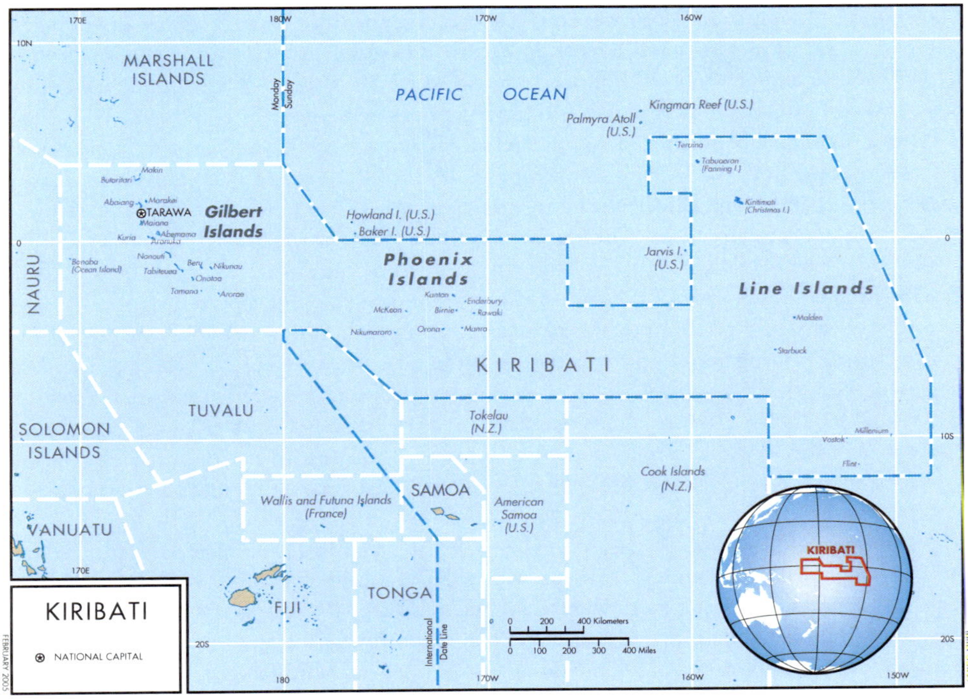

Kiribati's 33 atoll islands are spread among three groups: the Gilbert Islands, the Phoenix Islands, and the Line Islands. Most of the population lives in the Gilbert Islands, two-thirds of them in the capital, South Tarawa. Although the land area is relatively small, the country's exclusive economic zone covers a vast 3 million square kilometers. Climate change poses significant challenges for this low-lying island group.

Kiribati gained independence from the United Kingdom in 1979. The president is elected and is both the head of state and head of the government. Parliament has one chamber with 46 elected members.

SOURCES OF GROWTH AND ECONOMIC PROFILE

Main sources of growth. Growth on the expenditure side is driven by public sector spending (financed to a large extent by fishing license fees and drawdowns from the country's sovereign wealth fund), remittances, and development grants. By sector, the main contributors to growth are agriculture and fishing, the government sector, retail and wholesale trade, and tourism.

Production, employment, exports, and imports. Real GDP growth was below 2 percent a year on average over 2006–11 and this has been the trend since 1991. Growth has also been quite choppy because of the volatile output of some sectors, including agriculture, fisheries, and construction. In recent years, however, it has picked up as a result of record fishing license revenues and higher development grants. Even so, Kiribati's production opportunities are limited by lack of scale, remoteness, high transport costs, and insufficient infrastructure. Because of these constraints the private sector is small. The government sector is a major formal employer and plays a dominant role

---

Prepared by Ding Ding.

in the economy. The agricultural sector consists mainly of subsidized copra production and subsistence farming. Tourism, also small and constrained by the same issues holding back production opportunities, is dominated by niche game fishing. Merchandise exports are small (estimated at 5.1 percent of GDP in 2015) and largely limited to fish and copra. Given the narrow production base, Kiribati depends heavily on imports, which exceed 50 percent of GDP, and the country is highly exposed to fluctuations in world commodity prices.

External income. The major sources of external income are remittances, fishing license fees, and investment income from the country's sovereign wealth fund. The major share of remittances is from seamen working on foreign ships, averaging 6 percent of GDP in 2007–14. But these remittances have been on a declining trend. Fishing license fees, which averaged 20 percent of GDP over 2000–11, have been volatile. Thanks to the enforcement of the Parties to Nauru Agreement, fees increased from 16.8 percent of GDP in 2011 to a record high of 68.4 percent in 2014. Kiribati's sovereign wealth fund, the Revenue Equalization Reserve Fund, was established in 1956 and capitalized using phosphate mining royalties until the minerals were exhausted in 1979. The fund represented about 3.5 times GDP in 2013, but its real per capita value has declined significantly, from above $A9,350 in 2000 to about $A5,000 in 2013 in constant 2006 prices. This is mainly because of high withdrawals to finance the fiscal deficit (averaging 14 percent of GDP over 2007–12), but the global financial crisis also had an effect. In recent years, the fund's position has started to improve with the help of government reforms and income from fishing license fees.

Development aid. Kiribati is a large recipient of financial aid and technical assistance from multilateral and bilateral development partners, with aid accounting for about 34 percent of GDP on average in 2007–14. Most aid is provided as grants and directed at infrastructure, communication, energy, and climate adaptation projects, as well as education and training, and health. Technical assistance is provided in various areas, including public financial management, the fishing sector, and telecommunications.

Public finances. Current government expenditure (excluding grants) accounts for about 55 percent of GDP, after growing about 5 percent annually over 2007–14. Notwithstanding the fiscal surplus achieved from high fishing revenues in 2014, structural fiscal imbalances are significant and stem from insufficient tax revenue growth as well as expenditure pressures from significant infrastructure needs and nonperforming public enterprises. Fiscal adjustment is needed to reduce these imbalances and ensure the sustainability of the Revenue Equalization Reserve Fund.

Financial sector. The formal financial sector consists of a single foreign-owned commercial bank, a government-owned development bank, a provident fund, and an insurance company. Formal financial intermediation and access to credit for the private sector are very limited. Communal land and cumbersome access procedures restrict the use of land as collateral. That said, private sector credit as a percent of GDP has risen sharply since 2011, albeit from very low levels.

Investment and business climate. Infrastructure and business climate shortcomings curtail private and foreign direct investment. Improving infrastructure and communications is therefore essential. Enhancing regulations and training in the fishing sector will help expand the local fishing industry and better utilize Kiribati's vast marine resources. But accessing land and obtaining the necessary licenses are among the biggest impediments to starting a business. At the same time, enforcing business contracts can be quite a lengthy process. Better enforcement of land and other property rights and speedier resolution of court settlement procedures, in particular for those relating to land, should help strengthen the business and legal environment and promote private sector activity. Recent reforms to state-owned enterprises have improved transparency, though opportunities for private sector involvement need to continue.

Exchange rate and competitiveness. The Australian dollar circulates as legal tender. Kiribati has accepted the obligations of Article VIII and maintains an exchange system free of restrictions on payments and transfers for current international transactions. The real effective exchange rate is now close to but below its long-run average. The use of the Australian dollar as the official currency remains appropriate, as it has provided a strong nominal anchor and because of Kiribati's close links to Australia. Enhancing infrastructure and bolstering the business climate will be crucial to improving competitiveness.

GROWTH CHALLENGES, VULNERABILITIES, AND SPILLOVERS

Main growth challenges. Remoteness, dispersion, and small population have led to a lack of scale and high transportation costs, constraining growth and limiting employment opportunities. Climate change is exacerbating these constraints and causing additional costs. Insufficient infrastructure, business climate weaknesses, and limited financial intermediation hinder private-sector-led growth.

Main vulnerabilities. These include climate change, the Revenue Equalization Reserve Fund's exposure to global asset valuations, reliance on donor aid, and volatile fishing license revenues and import prices.

Global and regional economic spillovers. Australia and New Zealand have a significant impact on Kiribati's economy through aid and through the opportunities they provide to Kiribati nationals to work abroad. Australia is also important because of the use of its currency and the Revenue Equalization Reserve Fund's large exposure to Australian assets.

APPENDIX TABLE 2.1

Kiribati: Selected Economic Indicators, 2010–15

Nominal GDP (2014): US$186.1 million | **GDP per Capita (2014): US$1,656**
Main Export Products: Fish, Copra | **Population (2014): 112,334**
Remoteness (GDP-weighted distance): 8,210 km

	1991–2000 Average	2001–09 Average	2010–15 Average	2010	2011	2012	2013	2014	2015 Estimate
GDP, GDP growth, employment, and prices									
Real GDP (percent change)	1.4	1.0	1.9	–0.9	–0.2	3.4	2.4	3.7	3.1
Real GDP per capita (percent change)	–0.3	–0.4	–1.0	–3.9	0.9	–6.0	0.4	1.7	1.1
Real GNI (percent change)	3.2	–0.1	4.6	1.8	–5.8	14.3	11.5	13.6	–7.7
Consumer prices (percent change, average)	3.1	4.0	–0.6	–3.9	1.5	–3.0	–1.5	2.1	1.4
Consumer prices (percent change, end of period)	3.2	3.8	–0.2	–1.9	–0.8	–3.8	0.8	3.1	1.4
Unemployment (percent)									
Shares in GDP (percent)									
Largest sector (government)	27.5	25.4	26.9	27.3	27.3	26.7	26.4	...	...
Second largest sector (agriculture and fishing)	24.0	22.3	24.3	24.0	24.5	24.2	24.3	...	...
Third largest sector (wholesale and retail trade)	6.3	6.5	6.5	7.6	7.2	6.0	5.2	...	...
Hotel and restaurant	1.3	0.8	0.6	0.6	0.6	0.6	0.6	...	...
Agriculture									
Contribution to real GDP growth (percent)									
Government	0.4	0.6	0.2	0.5	0.4	0.0	0.0	...	...
Agriculture and fishing	0.0	0.5	0.6	–0.6	1.1	1.1	0.7	...	...
Wholesale and retail trade	0.3	0.2	–0.5	0.0	–0.2	–1.0	–0.9	...	...

(continued)

APPENDIX TABLE 2.1

Kiribati: Selected Economic Indicators, 2010–15 (*Continued*)

Nominal GDP (2014): US$186.1 million
Main Export Products: Fish, Copra
Remoteness (GDP-weighted distance): 8,210 km

GDP per Capita (2014): US$1,656
Population (2014): 112,334

	1991–2000 Average	2001–09 Average	2010–15 Average	2010	2011	2012	2013	2014	2015 Estimate
Share of GDP (percent)									
Private consumption and investment	65.6	59.1	53.3	58.3	59.8	54.7	60.1	43.1	43.6
Public consumption and investment	79.7	90.3	92.7	82.4	81.9	92.6	84.9	107.6	106.5
Public consumption	51.1	57.5	58.1	56.1	57.6	59.1	56.5	59.5	59.7
Public investment	28.6	32.7	34.6	26.3	24.3	33.5	28.4	48.1	46.8
Exports minus imports	–45.3	–49.4	–45.9	–40.7	–41.7	–47.4	–45.0	–50.7	–50.2
Exports	10.4	5.3	5.4	4.3	6.4	5.4	5.7	5.6	5.1
Imports	–55.7	–54.7	–51.3	–45.0	–48.1	–52.8	–50.7	–56.3	–55.2
Contributions to GDP growth (percent)[1]									
Nominal GDP growth	7.7	3.9	3.7	0.5	2.6	4.3	3.1	7.0	4.6
Private consumption and investment	7.0	0.3	–1.5	–4.9	3.1	–2.8	7.2	–14.0	2.6
Private consumption and investment (A$ million)	64.6	87.7	98.7	98.9	104.1	99.3	112.4	86.2	91.3
Public consumption and investment	6.7	4.8	8.0	2.9	1.6	14.7	–5.1	30.2	3.8
Public consumption	4.9	2.8	3.3	3.6	3.0	4.1	–1.0	7.2	2.9
Public investment	1.8	2.0	4.7	–0.7	–1.4	10.7	–4.2	23.0	0.9
Exports minus imports	–5.9	–1.1	–2.9	2.5	–2.1	–7.7	1.0	–9.2	–1.8
Exports	–0.1	0.2	0.1	–1.3	2.3	–0.7	0.4	0.3	–0.3
Imports	–5.8	–1.4	–3.0	3.8	–4.3	–6.9	0.5	–9.5	–1.4
Public finances									
Central government finance (percent of GDP)									
Revenue and grants	74.7	77.2	87.4	70.2	59.6	84.2	94.4	128.7	...
Total domestic revenue	50.9	46.9	56.5	46.2	35.6	50.3	65.6	84.9	...
Grants	23.8	30.3	30.9	23.9	24.1	33.9	28.8	43.8	...
Expenditure and net lending	78.0	90.9	84.1	82.4	80.0	86.0	79.5	92.3	...
Current (excluding grants)	49.6	57.5	52.8	56.1	55.8	52.5	51.1	48.5	...
Of which: wages and salaries	21.3	26.2	15.9	26.2	26.3	27.1	0.0	0.0	...
Development (capital)	27.9	32.7	31.3	26.3	24.3	33.5	28.4	43.8	...
Net lending	0.5	0.6	0.0	0.0	0.0	0.0	0.0	0.0	...
Current balance[2]	0.0	–8.3	1.9	–9.9	–22.0	3.4	9.1	25.4	5.8
Overall balance	–3.3	–13.7	2.8	–12.2	–20.4	–1.8	14.9	36.4	0.0
Financing	3.3	13.7	–2.8	12.2	20.4	1.8	–14.9	–36.4	0.0
Domestic assets (SWF, trust fund)	3.6	13.9	2.2	12.5	11.5	10.5	–9.5	–9.2	–2.4
Debt	0.3	–1.0	1.5	2.0	10.9	–14.6	–0.4	4.3	6.9
Domestic	0.0	–1.3	–0.6	–0.3	10.7	–14.2	0.0	0.0	0.0
Of which: external	0.4	0.3	2.2	2.3	0.2	–0.4	–0.4	4.3	6.9
Of which: concessional	0.4	0.3	2.2	2.3	0.2	–0.4	–0.4	4.3	6.9
Other	–0.6	0.8	–6.6	–2.3	–2.0	5.9	–5.0	–31.4	–4.5

(*continued*)

APPENDIX TABLE 2.1

Kiribati: Selected Economic Indicators, 2010–15 (*Continued*)

Nominal GDP (2014): US$186.1 million
Main Export Products: Fish, Copra
Remoteness (GDP-weighted distance): 8,210 km

GDP per Capita (2014): US$1,656
Population (2014): 112,334

	1991–2000 Average	2001–09 Average	2010–15 Average	2010	2011	2012	2013	2014	2015 Estimate
Balance of payments (percent of GDP, unless indicated otherwise)									
Current account including official transfers	–0.7	–8.0	0.9	1.3	–9.7	–1.0	8.6	9.2	–3.1
Current account excluding official transfers (US$ millions)	–9.6	–33.9	–34.0	–34.0	–61.9	–54.6	–20.1	–1.6	–31.7
Current account excluding official transfers	–14.7	–29.9	–19.4	–21.8	–34.4	–29.0	–11.1	–0.9	–19.3
Overall balance (US$ millions)	10.0	4.6	17.2	10.4	2.8	–17.3	10.7	66.1	30.2
Overall balance	15.0	5.6	5.8	4.5	1.1	–6.0	3.6	20.1	113
External debt service (US$ million)	0.2	0.6	0.4	0.6	0.5	0.5	0.5	0.3	0.3
External debt service (percent of exports of goods and services)	1.6	4.5	3.5	4.4	3.3	3.8	4.0	2.5	2.9
Foreign direct investment	0.1	0.4	–3.3	–8.7	–0.8	–4.9	–3.8	–4.6	3.1
External Income	86.2	68.5	59.8	48.9	39.8	53.9	67.9	83.8	64.7
Fishing license fees	37.8	31.6	39.6	24.8	16.8	32.2	47.6	68.4	47.8
Investment income	34.7	25.4	13.6	17.1	16.5	15.3	13.6	8.8	10.1
Remittances	13.7	11.5	6.6	7.0	6.5	6.4	6.7	6.6	6.8
External debt (US$ million)	7.2	12.2	15.4	14.3	14.3	14.3	14.3	14.3	20.8
External debt	11.9	11.5	8.9	9.2	8.0	7.6	7.9	7.9	12.7
Contributions to external income growth (percent)[1]									
External Income growth	13.6	1.2	12.7	10.2	–16.2	40.3	29.4	31.8	–19.2
External income (A$ millions)	60.2	73.4	113.3	82.9	69.2	97.7	126.9	167.5	135.3
Fishing license fees	7.4	0.8	13.5	8.5	–15.0	41.1	30.9	37.5	–21.9
Investment income	4.4	0.0	–0.9	2.8	–0.3	–1.2	–2.4	–6.2	2.1
Remittances	1.8	0.4	0.1	–1.1	–0.9	0.4	0.9	0.5	0.6
Exchange rate (Australian dollar to U.S. dollar period average)	1.4	1.4	1.1	1.1	1.0	1.0	1.0	1.1	1.3
Real effective exchange rate (period average)[3]	66.6	77.3	97.7	100.0	104.2	101.0	94.0	89.3	...
(percent change)	...	4.7	–1.8	1.7	4.2	–3.1	–6.9	–5.0	...
Money, credit, and financial sector									
Broad money (percent change)	...	...	...	...	...	...	...	...	...
Credit to private sector (percent of GDP)	...	...	13.3	8.4	14.1	13.3	17.2	...	...
(percent change)	...	...	16.3	–35.9	72.2	–5.1	34.0	...	...
Bank assets (percent of GDP)	...	...	27.8	26.3	27.5	28.5	28.8	...	...
Short-term treasury bill interest rate	...	...	...	...	...	...	...	...	...
Nonperforming loan ratio	...	...	0.3	0.4	0.2	0.7	...	...	...
Foreign bank market share (percent)[4]	...	...	80.8	79.9	81.7	78.2	...	...	...

(*continued*)

APPENDIX TABLE 2.1

Kiribati: Selected Economic Indicators, 2010–15 (*Continued*)

Nominal GDP (2014): US$186.1 million
Main Export Products: Fish, Copra
Remoteness (GDP-weighted distance): 8,210 km

GDP per Capita (2014): US$1,656
Population (2014): 112,334

	1991–2000 Average	2001–09 Average	2010–15 Average	2010	2011	2012	2013	2014	2015 Estimate
Business climate indicators									
Business environment rankings[5]									
Doing business (overall)	...	...	121	98	103	112	123	143	149
Construction permits	...	...	80	46	51	51	57	135	137
Getting electricity	...	...	160	143	147	159	169	170	173
Enforcing contracts	...	...	75.0	55.0	54.0	56.0	60.0	113.0	114
Getting credit	...	...	140	114	122	125	155	160	162
Human development index[6]	...	...	0.6	0.6	0.6	0.6	0.6	0.6	...
Memorandum									
Revenue Equalization Reserve Fund									
Closing balance (A$ million)	478.1	604.4	633.7	570.9	580.9	578.9	613.9	703.3	754.0
Per capita value (2006 A$)	7538.6	6757.4	5011.6	5040.0	4766.8	4869.5	5017.0	5112.9	5263.6
Public sector debt (percent GDP)	...	11.5	9.0	8.5	8.1	7.5	8.5	8.7	12.7
Nominal GDP (A$ million)	88.0	147.7	186.9	169.6	174.0	181.4	187.0	200.0	209.2
Nominal GDP (US$ million)	61.1	106.5	174.9	155.9	179.6	187.9	181.1	180.6	164.2

Sources: Kiribati authorities; and IMF, "Kiribati: 2015 Article IV Consultation–Staff Report" (Country Report No. 15/207, Washington).
Note: ... = data not available; SWF = sovereign wealth fund.
[1] In nominal terms.
[2] Current balance excludes grants and development (capital expenditure).
[3] Index, 2005 = 100.
[4] Share in total loans, not including small loan scheme.
[5] World Bank, *Doing Business* reports, Kiribati from 2006.
[6] United Nations Development Programme, Kiribati from 2011.

Appendix 3. Marshall Islands

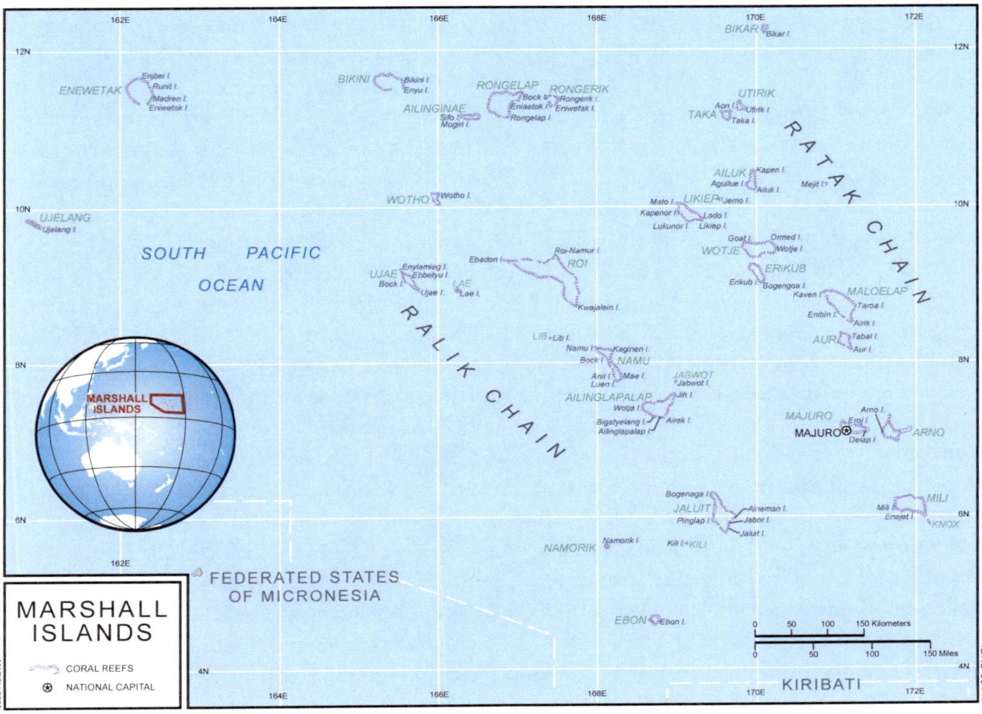

The 29 atolls and five isolated islands of Marshall Islands are spread over 1.9 million square kilometers in the north Pacific. As a small island country with a land area of just 181 square kilometers, Marshall Islands is highly dependent on external aid, mainly from the United States. The country has few accessible resources to sustain its population of about 60,000, which is concentrated in Majuro and Ebeye, the two main urban areas. With few accessible resources and vast distances, economic and development costs are high. In addition, the country's low elevation means that it is highly vulnerable to the effects of climate change, particularly sea level rise.

Marshall Islands achieved full sovereignty in 1986 under a Compact of Free Association with the United States. The government operates a mixed parliamentary-presidential system, with elections every four years.

SOURCES OF GROWTH AND ECONOMIC PROFILE

Main sources of growth. Public sector spending drives growth, financed to a large extent (about 60 percent) by grants from the United States under a renewed compact agreement effective since 2004. Fishing, copra production, and a limited services sector are the main economic activities. Tourism is modest, constrained by weak infrastructure and few flights.

Production, employment, exports, and imports. Growth is estimated to have declined to –1.1 percent in 2013/14 from 1.9 percent in the previous fiscal year, reflecting the earlier completion of important infrastructure projects and the postponement of some capital grants. The country's small size and isolation limit production opportunities. Public administration, education, and social services account for over 30 percent of GDP. Copra, coconut oil, and fish are the main

Prepared by Serkan Arslnalp and Mari Ishiguro.

exports in a narrow export base. Because Marshall Islands is almost completely reliant on imports for food, fuel, and other basic needs, it suffers a chronic trade deficit, and fluctuations in commodity prices pose a substantial risk to real incomes. Public sector employment accounts for almost half of total employment, and the U.S. military base on Kwajalein and foreign embassies for nearly another 10 percent. Unemployment is estimated at 30 percent.

Sources of external income. The main sources of external income are government grants, mainly from the United States, totaling about 50 percent of income receipts. Compact grants will expire in 2022/23 and a Compact Trust Fund has been set up to replace them. Compensation of employees working for the U.S. military base, rents to landowners around the base, and fishing license fees account for nearly another 35 percent of external income inflows.

Development aid. Aid averaged nearly 50 percent of GDP during 2007–12, mostly provided by the United States and Taiwan Province of China. This is directed especially to education and health, the energy and communication sectors, and infrastructure projects. Technical assistance is provided in public financial management, statistics, and state-owned enterprise reform.

Government finance. In 2012/13 government finances recorded a surplus of almost 0.7 percent of GDP; broadly on balance in 2013/14. The fiscal outlook is hindered by the financial positions of state-owned enterprises and limited budget planning. At the onset of the amended compact, Marshall Islands adopted a medium-term framework, but so far this has made no useful contribution to annual budget preparation. Authorities recently worked with the Pacific Finance Technical Assistance Centre to produce a comprehensive Public Financial Management Reform Road Map, which calls for the introduction of a medium-term budgeting framework. The prospective end of compact funding presents a key challenge to fiscal sustainability. Starting in 2023/24 the government will be able to withdraw from the existing Compact Trust Fund an amount not exceeding compact grant flows in 2022/23.

Financial sector. The commercial banking system consists of two private banks and a public development bank, which operates outside the regulatory framework. The banking system is profitable and liquid, with a loan-to-deposit ratio of less than 75 percent. However, vulnerabilities are emerging: consumer loans represent about 70 percent of private sector credit and the average household debt-to-income ratio is more than 80 percent. The publicly owned Marshall Islands Development Bank, which is outside the Banking Commission's oversight, is engaged in short-term consumer lending as well—an activity regarded as less risky and more profitable. Financial markets are underdeveloped and credit to the private sector is only 35 percent of GDP.

Business climate and investment. The geographic isolation and business climate shortcomings of Marshall Islands hinder private investment. Business entry is relatively easy, but the absence of a legislative framework for bankruptcy and the heavy presence of state-owned enterprises make business more difficult. Registering property appears to be particularly cumbersome, owing to complex land-ownership issues.

Monetary policy. The U.S. dollar is legal tender and Marshall Islands does not have a central bank.

Exchange rate and competitiveness. Past analysis has found no evidence of a significant misalignment in the real exchange rate.

GROWTH CHALLENGES, VULNERABILITIES, AND SPILLOVERS

Main growth challenges. Small size, geographic isolation, and institutional and human capacity constraints are the main obstacles to growth.

Main vulnerabilities. Heavy exposure to climate change, relatively high public and publicly guaranteed debt, sizable contingent liabilities from the social security system, a heavy reliance on donor aid, volatile import prices, and the Compact Trust Fund's exposure to global asset fluctuations are the main vulnerabilities.

Regional and global economic spillovers. The United States has a significant impact through aid and because of the use of the U.S. dollar. Marshall Islands has also developed close relations with Taiwan Province of China, which provides financial support.

APPENDIX TABLE 3.1

Marshall Islands: Selected Economic Indicators, 2010–15

Nominal GDP (FY2014): US$183.3 million | **GDP per capita (FY2014): US$3,410**
Main export products: Copra, Coconut oil | **Population (2014): 53,753**
Remoteness (GDP-weighted distance): 7,895 km

	1991–2000 Average	2001–09 Average	2010–15 Average	2010	2011	2012	2013	2014	2015 Estimate
GDP, GDP growth, employment, and prices									
Real GDP (percent change)	−1.1	1.4	2.2	6.2	1.3	4.0	1.9	−1.1	1.0
Real GDP per capita (percent change)	−1.7	1.2	1.9	4.9	0.8	3.6	1.5	−1.4	...
Unemployment (percent)	...	...	...	...	...	...	...	...	...
Consumer prices (percent change, average)	...	4.7	1.7	1.8	5.4	4.3	1.9	1.1	-4.0
Shares in GDP (percent)									
Public Administration	18.1	15.9	14.8	14.9	14.7	14.5	14.7	14.9	14.8
Education	11.6	13.5	14.9	14.4	14.9	15.2	14.8	15.2	15.3
Wholesale and retail trade and repairs	13.0	13.8	12.4	12.8	13.0	12.2	12.0	12.3	12.2
Tourism	...	...	...	...	...	...	...	...	...
Agriculture	3.4	3.0	2.8	2.9	2.6	2.9	2.9	2.6	2.6
Fishery	5.1	6.1	10.2	9.1	10.0	10.9	10.4	10.4	10.5
Contributions to GDP growth (percent, in real terms)									
Public administration	−0.3	0.1	0.1	0.0	0.0	0.3	0.5	0.1	0.0
Education	−0.2	0.5	0.5	0.8	0.7	0.9	−0.2	0.2	0.3
Wholesale and retail trade and repairs	0.4	0.1	0.2	0.7	0.4	−0.3	0.0	0.2	0.1
Agriculture	−0.2	0.1	0.0	−0.2	−0.2	0.4	0.1	−0.3	0.0
Fishery	0.6	0.2	0.8	2.7	1.0	1.3	−0.3	−0.1	0.1
Share in GDP (percent)									
Private consumption	...	...	...	...	...	...	...	...	...
Private investment	...	...	...	...	...	...	...	...	...
Public consumption	...	...	...	...	...	...	...	...	...
Public investment	...	...	...	...	...	...	...	...	...
Exports minus imports	−79.7	−71.9	−64.6	−83.7	−60.8	−56.6	−65.3	−61.5	−59.8
Contributions to GDP growth (percent, in nominal terms)									
Private consumption	...	...	...	...	...	...	...	...	...
Private investment	...	...	...	...	...	...	...	...	...
Public consumption	...	...	...	...	...	...	...	...	...
Public investment	...	...	...	...	...	...	...	...	...
Exports minus imports	−1.5	−1.8	1.1	−9.7	18.5	0.4	−10.5	5.0	2.8
Public finances									
General government finance (percent of GDP)									
Revenue and grants	65.7	63.9	55.3	61.6	57.8	51.4	54.1	54.5	52.3
Total domestic revenue	25.8	21.2	20.9	20.0	20.0	19.3	21.2	22.8	22.2
Grants	39.8	42.8	34.3	41.6	37.9	32.1	32.7	31.7	30.0

(continued)

APPENDIX TABLE 3.1

Marshall Islands: Selected Economic Indicators, 2010–15 (*Continued*)

Nominal GDP (FY2014): US$183.3 million
Main export products: Copra, Coconut oil
Remoteness (GDP-weighted distance): 7,895 km

GDP per capita (FY2014): US$3,410
Population (2014): 53,753

	1991–2000 Average	2001–09 Average	2010–15 Average	2010	2011	2012	2013	2014	2015 Estimate
Expenditure and net lending	59.4	63.2	54.2	58.2	55.7	52.2	53.4	53.9	51.9
Current (excluding grants)	47.7	52.4	46.8	45.7	44.6	45.5	47.2	49.6	48.1
Of which: wages and salaries	17.2	22.3	21.7	23.0	21.8	20.9	21.3	21.7	21.4
Development (capital)	11.7	10.8	7.4	12.5	11.2	6.7	6.2	4.3	3.8
Current balance[1]	-3.8	5.9	5.8	13.5	9.7	3.2	4.5	2.5	1.7
Overall balance	6.2	0.7	1.1	3.5	2.1	-0.7	0.7	0.6	0.4
Financing	-6.4	-0.7	-1.1	-3.5	-2.1	0.7	-0.7	-0.6	-0.4
Assets (SWF, trust fund)	5.2	-0.3	-1.6	-1.8	-6.6	2.0	-2.1	0.0	-1.1
Debt	-11.4	-0.4	0.5	-1.6	4.5	-1.3	1.3	-0.6	0.7
Of which: external	...	...	...	...	...	...	...	...	...
Of which: concessional	...	...	...	...	...	...	...	...	...
Other	...	...	...	...	...	...	...	...	...
Public-debt-to-GDP ratio (percent)	80.2	44.5	33.2	36.8	34.5	30.1	32.1	32.0	33.4
Sovereign wealth/trust fund	...	...	...	...	...	...	...	...	...
Balance of payments (percent of GDP, unless otherwise indicated)									
Current account including official transfers	-25.9	-5.8	-11.8	-26.5	-5.6	-9.3	-14.7	-7.3	-7.5
Current account excluding official transfers	-46.5	-39.2	-41.9	-60.3	-36.8	-38.6	-45.3	-36.5	-33.9
Overall balance	-3.9	11.8	3.9	4.8	11.5	2.9	-0.9	5.0	0.0
External debt service (percent of exports of goods and services)	127.2	33.1	13.8	18.6	23.2	9.6	8.9	10.1	12.3
Foreign direct investment	1.1	2.6	5.9	23.3	3.3	2.5	2.4	2.0	2.0
External debt	103.5	68.4	54.3	63.9	58.0	52.5	51.3	50.1	50.3
Main sources of external income (total)	44.6	59.0	50.5	55.7	51.9	48.7	49.8	49.2	47.4
Grants	20.6	33.4	30.0	33.8	31.2	29.4	30.6	29.2	25.9
Employee compensations	14.2	15.3	10.6	11.6	10.9	10.1	10.1	10.3	10.3
Rent for U.S. military base	9.8	10.3	9.9	10.2	9.8	9.2	9.1	9.6	11.2
Contributions to external income growth (percent)									
External income growth	5.5	5.1	-0.5	-0.2	-1.7	0.0	5.6	-3.0	-3.5
Grants	3.4	4.0	-1.0	1.3	-1.7	0.3	4.5	-3.8	-6.7
Employee compensations	2.1	0.2	-0.1	-1.1	-0.2	-0.4	0.7	0.1	0.0
Rent for U.S. military base	0.0	0.9	0.7	-0.4	0.2	0.1	0.4	0.7	3.2

(*continued*)

APPENDIX TABLE 3.1

Marshall Islands: Selected Economic Indicators, 2010–15 (*Continued*)

Nominal GDP (FY2014): US$183.3 million
Main export products: Copra, Coconut oil
Remoteness (GDP-weighted distance): 7,895 km
GDP per capita (FY2014): US$3,410
Population (2014): 53,753

	1991–2000 Average	2001–09 Average	2010–15 Average	2010	2011	2012	2013	2014	2015 Estimate
Exchange rate (local currency/U.S. period average)	1.0	1.0	1.2	1.0	1.0	1.0	1.0	1.0	2.0
Real effective exchange rate (period average)[2]	91.1	96.0	100.2	100.0	99.5	100.5	98.9	102.3	...
(percent change)	5.5	1.1	0.5	0.3	–0.5	1.0	–1.6	3.5	...
Money, credit, and financial sector									
Broad money (percent change)	...	...	...	...	...	...	...	...	...
Credit to private sector (percent of GDP)	29.6	33.8	35.3	38.6	34.8	32.2	35.3	35.3	...
(percent change)	4.6	2.4	–2.6	–5.3	–9.9	–7.4	9.7	0.0	...
Bank assets (percent of GDP)	52.1	70.6	72.1	81.5	76.3	64.5	69.8	70.2	70.5
Short-term treasury bill interest rate	...	...	...	...	...	...	...	...	...
Nonperforming loan ratio	2.0	1.8	1.1	1.1	1.1	1.1	1.1	1.1	1.1
Foreign bank market share (percent)[3]	...	...	...	...	...	...	...	...	...
Business climate indicators									
Business environment rankings[4]									
Doing business (overall)	...	...	123	102	112	116	128	137	140
Construction permits	...	...	25	5	6	8	4	62	63
Getting electricity	...	...	81	59	61	61	65	117	125
Enforcing contracts	...	...	57	51	51	54	58	65	65
Getting credit	...	...	74	64	68	74	88	71	79
Human development index[5]	...	...	...	...	...	...	...	...	...
Memorandum:									
Nominal GDP (US$ millions)[6]	110.7	137.2	180.2	163.9	173.0	184.4	190.2	186.7	183.3

Sources: Marshall Islands authorities; and IMF, World Economic Outlook database (April 2016).
Note: ... = data not available; SWF = sovereign wealth fund.
[1] Current balance excludes grants and development (capital expenditure).
[2] Index, 2005 = 100.
[3] Share in total loans, not including small loan scheme.
[4] World Bank, *Doing Business* reports.
[5] United Nations Development Programme.
[6] National currency is the U.S. dollar.

Appendix 4. Micronesia

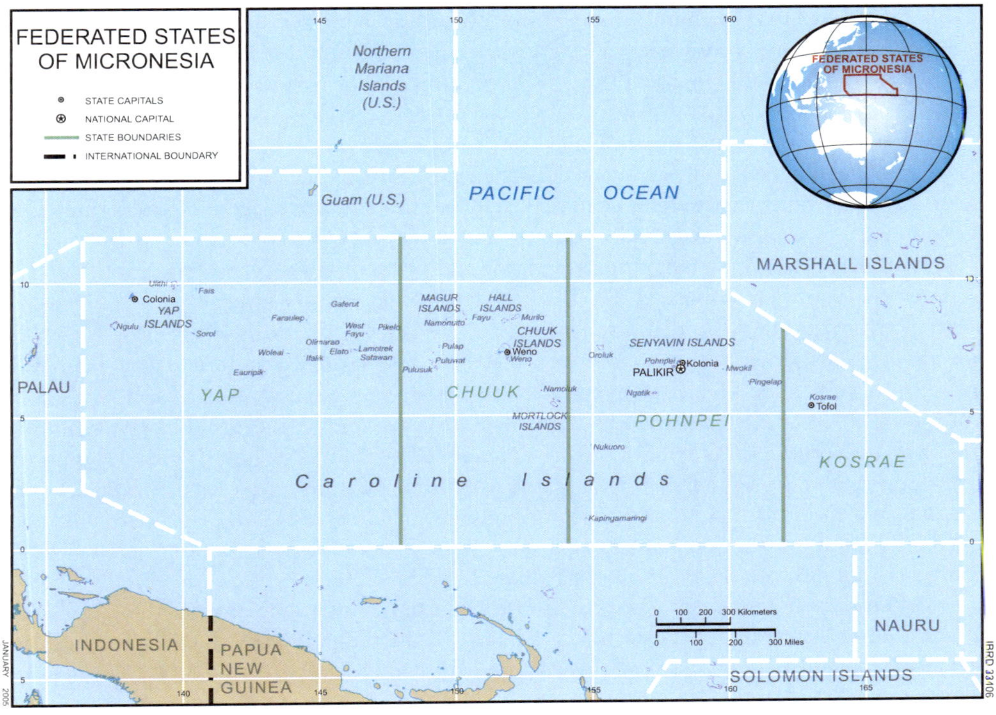

Micronesia's land area covers 700 square kilometers, dispersed over more than 600 islands. The country—with a population of about 100,000—is a microstate highly dependent on external aid, especially from the United States. Though small in land mass, Micronesia's exclusive economic zone covers an area close to the size of India and there is abundant tuna in these waters.

Micronesia's four states are grouped under a loosely federated structure, each with its own executive and legislative bodies. A president heads the national executive and is elected by a unicameral national congress.

SOURCES OF GROWTH AND ECONOMIC PROFILE

Main sources of growth. Micronesia's economy is largely dependent on a public sector sustained by foreign grants, mainly from the United States, and increasing revenue from fishing license fees. The private sector caters mostly to the needs of the public sector and its employees. Micronesia's pristine nature has potential for high-end tourism that preserves the ecology and cultural heritage. However, land tenure issues, combined with lengthy reviews of inward foreign direct investment applications, hinder the development of tourism facilities.

Production, employment, exports, and imports. The public sector provides half of total employment; subsistence farming and fishing dominate the private sector. Tourism is underdeveloped, with annual tourist arrivals of just 14,800 in 2013/14 (down from a peak of 16,000 in 2006/07 and 2007/08). Micronesia has few production facilities and imports most of its needs,

Prepared by Yasuaki Yoneyama.

including food. Fish exports account for more than 85 percent of total exports of goods (excluding the reexport of petroleum products for foreign aircraft refueling at the country's airports).

Sources of external income. Grants from abroad account for about 30 percent of GDP. Revenues from fishing license fees reached 15 percent of GDP in 2013/14, up from 6 percent in 2010/11. Remittances are quite small at 6–7 percent of GDP on a gross basis and 1–2 percent on a net basis.

Development aid. Grants from the United States are provided under its Compact of Free Association and other federal programs. Other bilateral donors include Australia and Japan. The Asian Development Bank has been providing concessional loans for investment projects, and the World Bank's International Development Association has provided grant financing since 2013.

Government finance. To better prepare for the end of compact grants, which expire in 2022/23, Micronesia's authorities established the Compact Trust Fund (mostly funded by the United States) and the FSM Trust Fund (funded through transfers from Micronesia's fiscal surplus). Even though state governments recently began fiscal consolidation under the Long-Term Fiscal Frameworks, returns from the trust funds are not expected to fill the revenue gap after 2023. To address the issue, Action Plan 2023, released in February 2015, includes a tax reform package to generate additional revenue of 4 percent of GDP by introducing value-added tax and replacing the gross revenue tax on corporations with a net income tax. The plan also calls for a further review of expenditures and for structural reforms to accelerate private sector growth, including addressing land tenure issues and enhancing inward foreign direct investment in tourism. Most of the policy actions require legislative approval, a complex task under Micronesia's loose federal structure.

Financial sector. Two commercial banks operate in the country, one of them the subsidiary of a U.S. bank. Both banks are supervised by the Banking Board and insured by the U.S. Federal Deposit Insurance Corporation. Authorities are preparing legislation to expand the Banking Board's supervisory mandate to credit unions.

Business climate and investment. The World Bank's *Doing Business* 2016 report ranks Micronesia 148th out of 189 economies globally. The difficulty of securing land leases—most property is held in family trusts and land use rights are passed from generation to generation within the extended family—has repeatedly been cited as a major hindrance to doing business in Micronesia.

Exchange rate and monetary policy. The U.S. dollar is the official currency and there is no central bank.

GROWTH CHALLENGES, VULNERABILITIES, AND SPILLOVERS

Main growth challenges. Disappointing economic growth has averaged just 1 percent since 2000, and the private sector remains largely dependent on the public sector. The 2023 Action Plan does include a number of policy actions to improve the business climate. But achieving a national consensus under the country's loosely federated structure will be essential.

Main vulnerabilities. The expiration of compact grants is a major challenge as this will result in a major loss of revenue. Micronesia's infrastructure and growth prospects are vulnerable to natural disasters. The country has been hit by five severe storms since 1980, each causing average damage of US$1.3 million (0.4 percent of GDP), and it was hit by Typhoon Maysak in 2015.

Regional and global economic spillovers. The Micronesian economy has been largely shielded from negative global spillovers, with the exception of higher imported food and fuel prices (the latter is mostly used for generating electricity and for interisland transport).

APPENDIX TABLE 4.1

Micronesia: Selected Economic Indicators, 2010–15

Nominal GDP (2015): US$318 million | **GDP per capita (2015): US$3,073**
Main export products: Fish (tuna) and fuel (re-export) to foreign aircraft | **Population (2015): 103,441**
Remoteness (GDP-weighted distance, 2003): 10,377 km

	1991–2000 Average	2001–05 Average	2006–11 Average	2010	2011	2012	2013	2014	2015 Estimate
GDP, GDP growth, employment, and prices									
Real GDP (percent change)	–0.1	0.6	0.3	3.5	1.8	–0.5	–3.6	–3.4	–0.2
Real GDP per capita (percent change)	–0.3	0.8	0.6	4.0	1.0	–0.7	–3.4	–3.3	–0.1
Consumer prices (percent change, average)	2.2	1.3	5.0	3.7	4.3	6.3	2.0	0.6	–1.0
Shares in GDP (in percent)									
Agriculture	14.2	14.2	15.6	15.6	15.5	15.4	16.1	17.0	16.3
Fisheries	11.1	10.1	10.6	10.7	11.2	12.4	11.4	11.5	11.1
Retail and wholesale	7.6	4.8	7.2	8.7	8.2	7.3	7.2	7.0	6.9
Construction	7.7	7.8	7.1	4.4	5.0	4.6	3.5	2.1	3.3
Contributions to GDP growth (percent of GDP)									
Agriculture	0.1	0.1	0.2	0.2	0.1	–0.1	0.1	0.4	0.0
Fisheries	–0.1	–0.2	0.2	0.4	0.6	1.1	–1.3	–0.2	0.0
Retail and wholesale	0.1	0.1	–0.2	0.4	–0.2	–0.6	–0.3	–0.3	0.0
Construction	–0.1	–0.1	0.5	1.2	1.0	–0.2	–1.7	–1.8	0.0
Public finances									
General government finance (percent of GDP)									
Revenue and grants	69.8	60.8	61.1	67.8	64.7	66.0	63.6	71.4	62.8
Total domestic revenue	24.5	20.5	20.9	21.5	20.7	22.9	27.7	42.7	34.7
Grants	45.3	40.3	40.1	46.3	44.1	43.2	36.0	28.7	28.2
Expenditure and net lending	69.4	60.2	60.8	65.7	63.5	63.8	59.4	58.7	58.3
Current (excluding grants)	55.5	52.4	48.2	45.0	43.6	42.8	45.1	50.3	51.3
Of which: wages and salaries	25.6	23.6	23.3	23.0	21.9	21.0	22.0	22.1	0.0
Development (capital)	13.9	7.9	12.6	20.7	19.9	21.1	14.4	8.4	7.0
Current balance[1]	0.2	–0.6	1.1	4.0	2.3	3.8	6.8	15.5	7.6
Overall balance	–1.2	–3.3	–1.4	0.5	–0.6	0.8	2.9	11.2	3.0
Overall balance (excluding grants)	–46.5	–43.6	–41.6	–45.8	–44.7	–42.4	–33.1	–17.5	–25.1
Public-debt-to-GDP ratio (percent)	41.7	24.6	28.1	29.2	28.9	27.7	27.0	26.1	26.3
Trust funds: per capita, in real terms (US$ million, 2013 prices)	. . .	0.8	1.7	2.2	2.2	2.6	3.2	3.8	4.3
Balance of payments (percent of GDP, unless otherwise indicated)									
Current account including official transfers	–19.1	–10.8	–15.3	–15.0	–17.8	–12.6	–10.0	6.8	1.0
Current account excluding official transfers	–59.5	–54.2	–52.6	–51.9	–51.2	–43.7	–41.1	–22.6	–29.4
Capital account	15.0	13.4	21.6	29.0	27.2	28.1	21.1	14.7	14.3

(continued)

APPENDIX TABLE 4.1

Micronesia: Selected Economic Indicators, 2010–15 (*Continued*)

Nominal GDP (2015): US$318 million
Main export products: Fish (tuna) and fuel (re-export) to foreign aircraft
Remoteness (GDP-weighted distance, 2003): 10,377 km
GDP per capita (2015): US$3,073
Population (2015): 103,441

	1991–2000 Average	2001–05 Average	2006–11 Average	2010	2011	2012	2013	2014	2015 Estimate
Financial account	6.1	4.9	7.1	14.0	9.8	17.7	12.8	16.5	16.4
External debt service (percent of exports of goods and services)	53.8	9.0	5.8	6.3	6.7	5.3	6.7	11.2	6.6
Foreign direct investment	–0.2	–0.1	0.2	–0.3	–0.3	–0.3	–0.2	–0.1	–0.1
External debt (stock, gross)	50.1	24.6	28.1	29.2	28.9	27.7	27.0	26.1	26.3
Main sources of external income (total)	49.9	52.2	49.2	48.8	45.4	45.2	48.7	51.2	56.2
Official transfers (current)	40.4	43.5	37.3	36.9	33.4	31.1	31.0	29.3	30.4
Fishing license fees	7.6	4.8	6.1	6.0	6.0	8.1	11.1	14.9	18.9
Household remittances (gross)	2.0	3.9	5.8	5.9	6.0	6.1	6.6	7.0	7.0
Contributions to external income growth (percent)									
External income growth	–1.4	5.0	0.6	2.1	–1.3	5.0	5.6	29.1	–8.9
Official transfers (current)	–0.6	4.5	–1.1	2.9	–3.5	–1.5	–2.1	–2.8	1.5
Fishing license fees	–1.1	–0.2	0.7	–1.6	0.7	5.0	5.4	7.5	5.8
Household remittances (gross)	0.7	0.7	0.8	0.4	0.7	0.8	0.7	0.7	0.0
Exchange rate (local currency to U.S. dollar period average)	1.0	1.0	1.0	1.0	1.0	1.0	1.0	1.0	1.0
Real effective exchange rate (period average)[2]	102.9	101.5	106.2	109.9	109.5	112.4	115.0	115.1	115.1
(percent change)	...	–0.5	1.5	–0.7	–0.4	2.7	2.3	0.0	0.0
Money, credit, and financial sector									
Credit to private sector (percent of GDP)	21.7	11.8	10.1	10.8	11.3	11.7	11.1	11.7	13.0
(percent change)	1.8	–14.1	4.1	17.5	5.0	2.9	–5.2	6.0	11.3
Bank assets (percent of GDP)	60.3	54.6	56.4	60.4	61.2	70.0	75.3	82.7	88.4
Business climate indicators									
Business environment rankings[3]									
Doing business (overall)	...	...	...	...	...	140	150	145	145
Construction permits	...	...	...	...	...	19	42	37	37
Getting electricity	...	...	...	...	...	40	53	125	30
Enforcing contracts	...	...	...	...	...	146	149	162	162
Getting credit	...	...	...	...	...	126	129	55	61

(*continued*)

APPENDIX TABLE 4.1

Micronesia: Selected Economic Indicators, 2010–15 (*Continued*)

Nominal GDP (2015): US$318 million
Main export products: Fish (tuna) and fuel (re-export) to foreign aircraft
Remoteness (GDP-weighted distance, 2003): 10,377 km
GDP per capita (2015): US$3,073
Population (2015): 103,441

	1991–2000 Average	2001–05 Average	2006–11 Average	2010	2011	2012	2013	2014	2015 Estimate
Human development index[4]	...	...	...	0.63	0.63	0.6	0.6	0.6	...
Memorandum:									
Nominal GDP (local currency)	220.1	242.9	276.0	295.6	310.4	325.8	315.7	318.1	317.8
Nominal GDP (millions of U.S. dollars)	220.1	242.9	276.0	295.6	310.4	325.8	315.7	318.1	317.8

Sources: Micronesia authorities; and IMF staff estimates as of April 2016.
[1] Current balance excludes grants and development assistance (capital expenditure).
[2] Index, 2003 = 100.
[3] Share in total loans. Does not include small loan scheme.
[4] World Bank, *Doing Business* reports.
[5] United Nations Development Programme.

Appendix 5. Palau

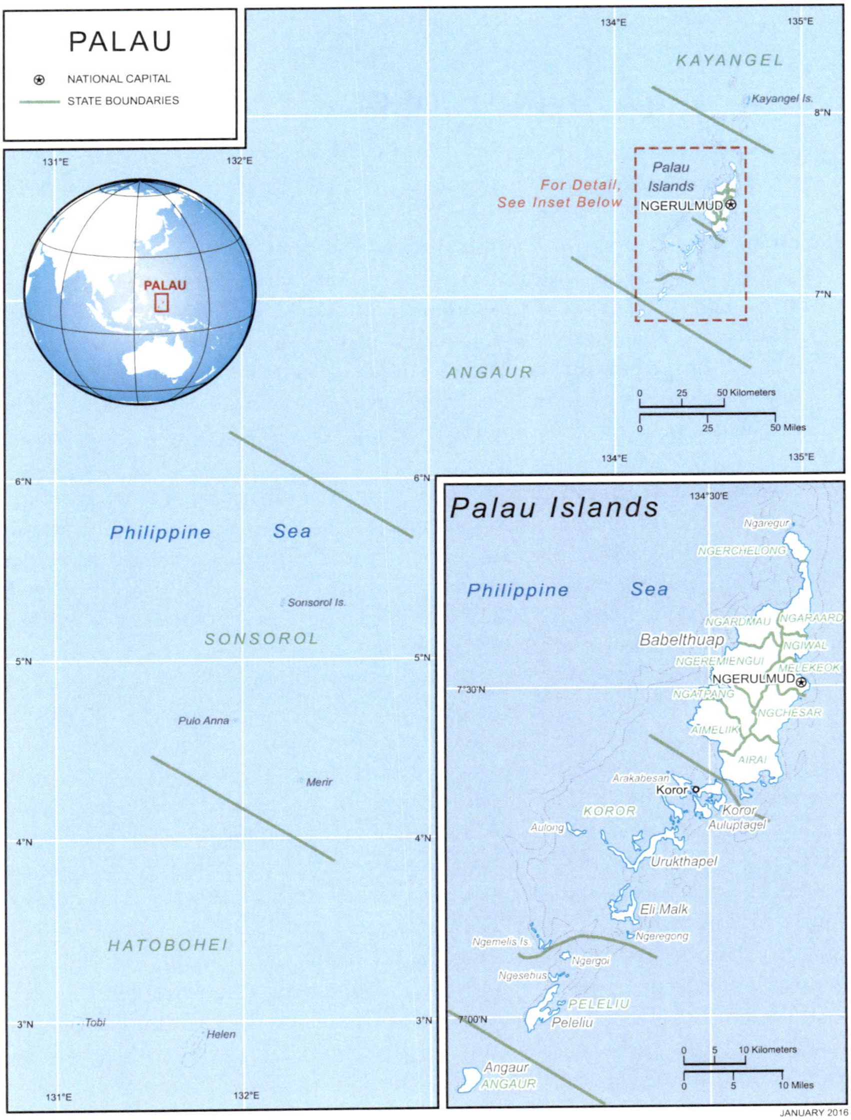

Palau, an archipelago of more than 560 islands occupying 460 square kilometers, is centered on the island of Koror. Based on 2012 census data, Palau's population was 17,500, including 4,500 non-Palauans.

Palau adopted its constitution in 1981 and became independent in 1994 after being part of a United Nations trust territory administered by the United States for 47 years. It entered into a Compact of Free Association with the United States in 1986.[1] The government structure is based broadly on the U.S. model, but there are no political parties. The legislative branch comprises an

Prepared by Jaime Guajardo.

[1] Under the compact agreement, the United States controls Palau's security and defense for 50 years and has exclusive access to waterways and certain land, in exchange for economic aid, security, and right of entry for Palauans to the United States for residence or work.

elected bicameral parliament of nine senators and 16 members of congress, representing each of the country's states. The president and vice president are elected on separate tickets for four-year terms. Per capita GDP is estimated at US$16,070 in 2014/15.

SOURCES OF GROWTH AND ECONOMIC PROFILE

Sources of growth. The main contributors to growth are tourism-related activities, including hotels and food services, and wholesale and retail trade. From the expenditure side, growth is driven by private consumption and service exports (tourism).

Production, exports, imports, and employment. GDP grew strongly at 9.4 percent in 2014/15, fueled by robust growth in tourism and construction. Reflecting the large increase in tourist arrivals and the decline in food and fuel prices, the current account deficit fell sharply to 0.5 percent of GDP in 2014/15. Tourism receipts account for about 52 percent of GDP, while goods exports are just 5 percent and largely limited to fish and reexports of fuel. Palau relies heavily on imports (55 percent of GDP), particularly of food and fuel. The labor force, 68 percent of the working-age population (including foreign labor), is mostly employed in the private sector. The unemployment rate was about 4 percent in 2011/12.

External income and development aid. Major sources of foreign income are government grants (15 percent of GDP in 2015), mainly from the United States, investment income from the Compact Trust Fund (CTF), and social security and pension funds.[2] Grants are directed to budget support, infrastructure, energy, and education. Financial aid under the country's compact with the United States, which is scheduled to provide US$229 million in grants until 2023/24, was renewed in 2010. The agreement is now pending ratification by the U.S. Congress, but Palau continues to receive advances. The CTF's balance stood at US$184 million (64 percent of GDP) at the end of the 2015 fiscal year. Drawdowns from the CTF are governed by the compact agreement and have been US$5 million annually since 2001/02. Technical assistance from multilateral and bilateral donors is provided in various areas, including public financial management and statistics.

Government finance. The fiscal deficit excluding grants was reduced sharply in 2014/15, but further fiscal adjustment is needed. A continued reduction in the current deficit excluding grants (5 percent of GDP in 2014/15) over the medium term—0.6 percentage point of GDP annually during 2016/17–2020/21—is needed to achieve long-term fiscal self-sufficiency. Otherwise, domestic revenue and investment income from the CTF will be insufficient to maintain steady public expenditure when compact grants expire in 2023/24. Reforming the tax system and containing spending growth are critical, and plans to implement the medium-term fiscal and budget frameworks are in place.

Financial sector. The financial sector consists of five commercial banks, a development bank, finance companies, and credit unions. Among the commercial banks, three are branches of U.S. chartered banks insured by the U.S. Federal Deposit Insurance Corporation. The U.S. bank branches hold 93 percent of the banking sector's loans and over 99 percent of the sector's deposits. The nonperforming loan ratio remained low at 2.1 percent at the end of 2014/15. Bank profitability is low despite a large interest rate spread. Total bank lending in U.S. dollars has remained low and has been declining relative to deposits. Loans are made mainly to construction, tourist, and commercial activities, as well as to mortgage and consumer loans.

Business climate and investment. Palau has great potential to develop a vibrant private sector and there is room to improve the business climate. For example, the World Bank's Doing Business indicators for 2016 show the difficulty in using land as collateral for securing loans, which limits access to finance. Other key obstacles include restrictions on foreign investment in certain sectors, such as wholesale and retail trade, transportation, tourism, and commercial fishing, and complex licensing arrangements.

---

[2] The purpose of the CTF is to provide income to replace Compact grants after 2023/24. The original compact agreement provided US$70 million to establish the CTF. The renewed agreement contributes an additional US$30 million.

Exchange rate and competitiveness. Palau uses the U.S. dollar as its legal tender, which remains appropriate given the close financial and trade links with the United States, and it maintains an exchange system free of restrictions on international payments and transfers. The U.S. dollar also provides an important nominal anchor. Annual average inflation was 2.2 percent in 2014/15 and the real effective exchange rate is broadly in line with its long-term average, indicating the country's external competitiveness and stability.

GROWTH CHALLENGES, VULNERABILITIES, AND SPILLOVERS

Main growth challenges. Palau faces a number of constraints common to small islands: an undiversified economy, geographical remoteness, small population, and a limited resource base. Insufficient infrastructure, weaknesses in the business climate, and limited access to credit hamper private sector growth. Here, the recent implementation of the secured transactions registry in the financial sector is a positive step. Further effort is needed to diversify the economy and attract foreign direct investment, including simplifying investment processes and making land leases more secure. Continued fiscal consolidation is crucial for achieving fiscal self-sufficiency and sustaining external stability.

Main vulnerabilities. Palau's heavy reliance on tourism, grants from the United States, and food and fuel imports carries substantial risk. Weak global growth could hurt tourism, and an increase in food or fuel prices could raise inflation, depress domestic demand, and weaken fiscal and external positions. Given the need for fiscal consolidation and the absence of monetary and exchange rate policies, Palau has limited policy space to react to any downside scenario. Palau's tourism prospects could also be affected by global climate change and weather-related disruptions such as typhoons.

Regional and global economic spillovers. The United States has a significant economic impact on Palau through the provision of grants and opportunities to study and work abroad. The CTF is also exposed to fluctuations in U.S. assets prices. Japan, Korea, Taiwan Province of China, and, recently, China provide the largest number of tourists.

APPENDIX TABLE 5.1

Palau: Selected Economic Indicators, 2010–15

Nominal GDP (FY2014): US$250.9 million
Main exports: Tourism, fish
Remoteness (GDP-weighted distance): 7,554 km
GDP per capita (FY2015): US$16,070
Population (FY2014): 17,708

	2001–09 Average	2010–15 Average	2010	2011	2012	2013	2014	2015 Estimate
GDP, GDP growth, employment, and prices								
Real GDP (percent change)	–0.5	3.8	3.3	5.0	3.2	–2.4	4.2	9.4
Real GDP per capita (percent change)	–0.4	4.5	5.3	7.0	5.2	–2.0	3.2	8.3
Unemployment (percent)	...	...	...	...	...	...	...	...
Consumer prices (percent change, average)	2.8	3.0	1.1	2.6	5.4	2.8	4.0	2.2
Shares in real GDP (percent)								
Accommodation and food services	8.0	12.0	9.6	11.6	12.4	11.9	12.8	13.6
Public administration	16.0	15.7	17.1	15.9	15.3	15.7	15.6	14.5
Wholesale and retail trade	12.2	12.7	12.6	12.2	12.5	13.1	13.1	12.8
Agriculture and forestry	1.5	1.3	1.5	1.4	1.3	1.3	1.2	1.1
Contributions to real GDP growth (percent)								
Accommodation and food services	0.2	1.2	0.7	2.6	1.1	–0.8	1.5	2.0
Public administration	0.1	0.0	–0.1	–0.5	–0.1	0.0	0.5	0.3
Wholesale and retail trade	–0.2	0.7	1.7	0.2	0.7	0.3	0.5	0.9
Agriculture and forestry	0.0	0.0	–0.1	0.0	0.0	0.0	–0.1	0.0

(continued)

APPENDIX TABLE 5.1

Palau: Selected Economic Indicators, 2010–15 (*Continued*)

Nominal GDP (FY2014): US$250.9 million
Main exports: Tourism, fish
Remoteness (GDP-weighted distance): 7,554 km

GDP per capita (FY2015): US$16,070
Population (FY2014): 17,708

	2001–09 Average	2010–15 Average	2010	2011	2012	2013	2014	2015 Estimate
Share in real GDP (percent)								
Private consumption	61.0	64.0	64.0	62.8	63.6	65.6	64.7	63.5
Private investment								
Public consumption	33.5	33.1	36.6	33.6	31.7	33.3	33.0	30.3
Investment	36.2	24.2	21.7	23.9	22.9	20.8	29.9	25.7
Exports minus imports	−30.7	−21.3	−22.2	−20.4	−18.2	−19.7	−27.6	−19.4
Contributions to real GDP growth (percent)								
Private consumption	−1.9	2.3	−0.4	0.4	4.1	3.1	0.9	6.0
Private investment								
Public consumption	−1.5	0.2	−0.3	−2.0	−0.3	2.1	0.6	0.8
Investment	−4.3	2.1	2.4	2.7	0.3	−1.3	10.0	−1.2
Exports minus imports	7.2	−0.8	1.6	4.0	−0.8	−6.4	−7.2	3.7
Public finances								
Central government finance (percent of GDP)								
Revenue and grants	41.7	43.7	47.4	44.5	45.2	41.0	43.3	40.5
Total domestic revenue	19.3	22.9	20.4	21.5	22.7	22.7	24.4	25.5
Grants	22.4	20.8	27.1	23.0	22.5	18.4	18.9	15.0
Expenditure	46.1	41.9	48.4	43.3	44.2	40.3	39.8	35.2
Current	36.7	35.3	37.5	36.0	36.1	36.1	35.4	30.6
Of which: wages and salaries	18.5	16.4	18.7	17.8	16.8	16.3	15.2	13.6
Capital	9.3	6.6	10.9	7.3	8.1	4.3	4.4	4.6
Current balance[1]	−17.4	−12.4	−17.1	−14.5	−13.4	−13.4	−11.0	−5.0
Overall balance	−4.3	1.9	−1.0	1.3	1.0	0.7	3.5	5.9
Financing	4.3	−1.9	1.0	−1.3	−1.0	−0.7	−3.5	−5.9
Assets	4.0	−1.8	−3.8	1.9	−4.7	2.7	−3.9	−3.0
Debt	0.4	−0.2	4.8	−3.2	3.7	−3.4	0.4	−3.6
Of which: external	−0.1	0.4	−0.9	−0.8	4.8	−1.5	1.7	−0.8
Public sector debt (percent of GDP)	34.4	29.3	36.2	31.2	32.0	28.4	25.6	22.5
Compact Trust Fund balance (percent of GDP)	80.8	77.0	82.2	73.3	80.2	82.9	79.4	64.0
Balance of payments (percent of GDP, unless otherwise indicated)								
Current account including official transfers	−20.5	−7.7	−6.7	−9.2	−8.7	−9.3	−11.8	−0.5
Current account excluding official transfers	−42.5	−26.9	−30.4	−30.4	−28.5	−27.6	−29.7	−14.7
Overall balance	−1.3	−0.4	6.4	−2.2	−6.4	−1.8	0.4	1.5
External debt service (percent of goods and services exports)	4.8	5.1	6.8	5.5	5.5	4.6	4.2	3.9
Foreign direct investment	−5.5	−4.8	−2.7	−3.3	−3.2	−3.4	−5.8	−10.2

(*continued*)

APPENDIX TABLE 5.1

Palau: Selected Economic Indicators, 2010–15 (*Continued*)

Nominal GDP (FY2014): US$250.9 million
Main exports: Tourism, fish
Remoteness (GDP-weighted distance): 7,554 km
GDP per capita (FY2015): US$16,070
Population (FY2014): 17,708

	2001–09 Average	2010–15 Average	2010	2011	2012	2013	2014	2015 Estimate
External debt	34.3	29.8	36.2	31.4	32.3	28.4	28.1	22.4
External income	22.9	21.9	25.1	23.1	22.5	20.6	20.6	19.4
Government current grants	18.5	16.1	19.5	17.6	16.5	14.8	14.8	13.6
Investment income	0.1	0.0	0.0	0.0	0.0	0.0	0.0	0.0
Fishing license fees, others	4.3	5.8	5.6	5.5	6.0	5.8	5.8	5.8
Contributions to external income growth (percent)								
External income growth	–0.2	3.2	7.7	0.6	4.8	–3.3	9.2	0.2
Government current grants	–1.4	1.6	8.7	–1.4	0.8	–3.7	6.6	–1.7
Investment income	0.0	0.0	0.0	0.0	0.0	0.1	0.0	0.0
Fishing license fees, others	1.3	1.6	–1.0	1.9	4.0	0.3	2.6	1.9
Exchange rate (U.S. dollar is the legal tender)	1.0	1.0	1.0	1.0	1.0	1.0	1.0	1.0
Real effective exchange rate (period average)[2]	122.7	124.5	126.1	119.2	122.4	127.1	128.0	...
(percent change)	1.4	–0.4	–4.0	–5.5	2.7	3.8	0.7	...
Money, credit, and financial sector[3]								
Broad money (percent change)	...	...	...	...	...	...	...	...
Credit to private sector (percent of GDP)	...	...	14.6	13.9	12.6	13.2	12.8	...
(percent change)	...	...	–16.4	3.8	–2.9	10.9	6.6	...
Bank assets (percent of GDP)	...	...	54.5	61.1	60.0	61.6	70.3	...
Average yield on banking sector loans	...	...	11.8	13.4	11.4	11.6	...	...
Nonperforming loan ratio	...	...	5.5	3.3	3.6	3.4	...	...
Foreign bank market share (percent)[4]	...	...	86.0	88.4	89.1	89.8	...	...
Business climate indicators								
Business environment rankings[5]								
Doing business (overall)	...	120	113	118	120	104	131	136
Construction permits	...	67	45	50	52	58	96	101
Getting electricity	...	102	77	80	85	92	137	138
Enforcing contracts	...	126	121	121	124	128	129	130
Getting credit	...	130	171	173	176	110	71	79
Human development index[6]	0.8	0.8	0.8	0.8	0.8	0.8	0.8	...
Memorandum:								
Nominal GDP (local currency)	180.8	227.5	183.8	199.9	214.2	228.7	250.9	287.4
Nominal GDP (US$ million)	180.8	227.5	183.8	199.9	214.2	228.7	250.9	287.4

Sources: Palau authorities; and IMF staff estimates as of May 2016.
Note: ... = data not available.
[1] Current balance excludes grants and capital expenditure.
[2] Index, 2005 = 100.
[3] Data are calendar year.
[4] Share in total loans.
[5] World Bank, *Doing Business* reports; Palau is included from 2006.
[6] United Nations Development Programme.

Appendix 6. Papua New Guinea

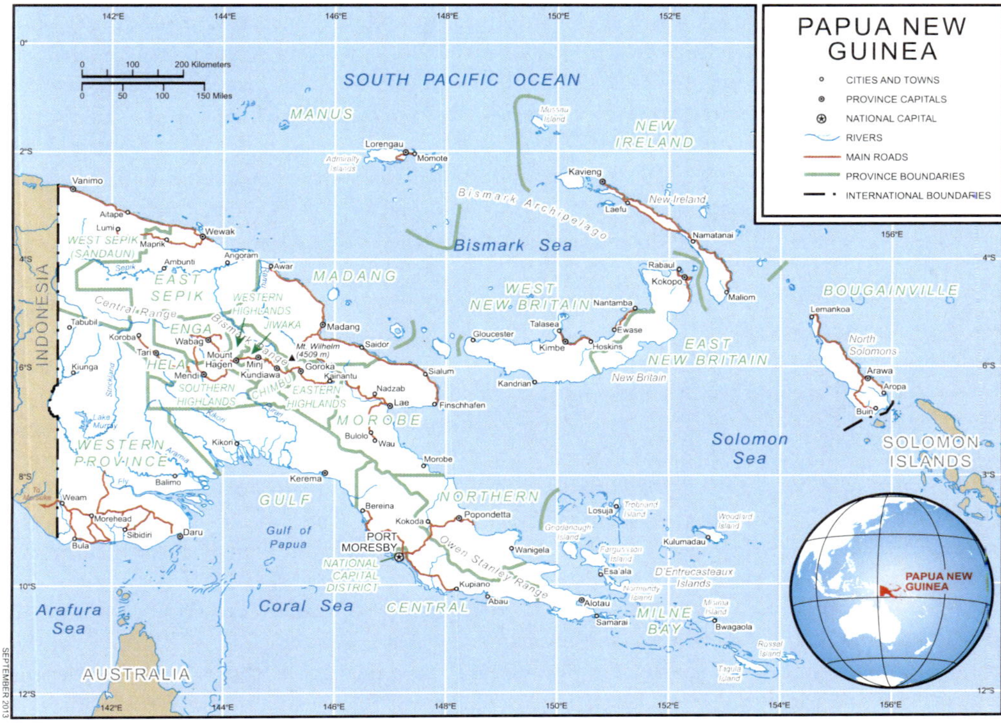

Papua New Guinea is the largest of the Pacific island countries, with a population of about 7.5 million and a land area of 462,800 square kilometers (about the size of Thailand). It occupies the eastern half of the island of New Guinea and approximately 600 offshore islands. The country is just south of the equator, making its climate moderate tropical with high seasonal rainfall.

Papua New Guinea gained independence in 1975 from an Australian-administered United Nations trusteeship and is a member of the Commonwealth of Nations. The national government includes three independent branches: the executive, the legislative, and the judiciary. Executive power is vested in the National Executive Council or Cabinet, composed of the prime minister and about 30 ministers.

SOURCES OF GROWTH AND ECONOMIC PROFILE

Main sources of growth. The mineral sector has been the main driver of growth since independence. But this source of growth has been volatile in the past decade, reflecting the pace of new discoveries and fluctuations in international commodity prices. More recently, extractive-industry-related construction has become one of the main sources of growth, particularly since the start of the construction of a large-scale liquefied natural gas (LNG) project in 2010. LNG production started in 2014 and reached full capacity in 2015, with the oil and gas extraction sector contributing to three-quarters of growth in 2014–15. With LNG production expected to stabilize from 2016 onward, however, agriculture (including fishing and logging), construction, and wholesale and retail trade will again become the main contributors to growth.

Prepared by Yongzheng Yang and Kumhwa Oh.

Production, employment, exports, and imports. Agriculture remains the dominant sector for household income and employment, generating about a third of GDP during 2006–13. The mineral and energy sector was also a large contributor to national income, contributing 9 percent of GDP over the same period. But as the economy undergoes major structural change in the next few years, this sector's contribution is expected to rise to about 19 percent of GDP by 2015. Minerals and petroleum currently dominate exports (72 percent of the total in 2013); the other main exports are cocoa, copra, coffee, palm oil, rubber, tea, and logs. The manufacturing sector accounts for only 6 percent of GDP and contributes little to exports. Papua New Guinea has been running a large current account deficit in recent years, but as LNG exports came onstream and LNG-project-related imports subsided, the deficit quickly declined and turned into a surplus in 2014.

External income. The country has very large outflows of investment income and remittances owing to foreign investments in the natural resource sector. Investment income and remittance outflows in net terms averaged 5.9 percent and 1.1 percent of GDP in 2006–13, respectively.

Development aid and technical assistance. Foreign grants averaged 14 percent of total government revenue in 2006–13. Australia is the biggest contributor to Papua New Guinea's development assistance program, with other major sources of financial and technical assistance from the European Union, Japan, the Asian Development Bank, and the World Bank. Newer development partners, such as China and Malaysia, are becoming more prominent. The IMF has provided substantial technical assistance recently in price and national accounts statistics, sovereign wealth fund management, and tax reform for extractive industries.

Government finance. Government expenditure represents about a third of GDP, of which about 40 percent is development spending. The government's fiscal framework is based on three medium-term economic strategies: the Medium-Term Fiscal Strategy, the Medium-Term Development Strategy, and the Medium-Term Debt Strategy. The Fiscal Responsibility Act further guides the fiscal framework, and limits public debt to below 30 percent of GDP. The current Medium-Term Fiscal Strategy focuses on development needs, with a commitment to allocate two-thirds of total budget resources to key areas such as health, education, infrastructure, and law and order by 2017. The government expects to have the sovereign wealth fund operational in 2016 to help manage resource revenues.

Financial sector. There are four commercial banks, seven authorized superannuation funds, and five life insurance companies and other nonbank financial sector institutions, all licensed and regulated by the Bank of Papua New Guinea, the central bank. The financial sector largely serves the formal sector and provides little reach to the very large informal, rural, and self-employed segments of the population. Total financial sector assets increased to K33 billion (about 100 percent of GDP) as of December 2012 from K9.5 billion at the end of 2005, with banking sector assets about 68 percent of total financial sector assets.

Business climate and investment. Much scope exists to improve private sector development through improved business conditions. Despite some improvements, the business environment remains challenging on many fronts. Papua New Guinea ranked 145th out of 189 countries in the World Bank's 2016 *Doing Business* report. Critical areas include law and order, governance, labor skills, land rights, transportation costs, and electricity supply, among others.

Monetary policy. The main objective of monetary policy is to achieve and maintain price stability. The Bank of Papua New Guinea largely relies on indirect instruments (that is, open market operations and the Kina Facility Rate) to conduct monetary policy, but other tools are also used, notably the cash reserve requirement. Semiannual statements set out the central bank's stance and conduct of monetary policy over the coming six months. Despite formal monetary policy instruments, however, the monetary policy transmission mechanism lacks effectiveness because of structurally high excess liquidity in the banking system.

Exchange rate and competitiveness. Papua New Guinea adopted a floating exchange rate system in 1994. Capital movements into and out of the country are largely unrestricted. However, in June 2014, the central bank introduced a trading band of 150 basis points around a de facto appreciated exchange rate target. Accordingly, the de facto arrangement was reclassified by the IMF from floating to a crawl-like arrangement, effective April 11, 2014. Since then, the exchange rate has depreciated gradually, but large foreign exchange shortages have continued. The external position is expected to improve in the medium term as new mineral and petroleum projects are developed.

GROWTH CHALLENGES, VULNERABILITIES, AND SPILLOVERS

Main growth challenges. Making the best use of natural resource revenues for inclusive growth while maintaining macroeconomic and debt sustainability is the main challenge. The government needs to ensure that resource revenue is channeled to the sovereign wealth fund and used effectively to foster inclusive growth in the face of weak capacity and governance challenges. Given the strong kina, improvements in the competitiveness of nonmineral tradable industries will require deeper structural reforms.

Main vulnerabilities. Risks to growth are tilted toward the downside, in particular over the longer term, reflecting uncertainty over commodity prices. Lower LNG and mineral prices are expected to continue to pressure government revenue, export earnings, and the kina. Depressed commodity prices may also reduce future inflows of foreign direct investment.

Regional and global economic spillovers. A weak global economy has dampened external demand and commodity prices. But reductions in quantitative easing in advanced economies are not expected to have a large impact, because the domestic financial market is not well integrated into the global market, with little capital inflow observed beyond foreign direct investment related to mineral projects. If risk factors were to materialize, however, funding costs for any future mining projects and the debt burden of the private sector could rise, which could reverberate on the economy.

APPENDIX TABLE 6.1

Papua New Guinea: Selected Economic Indicators, 2010–15

Nominal GDP (2014): US$16.8 billion[1]
Main export products: gold, copper, oil, palm oil, logs, coffee
Remoteness (GDP-weighted distance): 8,600 km
GDP per capita (2014): US$2,232[1]
Population (2014): 7.5 million

	1991–2000 Average	2001–09 Average	2010–15 Average	2010	2011	2012	2013	2014	2015 Estimate
GDP, GDP growth, employment, and prices									
Real GDP (percent change)	4.8	3.7	8.2	7.7	10.7	8.1	5.5	8.5	9.0
Mineral	20.2	−2.3	30.1	−2.0	−11.8	−7.4	7.2	134.2	60.2
Nonmineral	17.4	4.6	6.4	8.7	12.8	9.2	5.4	0.7	1.5
Real GDP per capita (percent change)	1.6	1.3	4.8	3.4	6.2	3.8	3.0	5.9	6.3
Consumer prices (percent change, average)	9.6	6.7	5.1	5.1	4.4	4.5	5.0	5.3	6.0
Shares in real GDP (percent)									
Agriculture	29.1	36.8	28.7	32.5	31.4	28.6	28.0	26.7	25.0
Construction	4.3	11.4	19.7	16.7	19.0	21.8	23.1	19.6	17.8
Mineral	14.7	12.1	9.7	8.5	6.8	5.8	5.9	12.7	18.7

(continued)

APPENDIX TABLE 6.1

Papua New Guinea: Selected Economic Indicators, 2010–15 (*Continued*)

Nominal GDP (2014): US$16.8 billion[1]
Main export products: gold, copper, oil, palm oil, logs, coffee
Remoteness (GDP-weighted distance): 8,600 km

GDP per capita (2014): US$2,232[1]
Population (2014): 7.5 million

	1991–2000 Average	2001–09 Average	2010–15 Average	2010	2011	2012	2013	2014	2015 Estimate
Contributions to real GDP growth (percent)									
Agriculture	3.1	0.7	0.9	1.1	2.3	–0.5	0.9	1.0	0.6
Construction	0.5	1.5	2.0	2.6	4.3	4.6	2.6	–1.9	–0.2
Mineral	1.7	–0.3	2.4	–0.2	–1.0	–0.5	0.4	7.9	7.7
Share in real GDP (in percent)									
Private consumption	...	...	...	...	...	...	...	...	...
Private investment	...	...	...	...	...	...	...	...	...
Public consumption	...	...	...	...	...	...	...	...	...
Public investment	...	...	...	...	...	...	...	...	...
Exports minus imports	...	...	...	...	...	...	...	...	...
Contributions to real GDP growth (percent)									
Private consumption	...	...	...	...	...	...	...	...	...
Private investment	...	...	...	...	...	...	...	...	...
Public consumption	...	...	...	...	...	...	...	...	...
Public investment	...	...	...	...	...	...	...	...	...
Exports minus imports	...	...	...	...	...	...	...	...	...
Public finances									
Central government finance (percent of GDP)									
Revenue and grants	28.8	31.8	28.5	31.3	30.4	29.2	28.2	27.3	24.7
Total domestic revenue	23.7	26.2	25.3	26.0	27.0	26.3	25.6	25.2	21.6
Grants	5.1	5.6	3.2	5.3	3.4	2.9	2.5	2.1	3.1
Expenditure and net lending[2]	31.6	31.4	32.0	28.2	28.7	32.4	36.1	34.5	32.3
Current (excluding grants)	24.4	19.9	21.2	15.8	17.5	19.3	26.4	26.3	22.1
Of which: wages and salaries	8.5	8.4	7.5	7.0	7.5	7.6	7.1	8.1	7.7
Development (capital)	7.2	11.5	10.8	12.4	11.2	13.0	9.8	8.1	10.2
Current balance[3]	–0.7	6.4	4.1	10.3	9.5	6.9	–0.8	–1.2	–0.5
Overall balance	–2.8	0.4	–3.5	3.1	1.7	–3.2	–8.0	–7.2	–7.6
Financing	2.7	–0.4	3.8	–3.9	–2.7	8.4	7.8	5.8	7.6
Assets (SWF, trust fund)	0.8	0.2	0.0	0.0	0.0	0.0	0.0	0.0	0.0
Debt	2.0	–0.4	3.8	–3.9	–2.7	8.4	7.8	5.8	7.6
Of which: external	0.0	–0.9	1.2	–0.3	0.1	0.5	1.0	0.9	4.7
Of which: concessional	–1.1	–1.4	0.5	–0.4	0.0	0.5	1.0	0.9	1.2
Other	–0.2	0.0	–0.3	0.8	1.0	–5.2	0.1	1.4	0.0
Public-debt-to-GDP ratio (percent)	61.4	49.2	30.7	25.6	23.0	26.7	34.0	35.6	39.4

(continued)

APPENDIX TABLE 6.1

Papua New Guinea: Selected Economic Indicators, 2010–15 (*Continued*)

Nominal GDP (2014): US$16.8 billion[1]
Main export products: gold, copper, oil, palm oil, logs, coffee
Remoteness (GDP-weighted distance): 8,600 km

GDP per capita (2014): US$2,232[1]
Population (2014): 7.5 million

	1991–2000 Average	2001–09 Average	2010–15 Average	2010	2011	2012	2013	2014	2015 Estimate
Balance of payments (percent of GDP, unless otherwise indicated)									
Current account balance	5.4	2.1	−21.7	−21.5	−23.6	−53.6	−31.8	−4.2	4.6
Excluding official transfers	0.5	−2.8	−24.3	−24.4	−26.8	−56.3	−34.4	−6.4	2.5
Overall balance	−0.1	4.3	0.2	4.8	9.6	−2.1	−8.6	−1.1	−1.2
External debt service (in percent of exports of goods and services)[4]	7.5	5.6	1.4	1.5	1.3	1.5	1.5	1.5	0.9
Foreign direct investment	4.0	3.9	7.2	5.7	8.0	12.2	5.9	5.1	6.1
External debt	58.2	47.3	118.7	69.5	89.9	144.6	157.9	129.2	121.2
Excluding Bank of Papua New Guinea	53.1	45.7	117.3	67.6	88.6	143.3	156.5	128.0	120.1
Main sources of external income (total)	−8.5	−8.8	−0.6	−5.4	−3.7	−5.4	−4.3	7.7	7.3
Investment income (net)	−7.4	−8.7	0.7	−4.5	−2.5	−3.4	−2.7	8.7	8.4
Remittances (net)	−1.1	−0.1	−1.3	−0.9	−1.2	−2.0	−1.6	−1.0	−1.1
Contributions to external income growth (percent)									
External income growth	−5.7	20.6	−44.3	−11.0	−8.0	71.2	−19.6	−295.5	−2.5
Investment income (net)	−4.0	17.4	−48.1	−9.6	−22.1	40.8	−12.4	−284.0	−1.3
Remittances (net)	−1.7	3.2	3.8	−1.4	14.0	30.4	−7.2	−11.6	−1.2
Exchange rate (kina to U.S. dollar period average)	1.5	3.2	2.4	2.7	2.4	2.1	2.2	2.5	2.6
Real effective exchange rate (period average)[5]	90.1	87.7	117.4	100.0	108.7	128.1	126.9	123.5	...
(percent change)	...	2.3	3.8	−3.7	8.7	17.9	−0.9	−2.7	...
Money, credit, and financial sector									
Broad money (percent change)	11.4	17.0	9.8	10.2	17.3	10.9	6.7	3.4	9.9
Credit to private sector (percent of GDP)	16.6	17.8	25.9	26.4	24.6	26.3	28.7	24.6	24.5
(percent change)	7.5	16.8	11.2	18.1	7.9	12.1	17.5	3.5	8.0
Bank assets (percent of GDP)	...	44.7	49.0	69.4	70.9	74.9	79.1	65.4	61.4
Short-term treasury bill interest rate (six-month)	...	8.4	5.4	5.2	4.3	5.8	5.0	5.1	6.7
Nonperforming loan ratio	...	4.8	1.7	1.7	2.0	2.0	1.2	1.6	1.5
Foreign banks market share (percent of total loans)[6]	...	6.4	6.1	5.6	4.8	6.9	7.3	...	...
Business climate indicators									
Business environment rankings[7]									
Doing business (overall)	...	...	123	106	115	119	114	141	145
Construction permits	...	...	124	119	115	119	131	130	127
Getting electricity	...	...	49	24	25	26	27	94	98
Enforcing contracts	...	...	170	165	167	170	181	169	169
Getting credit	...	...	139	122	143	146	88	165	167

(*continued*)

APPENDIX TABLE 6.1

Papua New Guinea: Selected Economic Indicators, 2010–15 (*Continued*)

Nominal GDP (2014): US$16.8 billion[1]
Main export products: gold, copper, oil, palm oil, logs, coffee
Remoteness (GDP-weighted distance): 8,600 km

GDP per capita (2014): US$2,232[1]
Population (2014): 7.5 million

	1991–2000 Average	2001–09 Average	2010–15 Average	2010	2011	2012	2013	2014	2015 Estimate
Human development index[8]	...	...	0.5	0.5	0.5	0.5	0.5	0.5	...
Memorandum:									
Nominal GDP (millions of kina)	6,466	15,966	35,090	26,421	30,522	32,070	34,595	41,668	45,262
Nominal GDP (millions of U.S. dollars)[1]	4,422	5,205	14,588	9,716	12,873	15,391	15,413	16,809	17,323

Sources: Papua New Guinea authorities; and IMF, "Papua New Guinea: 2015 Article IV Consultation–Staff Report" (Country Report No. 15/318).
Note: SWF = sovereign wealth fund.
[1] Based on period average exchange rate.
[2] Expenditure classification was changed in 2013.
[3] Current balance excludes grants and development expenditure (capital expenditure).
[4] Public external debt-service-ratio (in percent of exports).
[5] Index, 2005 = 100.
[6] Share of loans denominated in foreign currency.
[7] World Bank, *Doing Business* reports.
[8] United Nations Development Program.

Appendix 7. Samoa

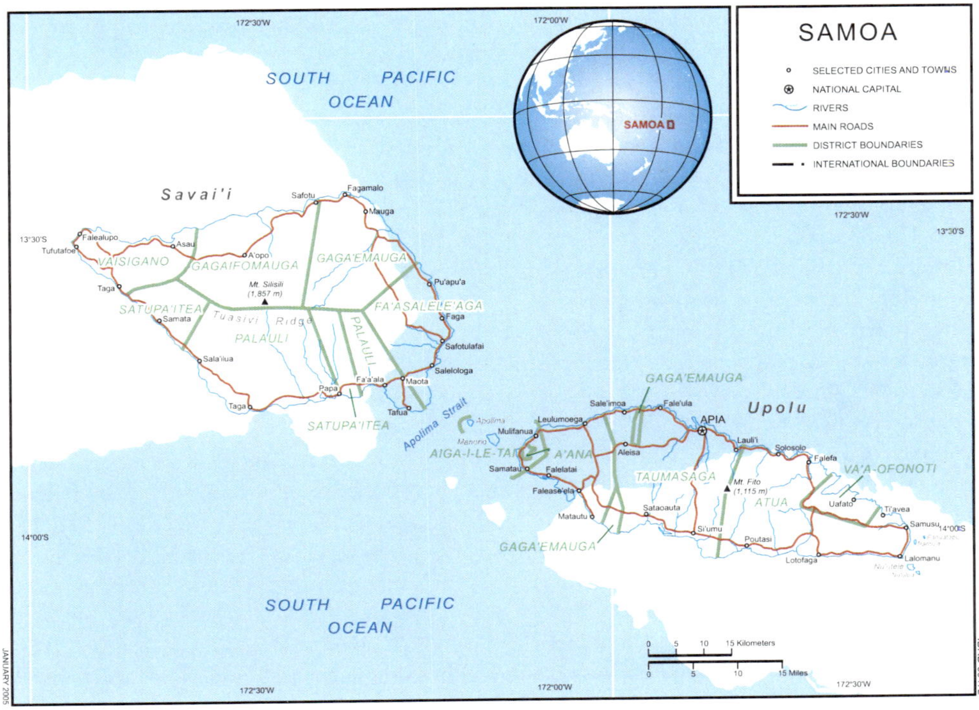

Samoa's 193,000 people live on four islands in the South Pacific about halfway between Hawaii and New Zealand and northeast of Fiji. The capital, Apia, is in Upolu, the most populous and developed of the country's islands, which also include five uninhabited ones. GDP per capita is about US$4,300. Natural disasters pose a significant risk.

As the first Pacific island country to achieve independence (from New Zealand in 1962), Samoa celebrated its fiftieth anniversary on June 1, 2012. The 49 members of the Fono, the legislative assembly, elect the head of state for a five-year term. Fono members are elected by universal suffrage, also for five-year terms. Samoa's cabinet consists of the prime minister and 12 ministers appointed by the head of state on the prime minister's advice.

SOURCES OF GROWTH AND ECONOMIC PROFILE

Main sources of growth. The economy has traditionally depended on development aid, remittances, agriculture, and fishing. Construction, commerce, and public administration have been the main sectors contributing to growth in recent years.

Production, employment, exports, and imports. Production growth has been led by sectors that are highly dependent on government spending, such as construction. Growth in labor-intensive sectors such as agriculture has been weak and unemployment remains widespread, with a high share of the labor force in the informal sector. The manufacturing sector mainly processes agricultural products. Tourism is expanding and accounts for about 18 percent of GDP. However, an earthquake and the resulting tsunami in September 2009 caused severe damage and losses equivalent to 25 percent

Prepared by Niamh Sheridan.

of GDP, and disrupted transportation and power generation. In December 2012 tropical Cyclone Evan caused damage and losses of 30 percent of GDP.

External income. Remittances are the major source of external income, mainly from New Zealand, and account for 20 percent of GDP. Australia and the United States are the next biggest source of remittances.

Development aid. Samoa depends largely on financial aid from multilateral and bilateral development partners, with aid directed to a variety of sectors including education, health, water, and energy. Two-thirds of external funding for reconstruction and rehabilitation after tropical Cyclone Evan came from grants and a third as concessional loans. The IMF provided financing under its Rapid Credit Facility of SDR 5.8 million in May 2013 (about 1.3 percent of GDP). Technical assistance is provided in a number of areas, including public financial management, financial sector supervision, and external sector statistics.

Public finances. Government current expenditure accounts for about 25 percent of GDP and grew at about 9 percent over 2006–11. Prior to the cyclone, Samoa had begun to consolidate its fiscal position after several years of high deficits to finance post-tsunami reconstruction, based on its medium-term fiscal framework. The cyclone's effects will delay this consolidation until reconstruction is completed. The government introduced a supplementary budget in January 2013 that raised expenditure by 0.8 percent of GDP to meet the immediate needs of postcyclone recovery. The government undertook additional rehabilitation using donor funds, costing 2.4 percent of GDP in 2012/13. For the medium term, the government is targeting a public-debt-to-GDP ratio of 50 percent by 2020. The medium-term fiscal plan in the 2015/16 budget maintains recent revenue efforts and contains current expenditure and the wage bill.

Financial sector. Four major commercial banks—ANZ, Bank South Pacific, National Bank of Samoa, and Samoa Commercial Bank—make up the banking sector in Samoa. The newly established Unit Trust of Samoa is attracting deposits away from commercial banks by offering higher interest rates. Along with the Development Bank of Samoa, a housing corporation, and a provident fund, there are a number of licensed money transfer/foreign exchange services. Banks remain well capitalized even though nonperforming loans rose after the cyclone and amid the slowdown in economic activity.

Investment and business climate. The World Bank's *Doing Business* 2016 report ranks Samoa at 96th out of 189 countries, above the average for the Asia and Pacific region (119th). Nevertheless, the country needs to address various structural impediments. The use of customary land as collateral for bank loans is a major constraint to lending, discouraging private investment and restricting the country's growth potential. The key task ahead is to build consensus on a legal framework and acceptable commercial practices and processes that would open up investment.

Exchange rate and competitiveness. The tala, which is pegged to a basket of industrial-country currencies, is not significantly overvalued, according to the current IMF staff assessment. Nevertheless, a gradual realignment of the exchange rate could help improve competitiveness and bolster reserves. Foreign reserves remain adequate (four months of prospective imports of goods and services) amid generous donor support, but the slow recovery in tourism and agriculture could put medium-term pressure on reserves. Enhancing infrastructure and bolstering the business climate will be crucial to improving competitiveness.

GROWTH CHALLENGES, VULNERABILITIES, AND SPILLOVERS

Main growth challenges. Samoa needs to improve external competitiveness and restore strong growth through structural reforms. Together with fiscal consolidation, this would help enhance fiscal and external sustainability and lay the foundation for higher growth in the long term. Enhancing resilience to natural disasters will also be essential to lift potential growth.

Main vulnerabilities. Possible delays in fiscal consolidation to restore debt sustainability and delays in structural reforms could represent a vulnerability. Samoa is also susceptible to natural disasters, which requires the country to maintain fiscal buffers.

Global and regional economic spillovers. Australia and New Zealand have a significant impact on the Samoan economy through aid and tourism, and because they provide opportunities to Samoans to work abroad. Derisking by global banks could reduce access to banking services, increase costs, and ultimately affect the flow of remittances, which currently amount to 20 percent of GDP.

APPENDIX TABLE 7.1

Samoa: Selected Economic Indicators, 2010–15

Nominal GDP (FY2015): US$838.0 million
Main export products: Tourism, Fish
Remoteness (GDP-weighted distance): 8,994 km

GDP per capita (FY2015): US$4,334
Population (2015): 193,337 million

	1991–2000 Average	2001–09 Average	2010–15 Average	2010	2011	2012	2013	2014	2015 Estimate
GDP, GDP growth, employment, and prices									
Real GDP (percent change)	3.0	3.1	0.9	−1.4	5.4	0.4	−1.9	1.2	1.7
Real GDP per capita (percent change)	2.6	2.4	0.1	−2.1	4.6	−0.3	−2.7	0.4	0.9
Unemployment (percent)	...	...	...	...	...	...	...	...	...
Consumer prices (percent change, average)	3.3	6.4	1.7	0.8	2.9	6.2	−0.2	−1.2	1.9
Shares in GDP (percent)									
Largest sector (commerce)	...	25.7	30.8	28.3	29.6	30.5	32.1	32.2	32.4
Second largest sector (construction)	...	8.5	10.6	9.6	11.4	11.1	10.5	11.6	9.7
Third largest sector (transport)	...	9.7	8.5	11.0	9.6	7.9	7.3	6.9	8.2
Tourism	...	16.0	18.7	21.3	19.0	19.0	17.1	17.8	18.1
Agriculture	...	9.3	7.2	8.5	7.1	7.1	7.3	6.9	6.4
Contributions to real GDP growth (percent)									
Commerce	...	1.3	0.8	−1.3	2.9	1.1	0.8	0.4	0.9
Construction	...	0.8	0.1	−1.1	2.4	0.1	−0.8	1.3	−1.4
Transport	...	0.5	−0.2	0.7	−0.8	−1.4	−0.6	−0.4	1.2
Agriculture	...	−0.3	−0.1	0.2	−0.2	−0.7	0.2	0.9	−1.0
Share in GDP (percent)									
Private consumption	...	...	...	...	...	...	...	...	...
Private investment	...	...	...	...	...	...	...	...	...
Public consumption	...	...	...	...	...	...	...	...	...
Public investment	...	...	...	...	...	...	...	...	...
Exports minus imports	...	-22.2	-24.5	-27.5	-24.2	-27.9	-20.3	-25.3	-22.1
Contributions to GDP growth (percent)									
Private consumption	...	...	...	...	...	...	...	...	...
Private investment	...	...	...	...	...	...	...	...	...
Public consumption	...	...	...	...	...	...	...	...	...
Public investment	...	...	...	...	...	...	...	...	...
Exports minus imports	...	-2.5	-1.6	-4.7	-2.0	-6.7	6.8	-5.5	2.6

(continued)

APPENDIX TABLE 7.1

Samoa: Selected Economic Indicators, 2010–15 (*Continued*)

Nominal GDP (FY2015): US$838.0 million
Main export products: Tourism, Fish
Remoteness (GDP-weighted distance): 8,994 km
GDP per capita (FY2015): US$4,334
Population (2015): 193,337 million

	1991–2000 Average	2001–09 Average	2010–15 Average	2010	2011	2012	2013	2014	2015 Estimate
Public finances									
Central government finance (percent of GDP)									
Revenue and grants	44.7	28.7	33.8	34.0	30.8	30.2	33.8	38.1	35.9
Total domestic revenue	32.6	21.9	24.2	24.6	22.6	22.6	24.1	25.4	26.1
Grants	12.1	6.8	9.5	9.4	8.1	7.6	9.7	12.6	9.8
Expenditure and net lending	35.4	29.7	38.9	39.8	36.0	37.3	37.6	43.3	39.2
Current	24.1	19.7	26.5	26.6	25.9	24.8	26.1	28.4	27.3
Of which: wages and salaries									
Development (capital)	11.3	8.7	12.4	13.2	10.2	12.5	11.5	15.0	11.9
Current balance[1]	–8.5	2.2	–2.3	–2.1	–3.3	–2.2	–2.0	–3.0	–1.2
Overall balance	–5.8	–1.1	–5.1	–5.8	–5.3	–7.2	–3.8	–5.3	–3.3
Financing									
Assets (SWF, trust fund)	...	...	...	...	...	...	...	...	...
Debt									
Of which: external	4.7	0.7	4.9	8.8	5.5	7.3	3.5	2.8	1.8
Of which: concessional	4.7	0.7	4.9	8.8	5.5	7.3	3.5	2.8	1.8
Domestic financing	1.0	0.4	0.2	–2.9	–0.2	–0.1	0.3	2.4	1.6
Central government debt to GDP ratio (percent)	...	38.7	51.6	45.2	49.1	52.1	53.5	54.4	55.5
Balance of payments (percent of GDP, unless otherwise indicated)									
Current account including official transfers	...	–7.7	–5.5	–7.8	–5.3	–8.6	–0.2	–7.6	–4.0
Current account excluding official transfers	...	–8.2	–5.8	–7.8	–5.3	–8.6	–0.9	–7.9	–4.2
Overall balance	...	–1.1	–5.1	–5.8	–5.3	–7.2	–3.8	–5.3	–3.3
External debt service (percent of exports of goods and services)	...	6.7	5.6	2.4	3.8	4.5	6.7	7.7	8.6
Foreign direct investment	...	1.1	2.2	7.1	0.2	1.2	0.9	1.3	2.7
External debt	...	...	49.3	41.6	46.6	49.9	51.6	51.8	54.4
Main sources of external income (total)	...	29.8	40.8	44.3	41.8	41.8	39.8	38.1	38.9
Private transfers	...	18.8	22.1	23.1	22.9	22.8	22.7	20.4	20.8
Tourism earnings	...	16.5	18.7	21.3	19.0	19.0	17.1	17.8	18.1
Contributions to external income growth (percent)									
External income growth	...	11.9	5.4	5.6	15.1	11.0	–1.4	–2.2	4.6
Private transfers	...	5.7	3.3	3.8	10.9	5.9	1.6	–4.7	2.5
Tourism earnings	...	6.2	2.1	1.8	4.2	5.1	–3.0	2.5	2.1

(continued)

APPENDIX TABLE 7.1

Samoa: Selected Economic Indicators, 2010–15 *(Continued)*

Nominal GDP (FY2015): US$838.0 million
Main export products: Tourism, Fish
Remoteness (GDP-weighted distance): 8,994 km

GDP per capita (FY2015): US$4,334
Population (2015): 193,337 million

	1991–2000 Average	2001–09 Average	2010–15 Average	2010	2011	2012	2013	2014	2015 Estimate
Exchange rate (tala to U.S. dollar period average)	...	2.9	2.4	2.5	2.4	2.3	2.3	2.3	2.4
Real effective exchange rate (period average)[2]	...	82.1	101.7	100.3	100.0	99.3	103.6	103.6	103.5
(percent change)	...	1.4	2.7	13.3	–0.3	–0.7	4.3	0.0	–0.1
Money, credit, and financial sector									
Broad money (percent change)	...	11.3	2.9	6.4	–6.1	–1.6	6.4	9.6	...
Credit to private sector (percent of GDP)	...	25.0	30.5	28.3	28.5	27.6	27.6	37.1	34.0
(percent change)	...	12.3	6.9	–0.7	9.5	1.4	–0.5	36.4	–4.4
Nonperforming loan ratio	...	8.4	6.2	6.1	4.4	4.7	7.5	8.3	...
Foreign bank market share (percent)[3]	...	...	...	...	...	...	...	...	...
Business climate indicators									
Business environment rankings[4]									
Doing business (overall)	...	...	65	43	47	49	60	92	96
Construction permits	...	...	56	34	38	39	42	92	93
Getting electricity	...	...	29	16.0	18	19	21	49	52
Enforcing contracts	...	...	79	78	76	77	83	79	79
Getting credit	...	...	124	98	106	108	128	150	152
Human development index[5]	...	...	...	0.7	0.7	0.7	0.7	0.7	...
Memorandum:									
Nominal GDP (Tala million)	...	1,317.1	1,813.9	1,632.2	1,765.1	1,843.4	1,838.9	1,866.4	1,946.3
Nominal GDP (US$ million)	...	455.7	748.7	570.3	695.5	772.1	799.2	816.9	838.0

Sources: Samoa authorities; and IMF, World Economic Outlook database (April 2016).
Note: ... = data not available; RGDP = real GDP; SWF = sovereign wealth fund.
[1] Current balance excludes grants and development (capital expenditure).
[2] Index, 2005 = 100.
[3] Share in total loans; not including small loan scheme.
[4] World Bank, *Doing Business* reports.
[5] United Nations Development Programme.

Appendix 8. The Solomon Islands

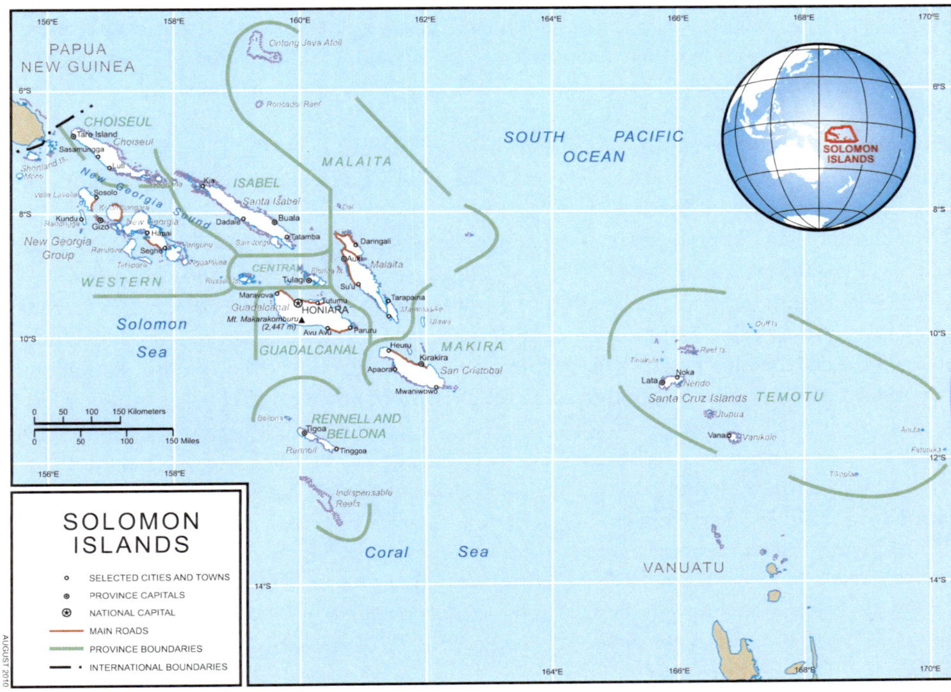

The Solomon Islands has the second largest land area among Pacific island countries after Papua New Guinea. Some 80 percent of the population of 615,000 lives in rural areas, and the population growth rate has been increasing at an annual rate of more than 3 percent in the past two decades, one of the fastest in the region. The capital, Honiara, has a population of about 69,000 and is the only urban center in the Solomon Islands.

The country gained independence in 1978 from the United Kingdom. It is a constitutional monarchy with Queen Elizabeth II as its head of state and a one-chamber parliament with 50 members elected for four years.

SOURCES OF GROWTH AND ECONOMIC PROFILE

Main sources of growth. Commodity production is a major component of economic activity, with agriculture, logging, and fishing collectively accounting for a third of GDP. Logging has been a major driver of growth for the last several years, although overexploitation of logging stocks is eroding the sector's long-term prospects. Mining had emerged as a major sector with the opening in 2011 of Gold Ridge, the country's only gold mine, which contributed more than half of economic growth in 2012. Gold Ridge's closure following severe floods in April 2014, as well as lower gold prices, disrupted production. As of May 2016, the mine was still closed, but the further development of nickel and bauxite extraction may see the mining sector reemerge.

Production, employment, and trade. The production base is narrow. The manufacturing sector accounts for about 6 percent of GDP share and contributes little to exports. Labor market data are limited, although the International Labour Organization puts unemployment in the Solomon Islands at above 30 percent, with a major concentration among the youth. Merchandise exports include logs, fish,

Prepared by Patrizia Tumbarello.

and, until recently, minerals, with logs accounting for around half of exports during 2006–14. The Solomon Islands is highly import-dependent and vulnerable to import price fluctuations. Imports of goods averaged about 45 percent of GDP during 2010–15. The main imported goods are manufactured goods, fuel, and food, with manufactured goods making up about 20 percent of GDP, and fuel and food imports about 9.5 percent of GDP each during 2010–15. The country's main trading partners are China and Singapore.

External income. External income accounted for 3.7 percent of GDP in 2014, lower than for several other Pacific island countries. The main sources of external income are remittances, fishing license fees, and investment income.

Development aid. The Solomon Islands is the largest recipient of multilateral and bilateral aid among non–micro states. After a period of civil unrest, the Regional Assistance Mission to Solomon Islands, a partnership between the people and government of the Solomon Islands and 15 contributing countries of the Pacific region, arrived in the country in July 2003 at the request of the government. Since then, the mission has been helping lay the foundations for long-term stability, security, and prosperity. The mission is expected to be totally wound down in 2017. Development aid flows, in general, are expected to decline steadily to less than 11 percent of GDP in the medium term from the peak level of 30 percent of GDP in 2010. Australia and New Zealand are the largest bilateral aid providers, with assistance programs focusing on health and education. Support from the World Bank Group has focused on improving the delivery of basic public services and strengthening economic resilience by maximizing sustainable growth in mining, agriculture, and fisheries, and tackling constraints to inclusive growth. The Asian Development Bank has provided $90 million in grants and technical assistance since the Solomon Islands became a member in 1973. These have focused on structural reforms to support private-sector-led growth, particularly by improving the business environment. In 2015, the European Union approved a national grant allocation of EUR 40 million for the period to 2020, focusing on water, sanitation and hygiene (WASH), and rural development. In addition, the European Union currently provides sector budget support in rural WASH of about EUR 2.5 million a year, for the next four years. This support depends on four general eligibility criteria, among them progress in public financial management and sectoral performance indicators. In response to the 2014 flood, with damages and losses equivalent to 9 percent of GDP, the World Bank Group approved US$10 million and the Asian Development Bank US$13 million in additional financing for the Solomon Islands. IMF support in the form of two back-to-back Standby Credit Facility arrangements during 2010–12 and an Extended Credit Facility arrangement from 2012 to March 2016 have been enhancing fiscal and monetary institutions and macroeconomic stability.

Public finances. Government expenditure accounts for nearly half of GDP. After the fiscal position deteriorated during the economic downturn in 2009, the government embarked on reforms to strengthen the fiscal position, with the support of consecutive IMF programs. Using the cash balance (which captures core deposits readily available for fiscal financing) as a fiscal anchor has helped strengthen the fiscal position and enhanced the budget plan's credibility. The government is currently implementing a multiyear budget framework, and the Public Financial Management Act, passed in October 2013, should strengthen public financial management. Public debt has fallen significantly since 2005 as a result of improved external debt management under the Honiara Club Agreement. In May 2012 the government introduced a new debt management strategy that allows the contracting of new concessional external debt within annual borrowing limits to ensure debt remains at a prudent level.

Financial sector. The Solomon Islands has two foreign commercial banks (ANZ and Bank South Pacific) and a domestically incorporated bank (Pan Oceanic Bank). Nonbank financial institutions, including credit unions, also operate in the Solomon Islands, along with a systemically important savings and retirement fund, the National Provident Fund, which holds the country's largest pool of savings. The country is one of the most underbanked in the Pacific. The private sector's access to credit is constrained by, among other things, customary land practices that limit the use of land as collateral. The Central Bank of Solomon Islands (CBSI) has been very proactive in promoting financial inclusion. In 2014, together with commercial banks, the CBSI introduced mobile banking services to deepen financial access in geographically dispersed and remote areas, making mobile banking well positioned to leapfrog conventional banking in providing financial services.

Investment, business climate, and competitiveness. The environment for private sector development has been weak, although structural reforms to improve the business environment have been undertaken, including in the context of the IMF's Extended Credit Facility arrangement. The Solomon Islands was 112th out of 189 countries in the World Bank's *Doing Business* 2016 report. Private investment has often been constrained by the high cost of financing, poor infrastructure, and cumbersome regulations and procedures.

Monetary policy and exchange rate. The Central Bank of Solomon Islands has the primary objective of achieving and maintaining domestic price stability. Its monetary policy tools include statutory reserve requirements, credit control measures, and open market operations in its own securities. The monetary transmission mechanism is weak as in other Pacific islands. In October 2012 the authorities moved from a de facto peg to the U.S. dollar to a basket peg using as weights the shares of the currencies of its main trading partners.

GROWTH CHALLENGES, VULNERABILITIES, AND SPILLOVERS

Main growth challenges. The Solomon Islands grapples with lack of scale and high transport costs from its remoteness from major export markets, dispersed population, and low level of urbanization. Growth has also been held back by poor infrastructure. Only 14 percent of households have access to electricity, while 75 percent of rural households have no access to piped water.

Main vulnerabilities. These include a narrow economic base, dependence on donor aid, and reliance on commodity exports. The country is vulnerable to natural disasters and climate change, particularly in the absence of climate-change-proof infrastructure.

Global and regional economic spillovers. China has been the largest trading partner since 2003, accounting for about 60 percent of the Solomon Islands' total exports. The country is closely linked with neighboring regional economies, specifically Australia and to a lesser extent New Zealand, while the European Union remains a key export market for the fishing industry. Contagion from negative external shocks would occur through a contraction in foreign direct investment, a drop in official development assistance, declining demand for commodities from Asia, and deterioration in the country's terms of trade.

APPENDIX TABLE 8.1

The Solomon Islands: Selected Economic Indicators, 2010–15

Nominal GDP (2014): US$1.15 billion
Main export products: Logs and fish
Remoteness (GDP-weighted distance): 8,702 km
GDP per capita (2014): US$1,931
Population (2015): 562,000

	1991–2000 Average	2001–09 Average	2010–15 Average	2010	2011	2012	2013	2014	2015 Estimate
GDP, GDP growth, employment, and prices									
Real GDP (percent change)	2.8	3.3	5.5	6.9	12.9	4.7	3.0	2.0	3.3
Real GDP per capita (percent change)	0.0	0.8	3.2	4.6	10.5	2.4	0.7	−0.3	1.0
Unemployment (percent)	. . .	. . .	. . .	. . .	. . .	. . .	. . .	. . .	. . .
Consumer prices (percent change, average)	10.5	9.4	4.1	0.9	7.4	5.9	5.4	5.2	−0.4

(continued)

APPENDIX TABLE 8.1

The Solomon Islands: Selected Economic Indicators, 2010–15 (*Continued*)

Nominal GDP (2014): US$1.15 billion
Main export products: Logs and fish
Remoteness (GDP-weighted distance): 8,702 km

GDP per capita (2014): US$1,931
Population (2014): 562,000

	1991–2000 Average	2001–09 Average	2010–15 Average	2010	2011	2012	2013	2014	2015 Estimate
Shares in GDP (percent)									
Largest sector (agriculture and hunting)	22.4	19.6	17.7	18.7	18.9	18.1	17.3	17.3	15.8
Second largest sector (forestry and logging)	16.8	8.8	10.1	11.3	9.4	9.3	9.1	10.3	11.2
Third largest sector (mining and quarrying)	0.7	6.7	4.8	5.7	5.7	5.7	5.5	5.9	0.1
Contributions to GDP growth (percent) (over real GDP)									
Largest sector (agriculture and hunting)	−2.5	0.5	0.4	1.8	1.6	−0.4	−0.3	0.3	−0.4
Second largest sector (forestry and logging)	−0.6	0.6	0.7	3.1	−1.2	0.1	0.0	1.4	1.0
Third largest sector (mining and quarrying)	−0.2	0.0	0.1	0.2	5.1	0.0	−0.7	−2.7	−1.4
Share in GDP (percent)									
Private consumption	...	69.7	66.2	66.8	64.6	65.5	66.3	67.9	...
Private investment	...	...	...	...	...	...	...	...	...
Public consumption	...	36.1	29.8	36.8	28.4	25.3	28.2	30.0	...
Public investment	...	...	...	...	...	...	...	...	...
Exports minus imports	...	−18.1	−14.3	−28.3	−10.0	−7.8	−10.7	−14.5	...
Contributions to GDP growth (percent) (based on real GDP)									
Private consumption	...	3.3	3.3	5.6	2.6	2.4	2.7	3.0	...
Private investment	...	...	...	...	...	...	...	...	...
Public consumption	...	4.6	0.2	3.7	−6.3	−2.6	3.7	2.4	...
Public investment	...	...	...	...	...	...	...	...	...
Exports minus imports	...	−3.2	−0.3	−14.0	17.6	2.0	−3.2	−4.1	...
Public finances									
Central government finance (percent of GDP)									
Revenue and grants	20.6	34.7	53.5	63.5	59.0	54.4	51.8	48.0	46.1
Total domestic revenue	16.7	20.8	33.1	32.4	32.5	33.6	34.1	33.2	34.7
Grants	3.9	13.9	20.4	31.1	26.6	20.8	17.8	14.8	11.5
Expenditure and net lending	18.1	33.6	49.8	57.7	50.2	50.6	47.6	46.3	46.4
Current (excluding grants)	18.3	20.6	27.7	28.6	25.1	27.7	27.8	28.1	28.7
Of which: wages and salaries	8.8	8.2	9.9	10.8	9.2	9.2	9.2	9.9	11.2

(continued)

APPENDIX TABLE 8.1

The Solomon Islands: Selected Economic Indicators, 2010–15 (*Continued*)

Nominal GDP (2014): US$1.15 billion
Main export products: Logs and fish
Remoteness (GDP-weighted distance): 8,702 km
GDP per capita (2014): US$1,931
Population (2014): 562,000

	1991–2000 Average	2001–09 Average	2010–15 Average	2010	2011	2012	2013	2014	2015 Estimate
Development (capital)	4.6	13.8	21.9	28.3	25.0	22.9	19.8	17.8	17.8
Unidentified	-4.7	-0.9	0.2	0.8	0.1	0.0	0.0	0.0	0.0
Current balance[1]	-1.0	2.0	9.7	11.2	11.0	10.2	9.9	7.1	8.7
Overall balance	2.5	1.2	4.0	5.9	8.8	3.8	4.2	1.7	-0.3
Financing									
Assets (SWF, trust fund)	...	...	...	...	...	...	...	...	...
Debt	...	...	...	...	...	...	...	...	...
Of which: external	...	...	...	...	...	...	...	...	...
Of which: concessional	...	...	...	...	...	...	...	...	...
Other (privatizations)	...	...	...	...	...	...	...	...	...
Public-debt-to-GDP ratio (percent)	44.4	53.2	17.9	28.9	21.7	17.6	15.5	13.3	10.4
Balance of payments (percent of GDP, unless otherwise indicated)									
Current account including official transfers	-6.3	-6.6	-8.4	-33.4	-8.7	1.8	-3.5	-4.3	-2.6
Current account excluding official transfers	-8.7	-15.1	-21.9	-58.5	-27.2	-9.5	-13.4	-13.0	-9.6
Overall balance	...	3.0	7.6	17.8	16.5	8.5	2.5	-1.1	1.6
External debt service (percent of exports of goods and services)	3.8	9.0	3.2	4.9	2.6	2.5	2.7	2.9	3.6
Foreign direct investment	-0.1	4.8	8.0	24.4	13.1	2.1	4.5	1.8	2.0
External debt	39.9	44.9	21.7	32.4	25.1	21.4	19.5	19.2	12.6
Main sources of external income	...	4.2	3.6	3.1	3.2	3.6	3.1	3.7	4.6
Remittances	...	3.0	2.0	1.8	1.7	2.1	1.8	1.7	2.7
Investment income	...	0.7	0.6	0.5	0.6	0.8	0.6	0.6	0.4
Fishing rent rights	...	0.5	1.0	0.8	0.9	0.7	0.7	1.4	1.5
Contributions to external income growth (percent)									
External Income growth	...	-0.9	14.1	-8.4	32.1	29.5	-9.7	21.0	20.3
Remittances	...	-1.7	4.8	-20.7	9.5	23.6	-6.1	-1.3	23.6
Investment income	...	-0.6	2.0	0.7	11.3	10.0	-5.8	0.1	-4.4
Fishing rent rights	...	1.4	7.4	11.6	11.3	-4.1	2.3	22.1	1.1
Exchange rate (local currency to U.S. dollar period average)	3.8	7.3	7.6	8.1	7.6	7.4	7.3	7.4	8.1
Real effective exchange rate (period average)[2]	111.1	98.1	115.9	100.0	103.1	112.6	121.1	128.2	130.1
(percent change)	-0.6	-0.2	3.4	-7.1	3.1	9.2	7.6	5.8	1.5

(continued)

APPENDIX TABLE 8.1

The Solomon Islands: Selected Economic Indicators, 2010–15 (*Continued*)

Nominal GDP (2014): US$1.15 billion
Main export products: Logs and fish
Remoteness (GDP-weighted distance): 8,702 km

GDP per capita (2014): US$1,931
Population (2014): 562,000

	1991–2000 Average	2001–09 Average	2010–15 Average	2010	2011	2012	2013	2014	2015 Estimate
Money, credit, and financial sector									
Broad money (percent change)	...	23.0	14.9	13.5	25.5	17.3	12.4	5.6	15.0
Credit to private sector (percent of GDP)	...	16.3	19.2	21.5	18.0	16.9	18.0	20.0	20.8
(percent change)	...	29.3	7.4	–4.7	4.7	4.1	15.1	16.4	16.7
Bank assets (percent of GDP)	...	38.8	48.5	43.6	44.1	45.9	49.5	49.9	58.0
Short-term treasury bill interest rate	...	4.6	1.5	3.7	2.5	1.4	0.4	0.2	0.5
Nonperforming loan ratio	...	2.1	5.6	7.9	5.9	3.7	7.2	4.7	4.1
Foreign bank market share (percent)[3]	...	...	...	...	...	...	...	...	...
Business climate indicators									
Business environment rankings[4]									
Doing business (overall)	...	73	98	90	89	88	100	109	112
Construction permits	...	36	39	30	28	30	30	58	58
Getting electricity	...	...	105	113	110	108	122	87	90
Enforcing contracts	...	105	148	138	139	142	150	160	160
Getting credit	...	141	74	64	68	74	88	71	79
Human development index[5]	...	0.5	0.5	0.5	0.5	0.5	0.5	0.5	...
Memorandum:				605.0	745.0	769.0	807.0	607	777
Nominal GDP (local currency)	1,660	3,285	7,553	5,416	6,774	7,540	8,109	8,530	8,948
Nominal GDP (US$ million)	414	445	999	672	887	1,025	1,111	1,154	1,147

Sources: Solomon Islands authorities; IMF, "Solomon Islands: 2016 Article IV Consultation and Fifth and Sixth Reviews Under the Extended Credit Facility Arrangement–Staff Report" (Country Report No. 16/90); and IMF staff estimates.

Note: ... = data not available; SWF = sovereign wealth fund.

[1] Current balance excludes grants and development (capital expenditure).

[2] Index, 2005 = 100.

[3] Share in total loans, not including small loan scheme.

[4] World Bank, *Doing Business* reports. Solomon Islands start in 2007.

[5] United Nations Development Programme; data only available for 2000 and after 2005.

Appendix 9. Timor-Leste

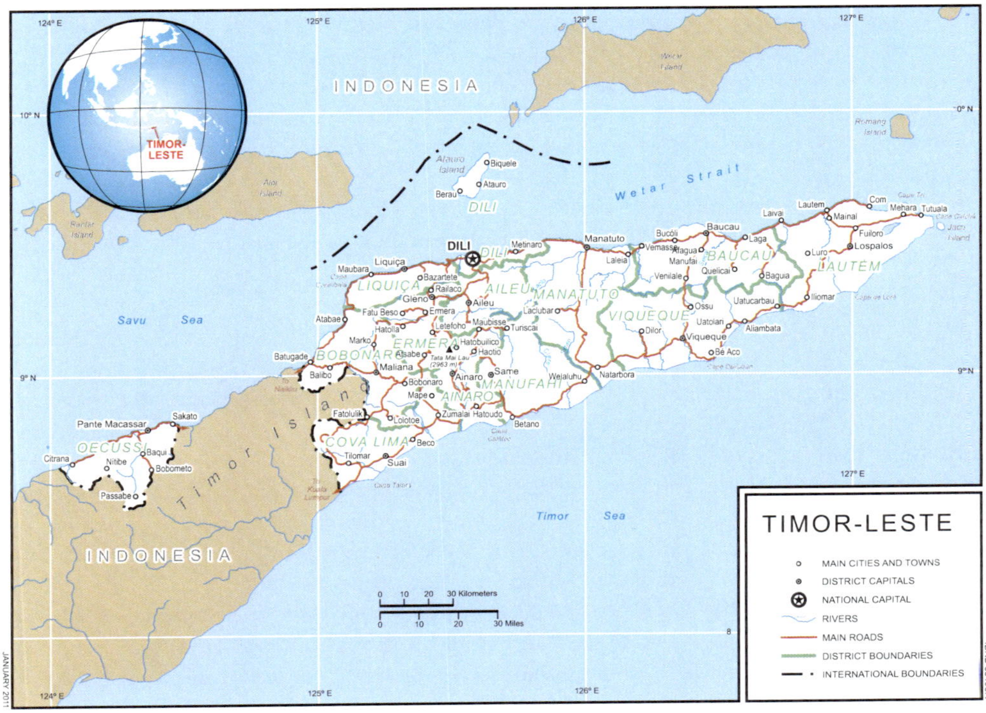

Timor-Leste, the eastern half of the island of Timor, has a land area of about 15,000 square kilometers. Its territory also includes the nearby islands of Atauro and Jaco, as well as Oecussi, an exclave in the Indonesian side of the island. Timor-Leste has a population of about 1 million.

A former Portuguese colony, Timor-Leste became a sovereign state in 2002 after gaining independence from Indonesia. The president is the head of state, elected for a five-year term. The president appoints the leader of the majority party or coalition as prime minister. The National Parliament's legislative chamber has 65 elected members.

Timor-Leste has made considerable progress in recent years, overcoming many severe challenges. It achieved lower-middle-income status in 2011 and the Strategic Development Plan (2011–2030) aims for upper-middle-income status and a substantial reduction in poverty by 2030. Nominal GDP per capita is US$4,974, but nonoil GDP per capita, in 2013, is significantly lower, at US$1,172.

SOURCES OF GROWTH AND ECONOMIC PROFILE

Main sources of growth. The economy is heavily reliant on the oil sector, which accounts for nearly 70 percent of total GDP and for almost all overseas-sourced income. Oil production started around 2005 and rapidly grew in importance; it now dominates the economy. High growth in nonoil GDP has been driven by public spending financed largely by withdrawals from the Petroleum Fund, the country's sovereign wealth fund. Construction, government services, and public administration have been the main sectors contributing to nonoil growth in recent years. Agriculture and manufacturing made only very small contributions.

Prepared by Yu Ching Wong and Fazurin Jamaludin.

Production, employment, exports, and imports. Sectors with a high dependence on government spending, such as construction, have led growth. Labor-intensive sectors such as agriculture have been weak and unemployment remains widespread, with a high share of the labor force either in informal or vulnerable employment (that is, unpaid family workers and the self-employed). A large current account surplus reflects the dominance of oil receipts but, given little domestic production, there is a heavy dependence on imported goods. Coffee exports account for about 90 percent of nonoil exports, but are small in absolute terms. There is a large structural deficit in the nonoil trade balance.

External income. Earnings from oil and gas reserves are Timor-Leste's major source of external income. Oil revenues are channeled into the Petroleum Fund, established in 2005, which stands at over US$16 billion (approximately four times the current estimate of GDP and 11 times the current estimate of nonoil GDP).

Development aid. Official development assistance was especially important in the years after independence, but has fallen in significance as oil revenues have grown. Development aid financed about 17 percent of expenditures in 2014. The major donors are Australia, United Nations agencies, the World Bank, the Asian Development Bank, and the European Union. Foreign aid is concentrated in governance, health, education, agriculture, and public works. Technical assistance has been provided by several institutions including the IMF as part of the international community's efforts to assist in the initial reconstruction and development of the economy. Technical assistance has focused on establishing key economic institutions and public financial management (including the fiscal regime for petroleum), and on developing statistical infrastructure.

Public finances. Government expenditure has grown sharply since independence, with the government focusing on development targets and nation building. Capital expenditure accounted for 20 percent of the budget in 2015, a reflection of severe infrastructure needs, and recurrent spending has risen strongly in recent years due to transfers and subsidies. Government finance is sourced primarily from oil and gas revenues, interest from the Petroleum Fund, and grants and concessionary loans. The Petroleum Fund Law requires the calculation of an estimated sustainable income level for each fiscal year; this represents the level of withdrawal that will ensure the stabilization of the real value of the fund. The law permits withdrawals in excess of this level if they are in the country's long-term best interest.

Financial sector. The financial sector remains small, with low penetration rates and limited access to finance for the private sector. The banking sector comprises four banks, two "other deposit-taking institutions" (supervised institutions that work on microfinance principles), a large number of small financial cooperatives, and two foreign-owned general insurers. Three of the banks are branches of international banks; the other is government owned and was recently upgraded from a microcredit institution. It is the only bank in Timor-Leste with its own capital base. Banks maintain substantial excess liquidity that is placed abroad, because lending is limited by a number of structural impediments. Reflecting high risks, interest rate spreads are wide. Safeguarding the banking system's soundness will become increasingly important as the financial sector develops.

Investment and business climate. The "organic" private sector, not linked to government, remains very small. Enhanced human capital, streamlined procedures, contract enforcement, and increased access to finance would greatly improve private sector development. The government has several initiatives underway to boost the private sector and stimulate entrepreneurship, including establishing a one-stop shop for new businesses and for developing public-private partnerships.

Exchange rate and competitiveness. The U.S. dollar was adopted as the currency in 2000, and Timor-Leste maintains an exchange system free of restrictions on payments and transfers for international transactions. Inflation pressure over 2011–13 (notwithstanding the decline in inflation over 2014) has resulted in a substantial appreciation in the real effective exchange rate, undermining diversification efforts.

GROWTH CHALLENGES, VULNERABILITIES, AND SPILLOVERS

Main growth challenges. Converting oil wealth into long-term sustainable growth, boosting the quality of growth, and creating sustainable jobs by catalyzing the private sector are the main growth challenges. Although the oil sector has supported government revenue and expenditure, it has not created a sufficient number of jobs. Social and physical development needs remain large. Good governance and accountability frameworks are in place, but public sector implementation capacity has been weak.

Main vulnerabilities. Key risks are fiscal spending above sustainable levels that boosts inflation and hampers economic diversification and poverty reduction; failure to develop new sources of growth amid falling production in existing oil fields and lack of inclusiveness and poverty reduction, which could result in social discontent and pressures for expansionary policies.

Global and regional economic spillovers. Timor-Leste's exposure to global financial conditions is limited by low levels of nonoil trade and capital account integration. However, fluctuations in global financial markets directly affect the investment returns of the Petroleum Fund, which will grow in importance as oil and gas receipts decline. Low oil prices would impact future investment and oil revenues and, hence, GDP growth.

APPENDIX TABLE 9.1

Timor-Leste: Selected Economic Indicators, 2010–15

Nominal GDP (2013): US$5.6 billion
Main export products: Oil, coffee
Remoteness (GDP-weighted distance): 8,339 km
GDP per capita (2013): US$4,974
Population (2015): 1.2 million

	1991–2000 Average	2001–09 Average	2010–15 Average	2010	2011	2012	2013	2014 Estimated	2015 Preliminary
GDP, GDP growth, employment, and prices									
Real GDP (percent change)	...	26.6	–2.6	–3.3	12.6	5.3	–13.9	–15.8	–0.6
Oil	...	88.1	–7.1	–18.7	14.6	–16.0	3.9	–23.6	–3.0
Nonoil	...	5.2	6.3	9.4	9.5	6.4	2.8	5.5	4.3
Real GDP per capita (percent change)	...	24.2	–4.2	–3.9	10.6	3.4	–15.4	–17.3	–2.4
Unemployment (percent)	...	...	...	...	...	...	...	...	...
Consumer prices (percent change, average)	...	4.5	6.7	5.2	13.2	10.9	9.6	0.8	0.6
Shares in real GDP (percent)									
Largest sector (oil)	...	59.7	69.2	74.6	75.9	60.6	73.1	...	...
Second largest sector (public administration)	...	5.5	6.2	4.3	4.3	4.6	5.9	...	...
Third largest sector (construction)	...	3.7	5.4	3.8	5.2	4.7	5.0	...	...
Tourism	...	...	...	...	...	...	...	...	...
Agriculture, forestry and fishing	...	11.0	4.7	4.7	3.3	3.9	4.6	...	...
Contributions to real GDP growth (percent)									
Largest sector (oil)	...	26.2	–5.8	–16.6	10.9	–12.2	2.4	...	...
Second largest sector (public administration)	...	0.7	0.7	0.5	0.5	0.5	0.5	...	...
Third largest sector (construction)	...	–0.3	0.2	0.2	2.0	–0.2	–0.4	...	...
Agriculture, forestry and fishing	...	0.3	0.0	–0.1	–0.9	0.8	0.0	...	...

(continued)

APPENDIX TABLE 9.1

Timor-Leste: Selected Economic Indicators, 2010–15 (*Continued*)

Nominal GDP (2013): US$5.6 billion
Main export products: Oil, coffee
Remoteness (GDP-weighted distance): 8,339 km

GDP per capita (2013): US$4,974
Population (2015): 1.2 million

	1991–2000 Average	2001–09 Average	2010–15 Average	2010	2011	2012	2013	2014 Estimated	2015 Preliminary
Share in real GDP (percent)									
Private consumption	...	...	...	...	...	...	...	...	...
Private investment	...	...	...	...	...	...	...	...	...
Public consumption	...	...	...	...	...	...	...	...	...
Public investment[1]	...	...	...	...	...	...	...	...	...
Exports minus imports	...	...	...	...	...	...	...	...	...
Contributions to real GDP growth (percent)									
Private consumption	...	...	...	...	...	...	...	...	...
Private investment	...	...	...	...	...	...	...	...	...
Public consumption	...	...	...	...	...	...	...	...	...
Public investment	...	...	...	...	...	...	...	...	...
Exports minus imports	...	...	...	...	...	...	...	...	...
Public finances									
Central government finance (percent of GDP)									
Revenue and grants	...	57.9	63.5	67.1	66.6	61.1	66.1	58.6	61.5
Domestic revenue	...	3.0	3.1	2.1	1.8	2.0	2.7	3.9	6.5
Petroleum revenue	...	22.6	54.8	57.5	59.8	55.5	58.7	48.5	48.9
Grants	...	32.4	5.5	7.6	4.9	3.7	4.7	6.2	6.1
Expenditure	...	41.4	31.8	26.3	24.0	22.0	24.0	37.4	57.3
Current	...	7.6	17.4	12.4	8.7	10.4	13.1	20.9	39.1
Of which: wages and salaries	...	2.3	3.1	2.2	1.9	1.9	2.5	3.7	6.5
Capital	...	2.6	8.8	6.2	10.4	7.9	6.3	10.2	11.7
Overall balance	...	16.5	31.7	40.8	42.6	39.1	42.1	21.2	4.2
Nonoil overall balance	...	−6.1	−23.1	−16.6	−17.3	−16.4	−16.6	−27.3	−44.7
Financing	...	6.1	23.1	16.6	17.3	16.4	16.6	27.3	44.7
Petroleum fund withdrawal	...	...	23.1	19.9	18.2	22.0	13.0	16.8	48.8
Borrowing	...	...	0.2	0	0	0	0.1	0.4	0.9
Of which: external	...	...	...	...	...	...	...	...	...
Of which: concessional	...	...	...	...	...	...	...	...	...
Public-debt-to-GDP ratio (percent)	...	...	...	0	0	0	0.1	0.5	1.8
Petroleum fund									
Closing balance (US$ million)	...	...	12,616	6,904	9,310	11,775	14,952	16,539	16,218
Closing balance (percent of GDP)	...	...	294.8	169.7	160.9	173.0	267.2	379.2	619.1

(continued)

APPENDIX TABLE 9.1

Timor-Leste: Selected Economic Indicators, 2010–15 (*Continued*)

Nominal GDP (2013): US$5.6 billion
Main export products: Oil, coffee
Remoteness (GDP-weighted distance): 8,339 km
GDP per capita (2013): US$4,974
Population (2015): 1.2 million

	1991–2000 Average	2001–09 Average	2010–15 Average	2010	2011	2012	2013	2014 Estimated	2015 Preliminary
Balance of payments (percent of GDP, unless otherwise indicated)									
Current account including official transfers	...	15.7	34.4	41.2	40.6	40.2	42.7	25.1	16.5
Current account excluding official transfers	...	−14.8	26.3	26.8	29.6	32.3	39.4	22.7	6.9
Overall balance	...	2.4	0.6	3.8	1.0	6.2	−3.5	−8.6	4.9
External debt service (percent of exports of goods and services)	...	...	...	...	...	...	...	...	...
Foreign direct investment	...	1.8	1.1	1.3	0.2	0.8	1.1	1.4	1.8
External debt	...	...	...	...	...	...	...	...	...
Main sources of external income (total)	...	25.9	56.8	59.6	61.9	57.1	61.0	49.9	51.3
Oil and gas	...	23.7	48.9	52.0	56.0	52.3	54.4	41.7	37.4
Investment income	...	1.6	6.1	4.9	3.8	3.0	4.9	7.6	12.5
Remittances	...	0.6	1.7	2.6	2.2	1.8	1.7	0.6	1.5
Contributions to external income growth (percent)									
External income growth	...	110.7	−0.7	26.3	47.8	8.4	−12.2	−36.3	−38.2
Oil and gas	...	106.7	−1.4	23.8	46.3	8.9	−13.3	−35.9	−38.5
Investment income	...	3.0	0.9	1.9	0.7	−0.3	1.7	1.6	−0.2
Remittances	...	1.0	−0.2	0.6	0.8	−0.2	−0.6	−2.0	0.5
Real effective exchange rate (period average)[2]	...	101.1	122.6	100.0	103.2	115.5	131.6	134.9	150.1
(percent change)	...	−0.9	6.7	−2.8	3.2	11.9	14.0	2.5	11.2
Money, credit, and financial sector									
Broad money (percent change)	...	30.2	15.9	9.9	9.3	26.2	22.9	19.9	7.1
Credit to private sector (percent of GDP)	...	4.2	3.8	2.7	2.3	2.4	3.2	4.4	8.1
(percent change)	...	...	12.8	5.9	21.1	20.5	13.6	5.5	10.5
Bank assets (percent of GDP)	...	...	14.9	8.3	7.0	8.2	11.9	18.5	35.4
Short-term treasury bill interest rate	...	...	...	...	...	...	...	...	...
Nonperforming loan ratio	...	...	32.7	41.7	36.3	30.8	28.0	26.8	22.9
Foreign bank market share (percent)[3]	...	...	...	...	...	...	...	...	...
Business climate indicators									
Business environment rankings[4]									
Doing business (overall)	...	...	164.5	150	159	164	174	167	173
Construction permits	...	...	115.2	85	91	99	109	153	154

(continued)

APPENDIX TABLE 9.1

Timor-Leste: Selected Economic Indicators, 2010–15 (*Continued*)

Nominal GDP (2013): US$5.6 billion
Main export products: Oil, coffee
Remoteness (GDP-weighted distance): 8,339 km

GDP per capita (2013): US$4,974
Population (2015): 1.2 million

	1991–2000 Average	2001–09 Average	2010–15 Average	2010	2011	2012	2013	2014 Estimated	2015 Preliminary
Getting electricity	...	...	39.7	10	15	15	14	89	95
Enforcing contracts	...	...	181.8	172	174	178	189	189	189
Getting credit	...	...	163.7	163	165	167	165	160	162
Human development index[5]	...	...	...	0.6	0.6	0.6	0.6	0.6	...
Memorandum:									
Nominal GDP (US$ million)	...	1,976.1	4,872.9	4,068.0	5,787.0	6,807.0	5,595.0	4,360.9	2,619.6
Oil	...	1,437.2	3,628.0	3,134.0	4,649.0	5,512.0	4,276.0	2,989.7	1,207.3
Nonoil	...	538.9	1,244.9	934.0	1,138.0	1,295.0	1,319.0	1,371.2	1,412.4

Sources: Timor-Leste authorities; and IMF staff estimates as of April 2016.
Note: ... = data not available.
[1] Public gross fixed capital formation.
[2] Index, 2005 = 100.
[3] Share in total loans, not including small loan scheme.
[4] World Bank, *Doing Business* reports.
[5] United Nations Development Programme.

Appendix 10. Tonga

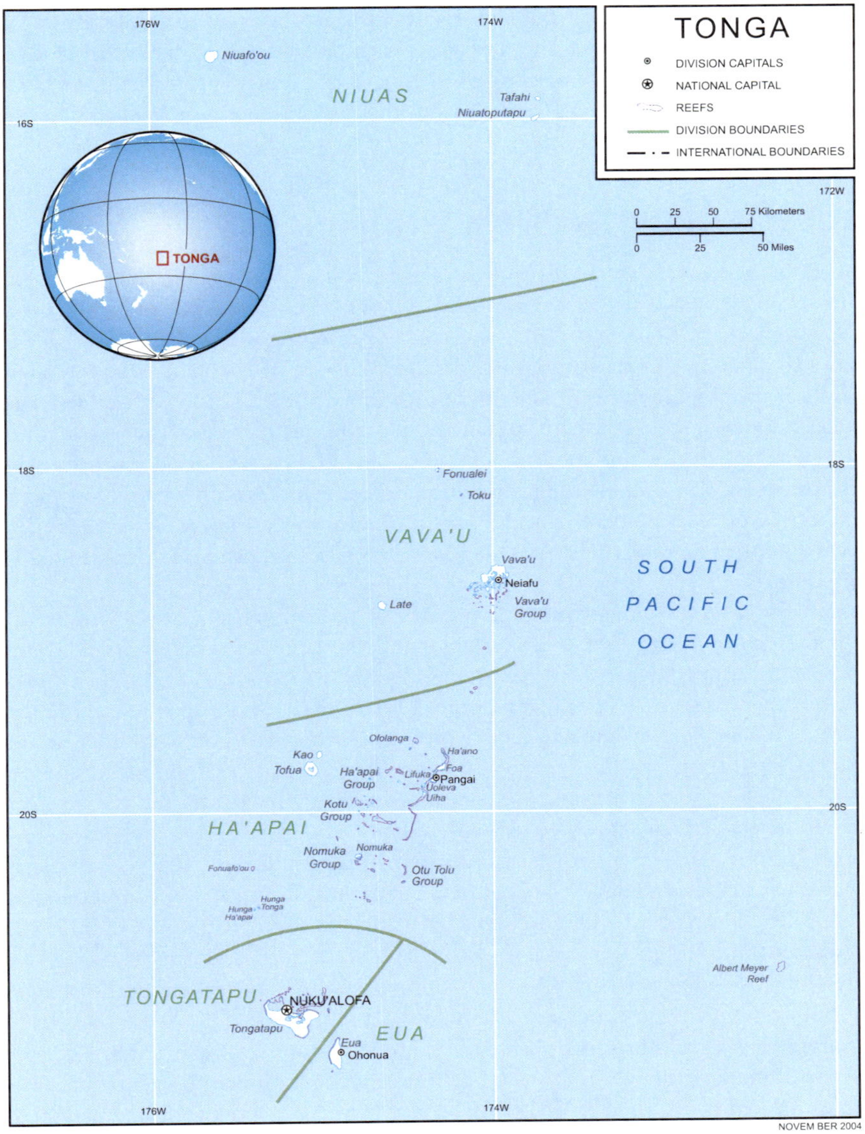

Tonga is a Polynesian state and an archipelago comprising 176 islands with a surface area of about 750 square kilometers scattered over 700,000 square kilometers of the southern Pacific Ocean. Fifty-two of these islands are inhabited by a population of about 104,000, out of which about 70 percent live on the main island, Tongatapu. Tonga is highly vulnerable to natural disasters.

Under the 2010 constitution, Tonga is a constitutional monarchy and a parliamentary democracy with the unicameral Legislative Assembly of Tonga consisting of 26 elected members, 9 of whom are elected by and from among the country's 33 hereditary nobles, and 17 by commoners. The prime minister is chosen by the legislative assembly and appointed by the monarch. The prime minister selects the

Prepared by Elena Loukoianova.

cabinet; its members are then appointed by the monarch. The prime minister may nominate up to four ministers from outside the assembly and on appointment they become members of the assembly.

All land belongs to the monarch and large estates have been allotted to nobles. By law, every male Tongan at age 16 is entitled to a small piece of agricultural land and a small town plot. In practice, there is not enough land and the majority of men have not been allocated land. Lately, objections have been raised to the exclusion of women from this process and, as a result, reform of the land tenure system has been under discussion.

SOURCES OF GROWTH AND ECONOMIC PROFILE

Main sources of growth. From the expenditure side, growth is driven mainly by private consumption and public spending, which are bolstered by official development assistance and remittances. Tourism has also increased its contribution in recent years, as has agriculture and retail and wholesale trade. As in most small states, the contribution of the public sector to the economy remains relatively large in Tonga.

Production, employment, exports, and imports. Since 2012/13 (Tonga's fiscal year ends on June 30), Tonga has been on a growth path supported by the reconstruction in the aftermath of Cyclone Ian in 2014, and by tourism and remittances. Tonga has also benefited from low prices globally.

As in most small island states, Tonga's production base is narrow. The share of its manufacturing sector in GDP is less than 10 percent and that of agriculture only 14 percent. Tonga's efforts to realize its deep-sea potential, both in fishery and mining, have not yet produced firm results. The fishing industry is surprisingly small and the extractive industry virtually nonexistent.

Although Tonga's unemployment rate is very low (1 percent), this is largely a result of low labor market participation, a high level of emigration, and the large share of subsistence workers, who generally do not earn cash wages. The labor market participation ratio is less than 56 percent.

The total export of goods was only 4 percent of GDP in 2013/14. Agricultural products such as vanilla, zucchini, and watermelon, and fishery products such as dried sea cucumber, account for the bulk of the exports. Tonga heavily depends on a wide range of imported products and services given the country's shallow manufacturing base, shortage of energy resources, and continued pattern of consumption diversification supported by remittances.

External income. Despite a decline relative to the previous decade, remittances remain Tonga's largest source of external income (21 percent of GDP during 2010–15). Tourism receipts are the second largest source (9 percent of GDP), followed by official transfers (5.6 percent) over the same period.

Development aid. Tonga receives both financial aid and technical assistance from multilateral and bilateral development partners. Most aid is provided as grants and directed toward infrastructure, communication, energy, education and training, and health.

Public finances. Government expenditure accounted for about 26 percent of GDP in 2013/14 and the ratio of public debt to GDP was 42 percent, up about 10 percentage points since 2008/09 as a result of the loans by China's EXIM Bank for reconstruction and infrastructure. While there are no explicit fiscal rules, Tonga intends to maintain usable cash balances equivalent to two months' cover of recurrent spending. The 2015 Joint IMF/World Bank Debt Sustainability Analysis indicates that Tonga remains at a moderate risk of debt distress.

Financial sector. The banking sector comprises five banks and is dominated by the local operations of two large foreign banks (ANZ and Bank South Pacific). It has gone through significant deleveraging since the abrupt end of the credit boom in the third quarter of 2008 from shrinking loan books and accumulating excess reserves. In 2014/15, the credit cycle turned. However, so far, rapid credit growth has not been a concern, because it started from a low level.

Investment and business climate. Tonga is the best performer among Pacific island countries rated by the World Bank's *Doing Business* 2016 report, ranking 78th out of 189 economies. However, Tonga's geographic disadvantage (long distance to the nearest key markets), small domestic market, and inadequate infrastructure have curtailed private investment.

Exchange rate and competitiveness. The pa'anga is the local currency. Tonga has accepted the obligations of Article VIII of the IMF's Articles of Agreement and maintains an exchange system that is free of restrictions on payments and transfers for current international transactions. The real effective exchange rate is broadly in line with Tonga's medium-term fundamentals.

GROWTH CHALLENGES, VULNERABILITIES, AND SPILLOVERS

Main growth challenges. As in other Pacific island countries, remoteness, a small population, and a narrow production base constrain growth. More recently, Tonga's trend growth has significantly weakened with the remittance-driven model of income convergence appearing to have reached its limit. The protracted balance sheet repair of Tongan banks is also an important challenge, as is enhancing resilience to climate change.

Main vulnerabilities. The devastation following Cyclone Ian in January 2014, which caused damage and losses equivalent to 10 percent of GDP, is a reminder of the country's vulnerability to natural disasters. The country's high dependence on Australia, New Zealand, and the United States as the major source of external income, particularly through remittances and tourism receipts, is another source of vulnerability.

Global and regional economic spillovers. The global financial crisis spilled over to Tonga mainly through weaker remittances and trade.

APPENDIX TABLE 10.1

Tonga: Selected Economic Indicators, 2010–15

Nominal GDP (FY2014): US$443.4 million
Main export products: Root crops, vanilla, squash, fish
Remoteness (GDP-weighted distance): 9,390 km

GDP per capita (FY2014): US$4,272
Population (2014): 103,802

	1991–2000 Average	2001–09 Average	2010–15 Average	2010	2011	2012	2013	2014	2015 Estimate
GDP, GDP growth, employment, and prices									
Real GDP (percent change)[1]	2.3	1.1	1.7	3.6	2.7	0.9	–3.1	2.1	3.7
Real GDP per capita (percent change)[1]	2.0	0.8	1.4	3.3	2.5	0.6	–3.4	1.7	3.4
Unemployment (percent)	...	...	...	...	...	...	...	...	...
Consumer prices (percent change, average)[2]	2.5	8.6	2.3	1.7	6.0	3.3	0.7	2.3	0.1
Shares in GDP (percent)[3]									
Largest sector (agriculture)	17.4	13.8	11.6	13.3	13.9	13.6	14.6	14.4	...
Second largest sector (public administration)	11.8	11.9	10.1	12.5	11.8	11.7	12.1	12.6	...
Third largest sector (trade services)	7.6	8.9	8.5	9.8	10.1	10.1	10.6	10.4	...
Tourism	5.1	5.3	8.5	7.0	7.9	8.3	9.7	10.0	...
Contributions to real GDP growth (percent)[1]									
Largest sector (agriculture)	0.1	0.5	0.8	1.4	1.7	0.2	0.6	0.3	...
Second largest sector (public administration)	0.4	0.6	0.5	1.1	0.4	0.3	0.1	0.8	...
Third largest sector (trade services)	0.1	0.7	0.3	–0.1	1.1	0.3	0.2	0.1	...
Share in GDP (percent)[3]									
Private consumption	93.6	98.3	80.7	97.2	91.4	93.4	100.1	101.9	...

(continued)

APPENDIX TABLE 10.1

Tonga: Selected Economic Indicators, 2010–15 (*Continued*)

Nominal GDP (FY2014): US$443.4 million
Main export products: Root crops, vanilla, squash, fish
Remoteness (GDP-weighted distance): 9,390 km

GDP per capita (FY2014): US$4,272
Population (2014): 103,802

	1991–2000 Average	2001–09 Average	2010–15 Average	2010	2011	2012	2013	2014	2015 Estimate
Private investment	...	...	...	...	...	...	...	...	...
Public consumption	17.8	18.0	16.2	21.9	17.3	18.9	19.7	19.4	...
Public investment	...	...	...	...	...	...	...	...	...
Exports minus imports	–33.6	–38.7	–33.6	–43.7	–43.0	–40.5	–36.7	–38.0	...
Contributions to GDP growth (percent)[1]									
Private consumption	1.7	5.6	3.1	0.2	1.8	4.3	5.1	4.3	...
Private investment	...	...	...	...	...	...	...	...	...
Public consumption	0.5	1.1	0.7	3.3	–2.9	2.2	0.3	0.4	...
Public investment	...	...	...	...	...	...	...	...	...
Exports minus imports	–0.9	–3.0	–0.3	–2.1	–2.9	1.1	4.9	–2.6	...
Public finances									
Central government finance (percent of GDP)									
Revenue and grants[4]	13.9	25.6	26.9	27.0	26.3	27.4	25.2	27.5	28.2
Total domestic revenue[4]	13.7	23.7	19.8	20.1	19.5	18.0	19.6	20.0	21.4
Grants[4]	0.2	2.0	7.1	6.8	6.8	9.4	5.6	7.5	6.7
Expenditure and net lending[4]	14.1	26.0	29.6	32.3	33.7	30.2	26.5	25.7	29.3
Current (excluding grants)[4]	13.9	23.1	24.6	25.8	22.7	23.5	24.9	25.0	25.8
Of which: wages and salaries[4]	7.5	11.4	11.4	11.6	11.8	10.4	10.8	11.5	12.0
Development (capital)[4]	0.7	1.3	3.8	2.6	9.6	5.6	1.6	0.9	2.4
Current balance[4,5]	–0.3	0.1	–4.9	–5.7	–3.4	–5.4	–5.4	–5.0	–4.3
Overall balance[4]	–0.3	–0.3	–2.7	–5.3	–7.4	–2.8	–1.3	1.7	–1.1
Financing[4]	0.3	0.3	2.7	5.3	7.4	2.8	1.3	–1.7	1.1
Assets (SWF, trust fund)	0	0	0	0	0	0	0	0	0
Debt[6]	...	...	3.0	3.5	8.4	5.1	0.2	0.3	0.6
Of which: external[6]	...	...	3.0	3.5	8.4	5.1	0.2	0.3	0.6
Of which: concessional	0	0	0.1	0.0	0.0	0.0	0.0	0.0	0.6
Other (government deposits)[4]	...	...	–0.3	1.9	–1.1	–2.4	1.0	–2.0	0.5
Public-debt-to-GDP ratio (percent)[7]	6.5	31.5	40.2	31.8	36.0	41.8	45.3	42.1	44.2
Sovereign wealth/trust fund (per capita ratio in real terms)	...	...	...	...	...	...	...	...	...
Balance of payments (percent of GDP, unless otherwise indicated)									
Current account including official transfers	–3.9	–5.5	–12.5	–20.2	–18.0	–12.4	–4.5	–7.9	–11.8
Current account excluding official transfers[3]	–6.1	–6.4	–18.0	–23.6	–23.4	–20.3	–11.3	–12.4	–17.2
Overall balance[8]	...	7.6	3.0	5.3	8.2	4.9	0.5	2.5	–3.7

(continued)

APPENDIX TABLE 10.1

Tonga: Selected Economic Indicators, 2010–15 (*Continued*)

Nominal GDP (FY2014): US$443.4 million
Main export products: Root crops, vanilla, squash, fish
Remoteness (GDP-weighted distance): 9,390 km

GDP per capita (FY2014): US$4,272
Population (2014): 103,802

	1991–2000 Average	2001–09 Average	2010–15 Average	2010	2011	2012	2013	2014	2015 Estimate
External debt service (percent of exports of goods and services)[7]	0.3	1.3	6.1	1.2	28.9	1.4	1.7	1.7	1.8
Foreign direct investment[3]	2.7	5.9	3.3	12.3	1.6	–0.3	1.2	2.6	2.7
External debt[7]	6.5	31.5	40.2	31.8	36.0	41.8	45.3	42.1	44.2
Main sources of external income (total)	19.1	33.8	34.7	29.3	29.4	32.6	40.3	37.7	39.0
Remittances	15.1	27.7	20.5	18.8	16.1	16.3	23.9	23.2	24.7
Tourism receipts	3.5	5.3	8.6	7.0	7.9	8.3	9.7	10.0	8.9
Official transfers	0.4	0.9	5.6	3.4	5.4	7.9	6.8	4.5	5.4
Contributions to external income growth (percent)									
External income growth	4.6	7.6	8.6	1.1	15.0	23.6	17.8	–7.8	1.6
Remittances	4.0	5.1	3.2	–6.8	–1.2	7.1	19.7	–2.6	3.0
Tourism receipts	0.8	1.9	1.6	–1.6	6.7	4.8	2.7	0.5	–3.5
Official transfers	–0.1	0.6	3.8	9.6	9.5	11.7	–4.6	–5.7	2.1
Exchange rate (local currency/ U.S. dollar period average)	1.4	2.0	1.8	1.9	1.8	1.7	1.7	1.8	1.9
Real effective exchange rate (period average)[9]	89.3	88.4	103.3	98.9	101.9	108.1	105.5	103.4	101.7
(percent change)	–3.0	1.3	0.6	0.8	3.1	6.1	–2.4	–2.1	–1.6
Money, credit, and financial sector									
Broad money (percent change)[4]	8.8	12.2	6.4	5.6	3.3	7.2	6.1	7.2	9.0
Credit to private sector (percent of GDP)[4]	...	0.4	0.3	0.4	0.3	0.3	0.3	0.3	0.3
(percent change)[4]	5.0	12.8	–4.8	–15.6	–9.9	–5.2	–7.5	0.7	8.6
Bank assets (percent of GDP)	...	...	...	...	...	...	...	...	...
Short-term treasury bill interest rate	...	...	...	...	...	...	...	...	...
Nonperforming loan ratio[10]	...	...	...	...	...	...	...	...	...
Foreign bank market share (percent)[11]	...	...	...	...	...	...	...	...	...
Business climate indicators									
Business environment rankings[12,13]									
Doing business (overall)	...	...	66	58	58	62	64	74	78
Construction permits	...	...	17	16	15	15	13	22	22
Getting electricity	...	...	42	34	31	33	35	60	61
Enforcing contracts	...	...	63	44	44	45	48	97	97
Getting credit	...	...	62	98	68	74	52	36	42
Human development index[14,15]	0.69	0.70	0.71	0.709	0.709	0.710	0.706	...	...

(continued)

APPENDIX TABLE 10.1

Tonga: Selected Economic Indicators, 2010–15 (*Continued*)

Nominal GDP (FY2014): US$443.4 million
Main export products: Root crops, vanilla, squash, fish
Remoteness (GDP-weighted distance): 9,390 km

GDP per capita (FY2014): US$4,272
Population (2014): 103,802

	1991–2000 Average	2001–09 Average	2010–15 Average	2010	2011	2012	2013	2014	2015 Estimate
Memorandum:									
Nominal GDP (T$ million)[3]	283.5	521.1	786.2	712.6	774.8	800.6	779.3	803.6	846.1
Nominal GDP (US$ million)[3]	205.1	257.5	432.2	369.4	422.9	472.3	449.5	443.4	435.4

Sources: Tonga authorities; and IMF staff estimates as of April 2016.
Note: ... = data not available; SWF = sovereign wealth fund.
[1] Data only available for the average of 1995–2000.
[2] Data only available for the average of 1996–2000.
[3] Data only available for the average of 1994–2000.
[4] Data only available for the average of 1998–2000.
[5] Current balance excludes grants and development (capital expenditure).
[6] Due to limited data availability, the average of 2006–11 only refers to data for 2009–11.
[7] Due to limited data availability, the average of 1991–2000 only refers to data for 1999–2000.
[8] Due to limited data availability, the average of 2001–05 only refers to data for 2004–05.
[9] Index, 2005 = 100.
[10] Due to limited data availability, the average of 2001–05 only refers to data in 2005.
[11] Share in total loans, not including small loan scheme.
[12] World Bank, *Doing Business* reports.
[13] Due to limited data availability, the average of 2006–11 refers to data for 2007–11. The average of 2006–11 for "Getting electricity" only refers to the year 2011.
[14] United Nations Development Programme.
[15] Due to limited data availability, the average of 1991–2000 refers to data for 2000 and the average of 2001–05 to data for 2005.

Appendix 11. Tuvalu

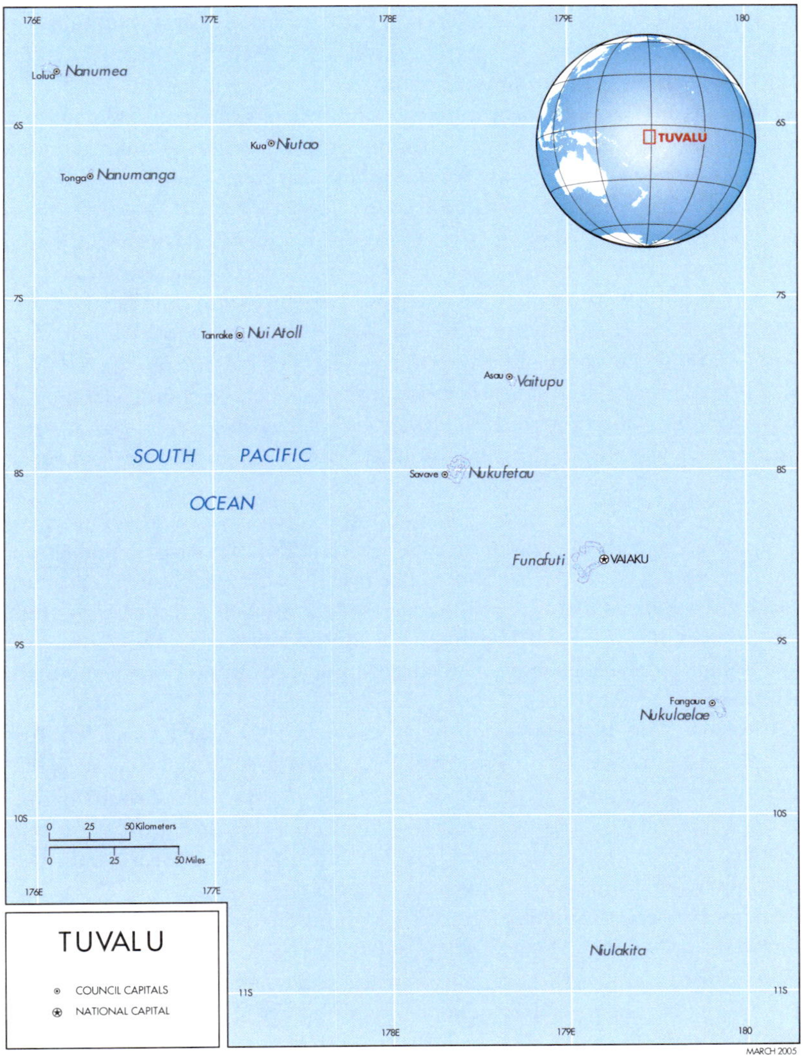

Tuvalu, a Polynesian island nation in the Pacific, has nine small coral islands with total land area of just 26 square kilometers. It has a population of about 11,000.

GDP per capita was US$3,452 in 2014. The country is a parliamentary democracy and member of the Commonwealth of Nations. As a low-lying group of islands, Tuvalu is highly vulnerable to climate change.

SOURCES OF GROWTH AND ECONOMIC PROFILE

Main sources of growth. Growth, estimated at 2.2 percent in 2014, remains weak. Inefficient public enterprises and weak bank lending are a drag on the economy, despite increasingly competitive private retail businesses and fisheries.

Prepared by Dan Nyberg.

Production, employment, exports, and imports. In 2014, agriculture accounted for 22 percent and industry 9 percent of output. The external sector has improved due to large fishing-related receipts and official aid, with Tuvalu registering a current account surplus of 24.3 percent of GDP in 2014, compared to a deficit of 61.3 percent of GDP in 2011. The current account is estimated to reach a surplus of about 8.2 percent of GDP in 2015.

External income. Overall, external income is estimated at more than 100 percent of GDP since 2013. Major sources of external income are fishing license fees, foreign aid, remittances, and TV Web domain license fees. Fishing license fees have more than doubled in just a few years and were at 32 percent of GDP in 2014. This income source remains volatile, however. Remittances have declined in importance since the global financial crisis. The Tuvalu Trust Fund holds most of the country's overseas assets, which stood at about 350 percent of GDP at the end of 2014.

Development aid. Financial support and technical assistance from multilateral and bilateral development partners have played an important role in strengthening capacity and facilitating growth and poverty reduction. Budget support and off-budget project financing averaged a combined 53 percent of GDP in 2006–12. On-budget grants have focused on budget support, public enterprise reform, infrastructure upgrades, education, and health. Extensive technical assistance has been provided by development partners to enhance tax administration, public financial management, and economic statistics.

Public finances. The authorities have taken important steps to strengthen budget monitoring by publishing a budget manual, strengthening the monitoring of outer-island budget operations, and releasing monthly reports of budget execution. The overall balance achieved a substantial surplus for the third consecutive year in 2014, as fishing license fees reached a record high and amid higher-than-expected foreign grants. The 2015 budget introduced a first step toward a medium-term fiscal framework to ensure fiscal sustainability and address procyclicality, and for accumulating savings to be used in the event of severe shocks.

Financial sector. The banking sector consists of the National Bank of Tuvalu and the Development Bank of Tuvalu, both state owned. The authorities are in the process of establishing a banking commission to improve oversight of the sector. About half of the banking sector's loan portfolio is nonperforming. While both banks have made substantial provisions, capital adequacy remains questionable given a lack of oversight. The Tuvalu National Provident Fund engages in lending to its members, with their contributions forming the collateral.

Investment and business climate. Tuvalu's geographical remoteness, outdated infrastructure, limited financial sector lending capacity, and small population have led to high transaction costs and lack of economies of scale, which have constrained business and investment. The government is committed to improving the investment climate, boosting private sector growth, and safeguarding macroeconomic stability.

Exchange rate and competitiveness. Tuvalu's legal tender is the Australian dollar, and there is no central monetary institution. The country has adopted transitional arrangements under Section 2 of Article XIV of the IMF's Articles of Agreement, but has not yet accepted the obligations under Article VIII. The real effective exchange rate depreciated over the past year, but has lately returned to its 20-year average on the back of a weakening Australian dollar.

GROWTH CHALLENGES, VULNERABILITIES, AND SPILLOVERS

Main challenges and vulnerabilities. Tuvalu faces tremendous challenges stemming from its remoteness, lack of economies of scale, weak institutional capacity, and climate change and rising sea levels. In March 2015 Tuvalu suffered significant damage from tropical Cyclone Pam, with damages and losses estimated at one-third of GDP, primarily to outer-island infrastructure such as sea walls, but also to housing and agriculture. In the medium term, risks to fiscal sustainability and vulnerabilities in the country's state-owned enterprise and banking sectors could cloud growth prospects.

Global and regional economic spillovers. Despite its geographical remoteness, the economy could suffer from external spillovers. The returns on the assets in the Tuvalu Trust Fund are dependent on global economic conditions, affecting the budgetary resources generated by the fund. Remittances by Tuvalu's seafarers and seasonal workers would be weakened further if there is a protracted growth slowdown in advanced and emerging market economies. Climate change and overfishing could undermine fishing license fees in the long term.

APPENDIX TABLE 11.1

Tuvalu: Selected Economic Indicators, 2010–15

Nominal GDP (2014): US$37.3 million[1]
Main export product: Fish
Remoteness (GDP-weighted distance): 8,745 km

GDP per capita (2014): US$3,452
Population (2014): 10,795

	1991–2000 Average	2001–09 Average	2010–15 Average	2010	2011	2012	2013	2014	2015 Estimate
GDP, GDP growth, employment, and prices									
Real GDP (percent change)	...	1.5	2.0	−2.7	8.5	0.2	1.3	2.2	2.6
Real GDP per capita (percent change)	...	−0.7	1.1	−4.0	7.1	−1.1	0.2	1.8	2.2
Unemployment (percent)	...	...	...	...	...	...	...	...	...
Consumer prices (percent change, average)	...	3.5	1.1	−1.9	0.5	1.4	2.0	1.1	3.3
Shares in real GDP (percent)									
Government	...	30.0	32.0	32.7	31.9	32.8	32.3	31.5	30.8
Agriculture	...	20.5	22.7	25.3	23.4	21.9	22.1	22.3	21.6
Finance and real estate	...	16.4	18.8	16.6	16.1	19.7	20.0	20.1	20.2
Trade, hotels and restaurants	...	9.5	9.1	8.0	8.3	9.4	9.4	9.4	9.9
Contributions to real GDP growth (percent)									
Government	...	1.0	0.6	0.6	1.8	1.0	−0.1	−0.1	0.1
Agriculture	...	0.3	0.5	3.1	0.1	−1.5	0.4	0.7	−0.1
Finance and real estate	...	0.0	1.0	0.0	0.8	3.7	0.6	0.6	0.6
Trade, hotels and restaurants	...	−0.4	0.6	0.7	0.9	1.1	0.2	0.1	0.8
Share in GDP (percent)									
Private consumption	...	...	...	...	...	...	...	...	...
Private investment	...	...	...	...	...	...	...	...	...
Public consumption	...	...	...	...	...	...	...	...	...
Public investment	...	...	...	...	...	...	...	...	...
Exports minus imports	...	...	...	...	...	...	...	...	...
Contributions to GDP growth (percent)									
Private consumption	...	...	...	...	...	...	...	...	...
Private investment	...	...	...	...	...	...	...	...	...
Public consumption	...	...	...	...	...	...	...	...	...
Public investment	...	...	...	...	...	...	...	...	...
Exports minus imports	...	...	...	...	...	...	...	...	...
Public finances									
Central government finance (percent of GDP)									
Revenue and grants	...	...	99.9	71.9	69.0	84.3	107.5	123.1	130.4
Total domestic revenue	...	...	71.1	55.5	47.8	56.6	82.9	74.1	108.4
Grants	...	...	28.9	16.4	21.2	27.8	24.6	49.0	21.8

(continued)

APPENDIX TABLE 11.1

Tuvalu: Selected Economic Indicators, 2010–15 (*Continued*)

Nominal GDP (2014): US$37.3 million[1]
Main export product: Fish
Remoteness (GDP-weighted distance): 8,745 km

GDP per capita (2014): US$3,452
Population (2014): 10,795

	1991–2000 Average	2001–09 Average	2010–15 Average	2010	2011	2012	2013	2014	2015 Estimate
Expenditure and net lending	...	...	88.8	95.7	77.9	75.0	81.1	86.8	130.1
Current	...	...	87.6	92.5	76.1	75.0	81.0	86.6	128.3
Of which: wages and salaries	...	...	34.0	33.8	31.3	31.9	32.2	36.1	34.4
Capital expenditure	...	...	1.2	3.2	1.8	0.0	0.2	0.2	0.1
Current balance[2]	...	...	-16.5	-37.0	-28.3	-18.4	1.9	-12.4	-21.5
Overall balance	...	...	11.2	-23.8	-8.9	9.3	26.3	36.3	0.3
Financing									
Assets (Consolidated Investment Fund)	...	...	-10.1	26.4	9.4	-9.2	-25.3	-35.9	1.2
Debt	...	...	-1.1	-2.7	-0.5	-0.2	-1.1	-0.4	-1.5
Of which: external	...	...	-1.0	-2.4	-0.5	0.1	-1.0	-0.4	-1.4
Of which: concessional	...	...	...	...	...	...	...	...	...
Other	...	...	...	...	...	...	...	...	...
Tuvalu Trust Fund									
Closing balance ($A million)	...	19.2	132.1	108.0	118.7	130.6	140.6	144.1	150.8
Closing balance (percent of GDP)	...	55.2	335.2	311.2	311.4	339.1	354.3	348.6	346.7
Per capita value ($A)	...	1,873	12,388	10,411	11,299	12,275	13,079	13,349	13,914
Public-debt-to-GDP ratio (percent)	...	50.8	48.6	55.6	45.3	43.0	41.1	58.5	64.1
Balance of payments (percent of GDP, unless otherwise indicated)									
Current account including official transfers	...	-11.6	6.1	-11.3	-36.5	25.3	26.4	24.3	8.2
Current account excluding official transfers	...	-54.2	-85.1	-58.8	-77.5	-30.7	-22.1	-42.8	-20.2
Overall balance	...	0.2	8.3	-9.5	-4.4	4.9	22.7	33.9	0.2
External debt service (percent of exports of goods and services)	...	7.1	12.7	7.8	19.4	11.2	11.6	11.5	10.7
Foreign direct investment	...	1.0	1.8	1.7	-0.3	4.2	1.8	1.8	1.8
External debt[3]	...	41.3	43.3	50.6	40.7	36.4	35.3	53.5	60.0
Main sources of external income (total)	...	62.4	93.5	76.2	63.4	89.4	107.3	103.8	120.9
Grants	...	44.9	49.7	48.2	42.4	57.1	49.8	59.7	41.3
Fishing license fees	...	17.6	33.1	20.6	14.9	21.8	45.4	32.0	64.0
TV domain license fees		7.9	9.4	5.8	4.9	9.6	11.0	10.9	14.4
Contributions to external income growth (percent)									
External income growth	...	...	6.5	-18.5	-16.8	41.0	20.0	-3.3	16.5
Grants	...	3.7	-2.0	-11.1	-7.6	23.1	-8.2	9.3	-17.8
Fishing license fees	...	...	7.0	-6.0	-7.5	10.9	26.4	-12.5	30.8
TV domain license fees	...	...	1.7	-0.9	-1.2	7.4	1.5	-0.1	3.4

(*continued*)

APPENDIX TABLE 11.1

Tuvalu: Selected Economic Indicators, 2010–15 (*Continued*)

Nominal GDP (2014): US$37.3 million[1]
Main export product: Fish
Remoteness (GDP-weighted distance): 8,745 km
GDP per capita (2014): US$3,452
Population (2014): 10,795

	1991–2000 Average	2001–09 Average	2010–15 Average	2010	2011	2012	2013	2014	2015 Estimate
Exchange rate (Australian dollar to U.S. dollar period average)	...	1.4	1.1	1.1	1.0	1.0	1.0	1.1	1.3
Real effective exchange rate (period average)[4]	...	88.2	99.6	100.0	102.5	103.8	102.1	97.3	91.9
(percent change)	...	2.6	–0.1	7.7	2.5	1.3	–1.6	–4.7	–5.5
Money, credit, and financial sector									
Broad money (percent change)	...	...	...	...	...	...	...	...	...
Credit to private sector (percent of GDP)	...	44.9	26.2	27.7	29.0	25.4	22.7	...	...
(percent change)	...	2.3	–0.8	0.9	15.1	–11.4	–7.7	...	...
Bank assets (percent of GDP)	...	118.6	118.7	118.5	112.2	115.1	129.2	...	...
Short-term treasury bill interest rate	...	...	...	...	...	...	...	...	...
Nonperforming loan ratio	...	...	...	...	...	50.8	55.1	...	...
Foreign bank market share (percent)[5]	...	...	...	...	...	...	...	...	...
Business climate indicators									
Business environment rankings[6]	...	...	...	...	...	...	...	...	...
Doing business (overall)	...	...	...	...	...	...	...	...	...
Construction permits	...	...	...	...	...	...	...	...	...
Getting electricity	...	...	...	...	...	...	...	...	...
Enforcing contracts	...	...	...	...	...	...	...	...	...
Getting credit	...	...	...	...	...	...	...	...	...
Human development index[7]	...	...	...	...	...	...	...	...	...
Memorandum:									
Nominal GDP ($A million)	...	30.4	39.3	34.7	38.1	38.5	39.7	41.3	43.5
Nominal GDP (US$ million)[1]	...	22.1	36.6	31.9	39.3	39.9	38.4	37.3	32.7

Sources: Tuvalu authorities; Tuvalu Trust Fund Advisory Committee; and IMF staff estimates.
Note: ... = data not available.
[1] Based on period average exchange rate.
[2] Current balance excludes grants and development (capital expenditure).
[3] External public debt.
[4] Index, 2005 = 100.
[5] Share in total loans.
[6] World Bank, *Doing Business* reports.
[7] United Nations Development Programme.

Appendix 12. Vanuatu

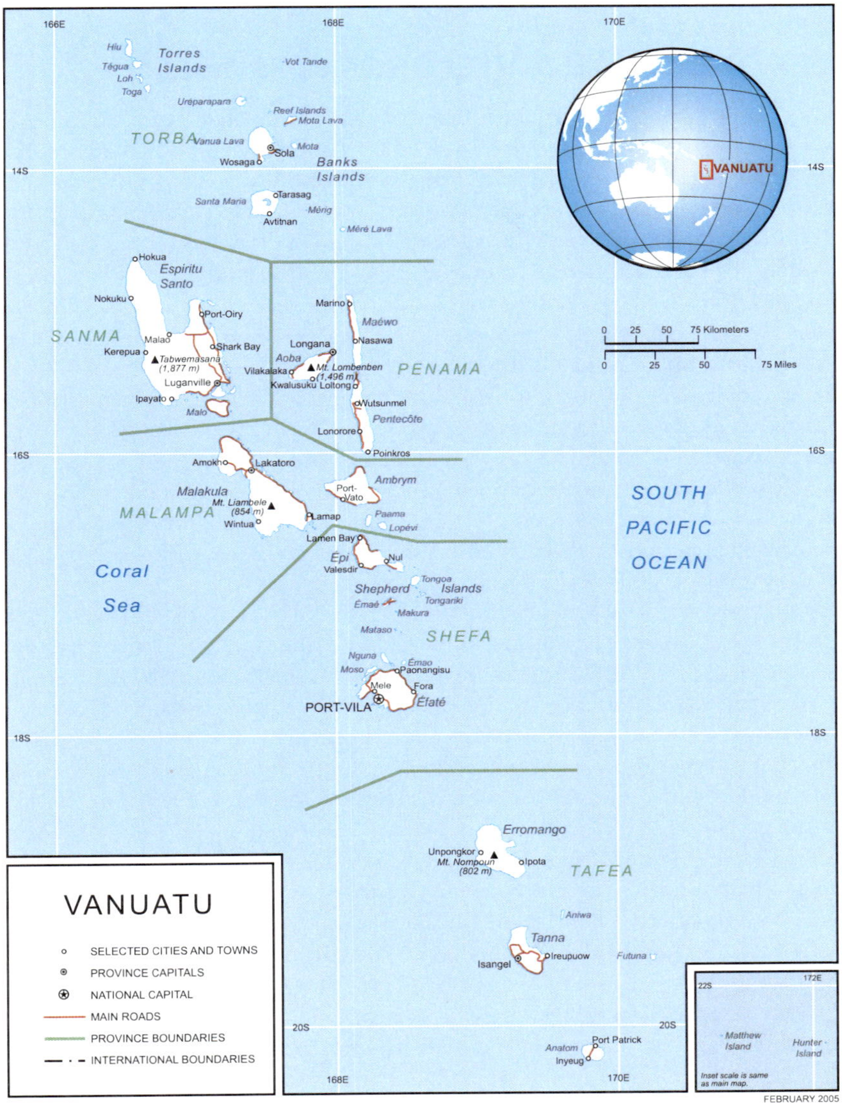

Vanuatu's 82 islands, 65 of them inhabited, cover a distance of some 1,300 kilometers separating the outermost islands. About a quarter of Vanuatu's estimated population of 270,000 lives in urban areas, including Port Vila, the capital. In March 2015, tropical Cyclone Pam destroyed or significantly damaged a large share of housing on several major islands, and caused severe damage to crops and tourist facilities. Estimated damage and losses to the economy exceed 60 percent of GDP.

A parliamentary republic, the country gained independence from France and the United Kingdom in 1980. The president is the head of state elected for a five-year term by an electoral college of members of parliament and the presidents of the regional councils. The government is led by

---

Prepared by Vladimir Klyuev.

the prime minister, who is elected by other members of parliament. The 52 members of parliament are elected by popular vote for four-year terms.

SOURCES OF GROWTH AND ECONOMIC PROFILE

Main sources of growth. Since the global financial crisis, primarily exports and private consumption have driven growth. Tourism has expanded particularly vigorously, with tourism receipts accounting for 30 percent of GDP. Most tourists come from Australia and New Zealand.

Production, employment, exports, and imports. Most of the population is employed in small-scale agriculture, and the main exports are agricultural commodities (coconut oil, copra, kava, beef) destined mainly for Asia. The services sector employs about a third of the labor force, but comprises about two-thirds of the economy's value added. Tourism receipts are the main source of foreign exchange, while goods exports—primarily agricultural commodities—bring in considerably less revenue. Merchandise imports, mainly from China, constitute about 30 percent of GDP and include machinery and equipment, food, and fuel. Industrial activity is nascent. The government sector is small compared to most other Pacific island countries.

External income. Remittances are also less important than in many other Pacific island countries. Despite considerable official transfers, current account deficits are sizable, amounting to about 6 percent of GDP on average during 2010–15. However, foreign direct investment and capital grants comfortably finance these deficits, with Australia the main source for both. Substantial international reserves provide a buffer against external shocks.

Development aid. Vanuatu benefits from considerable bilateral and multilateral aid, though the size of grants has been among the smallest in the Pacific island countries. Official grants amounted to about 5 percent of GDP on average during 2010–15; Australia, New Zealand, and, increasingly, China are the main sources of bilateral aid. The Asian Development Bank—focusing on private sector development and helping government address transport, urban development, and energy constraints—has provided 11 loans totaling $85.6 million and 62 technical assistance projects for $22.5 million, since Vanuatu joined the Asian Development Bank in 1981. The World Bank supports government efforts to extend electricity to lower-income households and is a major provider of technical assistance. The IMF provided SDR 17 million (100 percent of the quota) under the Rapid Credit Facility and the Rapid Financing Instrument in June 2015 to support Vanuatu's international reserves after Cyclone Pam. Technical assistance is provided in a number of areas, including tax administration, banking supervision, and national account and balance of payments statistics.

Government finance. The public sector is relatively small, with government expenditures at about 25 percent of GDP in recent years. Fiscal deficits and public debt are low, with the public debt ratio about 20 percent of GDP. At the same time, public finances would benefit from a medium-term fiscal framework and from better control over government business enterprises.

Financial sector. The onshore financial system includes four major banks. Three of these are foreign-owned branches and subsidiaries. Vanuatu has four insurance companies, two of which are local. Banks are well capitalized and profitable, but nonperforming loans are rather high.

Business and investment climate. Vanuatu ranked 94th out of 189 countries in the World Bank's 2016 *Doing Business* report, higher than most Pacific island countries. It has, however, considerably lower rankings in the categories of ease of starting a business and protecting minority investors. High energy and transportation costs, partly as a result of monopolistic market structures, raise the cost of doing business.

Monetary policy. Vanuatu pegs its currency, the vatu, to an undisclosed basket of currencies, which anchors monetary policy. The regime has served the country well, with inflation staying in the low single digits in the last few years. The main policy instrument is the Reserve Bank of Vanuatu's rediscount rate.

Exchange rate and competitiveness. The exchange rate is broadly in line with Vanuatu's fundamentals. The real effective exchange rate has been roughly stable, with currency movements against the U.S. dollar and against the Australian dollar offsetting one another.

GROWTH CHALLENGES, VULNERABILITIES, AND SPILLOVERS

Main growth challenges. Vanuatu faces considerable infrastructure bottlenecks, and the government has announced ambitious, largely debt-financed investment plans to overcome them. The government will need to ensure infrastructure projects align with the country's development priorities and that scale is commensurate with its implementation and debt repayment capacity.

Main vulnerabilities. Vanuatu's small size, as is the case for other Pacific countries, inhibits economic diversification and increases output volatility. It also shares the region's vulnerability to cyclones and tsunamis. Enhancing resilience against natural disasters will be important for long-term sustainable growth.

Regional and global economic spillovers. Vanuatu's dependence on tourism from Australia leaves it susceptible to that country's business cycle.

APPENDIX TABLE 12.1

Vanuatu: Selected Economic Indicators, 2010–15

Nominal GDP (2014): US$822.2 million
Main export products: coconut oil, copra, kava, beef
Remoteness (GDP–weighted distance): 9,175 km
GDP per capita (2014): US$3,132
Population (2014): 262,559.

	1991–2000 Average	2001–09 Average	2010–15 Average	2010	2011	2012	2013	2014	2015 Estimate
GDP, GDP growth, employment, and prices									
Real GDP (percent change)	...	4.0	1.4	1.6	1.2	1.8	2.0	2.3	-0.8
Real GDP per capita (percent change)	...	1.6	-0.9	-0.8	-1.1	-0.5	-0.3	0.0	-3.0
Unemployment (percent)	...	...	...	...	...	...	...	...	...
Consumer prices (percent change, average)	...	3.0	1.7	2.7	0.7	1.4	1.3	1.0	3.3
Shares in GDP (percent)									
Largest sector (tourism)	20.0	24.0	30.0	31.0	28.0	31.0	36.0	31.0	22.0
Second largest sector (crop production)	...	18.3	16.0	15.5	16.3	16.0	16.2	16.2	14.0
Third largest sector (public administration)	...	12.7	12.0	12.1	11.5	11.5	12.0	11.9	12.7
Agriculture									
Contributions to GDP growth (percent) (real based)									
Crop production	...	0.3	0.0	0.6	0.9	0.0	0.5	0.4	-2.5
Public administration	...	0.3	0.3	0.6	-0.5	0.2	0.7	0.2	0.6
Share in GDP (percent)									
Private consumption	...	64.5	61.0	59.3	60.4	61.1	61.9	63.1	60.4
Private investment	...	...	...	...	...	...	...	...	...
Public consumption	...	15.4	14.9	15.7	15.4	14.9	15.0	14.1	14.3
Public investment	...	...	...	...	...	...	...	...	...
Exports minus imports	...	-9.8	-8.9	-11.9	-5.9	-6.8	-8.2	-8.5	-12.2

(continued)

APPENDIX TABLE 12.1

Vanuatu: Selected Economic Indicators, 2010–15 (*Continued*)

Nominal GDP (2014): US$822.2 million
Main export products: coconut oil, copra, kava, beef
Remoteness (GDP–weighted distance): 9,175 km

GDP per capita (2014): US$3,132
Population (2014): 262,559.

	1991–2000 Average	2001–09 Average	2010–15 Average	2010	2011	2012	2013	2014	2015 Estimate
Contributions to real GDP growth (percent)									
(real terms)									
Private consumption	...	1.6	1.3	1.5	1.8	1.8	2.0	2.7	−2.3
Private investment	...	...	...	...	...	...	...	...	...
Public consumption	...	0.5	0.1	0.7	−0.1	−0.2	0.3	−0.5	0.3
Public investment	...	...	...	...	...	...	...	...	...
Exports minus imports	...	−1.1	0.1	1.5	5.9	−1.1	−1.6	−0.5	−3.8
Public finances									
Central government finance (percent of GDP)									
Revenue and grants	23.9	21.2	24.1	24.6	22.3	21.8	21.3	23.3	31.4
Total domestic revenue	20.6	18.3	19.0	18.1	18.1	18.8	19.2	19.2	20.5
Grants	3.3	2.8	5.2	6.5	4.2	3.0	2.2	4.1	10.9
Expenditure and net lending	26.7	21.8	25.3	27.1	24.4	23.4	21.5	22.3	32.9
Current (excluding grants)	19.1	19.2	22.5	22.2	21.9	21.8	20.6	21.4	27.2
Of which: wages and salaries	11.1	11.3	11.1	11.5	11.1	11.6	11.1	10.6	10.9
Development (capital)	6.6	2.6	2.8	4.9	2.7	1.6	0.9	0.9	5.8
Current balance[1]	1.5	−0.8	−3.6	−4.2	−3.7	−3.1	−1.5	−2.3	−6.7
Overall balance	−3.1	−0.6	−1.2	−2.5	−2.2	−1.6	−0.2	1.0	−1.5
Financing	1.4	0.6	0.2	2.5	2.2	1.6	0.2	−0.8	−4.8
Assets	0.0	−0.5	0.8	−0.9	−0.5	−0.2	−0.4	0.7	6.3
Debt	1.4	0.2	1.0	1.6	1.7	1.5	−0.2	−0.1	1.5
Of which: external	1.8	0.2	0.1	0.4	0.4	−0.5	−0.6	−0.4	1.5
Of which: concessional	1.8	0.2	0.1	0.4	0.4	−0.5	−0.6	−0.4	1.5
Other	...	...	...	...	...	...	...	...	...
Public-debt-to-GDP ratio (percent)	24.4	28.1	20.4	19.4	20.7	21.7	20.6	19.5	20.5
Balance of payments (percent of GDP)									
Current account	...	−7.0	−5.9	−6.5	−8.4	−9.4	−1.4	0.5	−10.1
Current account including official transfers	...	−11.8	−10.0	−9.5	−9.7	−11.2	−3.8	−2.9	−23.2
Overall balance	...	3.0	2.3	1.9	1.5	1.1	−0.6	0.6	9.2
External debt service (percent of exports of goods and services)	...	1.5	1.6	1.4	1.5	1.4	1.7	2.0	...
Foreign direct investment	8.1	7.1	5.6	5.7	7.5	4.9	4.2	2.6	8.9
External debt	19.2	19.9	13.4	14.5	14.7	14.0	12.7	11.7	12.9
Main sources of external income (total)	...	6.0	3.5	4.8	4.1	5.2	...	...	...

(continued)

APPENDIX TABLE 12.1

Vanuatu: Selected Economic Indicators, 2010–15 (*Continued*)

Nominal GDP (2014): US$822.2 million
Main export products: coconut oil, copra, kava, beef
Remoteness (GDP–weighted distance): 9,175 km
GDP per capita (2014): US$3,132
Population (2014): 262,559.

	1991–2000 Average	2001–09 Average	2010–15 Average	2010	2011	2012	2013	2014	2015 Estimate
Compensation of employees	...	1.4	1.9	1.7	2.7	3.4	...	...	...
Grants	...	4.6	1.6	3.1	1.4	1.9	...	...	...
Investment income	...	5.4	1.7	3.1	2.0	1.5	...	...	...
Contributions to external income growth (percent)									
External income growth	...	2.1	–22.4	2.9	–16.3	10.9	...	...	...
Compensation of employees	...	1.3	–5.2	–1.0	13.2	10.1	...	...	...
Grants	...	1.9	–10.0	–5.0	–18.5	7.5	...	...	...
Investment income	...	–1.1	–7.1	8.9	–11.0	–6.7	...	...	...
Exchange rate (vatu to U.S. dollar period average)	119.7	116.5	96.3	96.9	89.5	92.6	94.5	97.1	107.0
Real effective exchange rate (period average)[2]	90.81	95.58	104.31	100.0	102.5	104.9	104.9	105.8	107.8
(percent change)	...	5.3	9.1	2.1	2.5	2.3	0.0	0.8	1.9
Money, credit, and financial sector									
Broad money (percent change)	...	...	–1.8	–6.0	1.3	–0.6	–5.5	8.6	3.1
Credit to private sector (percent of GDP)	...	45.5	67.3	64.7	67.4	70.5	68.7	71.1	...
(percent change)	...	...	8.6	11.6	9.4	6.9	5.8	...	...
Bank assets (percent of GDP)		101.7	89.8	93.3	91.0	90.1	84.8	90.1	...
Short-term treasury bill interest rate	...	...	...	...	...	...	...	...	...
Nonperforming loan ratio			9.1	4.9	8.1	8.1	13.5	11.1	...
Foreign bank market share (percent)[3]	...	...	...	...	...	...	...	...	...
Business climate indicators									
Business environment rankings[4]									
Doing business (overall)	...	...	80	78	74	70	70	96	94
Construction permits	...	...	78	5	31	69	73	144	143
Getting electricity	...	...	110	142	149	102	109	77	82
Enforcing contracts	...	...	95	73	71	72	75	138	139
Getting credit	...	...	54	64	68	74	52	36	28
Human development index[5]	...	...	0.6	0.6	0.6	0.6	0.6	0.6	...
Memorandum:									
Nominal GDP (vatu million)	29,201	47,296	74,774	67,911	70,873	72,415	75,803	79,819	81,825
Nominal GDP (US$ million)	243	420	777	701	792	782	802	822	765

Sources: Vanuatu authorities; and IMF, "Vanuatu: Staff Report for the 2015 Article IV Consultation and Request for Disbursement Under the Rapid Credit Facility and Purchase Under the Rapid Financing Instrument" (Country Report No. 15/149).

Note: ... = data not available.

[1] Current balance excludes grants and development (capital expenditure).

[2] Index, 2005 = 100.

[3] Share in total loans, not including small loan scheme.

[4] World Bank, *Doing Business* reports.

[5] United Nations Development Programme.

Index

Page numbers followed by *b*, *f*, or *t* refer to boxes, figures, or tables, respectively.